Routledge International Handbook of Working-Class Studies

The *Routledge International Handbook of Working-Class Studies* is a timely volume that provides an overview of this interdisciplinary field that emerged in the 1990s in the context of deindustrialization, the rise of the service economy, and economic and cultural globalization. The *Handbook* brings together scholars, teachers, activists, and organizers from across three continents to focus on the study of working-class peoples, cultures, and politics in all their complexity and diversity.

The *Handbook* maps the current state of the field and presents a visionary agenda for future research by mingling the voices and perspectives of founding and emerging scholars. In addition to a framing Introduction and Conclusion written by the co-editors, the volume is divided into six sections: Methods and principles of research in working-class studies; Class and education; Work and community; Working-class cultures; Representations; and Activism and collective action. Each of the six sections opens with an overview that synthesizes research in the area and briefly summarizes each of the chapters in the section. Throughout the volume, contributors from various disciplines explore the ways in which experiences and understandings of class have shifted rapidly as a result of economic and cultural globalization, social and political changes, and global financial crises of the past two decades.

Written in a clear and accessible style, the *Handbook* is a comprehensive interdisciplinary anthology for this young but maturing field, foregrounding transnational and intersectional perspectives on working-class people and issues and focusing on teaching and activism in addition to scholarly research. It is a valuable resource for activists as well as working-class studies researchers and teachers across the social sciences, arts, and humanities, and it can also be used as a textbook for advanced undergraduate or graduate courses.

Michele Fazio is Professor of English and Coordinator of Gender Studies at the University of North Carolina at Pembroke, US.

Christie Launius is Associate Professor and Head of the Gender, Women, and Sexuality Studies Department at Kansas State University, US.

Tim Strangleman is Professor of Sociology in the School of Social Policy, Sociology and Social Research, SSPSSR, at the University of Kent, Canterbury, UK.

Routledge International Handbooks

The Routledge Handbook of British Politics and Society
Mark Garnett

The Routledge Handbook of Integrated Reporting
Edited by Charl de Villiers, Pei-Chi Kelly Hsiao and Warren Maroun

The Routledge International Handbook of Global Therapeutic Cultures
Edited by Daniel Nehring, Ole Jacob Madsen, Edgar Cabanas, China Mills and Dylan Kerrigan

Routledge Handbook of Street Culture
Edited by Jeffrey Ian Ross

The Routledge International Handbook of Simmel Studies
Edited by Gregor Fitzi

Routledge Handbook of Counter-Narratives
Edited by Klarissa Lueg and Marianne Wolff Lundholt

Routledge Handbook of Art, Science, and Technology Studies
Edited by Hannah Star Rogers, Megan K. Halpern, Kathryn de Ridder-Vignone, and Dehlia Hannah

Routledge Handbook of Bounded Rationality
Edited by Riccardo Viale

Routledge International Handbook of Charisma
Edited by José Pedro Zúquete

Routledge International Handbook of Working-Class Studies
Edited by Michele Fazio, Christie Launius, and Tim Strangleman

Routledge Handbook of Digital Media and Communication
Edited by Leah A. Lievrouw and Brian D. Loader

Routledge International Handbook of Religion in Global Society
Edited by Jayeel Cornelio, François Gauthier, Tuomas Martikainen and Linda Woodhead

The Routledge Handbook on the International Dimension of Brexit
Edited by Juan Santos Vara and Ramses A. Wessel; Assistant Editor, and Polly R. Polak

Routledge Handbook of Critical Finance Studies
Edited by Christian Borch and Robert Wosnitzer

For more information about this series, please visit: www.routledge.com/Routledge-International-Handbooks/book-series/RIHAND

Routledge International Handbook of Working-Class Studies

Edited by Michele Fazio, Christie Launius, and Tim Strangleman

Routledge
Taylor & Francis Group
LONDON AND NEW YORK

First published 2021
by Routledge
2 Park Square, Milton Park, Abingdon, Oxon OX14 4RN

and by Routledge
52 Vanderbilt Avenue, New York, NY 10017

Routledge is an imprint of the Taylor & Francis Group, an informa business

British Library Cataloguing-in-Publication Data
A catalogue record for this book is available from the British Library

Library of Congress Cataloging-in-Publication Data
A catalog record has been requested for this book

ISBN: 978-1-138-70982-9 (hbk)
ISBN: 978-0-367-61082-1 (pbk)
ISBN: 978-1-315-20084-2 (ebk)

Typeset in Bembo
by Newgen Publishing UK

Contents

List of images x
List of contributors xi
Acknowledgments xxii

Introduction 1
Michele Fazio, Christie Launius, and Tim Strangleman

PART I
Methods and principles of research in working-class studies 9
Section introduction: Methods and principles of research in working-class studies 11
Christie Launius

1 Class analysis from the inside: Scholarly personal narrative as a signature genre of working-class studies 20
Sherry Lee Linkon

2 Reconceiving class in contemporary working-class studies 32
Joseph Entin

3 Mediating stories of class borders: First-generation college students, digital storytelling, and social class 45
Jane A. Van Galen

4 The 'how to' of working-class studies: Selves, stories, and working across media 59
Christine J. Walley

PART II
Class and education **77**
Section introduction: Class and education **79**
Allison L. Hurst

5 Class Beyond the Classroom: Supporting working-class and first-generation students, faculty, and staff 91
Colby R. King and Sean H. McPherson

6 Working-class student experiences: Toward a social class-sensitive pedagogy for K–12 schools, teachers, and teacher educators 107
Colleen H. Clements and Mark D. Vagle

7 The pedagogy of class: Teaching working-class life and culture in the academy 118
Lisa A. Kirby

8 Being working class in the English classroom 130
Diane Reay

9 Getting schooled: Working-class students in higher education 141
Bettina Spencer

10 Learning our place: Social reproduction in K–12 schooling 151
Deborah M. Warnock

PART III
Work and community **161**
Section introduction: Work and community **163**
Tim Strangleman

11 Deindustrialization and its consequences 169
Steven High

12 Economic dislocation and trauma 180
Patrick Korte and Victor Tan Chen

13 Working-class studies, oral history and industrial illness 190
Arthur McIvor

14 Precarity's affects: The trauma of deindustrialization 201
Kathryn Marie Dudley

15 Feeling, re-imagined in common: Working with social haunting in the English coalfields 213
Geoff Bright

PART IV
Working-class cultures 225
Section introduction: Working-class cultures 227
Tim Strangleman

16 There is a genuine working-class culture 231
Jack Metzgar

17 Class, culture, and inequality 242
Jessi Streib

18 Post-traumatic lives: Precarious employment and invisible injury 252
Barbara Jensen

19 Activist class cultures 262
Betsy Leondar-Wright

20 The Australian working class in popular culture 274
Sarah Attfield

PART V
Representations 285
Section introduction: Representations of the working class 287
Michelle M. Tokarczyk

21 Writing Dubai: Indian labour migrants and taxi topographies 295
Christiane Schlote

22 The cinema of the precariat 313
Tom Zaniello

23 The 'body of labor' in U.S. postwar documentary photography: A working-class studies perspective 325
Carol Quirke

24 Mapping working-class art 343
Janet Zandy

25 'Things that are left out': Working-class writing and the idea of literature 359
Ben Clarke

26 Lit-grit: The gritty and the grim in working-class cultural production 371
Simon Lee

27 Mass incarceration, prison labor, prison writing 381
Nathaniel Heggins Bryant

28 Marketing millennial women: Embodied class performativity on American television 392
Jennifer H. Forsberg

PART VI
Activism and collective action 403
Section introduction: Activism and collective action 405
Scott Henkel

29 From stigma to solution: Centering the community college through activism in the classroom and the community 413
Karen Gaffney

30 Border crossing with day laborers and affordable housing activists 425
Terry Easton

31 Finding class in food justice efforts 442
Leslie Hossfeld, E. Brooke Kelly, and Julia F. Waity

32 The mutual determination of class and race in the United States: History and current implications 455
Michael Zweig

33 Documenting Lumbee working-class history: A service-learning approach 468
Michele Fazio

34 Precarious workers and social mobilization in Portuguese call centre assembly lines 480
Isabel Roque

35 Post-Fordist affect: Unions, the labor movement, and the weight of history 492
Joseph Varga

Conclusion 505
Michele Fazio, Christie Launius, and Tim Strangleman

Index *509*

Images

4.1 Charles William Walley, photograph by Chris Boebel 62
4.2 Image of lost industrial jobs used in the *Exit Zero* documentary, graphic by Sasha Goldberg 66
4.3 Baby shoes from the 1920s donated to the Southeast Chicago Historical Museum, photograph by Chris Boebel 70
4.4 Steelworkers union election, Local 1033, photograph courtesy of Southeast Chicago Historical Museum 71
14.1 Fire safety warning telling firefighters that there is nothing in the building to save 203
21.1 Dubai Gold Souq 299
21.2 Al Fahidi Street, Dubai 301
21.3 Sheikh Zayed Road, Dubai 304
21.4 Arabian Tea House, Dubai 305
23.1 Arthur Leipzig, 'Portrait of Axel Christiansen, 1955' 329
23.2 Arthur Leipzig, 'Daniél Dumouchel, 1953' 330
23.3 Arthur Leipzig, 'Dumouchel family, 1953' 331
23.4 Arthur Leipzig, 'Portrait of Axel Christiansen, inside the *Joan and Ursula*, 1955' 332
23.5 Arthur Leipzig, 'Work Portrait of Frenchy Maillet, 1955' 333
23.6 Arthur Leipzig, '*Joan and Ursula* Crew during Nor'easter, 1955' 334
23.7 Arthur Leipzig, 'Winter Storm on the Atlantic, 1955' 335
23.8 Dan Weiner, 'Willard Garvey, Head of Builders, Inc., Wichita Kansas,' 1952 337
23.9 Dan Weiner, 'Family Shopping for Modern Furniture, Brooklyn, Department Store,' 1952 338
30.1 Danny Solomon, Atlanta, Georgia, 2005 428
30.2 Dispatcher (right) talking to worker, 1988 429
30.3 Work secured at a street corner, Decatur, Georgia, 2005 431
30.4 Tisha Tallman (left) and Remedios Gomez Arnau (center) learn about day labor conditions, Sandy Springs, Georgia, 2005 432
30.5 Eva Villafañe, nonprofit hiring hall, Canton, Georgia, 2003 433
30.6 Marchers on the street, Doraville, Georgia, 2004 434
30.7 Imperial Hotel occupation with banner, Atlanta, Georgia, 1990 436
30.8 Supporters of the Imperial Hotel occupation, Atlanta, Georgia, 1990 437

Contributors

The editors

Michele Fazio is Professor of English and Coordinator of Gender Studies at the University of North Carolina at Pembroke where she teaches courses on American literature, contemporary US ethnic literature, and working-class studies. Her documentary film, *Voices of the Lumbee*, received the Studs Terkel Award for Media and Journalism and the North Carolina Folklore Society Brown-Hudson Award. She is a recipient of a BMI Woody Guthrie Research Fellowship and a Massachusetts Historical Society Fellowship to conduct research on her book project exploring the cultural legacy of Sacco and Vanzetti. Her research on family history, community, and memory has been exhibited at the Harvard Law School Library and the American Labor Museum. She has served as president of the Working-Class Studies Association and is currently a member of the editorial collective for the *Journal of Working-Class Studies*.

Christie Launius is Associate Professor and Head of the Gender, Women, and Sexuality Studies Department at Kansas State University. She has written extensively on narratives of upward class mobility achieved via education, and is co-author (with Holly Hassel) of the introductory women's and gender studies textbook *Threshold Concepts in Women's and Gender Studies: Ways of Seeing, Thinking, and Knowing*. She is a past president of the Working-Class Studies Association and serves as the book review editor of the *Journal of Working-Class Studies*.

Tim Strangleman is Professor of Sociology, in the School of Social Policy, Sociology and Social Research, SSPSSR, University of Kent, Canterbury, UK. He has researched and written widely on work identity, culture and meaning, traditional industries in decline and deindustrialization. He has a longstanding interest in working-class issues and was one of the founding members of the Working-Class Studies Association and one of the organization's past presidents. Tim is a historical sociologist who uses oral history and visual methods and approaches in his research. He has published articles in a range of journals including *Sociology*, *IJURR*, *Sociological Review* and *ILWCH*. He is the author of three books: *Work and Society: Sociological Approaches, Themes and Methods*, with Tracey Warren (Routledge); *Work Identity at the End of the Line? Privatisation and Culture Change in the UK Rail Industry*; and his new book, *Voices of Guinness: An Oral History of the Park Royal Brewery* (Oxford University Press, 2019).

The contributors

Sarah Attfield is a lecturer in communication in the Faculty of Arts and Social Sciences at the University of Technology Sydney, Australia. Sarah comes from a working-class background, and her work focuses on the representation of working-class people in the media, popular culture (film, TV, music), literature, and art. She has a book forthcoming from Palgrave, *Class on Screen: The Global Working Class in Contemporary Cinema*. Sarah is the co-founding editor of the *Journal of Working-Class Studies*.

Geoff Bright is a Research Fellow in the Education and Social Research Institute at Manchester Metropolitan University, UK. With a background as a rail union activist and community educator in the UK coalfields, his research focuses on the intersection of class, place, gender, and affect as it impacts on the political imagination of working-class communities. His most recent work uses a team of researchers/artists/activists and a repertoire of arts-based methods to carry out an original form of community co-research called 'working with social haunting'. This approach operates through a novel space called a 'Ghost Lab' to rearticulate heterodox historical narratives of collective resistance as a basis for re-imagining contemporary community futures. Dr. Bright is also an experimental musician, performance artist, and curator who is active in various projects and collectives in the north of England.

Nathaniel Heggins Bryant is Assistant Professor of English at California State University, Chico. He earned his PhD at the University of Pittsburgh, and he has published articles on the prison letters of George Jackson; the Soviet filmmaker Lev Kuleshov's adaptations of Jack London short stories; and the legal writing of the 1950s Death Row inmate Caryl Chessman. He regularly teaches courses on US and global prison writing, working-class literature, multicultural American literature and film, and science fiction. Outside of the classroom, he proudly serves as the chapter secretary of Chico State's California Faculty Association, the statewide faculty union; he helps coordinate the University Film Series; and he is on the steering committee of the Working-Class Studies Association. But, because life should not be defined entirely by one's labor, he also enjoys hiking, fishing, reading, watching films, playing video games, and, most importantly, being a new dad.

Victor Tan Chen is an assistant professor of sociology at Virginia Commonwealth University. He is the author of *Cut Loose: Jobless and Hopeless in an Unfair Economy* (University of California Press, 2015) and (with Katherine Newman) *The Missing Class: Portraits of the Near Poor in America* (Beacon Press, 2007), named by *Library Journal* as one of the Best Business Books of 2007. He received the 2017 Dunlop Outstanding Scholar Award from the Labor and Employment Relations Association. His work has been featured in *The Atlantic* and *The New York Times* as well as on NPR and BBC News. He also edits *In The Fray*, an award-winning magazine devoted to personal stories on global issues. With Katherine K. Chen, he is currently editing a forthcoming issue of the journal *Research in the Sociology of Organizations* focused on worker cooperatives and other collectivist-democratic alternatives to for-profit managerial firms.

Ben Clarke is Associate Professor of British Literature at the University of North Carolina, Greensboro. His research focuses on working-class writing, cultural studies, and the literature of the nineteen-thirties. He is the author of *Orwell in Context: Communities, Myths, Values* (Palgrave, 2007), co-author, with Michael Bailey and John K. Walton, of *Understanding Richard*

Hoggart: A Pedagogy of Hope (Blackwell, 2012), and co-editor, with Nick Hubble, of *Working-Class Writing: Theory and Practice* (Palgrave, 2018). He has published on authors including Jack Hilton, Edward Upward, Virginia Woolf, and H. G. Wells, and on subjects including the politics of literary experimentation, public houses, Englishness, the representation of mining communities, the idea of the public intellectual, and Western anthropological accounts of Taiwan.

Colleen H. Clements, PhD, is a lecturer in the Department of Curriculum and Instruction at the University of Minnesota. Dr. Clements' research focuses on social class and racialized identity and critical examination of the social foundations of education. Her scholarly work primarily concerns a critical examination of idealized white femininity as a racialized identity in white, hetero-normative, patriarchal US society and its relation to teaching in both formal and informal learning spaces. In much of her work, she draws on her background in theater, using performance studies in her inquiry to examine the cultural and social role of dominant and counter-narratives in shaping human experience.

Kathryn Marie Dudley is Professor of Anthropology and American Studies at Yale University. Her research focuses on regimes of labor that are marginalized by transformations in global capitalism. She is the author of *The End of the Line: Lost Jobs, New Lives in Postindustrial America*; *Debt and Dispossession: Farm Loss in America's Heartland*; and *Guitar Makers: The Endurance of Artisanal Values in North America*. She is a recipient of the Margaret Mead Award of the American Anthropological Association and the Society for Applied Anthropology, which recognizes ethnographic writing that reaches broadly concerned publics.

Terry Easton, former president of the Working-Class Studies Association, is Associate Professor of English at the University of North Georgia, where he teaches courses on multicultural, Appalachian, and working-class literature. His publications include essays on coal miners, deaf workers, and working-class literature pedagogy. In 2018, he was awarded a Faculty Undergraduate Summer Engagement Grant that resulted in a co-authored essay with an undergraduate student on Sherman Alexie's novel *Reservation Blues* that was published in an Indigenous Special Issue of *The Journal of Working-Class Studies*. His 2016 book, *Raising Our Voices, Breaking the Chain: The Imperial Hotel Occupation as Prophetic Politics*, documents struggles for affordable housing development in Atlanta since 1990. His dissertation on day laborers in Atlanta received the 2007 Constance Coiner Dissertation Award of the Working-Class Studies Association (*Temporary Work, Contingent Lives: Race, Immigration, and Transformations of Atlanta's Daily Work, Daily Pay*). His current research project explores music in Appalachian coal mining novels and films.

Joseph Entin teaches English and American Studies at Brooklyn College, City University of New York. He is author of *Sensational Modernism: Experimental Fiction and Photography in Thirties America* (2007) and co-editor, with Sara Blair and Franny Nudelman, of *Remaking Reality: U.S. Documentary Culture after 1945* (2018) and, with Leonard Vogt and Robert Rosen, of *Controversies in the Classroom: A Radical Teacher Reader* (2008). His current book projects include 'Living Labor: U.S. Fiction and Film after Fordism' (under contract, Class: Culture series, University of Michigan Press) and an anthology, co-edited with Elizabeth Duclos-Orsello and Rebecca Hill, on teaching American Studies.

Jennifer H. Forsberg earned her PhD in American literature from the University of Nevada, Reno, and is a lecturer at Clemson University, where she teaches American literature, business writing, and a graduate course in writing across the curriculum. Forsberg's research explores performativity, American identity, and the aesthetics of poverty in American literature and culture. Her work includes studies on hobo performativity in twentieth-century American narratives and, at present, examines class performativity as it modulates visibility across popular culture and visual art into the post-medium era. This work, of which her study of millennial women on television is a part, traces the forceful ideologies that reify hegemonic subject-positions in the cultural marketplace, continuing the work she has published in *Persona Studies*, the *Journal of Popular Culture*, and the *Journal of Working-Class Studies*.

Karen Gaffney, PhD, is an English professor at Raritan Valley Community College in New Jersey. She is the author of *Dismantling the Racism Machine: A Manual and Toolbox* (Routledge 2018), an accessible introduction to race and racism with tools for action. She addresses anti-racism through community workshops and organizations, her blog *Divided No Longer* (www.dividednolonger.com), and her role as a Public Scholar for the New Jersey Council for the Humanities. Karen has presented her work at academic and activist conferences alike, including the Working-Class Studies Association, the National Conference on Race and Ethnicity in American Higher Education, and the White Privilege Conference.

Scott Henkel is Associate Professor of English and African American and Diaspora Studies and Director of the Wyoming Institute for Humanities Research at the University of Wyoming. He received a PhD from Michigan State University and while there was the president of the Graduate Employees Union from 2002–2004. He is the past-president of the Working-Class Studies Association. His book, *Direct Democracy: Collective Power, the Swarm, and the Literatures of the Americas*, was published in 2017 in the Caribbean Studies Series by the University Press of Mississippi, and was the recipient of the Working-Class Studies Association's 2018 C. L. R James Award for Best Published Book for Academic or General Audiences.

Steven High is Professor of History at Concordia University's Centre for Oral History and Digital Storytelling. He is an interdisciplinary oral and public historian with a strong interest in transnational approaches to working-class studies, forced migration, and community-engaged research. He has published extensively on the deindustrialization of North America, including *Industrial Sunset* (2003), *Corporate Wasteland* (with David Lewis, 2007), *The Deindustrialized World* (with Lachlan Mackinnon and Andrew Perchard, 2017), and *One Job Town* (2018). He is currently leading a partnership project examining the relationship between deindustrialization and the rise of right-wing populism in Western Europe and North America.

Leslie Hossfeld, PhD, is trained in rural sociology from North Carolina State University. She has extensive experience examining rural poverty and economic restructuring and has made two presentations to the United States Congress and one to the North Carolina legislature on job loss and rural economic decline. Hossfeld was founding Director of the Mississippi Food Insecurity Project and serves on the US Department of Agriculture's Southern Extension Research Activity project to strengthen local and regional food needs and priorities in 13 Southern region states. Her current research focuses on multidisciplinary strategies and collaborative partnerships to understand and alleviate persistent poverty in the southeast, working to link US local food systems research and initiatives to nutrition, malnutrition (obesity), health outcomes, and health disparities in order to develop policy coherence that links health and agriculture policy. Hossfeld is Dean of the College of Behavioral, Social and Health Sciences at Clemson University.

Allison L. Hurst has been a proud member of the Working-Class Studies Association for many years and is currently serving as its current President (2020–21). She is Associate Professor of Sociology at Oregon State University, where she teaches courses on theory, qualitative research methods, and class and inequality. Her publications include *The Burden of Academic Success: Loyalists, Renegades and Double Agents* (2010), *College and the Working Class* (2012), *Working in Class: Recognizing How Social Class Shapes Our Academic Work* (2016, co-editor with Sandi Nenga), and *Amplified Advantage: Going to a 'Good' School in an Era of Inequality* (2019). She was one of the founders of the Association of Working-Class Academics, an organization composed of college faculty and staff who were the first in their families to graduate from college, for which she also served as president from 2008 to 2014. She also serves on the American Sociological Association Taskforce on First-Generation and Working-Class Persons in Sociology.

Barbara Jensen is a counseling and community psychologist in private practice in Minneapolis. She has worked and taught in a wide range of settings, including schools, homeless shelters, psychiatric residences, colleges, prisons, and mental health clinics, as well doing training and consultation for independent groups of therapists and the Minnesota Department of Health and Human Services. She has developed and taught a number of courses at Metropolitan State University, including Community Psychology, Working in America, and Psychology of Women. She helped found and is a past president of the Working-Class Studies Association, and she co-chaired its first annual conference in 2007 at Macalester College. She wrote *Reading Classes: On Culture and Classism in America*, published in 2012 by Cornell University Press.

E. Brooke Kelly is Professor of Sociology and Assistant Chair at the University of North Carolina at Pembroke, where she works on community-based research projects, often with students, to address food insecurity, poverty, and awareness about the circumstances of farmworkers. Through the Southeastern Consortium on Hunger, Poverty, and Nutrition, she is collaborating with others across the region to investigate and address food insecurity on college campuses. She has chaired the Southern Sociological Society's Committee on Sociological Practice, the Society for the Study of Social Problem's (SSSP) Poverty, Class, and Inequality Division, and SSSP's Program Committee. Dr. Kelly has also served as a fellow and research affiliate of the Rural Policy Research Institute's Rural Poverty Center. At Michigan State University, where she received her doctorate, she worked on a multi-state longitudinal study on the well-being of rural, low-income families with a state sample comprised of farmworkers. Her research and teaching continues to focus on inequalities, with a more recent focus on food and poverty.

Colby R. King teaches and studies social inequality and social class, urban sociology, work, and strategies for supporting working-class and first-generation college students. He is currently serving as Secretary of the Working-Class Studies Association and is a member of the American Sociological Association's Task Force on First-Generation and Working-Class People in Sociology. He is a co-principle investigator for the SEISMIC grant program at Bridgewater State University, funded by the National Science Foundation's S-STEM program (NSF-DUE 1643475). Dr. King has published research on post-recession shifts in occupational structures in the Pittsburgh and Detroit metropolitan regions, the geography and demographics of the working class, as well as DIY place branding in deindustrialized cities, and efforts to support development of students' social and cultural capital. He is also a regular contributor to the *Everyday Sociology* blog.

Lisa A. Kirby is Professor of English and Director of The Texas Center for Working-Class Studies at Collin College, where she teaches writing and American literature. Dr. Kirby completed her PhD in English at Texas Christian University. Her research areas include working-class studies, twentieth-century American literature, and the rhetoric of disaster. Along with Dr. Laura Hapke, she is co-editor of *A Class of Its Own: Re-envisioning American Labor Fiction* (Cambridge Scholars Publishing, 2008). Her work has also appeared in *Women's Studies: An Interdisciplinary Journal, Philip Roth Studies, The Journal of Popular Culture, Academic Exchange Quarterly*, and *Race, Gender, and Class*.

Patrick Korte is a graduate student of sociology and education at Virginia Commonwealth University and a rank-and-file education worker organizer.

Simon Lee is Assistant Professor of English at Texas State University. He specializes in working-class writing, specifically representations of working-class life in twentieth- and twenty-first-century British cultural production. He has published on authors such as John Osborne, Alan Sillitoe, Shelagh Delaney, Nell Dunn, and Colin MacInnes. His current research centers on the intersection of space and class in post-World War II British fiction and the impact of cultural production on articulations of working-class identities. In addition to appearing in a number of journals and anthologies on working-class writing, he is also a contributor for *The Los Angeles Review of Books*. Originally from the North East of England, he now splits his time between Austin and Los Angeles.

Betsy Leondar-Wright, PhD, is a long-time activist for economic justice. She teaches sociology at Lasell University. She authored *Missing Class: Strengthening Social Movement Groups by Seeing Class Cultures* (Cornell University Press, 2014) and *Class Matters: Cross-Class Alliance Building for Middle-Class Activists* (New Society Publishers, 2004), and co-authored *The Color of Wealth: The Story Behind the US Racial Wealth Divide* (The New Press, 2006).

Sherry Lee Linkon is a Professor of English and Director of the Writing Program and the American Studies Program at Georgetown University. Trained in American Studies, her research and teaching cover a wide range of fields, including American literature and culture, interdisciplinary teaching and learning, working-class studies, and writing studies. From 1997 to 2012, she was Co-Director of the Center for Working-Class Studies at Youngstown State University, where she also directed the American Studies Program. With John Russo, she co-authored *Steeltown USA: Work and Memory in Youngstown* (University Press of Kansas, 2002) and co-edited *New Working-Class Studies* (Cornell, 2005). Her latest book, *The Half-Life of Deindustrialization: Working-Class Writing about Economic Restructuring* (University of Michigan Press, 2018), examines contemporary writing that reflects the continuing effects of deindustrialization on ideas about work, place, and working-class culture. She was the founding president of the Working-Class Studies Association and editor of the *Working-Class Perspectives* blog.

Arthur McIvor is a labor and oral historian. He is Professor of Social History at the University of Strathclyde in Glasgow, Scotland, and Director of the Scottish Oral History Centre (SOHC) which he co-founded in 1995. He was brought up in a working-class community in Coventry, England, and his father worked on the assembly line at the Standard Triumph/British Leyland car factory in Coventry most of his life. His research interests lie in the history of work, occupational health and industrial heritage, and he has published widely in these areas, frequently deploying an oral history research methodology, including *Organised Capital* (Cambridge University Press, 1996), *A History of Work in Britain, 1880–1950* (Palgrave, 2000), *Lethal Work* (with Ronald Johnston; Tuckwell Press, 2000) and *Miners' Lung* (with Ronald Johnston; Ashgate, 2007). His most recent books are *Working Lives* (Palgrave, 2013) and *Men in Reserve* (with Juliette Pattinson and Linsey Robb; Manchester University Press, 2017). He is currently investigating the impacts of deindustrialization on health and well-being.

Sean H. McPherson teaches courses in global art and architectural history with a focus on the material and visual culture of Asia and the Asian diaspora in North America. His research explores Japanese popular religious art and architecture of the Edo through modern periods, Asian-American vernacular cultural landscapes, first-generation and working-class access to higher education, and issues of class, gender, and racial-ethnic diversity within the architectural profession. Dr. McPherson is a Fulbright Doctoral Dissertation Research Abroad grantee, recipient of a Gateways Grant from the Massachusetts Board of Higher Education for globalizing introductory art history surveys, a Global Architectural History Teaching Collaborative Grant to create an integrated history of East Asian Architecture, and a Korea Foundation grant for the introduction of Korean Language Studies at Bridgewater State University. He is a member of the Class Cultures Caucus of the Working-Class Studies Association, for which he has also served as a judge for the Studs Terkel and C. L. R. James Book Awards.

Jack Metzgar is Emeritus Professor of Humanities at Roosevelt University in Chicago. Jack was the founding Editor of *Labor Research Review*, and he was Director of Roosevelt's Labor Leadership Program, which is now at DePaul University. Over the years he has published numerous articles in both scholarly publications like *Labor Studies Journal*, *New Labor Forum*, and *Working USA* and in progressive political journals like *The Nation*, *Dissent*, and *In These Times*. He is the author of *Striking Steel: Solidarity Remembered* (Temple University Press, 2000)—in part a memoir of growing up in a steelworker family in the 1950s, in part a history of the 1959 steel strike. More recently, Jack was one of the organizers of the Chicago Center for Working-Class Studies, and he is a past president of the Working-Class Studies Association. He is a regular contributor to the *Working-Class Perspectives* blog.

Carol Quirke is Professor of American Studies at SUNY Old Westbury. Her historical scholarship focuses on photography and social movements; she investigates the political stakes of visual representation. She is currently exploring postwar representations of work, for which she interviewed Arthur Leipzig and Bill Owens, and has been awarded a grant from the Radcliffe Institute's Schlesinger Library to study photojournalist Bettye Lane as part of that project. Oxford University Press published her first book, *Eyes on Labor: News Photography and America's Working Class*, in 2012. Her *Dorothea Lange, Documentary Photography and Twentieth Century America: Reinventing Self and Nation* came out with Routledge in 2019. Her essays have appeared in the *American Quarterly*, the *Radical History Review*, and *History Now*, and her critical reviews in *Reviews in American History*, and *Labor Online*. Quirke is a former community organizer, working on public housing, immigrant rights, anti-racism efforts, and gender inequality.

Diane Reay grew up in a working class, coal mining community before becoming an inner city, primary school teacher for 20 years. She is now Visiting Professor at the LSE and Emeritus Professor of Sociology of Education at the University of Cambridge. Her main research interests are social justice issues in education and cultural analyses of social class, race and gender. She has researched extensively in the areas of social class, gender, and ethnicity across primary, secondary, and post-compulsory stages of education. She is author of *Miseducation: Inequality, Education and the Working Classes*, published by Policy Press in 2017.

Isabel Roque is a researcher at the Centre for Social Studies in the Project EmployALL and a member of the research group on Science, Economics and Society. She is also a social activist and a PhD candidate, completing her thesis in Sociology—*Labor Relations, Social Inequalities and Trade Unionism*—at the Faculty of Economics, Coimbra University, Portugal. Her research interests are involved with call and contact centers, digital labor, precarity, health and safety at work, psycho-social risks at work, social protest movements, trade unionism, and social inequalities.

Christiane Schlote teaches drama and postcolonial literatures and cultures at the University of Basel, Switzerland. She has published extensively on postcolonial and transnational theories and cultures (especially South Asia, Africa and the Middle East), contemporary British and Anglophone drama, war and commemoration, migration and refugee discourses, petrofiction, postcolonial cityscapes, and Latina/o American and Asian American culture. She is the author of *Bridging Cultures: Latino- und asiatisch-amerikanisches Theater in New York* (1997) and co-editor of *New Beginnings in Twentieth-Century Theatre and Drama* (with Peter Zenzinger, 2003), *Constructing Media Reality: The New Documentarism* (with Eckart Voigts-Virchow, 2008), and *Representations of War, Migration and Refugeehood: Interdisciplinary Perspectives* (with Daniel Rellstab, 2015). Current research projects include Anglophone literatures and human rights, in particular, literary and cultural representations of humanitarian aid, global working-class studies and British imperialism and the Edwardian era.

Bettina Spencer received her PhD in Social Psychology from the New School for Social Research and is currently an Associate Professor of Psychology and Chair of the Department of Psychological Sciences at Saint Mary's College, Notre Dame. She teaches courses in social psychology, cultural psychology, research methods, stereotyping and prejudice, and the psychology of violence. Her main research investigates issues of stereotyping and prejudice as they relate to low-income individuals. Specifically, she has examined the academic underperformance of low-income college students in testing situations, as well as perceptions of low-income women in the court system. She serves as the Education Chair of the American Psychological Association's Committee on Socioeconomic Status.

Jessi Streib is an Assistant Professor of Sociology at Duke University. Her research uncovers mechanisms and builds theories about how social class inequality is experienced, reproduced, and alleviated. She has written two books, *The Power of the Past: Understanding Cross-Class Marriages* (Oxford University Press, 2014) and *Privilege Lost: Who Leaves the Upper Middle Class and How They Fall* (Oxford University Press, 2020).

Michelle M. Tokarczyk is professor emerita of English and an emerita affiliate of Women's, Gender, and Sexuality Studies at Goucher College. She is the author of the critical works *Class Definitions: On the Lives and Writings of Maxine Hong Kingston, Sandra Cisneros, and Dorothy Allison* and *E. L. Doctorow's Skeptical Commitment*; and the poetry books *Bronx Migrations* and *The House I'm Running From*. Additionally, she edited *Critical Approaches to American Working-Class Literature* and *Working-Class Women in the Academy: Laborers in the Knowledge Factory*, which received the Susan Koppelman Award for Best Anthologies. Her article 'Toward an imagined solidarity in the working-class epic' received the 2014 Working-Class Studies Association's John Russo and Sherry Linkon Award for Best Academic Article. Tokarczyk has served as president of the Working-Class Studies Association and of the Northeast Modern Language Association. She lives and works in New York City.

Mark D. Vagle, PhD, is a professor in the Department of Curriculum and Instruction at the University of Minnesota and a former elementary and middle school teacher and administrator. Dr. Vagle is author of over 75 books, articles, book chapters, blogs, interviews, and invited lectures about powerful teaching philosophies and practices. His most current research examines the profound influence social class has on the ways in which teachers and students perceive (and engage with) one another and how particular social class-sensitive pedagogies can be enacted in classrooms.

Jane A. Van Galen is Professor Emeritus of Education at the University of Washington Bothell. Her teaching and research focus on social class and social mobility through education. Most recently, she has focused on ways in which new forms of participatory digital media enable the inclusion of more voices in deliberations about civic and cultural life. She is co-editor of two books on class, mobility, and education: *Trajectories: The Educational and Social Mobility of Education Scholars from Poor and Working Class Background* (Sense Publishers, 2009) and *Late to Class: Schooling and Social Class in the New Economy* (State University of New York Press, 2007). She also edits a book series for Sense Publishers: Mobility Studies in Education, and she is the facilitator of the First In Our Families project, in which first-generation college students create and share digital stories of being First.

Joseph Varga is Associate Professor of Labor Studies at Indiana University-Bloomington, where he has taught courses in the Department of Labor Studies since 2009. He is a former Teamster rank-and-file radical and a long-time labor movement activist. He currently teaches courses on US labor history, globalization, and the role of workers in US society. He has published work on urban and labor geography, 'right to work' laws, the decline of union power, and the rise of precarious labor. He is currently finishing a book on the changing political culture among the working class in the Midwest, tentatively titled 'Breaking the Heartland: Work and Precarity in South Central Indiana', and has just commenced a new research project on queer labor and the coal industry in the US and UK. He lives in beautiful Bloomington, Indiana, with his long-time partner and their five lovely cats.

Julia F. Waity is an Associate Professor of Sociology at the University of North Carolina Wilmington. Dr. Waity's research focuses on poverty, food insecurity and spatial inequality. She has presented her work at the American Sociological Association, the Society for the Study of Social Problems, the Southern Sociological Society, and the Research Innovation and Development Grants in Economics (RIDGE) Conference. She has received funding for her research from Indiana University, where she earned her PhD, the University of North Carolina Wilmington, the American Sociological Association, and the Southern Rural Development Center RIDGE Center for Targeted Studies. Her current research examines college food insecurity. Dr. Waity has experience teaching courses related to her research interests, including Sociology of Poverty, Social Problems, Public Sociology, The Community, Research Methods, and Introduction to Sociology.

Christine J. Walley is Professor of Anthropology at the Massachusetts Institute of Technology. In addition to an early book, *Rough Waters: Nature and Development in an East African Marine Park* (Princeton University Press, 2004), she is the author of *Exit Zero: Family and Class in*

Post-Industrial Chicago (University of Chicago Press, 2013). Walley and filmmaker Chris Boebel are the creators of a companion documentary film, *Exit Zero: An Industrial Family Story* (2017). They are currently collaborating with the Southeast Chicago Historical Museum on an online archive and storytelling site. The Exit Zero Project uses family stories from a declining steel mill region to explore the long-term impacts of deindustrialization and the transformation in what it means to be 'working class' in the United States.

Deborah M. Warnock is Sociology faculty at Bennington College. She holds a PhD in Sociology from the University of Washington and a BA in Psychology and German Studies from Vassar College. Her sociological imagination was awakened during her undergraduate education, where her experiences were indelibly shaped by her working-class background. Her scholarship, which has appeared in *Journal of Diversity in Higher Education*, *Journal of College Student Development*, *The Journal of Working-Class Studies*, and *Innovative Higher Education*, focuses on access to, and experiences of, higher education for underrepresented students, particularly students from working-class backgrounds. She co-founded Bennington College's FLoW (First-Generation, Low-Income, or Working-Class) Initiative, which seeks to raise awareness of social class diversity, identify and reduce classism in campus policies, and provide a community of support for FLoW students. She has provided guidance to multiple colleges and universities that seek to build and grow their own programs for first-generation, low-income, and working-class students.

Janet Zandy, emerita professor, Rochester Institute of Technology, is the author of *Hands: Physical Labor, Class, and Cultural Work* and editor of *Calling Home: Working-Class Women's Writings*; *Liberating Memory: Our Work and Our Working-Class Consciousness*; *What We Hold In Common: An Introduction to Working-Class Studies*; and co-editor (with Nicholas Coles) of the *Oxford Anthology of American Working-Class Literature*. Her latest book is *Unfinished Stories: The Narrative Photography of Hansel Mieth and Marion Palfi*. Her essay, 'Seeing Dirt, Seeing Beyond Dirt: Photographs by and about Workers,' received the Society for Photographic Education Conference Award for Excellence in Historical, Critical and Theoretical Writing. She was general editor of *Women's Studies Quarterly* from 1997 to 2001. She is a practicing artist, specializing in encaustics.

Tom Zaniello directed the Honors Program and taught film studies at Northern Kentucky University; he has also been an adjunct professor at the University of Maryland and the National Labor College of the AFL-CIO. He has been a film programmer on labor and other topics for film festivals in Washington DC, London, and Liverpool. He has published three guidebooks to labor films: *Working Stiffs, Union Maids, Reds, and Riffraff: An Expanded Guide to Films about Labor* (2nd edition), *The Cinema of Globalization: A Guide to Films about the New Economic Order*, and *The Cinema of the Precariat: The Exploited, Underemployed, and Temp Workers of the World*. His research into a corrupt criminal investigation at Stanford University and Palo Alto led to the publication of *California's Lamson Murder Mystery: The Depression-Era Case that Divided Santa Clara County*. His latest book, *Saints and Sinners in Queen Victoria's Courts* will be published in 2021. He is currently completing a 'psycho-cinematic biography' of Alfred Hitchcock.

Michael Zweig is emeritus professor of economics and founding director of the Center for Study of Working-Class Life at the State University of New York at Stony Brook, where he received the SUNY Chancellor's Award for Excellence in Teaching. He earned his PhD in economics in 1967 from the University of Michigan, where he was a founding member of Students for a Democratic Society and the Union for Radical Political Economics. Professor Zweig's books include *The Working Class Majority: America's Best Kept Secret*, *What's Class Got to Do with It: American Society in the Twenty-first Century*, and *Religion and Economic Justice*. He has a long history of social activism combined with scholarly work and has published widely in professional and general circulation journals. In 2014 Professor Zweig received the Working-Class Studies Association award for lifetime contributions to the field of working-class studies.

Acknowledgments

The idea for this project emerged from an early evening conversation in a bar in Madison, Wisconsin, during the 2013 Working-Class Studies Association conference. All three of us were conscious of the need to continue developing the field through a book that would showcase its work. This *Handbook* is the product of that conversation developed over the years in combination with many, many people.

First and foremost, we would like to acknowledge everyone who has organized, presented at, and attended Working-Class Studies Association events and conferences over the years, especially activists and organizers. The rich conversations during panel sessions, keynotes, in workshops, and at the bar inspired us to pursue this project, and they also spurred the field to move in critical new directions. We are grateful for the community of scholars, activists, and editors at presses who have dedicated their time and energy to the field, many since its inception. We are also grateful for the friendships we have developed.

To the pioneers of the field—Paul Lauter, Janet Zandy, Renny Christopher, Michelle Tokarczyk, Michael Zweig, Sherry Linkon, John Russo, and many others—we thank them for their expertise and support over the years.

We would especially like to acknowledge Jack Metzgar's imprint on this project. Without his unwavering belief in and support for this project, it might never have gotten off the ground. We have benefited immensely from his input.

Michele would like to thank Pamela Annas for introducing her to working-class literature as a graduate student at the University of Massachusetts at Boston and for suggesting that she attend the working-class studies conference at Youngstown State University. She is grateful to members of her family for their support as she worked on this project, especially Angelina, Sandra, Marlene, Michael, and Dan, the music maker. She would also like to thank her students for continuing to inspire her to confront class in the classroom. This book is for them.

Christie would like to acknowledge the institutional support of the Faculty Development program at the University of Wisconsin Oshkosh for granting her a sabbatical leave during the Fall 2017 semester, which allowed her to focus on this project. She would also like to thank her colleague Susan Rensing for taking over administrative duties as Director of the Women's and Gender Studies program during her sabbatical leave. Thanks go as well to her spouse and fellow traveler, Susan Rensing, for all the support and forbearance over the life of this project.

Tim would like to thank his colleagues at Kent for supporting running the Working-Class Studies Conference in Kent in September 2019; this gave added momentum to this project and illustrated its relevance internationally. In particular he would like to thank Sophie Rowland, Emma Pleasance, Triona Fitton, and especially David Nettleingham. Tim would also like to thank his family for their support—Claudia, Max, and Maddy.

We dedicate this volume to Felice Yeskel, Pepi Leistyna, and John Crawford, as well as to workers past and present in the struggle.

Introduction

Michele Fazio, Christie Launius, and Tim Strangleman

In 2013, the Working-Class Studies Association (WCSA), in conjunction with the Labor and Working Class Studies Project, met in Madison, Wisconsin (US)—the site of the 2011 Wisconsin Uprising—to present a joint conference and summit, Fighting Forward, in part to recognize the ongoing protests and activism against the state's plan to erode collective bargaining rights for public employees. Amid a rich program that explored the future of the labor movement, working-class solidarity and activism, and representations of class from across academic disciplines, folks from around the globe gathered, as one plenary session put it, not to mourn, but to organize. And so kindled the spark for this project, originating out of a spirited discussion among three working-class studies scholars who, not entirely coincidentally, would begin respective three-year terms as president-elect, president, and past president of the WCSA that year; first Christie, then Tim, and finally Michele.

In many ways, this project is an extension of our leadership roles in the organization; as such, it is both an intellectual project and an organizing project. Put differently, it represents our effort to build the field of working-class studies both by contributing to its published scholarship and by strengthening connections and relationships among its practitioners. In this volume, we not only present our vision of and for the field, but also bring together the work of colleagues we have gotten to know through our annual conferences along with many who submitted their work in response to the call for papers we circulated widely in 2017. In what follows, we briefly sketch out the origins and intellectual history of the field and the logistical and organizational milestones of its institutionalization before providing an overview of the volume's contents.

Why working-class studies?

German sociologist Ulrich Beck famously talked about class as one of his 'zombie' categories (2002). These were ideas and concepts that had no place in the modern, or should that be postmodern world. According to Beck, zombie concepts were kept alive but served no useful purpose: the living dead. Beck was writing in the wake of the fall of the Berlin Wall and the collapse of the communist system that had dominated Central and Eastern Europe since the end of the Second World War and the USSR since the end of the First. As politicians, journalists, and academics scrambled to make sense of the world they found themselves in, they saw class as rooted in that old order; a set of understandings as redundant as the wall itself. But just as these proclamations were being made, class analysis began to make a remarkable comeback; it even became, thanks to the application of French sociologist Pierre Bourdieu and his ideas of habitus and a variety of 'capitals', fashionable. The recession of 2007/08 and the age of austerity it engendered, as well as the Brexit vote, the election of Donald Trump, and other political developments, further made class and questions of class inequality timely and relevant.

Class, then, is back and, with it, attention to the working class. But why a field called working-class studies, and what does that field do? Working-class studies, in some respects, has had a long gestation period, or to frame it as Michele and Christie did in a roundtable they helped organize for the 2018 American Studies Association, the field has been in emergence for the past few decades. We can see intimations to it in the History Workshop movement in the UK, in the interest in so-called history from below, or peoples' history, which finds echoes as far back as the 1930s. We can see its seeds in liberation struggles of the past fifty years: civil rights and Black Power, second-wave feminism and the struggle for LGBTQ rights. And as John Russo and Sherry Linkon establish and trace out in detail in the introduction to their 2005 volume, *New Working-Class Studies*, the field has intellectual origins in labor studies, labor history, American studies, and British cultural studies, and in the work of key people in the fields of literary studies and composition, geography, sociology, anthropology, and economics. As a field, working-class studies began to coalesce during the 1990s, in part as a reaction to the kind of 'new world' globalization rhetoric espoused by neoliberals, but crucially as a reaction to the collapse of basic traditional industries in the Western economies such as the US, Canada, the UK and Western Europe. This process of industrial change had been occurring since the 1950s if not before, but was hidden by full employment and benign welfare regimes. From the mid-1970s onwards, the speed of job loss and factory closure accelerated to the point where US economists Barry Bluestone and Bennett Harrison could talk about the 'deindustrialization of America' in their 1984 volume of the same title. As they were quick to point out, this wave of closures was not accidental, but a planned attempt to move productive capacity away from the heartland to regions with a lower cost base. Crucially, Bluestone and Harrison stressed the need to blend economic analysis with detailed attention to the communities and families made obsolete by change.

The field of working-class studies also emerged out of a concern with those negatively impacted by these changes and with a sense of mission to find value in working-class culture more broadly. To some politicians and academics, working-class culture was either an oxymoron or, at best, a deficit culture. By contrast, those in working-class studies recognized value in everyday working-class life, in the culture of the factory, home, and community. In a sense this attention was made more urgent by the loss of huge swaths of industry and company towns that were supported by, and in turn supported, the economy now disappearing. In its beginnings, working-class studies could be seen as an attempt to find value at a point of loss, to memorialize that which was being eroded or already disappeared. While this strain continues, subsequent developments in the field have attempted to capture and theorize what is emerging in the aftermath of deindustrialization. The rapidly changing nature of work itself as seen with the increase of service industry jobs, migrant labor, and the gig economy, especially in today's digital world, points to the further decline of dignity and security in the workplace.

Working-class studies, then, originated at a time of crisis and insecurity for the working class, after a period where many working-class people had enjoyed both a measure of security and real and sustained wage growth over a thirty-year period from the 1940s through the 1970s. Of course, not all groups benefited equally from the 'Glorious 30', as it is sometimes called, and it was not coincidental that social movements for greater rights and freedom from (imperialist, racist, sexist, homophobic, etc.) oppression emerged during the latter part of those decades. The field, then, appeared at a fault line where the economic and political changes which had begun in earnest during the 1970s were becoming increasingly apparent, and the time elapsed had allowed a measure of critical distance by which unfolding events could be judged with some degree of perspective.

Starting in 1995, at a number of conferences and meetings based around the Center for Working-Class Studies at Youngstown State University, John Russo, Sherry Linkon, and a number of their colleagues built a community that reached out across multiple disciplines and fields and crucially beyond academia to artists, photographers, poets, activists, writers, and journalists, each with an interest in working-class culture beyond their particular silo and audiences. The conferences at Youngstown, at SUNY Stony Brook on Long Island, New York (starting in 2000), and in other locations in the Midwest and northeast US, have been crucial to building the field. In the UK, a group of academics including Tim, won funding from the Economic and Social Research Council for a high-profile seminar series, Spaces of Working Class Life, in 2003, which brought together in an interdisciplinary forum many of those in the field in the UK and beyond. The WCSA conference returned to the UK in 2019, hosted by the University of Kent in Canterbury; highlights included keynote addresses by Satnam Virdee, author of *Racism, Class, and the Racialized Outsider* (2014), and Diane Reay, author of *Miseducation: Inequality, Education, and the Working Classes* (2017).

At WCSA conferences, panels might include sociologists and historians alongside filmmakers and artists. Memorable sessions have included a laid-off steel worker reflecting on losing his job days before he would have made pension and a woman master electrician recounting the horrific sexism of her local and workmates. We have also heard from scholars and activists engaging in topics ranging from queer comics, environmental justice, healthcare, international union organizing, racial inequality, and many others. Conference programs dating back to 2001 have been archived and posted to the WCSA website, and, together, they provide a record of this vital, ongoing outlet for intellectual, creative, and activist work within the field.

Special journal issues and a number of anthologies began to appear in the mid-1990s, which can be seen as attempts to gather together some of the work starting to be produced, including a special issue of *Women's Studies Quarterly* in 1995, edited by Janet Zandy, that later morphed into *What We Hold In Common: An Introduction to Working-Class Studies* (2001), and another *Women's Studies Quarterly* issue in 1998 entitled 'Working Class Lives and Cultures' (edited by Christopher, Orr and Strom). Other notable edited collections include Michelle Tokarczyk and Elizabeth Fay's *Working-Class Women in the Academy: Laborers in the Knowledge Factory* (1993), Zandy's *Liberating Memory: Our Work and Our Working-Class Consciousness* (1994), Sherry Linkon's *Teaching Working Class* (1999), Michael Zweig's *What's Class Got to Do With It?* (2004), and Russo and Linkon's *New Working-Class Studies* (2005).

In addition, many single-authored books also appeared, some based in single disciplines and others crossing disciplinary boundaries. Many of these books lever off others, with a real sense of dialogue between them. Paired titles such as Janet Zandy's *Hands* (2004) and John Lennon and Magnus Nilsson's *Working-Class Literature(s): Historical and International Perspectives* (2017), Jack Metzgar's *Striking Steel* (2000) and Christine Walley's *Exit Zero* (2013), Betsy Leondar-Wright's *Missing Class* (2014) and Jeff Torlina's *Working Class* (2011), and Kathryn Dudley's *The End of the Line* (1994) and Steven High's *Industrial Sunset* (2003), to name but a few examples, have all helped to develop and build a significant body of work about class issues. These books come out of disciplines as diverse as literary studies, psychology, anthropology, social and labor history, politics, and business. Often these books rely in part on autoethnography, the authors drawing heavily on the experience of their family, friends, or themselves; this is, as Sherry Linkon observes in her excellent essay in this collection, one of the signature genres of the field—the ability, the need, to reflect on one's own experience to explore wider issues of class experience.

The field was further institutionalized by the launch of the WCSA in 2005 and by the creation in 2016 of the first online journal in the field, the *Journal of Working-Class Studies*, which currently publishes biannually. In addition, although not formally connected to the Association, the blog *Working-Class Perspectives* offers a weekly insight into an incredibly wide variety of working-class issues. As a field, working-class studies has somewhat fuzzy and porous boundaries, not unusual perhaps for an interdisciplinary field that strives to extend its boundaries beyond academia. The fuzziness and porosity certainly also relates to the history of its emergence, sketched above; without a dedicated journal until 2016, there was not a central, identifiable space for its knowledge production. Instead, key scholarship in the field has appeared in scattered disciplinary journals, authored both by people who have an explicit connection to and identification with the field as well as those who do not, but might have if there had been a journal. The field is small if measured solely by membership in its association, the WCSA, but larger if defined by participation in its conferences and larger still if one claims people teaching and/or writing about working-class people, their work, communities, politics, and culture across lines of race/ethnicity, gender, sexuality, and geographical location.

Definitional issues loom large in the field, but overall the focus has been on 'explor[ing] how class works, as both an analytical tool and a basis for lived experience', as opposed to 'struggl[ing] among scholars and theorists to reach agreement about what class is' (Russo and Linkon 2005, 11). This is not to say that there has been no disagreement in the field over how to define class, and the working class(es) in particular, but Russo and Linkon's insistence, at the Center for Working-Class Studies, on taking a 'big umbrella' approach had the positive effect of keeping those disagreements from taking center stage and hijacking the field's development and forward momentum. Within the field, one oft-cited definition comes from Michael Zweig in his book *The Working Class Majority* (2011). There and elsewhere Zweig focuses on class as 'mainly a question of economic and political power' (4). Zweig defines the working class as 'people, who, when they go to work or act as citizens, have comparatively little power or authority' (4). As the title of his book suggests, this definition leads to the conclusion that working-class people constitute over 60 percent of the labor force. Other approaches to these definitional issues focus on education level, social status, and cultural capital. As Nicholas Coles and Jandy Zandy assert in the introduction of *American Working-Class Literature: An Anthology*, 'Working-class identity is, of course, much more than a matter of one's economic position; it is also a lived experience, a set of relationships, expectations, legacies, and entitlements (or the lack of them)' (2007, xx).

The field also privileges intersectional analyses—that is, analyses that emphasize how class intersects and is inflected by race, gender, and sexuality—and acknowledges how place and location shape class. More broadly, practitioners in the field attend to the wide diversity of identities represented in the working class. As Keeanga-Yamahtta Taylor asserts in her 2016 book, *From #BlackLivesMatter to Black Liberation*, 'In fact, the American working class is female, immigrant, Black, white, Latino/a, and more. Immigrant issues, gender issues, and antiracism *are* working-class issues' (216). Taylor and many others reject the political and media narratives that (willfully?) misconstrue the working class by representing it explicitly and/or implicitly as largely white and male. In the final chapter of her book, she makes the case that 'there is a basis for solidarity among white and nonwhite working-class people' (211) and that

> Solidarity is only possible through relentless struggle to win white workers to antiracism, to expose the lie that Black workers are worse off because they somehow choose to be,

> and to win the white working class to the understanding that, unless they struggle, they too will continue to live lives of poverty and frustration, even if those lives are somewhat better than the lives led by Black workers. Success or failure are contingent on whether or not working people see themselves as brothers and sisters whose liberation is inextricably bound together.
>
> *(215)*

Though the field privileges intersectional analyses, this is not the same as saying that the field's practitioners are broadly diverse, particularly with regard to race/ethnicity. The majority of those who explicitly see themselves as working in the field are white, and this whiteness, regrettably, is reflected in the list of contributors to this volume. Even as there has been a rise in white nationalism and anti-immigration rhetoric sweeping the globe, there has also been a progressive response from academics and activists—the WCSA conferences certainly reflect that such work is happening across many lines of difference. It is our hope that this volume, then, serves as a point of departure to encourage continued linkages among class, race, and ethnicity as we move forward. Antiracist white people in the field have more to do to forge those linkages and be a part of the resistance to the mainstream media narrative that codes the working class as white and male.

Another key value of the field is the insistence that its intellectual output have political impact. Janet Zandy describes working-class studies as 'a democratic force as well as a curricular and cultural movement' (2001, x) while Russo and Linkon assert that the field 'is not just an academic exercise. Rather, we strive to advance the struggle for social and economic justice for working-class people' (2005, 15). It is this push for what they call 'intellectual activism' that drives scholars across many disciplines to design projects centered around the subject of class.

What makes working-class studies distinct may be difficult to boil down into a single characteristic—always a dangerous task—so we offer the following to sum up the field: a strong, generous interdisciplinary focus on working-class life and culture and a desire to combine the insights of academics, activists, journalists, artists, photographers, and writers of all kinds in the exploration of the lived experience of class. In part, it offers a space and legitimacy for those of working-class origin to reflect on their experience and practice as educators. It also offers a set of concepts, ideas, and methods for looking at class and, we think, a strong commitment to social justice issues around class. All of these are often seen in other fields, but we feel they are especially present in working-class studies.

Why then a *Handbook of Working-Class Studies*? As editors, we recognize that a handbook has many roles and uses. It also has a wide variety of potential audiences. As a field, working-class studies is now into its third decade. One of our purposes here is to put down a marker as to how the field has developed up until now, to act as a 'state of the field'-type statement and in turn to offer some insights as to how it might develop in the future. It has been over fifteen years since Russo and Linkon's *New Working-Class Studies* was published; that volume continues to be enormously useful, and our aim is to follow in its footsteps and provide a forum for work that builds from it while capturing how the field has developed since its publication. As 2020 marks a quarter of a century since the initial Youngstown conference, it is worth taking time to reflect on developments over that time. Finally, this volume has come into being against the Brexit vote in the UK, the election of Donald Trump in the US, and the wider rise of populism in Europe. In each of these cases, the working class is bound up with explanations of political shifts, whether accurately or not. This handbook, then, not only seeks to bring readers up to date on developments in the field, but also hopes to create a clear path forward by setting an agenda and inspiring the work of both well-established and up-and-coming voices in working-class studies.

Organization of the *Handbook*

We have organized the volume to recognize these various needs, arranging our chapters across six major themes: methods and principles of research in working-class studies; class and education; work and community; working-class cultures; representations; and activism and collective action. Clearly there are many points of connection between and among these themes, and to some extent the boundaries between them are permeable, which reflects the innate cross-disciplinary nature of the field. Each strand has an introductory essay which clears the ground for the individual area, looking at how that particular subfield is located within the larger field. These essays act to provide historical background, an introduction to the section, and at times a more speculative account of how the area might develop.

The first section, 'Methods and principles of research in working-class studies', considers how those working in the field use and adapt a variety of theories and methods to engage in multi- or interdisciplinary research that sheds light on social class in general as well as working-class lives, consciousness, and cultures more specifically. The contributors to this section cover significant ground; they variously attempt to describe and analyze their own methods and those of the field more broadly, and they make a series of arguments about the methods that are well-suited to the field, as well as those that are perhaps ill-suited. They offer reflections about what the field has done well and what it could do better and do some thinking about the future of research in the field.

The second section, 'Class and education', reflects the field's longstanding and varied interest in this topic. For many practitioners in the field, education was the means through which they achieved upward class mobility, which gives them a unique perspective on the educational system as a societal institution. This section captures and explores how education functions as a means to maintain class inequality for most, even as it is a site of mobility for a few. It documents the efforts of those in the field who are attempting to make schools a more welcoming place to working-class students by changing the culture and policies of schools as well as the teaching practices and content of the curriculum. Sociologist Allison L. Hurst's overview of the section reveals a desire and vision to move beyond conceptualizing education as either a gatekeeper or an escalator and, instead, imagine it as a collaborator for progressive social change.

The workplace is a fundamental arena for understanding working-class life. Historians, sociologists, anthropologists, and literature scholars, among others, each in their different ways study work and employment and how it both shapes and is in turn shaped by class cultures. The third section, 'Work and community', explores class cultures in and around the workplace, including how they have been conceptualized, discussed, and represented. It also explores how these work cultures have been eroded or destroyed by job loss and full-scale deindustrialization over the last four decades or more, paying attention to the wider issue of communities created by and through working-class employment and the multiple effects job loss has had on working-class communities. In addition, this section considers new sites of industrialization in the global economy and newly emerging precarious work. Here issues of gender, ethnicity, and race are addressed with their intersections with class.

'Working-class cultures' examines how distinct that culture is in comparison with the middle-class mainstream, taking time to examine in turn the hidden injuries of class as well as its rewards. As Barbara Jensen and others have argued, working-class culture has strengths and positive aspects. Chapters explore how the field relates to wider debates about stratification, especially within sociological understandings, focusing on how class differences shape people's attitudes, beliefs, and values, as well as how class impacts experiences of marriage, parenting, schooling, and activism.

The working class has been represented through various media. From novels, poetry, television, and film to photography, song, and sculpture, working-class identity has been explored, projected, and demeaned. Contributions in the fifth section, 'Representations', examine how working-class studies' perspectives can help to unlock some of the meanings embedded in a variety of media and literature, critically asking questions of the producers, consumers, and audiences of historical and contemporary representations of working-class people, issues, movements, and culture.

Our final section, 'Activism and collective action', explores how working-class studies has looked at class-based interventions and is itself an intervention into class-based debates. Effective change, whether in the workplace, in the academy, or in everyday life, takes many forms. This section explores past and present initiatives that have given voice to working-class people's struggles and their efforts to mobilize movements across cultures, geographical borders, periods, and generations, ultimately expanding notions of the efficacy of protest and collectivity in advocating for economic, political, and social justice.

Together, the *Handbook* showcases the kind of work the field has come to be known for, along with the range of practices and approaches in the field, especially emerging trends. There is no consensus on how to do working-class studies nor is this an exhaustive representation; rather, these chapters serve as examples to provide options for scholars, students, practitioners, artists, activists, and others to see how their work adds to the growing dialogue on class in contemporary society today. We hope you see this book as an invitation to consider the ways in which the study of working-class history and culture functions comparatively, creating new interventions as we look forward to future developments in the field.

References

Beck, U. (2002) 'The Cosmopolitan Society and its Enemies', *Theory, Culture and Society*, 19, 1/2, pp. 17–44.

Bluestone, B. and Harrison, B. (1984) *The Deindustrialization of America: Plant Closings, Community Abandonment, and the Dismantling of Basic Industry*, New York, Basic Books.

Christopher, R., Orr, L. and Strom, L. (eds.) (1998) Working-Class Lives and Cultures [special issue], *Women's Studies Quarterly*, 26, 1/2.

Coles, N. and Zandy, J. (eds.) (2007) *American Working-Class Literature: An Anthology*, New York, Oxford University Press.

Dudley, K. (1994) *The End of the Line: Lost Jobs, New Lives in Postindustrial America*, Chicago, University of Chicago Press.

High, S. (2003) *Industrial Sunset: The Making of North America's Rust Belt, 1969–1984*, Toronto, University of Toronto Press.

Lennon, J. and Nilsson, M. (2017) *Working-Class Literature(s): Historical and International Perspectives*, Stockholm, Stockholm University Press.

Leondar-Wright, B. (2014) *Missing Class: Strengthening Social Movement Groups by Seeing Class Cultures*, Ithaca, ILR Press.

Linkon, S. L. (ed.) (1999) *Teaching Working Class*, Amherst, University of Massachusetts Press.

Metzgar, J. (2000) *Striking Steel: Solidarity Remembered*, Philadelphia, Temple University Press.

Reay, D. (2017) *Miseducation: Inequality, Education, and the Working Classes*, Bristol, Policy Press.

Russo, J. and Linkon, S. (2005) 'What's New about New Working-Class Studies?', in Russo, J. and Linkon, S. (eds.) *New Working-Class Studies*, Ithaca, NY, Cornell University Press.

Taylor, K.-Y. (2016) *From #BlackLivesMatter to Black Liberation*, Chicago, Haymarket Books.

Tokarczyk, M. and Fay, E. (eds.) (1993) *Working-Class Women in the Academy: Laborers in the Knowledge Factory*, Amherst, University of Massachusetts Press.
Torlina, J. (2011) *Working Class: Challenging Myths about Blue-Collar Labor*, Boulder, Lynne Rienner Publishers.
Virdee, S. (2014) *Racism, Class, and the Racialized Outsider*, London, Red Globe Press.
Walley, C. (2013) *Exit Zero: Family and Class in Postindustrial Chicago*, Chicago, University of Chicago Press.
Zandy, J. (1994) *Liberating Memory: Our Work and Our Working-Class Consciousness*, New Brunswick, Rutgers University Press.
Zandy, J. (1995) (ed.) Working-Class Studies [special issue], *Women's Studies Quarterly*, 22, 1/2.
Zandy, J. (2001) 'Preface to the New Edition', in Zandy, J. (ed.) *What We Hold In Common: An Introduction to Working-Class Studies*, New York, Feminist Press.
Zandy, J. (2004) *Hands: Physical Labor, Class, and Cultural Work*, New Brunswick, Rutgers University Press.
Zweig, M. (2004) 'Introduction—The Challenge of Working Class Studies', in Zweig, M. (ed.) *What's Class Got to Do with It? American Society in the Twenty-First Century*, Ithaca, Cornell University Press.
Zweig, M. (2011) *The Working-Class Majority: America's Best-Kept Secret*, 2nd ed., Ithaca, ILR Press.

Part I

Methods and principles of research in working-class studies

Section introduction

Methods and principles of research in working-class studies

Christie Launius

The four chapters in this section aim to break new intellectual ground in the field of working-class studies by offering metalevel reflections on and insights into the methods used in working-class studies research, as well as the principles that inform and guide that research. In the years since the field's founding in the mid-1990s, there have been several broad, 'big picture' discussions of the defining features of working-class studies and what sets the field apart from other fields, but not much explicit attention to questions of research methods or methodologies. Twenty plus years in, the field is poised to move that metalevel discussion forward; this section, then, seeks to suggest an agenda for the field and invite others to offer responses of their own. My introduction to this section offers some observations about methods in working-class studies and the principles that guide them, grounded in what has been written on the subject. It situates these four chapters in the larger context of the field and places them in conversation with one another.

It is my hope that the collective work contained in this section of the *Handbook*, which does a lot of intellectual 'heavy lifting', will clear a path forward for working-class studies practitioners, particularly its next generation, to take up some of the following questions, as well as pose new ones: How are researchers' choices regarding methods guided by the ethos of the field? What method(s) help shed light on working-class lives, experiences, and cultures, and 'bridge the gap between the concrete, material world of the majority class, the working class, and the more sequestered scholarly practices of the academy?' (Zandy 1997, 159). Conversely, do some research methods potentially make that work more difficult? What tools and methods do we need in order to gain a better understanding of how class works two decades into the 21st century? What tools do we need as scholars to capture the changing nature of work and capitalism, new types of work and workers, and how people understand their own class position?

In considering these questions, an apt point of comparison comes from the interdisciplinary field of women's and gender studies, which has generated a robust literature on epistemology, method, and methodology.[1] In women's and gender studies, researchers use a variety of methods, both quantitative and qualitative, including survey research, in-depth interviewing, ethnography, focus groups, oral history, and textual analysis. A consistent point in discussions of methods within the field is that the methods themselves are not unique to the field, and not inherently feminist or anti-feminist, but instead are *used* in particular ways by feminist researchers. As such, exploring questions related to what tools and methods working-class studies practitioners need entails a consideration of *how* to use them, ethically speaking. For practitioners of working-class studies, choices about research methods and how to use them tend to follow from and be in line with the ethos of the field.

As a knowledge project, perhaps the most basic and key aspect of working-class studies is that it puts the working class at the center. As John Russo and Sherry Linkon assert, 'working-class people and their lives take center stage' (2005, 11), and the field tries to 'make working-class voices a primary source for the study of working-class life' (2005, 12). Likewise, Janet Zandy states that 'The subjectivity of working people is at the center of working-class studies' (1997, 162); working-class people are the subject, not only the object, of study in the field. Overall, a focus on the lived experience of class is at the heart of working-class studies, a feature which helps distinguish it from the way other academic disciplines have and continue to study class, and the working classes more specifically.

The centering of working-class people and their subjectivity is connected to the assertion made by Janet Zandy and Jack Metzgar, among others, that there is a working-class epistemology. Zandy, for example sees working-class studies as an 'academic frame for working-class culture, history, language, stories, bodies—all forms and expressions of working-class knowledge, an epistemology that is generally excluded from institutional constructions of knowledge' (2001, 159). Jack Metzgar sketches out a working-class epistemology that he sees as distinct from the 'standard educated middle-class one', and he somewhat playfully suggests that the differences between the two, in terms of how their respective knowledge claims are presented rhetorically, can be captured by the phrases 'by my lights' and 'studies have shown' (2012). Metzgar asserts that both working-class and middle-class epistemologies have limitations when taken alone, but that bringing these two 'contrary, but potentially complementary epistemologies' together dialogically can be fruitful and productive (Metzgar 2012). Within the field, this can take several forms. At base, practitioners of working-class studies grasp that working-class epistemology is not granted authority in academic settings, and as such, a key part of the field entails granting and asserting that working-class people are knowers who potentially have valuable insights into and perspectives on their own experiences and the world around them that can and should shape our understanding of social class. Working-class studies scholars, then, intervene in academic discourse by granting the epistemic authority of working-class people and integrating their perspectives into scholarly work, thereby expanding scholarly understanding of the working class, which provides a corrective to previous omissions and/or distortions.

A related way that working-class and middle-class epistemologies are brought into dialogue is by working-class studies practitioners who are themselves class straddlers and who write about their own experiences navigating or toggling between middle-class and working-class epistemological frameworks.[2] In her contribution to this section, Sherry Linkon argues that scholarly personal narratives by working-class academics are the signature genre of the field of working-class studies, and that these texts 'make working-class people visible and central, as subjects and storytellers but also as *interpreters*, not only as objects of study' (emphasis added). Authors of these scholarly personal narratives bring together working-class and middle-class epistemological frameworks through metalevel reflections on their own lives and through their discussions of working-class people they know.

Christine J. Walley's chapter in this section also picks up on this thread about the interplay between working-class and middle-class epistemologies; her formulation of the contrast is characterized in terms of 'stories' and 'theory', and she asks whether stories can 'be the stuff of rigorous scholarly work, and in what ways do they count as evidence and relate to theory?' (65).

Walley suggests that one way out of seeing stories and theory as opposites and mutually exclusive is to instead emphasize analysis.

> Analysis, after all, more firmly builds upon concrete engagement with the world and is as much part of everyday storytelling as it is of academic theory. Emphasizing analysis can further open such conversations to working-class voices, potentially providing alternative analyses to those commonly found in academia.
>
> *(p. 68)*

Both Linkon and Walley explore these epistemological issues alongside and in relation to their discussions of methods in the field.

A second defining feature of the field has to do with definitions of class. For many reasons, working-class studies has no single, agreed-upon definition of class; its practitioners embrace 'diverse and even contradictory ideas about how class works, why it matters, and how we can best understand it' (Russo and Linkon 2005, 10). Linkon and Russo assert that 'What do we mean by class?' is one of four central questions that shape the field. The field 'embraces this question but refuses to provide a simple answer' (2016, 5). A practitioner's understanding and definition of class, whether 'class as a category of analysis' or 'class as a social category and a culture', to use Linkon and Russo's shorthand, surely shapes their choice of method (2016, 5). More broadly, the willingness to keep the question in play rather than trying to pin down a definitive answer speaks to another aspect of the ethos the field. In this section, Joseph Entin's chapter explores this terrain, as clearly broadcast by his title, 'Reconceiving class in contemporary working-class studies'. In Linkon and Russo's formulation, Entin squarely situates himself in the 'class as a category of analysis' camp, though he shares with Linkon and Russo a desire to eschew 'drawing lines between theoretical approaches and traditions', instead advocating for the adoption of 'a willfully creative and promiscuous approach to conceptualizing class formation and class struggle—one that embraces intersectional, post-colonial, and poststructuralist approaches, and a wide range of Marxisms' (p. 34).

A third defining feature of the field has to do with how class is understood and taken up in relation to other categories of analysis, as alluded to by Entin's quote above that invokes the framework of intersectionality. From its beginnings, practitioners of working-class studies have defined the field as focusing on the intersections between class and other categories of identity. The assertion of this focus has often operated on a dual level: as a positive description of what the field is and does, and as a corrective to misperceptions of it. As Janet Zandy puts it in 'Toward Working-Class Studies', 'Working-Class Studies is *not* white studies; it *must* be multicultural' (1997, 161). Twenty years later, Sara Appel uses the theoretical framework of intersectionality rather than multiculturalism in posing the question, 'How can working-class studies *be* a form of intersectional studies…?' (2017, 408). She writes,

> We don't assume that the complexities of socioeconomic inequality, labor relations, or class identity can be understood merely by examining class in isolation; we've adopted a multi-faceted way of seeing and reading that recognizes the interconnectedness of class with race, gender, sexuality, and other categories of experience.
>
> *(2017, 406)*

In two early pieces, Janet Zandy refers to this as a critical practice of 'reciprocal visibility' (2001, 250) and an 'expanded relational vision' (1997, x). A commitment to intersectionality is frequently reflected in practitioners' choice and use of research methods.

A final core principle of the field is that it has a social justice component; as Russo and Linkon assert, working-class studies is 'not just an academic exercise' (2005, 15). Janet Zandy is prescriptive in her assertion that 'If Working-Class Studies becomes merely an object of study, and not a means of struggle, then it would lose purpose. Working-Class Studies is intended to continue the struggle of earlier generations for an economically just society for us all' (1997, 162). Since its beginnings, the 'big tent' approach to the field has explicitly included activism and activists outside academia, but as both Russo and Linkon and Zandy make clear, there is also an expectation that the scholarly work produced by its academic practitioners be a type of praxis—that is, that it support the aim of social justice.

This part of the ethos of the field can be seen in all four chapters in this section, though it is perhaps attended to most explicitly by Jane Van Galen and Christine Walley. In 'Mediating stories of class borders: First-generation college students, digital storytelling, and social class', Van Galen uses the work of Vivienne to discuss four levels of social change that are potential outcomes of her digital storytelling project. She writes about 'the potential of these stories to provoke change' (p. 53), starting from the individual level (i.e. how the students are personally changed by the experience of participating in the workshop), then outward to change that occurs from them sharing their stories both with their fellow students and their friends and families, and finally with a public audience, potentially resulting in institutional-level change. While Walley isn't as explicit about overt social justice aims, she writes extensively in her chapter about her commitment to diversifying the audience for her work and further incorporating working-class perspectives into academic conversations and scholarship through her creation of multimedia work in tandem with a variety of collaborators. She writes of making a documentary film as an extension of her monograph, *Exit Zero: Family and Class in Postindustrial Chicago* (2013), as well as developing an online archive and storytelling site for the Southeast Chicago Historical Museum.

Working-class studies scholars use a variety of methods; practitioners with training and interests in the humanities have focused on finding adequate methods for analyzing and interpreting working-class texts (literature, film, art, photography, etc.), while those in the social sciences have focused, for example on adapting methods for interviewing working-class people and studying working-class communities through ethnography, as well as interviewing and/or surveying people *about* social class. Historians with interests in studying working-class people, places, and movements have also discussed how best to adapt their field's methods to this area. And across disciplines, those in working-class studies have adapted models of service learning and civic engagement to bridge the divide between their classrooms and the community.

As the above description suggests, most working-class studies practitioners utilize methods that stem from their primary disciplinary training; a much smaller number engage in research that spans disciplines and/or would be considered truly interdisciplinary. Linkon and Russo are among that number; in 'Border crossings: Interdisciplinarity in new working-class studies', Linkon and Russo describe and advocate the use of a method of 'comparative, connective textual analysis' that, they argue, can aid working-class studies practitioners who want to engage in interdisciplinary research. This method is grounded in the belief that 'texts of all kinds can and should be read as historically grounded, socially constructed, purposeful, rhetorical, and influential' (2012, 375). They employed this method in their book *Steeltown USA: Work and Memory in Youngstown* (2002) and subsequently began teaching the method to their students using a text analysis rubric.

Whether the project is disciplinary, multidisciplinary, or interdisciplinary, the emphasis in the field is on adapting and using methods in ways that are consistent with the four principles outlined above. In this section, Walley, Van Galen, and Linkon all exemplify this tenet in their respective chapters. Van Galen focuses on digital storytelling and multimedia authoring, arguing that it offers the potential 'to foster deep reflection and to amplify the voices of first-generation students on their own campuses' (p. 45). She offers three-day digital storytelling workshops to first-generation college students during which they explore their student experience and present first-person multimedia stories; she subsequently interviews the participants about their authoring process as well as their experiences in the workshop itself. What the three-day process seems to offer is the chance to 'explore as well as explain' their stories, as Van Galen puts it (p. 47); more specifically, not only the method of digital storytelling but also the three-day workshop process gives students the space to move out of the silence and shame that many of them experience and into a fuller and more complicated understanding of their own positioning as first-generation college students.

Walley argues that ethnographic fieldwork, the 'trademark method' of anthropology is 'well-suited to exploring how social class works' (p. 60). As a method, she asserts, it is '"good to think with" ... for working-class studies scholars' because of its 'focus on the complexity of daily life', its ability to uncover 'the contours of—and contradictions and ambiguities in—our beliefs, identities, practices, and interests', as well as its ability to capture 'how people's everyday improvisations respond to the structured constraints and unequal opportunities (including class-based ones) that make up our lives' (p. 59–60).

As previously mentioned, Sherry Linkon's contribution to this section focuses on scholarly personal narratives, a genre of writing that is by no means unique to the field of working-class studies, but that has nonetheless emerged as central to the knowledge project of the field. But more than just a genre of writing, Linkon sees within these texts a type of method used in the service of the knowledge project of working-class studies, a method which 'link[s] personal narrative with historical, theoretical, representational, and other approaches to examine working-class life from the inside' (p. 21). Linkon sees, in these scholarly personal narratives, a mapping of 'the dialogic relationship between experience and evidence' (p. 26).

These three chapters share a focus on and commitment to analytical narrative. Walley reflects on her use of the method in the context of her ethnographic fieldwork. Linkon offers an analysis of and series of arguments about texts in the genre (including Walley's) and the genre as a whole, while Van Galen discusses her process of working with first-generation working-class students to author their own analytical narratives.

If we imagine the chapters in this section to be in conversation with one another, Joseph Entin's chapter, then, is the provocateur in this quartet, in that he champions the relevance and importance of theory, more traditionally understood, for the field of working-class studies. Whereas Linkon, Van Gallen, and Walley explore and champion the value of stories (and the analysis generated from them) to the knowledge project of the field, even as they grant the downsides or risks of doing so, Entin instead takes up the cause of Marxist theories, which he sees as having been sidelined in the field's development. Entin's chapter is more about methodology than about method; that is, his focus is not on techniques for gathering evidence, or a particular mode of scholarly inquiry, but instead on a theoretical framework that he believes can and should guide the field. As Entin argues, 'working-class studies would benefit from more actively embracing Marxist and other more abstract theoretical paradigms' (p. 33). Entin notes that scholars in the field often don't engage with the 'wealth of stellar critical work on capitalism', 'in part due to the wariness about post-structuralism that has been woven (in some ways understandably) into the field, given its historic emphasis on the lived experience of working-class people' (p. 33). His is a compelling argument, particularly when he sketches out how embracing these theoretical paradigms would provide a route to more active political engagement and alliances with other progressive movements.

The assertion that some methods and theoretical frameworks are particularly useful—that is, in line with the values and ethos of the field—raises the possibility that other methods are *less* useful and/or that some ways of using those methods should be avoided. Among these four chapters, Van Galen explores this ground most explicitly; she discusses her choice of multimedia authoring and digital storytelling in terms of her desire to avoid more conventional methods that rely on 'self-reflection and self-disclosure' (p. 47). These more conventional methods were 'likely to fall short of capturing students' *embodied* experiences of *living* class ... when *living* class stratification likely feels instead like shame over the sense that one is simply not good enough to make it in college' (p. 47). Her choice of digital storytelling and the three-day workshop structure gives students an opportunity to 'question, affirm, craft, and eventually share first-person multimedia stories of being "first"' (p. 47). The method and the workshop structure give students a chance to work through their silence and shame and to arrive at a different place. This quote also suggests the importance Van Galen places on the ethical dimensions of her research, which entails working with a somewhat vulnerable population. She writes, 'In contrast to more conventional researcher/subject relationships, artistic production also positions the creator as an active participant in inquiry' (p. 52).

A smattering of other articles[3] have taken up these issues; not surprisingly, these reflections on the ethical issues involved in research come from social scientists who work directly with research participants in studies that require institutional review board approval. For example in '"Oh goodness, I *am* watching reality TV": How methods make class in audience research', Skeggs, Thumim, and Wood (2008) argue, as their title implies, that methods *make* class. They argue that in-depth interviews, as a method, are more familiar and comfortable for middle-class research subjects, while other methods, including what they call 'text-in-action' (which entails having the researcher observe and record the research subject while watching television), as well as focus groups, can help give greater voice to working-class research subjects. They make the case for using mixed methods in a project that seeks to generate knowledge about the television viewing practices of both working-class and middle-class women. They conclude that 'our methodological design enabled different kinds of knowledge to be displayed, and offered a more transparent account of that process than is often rendered in research' (2008, 21) and that there is a pressing 'need to explore how different techniques reproduce what is in fact a demonstration of unequal access to cultural resources, while appearing as if neutral and value-free' (2008, 21).

Other social science researchers have reflected on how their own class position has inevitably shaped their research and their use of particular methods. In these reflections, the focus is not on evaluating and making claims about the suitability of particular methods over others, but rather that there are (perhaps unavoidable) issues that arise as a result of the class position of the researcher, the class position of the subjects of the research, and/or the interaction between the two.

Sociologists Diane Reay and Allison L. Hurst (both contributors to the 'Class and education' section of this volume) have reflected on the difficulty of reconciling their positions as class straddlers and how it impacted their doctoral research. Reay's research entailed interviewing both working-class and middle-class women, while Hurst's focused on first-generation college students across gender lines. In 'Insider perspectives or stealing the words out of women's mouths: Interpretation in the research process', Reay reflects on her growing recognition that her own class background shaped how she responded to both groups, and asserts that her multiple class positionings 'spilled over into both the interviewing process and the interpretation of my data' (1996, 60). When interpreting the interviews of the working-class women, she fears the 'dangers of proximity' and set out to

> address the issue of whether I was conflating their many varied experiences with my own. Was I finding in the field the slights, reflections and silencings I had experienced in my own educational career? There is a thin dividing line between the understandings that similar experiences of respondents bring to the research process and the element of exploitation implicit in mixing up one's own personal history with very different working-class experiences.
>
> *(1996, 65)*

Hurst offers similar reflections in 'A healing echo: Methodological reflections of a working-class researcher on class' (2008). Hurst worried about the danger of projecting her own experience onto that of her straddler interviewees, running the risk of only hearing what she expected to hear—that is, what echoed her own experiences and the conclusions she had drawn from them. Both Reay and Hurst think carefully about their insider/outsider status relative to their interviewees, and both document the struggle to honor the voices and perspectives of working-class people whose perspectives differ from their own, or differ in ways that confound their expectations for what they would hear. Ultimately, both Reay and Hurst offer their reflections in an attempt to be rigorously reflexive about their research process and to gain insight into the difficulties of engaging in research that entails use of the method of interviewing.

A variation on these ethical considerations comes from Iben Charlotte Aamann, who offers some interesting insights about how her middle-classness impacted her research subjects' relationship to her. The quote from a research subject that opens her title, '"Oh, Iben's here now, so we better behave properly": The production of class as morality in research encounters' (2017), gets at the realization she had while conducting 'ethnographic fieldwork among ethnic Danish middle- and working-class parents at three Danish primary schools' (par. 1); namely, that in her capacity as a middle-class researcher, she 'was being interpreted as a "judge", authorized and with an institutionalized power to make judgments on the participants' (par. 9). Furthermore, Aamann argues that 'I was being interpreted in the same way by [both the working-class and middle-class] participants, who then positioned themselves differently toward this interpretation of my presence' (par. 7). Aamann finds that the middle-class parents tended to either try to elicit a positive judgment of them from her or position themselves as peers with an equal authority to judge, while the working-class parents engaged in what Aamann calls 'class resistance': they rejected her attempts to engage them and 'simply refused to be judged by avoiding contact with me' (par. 60). Aamann extrapolates from her research experiences to suggest that researchers 'need to develop qualitative approaches that are sensitive toward the fuzzy and subtle character of class and its cultural and subjective dimensions' (par. 2). Aamann goes beyond points made by Reay and Hurst about the importance of reflexivity to suggest that the class relationships between researchers and their subjects and the 'distortion, discomfort and disharmony' (par. 70) that can arise as a result are part of the data that is produced in the study.

The assertions made both by the contributors to this section as well as other researchers about the suitability or lack thereof of particular methods, and about the thorny ethical issues raised by the class positioning of the researcher vis-à-vis their subjects, are particularly intriguing. As stated at the outset, it is my hope that these assertions and my framing of them will spark future projects that will test, affirm, refine, and/or refute them.

Linkon's chapter concludes by wondering whether a new generation will take up the signature genre of the field, writing scholarly personal narratives. She writes,

> I hope so, because working-class culture is being reshaped by globalization, mobility, neoliberal ideologies, and contingent employment. Much as we have learned from stories of

> working-class lives in the second half of the twentieth century, we need now to hear from those who are coming of age and navigating the early twenty-first century.
>
> *(p. 29–30)*

The notion, presumably, is that the narratives of a younger generation will be shaped by these forces and that the works they produce will shed light on them and help us understand them in new and more nuanced ways, and in so doing, these works will move the field of working-class studies forward. Entin, too, is deeply invested in seeing the field move forward, but sees engagement with theory as the key to this forward movement. Without that sustained engagement with theory, Entin might say, scholarly personal narratives even by the next generation of scholars will run the risk of remaining stuck in the past, anachronistic in their intellectual practices, and not accurately reflecting the present reality. I would argue that this tension between stories and theory is a productive one; both are needed and important. In the spirit of 'both/and', I look forward to a proliferation of voices contributing to working-class studies' consideration of epistemology, method, and methodology.

Notes

1 See, for example Hesse-Biber (2012) and Ramazanoglu and Holland (2002).
2 This process is not infrequently fraught with difficulty for working-class academics. Judith Barker, for instance, writes of the problems that arise when 'translating our working-class knowledge and understanding into a format, structure, and language that was designed to deny our knowledge, experiences, realities, and values' (1996, 104).
3 See Payne and Grew (2005) and Pilon (2015) for additional discussion of how class shapes research findings.

References

Aamann, I. C. (2017) '"Oh! Iben's Here Now, So We Better Behave Properly": The Production of Class as Morality in Research Encounters', *Forum Qualitative Sozialforschung*, 18, 3, Article 7.

Appel, S. (2017) 'A Turn of the Sphere: The Place of Class in Intersectional Analysis', in Coles, N. and Lauter, P. (eds.) *A History of American Working-Class Literature*, Cambridge, Cambridge University Press.

Barker, J. (1996) 'A White Working-Class Perspective on Epistemology', *Race, Gender, & Class*, 4, 1, pp. 103–118.

Hesse-Biber, S. (2012) *Handbook of Feminist Research: Theory and Praxis*, Thousand Oaks, Sage Publishing.

Hurst, A. (2008) 'A Healing Echo: Methodological Reflections of a Working-Class Researcher on Class', *The Qualitative Report*, 13, 3, pp. 334–352.

Linkon, S. and Russo, J. (2002) Steeltown USA: Work and Memory in Youngstown, Lawrence, University Press of Kansas.

Linkon, S. and Russo, J. (2012) 'Border Crossings: Interdisciplinarity in New Working-Class Studies', *Labor History*, 53, 3, pp. 373–387.

Linkon, S. and Russo, J. (2016) 'Twenty Years of Working-Class Studies: Tensions, Values, and Core Questions', *Journal of Working-Class Studies*, 1, 1, pp. 4–13.

Metzgar, J. (2012) '"By My Lights" and "Studies Have Shown"', *Working-Class Perspectives*. Available at: https://workingclassstudies.wordpress.com/2012/09/24/by-my-lights-and-studies-have-shown/ Accessed November 10, 2017.

Payne, G. and Grew, C. (2005) 'Unpacking "Class Ambivalence": Some Conceptual and Methodological Issues in Accessing Class Cultures', *Sociology*, 39, 5, pp. 893–910.

Pilon, D. (2015) 'Researching Voter Turnout and the Electoral Subaltern: Utilizing "Class" as Identity', *Studies in Political Economy: A Socialist Review*, 96, 1, pp. 69–92.

Ramazanoglu, C. and Holland, J. (2002) *Feminist Methodology: Challenges and Choices*, London, Sage Publishing.

Reay, D. (1996) 'Insider Perspectives or Stealing the Words out of Women's Mouths: Interpretation in the Research Process', *Feminist Review*, 53, pp. 57–73.
Russo, J. and Linkon, S. (eds.) (2005) *New Working-Class Studies*, Ithaca, Cornell University Press.
Skeggs, B., Thumim, N. and Wood, H. (2008) '"Oh goodness, I *am* watching reality TV": How Methods Make Class in Audience Research', *European Journal of Cultural Studies*, 11, 1, pp. 5–24.
Zandy, J. (1997) 'Toward Working-Class Studies', in Smith, L. (ed.) *The Heartlands Today: The Urban Midwest*, Huron, Ohio, Firelands Writing Center.
Zandy, J. (2001) 'Traveling Working Class', in Zandy, J. (ed.) *What We Hold In Common: An Introduction to Working-Class Studies*, New York, The Feminist Press.

1

Class analysis from the inside

Scholarly personal narrative as a signature genre of working-class studies

Sherry Lee Linkon

Autobiographical writing by working-class academics has helped to inspire and shape working-class studies as a field. Books like Jake Ryan and Charles Sackrey's 1984 *Strangers in Paradise: Academics from the Working Class* raised questions about how class background influenced academic life, as did two later collections, Michelle M. Tokarczyk and Elizabeth A. Fay's 1993 *Working-Class Women in the Academy: Laborers in the Knowledge Factory* and C. L. Barney Dews and Carolyn Leste Law's 1995 *This Fine Place So Far from Home: Voices of Academics from the Working Class*. Through their stories about moving from working-class communities into the professional world of the academy, contributors to these collections described working-class culture but also critiqued the way class shaped institutions, social relations, and identities. They made working-class experience visible and argued for its significance. These personal essays illustrated how the structural hierarchies and cultural patterns of class played out in social and institutional life and in the day-to-day experiences of individuals. By sharing their stories and treating them as sources for analysis, these writers helped to create a field.

While the scholarly personal narrative of working-class life has a longer history, dating back (at least) to two books by British academics – Richard Hoggart's 1957 *The Uses of Literacy: Changing Patterns in English Mass Culture* and Carolyn Steedman's 1987 *Landscape for a Good Woman: A Story of Two Lives* – the anthologies published in the 1980s and 1990s provided a foundational core of primary and analytical texts for working-class studies. Alongside the essay collections mentioned above, Janet Zandy's anthologies of working-class writing, especially her 1995 volume *Liberating Memory: Our Work and Our Working-Class Consciousness*, positioned the voices and experiences of working-class people not simply as sources for study but as offering critical insights in themselves. Similarly, in *A Carpenter's Daughter: A Working-Class Woman in Higher Education*, Renny Christopher (2009) offered her own education narrative as a means of critiquing the American ideal of upward mobility. Other scholars followed with analytical monographs that drew on personal memory to examine class, culture, and politics. Jack Metzgar's 2000 *Striking Steel: Solidarity Remembered* links recollections of growing up in a steelworker household in Johnstown, Pennsylvania, with historical analysis of labor activism and working-class culture in the 1950s and the erasure of that culture and memory over time. Zandy followed in 2004 with *Hands: Physical Labor, Class, and Cultural Work*, a collection of critical essays that combined reflections on her family's experience, her perspective as a working-class critic, and analysis of representations of the physicality of working-class labor. Barbara Jensen's *Reading Classes: On Cultures and Classism in America* appeared in 2012, offering a comparison between working-class and middle-class cultures based on personal narrative and scholarly sources from psychology, education, and sociology. Christine Walley's *Exit Zero: Family and Class in Postindustrial Chicago*, published in 2013, centered on her family's experiences with steelwork and deindustrialization. Like the essay collections, these books link personal narrative with historical, theoretical, representational, and other approaches to examine working-class life from the inside. Although these books represent only part of the scholarly and creative work emerging from working-class studies, they have been particularly influential, both for their insights on how class works and for their approach. For these reasons, I would argue, the scholarly personal narrative has become the signature genre of working-class studies.

I borrow the term "scholarly personal narrative" from the work of Robert J. Nash, an education scholar whose 2004 book, *Liberating Scholarly Writing: The Power of Personal Narrative*, advocates for its use in social science research. He writes that "the best way to make sense of the 'truth' of what is 'out there' is through the construction, and telling, of stories, both to ourselves and to others" (2004, 7). Others have referred to this hybrid genre as "scholarly memoir" or "autoethnography," but Nash's term seems to me usefully flexible, because it highlights personal stories as tools rather than as the primary focus of a text and avoids identification with any particular method or discipline. One of the challenges but also one of the strengths of working-class studies has been the centrality of the personal, and our work is strongest when it balances along the edge between memory and analysis. Unlike memoir, a scholarly personal narrative is not about one's own story. It uses individual experience as a source of insight, and in the process, it maps the intersection between identity, social structure, perspective, and politics that makes working-class studies a compelling and important field.

Scholarly genres reflect and shape the cultures of academic fields. Scholars share ideas and shape knowledge through writing, and their articles and books are produced and distributed within communities of practice. But disciplinary cultures are constructed not only through what scholars say but also through forms and styles that align with the core values and epistemologies of our fields. As Ken Hyland and Marina Bondi argue, scholarly genres are "systematic expressions of institutional meanings and values" that are also "socially produced in particular communities and depend on them for their sense" (2012, 8). Most analyses of disciplinary genres focus on traditional fields with well-defined methods and communication practices, and disciplinary experts have produced hundreds of articles and guides to writing in various fields.[1] Nothing like that exists in working-class studies. Like other interdisciplinary fields, working-class studies integrates varied ideas about knowledge production, significance, and validity. Add to the mix the contested history of theorizing class, especially debates over whether class should be defined as an economic relationship or as an element of culture, and the challenges facing the diverse scholars who have been building working-class studies become clear. In the context of a contested, diverse, and emerging field, scholarly personal narratives have defined core concepts, modeled scholarly practices, and helped to define working-class studies as an interdisciplinary academic field.[2]

Scholarly personal narratives have made several key formative contributions to working-class studies. First, they foreground and validate working-class voices and perspectives. Part of what distinguishes working-class studies from the long-established bodies of research on the working class is that the field locates individuals at the center, using their experiences and responses to shed light on larger patterns and groups, rather than focusing primarily on social institutions like unions or schools. Where labor historians study, for example, organizing campaigns, working-class studies scholars focus on how working people navigate the relationship between work, union, family, and neighborhood.[3] In the process, these texts respond to, counter, and complicate existing concepts of class and ideas about working-class life. They also articulate and model a grounded approach that uses experience to translate the "structure of feeling" of working-class culture into analyses that treat working-class subjects with respect, empathy, and critique. These intellectual moves generate new material and articulate a conceptual but also ethical approach to the study of working-class life. At the same time, personal narratives serve social functions, building community within the field and advocating for the value of working-class people and perspectives in ways that reach beyond the field of working-class studies.

Claiming and complicating working-class perspectives

While working-class studies has long argued that working-class people have been ignored, misrepresented, or denigrated in American culture, scholarly personal narratives make working-class people visible and central as subjects and storytellers but also as interpreters, not only as objects of study. As Carol Faulkner writes in her essay in *Liberating Memory*, "Telling our story is, for me, a matter of recovering the reality of the working-class existence" (1995, 205). Reviewers identify this inside view as a key strength of these books. Mary Patillo writes that *Exit Zero* reveals aspects of working-class life that are "unseen and unrecognized" (2014, 751), while Jim Barrett praises *Striking Steel* for the way it "reconstruct[s] the hidden world … the internal values, motivations, and worldviews of common people" (2005, 117). By taking readers inside working-class experience, these books provide both intimacy and interpretation. They explain and validate working-class culture both for those who have experienced it and for those who have not.

Even more important, these narratives emphasize working-class perspectives, not just the conditions of working-class life. Early in *Reading Classes*, Jensen writes that she uses stories because they "show what may not be visible when one looks through the lens of middle class culture" (2012, 27). Instead of opening with this claim, though, she first outlines her own story, focusing on the experiences that helped her begin to see how class shaped her life. In other words, Jensen first invites readers into her world, framing the book in personal terms that enact the goal she then articulates. She makes her experience visible in order to make a case for its value as scholarly material. Walley (2013) also begins in the personal, opening *Exit Zero* with the memory of the morning Wisconsin Steel, where her father worked, shut down. She then reflects on her decision to write about her family, and like Jensen, Walley makes clear that she is using the personal strategically. She acknowledges her own attachment to the story of deindustrialization in southeast Chicago, but she argues that this attachment is not "simply personal." Rather, it represents "in unusually stark terms something larger and more troubling" – the "costs" of "class divisions" and "increasing economic inequalities" in the US (2013, 2). Jensen and Walley both use stories to make working-class lives visible by locating working-class perspectives at the center, a move that decenters dominant – middle-class but also academic – notions about class even as it claims the right of working-class people to tell their own stories and, crucially, to develop their own interpretations. This practice of locating working-class perspectives, not just working-class people, at the center has been a defining aspect of working-class studies as a field, but it is perhaps most fully and actively performed in scholarly personal narratives.

By foregrounding working-class perspectives, these narratives also challenge academic analyses of the working class, which often misread class culture because they begin with theoretical assumptions rather than with experience. As Nash notes, scholarly personal narratives approach their subjects by asking "personal, narrative-grounded, contextual questions that are too often ignored by researchers who use the more established frameworks" (2004, 5). For Walley, personal narrative offers an alternative to scholarly analyses that seem "inaccessible and distant … from the working-class lives" they describe (2013, 12). Stories bring us closer to working-class experience, and in the process they also "challenge the tendency of elites to make abstract and authoritative generalizations in ways that seek to define the world from their vantage point without appearing to do so" (2013, 13). By reading working-class culture from the inside, through memory and experience as well as interviews with family and friends – an especially personal version of ethnography – Walley offers a more grounded and more nuanced analysis than what she found in the scholarly literature.

Writing from within working-class experience can highlight gaps and oversimplifications. As Walley writes, the fact that her family's stories do not fit the standard scholarly explanations enables her to "wrestle with more dominant understandings" and offer a more accurate and complex version of working-class experience (2013, 6). Steedman makes a similar case in *Landscape for a Good Woman*, but unlike Walley, whose critique is aimed at traditional scholarly studies, Steedman explicitly challenges the work of male scholars whose accounts of their own working-class worlds erased the agency of people like her mother (1987, 10–11). She explicitly positions her mother's life – a single mother and a Conservative voter – as separate and different from the working-class households that earlier books, like Hoggart's *Uses of Literacy*, had presented. Unlike the "psychological simplicity" that Steedman sees in previous narratives of British working-class life, her mother's experiences, and her own, were marked by complexity and conflict (1987, 7). Like Walley, Steedman presents her book as offering an analysis that other scholars have missed, but neither claims that her analysis is the only "true" version of the story of working-class life. Rather, both suggest that scholarly personal narratives expand and enrich our understanding of how class works.

Where Steedman and Walley position their work as counternarratives to dominant academic discourses, Metzgar identifies a different kind of opposing narrative – the amnesia of the working-class community where he grew up and, by extension, of American culture. He opens *Striking Steel* with a story of arguing with his father, a former steelworker and union steward who had been deeply involved in battles for worker power two decades earlier but was now complaining about striking miners driving "brand-new trucks" and getting food stamps (2000, 3). That story sets up the question that lies at the heart of Metzgar's book: How could his father and so many others forget the history and the importance of unions? Metzgar's answer is clear: middle-class culture had, as he puts it, "reach[ed] right into your memory" to offer an inaccurate and problematic story about unions as contributing to rather than trying to solve problems of inequity (2000, 7–8). To understand how that happened, Metzgar suggests, requires not only labor history but also sharing and analyzing family stories. By weaving critical analysis together with memory, Metzgar offers a study of mid-century working-class politics that challenges simplistic claims about the meaning of class and organized labor.

As Metzgar demonstrates, individual narratives can provide insight into social patterns, including the complexity of class identity. An approach to class built on personal narratives recognizes the tension between specificity and generalization. Walley argues that "our lives only exist and take on meaning within the social worlds that have shaped us and through which we negotiate our paths in life. Our individual stories are also always communal ones." (2013, 5). As they tell their own stories, writers also "trac[e] the links and relationships that shape and define not only who we are as individuals but also the broader social worlds of which we are a part" (2013, 5). Stories cannot help but acknowledge the particulars of place, time, and specific structures of labor, family, and community, and by doing so they also draw attention to the messiness of class identities. As Walley demonstrates by tracing the immigrant and migrant narratives and the different experiences of the women and men in her family, stories reveal class intersections, the way people speak not only as members of the working class but also as "women and men, African-Americans, whites, Mexicans, immigrants, natives, gays, and straights in addition to our class backgrounds" (2013, 13). Indeed, while these narratives focus on class, the writers also acknowledge how their lives and perspectives reflect gender, racial, ethnic, geographical, and religious elements of their identities. This multiplicity does not take away from class; it makes clear how class is inflected by and plays out through other social categories.

Personal narratives also emphasize the way class is embodied and reproduced not only in the workplace or economic relations but also in interpersonal relationships and internal struggles. As Rita Felski suggests of Steedman's *Landscape for a Good Woman*, shifting the focus from the workplace and labor, which have occupied center stage in Marxist models of class consciousness, reveals how class "is ingrained from an early age in the psychological rhythms and flows of the mother-child relation" (Felski 2000, 39). While labor is always present in these narratives, most of these writers' stories take place at home, at school, and in the neighborhood. Metzgar remembers the labor struggles of the 1950s through the lens of his household, and Walley focuses her stories on the effects of deindustrialization. Class struggle plays out in daily life and sense of self, not only labor conflict. Jensen traces the challenges working-class students face as they make their way through the educational system. Walley recalls her conflicted feelings about leaving home to attend an elite private boarding school as a scholarship girl, as well as her later battle with cancer, which she ties to pollution from the steel plant where her father worked. Felski reads Steedman's story as evidence of how "class-based attitudes of fatalism, resentment, envy, and shame are inexorably transmitted from the working-class mother to her child" (2000, 39). Through personal stories, these writers explicate the diversity of class as well as its multiple forces and operations, offering a layered, contested view of working-class culture.

These narratives also articulate positive aspects of working-class culture, which is too often represented primarily in terms of struggle and hardship. In telling their stories, these writers identify what Jensen describes as the "humane, healthy, and life-giving qualities" (2012, 174) of working-class culture. Both Jensen and Metzgar identify working-class values of "being and belonging" (Jensen 2012, 63; Metzgar 2000, 202–203), which, as Jensen explains, play out in "peer relationships" that are free from "hidden power agenda[s]" (2012, 63). This value facilitates solidarity and collective action, as Zandy argues, noting that working-class consciousness (which she differentiates from working-class identity) offers "myriad possibilities for acting on and in the worlds we inherit" (1995, 2). Yet even as they identify the transformative potential of class solidarity, these writers also attend to the real hardships of working-class life. In this way, they resist romanticizing class-based struggles. Instead of revising the story to, as Faulkner puts it, "transform oppression into character-building experience" (1995, 205), these writers present working-class experience through both struggle and strength.

This complex understanding provides a foundation for scholarship that is at once critical and empathetic. Scholarly personal narratives model a subject-oriented approach to the study of class, putting individuals and their stories, including their interpretations of their experiences and of the social worlds in which they live, at the center of the field. The genre defines working-class people not as an undifferentiated object of study but as individuals who are part of a diverse collective of subjects. This approach resists two common tendencies. First, by offering varied narratives and analyses grounded in the perspectives of individuals with particular identities and experiences, the scholarly personal narrative makes clear that the working class is not a homogeneous group. Second, instead of considering class only as a social force or focusing, as much important research does, on class formation and activism,[4] the genre encourages us to also consider how class is lived. Scholarly personal narratives remind us that class matters even when working-class people do not exhibit the kind of collective consciousness than enables collective class-based action. By examining how class works through the lens of memory and stories, they suggest a theory of class that integrates the individual and the collective, specific experience and widespread patterns.

Positional authority as a working-class scholarly ethos

Along with offering new ways of understanding the working class, scholarly personal narratives articulate a theory of working-class scholarship that embraces grounded, engaged analysis. Like the scholarly personal narrative itself, models of scholarship from the ground up are not unique to working-class studies, of course. Feminist, queer, and ethnic studies critics have long advocated for not only recognizing the scholar's perspective but also viewing experience and positionality as sources of insight.[5] Positional authority has become a central tenet of working-class studies as well. To be clear, while most scholars in the field do not claim that one must be working class in order to understand or analyze the working class, working-class studies research usually incorporates self-reflexivity about class positionality, as scholars note how their experiences inform the questions they study as well as their approaches.

Most working-class studies scholars identify themselves either as professionals who come from working-class backgrounds or as straddlers with dual affiliations and identities.[6] Jensen describes herself as "culturally (if not economically)" in the upper middle class (2012, 24), a position that, she argues, allows her to understand class from both sides. Metzgar writes that "only a professional middle-class son" could draw on both experience and historical analysis to restore the memory of "what had been basic" to his father's working-class "way of looking at things" (2000, 8). In an essay reflecting on the Exit Zero Project, Walley describes her book as a "conversation between two parts of myself—the daughter of a steelworking family and the professional anthropologist" (2015, 627). While these scholars are, as Felski notes, "distanced" from working-class life in significant ways (2000, 42), they claim authority on a dual basis: as people who remember their working-class histories and retain ties to working-class communities but also as trained scholars with the expertise and distance to enable critical analysis.

Explicitly acknowledging the scholar's positionality has become a common practice in working-class studies, even in texts that do not center on the writer's own story. Tim Strangleman opens his essay on autobiographical writing by British railway workers by recalling his first job as a signalman on the London Underground (2006, 137). In writing about the class dynamics of community organizing, Betsy Leondar-Wright (2005) draws on interviews with dozens of activists, but she also incorporates her own experiences as an organizer and scholar who grew up in the middle class. The practice of identifying one's class-based positionality is not universal in working-class studies, but it has become a common rhetorical gesture because it establishes the nature of one's authority and investment in the working class.

It also embraces the productive value of subjectivity. These writers do not merely tell their stories; they present them in ways that draw attention to and advocate for the significance of subjectivity. In *Striking Steel*, Metzgar describes how reading the *Johnstown Tribune-Democrat*'s reports on the 1959 strike brought back a "flood of memories," not about the strike but about high school baseball games and a Saturday night date. Realizing how little he remembers about that year's strike allows him to articulate the difference between his parents' lives and his own, and it emphasizes the link between stories and research (2000, 85). Memory takes us into the Metzgar household, where Johnny taught his children about the value of the union along with other life lessons, while other sources fill in the gaps in memory and provide context. Neither, Metzgar suggests, can stand alone, especially in a book intent on figuring out why so many people have forgotten so much. Memory may not be reliable or complete, in other words, but the positionality that it reflects is necessary if we are to understand and appreciate labor history and the significance of social class. "Pretending that we are not a part of the picture," Metzgar argues, "distorts our self-understanding" (2000, 12).

Zandy makes a more specific claim for the value of positionality in studying working-class culture in particular. Scholarly work rooted in a working-class perspective enables "ambiguity, imprecision, and contradiction in confronting definitions of the working class" while also "recognizing the common working-class ground of *struggle*, a visceral and material and psychic state not easily or theoretically translatable" (Zandy 2004, 146). She defines such work as "*grounded*" (2004, 145), a term that suggests multiple meanings: ground refers to the materiality of the earth but also "what is unstable and open to cultivation and destruction. To grind is to reduce to small particles, to roughen. Any kind of work can be a grind. Metaphorically, ground is capacious, especially as linked to verbs. One *holds* one's ground, or *gives* ground, or *breaks* ground. But, whose ground?" (2004, 146, ital. original). Working-class academics, Zandy suggests, must claim their ground in working-class experience. She illustrates this in a discussion that moves from describing a Lewis Hine photograph of working children to asking about the experience of those children to comparing their lives with her own childhood and then to the memory of watching her father, lying in bed in the middle of a work day, recovering from a workplace injury (2004, 38–39). Through her shifting perspective, Zandy demonstrates that we cannot look at evidence without drawing on our own classed experiences, regardless of our backgrounds. As she writes, "All of us (even the owning class) carry within us traces of our family's work histories" (2004, 40). Memory, Zandy suggests, shapes the way we see evidence in productive ways. All of these writers demonstrate this as they map the dialogic relationship between experience and evidence. In the process, they model a scholarly practice that emerges from working-class culture, provides strategies for capturing its nuances, and embraces positional authority as well as subjectivity.

Building a community of practice

Scholarly personal narratives have not only shaped the ethos of working-class studies as an interdisciplinary academic field, but have also helped to build a community of practice. Academics in all fields organize themselves into subgroups clustered around key questions, themes, methods, or bodies of evidence, and academics often build important social bonds with their colleagues. To identify a field as a community of practice suggests something deeper, built around a sense of shared purpose and belonging. In defining the core elements of a community of practice, Etienne and Beverly Wenger-Trayner describe one such group: "new members were warmly welcomed into 'the family', ... many people stepped up to take initiative or share their war stories. ... Evening events, organized by the host country, were always lively – with singing, dancing and a hymn composed and sung by members" (2015, 1). The description comes from a report on a community of practice of internal auditors, but it will sound familiar to those who attend Working-Class Studies Association conferences. As a field, working-class studies does not merely share commitment to understanding working-class life and a critical ethos for studying class; it has also generated significant interpersonal connections, creating a structure of feeling within an academic community.

This sense of community does not simply reflect the warmth and generosity of individuals in this field. As Jensen and Metzgar have argued, belonging is a core value of working-class culture, so we should not be surprised that it is also valued in an academic community with many members from working-class backgrounds. The field's scholarly ethos encourages storytelling and egalitarian rather than hierarchical relationships. But as scholarly personal narratives remind us, academic fields and organizations have not always welcomed working-class people or perspectives, and few facilitate the kind of sharing and mutuality that we see in this field. By telling, reflecting on, and analyzing their own stories, working-class studies scholars have created an intellectual practice that also generates social connections. Because many contributors to this field include personal stories in their scholarly work, their colleagues know not only their analyses of class but also what their childhoods were like, how they have navigated the obstacles of higher education, or how their family relationships reflect class dynamics. Personal narrative fosters familiarity, even intimacy, sometimes even before people have met face to face.

The themes and insights embedded in scholarly personal narratives also contribute to this sense of belonging, especially narratives about leaving home and navigating the academic world. As Carolyn Leste Law writes in *This Fine Place So Far from Home*, autobiographical writing "develop[s] community" (1995, 10) by inviting working-class academics to recognize the value of their class origins and to tell their own stories despite any shame or anxiety they may feel. In telling and analyzing their stories, working-class academics identify common challenges and offer critiques of higher education and of middle-class culture that enable readers to make sense of their own experiences. Part of the power of these personal narratives lies in their familiarity; many working-class academics have found echoes of their own struggles in each other's stories. In a review essay, Ray Mazurek recalls how, in *Strangers in Paradise*, he encountered "people talking about my working life in ways that, retrospectively, seemed obvious, but which I had never understood so clearly before" (2009, 151). They also encourage readers to resist pressure to erase or revise their perspectives in order to fit into academic culture, a lesson Kathryn Hughes finds in Steedman's *Landscape for a Good Woman*: "if your story doesn't fit the universal formulae – whether feminism, Marxism, or psychoanalysis – then there's something wrong not with your story but with those who think they know what it means" (2000, 54). By modeling alternative academic practices and perspectives and by sharing stories of struggle within the academy, these writers challenge the isolation and exclusion that many working-class academics feel. This sense of shared struggle and resistance also contributes to the working-class studies community of practice. In a seminal essay on the study of genres, Carolyn R. Miller argues that what matters most about a genre is not "the substance or the form of discourse," but "the action it is used to accomplish" (1984, 151). In scholarly personal narratives in working-class studies, substance and action work together. They recount and analyze the centrality of belonging in working-class culture, and they also help to create it.

Personal narrative as agency

Yet scholarly personal narratives do not serve only academic purposes or audiences. Having engaged in what Walley describes as a "dialogic" research process that includes many conversations with family and friends (2015), many of these authors also imagine continuing the conversation in their writing. Margaret Willard-Traub describes how becoming an academic involved a "distancing from family and friends, and exclusion from the working-class culture of [her] childhood," but envisioning her working-class family, friends, and students as potential audiences helped her "feel less isolated in [her] work" (2001, 49). In an essay articulating the multiple modes and purposes of the Exit Zero Project, "Transmedia as experimental ethnography: The Exit Zero Project, deindustrialization, and the politics of nostalgia," Walley suggests that the "call-and-response mode of storytelling extends an invitation to others to join in the discussion" (2015, 628), though as Jensen acknowledges, the ideal of reaching both working-class and academic readers can be elusive (2012, 226). Despite the challenge, the goal of writing not only about but for working-class people is common in working-class studies, and rooting scholarly work in the personal offers a strategy for bridging the gap.

Using narrative to complicate and correct misrepresentations of the working class matters not only for the scholarly record but also for working-class people and communities. Personal narratives serve analytical and political ends, offering "public political statements" that critique the dominant culture and invite readers to join in "confronting" injustice (Mazurek 2009, 174). Walley argues that the more complex "concept of class" that her autoethnography explores can provide a "frame of action" for social change (2013, 168). Near the end of *Reading Classes*, Jensen describes a conversation with several aunts who seem "puzzled" when she tries to explain why she's writing the book. She thinks, but doesn't say to them, "Look, I am writing for you, to defend you" (2012, 209), and she suggests that analyses such as hers could enable cross-class alliances "that could provide some much-needed common ground" for fighting growing inequality (2012, 225). Similarly, Metzgar explains that he is telling the story of the era "when unions were strong" and workers "banded together to get a say in their lives" because he wants to "mak[e] it so again" (2000, 15). Of course, it is not unusual for academic writers to hope that their work will make a difference in the world. We would not do this work if we didn't believe that it mattered. What marks the writing of these working-class academics is that they locate that hope in the power of memory and stories.

Foregrounding personal narratives and perspectives also challenges dominant power structures by claiming authority from a position of otherness. As Jeffrey Gray argues, personal narrative can "link the 'I' to a collective which becomes rhetorically empowered to the degree that it appears decentered" (2001, 53). As Gray suggests, such narratives deploy the personal not to complain but to claim agency. Zandy makes a similar argument. By telling their stories, she writes, working-class writers not only "resist class amnesia" but also "illustrate agency" (1995, 1). The phrasing here is productively ambiguous, since "illustrating" could mean telling stories about people taking action but also writing one's story as a form of agency and using stories to generate activist responses. Memory may be personal, Zandy acknowledges, but it has the potential to "lead out to a more expansive understanding of class identity" that can be "practiced in the classroom, in political activism, in the shaping of culture" (1995, 5). In other words, these narratives model an activist response to classism. As Lois Rita Helmbold writes, the essays in Zandy's collection "inspire me and reaffirm my struggles" (1995, 23).

Personal problems

Using personal narrative in scholarly writing presents real challenges, however. Given the field's commitment to treating working-class people with respect, we must consider the ethics of how we use other people's stories as we recount our own. In her book, *The Ethics of Working-Class Autobiography: Representation of Family by Four American Authors*, Elizabeth Bidinger (2006) considers the tensions that underlie some personal stories, in part because the writers – who despite their continuing identification with their working-class families are nonetheless also separate from them by virtue of education and professional roles – reveal to outsiders aspects of family life that might otherwise have remained private. Even more troubling, Bidinger suggests, writers sometimes emphasize how they are different from their family members. For example stories of leaving home for college and becoming an academic can represent the narrator as a "family redeemer," whose success "vindicate[s] the family's hardship, sacrifice, or, simply, its ordinariness," even when the central emphasis is on "the authors' ambivalence about the power disparity between themselves and their families" (2006, 17). For Bidinger, power is a core issue in working-class autobiography, because our narratives include the stories of others who may not share our purposes. Commenting on memoirs by Mary Karr and Jacki Lyden, Bidinger asks what the writers' mothers, "women with very difficult and marginal lives, gain from their willingness to offer up their humiliation and pain to their successful daughters' book projects" (2006, 11). She encourages scholars to "be scrupulous in exploring the socioeconomic and cultural factors that shape their subjects' lives" and understand that readers may "be prejudiced against the poor and the working class" (2006, 17) – strategies that are common in working-class studies. Most scholarly personal narratives about working-class life make clear the authors' awareness of their conflicted positions, their concern for representing others fairly, and their commitment to contextualizing and analyzing working-class experience in ways that validate rather than simply expose it.

In addition, their emphasis on perspective and subjectivity can open scholarly personal narratives to critiques focused on the authors rather than their ideas. Reviewers commonly identify gaps in or disagreements with other scholars' arguments, but reviews of scholarly personal narratives sometimes attribute these to bias rather than to differences of academic opinion. For example in his critique of *Liberating Memory*, Anthony Dawahare attributes Zandy's lack of attention to "how the class consciousness and the left-leaning political sensibilities of her working-class contributors were formed" to a "repression of memory" (1997, 162). A review of *Reading Classes* suggests that "numerous swipes at the middle class as insensitive over-achievers" and Jensen's "valorizing" of her working-class family "exposes" her "own unresolved tensions" (Latham 2013, 254). While such personal jabs are happily rare, they suggest the importance – and the challenge – of balancing perspective with critical analysis. They also remind us that academics who choose to incorporate personal stories may be more likely to encounter personalized critique.[7]

Finally, while storytelling and memory have been rich resources for scholarship in working-class studies, we must resist the temptation to claim that they are better or more important than other kinds of sources. In their study of how scholars use other people's personal stories, Mary J. Maynes, Jennifer L. Pierce, and Barbara Laslett remind us that it is "an illusion to view individual biographical and autobiographical sources as in and of themselves deeper, truer, or more authentic than accounts based on other sources and methodologies" (2008, 41). What stories offer is not better evidence but different evidence. In reflecting on why she chose to write an autoethnography, Walley explains that the stories she tells "do not provide unmediated access to experience or a window onto daily life," and they are "bound up with power and power-laden conventions in the style, content, and contexts of their telling." They may not even bring us "closer to 'the people'". They can, however, "expose dominant viewpoints as particularistic rather than universalistic" (2015, 627). This view has been central in working-class studies, but the field has also generated significant work that eschews the personal. In nominating the scholarly personal narrative as the signature genre of this field, I do not intend to denigrate or exclude other forms. To do so would marginalize important research, and it could seem to exclude colleagues who come from other class positions. While some in working-class studies do view scholars who come from privileged backgrounds with suspicion, scholarly personal narratives by people from middle-class backgrounds about how and why they have become engaged with working-class studies might offer useful insights. As a field, we need diverse voices and approaches.

Working-class studies remains a varied and emerging field, taking many forms. As the signature genre of the field, scholarly personal narratives have laid the foundation for an interdisciplinary field of study that puts working-class people at the center as a complex subject for analysis, as a subject position from which to analyze class, as a community of practice, and as active, critical agents within social, political, and cultural worlds. Will younger scholars recognize the potential not only in the ideas but in the scholarly strategies of writers like Jensen, Metzgar, Steedman, Walley, and Zandy? I hope so, because working-class culture is being reshaped by globalization, mobility, neoliberal ideologies, and contingent employment. Much as we have learned from stories of working-class lives in the second half of the twentieth century, we need now to hear from those who are coming of age and navigating the early twenty-first century.

Notes

1 The Writing Across the Curriculum Clearinghouse provides links to many of these (see https://wac.colostate.edu/). They can also be found through online writing centers and on the websites of many college writing programs.
2 Working-class studies is neither the first nor the only field to embrace personal scholarly narrative. Since the 1970s, scholars in women's and gender studies and ethnic studies have advocated for the personal as a valid and important source for understanding difference and inequality.
3 For an overview of the scholarly traditions upon which working-class studies builds but from which it also differs, including labor studies, labor history, and cultural studies, see the "Introduction" to *New Working-Class Studies* (Russo and Linkon 2006).
4 See, for example Ira Katznelson and Aristide R. Zolberg's *Working-Class Formation: Nineteenth-Century Patterns in Western Europe and the United States* (1986) as well as Stanley Aronowitz's updated discussion of class as a social force, *How Class Works: Power and Social Movement* (2003) and Michael Zweig's *The Working-Class Majority: America's Best Kept Secret* (2000). All are significant, even essential, books in working-class studies, but they also take a distinctly different approach from the scholarly personal narrative.
5 Sandra Harding's edited collection, *The Feminist Standpoint Theory Reader: Intellectual and Political Controversies* (2004), provides a useful introduction. For a thoughtful review and critique of the uses of the personal in scholarly writing in the humanities, see *Personal Effects: The Social Character of Scholarly Writing*, edited by Deborah H. Holdstein and David Bleich (2001).
6 The term "straddlers" comes from journalist Al Lubrano's 2004 book, *Limbo: Blue-Collar Roots, White-Collar Dreams*, which examines the class identifications and perspectives of professionals in a variety of fields who come from working-class families.
7 The riskiness of self-revelation may explain why the texts discussed here were written by scholars who were either not in traditional academic positions or had tenure. While scholars in more precarious positions may engage the personal in conference presentations or in essays contributed to collections focused on the experiences of working-class academics, they may feel pressure to produce more traditional research early in their careers in order to secure jobs or win tenure.

References

Aronowitz, S. (2003) *How class works: Power and social movement*, New Haven, CT, Yale University Press.
Barrett, J. R. (2005) 'Striking steel: Solidarity remembered', *Labor*, 2, 1, pp. 116–118.
Bidinger, E. (2006) *The ethics of working class autobiography: Representation of family by four American authors*, Jefferson, NC, McFarland.
Christopher, R. (2009) *A carpenter's daughter: A working-class woman in higher education*, Boston, Sense Publishers.
Dawahare, A. (1997) 'The remembering and remaking of American working-class life and literature', *College Literature*, 24, 3, p. 158–163.
Dews, C. L. B. and Law, C. L. (1995) *This fine place so far from home: Voices of academics from the working class*, Philadelphia, Temple University Press.
Faulkner, C. (1995) 'My beautiful mother', in Zandy, J. (ed.) *Liberating memory: Our work and our working-class consciousness*, New Brunswick, NJ, Rutgers University Press.
Felski, R. (2000) 'Nothing to declare: Identity, shame, and the lower working class', *Profession*, 115, 1, pp. 33–45.
Gray, J. (2001) 'In the name of the subject: Some recent versions of the personal', in Holdstein, D. H. and Bleich, D. (eds.) *Personal effects: The social character of scholarly writing*, Logan, Utah State University Press.
Harding, S. G. (2004) *The feminist standpoint theory reader: Intellectual and political controversies*, New York, Routledge.
Helmbold, L. R. (1995) 'Class actions, class reactions', *The Women's Review of Books*, 13, 2, p. 23.

Hoggart, R. (1957) *The uses of literacy: Changing patterns in English mass culture*, London, Chatto and Windus.
Holdstein, D. H. and Bleich, D. (2001) *Personal effects: The social character of scholarly writing*, Logan, Utah State University Press.
Hughes, K. (2000) 'On Carolyn Steedman's *Landscape for a good woman*', *New Statesman*, November 27. www.newstatesman.com/node/152461.
Hyland, K. and Bondi, M. (2012) *Academic discourse across disciplines*, Bern, Peter Lang AG.
Jensen, B. (2012) *Reading classes: On culture and classism in America*, Ithaca, NY, Cornell University Press.
Katznelson, I. and Zolberg, A. R. (1986) *Working-class formation: Nineteenth-century patterns in western Europe and the United States*, Princeton, Princeton University Press.
Latham, J. M. (2013) 'Reading classes: On culture and classism in America', *Journal of American Culture*, 36, 3, pp. 253–254.
Law, C. L. (1995) 'Lives are not essays', in Dews, C. L. B. and Law, C. L. (eds.) *This fine place so far from home: Voices of academics from the working class*, Philadelphia, Temple University Press.
Leondar-Wright, B. (2005) *Class matters: Cross-class alliance building for middle-class activists*, Gabriola Island, British Columbia, New Society Publishers.
Lubrano, A. (2004) *Limbo: Blue-collar roots, white-collar dreams*, Hoboken, NY, Wiley.
Maynes, M. J, Pierce, J. L. and Laslett, B. (2008) *Telling stories: The use of personal narratives in the social sciences and history*, Ithaca, NY, Cornell University Press.
Mazurek, R. A. (2009) 'Work and class in the box store university: Autobiographies of working-class academics', *College Literature*, 36, 4, pp. 147–178.
Metzgar, J. (2000) *Striking steel: Solidarity remembered*, Philadelphia, Temple University Press.
Miller, C. R. (1984) 'Genre as social action', *Quarterly Journal of Speech*, 70, 2, pp. 151–167.
Nash, R. J. (2004) *Liberating scholarly writing: The power of personal narrative*, New York, Teachers College Press.
Patillo, M. (2014) 'Exit zero: Family and class in postindustrial Chicago', *Contemporary Sociology*, 43, 5, pp. 749–751.
Russo, J. and Linkon, S. (2006) 'Introduction', in Russo, J. and Linkon, S. (eds.) *New working-class studies*, Ithaca, Cornell University Press.
Ryan, J. and Sackrey, C. (1984) *Strangers in paradise: Academics from the working class*, Boston, South End Press.
Steedman, C. (1987) *Landscape for a good woman: A story of two lives*, New Brunswick, NJ, Rutgers University Press.
Strangleman, T. (2006) 'Class memory: Autobiography and the art of forgetting', in Russo, J. and Linkon, S. (eds.) *New working-class studies*, Ithaca, Cornell University Press.
Tokarczyk, M. and Fay, E. A. (1993) *Working-class women in the academy: Laborers in the knowledge factory*, Amherst, University of Massachusetts Press.
Walley, C. J. (2013) *Exit zero: Family and class in postindustrial Chicago*, Chicago, University of Chicago Press.
Walley, C. J. (2015) 'Transmedia as experimental ethnography: The Exit Zero Project, deindustrialization, and the politics of nostalgia', *American Ethnologist*, 42, 4, pp. 624–639.
Wenger-Trayner, E. and Wenger-Trayner, B. (2015) 'Introduction to communities of practice: A brief overview of the concept and its uses', *EB Wenger-Trayner*. Available at https://wenger-trayner.com
Willard-Traub, M. (2001) 'Scholarly memoir: An un-"professional" practice', in Holdstein, D. H. and Bleich, D. (eds.) *Personal effects: The social character of scholarly writing*, Logan, Utah State University Press.
Zandy, J. (1995) *Liberating memory: Our work and our working-class consciousness*, New Brunswick, NJ, Rutgers University Press.
Zandy, J. (2004) *Hands: Physical labor, class, and cultural work*, New Brunswick, NJ, Rutgers University Press.
Zweig, M. (2000) *The working-class majority: America's best kept secret*, Ithaca, ILR Press.

2

Reconceiving class in contemporary working-class studies

Joseph Entin

An 'infinite fragmentation of interests and position'

In the final, unfinished pages of *Capital, Volume Three*, Karl Marx turns to address the question, 'what constitutes a class?' 'At first glance', he says, the three major classes—laborers, capitalists, and property owners—are defined by each group's respective source of income: wages, profit, or rent. Yet the clarity of this formulation quickly dissolves, as Marx acknowledges the 'infinite fragmentation of interests and position into which the division of social labor splits laborers as well as capitalists and landlords' (1981, 1026). Class, Marx seems to realize, is not reducible to income and cannot be read easily from economic condition. Rather than generating secure class affinities, both class 'position' and class 'interests' are subject to what he calls 'infinite fragmentation'—a seemingly endless multiplication that challenges the stability and certainty of class as a category of sociological understanding and critical analysis.

I want to take Marx's emphasis on the contingency of class and the multiplicity of class determinations as a starting point for thinking about how to theorize the 'working class' in working-class studies under conditions of contemporary, late capitalist globalization. And one of my arguments here is that current conditions present a vital opportunity for such theoretical rethinking. More specifically, I think the global expansion and diversification of capitalist production and the laboring population since the 1970s make it imperative to develop new ways to conceptualize the social *differences, tensions, and contradictions* that have in fact *always been* constitutive of working-class collectivity. As I indicate below, such conceptual rethinking can help us more fully grasp the heterogeneity of work and workers, the always-shifting nature of class composition, and the relationality of class with other dimensions of capitalist power and collective identity.

Let me say at the outset that such rethinking is important for at least two reasons. First, the field of working-class studies is, to its credit, an interventionist field that has a vital role to play in contemporary political debates in the United States and elsewhere (see, in particular, the *Working-Class Perspectives* blog). To advance—as I think working-class studies should—an anticapitalist, anti-imperialist politics of solidarity organized by the intersections of class with race, gender, ethnicity, nation, and other axes of power and oppression, we need a more socially, economically, and culturally diverse vision of the working class. This is especially urgent right now, when a great deal of public discourse in the United States continues to privilege an outmoded, politically conservative image of the working class. In the wake of the 2016 presidential election, in particular, the news media exploded with stories about 'the white working class' and its role in Donald Trump's victory. Many scholars, too, have turned to white, rural workers and voters to dissect the contemporary cultural conflagration (Hochschild 2016; Vance 2016; Isenberg 2016; Williams 2017; Cramer 2016). In reality, however, white workers, and white male industrial workers especially, occupy a shrinking proportion of America's working-class labor force. The US working class is, in the words of a recent report from the Center for American Progress, 'more diverse than ever and growing more so' (Rowell 2017, 1). To help develop a viable critical and political diagnosis of the present, working-class studies needs to foreground the constitutive heterogeneity of labor and the 'intimate and plural relationships' workers have to capital (Chakrabarty 2000, 66).

The second reason rethinking class is crucial is because working-class studies would benefit from more actively embracing Marxist and other more abstract theoretical paradigms. There is a wealth of stellar critical work on capitalism—on racial capitalism, on settler colonial capitalism and what Marx called primitive accumulation, on reproductive labor and capitalism's gendered dynamics—that working-class studies could engage but often does not, in part due to the wariness about poststructuralism that has been woven (in some ways understandably) into the field, given its historic emphasis on the lived experience of working-class people. As a field, working-class studies has a lot to contribute to cultural theory, and a lot to learn from it. The engagement with theory is a challenge that working-class studies students, scholars, and activists should welcome.

As the editors of this volume explain in the introduction, the field of working-class studies took formal shape in the early to mid-1990s, when the Fordist regime of mass industrial production was unraveling in the face of corporate globalization, deindustrialization, and the rise of neoliberal policies. Initially, however, the field's class imaginary was grounded largely in a Fordist notion of the working class that was in the early stages of being eroded (and, as I argue above, this image of the working class is still monopolizing public discourse in the United States today). Under Fordism, class often seemed like a relatively stable category, and the working class itself both self-evident and familiar, often personified by a white, male breadwinner working in an auto plant or a coal mine. As such, the working class was often presumed to be an a priori subject, a known and recognizable entity: organized around large-scale industrial labor and the Congress of Industrial Organizations unions, it seemed to have a discrete culture and distinct values that reflected a fixed and coherent identity. Early on in its formation, working-class studies adopted the logic of multiculturalism, asking, as did an early grant proposal that helped found the Center for Working-Class Studies at Youngtown State, 'Where is class at the diversity banquet?' In the logic of multicultural inclusion, the emphasis fell on class as an identity—shaped by economics and exploitation, to be sure, but most urgently understood as a form of belonging. This way of thinking framed class less as a systemic process or social relation and more as a product of shared norms and lifestyle—an organic, integrated way of life that needs to be intellectually recovered and validated.[1]

However, several economic and social transformations—including the growing significance of transnational corporations; the global restructuring of work around more contingent, flexible forms of production and precarious labor; a surge in global migrations; the rise of neoliberal economic policies; and new forms of racial formation, struggle, and resistance—have challenged established conceptions of the working class and class as an analytic category. Global forms of lean production and 'flexploitation' have produced what Andrew Ross describes as 'a new landscape of irregular work' across job categories, from seasonal and day labor to part-time retail and service work, to skilled flex work and freelance work in the 'creative' and high-tech sectors (2009, 4, 9). Ross, and others, suggest that precarity is not only a labor condition, but also a 'new experiential norm' (2009, 9), perhaps even the basis for a new class, 'the precariat' (Standing 2011) or the 'multitude' (Hardt and Negri 2000).

Globalization has also expanded and diversified the wage-labor population, both in the United States, where post-1965 immigration has brought millions of workers from Latin America, the Caribbean, and Asia into the country, and around the world, where the planet's wage labor force has more than doubled in size.[2] These conditions have created what Saskia Sassen (2001) and David Harvey (2000) describe as a new 'transnational working class—heavily dependent on women', many of them 'living under conditions of poverty, violence, chronic environmental degradation, and fierce repression' (Harvey 2000, 42). As a result of these economic, social, and demographic transformations, the icon of America's mid-century labor imaginary—a male, blue-collar worker supporting a family on a single wage—is now almost extinct. At the dawn of the twenty-first century, historian Joshua Freeman notes, 'sales clerks, hospital aides, and school teachers were more representative of the working class than the steelworkers, coal miners, autoworkers, and railroad men who dominated images of twentieth-century labor' (2006, 205).

The economic and demographic transformations to labor and the laboring population over the last several decades present a substantial challenge for working-class studies: given the rise (or, one can argue, the return to prominence) of precarious labor and the expansive social and cultural heterogeneity of the world capitalist labor force, is there a discrete or coherent working class? Class remains an indispensable category of analysis and social condition, but it is less than ever a secure or stable form of collective or individual identity. How do neoliberal globalization, transnational migration, and the growing insecurity of labor conditions ask us to reconsider the assumptions we've made about class and the working class? Further, how is our understanding of class and class struggle reshaped by the emergence of new social movements, including Occupy, Black Lives Matter, Critical Resistance, #NoDAPL, and others? What resources can we draw on to complicate and enrich our conceptualization of class and the working class in light of current transformations? What kinds of working-class studies do we, as scholars, teachers, and activists, need in the present moment?

I propose that the challenge before working-class studies today is to reimagine and re-theorize its object of study—class, and the working class in particular—in ways that can give the field new analytic and activist purchase in the contemporary world. We must take class not as the ground on which we conduct our work, not as a preexisting category we use to crack open various aspects of history, culture, and society. Rather, we should approach class as a *problem* that must be continually interrogated and recast in the context of particular struggles. Class is a process and relation; the working class is not now and never has been a stable, singular, organic entity, identity, or formation. Our job is not simply to bust the myth of classlessness and reveal that class exists; we must also produce new and more nuanced understandings of the way that class comes into being, operates, and intersects with other axes of identification, collectivity, and conflict. Rather than drawing lines between theoretical approaches and traditions, working-class studies should adopt a willfully creative and promiscuous approach to conceptualizing class formation and class struggle—one that embraces intersectional, postcolonial, and poststructuralist approaches, and a wide range of Marxisms. This approach reveals that the working class is (and has been) larger, and more multifarious and shifting, than is often presumed. In what follows, I direct attention to lines of thought and theory that complicate class by underscoring the contingency of class formation, the social divisions and differences internal to the working class, and the larger circuits of social life and struggle beyond the workplace. My examples are weighted toward, but by no means exclusively drawn from, my home discipline of literary studies; I am convinced that the larger conceptual issues these sources raise about the diversity and contingency of the contemporary working class, and the place of theory in working-class studies, are relevant across disciplinary lines.

'Under construction'

Certainly, much of the best scholarly work in working-class studies has long argued for a complex, multifaceted view of class and its cultural manifestations. Paul Lauter's foundational 1980 *Radical Teacher* essay on working-class women's writing, for instance, opens not with an axiomatic *statement* about class, but with a series of provocative *questions* about how working-class literature might be defined. 'Writing - and indeed thinking - about working-class literature presents a number of unique problems', Lauter explains. 'To begin with, what do we mean by "working-class literature"? Literature *about* working-class people, literature by them, or literature addressed to them?' (1980, 16). Defining the working class itself, he contends, raises similarly thorny definitional issues, as traditional conceptions often exclude as many people—women, people of color, unwaged workers—as they include. As Lauter puts it in his contribution to Sherry Linkon and John Russo's 2005 anthology *New Working-Class Studies*, the relationship between class and literature is never definitive or final, but always 'under construction'.

The question of determination to which Lauter alludes—the manner and extent to which economic conditions shape cultural expression—has long been a critical concern in working-class studies. Literary historian Peter Hitchcock proposes the concept of answerability to theorize the relationship between representation and 'discontinuous histories of working-class culture' (2000, 29). Stressing 'the elusive and unstable nature of class itself' (2000, 20), Hitchcock argues that art does not simply 'express' working-class 'experience' or 'reflect' economic conditions, but rather answers it through a process of active, uncertain negotiation. Similarly focusing on the uneasy crossroads of class and culture, Janet Zandy's pioneering book *Hands: Physical Labor, Class, and Cultural Work*, which examines how physical labor gets encoded in literary forms, aims to create a never-quite-finished dialogue between 'the tactile world of work and the textured world of the academy' (2004, 2). Working-class studies, she argues, occupies the space *between* materiality and theory, the body and epistemology, labor and culture. Zandy rejects the poststructuralist theory that Hitchcock embraces, but like him, she aims to produce a non-reductive poetics to think through the intersection of class and representation.

In 1963, British historian E. P. Thompson famously argued that class is 'a relationship, not a thing'. It is, he insisted, not an ideal or static interest, but rather a 'social and cultural formation' that is 'defined by men [sic] as they live their own history' (1963, 11). Exemplary scholarship in working-class studies has always adopted Thompson's insight that class is a fluctuating, historically realized relation, extending it to underscore the culturally variegated quality of the US and global working class. Sherry Linkon and John Russo, cofounders of the Center for Working-Class Studies at Youngstown State University, have long insisted that we think expansively about how the working class is conceived. Linkon (2016) writes:

> Too often, references to 'the working class' imply white, male industrial workers. Yet the working class has always included men and women of all races, ethnicities, and sexualities, who work in a wide range of jobs at factories, farms, stores, offices, and homes. Within this large and multifaceted working class, individuals and groups have rarely defined themselves solely in terms of class, and the working class has fought bitter battles across divides of race, gender, and nationality.

Linkon's emphasis on the working class as diverse and internally divided is a crucial starting point for retheorizing class in working-class studies. More recent scholarship, such as Sonali Perera's *No Country: Working-Class Writing in the Age of Globalization*, to take one example, is pushing the field in new directions. Perera's book asks how working-class literature from across several national traditions imagines collective identification in an era when globalization is generating not labor unity, but an exacerbation of social, cultural, and geopolitical divisions. Exploding the idea that the working class can be constituted by 'alibis of origins and identity', she argues for class as a 'unity-in-dispersal' (2014, 3) and defines working-class literature not as a self-evident, stable tradition, but as a serially interrupted form that can 'only be understood in terms of its interrelationships and dialogic tensions' (2014, 4).

Taking inspiration from Perera and others, I want to suggest some theoretical resources for helping us understand the fluctuating, unpredictable, and complex way that class comes into being, which can help us further complicate and enrich the way we understand what Perera calls the 'interrelations and dialogic tensions' between class and culture in the tumultuous, global present.

'Multiplication of the proletariat': for Marxism in working-class studies

One place to start is with Karl Marx, whose writing has been given surprisingly scant attention in US-based working-class studies. This reluctance to engage deeply with Marxism is not uniform within working-class studies, and its origins are complex, traceable in part to the lingering power of Cold War anti-communism and the 'special conditions' of US cultural studies, which has been shaped by the durable ideology of American exceptionalism (see Denning 2004; for a lively debate about Marxism's place in working-class studies, see Schocket 2002). This resistance to Marxism continues into the present. For instance, in her introduction to *Critical Approaches to American Working-Class Literature*, Michelle Tokarczyk suggests that Marxism's putatively rigid conception of economic determination makes it an unworthy companion for contemporary scholarship on working-class culture: 'Marxist scholars see class as a defining status that supersedes identities such as gender and race. Working-class scholars, in contrast, practice intersectional analysis' (2012, 3). This oppositional rendering not only misrepresents Marxism, but also cuts a damaging divide between Marxism and working-class studies as allied fields of critical thought.

Indeed, for working-class studies to flourish in the era of neoliberal globalization, it is more urgent than ever to engage, rather than avoid or defame, Marxian thought and theory. And the first step in that direction is to revisit Marx himself. While Marx is often blamed for a reductive conception of class, much of his writing—like the passage from the end of *Capital* that is cited at the beginning of this chapter—in fact suggests the complex fluidity of class as an analytic and experiential category. In a well-known formulation at the beginning of Chapter 25 of *Capital*, for instance, Marx asserts: 'Accumulation of capital is therefore multiplication of the proletariat' (1976, 764). 'Multiplication' here is not only a reference to the size of the proletariat, but also, as Sandro Mezzadra and Brett Neilson assert, to its cultural and social composition, for as capital expands, generating new modes of production and labor capture, it absorbs an increasingly heterogeneous population into the accumulation process (2013). As a result, even as labor is consolidated, it becomes, as Marx argues in the *Grundrisse*, 'more diverse, more internally differentiated' (1973, 408). Capital's extension thus entails the expansion and diversification of both work and the working population.

In the emerging post-Fordist era, as 'labor positions are being multiplied from the point of view of tasks and skills', as well as 'legal statuses and conditions', Mezzadra and Neilson insist there is a 'widening of the concept of the working class' (2013, 100). Under these conditions, they argue, 'relations of social solidarity become more fluid' (2013, 88). The working class is no longer, if it ever was, a cohesive collective subject, but is in a process of uncertain becoming. 'Far from looking for old or new universal subjects', Mezzadra notes, 'we should rather investigate the tense and often conflict-ridden processes of production of common conditions that can make way for new inhabitants of the world' (2011, 166). Class is a relation and a process, and classes are continually being unmade and remade under shifting historic, social, and economic pressures and transformations (Silver 2016).

These insights are echoed in some of the most compelling historical and theoretical work on the working class by scholars such as Peter Linebaugh and Marcus Rediker (2000), Silvia Federici (2004), George Lipsitz (1994), Robin Kelley (1997, 2015), and others, which reminds us that the process of capital accumulation not only entails the consolidation and expansion of capital and exploitable workers, but also, as Federici explains, 'an accumulation of differences and divisions within the working class' (2004, 64). The working class is always polyglot, always internally riven with tensions and differences, even as and when it comes together in moments of solidarity and collective action. In the age of late capitalist globalization and global migration—when the extension of what Marx called the 'world market' is wider than ever and the working population is in remarkable flux, as hundreds of millions are on the move in search of work, sustenance, and safety—now, more than ever, we need to take seriously the heterogeneity of working peoples and the unfinished, always contested quality of class formation, even as we insist on the centrality of capitalist accumulation and exploitation to the shaping of contemporary world experience, and the acuteness of class as a category of analysis.

Further complicating any static notion of the working class, Marx underscores the instability and precarity of labor under capital and the porousness of the working class as a social formation. As capitalist production accelerates and intensifies, the living and laboring conditions of working people tend to become less secure. '[T]he higher the productivity of labor', Marx argues in *Capital*, 'the greater is the pressure of the workers on the means of employment, the more precarious therefore becomes the condition of their existence' (1976, 798). Marx notes that even as capital aims to concentrate workers at the point of production, consolidating the labor force, it also undercuts the predictability and stability of working-class life: 'large-scale industry, by its very nature, necessitates variation of labour, fluidity of functions, and mobility of the worker in all directions' (1976, 617). He continues, asserting 'an absolute contradiction' between the development and centralization of industry, through which capital seeks to reaffirm the 'ossified particularities' of the 'division of labour', and the unstable, precarious position of workers which 'does away with all repose, all fixity and all security as far as the worker's life-situation is concerned' (1976, 617–618). Far from being a new phenomenon, precarity is in fact the norm under capitalism.

There is thus a profound paradox at the heart of working-class conditions: in the process of generating capital's wealth, the proletariat is continually displaced, or as Marx puts it, 'thrown into the street as soon as [it] becomes superfluous to the need for valorization' (1976, 764). As production accelerates and intensifies, capital can produce more with less labor, the population of surplus labor continually grows, and workers' chances of poverty, or pauperism, increase. Workers are always threatened with nonwork as the line between employment and unemployment, between waged and unwaged labor, becomes increasingly blurred. 'It is already contained in the concept of the *free labourer*', Marx writes in the *Grundrisse*, 'that he is a *pauper*: virtual pauper' (1973, 604). If the working-class is defined by its separation from the means of production, it is thus always vulnerable to immiseration. 'The greater the social wealth', Marx asserts, 'the greater is the industrial reserve army. … *This is the absolute general law of capitalist accumulation*' (1976, 789). To account for this, we need to expand and complicate our conception of the working class to include both the employed and the unemployed; both formal and informal, and paid and unpaid, work; and both the possibility of conceptual universality and the intractable realities of political particularity.[3]

Seriality, living labor, and social reproduction

In the remainder this essay, I want to gesture to three different modes of theorizing class, and the relationship between class and culture, that can help us to think creatively about working-class formation and struggle in the global present: seriality, living labor, and social reproduction.

One way to think about class that exceeds the rigidity of many conventional definitions is Jean-Paul Sartre's notion of seriality, particularly as it has been taken up by feminist scholars Iris Marion Young and Sonya Rose. Seriality denotes a loose or passive form of social collectivity that does not rise to the level of self-conscious commitment and identity which marks what Sartre calls a 'group'. Unlike a group, a series refers to a collective whose members face common circumstances due to historically-sedimented material objects and social forces, which Sartre calls the 'practico-inert reality', or 'milieu of action', but do not necessarily share a deeply felt sense of unity and identity. Indeed, a series is not an identity, but a more open configuration; membership in a series is defined not by one's being, but by the fact that one's 'diverse existences and actions are oriented' around a common set of forces and structures (Young 1994, 728). Sartre contends that class as a series constitutes a 'unity … which is ever present but always elsewhere' (1991, 267). In response to changing conditions, a series may become unified by a set of collective aims as a group, an integrated collective in which members adopt deliberate membership. 'There is *identity*', Sartre explains, 'when the *common* interest … is made manifest, and when the plurality is defined just *in relation to this interest*' (1991, 260). The shared conditions that create serial relations establish a 'complex of possibilities'; group unity is created out of these possibilities only through 'praxis' (1991, 263, 265). Seriality is an experience of being with others *before* identity. A series is thus a way to imagine a class in itself, while a class that has achieved a self-conscious sense of identity through active struggle—a class for itself—would represent a group.

Seriality is a relation defined by a fundamental tension between commonality and separation. Indeed, seriality refers to the loose and unstable, even unconscious, unity of a collective that is experienced largely through isolation. As opposed to the group, Sartre insists, seriality is 'a plurality of isolations' that demonstrates 'the impossibility of uniting with Others in an organic totality' (1991, 256). The conditions of wage labor have a paradoxical effect on workers, uniting them in competition with one another as 'alienated others', in the words of Iris Marion Young (1994, 727). Sartre puts it this way: 'the existence of a labour market create[s] a link of *antagonistic reciprocity* between workers' (1991, 311, my emphasis). The idea of 'antagonistic reciprocity', of a relation marked by both mutuality and conflict, suggests that class is a contested, uneven category brought into being through struggle. Sonya Rose notes that Sartre's ideas about class 'do not presume that one level of practice leads to another in any simple way or in any predefined narrative of class development' (1997, 154). Under the sign of seriality, then, class formation becomes an uncertain process undertaken by a collective brought together in what frequently feel like antagonistic relations. Seriality helps us grasp the contingency of working-class composition both as a process without guarantees and as one mode of collective organization and struggle among many.

One benefit of seriality is that it allows for the idea that individuals participate in several series simultaneously. These series may overlap or contradict one another, creating layered or conflicting lines of social allegiance and possibility. Seriality fosters a conception of class that is at once determinative and conditional, grounded in material circumstances yet fluid and open-ended—a notion of class that can accommodate a sense of internal contradiction and intersection with other axes of conflict, identity, and struggle; a notion of class that is thus never stable, discrete, whole, or complete, but always internally riven with tensions and differences.

Seriality thus provides a flexible notion of class as a process of continual becoming that undercuts more static or identity-based notions. But how can we think about class beyond class—about the ways that economic relations and structures shape and are shaped by experiences, identities, and cultures outside the workplace? And how do we conceive the working class when more and more laboring people are being rendered redundant, actively excluded from the formal economy through unemployment, underemployment, mass incarceration, and other mechanisms of social and economic exclusion?

We might start with Marx's concept of living labor, which he defines alongside and in tension with the 'dead' labor objectified in tools and machines, and with capital's norm of abstract labor. Abstract labor is capital's measure of general labor to which all labor can be reduced, independent of specific working persons and their individual capacities. Abstract labor is capital's effort to lend homogeneity to the diversity of actual laboring bodies, to produce what Marx describes as 'a continuity, a uniformity, a regularity, an order … of labor' (1976, 465). By contrast, living labor is concrete labor 'as it exists in the personality of the worker' (quoted in Chakrabarty 1997, 53), or what Marx calls 'labor as subjectivity' (1973, 272). This latter phrase is especially evocative, suggesting that labor shapes one's sense of self and that workers bring to their labors not only their labor power but also their individual histories, capacities, limitations, and desires. Capital may have an interest in reducing workers to abstract quantities of pure laboring force, which the capitalist class can direct as it chooses, but in fact workers are always complex and embodied subjects that can never be fully contained, controlled, or subsumed during the accumulation process (Ong 1997).

Can we theorize, historicize, and analyze the manifold relationships workers—across a global range of social positions and laboring contexts—have to capital? Addressing this would be one way to circumvent the misleading opposition between class and cultural difference (race, gender, ethnicity) that all too often shapes critical discourse. Historian Dipesh Chakrabarty argues that the tension between living and abstract labor, between capital's drive to reduce all labor to a quantifiable unit and the individual particularities of the human beings who perform that labor, is one key place where social and cultural differences enter, and have the capacity to disrupt, capitalism. 'Difference', Chakrabarty concludes, 'is not something external to capital. Nor is it something subsumed into capital. It lives in intimate and plural relationships to capital' (2000, 66).

Chakrabarty's position, however, may underestimate the extent to which capital itself thrives on 'differences', exploiting them to expand its markets and divide working people from one another. As Lisa Lowe notes, 'in the history of the United States, capital has maximized its profits not through rendering labor 'abstract' but precisely through the social productions of 'difference', of restrictive particularity and illegitimacy marked by race, nation, geographical origins, and gender' (1996, 27–28). Working-class composition, then, does not occur beyond or above the stubborn particularities of social life and cultural difference. Rather, contradictions, divisions, and inequalities are structured within the working class in the very process of its constitution.

Putting stress on the social and economic divisions *internal* to the working class opens avenues to explore the ways that the working and nonworking populations are always organized by categories such as race, gender, and sexuality. For instance, Black radicals have long realized that a substantial challenge to the racist structures of US and global society requires a simultaneous challenge to capitalism. To cite one notable example, in 1967, Martin Luther King argued that the civil rights movement must 'address itself to the question of restructuring the American society', focusing on 'the economic system' and the 'distribution of wealth'. When you start to ask how racism relates to the control of material resources, he noted, 'you begin to question the capitalistic economy' (quoted in Taylor 2016, 198). King's often overlooked embrace of an anticapitalist, anti-militarist stance in the years before his death are significant, but by no means unprecedented. In fact, this thinking is in accord with a long line of Black revolutionary thinkers, from W. E. B. DuBois to Claudia Jones, C. L. R. James, the Black Panthers, Angela Davis, and many others who have understood the interdependency of racism and capitalist exploitation. The Panthers' Ten-Point Program (1966), for instance, calls not only for the right to political self-determination, an end to police brutality, and adequate education, but also for economic reparations, full employment, decent housing, and 'An End To The Robbery By The Capitalists Of Our Black Community'. Echoing this, the Economic Justice platform published by the Movement For Black Lives (n.d.) includes a robust set of demands for economic justice, including the right of workers to organize collectively, progressive taxation, and 'a reconstruction of the economy to ensure Black communities have collective ownership, not merely access'.

Capitalism is, and always has been, racial capitalism—a world system dependent on slavery, imperialism, and genocide that facilitates the super-exploitation, and the premature exposure to death, of racially marked populations.[4] As a result, addressing racial injustice requires addressing issues of economics and class, and vice versa. We must realize, as Keeanga-Yamhatta Taylor puts it, that '[i]mmigrant issues, gender issues, and antiracism *are* working-class issues' (2016, 216).

Finally, let me suggest that a focus on living labor, on the everyday life struggles and capacities integral to the production of value under capitalism, also directs us to the processes and politics of social reproduction. In *Capital*, Marx insists that the continuation of capitalist production requires incessant *re*production—the perpetuation of workers as workers as well as the terms and conditions of capitalist labor exploitation. Or, as he puts it: 'every social process of production is at the same time a process of reproduction' (1976, 711). Significantly, social reproduction points us beyond the workplace to the realms of social life through which workers sustain themselves and attend to their own needs. Historically, much of the labor required in these areas—childrearing, educating, and caretaking—has been the province of women. And while much of this labor has traditionally been unwaged, it is in fact crucial to capital accumulation and, therefore, a site of capitalist control and resistance, as a long line of Marxist- and socialist-feminist writers have contended (see, among many others, Dalla Costa and James 1973; Mies 1986; Vogel 1983). On Black radical theories of reproduction, especially, see Mullen (2017).

Attending to questions of reproduction has several benefits. Perhaps most important, it connects the analysis of capital to what theorist Bue Rübner Hansen describes as 'individual and collective strategies of life and survival' (2015)—not only exploitation on the job, but also personal and communal livelihood in the broadest sense. Social reproduction helps us see that labor in all its forms, as well as the capital-labor relation itself, needs to be continuously recreated and reinforced, and that it can also be resisted. The reproduction of labor and its conditions takes place every day, and the social and civic institutions—families, schools, religious organizations, systems of policing and incarceration—responsible for that reproduction are thus all shaped by (and in turn shape) capital's imperatives and are part and parcel of class composition and conflict. All the practices and systems of childrearing, race, gender, ethnicity, sexuality, and citizenship involved in the reproduction of human life under capitalism play a role in class formation, and vice versa. As Tithi Bhattacharya (2015) explains:

> Beyond the two-dimensional image of the individual … producer locked in wage labor, we begin to see emerge myriad capillaries of social relations extending between workplace, home, schools, hospitals – a wider social whole, sustained and co-produced by human labor in contradictory yet constitutive ways.

Thinking along these lines allows us to conceive manifold conflicts over the reproduction of everyday life—over food, health, housing, and well-being—*as* class struggles.

Social reproduction, then, allows an expansive, integrative, relational view of capitalism, class struggle, and working-class formation as, in Marx's words,'a total, connected process' (1976, 724). Class is no longer simply a matter of labor, but also of race, gender, ethnicity; it is no longer a matter merely of the conventional workplace—the shop floor—but also the home, the school, the street; it is no longer only a question of waged labor, but also of unwaged labor and all the work entailed in the full and complex reproduction of social life. Thinking through social reproduction allows us to see the false opposition between so-called 'identity politics' and class politics; in fact, contemporary struggles around so-called 'identity' issues—around immigration policies, around police killings and mass incarceration, around gender- and sexuality-based violence, around urban redevelopment and gentrification, around the Dakota Access Pipeline and other environmental injustices and matters of indigenous sovereignty—can all be understood as elements of a larger challenge to the capitalist organization of social and economic life.

Abandoning an image of the working class as a homogenous social or economic subject, we can, through attention to seriality, living labor, and reproduction, more fully grasp the continuous, contested process of formation, deformation, and reformation through which classes come into being and acquire social meaning in relation to multiple struggles under capitalism (Therborn 1983). This is, I submit, an important step in forging a notion of class adequate to an analysis of present conditions and the historic realities of capitalist society. My hope is that working-class studies will embrace this project in all of its complexity.[5] Doing so would forge a field marked by at least three qualities. First, it would be more engaged not only with the historical and cultural, but also with the conceptual study of class. The strength of working-class studies has been its focus on the traditions, texts, and values that have historically created a sense of cultural identity for working peoples in the United States. Moving forward, let us attend equally to the systemic, structural, and theoretical dimensions of class as a category and capitalism as a mode of accumulation and exploitation. Second, retheorizing class provides an opportunity for working-class studies to be even more active and visible politically, especially in pushing a politics that puts race, ethnicity, and gender at the center of a progressive economic agenda. Third, and relatedly, a more expansive and rigorously theorized notion of class can help the field craft more lines of alliance and affiliation to other intellectual and political struggles, including the fight to end white supremacy; struggles against settler colonialism and for indigenous sovereignty; struggles against mass incarceration and to make Black Lives Matter; the fight for women's, queer, and transgender rights, and the rights of all gender non-normative peoples; struggles for justice for the undocumented, and refugees and migrants; challenges to militarism and against empire and imperialism; and more. All of these struggles *are* class struggles—both because working-class people are already engaged in all of these struggles and because a capitalist system organized around economic exploitation and class hierarchies can only truly be abolished when all other forms of social and cultural violence and injustice are likewise overturned.

Notes

1 For example, Renny Christopher and Carolyn Whitson describe working-class culture as 'a culture that differs in values and aesthetic from the nation's dominant middle-class culture' (1999, 71). The essay claims that there is a discrete 'working-class aesthetic' (1999, 75) that reflects, in a seemingly straightforward manner, the terms of working-class existence: 'Working-class literature reproduces, in literary form, the conditions of the working class' (1999, 73). Christopher and Whitson's essay is a powerful piece that exposes and challenges the bias against working-class literature in both the canon and literary scholarship, but the ideas about culture and class that animate their analysis have trouble, I think,

accounting for the diversity and complexity of working-class formation, and the interrelations between class and culture, outside an identity-based framework. For an excellent discussion of these issues, to which I am indebted, see Hanley (2003). Other examples of the culturalist and identity-based model of class include the introduction to the seminal 1999 volume *Teaching Working Class*, which frames class as a matter of multicultural diversity: 'the principles of inclusion and recognition that have been so important in creating spaces for gender studies, Black studies, queer studies, and ethnic studies in colleges and universities have not generally been extended to class. … Bringing class into the classroom is an important step both to benefit our working-class students and to expand our institutions' recognition of diversity' (Linkon 1999, 2–3). Similarly, Laura Hapke framed her magisterial book *Labor's Text: The Worker in American Fiction*, in part as an exercise in multicultural restoration and affirmation, as an effort to 'recover' (2000, 4) and 'restor[e] knowledge lost and scattered' (xiii). For a strong critique of the emphasis on "experience", "culture" and "identity" as grounds for critical analysis in working-class studies, see Foley (2002) and Mullen (2002).

2 According to the United Nations, the number of global migrants increased from 84 million in 1975 to 215 million in 2010 (cited in Wise 2013). Sociologists William Robinson and Xuan Santos assert that in recent decades, '*[i]mmigrant workers [have] become the archetype of the new global class relations[,] the quintessential workforce of global capitalism*' (2014, 8, emphasis in original).

3 For more, see Denning (2010) as well as the growing scholarship on labor precarity, such as Neilson and Rossiter (2005, 2008); Standing (2011). Innovative work on labor precarity can also be found in anthropology; see, for example, Millar (2014). For an expansion of the proletariat beyond wage laborers, see Kreiner: 'At its root, proletarian is a Roman legal term. It refers to those with nothing to lose but their children, or *proles*. … Historically, moreover, *proletariat* gathered together—however rudely, and with no shortage of internal divisions too numerous to enumerate here—all those *both shackled by and excluded from* the wage relation. A proletarian is not a wage laborer per se. The proletariat encompasses all those for whom the fate of more or less miserable and immiserated wage-labor is the only available dream' (2017, my emphasis).

4 See, among many others, Kelley (2017) and Robinson (1983).

5 My own recent work on working-class literature and photography adopts some of the theoretical insights outlined in this essay. My 2017 essay, for instance, argues that migration becomes a metaphor in contemporary literature for imagining the ways that class formation is always in motion, in the process of becoming; my 2018 essay contends that in the hands of Milton Rogovin and Alan Sekula, the photographic series serves as an allegory for the contingency of class, as a relation and process that is at once material and representational.

References

Bhattacharya, T. (2015) 'How Not to Skip Class: Social Reproduction of Labor and the Global Working Class', *Viewpoint Magazine*, October 31. Available atwww.google.com/search?q=tithi+bhattacharya+viewpoint+magazine&oq=tithi&aqs=chrome.1.69i57j69i59l3j69i60j0.2208j0j7&sourceid=chrome&ie=UTF-8. Accessed July 15, 2017.

Chakrabarty, D. (1997) 'The Time of History and the Times of Gods', in Lowe, L. and Lloyd, D. (eds.) *The Politics of Culture in the Shadow of Capital*, Durham, Duke University Press, pp. 35–60.

Chakrabarty, D. (2000) *Provincializing Europe: Postcolonial Thought and Historical Difference*, Princeton, Princeton University Press.

Christopher, R. and Whitson, C. (1999) 'Towards a Theory of Working-Class Literature', *NEA Higher Education Journal*, 15, 1, pp. 71–81.

Cramer, K. (2016) *The Politics of Resentment: Rural Consciousness in Wisconsin and the Rise of Scott Walker*, Chicago, University of Chicago Press.

Dalla Costa, M. and James, S. (1973) *The Power of Women and the Subversion of the Community*, Bristol, Falling Wall Press.

Denning, M. (2004) '"The Special American Conditions": Marxism and American Studies', in *Culture in the Age of Three Worlds*, New York, Verso, pp. 169–191.

Denning, M. (2010) 'Wageless life', *New Left Review*, 66, pp. 79–97.

Entin, J. (2017) 'Globalization, Migration, and Contemporary Working-Class Literature', in Coles, N. and Lauter, P. (eds.) *A History of American Working-Class Literature*, Cambridge, Cambridge University Press, pp. 376–391.

Entin, J. (2018) 'Working Photography: Labor Documentary and Documentary Labor in the Neoliberal Age', in Blair, S., Entin, J. and Nudelman, F. (eds.) *Remaking Reality: U.S. Documentary after 1945*, Chapel Hill, University of North Carolina Press, pp. 151–171.

Federici, S. (2004) *Caliban and the Witch: Women, the Body, and Primitive Accumulation*, New York, Autonomedia.

Foley, B. (2002) 'Ten Propositions on the Role Played by Marxism in Working-Class Studies', *Rethinking Marxism*, 14, 3, pp. 28–31.

Freeman, J. (2006) 'Labor during the American Century: Work, Workers, and Unions since 1945', in Agnew, J.-C. and Rosenzweig, R. (eds.) *A Companion to Post-1945 America*, Hoboken, Wiley & Sons, pp. 192–210.

Hanley, L. (2003) 'Working-Class Cultural Studies in the University', *Radical Teacher*, 68, pp. 26–31.

Hansen, B. (2015) 'Surplus Population, Social Reproduction, and the Problem of Class Formation', *Viewpoint Magazine*, October 31. Available atwww.viewpointmag.com/2015/10/31/surplus-population-social-reproduction-and-the-problem-of-class-formation/. Accessed July 15, 2017.

Hapke, L. (2000) *Labor's Text: The Worker in American Fiction*, New Brunswick, Rutgers University Press.

Hardt, M. and Negri, A. (2000) *Empire*, Cambridge, Harvard University Press.

Harvey, D. (2000) *Spaces of Hope*, Berkeley, University of California Press.

Hitchcock, P. (2000) 'They Must Be Represented? Problems in Theories of Working-Class Representation', *PMLA*, 115, 1, pp. 20–32.

Hochschild, A. (2016) *Strangers in Their Own Land: Anger and Mourning on the American Right*, New York, New Press.

Isenberg, N. (2016) *White Trash: The 400-Year Untold History of Class in America*, New York, Viking.

Kelley, R. (1997) *Yo' Mama's Disfunktional! Fighting the Culture Wars in Urban America*, Boston, Beacon Press.

Kelley, R. (2015). *Hammer and Hoe: Alabama Communists During the Great Depression*, Chapel Hill, University of North Carolina Press.

Kelley, R. (2017) 'What Did Cedric Robinson Mean by Black Marxism?' *Boston Review*, January 12. Available at: http://bostonreview.net/race/robin-d-g-kelley-what-did-cedric-robinson-mean-racial-capitalism. Accessed July 15, 2017.

Kreiner, T. (2017) 'The Fate of the Fast Against the Slow', *Viewpoint Magazine*, June 1. Available at: www.viewpointmag.com/2017/06/01/the-fate-of-the-fast-against-the-slow/. Accessed July 15, 2017.

Lauter, P. (1980) 'Working-Class Women's Literature: An Introduction to Study', *Radical Teacher*, 15, pp. 16–26.

Lauter, P. (2005) 'Under Construction: Working-Class Writing', in Linkon, S. and Russo, J. (eds.) *New Working-Class Studies*, Ithaca, Cornell University Press, pp. 63–77.

Linebaugh, P. and Rediker, M. (2000) *The Many-Headed Hydra: The Hidden History of the Revolutionary Atlantic*, London, Verso.

Linkon, S. (ed.) (1999) *Teaching Working Class*, Amherst, University of Massachusetts Press.

Linkon, S. (2016) 'Redefining the Working Class', *Working-Class Perspectives*, March 21. Available at: https://workingclassstudies.wordpress.com/2016/03/21/redefining-the-working-class/. Accessed July 15, 2017.

Lipsitz, G. (1994) *Rainbow at Midnight: Labor and Culture in the 1940s*, Urbana and Chicago, University of Illinois Press.

Lowe, L. (1996) *Immigrant Acts: On Asian American Cultural Politics*, Durham, Duke University Press.

Marx, K. (1973) *Grundrisse*, translated by Martin Nicolaus, London, Penguin Books.

Marx, K. (1976) *Capital, Volume One*, translated by Ben Fowkes, London, Penguin Books.

Marx, K. (1981) *Capital, Volume Three*, translated by David Fernbach, London, Penguin Books.

Mezzadra, S. (2011) 'How Many Histories of Labour? Towards a Theory of Postcolonial Capitalism', *Postcolonial Studies*, 14, 2, pp. 151–170.

Mezzadra, S and Neilson, B. (2013) *Border as Method, or, The Multiplication of Labor*, Durham, Duke University Press.

Mies, M. (1986) *Patriarchy and Accumulation on a World Scale: Women in the International Division of Labor*, Atlantic Heights, Zed Books.

Millar, K. (2014) 'The Precarious Present: Wageless Labor and Disrupted Life in Rio de Janeiro, Brazil', *Cultural Anthropology*, 29, 1, pp. 32–53.

Movement for Black Lives (n.d.) 'Economic Justice'. Available at: https://m4bl.org/policy-platforms/economic-justice/.

Mullen, B. (2002) 'Working-Class Studies Without Borders', *Rethinking Marxism*, 14, 3, pp. 38–41.

Mullen, B. (2017) 'The Russian Revolution, Black Bolshevichki and Social Reproduction', *Viewpoint Magazine*, December 14. Available atwww.viewpointmag.com/2017/12/14/russian-revolution-black-bolshevichki-social-reproduction/#fn23-8568. Accessed January 5, 2018.

Neilson, B. and Rossiter, N. (2005) 'From Precarity to Precariousness and Back Again: Labour, Life and Unstable Networks', *Fibreculture Journal*. Available at: http://five.fibreculturejournal.org/fcj-022-from-precarity-to-precariousness-and-back-again-labour-life-and-unstable-networks/. Accessed January 7, 2018.

Neilson, B. and Rossiter, N. (2008) 'Precarity as a Political Concept, or, Fordism as Exception', *Theory, Culture & Society*, 25, 7–8, pp. 51–72.

Ong, A. (1997) 'The Gender and Labor Politics of Postmodernity', in Lowe, L. and Lloyd, D. (eds.) *The Politics of Culture in the Shadow of Capitalism*, Durham, Duke University Press, pp. 61–97.

Perera, S. (2014) *No Country: Working-Class Writing in the Age of Globalization*, New York, Columbia University Press.

Robinson, C. (1983) *Black Marxism: The Making of the Black Radical Tradition*, Chapel Hill, University of North Carolina Press.

Robinson, W. and Santos, X. (2014) 'Global Capitalism, Immigrant Labor, and the Struggle for Justice', *Class, Race and Corporate Power*, 2, 3, pp. 1–16.

Rose, S. (1997) 'Class Formation and the Quintessential Worker', in Hall, J. (ed.) *Reworking Class*, Ithaca, Cornell University Press, pp. 133–168.

Ross, A. (2009) *Nice Work if You Can Get It: Life and Labor in Precarious Times*, New York, New York University Press.

Rowell, A. (2017) *What Everyone Should Know about America's Diverse Working Class*, Center for American Progress Action Fund. Available at: https://cdn.americanprogress.org/content/uploads/sites/2/2017/12/11045153/What_Everyone_Should_Know_About_Americas_Diverse_Working_Class.pdf. Accessed December 30, 2017.

Sartre, J.-P. (1991) *Critique of Dialectical Reason, Volume One: Theory of Practical Ensembles*, London, Verso Books.

Sassen, S. (2001) *Globalization and its Discontents: Essays on the Mobility of People and Money*, New York, The New Press.

Schocket, E. (2002) 'Marxism and Working-Class Studies', *Rethinking Marxism: A Journal of Economics, Culture, and Society*, 14, 3, pp. 25–48.

Silver, B. (2016) 'The Remaking of the Global Working Class', *ROAR Magazine*. Available at: https://roarmag.org/magazine/the-remaking-of-the-global-working-class/ Accessed September 15, 2017.

Standing, G. (2011) *The Precariat: The New Dangerous Class*, London, Bloomsbury Academic.

Taylor, K.-Y. (2016) *From #BlackLivesMatter to Black liberation*, Chicago, Haymarket Books.

Therborn, G. (1983) 'Why Some Classes are More Successful than Others', *New Left Review*, 138, pp. 37–55.

Thompson, E.P. (1963) *The Making of the English Working Class*, London, Vintage.

Tokarczyk, M. (2012) *Critical Approaches to American Working-Class Literature*, New York, Routledge.

Vance, J.D. (2016) *Hillbilly Elegy: A Memoir of a Family and Culture in Crisis*, New York, Harper.

Vogel, L. (1983) *Marxism and the Oppression of Women*, London, Pluto Press.

Williams, J. (2017) *White Working Class: Overcoming Class Cluelessness in America*, Cambridge, Harvard Business Review Press.

Wise, R. (2013) 'The Migration and Labor Question Today: Imperialism, Unequal Development, and Forced Migration', *Monthly Review*, 64, 9. Available at: https://monthlyreview.org/2013/02/01/the-migration-and-labor-question-today-imperialism-unequal-development-and-forced-migration/. Accessed July 15, 2017.

Young, I. (1994) 'Gender as Seriality: Thinking Women as a Social Collective', *Signs*, 19, 3, pp. 713–738.

Zandy, J. (2004) *Hands: Physical Labor, Class, and Cultural Work*, New Brunswick, Rutgers University Press.

3

Mediating stories of class borders

First-generation college students, digital storytelling, and social class

Jane A. Van Galen

First-generation college students occupy a distinctive social class position. Most, by far, are from poor and working-class backgrounds; their college ambitions are inextricably entangled with hopes for social class mobility through success in school. Yet the odds are firmly against them: decades of evidence indicates that higher education replicates rather than eradicates inequalities (e.g. Armstrong & Hamilton 2013; Goldrick-Rab 2016; Hamilton 2016; Lee 2016; Weis, Cipollone, & Jenkins 2014).

In this chapter, I make the case for multimedia authoring as a participatory research method for unpacking the complex ways in which social class shapes the experience of poor and working-class college students as they navigate college against the odds. Within the interdisciplinary, activist, and intersectional traditions of working-class studies, I was drawn to the distinctive potential of digital storytelling to foster deep reflection and to amplify the voices of first-generation students on their own campuses and beyond. I expected their stories to reveal nuanced and diverse experiences of students on the margins of colleges and universities, as they also complicate meritocratic notions of education.

As a first-generation college student myself, who didn't learn to name the social class constraints in my education until long after finishing college, I brought both personal and intellectual commitments to this work.

First-generation students' pathways to college are etched within class stratification. They are less likely to have access to admissions test preparation, college counseling while in high school, advanced high school coursework, and information about academic requirements for college degrees. They are more likely to enroll in two-year, rather than four-year, colleges; first-generation students are four times more likely than peers to leave college after their first year. Nearly half leave college without graduating (Banks-Santilli 2014; Engle, Bermeo, & O'Brien 2006; Pell Institute 2011; Stephens, Fryberg, Markus, Johnson, & Covarrubias 2012).

The literature written for and by those who work directly with first-generation students is typically focused on fixing students. This body of work often attributes their challenges to intellectual, social, financial, and emotional deficits of the students and their families (e.g. Ishitani 2003; Woosley & Shepler 2011). Ward, Siegel, and Davenport, for example, write:

> For many first-generation students, lacking college-related cultural capital as they do, these aspects of college life are not well understood, and for that reason their levels of engagement and integration may be different from those of their better-prepared peers. The academic aspects of college life often overwhelm first-generation students. In particular, they are frequently unaware of the level of rigor they will face in their classes and are surprised by the expectations and behaviors of their instructors.
>
> *(2012, 49)*

Beyond mention of 'cultural capital' (often, as in this case, as an individual attribute rather than hierarchical judgments of presumed worth), this professional literature rarely considers social class stratification as foundational to the experiences of first-generation students. These authors do not explain why the basic ground rules for success in college are not simply made explicit, why financial aid cannot be simple and adequate (Kelly & Goldrick-Rab 2014), why many students are consigned to K–12 schools with inadequate resources, or how the daily social interactions of campus life convey to academically capable poor and working-class students that they do not 'belong' (Mallman 2017; Reay 2015; Ward, Siegel, & Davenport 2012, 75).

Denied the resources needed for success in college, newcomers are excluded from the high-stakes credentialing systems of higher education (e.g. Lamont & Fournier 1992; Bourdieu 1984). As Gans writes, 'Many boundaries, especially guarded and closed ones, exist to protect inequalities and to make sure that the less than equal cannot enter or can do so only by paying proper deference' (1992, xiii). The boundaries are not absolute; first-generation students are the 'ones who got away' (Reay 1997, 21) from highly stratified systems of schooling that function to 'inscribe failure' (Reay 2015, 21) on poor and working-class children.

As such, their experiences offer potentially rich insights into the opportunities and the formidable constraints of social class, mobility, and schooling. Yet as Renny Christopher (2009) has written, class in the U.S. is essentially invisible until one is poised at the very threshold of crossing class boundaries. Given the silence about class in education (hooks 2000), academically ambitious students from poor and working-class communities may not fully recognize the depths of structural inequalities within which they have been educated (Armstrong & Hamilton 2013) or the familial and social resources that middle- and upper-class students have taken for granted as they prepared for college (Calarco 2011, 2014–2015; Lareau 2000, 2011; Reeves 2017).

They may be even less conscious of how social class hierarchies become 'embodied and turned into a second nature' (Bourdieu 1990, 63), shaping their very sense of themselves and their place in the social world. Indeed, a long sociological literature documents the embodied 'ease' of privileged students among those in power (including academic researchers) and the parallel embodied unease of poor and working-class students in classed interactions (e.g. Bottero 2004; Bourdieu 1984; Holland, Lachiocotte, Skinner, & Cain 1998; Reay 2003, 2005, 2015; Skeggs 2005; Sayer 2005a; Walkerdine, Lucey, & Melody 2001).

More privileged students may understand that hours of admissions test prep, private tutoring, and private college admissions counselors are simply strategies to get them into colleges where they deserve to be. Being raised to believe that adults are interested in their questions and opinions (Lareau 2011) and that college is their right, privileged students are more likely to expect faculty and staff to support their success (Armstrong & Hamilton 2013; Hamilton 2016; Rivera 2016). Poor and working-class students, in contrast, may be proud of having gotten themselves into college on their own, but once within the new social landscape of academia, begin to doubt whether they belong. They may believe that success depends on proving their independence and resilience rather than on finding and accessing campus resources, and then blame themselves when things go wrong.

Thus, the 'heavy psychic costs' of deeply inequitable systems of education fall solely on the shoulders of poor and working-class students (Reay 2015, 13). In Mallman's words, first-generation student experiences represent 'the emotional embodiment of class distinctions' (2017, 241). Reay (2005, 924) writes that for first-generation students, college is often marked by shame and by fear of reaching and failing. Shame, Sayer writes (2005b, 955) is 'likely endemic to the experience of class'. He elaborates:

> Within the educational systems of class societies, the shaming of those who fail is a structurally generated effect, as Bourdieu's extensive research on such systems demonstrates, even though it is felt as an individual failure (e.g. Bourdieu, 1996). Those who believe that society is basically meritocratic are most vulnerable to shame.
>
> *(959)*

Students' sense that they don't belong in college may have less to do with their academic preparedness than with this 'structurally generated' shame (Mallman 2017; Reay 2005). When students have inequitable access to the 'social bases of respect' as college students, when they face judgment not over what they have done, but what they lack (Sayer 2005b, 954), their shame may lead to a complicated silence: 'Low-level shame often cannot be articulated, indeed it can lead to withdrawal and inarticulacy in terms of feeling a lack of authority to speak and hence lack of practice in articulating one's situation' (Sayer 2005a, 157).

While their colleges may provide students with remedial coursework or personal counseling, few first-generation students have had access to explicit discourse about structurally generated failure grounded in class stratification.[1] Their success in getting to college is entangled within ideologies of meritocracy that mask deep educational inequalities. I expected, then, that research into the lived experiences of first-generation students would require methods that could capture their experiences 'as situated, partial, constructed, multiple, embodied, and enmeshed in power relations' (Ellingson 2009, 10). Conventional research methodologies dependent on self-reflection and self-disclosure were likely to fall short of capturing students' *embodied* experiences of *living* class (Reay 2005), when *living* class stratification likely feels instead like shame over the sense that one is simply not good enough to make it in college. Given their positions at the borderlands of class mobility, I sought research methods through which students could explore as well as explain their stories. I sought ways for them to interrogate embodied knowledge, knowing that class subordination may well be felt as individual inadequacy rather than as critique of campus policies and practices (Mallman 2017; Reay 2015; Sayer 2005a).

Digital storytelling, voice, and power

Drawing from the methodologies of Story Center (Lambert 2010, 2012), I began facilitating three-day digital storytelling workshops in which first-generation students question, affirm, craft, and eventually share first-person multimedia stories of being 'first'. To date, more than 60 students and former students across the U.S. have created digital stories. Several weeks after the workshop, I interview the students about decisions made in composing their stories and about their experiences of working side by side with other first-generation students. Public stories from the workshop are available at the First in Our Familes website (firstinourfamilies.org). The project is a partnership with Class Action, a nonprofit dedicated to ending classism and extreme inequalities. In supporting students' dialogue with one another and then foregrounding the voices of poor and working-class students, we envisioned this partnership as one step toward making higher education more equitable and just.

The project draws from and extends theoretical work on narrative, silence, and power in the lives of students marginalized by inequitable systems of education. As Bourdieu (1999, 716) argues, accounts of 'the most personal difficulties and apparently subjective tensions and contradictions reflect the deepest structures of the social world and their contradictions'. With Vivienne (2015, loc 2953), I have found that digital stories locate 'heartfelt descriptions of everyday life' within broader questions of equity and justice.

Participants in the First in Our Families workshops develop first-person story scripts, typically around 350 words in length. The focus is on the genre of *story* in which the students are protagonists in their own lives. It typically takes hours of writing and revision for students to create their scripts; the constraints of the short script require them to be clear about the meaning of the stories and, thus, the narrative core of their story. These scripts are audio recorded and imported into video editing software. Images, video clips, sound, and music are then woven together in three- to five-minute productions that are collectively screened on the final afternoon.

The workshops are designed to support deep and collaborative reflection. On the first day of the workshop, we do writing exercises and then compile a shared list of descriptive words representing the dailiness of life as a first-generation student. We then go on a photowalk through campus, with each student shooting multiple, intuitive metaphorical images of the emotion words we've listed together. Back in our workspace, each student shares an image they've taken along with a brief account of the connection that they see to the first-generation experience. A steep stair familiar to most of the students may be framed as a metaphor for exhaustion; a short video clip of swirling autumn leaves evokes stories of trying (and failing) to find a major. As stories begin to develop, as we explore visual metaphors, as we create an affirming community, the students begin adding depth and detail to their own narratives, supported by peers and facilitators. Then, each student presents a working draft of their story during a 'story circle'. Stories beget stories, as memories are rekindled and students begin to see their collective experiences in what they'd understood to be personal challenges. Tears and laughter are common, in equal measure.

Over the hours of video editing (each three-minute story represents approximately ten hours of editing), the students listen to their own recorded narration multiple times and make hundreds of creative decisions in anticipation of their audience (Coventry 2008; Leon 2008; Luschen 2014; Opperman 2008). As such, digital stories are 'conversational media' (Lambert 2012, 14), as the creative work of authoring enables stories to become 'a place of reconciliation with difficult experiences' (Gubrium & Harper 2013, 58).

The multiple layers of story production enable students to represent what they understand, as well as the complexity and uncertainties of their experiences (Kara 2015, loc 2087). Family photos evoke personal memories but also are positioned as acts of defiance within stories of patronizing faculty. An image of a lone lit window in an otherwise dark dorm building, juxtaposed against narration of a family feast, powerfully conveys what is lost when poor and working-class students leave family for the isolation of college. Abstract images of elements of campus landmarks symbolize a storyteller's distance from the meaning that these landmarks may have for other students. Visual media are layered with driving – or plaintive – soundtracks, with transitions that superimpose images upon one another, or with ambient sounds from home. Students work intensely on every detail.

Thornburg, Booker, and Nunez-Janes describe this work as simultaneously inwardly reflective and outward facing.

> The practice of digital storytelling provides an entry point to people's theorizing processes as they attempt to make sense of their multiple and sometimes contradictory lives. In this

> sense, digital storytelling can identify borderlands and challenge or blur instantiations of state and institutional power that demarcate borders and invalidate the hybrid experiences of those who inhabit them.
>
> *(2017, 7)*

This distinctive semiotic power of multimodal composition supports the goal of 'crafting an agentive self' (Hull & Katz 2006) during the intensive production process. Hull and Nelson explain that 'a multimodal text can create a different system of signification, one that transcends the collective contribution of its constituent parts' of words, images and music (2005, 225). In short, digital stories hold the potential to convey the experiences of *feeling* power, even when those experiences are as yet 'beyond the reach of articulation' (Boler 1999, loc 573). Students may spend hours finding the exact image to metaphorically convey a moment in their stories, and then invest even further in refining the timing of the image on screen and the transitions between visual elements. Over meals and breaks, they tell peers and facilitators about the back-stories of these moments and find even more connections with each other's stories. In this work, they simultaneously come to deeper understanding of their stories while striving to represent their significance to others.

Vivienne elaborates:

> Every element of a digital story represents a directorial choice, from which story to tell, which characters to include, what images to use, how they are framed, how quickly or slowly they will be edited together, transitions and visual effects and whether to include music and sound effects. These textual decisions constitute material negotiations of privacy and publicness that are laden with richly evocative cultural significance.
>
> *(2015, loc 3053)*

Thinking 'through and with' images, sound, and video (Alexandra 2017, 120) enables both storytellers and audience to feel 'the multi/con/textual digital story and [to develop] a multisensory relationship with the story' (Gubrium & Harper 2013, 63). Benmayor notes that digital story production 'involves the skills of conceptualizing, writing, performing, selecting, imagining, integrating, and signifying' (2008, 194), all complex forms of conveying deeply embodied stories.

In facilitating these workshops, I perform multiple roles: Throughout the workshop, I share my own stories of being a first-generation student and now faculty member, openly conveying both my frustration and my joy within academia. In the facilitated story circle in which students share drafts of their stories, I listen diligently for clues to stories-within-stories that students may be seeking permission to tell and for connections among the students' stories. I model and encourage collaborative affirmation of emerging stories and lead brainstorming sessions about how each student might integrate visual elements into their production. I individually workshop scripts with each student, focusing on deepening the students' own understanding of the meaning of the story and supporting their decisions about what to represent and what to still hold to themselves. During the hours of production, I circulate among students to offer ideas, feedback, technical advice, and encouragement to own yet more of their wisdom about the circumstances of their lives. After the culminating screening of stories on the last afternoon, I facilitate conversations about what the students learned from one another about 'being first' and about what they, collectively and individually, might now like to do with these stories. In all of this work, I acknowledge the institutional obstacles that have been placed in their way, raise questions about classist policies and practices of their institutions, and applaud their insights. I supply copious amounts of chocolate and tissues.

Breaking silences on class

For most students, the workshop was the first time that they had told their stories. Silence around class, Lindquist (2004, 190) cautions, is grounded in the emotional labor of 'living class' (Reay 2005). Lindquist writes that

> pedagogies informed by critical and cultural theory have treated class less as a complex affective experience than as a set of social issues to be addressed through systematic analysis. [...] We understand class as a problem of distribution of resources, but we experience it affectively, as an emotional process.
>
> *(2004, 190, 192)*

Alison Jaggar (1989) argues that such emotion signals an *evaluative* stance. Megan Boler (1999, loc 164) elaborates that within inequitable social relationships, injustice is not simply rationally analyzed but is instead experienced viscerally. She writes: 'We "feel power" in the sense that we understand and enact our appropriate roles of subordination and domination significantly through learned emotional expressions and silences.' Within Western intellectual traditions, however, emotions have been framed within false binaries of rationality/irrationality, with emotion dismissed as evidence of feminine frailty and therefore silenced (Boler 1999; Zorn & Boler 2007).

This social control of emotions, Boler writes (1999), is at the core of social processes that frame injustices such as educational inequality as inevitable. She cautions particularly that gendered silence is too often interpreted as 'a willing agreement to their subordination', noting that Western intellectual traditions teach students not to articulate affect. She also argues (1999, loc 2274) that conventional scholarship misses the gendered, classed, and raced powerlessness felt by many students, particularly

> how powerlessness functions, affects, feeds on, and drains our sense of agency and power *as active creators of self- and world-representations*. By powerlessness I mean a state that is usually silent and mutates into guilt and denial that gnaw at us.
>
> *(Italics added)*

It would be challenging for any conventional research methodologies to break these silences, embodied as they are within shame for falling short of goals that have been placed beyond one's reach. Within analytical cultures of college, students learn instead 'to view emotions as their private problem rather than as a sign that something is wrong with the outside world' (Boler 1999, loc 68). Drawing from Foucault's analysis of embodied social control, Boler continues: 'emotions are a prime site for developing pastoral power, as emotions are already discursively constructed as "private" "individualized" and "natural", exceeding language and thus sometimes beyond the reach of our articulation.' Yet as students are invited to tap the emotional narrative arcs within the stories they tell one another in the workshop, they begin to break long-embodied silences.

Jaggar describes such moments as a reframing of 'outlaw' emotions experienced by subordinated individuals who 'pay a disproportionately high price for maintaining the status quo' (1989, 166). Jaggar sees 'outlaw emotions' in 'dialectical relation to critical social theory'. She elaborates:

> When unconventional emotional responses are experienced by isolated individuals, those concerned may be confused, unable to name their experience. … When certain emotions are shared and validated by others, however, the basis exists for forming a subculture defined by perceptions, norms, and values that systematically oppose the prevailing perceptions, norms, and values. By constituting the basis for such a subculture, outlaw emotions may be politically because epistemologically subversive.
>
> *(166)*

Given how few social spaces are available for first-generation students to acknowledge the powerlessness, shame, fear, guilt, doubt, or frustration of living and working within unjust social spaces, multimodal composition in collaboration with other first-generation students offers a distinct way to represent their experiences as something very different from prevailing narratives of college life. First, though, they have to create a narrative arc through those experiences.

Narratives as subversive stories

Narrative has long been recognized by scholars as a tool of critical reflection and identity construction (e.g. Bruner 1994; Clandinin & Connelly 1998; Miller 1994; Ochs & Capps 2001; Witherell & Noddings 1991). In constructing narratives, actors do not simply remember, but instead socially create the 'perpetually rewritten story' of self (Bruner 1994, 53). In that narratives are constructed and co-constructed for particular audiences, those writing them also anticipate the 'interpretive grids' that audiences will bring to listening (Ochs & Capps 2001, loc 2250).

Thus, narrators who have embodied class distinctions perform 'an evaluation of the self by the self' (Sayer 2005b) in anticipation of more powerful others' judgment of them (Skeggs 1997). Thus, I knew that students living at complicated social borderlands might well tell only stories that reflect rather than challenge power relationships (Boler 1999; Ewick & Silbey 1995, 2003; Ochs & Capps 2001; Orbuch 1997; Zorn & Boler 2007) or that would serve as rituals of 'impression management' (Goffman 1984) rather than reflection. Drawing from Bourdieu, Reay (2015, 12) cautions that 'the learning that comes through inhabiting pathologised spaces within the [social] field often results in a predilection for shame, fear, anxiety, and even righteous indignation' rather than expectations of respect. Thus, as social practices, narratives may 'bear the imprint of dominant cultural means and practices as any other social practice' (Ewick & Silbey 1995, 211).

The workshops instead intentionally create support for the emergence of subversive stories (Ewick & Silbey 1995, 220–222). Multimodal authoring provides marginalized individuals the opportunities to articulate 'agentive stances toward their present identities, circumstances, and futures' (Hull & Katz 2006, 44). The social space of the workshop within which they create their stories takes this even further.

Ewick and Silbey (1995, 220–222) elaborate on the conditions under which 'subversive stories' that appropriate and transcend cultural norms can be told.

a. The lives of the narrators are otherwise not visible. Subversive stories break silences.
b. Subversive stories are told by those who *know* the rules of the system and can appropriate them. The very visibility of marginalized narrators within settings that deny their presence helps to reveal power and inequities that may otherwise be concealed.
c. The narratives locate particular individuals within the 'encompassing web of social organization': subversive stories disrupt hegemonic collective narratives and offer possibilities for reshaping the social world.

First-generation student narratives become 'subversive' to the extent that they articulate their resilience as well as shame, name the barriers they face as well as their tenacity, and convey their anger as well as their joy – even while they may not yet frame their narratives within formal class analyses. Ewick and Silbey (2003, 1342) write of narrative functioning as 'lay sociology' that can 'locate characters in time and space, describing both what enables and what constrains action'. As such, stories composed by 'the ones who got away' (Reay 2005) are vividly located within barriers constructed against their success.

Novel, creative genres of narrative uniquely support more complex, reflective, and subversive stories than the mere verbal accounts of conventional academic research. With other scholars calling for more creative, participatory modes of inquiry, Kara (2015, loc 247) argues that 'multiple, partial, context-dependent and contingent' truths call for research methods that can capture complexity beyond more linear accounts. She argues instead for art as knowledge production:

> The processes involved in making art can be surprisingly similar to the processes involved in doing research. Higher level thinking (as we like to call it) demands connections, associations, linkages of conscious and unconscious elements, memory and emotion, past, present and future merging in the processes of making meaning.
>
> *(loc 469)*

In contrast to more conventional researcher/subject relationships, artistic production also positions the creator as an active participant in inquiry. Gubrium and Harper (2013, 78) argue that within multimedia production: 'the interpretive aspect does not just fall in the lap of the academic researcher. The process lends itself to positioning participants in a far more analytic mode as far as discussing representations and meanings' of their experiences. On the first morning of one workshop, a woman asked 'Is it ok to be angry?' I affirmed that it was indeed ok, and her story eventually conveyed anger in multiple ways: in images stripped of color, in harsh transitions between visuals elements, and in the clipped tone of her voice as she narrated a story of faculty condescension. Her final, full-color image, held on the screen for some time, showed her smiling student cohort reaching a milestone in their academic program, but included no faculty.

The production of stories in the First in Our Families workshops are positioned squarely at the intersections of creativity, analysis, and reflection as students compose 'objects for thinking with and through lived experiences' (Gubrium & Harper 2013, 59). The creative work serves students well at multiple levels. One student who came to the workshop only reluctantly on the advice of her campus mentor (she was part of a scholarship program for homeless students) explained that she proudly showed her story to multiple faculty members after the workshop. In our interview, she said, 'I cannot believe that I created something this beautiful. I had no idea that I could do that'. She was simultaneously proud of her story *and* the digital story that she had created.

It is not surprising, then, that students describe the three days that they spend in the workshop as 'therapeutic'. By the second day, I have to remind students to take breaks, to get snacks, to step away from their projects for a time. They immerse themselves in experimenting with multiple versions of their stories and typically stop editing only when we're out of time. The screenings on the final afternoon are deeply engaging; a story that began in story circle two days before as tearful, fragmented memories now culminates with the image of a young woman on the big screen gazing directly at the audience. Families are visually brought into the room; strong student voices are amplified through the speakers.

The ease with which digital projects can be disseminated also represents a cultural shift in the capacity of marginalized individuals to connect and network with others sharing their experiences and identities, potentially enabling significant shifts from individual shame to collective voice (Bennet & Segerberg 2016; Castells 2014; Livingstone & Blum-Rose 2017; Zuckerman 2016). Hull and Katz thus describe digital stories as 'acts of control, agentive and constructive performative moments' (2006, 71).

Stories for equity and justice

Beyond the reflective power of story production is the potential of these stories to provoke change. Vivienne (2015, loc 461) has examined the four levels of change that can potentially emerge from the digital storytelling workshops themselves.

First, first-generation students come to understand that they have a story worth sharing. Students frequently come to the workshops having 'no idea' what story they may want to tell. Conversations are rich on the first day as we consider the creative possibilities in sample stories that we view together, especially during the facilitated story circle. In a break during one workshop, several students began talking about the foods that their families sent with them back to the dorms. Eventually, two students from very different backgrounds drafted moving stories of familial love conveyed through food when parents could no longer fully understand what their sons and daughters were experiencing. The stories implicitly questioned why success in college requires them to distance themselves from poor and working-class families when for many peers, college is a family rite of passage.

Second, Vivienne (2015, loc 461) observes, change happens among 'familiars'. The students often show their stories to peers and to trusted faculty or staff, or they post them on social media. They report unanimously positive feedback. A young woman whose story of self-doubt was created early in her sophomore year was amazed when a faculty member who'd attended a campus screening asked for her advice on being more supportive. Significantly, students who do create stories about parents had rarely shared their stories with family when I interviewed them weeks later. These students had at least tacit understanding that their families would be wary of the judgment of more powerful others in their students' lives, yet creating stories of family deepened their self-understanding of these dynamics, and sharing stories with others on campus opened conversations about students' class backgrounds.

A third level of change (Vivienne 2015, loc 461) that comes from digital storytelling workshops is the support that students experience from one another. At the end of the first day of a workshop on the large campus of a state school, a young woman asked: 'Where have you all been? I thought I was the only one!' In interviews, students consistently speak of reframing their stories after realizing that others were experiencing what they had assumed were deeply personal experiences. In debriefings at the end of the workshops, the most common insight conveyed by students is that they could identify with something in every single other story, even while the students typically come from very different backgrounds. As Jaggar (1989) would argue, their 'outlaw' emotions were being transformed into counter-narratives about the institution.

Finally, change happens when stories are screened for more distant and possibly unknown audiences who may influence institutional change (Vivienne 2015, loc 528). At one small liberal arts college, students screened stories for faculty, staff, and students at an open campus event. Faculty then publicly asked the students for their thoughts on how the college could become more equitable, positioning the students as experts on their own experience. Having started this conversation in the workshop, the students had concrete recommendations to make. Later, staff called to tell me that financial aid administrators referenced specific student stories as they finally agreed to policy changes that had been stalled for some time. Other students at a large research university screened stories at a social gathering for first-generation graduate students and then facilitated a panel discussion about the power of being vocal about the first-generation experience. Students who agree to publish their stories on the First in Our Families website often explain that they're motivated by the hope that high school students or students just starting college will be inspired by knowing that they're not alone.

Vivienne summarizes how the experience of workshop participation and subsequent publishing of stories become agentive acts:

> First, they develop technical skills and social capital. Second, they feel entitled to speak as a representative (of self, or 'people like me'). Third, they fulfill a sense of duty ('I hope that sharing my story helps others'). Fourth, they negotiate confidently with publics (familiar, intimate, counter and unknown). Empowerment in this context might also be defined as a combination of agency (to define and create a congruent self) and ownership (the right to curate identity on own terms). Through networked identity work, storytellers build bridges across personal and social differences and this activity confers agency.
>
> *(2015, loc 3879)*

The networked identity work was evident at the start of one recent workshop when, in their introductions, two storytellers explained that they'd viewed the stories on the First in Our Families website and then declared that there were stories not yet being told. They insisted that they'd be telling some of those missing stories. They crafted deeply personal stories while also consciously anticipating their contributions to the collective representation of being first-generation.

Conclusions

While first-generation students deeply 'live class' as an embodied element of their identities as college students, Dorothy Holland and her colleagues (Holland, Lachicotte, Skinner, & Cain 1998) argue against 'simplistic notions that identities are internalized in a sort of faxing process that unproblematically reproduces the collective upon the individual, the social upon the body' (169). Holland's work suggests an 'alternative vision, organized around the conflictual, continuing dialogic of an inner speech where active identities are ever forming' (169).

In the First in Our Families workshops, students' 'dialogic of inner speech' is translated into a digital project that is both an object for ongoing reflection and a subversive story told to those responsible for creating a more just system of education. Sayer (2005a, 35), writing of the place of resistance within Bourdieu's work on embodied social hierarchies, elaborates:

> Acknowledging internal conversations and longing helps to make sense of the obvious point that our relationship to the world is not simply one of accommodation or becoming skilled in its games, but, at least in some ways, one of wanting to be different and wanting the world and its games to be different.

The participants in these workshops have longed to be seen, to be heard, and to succeed in college without losing their place in their own communities. They have also begun to articulate how they want the 'games' of college to become more just and equitable.

The students are overwhelmingly positive about their experiences in the workshop. While data analysis of the stories and interviews is ongoing,[2] students describe their work in story creation as deeply meaningful. Asked what they'd tell others about what they'll learn during the three days, they speak of the profound experience of being heard.

- You'll feel vulnerable at first and when you are done, you'll be like, damn I rule.
- I had an amazing experience doing this workshop. It not only allowed me to dive into my creative part, but also to reflect about my story. I cried a lot internally and I also celebrated. It felt as a profound spiritual milestone.
- It is powerful. It is creative. It helps you feel like you are not alone in your experience as a first-gen but that your story is unique and has value in telling.
- It is an amazing way to individually contribute your story to counter a generic narrative about first-gen college students as just 'hard-working kids who wanted to have a different life'. Our stories matter, and are not frequently shared with others. It's a great tool to help professors and peers understand you and also reflect on their own lives.

Before the workshops, few of the students had ever talked to anyone on their campuses about being first-generation. Those who could explain their silence spoke of their fear of being judged and their sense of vulnerability, yet they were often hard-pressed to explain where that embodied fear of judgment came from. For most of the students, the workshop was the first opportunity to talk with other first-generation students about their experiences and their only opportunity to intentionally reflect on the meaning of their own stories within the contexts of social class. The students had been living with the silences about social class in education about which bell hooks (2000) writes. The stories began to break those silences in poignant ways. With access to the means to explore and to explain their stories, they've in turn given scholars deeper insights into the multilayered experiences of poor and working-class students in higher education.

To be clear, these stories of poor and working-class students, though now visible, remain on the margins of the 'central stories' (Steedman 1986, 144) of college life. As Reay (2001, 342) notes, there is currently no framework that holds the two versions together. Yet the creation of 'subversive' digital stories may be one step in normalizing socioeconomic diversity in higher education, one way of opening dialogue about how to shift the burden of navigating social class barriers from students to the institutions that claim to be engines of opportunity.

Francis Polletta (2009) argues that storytelling has always helped to drive social change: 'And people do things with stories. They entertain and persuade, build social bonds and break them, make sense of their worlds and, in the process, create those worlds' (loc 318). She argues that stories are 'critical to collective action' (loc 215).

The poor and working-class students who have created and shared their stories are better prepared to be part of the collective action of building institutions that honor all stories. They are no longer silent. Within working-class studies, facilitated multimedia production holds great potential as a research method for bringing participants into dialogue with one another, for simultaneously fostering reflection and voice, and for decentering the academic voice as we instead amplify the voices of poor and working-class people in deliberations about public life.

Notes

1 Student activists at some elite colleges have begun 'class confessions' events and social media campaigns. See Northwestern's Class Confessions http://nuclassconfessions.tumblr.com/, Stanford's Class Confessions http://stanfordclassconfessions.tumblr.com/, and Columbia Class Confessions http://columbiaclassconfessionsflip.tumblr.com/. Stephens, Hamedani and Destin (2014) also found that after college seniors talked at a first-year orientation about how social class backgrounds can shape college experiences, first-generation students were more likely to seek assistance from professors and other campus resources and to narrow academic achievement gaps between themselves and peers. Yet explicit acknowledgement of class in first-generation experiences is rare.

2 In addition to conference presentations and journal articles, I am working on a book from this project.

References

Alexandra, D. (2017) 'More than words: Co-creative visual ethnography', in Thornburg, A., Booker, A. and Nunez-Janes, M. (eds.) *Deep Stories*, Warsaw, Poland, De Gruyter Open.

Armstrong, E.A. and Hamilton, L.T. (2013) *Paying for the Party: How College Maintains Inequality*, Cambridge, MA, Harvard University Press.

Banks-Santilli, L. (2014) 'First-generation college students and their pursuit of the American Dream', *Journal of Case Studies in Education*, 5, 1.

Benmayor, R. (2008) 'Digital storytelling as a signature pedagogy for the new humanities', *Arts and Humanities in Higher Education*, 7, 2, 188–204.

Bennett, W. L. and Segerberg, A. (2016) 'The logic of connective action: Digital media and the personalization of contentious politics', in Gordon, E. and Mihailidis, P. (eds.) Civic Media: Technology, Design, Practice, Cambridge, MA, MIT Press.

Boler, M. (1999) *Feeling Power: Emotions and Education*, London, Routledge.

Bottero, W. (2004) 'Class identities and the identity of class', *Sociology*, 38, 5, 985–1003.

Bourdieu, P. (1984) *Distinction: A Social Critique of the Judgement of Taste*, Cambridge, MA, Harvard University Press.

Bourdieu, P. (1990) *In Other Words: Essays Toward a Reflexive Sociology*, Cambridge, Polity Press.

Bourdieu, P. (1999) 'The contradictions of inheritance', in Bourdieu, P. and Accardo, A. (eds.) *The Weight of the World: Suffering in Contemporary Society*, Stanford, Stanford University Press.

Bruner, J. (1994) 'The "remembered" self', in Neisser, U. and Fivush, R. (eds.) *The Remembering Self: Construction and Accuracy in the Self-Narrative*, Cambridge, Cambridge University Press.

Calarco, J. M. (2011) '"I need help!" Social class and children's help-seeking in elementary school', *American Sociological Review*, 76, 6, 862–882.

Calarco, J. M. (2014–2015) 'Help seeking and silent strugglers', *American Educator*, Winter, 24–45.

Castells, M. (2014) 'Foreword', in Costanza-Chock, S. *Out of the Shadows and into the Streets*, Cambridge, MA, MIT Press.

Christopher, R. (2009) *A Carpenter's Daughter: A Working Class Woman in Higher Education*, Boston: Sense Publishing.

Clandinin, D. J. and Connelly, M. (1998) 'Stories to live by: Narrative understandings of school reform', *Curriculum Inquiry*, 28, 2, 149–164.

Coventry, M. (2008) 'Engaging gender: Student application of theory through digital storytelling', *Arts and Humanities in Higher Education*, 7, 2, 205–219.

Ellingson, L. L. (2009) *Engaging Crystallization in Qualitative Research*, Thousand Oaks, CA, Sage Publications.

Engle, J., Bermeo, A. and O'Brien, C. (2006) *Straight from the Source: What Works for First-Generation College Students*, Washington, DC, Pell Institute for the Study of Opportunity in Higher Education. Available at https://eric.ed.gov/?id=ED501693.

Ewick, P. and Silbey, S. (1995) 'Subversive stories and hegemonic tales: Toward a sociology of narrative', *Law and Society Review*, 29, 2, 197–226.

Ewick, P. and Silbey, S. (2003) 'Narrating social structure: Stories of resistance to legal authority', *American Journal of Sociology*, 108, 6, 1328–1372.

Gans, H. J. (1992) 'Preface', in Lamont, M. and Fournier, M. (eds.) *Cultivating Differences: Symbolic Boundaries and the Making of Inequality*, Chicago IL, University of Chicago Press.

Goffman, E. (1984) *The Presentation of Self in Everyday Life*, Harmondsworth, Penguin Books.

Goldrick-Rab, S. (2016) *Paying the Price: College Costs, Financial Aid, and the Betrayal of the American Dream*, Chicago, University of Chicago Press.

Gubrium, A. and Harper, K. (2013) *Participatory Visual and Digital Methods*, Walnut Creek, CA, Left Coast Press.

Hamilton, L. T. (2016) *Parenting to a Degree: How Family Matters for College Women's Success*, Chicago, University of Chicago Press.

Holland, D., Lachicotte, W. J., Skinner, D. and Cain, C. (1998) *Identity and Agency in Cultural Worlds*, Cambridge, MA, Harvard University Press.

hooks, B. (2000) *Where We Stand: Class Matters*, New York, Routledge.

Hull, G. A. and Katz, M. (2006) 'Crafting an agentive self: Case studies of digital storytelling', *Research in the Teaching of English*, 41, 1, 43–81.

Hull, G. A. and Nelson, M. E. (2005) 'Locating the semiotic power of multimodality', *Written Communication*, 22, 2, 224–261.

Ishitani, T. T. (2003) 'A longitudinal approach to assessing attrition behavior among first-generation students: Time-varying effects of pre-college characteristics', *Research in Higher Education*, 44, 4, 433–449.
Jaggar, A. M. (1989) 'Love and knowledge: Emotion in feminist epistemology', *Inquiry*, 32, 2, 151–176.
Kara, H. (2015) *Creative Research Methods in the Social Sciences: A Practical Guide*, Bristol, The Policy Press.
Kelly, A. and Goldrick-Rab, S. (eds.) (2014) *Reinventing Financial Aid: Charting a New Course to College Affordability*, Cambridge, MA, Harvard Education Press.
Lambert, J. (2010) *Digital Storytelling Cookbook*, Berkeley, CA, Digital Diner Press.
Lambert, J. (2012) *Digital Storytelling: Capturing Lives, Creating Community* (3rd edition), Berkeley CA, Digital Diner Press.
Lamont, M. and Fournier, M. (eds.) (1992) *Cultivating Differences: Symbolic Boundaries in the Making of Inequality*, Chicago, University of Chicago Press.
Lareau, A. (2000) *Home Advantage: Social Class and Parental Intervention in Elementary Education*, Lanham, MD, Rowman and Littlefield Publishers.
Lareau, A. (2011) *Unequal Childhoods: Class, Race, and Family Life*, Berkeley CA, University of California Press.
Lee, E. M. (2016) *Class and Campus Life: Managing and Experiencing Inequality at an Elite College*, Ithaca, ILR Press.
Leon, S. M. (2008) 'Slowing down, talking back and moving forward: Some reflections on digital storytelling in the humanities curriculum', *Arts and Humanities in Higher Education*, 7, 2, 220–223.
Lindquist, J. (2004) 'Class affects, classroom affectations: Working through the paradoxes of strategic empathy', *College English*, 67, 2, 187–209.
Livingstone, S. and Blum-Rose, A. (2017) 'Researching children and childhood in the digital age', in Christensen, P. and James, A. (eds.) *Research with Children: Perspectives and Practices* (3rd edition) Abingdon, UK, Routledge.
Luschen, K.V. (2014) 'Exploring (dis)connection through digital storytelling: Toward pedagogies of critical co-learning', in Carmona, J. F. and Luschen, K. V. (eds.) *Crafting Critical Stories: Toward Pedagogies and Methodologies of Collaboration, Inclusion, and Voice*, New York, Peter Lang.
Mallman, M. (2017) 'The perceived inherent vice of working-class university students', *The Sociological Review*, 65, 2, 235–250.
Miller, P. J. (1994) 'Narrative practices: Their role in socialization and self-construction', in Neisser, U. and Fivush, R. (eds.) *The Remembering Self: Construction and Accuracy in the Self-Narrative*, Cambridge, Cambridge University Press.
Ochs, E. and Capps, L. (2001) *Living Narrative: Creating Lives in Everyday Storytelling*, Cambridge, MA, Harvard University Press.
Opperman, J. (2008) 'Digital storytelling and American studies: Critical trajectories from the emotional to the epistemological', *Arts and Humanities in Higher Education*, 7, 2, 171–187.
Orbuch, T. L. (1997) 'People's accounts count: The sociology of accounts', *Annual Review of Sociology*, 23, 455–478.
Pell Institute (2011) *Pell Institute Fact Sheet: 6-Year Degree Attainment Rates for Students Enrolled in a Post-Secondary Institution*. Washington, DC, The Pell Institute.
Polletta, F. (2009) *It was Like a Fever: Storytelling in Protest and Politics*, Chicago, University of Chicago Press.
Reay, D. (1997) 'The double-bind of the "working class" feminist academic: The success of failure or the failure of success', in Mahony, P. and Cmroczek, C. (eds.) *Class Matters: 'Working Class' Women's Perspectives on Social Class*, London, Taylor and Francis.
Reay, D. (2001) 'Finding or losing yourself? Working-class relationships to education', *Journal of Education Policy*, 16, 4, 333–346.
Reay, D. (2003) 'A risky business? Working class women students and access to higher education', *Gender and Education*, 15, 3, 301–317.
Reay, D. (2005) 'Beyond consciousness? The psychic landscape of social class', *Sociology*, 39, 5, 911–928.
Reay, D. (2015) 'Habitus and the psychosocial: Bourdieu with feelings', *Cambridge Journal of Education*, 45, 1, 9–23.
Reeves, R.V. (2017) *Dream Hoarders: How the American Upper Middle Class is Leaving Everyone Else in the Dust, Why that is a Problem, and What to do about it*, Washington, DC, Brookings Institution.
Rivera, L. A. (2016) *Pedigree: How Elite Students Get Elite Jobs*, Princeton, Princeton University Press.
Sayer, A. (2005a) *The Moral Significance of Class*, Cambridge, Cambridge University Press.
Sayer, A. (2005b) 'Class, moral worth and recognition', *Sociology*, 39, 5, 947–963.
Skeggs, B. (1997) *Formations of Class and Gender: Becoming Respectable*, London, Sage Publications.

Skeggs, B. (2005) 'The making of class and gender through visualizing the moral subject', *Sociology*, 39, 5, 965–982.

Steedman, C. (1986) *Landscape for a Good Woman*, London, Virago Press.

Stephens, N. M., Fryberg, S. A., Markus, H. R., Johnson, C. S. and Covarrubias, R. (2012) 'Unseen disadvantage: How American universities' focus on independence undermines the academic performance of first-generation college students', *Journal of Personality and Social Psychology*, 102, 6, 1178–1197.

Stephens, N. M., Hamedana, M. G. and Destin, M. (2014) Closing the social-class achievement gap: A difference-education intervention improves first-generation students' academic performance and all students' college transition, *Psychological Science*, 25, 4, 943–953.

Thornburg, A., Booker, A. and Nunez-Jones, M. (eds.) (2017) *Deep Stories*, Warsaw, Poland, De Gruyter Open.

Vivienne, S. (2015) *Digital Identity and Everyday Activism: Sharing Private Stories with Networked Publics*, London, Palgrave Macmillan.

Walkerdine, V., Lucey, H. and Melody, J. (2001) *Growing Up Girl: Psychosocial Explorations of Gender and Class*, Basingstoke, Palgrave.

Ward, L., Siegel, M. J. and Davenport, Z. (2012) *First-Generation College Students: Understanding and Improving the Experience from Recruitment to Commencement*, Hoboken, NJ, John Wiley and Sons.

Weis, L., Cipollone, K. and Jenkins, H. (2014) *Class Warfare: Class, Race and College Admissions in Top-Tier Secondary Schools*, Chicago, University of Chicago Press.

Witherell, C. and Noddings, N. (eds.) (1991) *Stories Lives Tell: Narrative and Dialogue in Education*, New York, Teachers College Press.

Woosley, S. A. and Shepler, D. K. (2011) 'Understanding the early integration experiences of first-generation college students', *College Student Journal*, 45, 4, 700–714.

Zorn, D. and Boler, M. (2007) 'Rethinking emotions and educational leadership', *International Journal of Leadership in Education*, 10, 2, 137–151.

Zuckerman, E. (2016) 'Effective civics', in Gordon, E. and Mihailidis, P. (eds.) *Civic Media: Technology, Design, Practice*, Cambridge, MA, MIT Press.

4

The 'how to' of working-class studies

Selves, stories, and working across media

Christine J. Walley

How do those of us involved in working-class studies go about doing the kind of work that we do? Given that working-class studies is an interdisciplinary field that spans history, American studies, cultural studies, literature, geography, sociology, economics, and anthropology, among other disciplines, there is no single answer to this question.[1] But questions about methodology and methods – the 'how to' practical realities of how we conduct our research – raise key issues for all those interested in working-class studies: What do we count as evidence about working-class lives? What is the relationship between theory and evidence in thinking about class? What role does who we are as researchers (including our class backgrounds) play in how that research is conducted and the results we end up with? And how does the fact that we're living in an increasingly media-centric world shift possibilities not only for *how* we do our research but also to *whom* it is addressed and *how* we engage others?

My home discipline of cultural anthropology has been a less central player within working-class studies, perhaps because 'class' has historically been a less dominant concept for anthropology than for our partner discipline, sociology.[2] Nevertheless, anthropology's defining method of ethnographic fieldwork has influenced a range of other fields, and I would argue, it is 'good to think with' (as anthropologists say) for working-class studies scholars. In this chapter, I use my anthropological training and involvement in the 'transmedia' Exit Zero Project as a vantage point for reflecting on questions of method.[3] In particular, I ask: Why is writing in the first person so common in working-class studies scholarship, and what is the nature of this authorial 'self'? Can 'stories' count as evidence in rigorous social science analysis, and how do they relate to theory? And, in our media-saturated world, how might combining analysis of texts, objects, and images and working across media increase opportunities to address and collaborate with non-academics, including those from working-class backgrounds?

Working ethnographically

Anthropology is a discipline awkwardly, but productively, positioned between the humanities and social sciences. As such, it shares with the interdisciplinary field of working-class studies the conundrum of how to express the richness, particularity, and malleability of everyday experiences *and* the structured patterns by which history unfolds. In particular, working-class studies seeks a dual perspective that simultaneously conveys working-class realities up close and personal while underscoring the links between those realities and the power-laden workings of capitalism, governance, and class-stratified societies.

Anthropology's trademark method of ethnographic fieldwork, known as 'participant observation', is well-suited to exploring how social class works. Historically, ethnographic research has entailed fieldworkers living and working alongside research participants for extended periods of time and sharing in their daily life activities.[4] This mode of engagement is sometimes referred to as 'deep hanging out', a term that Hugh Gusterson (2008) notes colorfully captures both the method's informality and its seriousness. 'Participant observation' is characterized by a heightened sense of attunement to daily life and is also improvisational. Instead of rigidly following preordained research questions formulated from the academic literature, researchers are encouraged to let the ideas, interests, and understandings of our research participants challenge our own thinking and direct our questions. Consequently, Sharon Hutchinson characterizes ethnographic fieldwork in dialogical terms as the 'art of perfecting conversation' (1996, 45), a mode of working, I might add, that places a particular premium on the often-neglected art of listening. As a result, ethnographic research is not only *interactive* but potentially *transformative* for subjects and researchers alike – there is no 'objective' space to be as an ethnographer outside these relationships, and both parties may emerge from these encounters different than when they began (Gusterson 2008).

Ethnographic methods are particularly adept at getting at certain things. First, ethnography excels at capturing and emphasizing questions of meaning (including those relating to class), or how we are caught in 'webs of significance' that we have ourselves spun, as influential anthropologist Clifford Geertz famously put it (Geertz 1973). Second, up-close ethnographic encounters underscore the complexity, contradictions, and ambiguities of everyday life. Ethnographers are well positioned to recognize that what people say and do are not always the same thing and that all of us are capable of holding contradictory beliefs and values simultaneously.[5] Ethnography's holistic focus on the complexity of daily life also offers insight into how class, race, and gender come to be mutually constituted in everyday encounters, sometimes in unanticipated ways.[6] In sum, ethnographic methods are adept at uncovering the contours of – and contradictions and ambiguities in – our beliefs, identities, practices, and interests, including those relating to class, as they play out in daily life. And, they do so while capturing how people's everyday improvisations respond to the structured constraints and unequal opportunities (including class-based ones) that make up our lives. In short, the kind of 'knowledge' that emerges from ethnographic encounters is not 'information', or discrete items that might be gathered, for example, from surveys. Instead, it offers a complex sense of how people understand and act in the world in ways that emerge out of the flux of everyday experience and encounters.

While doing ethnography is sometimes characterized as an 'art', it is an art tied to an analytic project. Ethnographers spend long periods of time working closely with particular groups of people because they want to comprehend not only *what* the world looks like from different points of view but also the reasons, both structured and unstable, *why* it looks that way. It is an 'experience-near' research perspective, in Geertz's terms, that attempts to understand power-laden, if open-ended, social patterns. For these reasons, ethnographic methods are useful in tackling the broad range of questions in which working-class studies practitioners are collectively interested. Such questions include: How do we understand the intertwined material, symbolic, and identity-related dimensions of social class? How is class mutually constituted with other structuring principles like gender and race? How are contemporary neoliberalism and expanding forms of economic precarity leading us to rethink the nature of capitalism itself?

Since its founding in the colonial era as a discipline that looked at cross-cultural differences across geographic regions, anthropology has undergone widespread efforts to self-critique and 'decolonize'. While much of anthropology has changed (and anthropologists now are as likely to 'study' scientists in Paris as tech entrepreneurs in Mumbai, farmers in Indiana, or miners in rural Papua New Guinea), ethnographic methods remain at the core of the discipline, even as they too have transformed over time. Once conducted in a single geographic location, ethnographic fieldwork may now happen across multiple sites in ways that suggest how people, things, and processes circulate or are linked across regions (Marcus 1995). Ethnographic fieldwork also no longer relies for scholarly authority simply on the trope of 'being there' in a field site, but regularly supplements participant observation with other kinds of research methods, including formal interviews, archival research, and analysis of discourse, texts, or visual images. Finally, anthropology continues a longstanding tradition of openness to experimentation, which, as discussed below, includes a growing interest in 'auto-ethnography', collaborative research ventures, and multimedia projects with roots in older ethnographic filmmaking traditions.

The Exit Zero Project, the 'transmedia' anthropological research initiative that I have collaborated with others on for over a decade, combines these anthropological interests with those of working-class studies. The project as a whole explores the long-term impacts of deindustrialization within the former steel mill region of Southeast Chicago (Walley 2009, 2013, 2015; *Exit Zero*, dir. Boebel 2017). It thereby parallels the centrality of deindustrialization as a key topic within working-class studies (Russo and Linkon 2005, 8; Linkon and Russo 2002; Strangleman 2004, 2019; Cowie 1991; Cowie and Heathcott, 2003; Dudley 1994, this volume; Pappas 1989; Doukas 2003; Modell 1998; Taft 2016; Bright 2015).[7] Organized around multigenerational family 'storytelling', the Exit Zero Project's focus on Southeast Chicago serves as an entry point for discussing the changing nature of work and expanding class inequality in the United States as well as how Americans talk – and fail to talk – about social class. The project offers an extended examination of what Linkon (2014, 2018) refers to as the long 'half-life' of deindustrialization, underscoring how the systematic loss of industrial jobs has not been a discrete historical event, but a checkered, uneven, sometimes contradictory process that has contributed to profound and lasting social transformations with impacts extending across generations. Deindustrialization has also contributed to an upending of scholarly theory given the centrality of industry and industrial labor to 19th- and 20th-century definitions of social class and capitalism.

The Exit Zero Project (www.exitzeroproject.org) includes a book, *Exit Zero: Family and Class in Postindustrial Chicago*, authored by myself, and a documentary film, *Exit Zero: An Industrial Family Story*, directed by filmmaker Chris Boebel and produced by Boebel and myself. Both are 'auto-ethnographic' and use my own family's experiences in Southeast Chicago as the point of departure. The project also includes a collaborative website project being made with the community-based Southeast Chicago Historical Museum (http://sechicagohistory.org). The website involves building an online archive of materials donated by area residents and using the stories that people tell about – and through – those objects to understand working-class engagements with history and the transformations entailed by deindustrialization. The Exit Zero Project overall combines a focus on 'stories' with efforts to work both collaboratively and across media, thereby raising key methodological questions explored below.

Rethinking methods: Getting personal

> Although the intense depression that followed the mill's shutdown had lessened over the years, [my father; Image 4.1] continued to exude the deep-seated bitterness of a man who felt that life had passed him by.
>
> [He] retained this bitterness for the rest of his life, just as he retained a sense of identity as a steelworker. Once, when he was still working as a security guard downtown, he found an

> abandoned painting in the garbage. It was an acrylic rendering of an early mill with furnaces aglow. My dad dusted it off and brought it home where it hung in our dining room for years, a fitting reminder of a lost world.
>
> *(Walley 2013, 74)*

Sherry Lee Linkon has described first person narrative as the 'signature genre' of working-class studies (2014, this volume); how should we understand the positioning of 'self' in such accounts? Within anthropology, working in the first person has also become an increasingly recognized genre. However, it is instructive to tease apart the different *ways* that writing in the first person happens and the different intellectual *reasons* scholars might give for it. Anthropology, for example, has a long history of incorporating 'reflexivity', or an acknowledgement of anthropologists' relationships with research participants within written ethnographies. This trend emerged during the 1960s to 1990s from attempts to 'decolonize' the discipline by acknowledging the power-laden positioning of often white, middle-class Western researchers in relation to their often non-Western, formerly colonial, subjects. In this sense, positioning the 'self' as a researcher was crucial to contesting a disembodied 'God's-eye view' rendering of scholarly knowledge. Feminist anthropologists and theorists, in particular, emphasized that knowledge production is always 'situated'; in other words, knowledge is never transcendental but is inevitably generated within existing social relationships, meaning it can only ever offer a partial perspective (Haraway 1988; Abu-Lughod 1991; Okely and Callaway 1992).

For this reason, the idea that there should be a least a modicum of scholarly reflexivity is widely accepted within anthropology. Such reflexivity, however, is distinct from the use of the first person in auto-ethnography, a form of scholarship that explicitly uses the self as a terrain for research and which has since emerged as a distinct anthropological sub-genre.[8] It is a truism that the 'self' can only be constituted through relationships with others, and,

Image 4.1 Charles William Walley
Source: Photograph by Chris Boebel

unsurprisingly, auto-ethnography is more often about an ethnographer's relationships with those others, often intimate family members, than about the self (Okely and Callaway 1992; Reed-Danahay 1997; Waterston and Rylko-Bauer 2006). Within anthropology, for example, recent auto-ethnographies include attempts to make sense of the emotional trauma experienced by prior generations in response to events like the Holocaust (Slyomovics 2014; Waterston 2014), the Nakba for Palestinians (Abu-Lughod 2007), colonialism (Pandian and Mariappan 2014), related forms of displacement and migration (Behar 2007), or, in my own case, deindustrialization (Walley 2009, 2013). Other auto-ethnographies have explored complex ethnic, racial, class, or gendered identities within families (Narayan 2008; Chin 2016; Moran-Thomas 2017), using, in Elizabeth Chin's work, relationships to consumer objects to do so.

In my own case, the inspiration to write in the first person did not emerge from anthropology's scholarly concerns (although anthropology's openness to experimentation allowed the professional space to do so). Instead, the desire to write a personal account came from a deep-seated psychological need to explore the class tensions that had marked my own life. The idea that it might be possible for an academic to write in this way came from reading works that would now be thought of under the rubric of 'working-class studies' (although mostly written before that rubric existed). For me, it was books like historian Carolyn Steedman's *Landscape for a Good Woman: A Story of Two Lives* (1986) about the complex class positioning of Steedman's white working-class but aspirational mother in post-World War II Britain, the (politically controversial) account of being an upwardly mobile Mexican-American youth in Richard Rodriguez's *Hunger of Memory: The Education of Richard Rodriguez* (1982), and the personal narratives in edited volumes like *Strangers in Paradise: Academics from the Working Class* (Ryan and Sackrey 1984), *Working Class Women in the Academy: Laborers in the Knowledge Factory* (Tokarczyk and Fay 1993), and *This Fine Place So Far From Home: Voices of Academics from the Working Class* (Dews and Law 1995).[9]

If personal narrative is the 'signature genre' of working-class studies, as Linkon argues, where does the need to write in this fashion stem from, and why is it an important style for working-class studies to own? Many of those who write in a personal vein appear to do so because of a visceral need to convey their own stories in cases where hegemonic narratives fail to account for lives on the margins, leading to a felt need to understand how and why their own experiences might differ from dominant accounts. Such concerns appear not only in literature about class, but within feminist scholarship as well as literatures on race and post-coloniality. Richard Delgado, for example, characterizes the telling of counterstories by the 'oppressed' (Delgado 1989) as a necessary 'survival strategy' (Diawara 1999, 316). Creating counternarratives about *class* might be particularly important in regions like the United States where discussions of class are often either muted or conflated with, or displaced onto, other structuring principles such as race and gender (Ortner 1991; Bettie 2003). In the United States, this includes the use of gendered or sexualized language to reference class dynamics and, even more so, the tendency to conflate being African-American with poverty and whiteness with wealth or middle-classness (obscuring the experiences of wealthy and middle-class African-Americans as well as the white working-class and poor in the process) (Lacy 2007; Ortner 1991; Bettie 2003). As Julie Bettie notes, race and class are 'always already mutually implicated and read in relationship to one another. But when class is couched in race and ethnicity, and vice versa, it impairs our understanding of *both* social forces' (2003, 86). In other words, we need to be able to distinguish analytically among the distinct workings of race, class, and gender in order to understand how they come to be 'co-constituted' in daily life.

Working-class studies scholarship recognizes that personal narratives can help to make sense of both individual and collective social trajectories and often underscores the ways that class, race, gender, and sexuality come together in daily experience (with the impossibility of privileging any one) (Russo and Linkon 2005; Roediger 2005). In this way, working-class studies can contribute to discussions of 'intersectionality' that have sometimes given less attention to class dynamics (Russo and Linkon 2005, 4; Bettie 2003).

In addition, many working-class studies scholars themselves hail from working-class backgrounds, and writing in the first person potentially offers a way to acknowledge the complex relationships such scholars might have with both middle-class academic social norms and their home communities. French intellectual Didier Eribon's book *Returning to Reims* (2013), although outside the U.S.-based 'working-class studies' tradition, offers one example of the latter. The book centers upon his estranged relationship with his white working-class family and his attempts to understand their shifting political allegiances from Communist Party to National Front. Eribon suggests that, for him, 'coming out' as a gay public intellectual happened more readily than 'coming out' as someone from a working-class background. He offers a poignant account of how, at a time when he was 'passing' as a bourgeoisie intellectual, he felt such class shame when he encountered a working-class relative on the streets of Paris that he ignored him. Intriguingly, Eribon also persuaded famed sociologist Pierre Bourdieu to write his posthumously published memoir, *Sketch for a Self-Analysis* (2008) (which Bourdieu refused to call an 'autobiography'), that contains guarded moments of insight into his relationship with his own working-class background.[10] Periodically, the 'I' in *Sketch for a Self-Analysis* breaks through the notorious density of Bourdieu's scholarly prose, which appears as a kind of class-laden armor against the hierarchical world of French academia. In short, writing in the first person, as emotionally fraught as it might be, is more than a stylistic choice; it is one with particular analytical and sometimes political goals and one that holds out possibilities for generating alternative thinking, new political visions, and expanded conceptions of how to live.

My own approach to actually doing 'auto-ethnography' when working on the *Exit Zero* book entailed a variety of methods. I created the stories at the core of the book through 'stream of consciousness' writing – what the surrealists called 'automatic writing' and what they viewed as a tool to tap the unconscious. I focused on painful moments associated with class encounters in my own and my family's past and holed myself up with my computer and tried to 'get out' those stories in as unfiltered a way as possible. Later, I would go back and work with them, trying to ride the line between accessing the emotion felt at the time and critically analyzing. I consciously used my anthropological training to help create distance from these stories and to treat them as I would the stories of others, especially when what emerged surprised or embarrassed me, such as the sometimes-repressed recognition that I had hated as well as identified with the Southeast Chicago of my childhood. In this early stage of writing, I avoided academic literature to prevent the voices of others from drowning out the semi-submerged memories and feelings that I was trying to reconstruct (although academic accounts were later instrumental in making sense of those memories).

My previous experience doing ethnographic research in Tanzania helped provide the discipline to conduct this more personal research. It helped generate the heightened sense of awareness characteristic of 'participant observation' as I observed taken-for-granted daily interactions in Southeast Chicago. It gave me the discipline to take nightly fieldnotes on seemingly mundane family interactions, everyday storytelling, or community events. It also led me to conduct numerous formal interviews and oral histories over the years, to carry out archival research, and to analyze and collect visual materials and objects. Together, Chris Boebel and I taped over a hundred hours of video footage, often on everyday family encounters. I also regularly tacked back and forth between the particulars of my family's and Southeast Chicago's experiences and those of other families or regions as captured in the secondary literature or in materials from the Southeast Chicago Historical Museum. This tacking back and forth underscored which particulars were commonplace and which were seemingly idiosyncratic, highlighting the need to account for both. Although much of this scholarly background work never made it into the final products (or ended up relegated to extensive endnotes to make the book more accessible), it offered a disciplined path to using the 'personal' as a way to understand broader patterns and, as such, profoundly shaped the resulting work.

Many have noted the tendency for academic accounts written in the first person to be judged as solipsistic or lacking rigor (Vesperi and Waterson 2011; Okely and Callaway 1992). However, as oral historian Alessandro Portelli (1981, 1991) argues, intellectual rigor does not come from the voice or form in which accounts are presented – whether written, oral, first person or third – but from constant cross-checking across a range of sources or literatures and by accounting for the parallels and differences among them. All such accounts, in the end, hold the potential for blind spots, mistakes, and distortions – as well as for crucial insights.

Rethinking methods: What stories can contribute to theory

Many theoreticians and social scientists express skepticism, not just about personal narratives but about 'stories' more broadly. Can 'stories' – whether in working-class studies or elsewhere, first person or otherwise – be the stuff of rigorous scholarly work, and in what ways do they count as evidence and relate to theory? While narratives are bread and butter for literary scholars, among social scientists, 'stories' are widely critiqued for being 'anecdotal', by which it is meant that they are too particularistic to allow for generalizations, making it impossible to make broader scholarly claims. This characterization reflects the longstanding tension between what scholars call idiographic work, based on detailed description, and nomothetic, or rule-oriented, models for research. However, as is generally the case for narrative-based, historical, and ethnographic work (including the *Exit Zero* book and documentary), the goal is different. It is not to make generalizing claims, but to dig deeply into particulars in a way that allows for depth of understanding that enables others to claim points of recognition.

In the case of the Exit Zero Project, there have been two goals. One is to provide a sense of what experiencing deindustrialization or a certain kind of class positioning might *feel* like in a way that statistics cannot convey. The second is to flip how deindustrialization is customarily discussed. Instead of relying upon statistics, economic indicators, or policy debates that begin from an abstracted 'top-down' point of view (one that relegates the 'stories' of particular individuals or communities to being mere illustrations or case studies), the goal is to instead start with the particulars of individual lives and trace their connections outward in ways that call attention to larger patterns and developments. The way to gain sight of the 'big picture' in such accounts is not through generalizations that risk stereotyping or flattening human experience (with the little-known realities of working-class experiences being easily susceptible to distortion). Instead, the goal is for the larger patterns to emerge through the act of making connections, identifying commonalities and differences, and following linkages based on the socially and historically grounded particularities that comprise daily realities. While the point of view offered by statistical abstractions can helpfully suggest a sense of scale, areas to probe more deeply, or questions that should be asked, it cannot convey what social phenomena *mean* in everyday life.

Here, I offer an example of how, within the *Exit Zero* documentary film, we attempted to suggest a big-picture perspective by means of particularity and connection. The film details how Wisconsin Steel, the mill where my father had worked as a shear operator, was chaotically shut down in questionably legal ways. My father's voice is heard saying, 'People were losing homes, killing themselves, getting divorced. Everything happened. Everything!' (an assessment supported in studies done on the region). There is then a jump to a Google Maps image of Southeast Chicago that offers the estimated number of jobs lost for each of the local steel mills since peak employment in the 1960s. The camera then zooms out from Southeast Chicago to the Midwest to the entire United States, with colored shading for each county specifying the numbers of industrial jobs lost between 1960 and 2000. In creating the graphic, the difficulties of statistical rendering of deindustrialization became abundantly clear given the difficulty of finding data sets that are consistent across time periods and regions of the U.S.[11] Yet, the graphic helps to visually convey the extent of industrial jobs lost across the United States in recent decades – thereby intimating the number of 'stories' in other regions there are to tell – even though the *Exit Zero* documentary itself delves into only one family's story (Image 4.2). We also plan to convey a 'larger picture' for the Southeast Chicago Historical Museum website project in the future by linking it to other websites about deindustrialized communities, thereby creating a sense of scale through concrete linkages across time and space while simultaneously drawing attention to regional commonalities and differences.

While 'stories' are often symbolically positioned as the opposite of theory, I would like to suggest that there is more room for parallels and connections between them than is commonly recognized. First, we must ask: are stories indeed the opposite of theory? 'Stories' can range from formal narrative performances to the kind of minimalist everyday speech acts identified by Elinor Ochs and Lisa Capps (1996, 2001) as the basic building blocks for ordering and making sense of the world. Ochs and Capps have argued that narrative is a fundamental and universal genre, one that gives shape and meaning to experience, is essential to self-making, and is co-produced between listeners and tellers. Narratives, in their view, order our experiences, not necessarily in a chronological sense, but in a moral one. They morally order past, present, and possible experiences, and they often focus on unexpected or troubling turns of events as

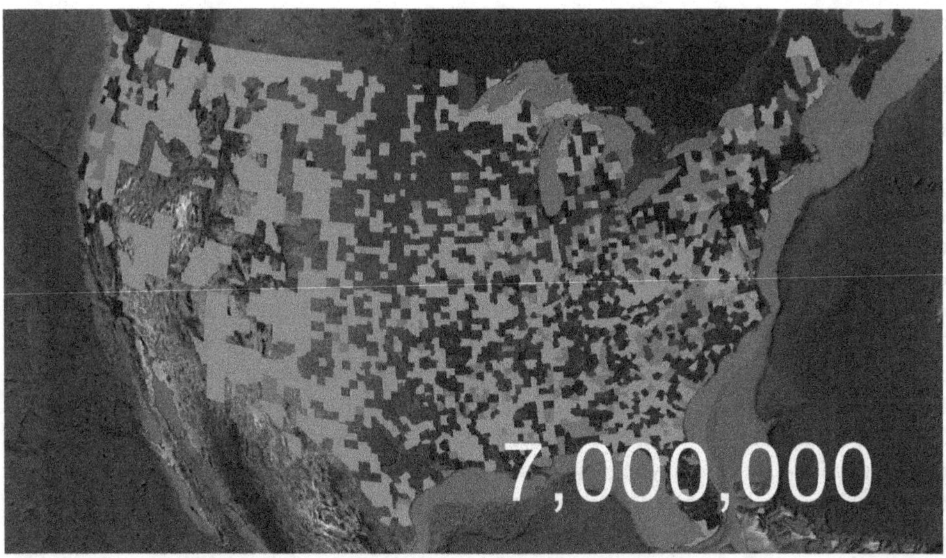

Image 4.2 Image of lost industrial jobs used in the *Exit Zero* documentary
Source: graphic by Sasha Goldberg

narrators try to resolve discrepancies between what was expected and what transpired. In short, narratives are a way to order our thought and emotions and to make sense of the world.

'Stories' in this sense, whether taking basic or highly elaborated forms, suggest a means for engaging the world by ordering and analyzing it. Growing up in Southeast Chicago, stories were powerful to me because they represented the commonplace medium for analyzing everyday life. When I would come home from college and talk with my (then unemployed) dad about 'big issues', often using the abstracted language I had learned in school, my father would always counter such rhetorical moves with a story. Whether talking about politics, the mills, or the state of the country, he would poke me on the leg and begin, 'Let me tell you, Peanut … '. And then, he would launch into some story that illustrated how he viewed the world.

One story that my father obsessively told just before he passed away was about an uninsured middle-aged couple who were 'kicked out' of the nearby hospital where he was undergoing cancer treatment because they could not afford to pay. My father (insured under Medicare after going for years without health insurance) repeatedly told this story to his doctors and nurses as well as to neighbors and family friends coming to bid him farewell, anyone who would listen. Usually, he just told the story. Occasionally (I suspect if he thought his audience was being obtuse), he would make its moral explicit: 'Can you believe it', he would ask, 'in a country as rich as this?' (The fact that the couple was African-American was significant in that the story symbolically transcended the longstanding racial animosity of many old industrial areas like Southeast Chicago where mill management had historically pitted ethnic and racial groups against each other, using newer arrivals to undermine wage scales). To me, the story suggested my father's recognition of the vulnerability of so many like him in the wake of the steel mills' closures as well as an underlying feeling that a sense of basic humanity was being violated in this economically crueler era.

Analysis, for my father as well as for so many others, was always in the stories. While all people might tell 'stories', stories might be particularly central to accounts from working-class communities. Shirley Brice Heath's research (1982), for example, has suggested that those from different class and racial backgrounds might teach their children diverse reasoning and narrative styles. While middle-class parents emphasize teaching their children to abstract from particulars – a skill valorized in schools – others might teach their children through stories or actions grounded in the particular, a less scholastically valued but equally adept way to make sense of the world (Heath 1982). My goal here is not to romanticize storytelling or the analysis that comes out of it. Academics have long recognized that stories are bound up with power-laden conventions in the style, content, and contexts of their telling; and their absences and erasures are just as important as what they contain (Ewick and Silbey 1995). Yet, we should also not underestimate the power of stories as building blocks for analysis of the worlds in which we live.

But how do stories relate to the 'theory' of academics? Might they, at least sometimes, serve as parallel kinds of activity? Before answering, we must consider what 'theory' is. Anthropologist Cathy Lutz in 'The gender of theory' (1995) has offered an irreverent feminist critique of theory. She argues there are gender-based differences in what gets 'counted' as theory and how it is signaled to others, with male anthropologists more often being associated with theory and female anthropologists more often with lower-status ethnography. Lutz notes that rendering something 'theoretical' in academic texts often revolves around such stylistic choices as self-labeling (i.e. incorporating the term 'theory' in titles such as Bourdieu's (1977) *Outline of a Theory of Practice*) or by suggesting a general applicability across multiple cases by denuding statements of their origins in specific experiences or historical contexts. Theory might also be signaled by use of abstract language coupled with difficult jargon or with citational practices that ignore contemporary scholars and cite further back in history, often to male theorists.

At the core of 'theory', then, is a distancing from the kind of interactive encounters heavily emphasized in ethnographies as well as in oral histories and feminist theories of 'situated knowledges' (Haraway 1988). As Lutz argues,

> theory has traditionally allowed for the erasure of the subject – both the subject that writes and the human subjects who are written about. It allows the theorist to avoid the roots of statements in real-world encounters, to speak for or appear to speak for the whole and to speak from a transcendental vantage point.
>
> *(1995, 260)*

She notes that feminist theory has often shown a certain skepticism about its own role, questioning the universal voice behind the bird's-eye view of theory and pushing back against the presumed dualisms of theory versus practice while emphasizing the intimate connections between the personal and the political, the local and the abstract (Lutz 1995, 258; see also Haraway 1988; Abu-Lughod 1991; Gluck and Patai 1991).

Anthropologist Joao Biehl (2013) also argues for the potential of stories to further academic discussion and theory-making. He suggests that contemporary anthropologists have deferred too readily to philosophers and theorists and that ethnography should not be seen as lower-order fodder for philosophy (nor, I might add, simply as 'case studies' for the social sciences). Rather, he contends, we should imagine ethnography *in the way of* theory, with theory and ethnography each pushing the other forward, and with philosophy learning in turn from ethnography. It is from doing ethnography, Biehl argues, that anthropologists learn to engage with the everyday theories of our interlocutors. At the same time, he stresses that we all tell stories: anthropologists tell stories of 'human becomings'; philosophers tell stories with concepts; filmmakers tell stories 'with blocks of movement and duration'. This storytelling, he emphasizes, is not simply an act of communication, but also one of invention, creativity, and engagement with the world.

What brings together academic theory and stories for me is that both represent forms of conversation that push forward our thinking. As historian William Sewell Jr. writes,

> Scholarship, which may seem a lonely occupation to those who do not pursue it, is in fact profoundly social. Our ideas are produced within the socially constructed network of puzzles, problems, and obsessions that are the stuff of intellectual communities, and they are advanced by endless discussion and argument.
>
> *(2005, x)*

When we think of theory as a form of social practice rather than as abstracted concepts, it becomes clear that it is a form of conversation, albeit one that occurs across disjunctures of time and space. Perhaps the key significance of academia is its ability to institutionalize and value such conversations in ways that offer possibilities to challenge and refine our thinking. Might we, however, need to broaden what counts as theoretical or, at least, offer greater recognition of the parallel tracks along which other analytical conversations about the world might run? Instead of enshrining theory as the highest form of conversation (one that excludes by presuming readers' familiarity with key academic texts and the time and money to master them), I would like to suggest we might do better to emphasize *analysis*. Analysis, after all, more firmly builds upon concrete engagement with the world and is as much part of everyday storytelling as it is of academic theory. Emphasizing analysis can further open such conversations to working-class voices, potentially providing alternative analyses to those commonly found in academia.

In conversation, it is important to acknowledge to whom one is speaking and who has been invited or excluded from the conversation. As someone from a working-class background, one of things that troubled me as a youth reading academic accounts of Southeast Chicago was the sense that such works were written *about* us rather than *for* us (much less *by* us). As a result, at the heart of the Exit Zero Project (successful or otherwise) has been a desire to emphasize stories, because they are more likely to establish a common ground for conversation and analysis among those from different class backgrounds.

Rethinking methods: Multimedia conversations

Another way to create common ground and further incorporate working-class perspectives into academic conversations and scholarship is by taking full advantage of newer possibilities for multimedia work, or what some call multiplatform or transmedia work (i.e. accounts that unfold across multiple media with each component adding a different element to an overall project). In an increasingly 'mediated' world, such work offers possibilities for combining text-based, object-based, or visual analysis in ways that engage multiple sensory modalities while expanding options for research, collaboration, and the diversification of audiences. Such developments can build upon the fact that working-class studies already supports scholars working in multiple media and has long encouraged practitioners to speak to those beyond the academy, whether through collaboration with community activists, labor leaders, or artists oriented to class issues. For example, sociologist Tim Strangleman's work on deindustrialization ranges from the photo-laden book *Voices of Guinness: An Oral History of the Park Royal Brewery* (2019) on the closing of London's Guinness brewery to participation in a documentary film *Watermark* on the demise of a Dover paper mill,[12] while literary scholar Michele Fazio has created a multimedia family-based research project that includes a museum exhibit exploring her Italian-American immigrant family's long-denied relationship to radical politics in the wake of the Sacco and Vanzetti trials. Digital projects include Jane Van Galen's digital storytelling project with first-generation students and the Class Action website, that offers resources for exploring class-related issues.[13] The Center for Working-Class Studies at Youngstown State University and the Center for the Study of Working-Class Life at SUNY-Stonybrook, the two founding institutions of the working-class studies field, have also strongly advocated for community outreach efforts, including an oral history collection, Steel Valley Voices, about Youngstown.[14]

Even apart from online initiatives, film and video have long offered possibilities for understanding class-related phenomena through different sensory modalities. This reality was highlighted for me while shooting the *Exit Zero* documentary film with Chris Boebel. Attempting to visually capture the wetlands, brownfields, and garbage landfills of Southeast Chicago's post-industrial landscape encouraged us to explore this region in a very different way than if we had been working in a text-based medium. Film and video are also well-suited to capturing the minutiae of daily life, including what Bourdieu called class 'habitus', or the embodied expression of power-laden social dispositions potentially conveyed through a look, a hand gesture, a joke, a body posture, or a style of speech. In the *Exit Zero* documentary, I think of my grandfather's audiotaped voice, with his heavily class-inflected 'hillbilly' accent, as he described being present at the landmark labor event, the 1937 Memorial Day Massacre. In addition, filmed images readily convey the centrality of material artifacts in daily experience, leading Chris Boebel to meticulously film my mother's carefully preserved antique dining room, with its glass teacups and family heirlooms, in order to underscore the symbolic dimensions of a gendered home space that for decades had served as a buttress against a chaotic post-mill shutdown world.

Online documentary work similarly allows exploration through multiple sensory modalities while also adding opportunities to enhance research by means of multilinear approaches and by allowing expanded forms of engagement with collaborators and audiences. Here, I use my and Chris Boebel's in-progress website collaboration with the Southeast Chicago Historical Museum as an example. After being inspired by an emergent body of online interactive documentaries and MIT's Open Documentary Lab, we approached the Southeast Chicago Historical Museum in 2014 about a collaborative project that would use their materials to create an online archive and storytelling site about the region's industrial to postindustrial transformation. The museum, an unassuming room in a park field house located mere yards from the region's massive industrial brownfields, was founded in the early 1980s as the steel mills were closing. It has survived on volunteer labor for nearly 40 years, serving as a community repository where residents could donate materials they found meaningful about the region's past. Despite gaps in its collections, the wealth of materials is remarkable. Crammed to the rafters, the museum holds over 300 videotapes and film reels of home movies and community events, approximately 10,000 still images, 180 oral histories, 85 scrapbooks, 250 items of clothing, and countless documents and material artifacts, ranging from domestic items like a clothing iron and cradle to religious icons to steel bars rolled at the mills (see Image 4.3) After digitizing a large portion of the museum's collections, we are currently designing the website. The website is intended to allow audiences to explore the region's working-class history through its artifacts, either by direct searching or by choosing curated, 'story'-laden pathways based on themes drawn from the museum's collections.

The online project appealed to Chris Boebel and myself for a variety of reasons, including its possibilities for multilinear storytelling. If the auto-ethnographic focus of the *Exit Zero* book and documentary film allowed a deep dive into my own (white) family's experience of deindustrialization, that storyline (and the more linear narrative expectations of academic book-writing and filmmaking) made it difficult to explore fully the diversity of working-class experiences across racial, ethnic, gender, and neighborhood divides within Southeast Chicago. If the *Exit Zero* book and film were built on the fragments of a single family 'archive', the website project, in contrast, is being built upon an archive collectively curated by a wide range of Southeast Chicago residents. The relative ease of working in multilinear fashion and the ability to include a multitude of stories and artifacts online makes it an ideal medium for exploring this diversity.

Image 4.3 Baby shoes from the 1920s donated to the Southeast Chicago Historical Museum
Source: photograph by Chris Boebel

However, just as with other kinds of methodological approaches, there are limitations as well. As with written or spoken stories, the silences and absences among the museum's artifacts are as revealing as what is present (Trouillot 1995). The gaps and imbalances, which we are currently addressing, run along power-laden fault lines of race and gender as well as more subtle internal class differentiation within the old steel mill communities. The most crucial concern race. The fact that Mexican-Americans and African-Americans worked in the region's steel mills in large numbers beginning in the World War I era helps counter tenacious stereotypes that depict white men as the archetypal industrial workers (see Image 4.4). The museum, however, was historically founded in what was then a majority white ethnic neighborhood, and the preponderance of non-industry-related museum artifacts relate to various European immigrant groups. The museum does hold a substantial collection on Mexican-American history in what is now a majority Latinx region;[15] however, material on African-Americans is sparser, in part because of virulent housing discrimination in the past that meant that African-American steelworkers often lived in other parts of the city.

Although women are central to the museum's collections in many ways, men's work experiences (regardless of race) are far more fully represented than either women's domestic labor or their past work running boarding houses, taking in laundry and sewing, or working in mills and service industries (an exception being 'Rosie the Riveter'-style depictions of women steelworkers from the World War II era). Museum artifacts also suggest internal status divisions,

Image 4.4 Steelworkers union election, Local 1033
Source: photograph courtesy of Southeast Chicago Historical Museum

as more prosperous industrial workers and families are more fully represented than poorer ones. Addressing these gaps and imbalances has meant selective curation of the museum's extensive collections and, in some instances, additional outreach and collecting.

In general, the website project is premised upon two orientations to working-class history that are intended to encourage broader engagement with regional and general audiences. First, the construction of the website is premised on the recognition that many people do not engage with 'history' primarily through written academic accounts (Trouillot 1995). Such engagement (in addition to that gleaned from media) often happens through family objects saved, images kept, or stories told. Second, the website is concerned not only with the historical *content* of museum artifacts, but also *why* people chose to save certain artifacts, what stories were told about – and through – them, and what this conveyed about social class in everyday industrial and postindustrial settings. In short, this approach combines the disciplinary perspectives of history, anthropology, and working-class studies by seeking to understand and interpret what happened in the past, why it was meaningful to people, and what these histories might tell us about social class.

The meanings of material objects extend to the ways such objects as photographs and family heirlooms circulated through social networks, producing or maintaining relationships in the process (Edwards 2006). For example, among the immigrant and migrant communities that dominated Southeast Chicago's history, photographs often circulated across oceans and borders as indexical images that offered the 'magic' of connection to family members in the 'old country' as well as a sense of multigenerational continuity across experiences of rupture (see also Barthes 2010[1981]; Hirsch 1997). In other cases, museum items reflect genres of collecting specific to deindustrialized communities, that served to ritually mark or reflect upon historical changes. For example, the museum's collection of home movies, an increasingly recognized form of 'bottom-up' history in its own right (Zimmerman 2008), includes videos that steelworkers took during the 1980s and 1990s, poignantly depicting the demolition of the steel mill structures where they had once worked.

In short, the website project recognizes museum artifacts as embedded in social worlds and interwoven with 'stories' in ways that we hope will help make those worlds compelling and approachable. These stories occur at multiple levels. Residents, for example, may have saved items like World War II or Vietnam War artifacts because they deemed them 'historical' in ways that accorded with larger national narratives. In another sense, 'narratives' emerge directly from the artifacts themselves, as when the creators of home movies, photos, or scrapbooks deemed certain things worthy of recording (while neglecting others) or when they framed or juxtaposed content in particular ways (Zimmerman 2008; Hirsch 1997; Trachtenburg 1990). Donors also often told stories about why they saved and donated particular objects, as recorded in decades' worth of museum newsletters. In addition, the museum's extensive oral history collections offer even more elaborate stories, touching upon topics relating to work, immigrant experiences, family and neighborhood life, and reflections on labor and civil rights struggles, among others. And, finally, there are the narratives that my collaborators and I are bringing to the project as we design and piece together the website, as well as the stories and artifacts that future website viewers will themselves offer. (Interested website users will also be directed toward the museum's lively 5,000+ member Facebook group where interactive sharing of artifacts and conversation is already well established). To paraphrase Clifford Geertz, it is 'stories' all the way down.

In contrast to most anthropological and ethnographic accounts of 'archives' that have focused on government or colonial archives (Zeitlyn 2012; Stoler 2010; Dirks 2014; Weld 2014), this project centers upon a very different kind of repository, one generated by working-class interlocutors responding to a transformed industrial world. Like other forms of public anthropology or public history, the goal is to engage a broader public, in this case with a collection that puts working-class accounts at the center. Analysis in this project emerges through the juxtapositioning of artifacts, stories, and accounts (with just enough historical context to allow for interpretation of competing accounts). The 'methods' involved have also been quite different from the individualistic ones of classical anthropological scholarship and entail working in a team that includes not only museum volunteers and area residents but also an archivist, a web designer, museum and media professionals, and technologists.[16] While the methodological and funding hurdles to working in this way are significant (and multimedia work should not be a goal of all scholarship any more than working in the first person should), we believe that selectively utilizing its possibilities holds crucial opportunities for research as well as for engagement with working-class interlocutors and audiences.

Conclusion

This chapter has put working-class studies in deeper conversation with anthropology (and anthropological engagements with history) in order to explore key methodological questions that have emerged in these fields, including how and why the self comes to be incorporated into scholarly research, how using 'stories' as a medium of scholarship can relate to theory, and possibilities for research, collaboration, and outreach offered by multimedia approaches. As discussed at the outset, the collective project of working-class studies, like anthropology, is one that simultaneously attempts to capture the richness of daily life *and* the larger structural realities that shape historic and contemporary power relations. Exploring such methodological questions helps clarify how we can simultaneously achieve analytical rigor and remain open to the ambiguity, improvisations, and emotional resonances of everyday encounters. In a contemporary moment of increasingly toxic inequalities and related political upheavals, there is an urgent need to return to questions of social class. Working-class studies can help expand conversations about social class both outside and within academia while emphasizing a diversity of working-class viewpoints. Explicitly addressing questions of *how* we work as working-class studies practitioners is key to clarifying the directions we would like research to head and with whom we would like to collaborate and engage along the way.

Notes

1 For discussion of the relationship among various disciplines in the founding of working-class studies, see Russo and Linkon (2005).

2 Anthropology, as a discipline that historically studied non-Western, often colonized, parts of world, has tended to emphasize questions of cultural difference, ethnicity, and identity rather than social class (Ortner 1991). For additional discussion of anthropology's relationship to working-class studies, see Kate Dudley (this volume).

3 'Transmedia' refers to work in which story elements or analytical content unfolds *across* multiple media or platforms (rather than, for example, merely supplemental information being shared on a website).

4 For reflections on ethnographic fieldwork, see Gusterson (2008), Goffman (1989), and Geertz (1973), among many others; see Marcus (1995) for discussions of multi-sited fieldwork.

5 Qualitative sociologists often use similar ethnographic methods and emphases – for example, the tensions between what is said and done in formal 'front stage' settings and the more informal or 'backstage' settings (Goffman 1989).

6 For a few discussions of either class or working-class studies in relation to the voluminous literature on 'intersectionality', see Bettie (2003), Lacy (2007), Russo and Linkon (2005), Roediger (2005), Hubbs (2014), and Hartigan (1991).

7 This work also includes accounts by other anthropologists. In general, deindustrialization is key to thinking about changing class dynamics for working-class populations in the United States. Although predating working-class studies, William Julius Wilson's (1996) work on the impact of deindustrialization on African-Americans remains a foundational text. In terms of the field of working-class studies itself, not surprisingly, one of its founding institutions, the Center for Working Class Studies, is located in deindustrialized Youngstown, Ohio. Although the scholarly work of Jack Metzgar (2000), another founding figure, was not directly about deindustrialization (although it was about manufacturing), he has been a key figure in supporting research and theorizing on deindustrialization within the discipline.

8 Although the emergence of 'auto-ethnography' as a distinct sub-genre is quite recent, there are precedents in the history of anthropology – perhaps most famously, Zora Neale Hurston's *Dust Tracks on a Road: An Autobiography* (1942).

9 A later account of class 'straddling' can be found in Alfred Lubrano's *Limbo: Blue Collar Roots, White Collar Dreams* (2004).

10 The analysis of Eribon's relationship to Bourdieu comes from MIT Professor Bruno Perreau, personal communication, October 25, 2017.

11 Although the 'number ticker' for total jobs lost at the bottom of the graphic eventually reaches 7 million – the number of industrial jobs estimated to have been lost between 1980 and 2014 – the color shading of the graphic artificially ends at 2000, when information on this loss by county ceased to be available.

12 www.dadonline.eu/projects/watermark/

13 https://firstinourfamilies.org/about/; https://classism.org

14 http://steelvalleyvoices.ysu.edu/events/

15 The Mexican-American History Project within the museum was spearheaded by Director Rod Sellers, who worked with area high school students to expand this collection. The museum also received an important infusion of materials from Columbia College's Southeast Chicago Historical Project in the 1980s.

16 This project http://sechicagohistory.org was funded by National Endowment for the Humanities, Donnelly Foundation, and MIT.

References

Abu-Lughod, L. (1991) 'Writing against Culture', in Fox, R. (ed.) *Recapturing Anthropology*, Santa Fe, School of American Research.

Abu-Lughod, L. (2007) 'Return to Half-Ruins: Memory, Post-Memory, and Living History in Palestine', in Sa'di, A. and Abu-Lughod, L. (eds.) *Nakba: Palestine, 1948, and the Claims of Memory*, New York, Columbia University Press.

Barthes, R. (2010 [1981]) *Camera Lucida: Reflections on Photography*, New York, Hill and Wang.

Behar, R. (2007) *An Island Called Home: Returning to Jewish Cuba*, New Brunswick, NJ, Rutgers University Press.

Bettie, J. (2003) *Women Without Class*, Berkeley, University of California Press.

Biehl, J. (2013) 'Ethnography in the Way of Theory', *Cultural Anthropology*, 28, 4, pp. 573–597.

Bourdieu, P. (1977) *Outline of a Theory of Practice*, Cambridge, Cambridge University Press.

Bourdieu, P. (2008) *Sketch for a Self-Analysis*, Chicago, University of Chicago Press.

Bright, G. (2015) '"The Lady is Not Returning!" Educational Precarity and a Social Haunting in the UK Coalfields', *Ethnography and Education*, 11, 2, pp. 142–157.

Chin, E. (2016) *My Life with Things*, Durham, Duke University Press.

Cowie, J. (1991) *Capital Moves: RCA's Seventy Year Quest for Cheap Labor*, Ithaca, Cornell University Press.

Cowie, J. and Heathcott, J. (eds.) (2003) *Beyond the Ruins: The Meanings of Deindustrialization*, Ithaca, ILR Press.

Delgado, R. (1989) 'Storytelling for Oppositionists and Others: A Plea for Narrative', *Michigan Law Review*, 87, 8, pp. 2411–2441.

Dews, C. L. and Law, C. (1995) *This Fine Place So Far From Home: Voices of Academics from the Working Class*, Philadelphia, Temple University Press.

Diawara, M. (1999) 'The "I" Narrator in Black Diaspora Cinema', in Klotman, P. and Cutler, J. (eds.) *Struggles for Representation: African American Film and Video*, Indianapolis, Indiana University Press.

Dirks, N. (2014) *Autobiography of an Archive*, New York, Columbia University Press.

Doukas, D. (2003) *Worked Over: The Corporate Sabotage of an American Community*, Ithaca, Cornell University Press.

Dudley, K. (1994) *The End of the Line: Lost Jobs, New Lives in Post-Industrial America*, Chicago, University of Chicago Press.
Edwards, E. (2006) 'Photographs and the Sound of History', *Visual Anthropology Review*, 12, 1 & 2, pp. 27–46.
Eribon, D. (2013) *Returning to Reims*, Los Angeles, Semiotext(e).
Ewick, P. and Silbey, S. (1995) 'Subversive Stories and Hegemonic Tales: Towards a Sociology of Narrative', *Law and Society Review*, 29, 2, pp. 197–226.
Exit Zero: An Industrial Family Story, Director Chris Boebel, 2017.
Geertz, C. (1973) *Interpretation of Cultures*, New York, Basic Books.
Gluck, S. B. and Patai, D. (eds.) (1991) *Women's Words: The Feminist Practice of Oral History*, New York, Routledge.
Goffman, E. (1989) 'On Fieldwork', *Journal of Contemporary Ethnography*, 18, 2, pp. 123–132.
Gusterson, H. (2008) 'Ethnographic Research', in Klotz, A. and Prakash, D. (eds.) *Qualitative Methods in International Research*, London, Palgrave McMillan.
Haraway, D. (1988) 'Situated Knowledges: The Science Question in Feminism and the Privilege of Partial Perspective', *Feminist Studies*, 14, 3, pp. 575–599.
Hartigan, J., Jr. (1991) *Racial Situations: Class Predicaments of Whiteness in Detroit*, Princeton, Princeton University Press.
Heath, S. B. (1982) 'What No Bedtime Story Means: Narrative Skills at Home and School', *Language in Society*, 11, 1, pp. 49–76.
Hirsch, M. (1997) *Family Frames: Photography, Narrative, and PostMemory*, Cambridge, Harvard University Press.
Hubbs, N. (2014) *Rednecks, Queers, and Country Music*, Berkeley, University of California Press.
Hurston, Z. N. (1942) *Dust Tracks on a Road: An Autobiography*, New York, Harper Perennial.
Hutchinson, S. (1996) *Nuer Dilemmas*, Berkeley, University of California Press.
Lacy, K. (2007) *Blue Chip Black: Race, Class, and Status in the New Black Middle Class*, Berkeley, University of California Press.
Linkon, S. L. (2014) 'Book Review: *Exit Zero: Family and Class in Postindustrial Chicago*', *Working Class Studies Association Newsletter*.
Linkon, S. L. (2018) *The Half-Life of Deindustrialization: Working-Class Writing about Economic Restructuring*, Ann Arbor, University of Michigan Press.
Linkon, S. L. and Russo, J. (2002) *Steeltown U.S.A.: Work and Memory in Youngstown*, Lawrence, University Press of Kansas.
Lubrano, A. (2004) *Limbo: Blue Collar Roots, White Collar Dreams*, Hoboken, NJ, John Wiley and Sons.
Lutz, C. (1995) 'The Gender of Theory', in Behar, R. and Gordon, D. A. (eds.) *Women Writing Culture*, Berkeley, University of California Press.
Marcus, G. (1995) 'Ethnography in/of the World System: The Emergence of Multisited Ethnography', *Annual Review of Anthropology*, 24, pp. 95–117.
Metzgar, J. (2000) *Striking Steel: Solidarity Remembered*, Philadelphia, Temple University Press.
Modell, J. (1998) *A Town Without Steel: Envisioning Homestead*, Pittsburgh, University of Pittsburgh Press.
Moran-Thomas, A. (2017) 'Mine', Hot Spots, *Fieldsites*. Available at https://culanth.org/fieldsights/1030-the-rise-of-trumpism
Narayan, K. (2008) *My Family and Other Saints*, Chicago, University of Chicago Press.
Ochs, E. and Capps, L. (1996) 'Narrating the Self', *Annual Review of Anthropology*, 25, pp. 19–43.
Ochs, E. and Capps, L. (2001) *Living Narrative: Creating lives in Everyday Storytelling*, Cambridge, Harvard University Press.
Okely, J. and Callaway, H. (1992), *Anthropology and Autobiography*, New York, Routledge.
Ortner, S. (1991) 'Reading America: Preliminary Notes on Class and Culture', in Fox, R. G. (ed.) *Recapturing Anthropology: Working in the Present*, Santa Fe, School of American Research.
Pandian, A. and Mariappan, M. P. (2014) *Ayya's Accounts: A Ledger of Hope in Modern India*, Bloomington, Indiana University Press.
Pappas, G. (1989) *The Magic City: Unemployment in a Working-Class Community*, Ithaca, Cornell University Press.
Portelli, A. (1981) 'The Peculiarities of Oral History', *History Workshop*, 12, Autumn, pp. 96–107.
Portelli, A. (1991) *The Death of Luigi Trastulli and Other Stories: Form and Meaning in Oral History*, Albany, State University of New York Press.
Reed-Danahay, D. (1997) *Auto/Ethnography: Rewriting the Self and the Social*, London, Bloomsbury.
Rodriguez, R. (1982) *Hunger of Memory: The Education of Richard Rodriguez*, New York, Bantam Dell.

Roediger, D. (2005) 'More than Two Things: The State of the Art of Labor History', in Russo, J. and Linkon, S. L. (eds.) *New Working-Class Studies*, Ithaca, Cornell University Press.
Russo, J. and Linkon, S. L. (eds.) (2005), *New Working-Class Studies*, Ithaca, Cornell University Press.
Ryan, J. and Sackrey, C. (1984) *Strangers in Paradise: Academics from the Working Class*, Boston, South End Press.
Sewell, W., Jr. (2005) *The Logics of History*, Chicago, University of Chicago Press.
Slyomovics, S. (2014) *How to Accept German Reparations*, Philadelphia, University of Pennsylvania Press.
Steedman, C. (1986) *Landscape for a Good Woman*, New Brunswick, Rutgers University Press.
Stoler, A. (2010) *Along the Archival Grain*, Princeton, Princeton University Press.
Strangleman, T. (2004) *Work Identity at the End of the Line? Privatisation and Culture Change in the UK Rail Industry*, London, Palgrave McMillan.
Strangleman, T. (2019) *Voices of Guinness: An Oral History of the Park Royal Brewery*, New York, Oxford University Press.
Taft, C. (2016) *From Steel to Slots: Casino Capitalism in the Postindustrial City*, Cambridge, Harvard University Press.
Tokarczyk, M. M. and Fay, E. A. (eds.) (1993) *Working Class Women in the Academy: Laborers in the Knowledge Factory*, Amherst, University of Massachusetts Press.
Trachtenberg, A. (1990) *Reading American Photographs: Images as History, Matthew Brady to Walker Evans*, New York, Hill and Wang.
Trouillot, M. R. (1995) *Silencing the Past: Power and the Production of History*, Boston, Beacon Press.
Vesperi, M. and Waterston, A. (2011) *Anthropologists Off the Shelf: Anthropologists on Writing*, New York, Wiley-Blackwell.
Walley, C. J. (2009) 'Deindustrializing Chicago: A Daughter's Story', in Gusterson, H. and Besteman, C. (eds.) *The Insecure American*, Berkeley, University of California Press.
Walley, C. J. (2013) *Exit Zero: Family and Social Class in Postindustrial Chicago*, Chicago, University of Chicago Press.
Walley, C. J. (2015) 'Transmedia as Experimental Ethnography: The Exit Zero Project, Deindustrialization, and the Politics of Nostalgia', *American Ethnologist*, 42, 4, pp. 624–639.
Waterston, A. (2014) *My Father's Wars: Migration, Memory and the Violence of a Century*, New York, Routledge.
Waterston, A. and Rylko-Bauer, B. (2006) 'Out of the Shadows of History and Memory: Personal Family Narratives in Ethnographies of Rediscovery', *American Ethnologist*, 33, 3, pp. 397–412.
Weld, K. (2014) *Paper Cadavers: The Archives of Dictatorship in Guatemala*, Durham, Duke University Press.
Wilson, W. J. (1996) *When Work Disappears: The World of the New Urban Poor*, New York, Vintage Books.
Zeitlyn, D. (2012). 'Anthropology in and of the Archive', *Annual Review of Anthropology*, 41, pp. 461–480.
Zimmermann, P. (2008) 'Introduction', in Ishizuka, K. and Zimmermann, P. (eds.) *Mining the Home Movie*, Berkeley, University of California Press.

Part II

Class and education

Section introduction

Class and education

Allison L. Hurst

> We cannot teach our way out of inequality.
>
> *(Marsh 2011)*

There are two constant themes that come up in the literature on the working class and education – social reproduction and social mobility; which I'll call here the gatekeeper and escalator models of education systems. Many people presume that education is a pathway to social mobility for people from the working class. It works like a magic escalator. Indeed, many models of class use education as the primary boundary marker between the working class and the middle class, implying that once a person has become educated, that person is no longer working class. This is highly problematic, as will be discussed later. There is another problem here, one we can call the gatekeeper problem. Because education has become a marker of class and therefore *moral worth* and deservingness (at minimum, of a salary versus a wage), success in education cannot be open to all (Hurst 2010). Students are sorted and graded continuously (notice the eerie concordance of double words like 'grade' and 'class').

Much scholarly literature highlights the ways in which working-class kids are disadvantaged at school by teacher biases (Brantlinger 2003), barriers to access/unequal resources (Sacks 2007), lowered aspirations and expectations (Fordham 1996), and internalized classism (and racism) (Willis 2017) to name just a few. In this view, schools reproduce the unequal social system, transferring one generation's advantages (or disadvantages) on to the next. For many of these scholars, the ultimate goal is to get schools operating less like gatekeepers and more like escalators, especially given the (supposed) needs of a highly advanced technological society (Stevens, Armstrong, and Arum 2008). The reasoning goes as follows: if we could only get more students to college, we could solve both labor market shortages and social inequality. Other scholars, including myself (Hurst 2012), call this into question. It is a lazy answer to a bigger problem. While we would like everyone to have equal opportunities to succeed in school, we are already seeing too many of our graduates fail to find safe places in the middle class (Brinton 2011; Brown, Lauder and Ashton 2011; Burke 2016; Wolff 2006). Cappelli's (2015) sobering answer to the question 'will college pay off?' is largely that 'it depends' (on where you go to college, what you study, and, to a very large extent, who your parents are). It is time to recognize that we simply 'cannot teach or learn our way out of inequality' (Marsh 2011).

In this context, universal access to a college degree will only make further gradations (Which college? Which degree?) more salient. Nevertheless, this mantra of 'college for all' guides much current policy and research today, both in the US and globally (Rosenbaum 2001). We are stuck in the framework of thinking of college as an escalator to the middle class, even as many researchers point out that the goal line keeps moving for the working class, from getting a high school degree to getting a college degree to, increasingly, getting a college degree from the right program and/or getting a graduate degree (thus bringing us back to the gatekeeper function). I will discuss the consequences of using these two models, gatekeeper and escalator, to think about higher education, before turning to working-class studies as an alternative way forward. The following chapters demonstrate the need for an alternative way of thinking about education. If we are to send many more students to college than ever before, we need an educational system that works in collaboration with all its students, in projects that reimagine, rather than simply reinscribe, the larger social systems in which we find ourselves embedded.

The rise and consequences of the escalator model

The notion of education as an escalator is a historical one. The desire to reduce inequality by broadening access to salaried careers and professions has animated all the great educational reform movements of the modern era (Hochschild and Scovronick 2003; Lucas 1999; Rudolph 1962; Pritchard 1990; Sacks 2007). In the US, the Morrill Act (the enabling act of the Land Grant colleges) was said to have 'made possible the higher instruction of the children of workers and farmers and thus enabled social mobility and the equality of educational opportunity to become realities in a political democracy' (Brickman and Lehrer 1962, 11). The rise of a public university system was, in turn, predicated on earlier reform movements for public primary and secondary education, movements led by and for working-class people (Neem 2017). The conversations we have today about increasing access to college mirror those we were having in the nineteenth century about increasing access to high school.

These reform movements worked, to a point. As late as 1947, most adult Americans (76%) did not even have a high school degree, while less than 5% had a four-year college degree. Today, almost everyone eventually earns a high school degree, and one-third of all adults have earned a four-year college degree (US Census Bureau). Note that these figures are still far from the ideal of a thoroughly educated populace. Other industrialized countries have similar (or lower) rates of college participation (Shavit, Müller, and Tame 1998; Smeeding, Jäntti, and Erikson 2011), although almost everyone graduates from secondary school.

Despite the fact that we have in no way reached 'universal access' to post-secondary education, higher education is perversely seen as the near exclusive path to upward social mobility. Education generally is no longer supposed to function as a gatekeeper, barring the *hoi polloi* from elite positions. This belief in the escalator function comes with a price, however, as those who *do not succeed* academically have no one to blame but themselves. You want to do well in life? Stay in school. Growing up in such a culture, we tend to take the normalcy of this for granted. 'The rise of education as the near sole arbitrator of access to adult status has been so complete that former processes [of social advancement] – sinecure, occupational inheritance, religious charisma, guild training, patronage, caste – appear now as exotic social relics' (Baker 2014, 54). Increasingly, one's level of education defines one's social position.

A great curiosity of the current system is that despite all the reforms, the end result has generally been a rising of the educational expectations without an equalizing of life opportunities. Those who receive more (and better) forms of higher education monopolize the good positions. This was noted as early as the 1970s in France.

> The net result is that the relation between education and occupational status described changes very little over time. What does change is the number of years of schooling associated with each educational class. ... As a result, lower-class people become progressively better educated on the average, but their status expectations remain more or less constant.
>
> *(Boudon 1974, 183)*

The phenomenon has been noted many times since. In one cross-national study of mass educational systems, the authors found that 'nonelite students are never able to displace elite students; they gain access only when additional openings are generated and only after the more advantaged social stratum has accessed the most valued level of education' (Attewell and Newman 2010, 17). Across the world, 'higher education overall became more unequal as participation rates went up' (in Rhoten and Calhoun 2011, 16). Most of us are running faster to fall further behind.

Actually, there are only two examples that I know of in which educational reforms did make a clear difference in breaking down inequalities, and these are the cases of the Soviet Union (Fitzpatrick 1979) and Communist China during its Cultural Revolution (Deng and Treiman 1997). Communist ideology allowed for affirmative action programs for children of peasants and workers, turning the customary class advantages on their head. It need hardly go mentioned that these programs were bitterly contested, often shattering to the individuals involved, and have largely disappeared. These examples highlight the point made by Andy Green, in his comparative study of the educational systems of the US, France, and England, that it is the class relations of society which ultimately determine the purposes of schooling.

> It was the different forms of hegemony operating between the dominant and subordinate classes which was ultimately responsible for what schools did, for who they allowed to go to what type of school and for what they taught them when they were there.
>
> *(Green 1990, 311)*

To break down the inequalities reproduced through education, in other words, takes a lot more than getting more people educated. It requires major tinkering in society itself.

More often, however, the problem of universal education programs is not that they are too effective (and therefore incredibly destructive to accustomed privileges, including to the people who bear them), but that they are not nearly effective enough. Or, more exactly, that they *appear* effective when really they do very little to alter the fundamental classed system in place. For one, universal education programs appear to reward those with merit through advancement up the educational ladders. What this means on the ground is that those who *do not* go to college are more likely to be blamed individually. And since we know that educational programs are not autonomous from the larger social systems in which they are embedded, this means that current class positions are *legitimated* through the educational system (Bourdieu and Passeron 1977).

Martin Trow, the person who gave us the boosterish concept of successive eras of education from elite (early twentieth century) to mass (mid twentieth century) to universal (late twentieth century), penned a series of critical essays in his later years. He argued that 'failure to go on to higher education from secondary school is increasingly a mark of some defect of mind or character that has to be explained or justified or apologized for' (Trow, in Burrage 2010, 95). This holds as true, if not truer, for students from middle- and upper-class families as it does for working-class students. But universal education has had a particularly negative impact on the working class, as a class. Trow pointed to the impact of a 'brain drain' on the working class, arguing that this 'drain through education out of the unions of their best and brightest young members is one of the mechanisms' of loss of union power today (219). Ultimately, he argued, 'if we have any national policy regarding social or economic class, it is an educational policy designed not to strengthen the working class, or ameliorate its conditions, but to abolish it' (225). The escalator may carry a few individuals upwards, but most of the class, as a class, remain milling around at the bottom, often relatively worse off than before the escalator began carrying away their best and brightest stars.

Interestingly, Trow's comments here echo some of the early criticisms of mass education by social conservatives. In nineteenth-century France, for example, it was widely held that education should be confined to the rich, 'for, if it were extended to the poor, it would turn them against manual labor and make social misfits of them' (Ariés 1962, 309). Actually, Ariés points out that this critique has very long roots, and quotes a seventeenth-century critic of local town schools.

> How are we to stop this flood of education which is submerging so many cottages, depopulating so many villages, producing so many charlatans, intriguers, envious, angry and unhappy people of all sorts, and introducing confusion into every class and condition?
>
> *(311)*

One thing that these conservative writers seemed to recognize was that access to education was not the same thing as access to position. We have forgotten that in our rush to send everyone to college, but more on that later.

Whereas the nineteenth-century reform movement was rooted in ideas of progressive education for advancing civic participation (as in Horace Mann's common school movement), the twentieth-century push for education was increasingly tied to individual advancement. Since World War II, 'very little has been heard of "rising with your class," and a great deal about the need to create more truly equal opportunities for individual advancement for all through education – and especially through higher education' (Trow, in Burrage 2010, 223). Eventually, this led to today's policies of privatization and the defunding of public institutions. If the only benefit is personal, why should the public get involved at all? Education reforms under Secretary of Education DeVos are likely to intensify the trend toward individual purchase of educational packages that are then used to help secure access to the 'best' colleges. Any notion of education 'for the public good' seems to have been lost.

Indeed, it is hard to discuss education today other than in terms of individual success within a capitalist society. By the late twentieth century, in both the US and the UK, the purpose of education was squarely linked with gaining access to jobs, but as the underlying capitalist system in which these jobs were located was never questioned, getting an education became a credential for managerial and professional positions, exacerbating divisions within the labor force. The goal may be 'universal education', but how this is supposed to square with a continued need for a brutalized and dominated working class goes undiscussed. The contradictions of such a setup are becoming more pronounced. 'The notion of an overwhelming surge in educational requirements for jobs is absurd, and the promotion of college for all is in some ways dishonest' (Grubb and Lazerson 2004, 19). As the costs of higher education have mounted and public support has withered, it is harder to overlook the classing and sorting taking place. We may be getting more students through high school and into college, but many of them are failing to gain a degree and/or graduating with great debt, leaving them in a more precarious position than they would have been had they never continued education (Collinge 2010; Goldrick-Rab 2016; Hurst 2012, 2019). The size of this debt, nationally speaking, is also something policymakers are taking note of, as it threatens to spill over into the broader economy (Mettler 2014; Rothstein and Rouse 2007).

Understanding how education remains a gatekeeper

> The American dream is egalitarian at the starting point in this 'race of life,' but not at the end. That is not a paradox; it is simply an ideological choice. ... The paradox lies in the fact that schools are supposed to equalize opportunities across generations and to create democratic citizens out of each generation, but people naturally wish to give their own children an advantage in attaining wealth or power, and some can do it. When they do, everyone does not start equally, politically or economically. This circle cannot be squared.
>
> *(Hochschild and Scovronick 2003, 2)*

Researchers follow the story, while theorists take a step back and look at bigger structures in which the story is unfolding. Taking a big picture here means noting what gets discussed and what doesn't. A rising area of sociological research in education examines the impact and power of *parents* on maximizing and leveraging school success (Cucchiara 2013; Devine 2004; Johnson 2006; Goyette and Lareau 2014; Hamilton 2016; Lareau 1989, 2003; Smeeding, Jäntti, and Erikson 2011). From a theoretical perspective, this is a giant signpost warning: 'Danger ahead! Our inequality is in danger of spilling into caste-like territory!' It also marks the limits of an individualistic focus. Students are not succeeding on their individual merits, but through a confluence of classed resources. Phil Brown calls this wave of socio-historical development of education, 'parentology', and it is characterized by 'a shift away from the "ideology of meritocracy" to ... the "ideology of parentocracy"' (Brown 1990).

Neoliberalism and its focus on markets and individual choice favor highly resourced parents. 'Within the market rules of exclusion both consumers and producers are encouraged by the rewards and disciplines of market forces, and are legitimated by the values of the personal standpoint in their quest for positional advantage over others' (Ball 2003, 21). As the commitment to public education vanishes, middle-class and upper-class parents are wielding their know-how, social networks, and money to ensure that their children access the right kinds of schools at the right times. The involvement of parents has been noticed from preschool through college and beyond. Hamilton (2016) demonstrates how privileged parents leverage contacts and provide financial support to help their children successfully transition from college to career. Graduating from the same college with the same degree can lead to drastically unequal outcomes, dependent on the power and resources of one's parents. At the same time, the stress on middle-class parents to produce successful middle-class children is intense (Heiman 2015; Power et al. 2003). We are a far place today from seeing schools as a public good, rather than as helping the material interests of particular parents (Cucchiara 2013, 203). Further damaging is research that shows that 'parental involvement' is only effective when it is involves highly resourced parents, so encouraging working-class parents to attend PTA meetings and open houses is really not going to make a difference (Robinson 2014).

Sometimes, it is those who have experienced social mobility against the odds that have the greatest insight into how the system works. This is certainly the case with the brilliant social theorist Pierre Bourdieu. Himself the provincial son of a postal clerk and grandson of peasants, Bourdieu catapulted to the very top of the French academic hierarchy (Bourdieu 2008). His work has influenced multiple disciplines from sociology to literature, anthropology to architecture, political science to art to education. In the 1970s and 1980s, the English-speaking world mostly knew Bourdieu as a social reproduction theorist, one who argued that schools maintained social inequality by privileging and rewarding the cultural capital of its higher-classed students. For example, an early study by Bourdieu compared how primary school teachers used different language when describing 'A'-grade work by students, depending upon what was known of their parents' occupations. Bourgeois students were praised as 'innately talented' or 'brilliant', while working-class students were described as 'hard-working' and, sometimes, as merely imitative (Bourdieu and Passeron 1977). Over time, he argued, working-class students, even those of high ability, took the lesson to heart that school was 'not for them' and left early, thus reproducing inequality inter-generationally without any need for overt or explicit limits on working-class access to higher levels of education. This accords well with a recent study of high school valedictorians that found many working-class high achievers never even apply to college (Radford 2013).

Some American scholars who read Bourdieu's early work on education criticized him for being pessimistic and deterministic. There seemed little possibility of school as an escalator. But this, I would argue, was a serious misreading. Having himself been helped up the class ladder by education, Bourdieu was aware that reproducing class inequalities does not mean that any one individual's fate is determined at birth. Instead, the tendency is to advance those whose habits and worldviews fit them for advancement and to subvert all others to different pathways. Being fit for advancement had much less to do with intrinsic merit or aptitude than sharing the cultural norms and expectations of those already advanced, but this is not *biological* or inherent to a person. Indeed, Bourdieu was aware of the costs of so-called upward social mobility, leading those who experienced this social dislocation divided in both loyalties and habits, caught between two worlds, as so ably described by many working-class academics. Additionally, 'controlled mobility of a limited number of individuals' has the advantage of strengthening the system, making it appear more fair and open than it actually is (Bourdieu and Passeron 1977, 54). Unlike many who see universal access as a precondition to a more fair and open society, Bourdieu saw education, especially at the higher levels, as inextricable from a dominant position and worldview – one could join, but he or she would have to change to do so. The escalator was there for a few to use, if they were willing to take it where it was headed.

The truth is, not everyone is willing to take the escalator into the middle class. Even smart working-class kids who are encouraged by teachers might choose not to get on the escalator, because they know that escalator will take them away from the people they love. The failure of so many talented kids to continue their schooling has led some researchers to argue they have 'stunted aspirations' (Bradley and Ingram 2012; Roberts and Evans 2012; Beasley 2011; Davidson 2011) or internalized classist (and racist) conceptions of their self-worth (Fordham 1996; Ochoa 2013), or that they actively resist what they see as middle-class culture (Willis 2017; Perry 2002). I think a lot of this misses the heart of the problem. Succeeding in a stratified society means joining the other team. This can cause a lot of ambivalence, to say the least. Valerie Walkerdine describes her own experience thusly:

> They held out a dream. Come, they told me. It is yours. You are chosen. They didn't tell me, however, that for years, I would no longer feel any sense of belonging, nor any sense of safety. That I didn't belong in the new place, any more than I now belonged in the old. So, around every corner of apparent choice lurked doubt and uncertainty.
>
> *(Quoted in Bourke 1994, 120)*

In my own research with working-class college students, I found that they develop different strategies for dealing with the mismatch between class cultures and the attendant discomfort with learning in a middle-class space (Hurst 2010). Some remain stubbornly attached to their working-class roots, even to the detriment of their academic and social success (I called these 'Loyalists'), while others go so far as rejecting their pasts in a bid at assimilation into the middle class (I called these 'Renegades'). A lucky few are able, like 'Double Agents', to move freely between class cultures and social groups. Actually, this insight was not new, as working-class academics (college faculty with working-class roots) have long published accounts descriptive of the experience of being a 'stranger in paradise' (Ryan and Sackrey 1984) and how one deals with this experience. Similar to my typology, for example, Barb Jensen (2012) notes three coping strategies for what she calls 'crossovers': distancing, resisting, and building bridges.

Working-class academics are proof of much of Bourdieu's commentary on the relationship between class and education. These are scholars who have advanced on the escalator of education but who can be deeply ambivalent about the value of this so-called advancement (Dews and Law 1995; Grimes and Morris 1997; Matthys 2012; Muzzatti and Samarco 2005; Oldfield and Johnson 2009; Ryan and Sackrey 1984; Welsch 2005; Yates 2007). Many would like to reorient the system to the needs and value of working-class persons (hooks 1994; Linkon 1999). As a group, working-class academics may point us toward an alternative way of thinking about what education is for, one that not only allows working-class people in but also works with and for them and their communities, rather than presuming to 'escalate' them out of the working class entirely.

College as a collaborator

We need not remain stuck between the two-sides-of-the-same-coin escalator and gatekeeper models of higher education. Both are premised on college's relationship with the class system, and neither presume to alter this substantially. While 'college as gatekeeper' keeps out working-class students, 'college as escalator' brings them in only to change them, or even worse, changes them but still doesn't help them get the kind of well-paid, rewarding work they hoped to get by earning a degree. But we can envision an alternative model in which college collaborates with the working class. How might this work? First, colleges can and sometimes are places of reorientation and democratic training. Although this is not an easy task in today's austerity climate, harsh times open up previously foreclosed spaces. A growing backlash against the costs of college and skepticism over whether it delivers what it has been promising means the link between higher education and the middle class is loosening. Let us rethink what we want out of our educational systems now. Let us draw from the strengths working-class people provide to reorient our systems in a way that better serves not them specifically, but all of us.

Including working-class students in the academy can contribute to a better system for all. First, these students generally have a greater awareness of alternative or multiple perspectives. Second, they are particularly sensitive to issues of oppression and sympathy toward other marginalized groups. Third, they have shown a great deal of resourcefulness in their lives already, as well as an immense reservoir of tenacity, discipline, and hard work. They really want to be in college! As outsiders, working-class college students can produce real insights into the nature, limitations, and discourse of academia. Working-class college students not only bring diversity (as in diverse opinions, viewpoints, and experiential bases) with them to school, but might also encourage a different vision of education – one premised on equality and social justice as much as or more than individualism and competitiveness. As Bourdieu once noted, 'out-of-place people, *déclassé* upwards or downwards, are the troublemakers who often make history. [...] [T]he greatest contributions to social science have been made by people who were not perfectly in their element in the social world as it is' (Bourdieu 1993, 47).

In order to welcome these students, to truly make them feel at home in the academy and full participants, we need more working-class studies programs. Working-class studies programs are very important for reclaiming education's public mission (both in the sense of education for all and training for democratic participation), but also for a deeper reconceptualization of what education can be. Working-class studies is one of the only 'disciplines' which centers class relations at its core of what is to be explained. Whereas class relations are often the backdrop to many fields of study, they operate more like the air we breathe, taken for granted and unrecognized. 'Class has a color. It is what you eat; it is how you eat. ... It shapes reputation. It opens and closes doors. ... And though seemingly omnipresent, it remains strangely absent from the collective conscious' (Stich 2012, 105). Working-class studies puts relations of power and inequality squarely at the center of our attention, thus allowing us to question and contest the structures that produce such relations.

The chapters included here all grapple, in one way or another, with the issue of schools as gatekeepers or escalators. In 'Learning our place: Social reproduction in K–12 schooling', Deborah M. Warnock focuses on social class inequalities in educational experiences and outcomes among K–12 students in the US. Mostly following a social reproduction lens, Warnock discusses the key landmarks of scholarship on socioeconomic stratification in schooling in the past fifty years, as well as the constant tension of projects to reform school to make them function as escalators rather than gatekeepers. The second article, 'Being working class in the English classroom', by Diane Reay, turns attention to working-class students themselves. Reay argues '[t]he working-class experience of education has traditionally been one of educational failure, not success' (p. 130). What is this experience of failure like from the perspective of those living it? For one thing, many aspects of education appear 'pointless and irrelevant' (p. 131). In most schools, working-class knowledge is denigrated, and working-class kids struggle for some form of recognition. Reay's interviews with working-class students in the English school system speak volumes about the ways that the gatekeeping mechanism of education persists. A note in passing, here. Although Warnock's article focuses on US scholarship on social reproduction, and Reay's on students in the UK system, what they report echoes similar scholarship on both sides of the pond. Like the US, the UK has spent the past several decades trying on reforms to promote social mobility. Like the UK, working-class students in the US often feel alienated and marginalized, and dropout rates are much higher than those of their peers. This cross-national concordance is further evidence that the relationship between education and class is a highly structured one, working at a macro-historical level that transcends national boundaries.

What happens when working-class students do go to college? Are their experiences and outcomes similar to their peers? Does higher education lead to social mobility? Bettina Spencer's 'Getting schooled: Working-class students in higher education' takes a deeper look at working-class students in higher education. Drawing on psychological literature, she explores how classist stereotypes influence academic performance and how working-class culture influences a student's sense of belonging. She ends the chapter describing prejudice-reduction techniques which may make college feel more inclusive for students from the working class.

One of the reasons working-class students may feel alienated from the academy is its focus on middle-class issues and concerns. Janet Zandy once asked us to imagine 'what it would be like if the history and culture of working-class people were at the center of educational practices' (2001, xiv). Lisa A. Kirby takes this to heart in her chapter, 'The pedagogy of class: Teaching working-class life and culture in the academy.' She explores strategies for teaching working-class culture and experience through literature, popular culture, and history. Introducing these topics will help *all* students better understand and appreciate the diversity of American experience.

Colleen H. Clements and Mark D. Vagle take this focus on diversity further in their chapter, 'Working-class student experiences: Toward a social class-sensitive pedagogy for K–12 schools, teachers, and teacher educators'. They focus particularly on the ways that 'working class' as an identity is racialized as white and what the implications for this are in our teaching and broader culture. In what ways do embodied experiences of being working-class intersect with racialized identity in educational spaces? How are current social hierarchies created and maintained at the intersections of race and class, and what is the role of education in reinforcing those hierarchies? Like Kirby and Spencer, the authors conclude with suggestions for helpful educational practices.

How can we support our working-class students on campus? Colby R. King and Sean H. McPherson discuss a program they helped organize at Bridgewater State University in 'Class Beyond the Classroom: Supporting working-class and first-generation students, faculty, and staff'. Consisting of working-class faculty and staff or those first in their families to attend college, the Class Beyond the Classroom project employs a variety of activities, including story-sharing panel discussions, to break down classism and provide support for working-class and first-generation college students. Their program, especially the idea of telling 'stories' has been widely imitated on other campuses and could serve as a useful model for others to follow. They conclude with suggestions for how to develop a similar program at one's own campus.

So, what is the relationship between education and the working class? Is that relationship the same now, under late capitalism, as in the years immediately following World War II, when 'mass' and 'universal' education first became the objective of college administrators and policymakers (in both the US and UK)? And is this different from the great era of the founding of land-grant public colleges in the US? Perhaps we should ask what *should* be the relationship between education and *the class system*?

We need to think clearly about what we want. The pieces here help us understand more about the relationship between education and the working class. But they also help us ask what the relationship *should* be. What are the contradictions of education within a capitalist system? Do we want to provide an escalator for working-class students, or teach working-class students to dismantle the building altogether? How might education work to help produce rather than maintain an unequal social system? What insights can we learn from the experiences in the academy of our working-class college students and working-class academics? Will our existence provide a critical mass for change? How can we make the institution less middle class? How might this help everyone?

For example, what if schools taught us how to make new places, rather than taking the one provided for us? What would happen if we incorporated working-class knowledge into our schools? Perhaps if our schools were less classist and psychologically damaging to so many of our learners, less than half of Americans would think colleges were detrimental to the nation. Learning about working-class history and past social movements (including the fight for public education) could provide a vision of a better future. An inclusive vision can only happen (according to the old Marxist in me) by breaking through the racial, gender, and national divisions that have contained working-class solidarity. Regardless of our own backgrounds, we can model class sensitivity, awareness, and desire for change for our students. By telling our stories, we link the past to the present and articulate the future. And, yes, we need to resist 'becoming the man'. Figure out what you are doing in academia. What role are you playing? What is your vision of education? Fight for it.

This is why working-class studies is so important and the chapters in this book so instructive. For too long, working-class people were left out of the academy. Studies of working-class life, literature, and politics were rare. This has been changing, especially since the era of 'mass education' following World War II. And yet, too often the academy has seen these studies as tangential to the reproduction of the next generation of middle-class professionals. But working-class studies has the potential to transform the academy as a place in which alternative futures and less classist social systems can be imagined and practiced. Far from being a gatekeeper, or even an escalator to the middle class, the academy can be a collaborator with all its diverse citizens, allowing the free development of each for the benefit of all. Working-class studies can aid in this endeavor, opening up the academy to new ways of thinking about its place in the larger social system, breaking or questioning its ties to the reproduction of class privilege.

References

Ariés, P. (1962) *Centuries of Childhood: A Social History of Family Life*, New York, Vintage.

Attewell, P. A. and Newman, K. S. (2010) *Growing Gaps: Educational Inequality Around the World*, New York, Oxford University Press.

Baker, D. (2014) *The Schooled Society: The Educational Transformation of Global Culture*, Stanford, Stanford University Press.

Ball, S. J. (2003) *Class Strategies and the Education Market: The Middle Classes and Social Advantage*, New York, Routledge.

Beasley, M. A. (2011) *Opting Out: Losing the Potential of America's Young Black Elite*, Chicago, University of Chicago Press.

Boudon, R. (1974) *Education, Opportunity, and Social Inequality; Changing Prospects in Western Society*, New York, Wiley.

Bourdieu, P. (1993) *Sociology in Question*, Thousand Oaks, Sage.

Bourdieu, P. (2008) *Sketch for a Self-Analysis*, Chicago, University of Chicago Press.

Bourdieu, P. and Passeron, J. C. (1977) *Reproduction in Education, Society and Culture*, Beverly Hills, Sage Publications.

Bourke, J. (1994) *Working-Class Cultures in Britain: 1890–1960*, London, Routledge.

Bradley, H. and Ingram, N. (2012) 'Banking on the Future: Choices, Aspirations and Economic Hardship in Working-Class Student Experience', in Atkinson, W., Roberts, S. and Savage, M. (eds.), *Class Inequality in Austerity Britain*, London, Palgrave Macmillan.

Brantlinger, E. A. (2003) *Dividing Classes: How the Middle Class Negotiates and Rationalizes School Advantage*, New York: Routledge.

Brickman, W. W. and Lehrer, S. (1962) *A Century of Higher Education*, New York, Society for the Advancement of Education.

Brinton, M. C. (2011) *Lost in Transition: Youth, Work, and Instability in Postindustrial Japan*, Cambridge, Cambridge University Press.

Brown, P. (1990) 'The "Third Wave": Education and the Ideology of Parentology', *British Journal of Sociology of Education*, 11, 1, pp. 65–85.

Brown, P., Lauder, H. and Ashton, D. (2011) *The Global Auction: The Broken Promises of Education, Jobs, and Incomes*, New York, Oxford University Press.

Burke, C. (2016) *Culture, Capitals, and Graduate Futures: Degrees of Class*, London, Routledge.

Burrage, M. (2010) *Trow, M. A.: Twentieth-Century Higher Education: Elite to Mass to Universal*, Baltimore, Johns Hopkins University Press.

Cappelli, P. (2015) *Will College Pay Off? A Guide to the Most Important Financial Decision You Will Ever Make*, New York, Public Affairs.

Collinge, A. (2010) *The Student Loan Scam: The Most Oppressive Debt in U.S. History and How We Can Fight Back*, Boston, Beacon Press.

Cucchiara, M. B. (2013) *Marketing Schools, Marketing Cities: Who Wins and Who Loses When Schools Become Urban Amenities*, Chicago, University of Chicago Press.

Davidson, E. (2011) *The Burdens of Aspiration: Schools, Youth, and Success in the Divided Social Worlds of Silicon Valley*, New York, New York University Press.

Deng, Z. and Treiman, D. J. (1997) 'The Impact of Cultural Revolution on Trends in Educational Attainment in the People's Republic of China', *American Journal of Sociology*, 103, 2, pp. 391–428.

Devine, F. (2004) *Class Practices: How Parents Help their Children Get Good Jobs*, Cambridge, Cambridge University Press.

Dews, C. L. B. and Law, C. L. (1995) *This Fine Place So Far from Home: Voices of Academics from the Working Class*, Philadelphia, Temple University Press.

Fitzpatrick, S. (1979) *Education and Social Mobility in the Soviet Union, 1921–1934*, Cambridge, Cambridge University Press.

Fordham, S. (1996) *Blacked Out: Dilemmas of Race, Identity, and Success at Capital High*, Chicago, University of Chicago Press.
Goldrick-Rab, S. (2016) *Paying the Price: College Costs, Financial Aid, and the Betrayal of the American Dream*, Chicago, University of Chicago Press.
Goyette, K.A. and Lareau, A. (2014) *Choosing Homes, Choosing Schools: Residential Segregation and the Search for a Good School*, New York, Russell Sage Foundation.
Green, A. (1990) *Education and State Formation: The Rise of Education Systems in England, France, and the USA*, New York, St. Martin's Press.
Grimes, M. D. and Morris, J. M. (1997) *Caught in the Middle: Contradictions in the Lives of Sociologists from Working-Class Backgrounds*, Westport, Praeger.
Grubb, W. N. and Lazerson, M. (2004) *The Education Gospel: The Economic Power of Schooling*, Cambridge, Harvard University Press.
Hamilton, L. T. (2016) *Parenting to a Degree: How Family Matters for College Women's Success*, Chicago, University of Chicago Press.
Heiman, R. (2015) *Driving after Class: Anxious Times in an American Suburb*, Berkeley, University of California Press.
Hochschild, J. L. and Scovronick, N. B. (2003) *The American Dream and the Public Schools*, New York, Oxford University Press.
hooks, b. (1994) *Teaching to Transgress: Education as the Practice of Freedom*, New York, Routledge.
Hurst, A. L. (2010) *The Burden of Academic Success: Loyalists, Renegades, and Double Agents*, Lanham, Lexington Books.
Hurst, A. L. (2012) 'The Different Meanings of "Living Beyond Your Means": Distinguishing Debtors in Undue Hardship Bankruptcy Cases', *Michigan Sociological Review*, 26, pp. 16–41.
Hurst, A.L. (2019) *Amplified Advantage: Going to a "Good" College in an Era of Inequality*, Lanham, Lexington Books.
Jensen, B. (2012) *Reading Classes: On Culture and Classism in America*, Ithaca, ILR Press.
Johnson, H. B. (2006) *The American Dream and the Power of Wealth: Choosing Schools and Inheriting Inequality in the Land of Opportunity*, New York, Routledge.
Lareau, A. (1989) *Home Advantage: Social Class and Parental Intervention in Elementary Education*, New York, Falmer Press.
Lareau, A. (2003) *Unequal Childhoods: Class, Race, and Family Life*, Berkeley, University of California Press.
Linkon, S. L. (1999) *Teaching Working Class*, Amherst, University of Massachusetts Press.
Lucas, S. R. (1999) *Tracking Inequality: Stratification and Mobility in American High Schools*, New York, Teachers College Press.
Marsh, J. (2011) *Class Dismissed: Why We Cannot Teach or Learn our Way Out of Inequality*, New York, Monthly Review Press.
Matthys, M. (2012) *Cultural Capital, Identity, and Social Mobility: The Life Course of Working-Class University Graduates*, New York, Routledge.
Mettler, S. (2014) *Degrees of Inequality: How the Politics of Higher Education Sabotaged the American Dream*, New York, Basic Books.
Muzzatti, S. L. and Samarco, C.V. (2005) *Reflections from the Wrong Side of the Tracks: Class, Identity, and the Working-Class Experience in Academe*, Lanham, Rowman & Littlefield.
Neem, J. (2017) *Democracy's Schools: The Rise of Public Education in America*, Baltimore, Johns Hopkins University Press.
Ochoa, G. L. (2013) *Academic Profiling: Latinos, Asian Americans, and the Achievement Gap*, Minneapolis, University of Minnesota Press.
Oldfield, K. and Johnson, R. G. (2009) *Resilience: Queer Professors from the Working Class*, Albany, State University of New York Press.
Perry, P. (2002) *Shades of White: White Kids and Racial Identities in High School*, Durham, Duke University Press.
Power, S., Edwards, T., Whitty, G. and Wigfall, V. (2003) *Education and the Middle Class*, Buckingham, Open University Press.
Pritchard, R. M. O. (1990) *The End of Elitism? The Democratisation of the West German University System*, New York, Berg.
Radford, A. W. (2013) *Top Student, Top School? How Social Class Shapes Where Valedictorians Go to College*, Chicago, University of Chicago Press.
Rhoten, D. and Calhoun, C. J. (2011) *Knowledge Matters: The Public Mission of the Research University*, New York, Columbia University Press.

Roberts, S. and Evans, S. (2012) 'Aspirations and Imagined Futures: The Im/possibilities for Britain's Young Working Class', in Atkinson, W. (ed.), *Class Inequality in Austerity Britain*, London, Palgrave Macmillan.

Robinson, K. (2014) *The Broken Compass: Parental Involvement with Children's Education*, Cambridge, Harvard University Press.

Rosenbaum, J. E. (2001) *Beyond College for All: Career Paths for the Forgotten Half*, New York, Russell Sage Foundation.

Rothstein, J. M. and Rouse, C. (2007) *Constrained after College: Student Loans and Early Career Occupational Choices*, Cambridge, National Bureau of Economic Research.

Rudolph, F. (1962) *The American College and University: A History*, New York, Knopf.

Ryan, J. and Sackrey, C. (1984) *Strangers in Paradise: Academics from the Working Class*, Boston, South End Press.

Sacks, P. (2007) *Tearing Down the Gates: Confronting the Class Divide in American Education*, Berkeley, University of California Press.

Shavit, Y., Müller, W. and Tame, C. (1998) *From School to Work: A Comparative Study of Educational Qualifications and Occupational Destinations*, Oxford, Clarendon Press.

Smeeding, T. M., Jäntti, M. and Erikson, R. (2011) *Persistence, Privilege, and Parenting: The Comparative Study of Intergenerational Mobility*, New York, Russell Sage Foundation.

Stevens, M., Armstrong, E. A. and Arum, R. (2008) 'Sieve, Incubator, Temple, Hub: Empirical and Theoretical Advances in the Sociology of Higher Education', *Annual Review of Sociology*, 34, pp. 127–151.

Stich, A. E. (2012) *Access to Inequality: Reconsidering Class, Knowledge, and Capital in Higher Education*, Lanham, Lexington Books.

US Census Bureau (various) (1952–2002) March Current Population Survey, 2003–2012 Annual Social and Economic Supplement to the Current Population Survey; 1940–1960 Census of the Population www.w3.org/2013/04/odw/EducationalAttainment.pdf

Welsch, K. A. (2005) *Those Winter Sundays: Female Academics and their Working-Class Parent*, Lanham, University Press of America.

Willis, P. (2017) *Learning to Labour: How Working-Class Kids Get Working-Class Jobs*, New York, Columbia University Press.

Wolff, E. N. (2006) *Does Education Really Help? Skill, Work, and Inequality*, New York, Oxford University Press.

Yates, M. D. (2007) *More Unequal: Aspects of Class in the United States*, New York, Monthly Review Press.

Zandy, J. (2001) *What We Hold In Common: An Introduction to Working-Class Studies*, New York, The Feminist Press.

5

Class Beyond the Classroom

Supporting working-class and first-generation students, faculty, and staff

Colby R. King and Sean H. McPherson

Introduction

Working-class and first-generation (WCFG) status can be both invisible and stigmatized on college campuses, and these statuses can make success more difficult for students, faculty, and staff (Hurst & Nenga 2016; Pascarella et al. 2004; Warnock 2014; Warnock & Appel 2012; Warnock & Hurst 2016). People from WCFG backgrounds are also more likely to represent other marginalized groups on campus (Chen & Carroll 2005; Hurst & Nenga 2016; Jehangir et al. 2015). State comprehensive university missions focus on increasing public access to higher education, inspiring Henderson (2009) to describe them as the 'people's university'. These universities often enroll and employ many people from WCFG backgrounds. State comprehensive universities can therefore be a pivotal location from which to develop efforts that support WCFG students, faculty, and staff.

Beginning in fall 2014, a group of faculty and staff at Bridgewater State University (BSU) organized Class Beyond the Classroom (CBtC) around a shared interest in supporting individuals from WCFG backgrounds. Following Christopher's (2005) call to transform higher education to work for the working class, CBtC pursued our purposes through a wide variety of activities. Inspired by our shared WCFG backgrounds and our institution's mission, and informed by discussions at the 2014 Working-Class Studies Association (WCSA) conference, CBtC organized around two central purposes: we were motivated to support the success of students from WCFG backgrounds and to support the success of our colleagues from these backgrounds. With these purposes in mind, we organized and created programming that supported students by encouraging their sense of belonging, validating their life experiences, and nurturing the growth of their social and cultural capital. We also held discussions and activities that worked against classism on campus and supported solidarity among group participants.

In this chapter we describe the context for our work with CBtC, first by reviewing literature on supporting the success of WCFG students and discussing how struggles of working-class people in academia emerge from mismatch between social class cultures, and then by pointing to other programs across the US supporting WCFG students. We then describe CBtC's institutional context and how the group's specific efforts supported students, faculty, and staff and generated solidarity and esprit de corps. We suggest that CBtC efforts had the positive impact of creating spaces for WCFG students to share their experiences, increasing awareness of common struggles and nurturing a sense of agency within and beyond academia.

Mismatch between social class cultures: Struggles of the working class in academia, and supporting success

As Warnock (2014) explains, social class identity is unlike most other identities in that it can change. Often, she explains, 'the whole point of attending college IS to change one's social class identity'. The implicit value placed on class mobility seems to suppress discussion of class issues in higher education. Education is one of the primary institutions through which members of the middle class create and maintain their social advantages (Ball 2003). Middle-class cultural norms so permeate academia that Wakeling (2010, 35) asked, 'Is there such a thing as a working class academic'? The lack of explicit discussion of social class issues on campus can be seen, then, as a microcosm of a broader, uncritical assumption of privilege. Ironically, the recent corporatization of higher education has shaken the assumptions of class privilege long associated with college teaching. Riederer (2014) argues that with the expansion of adjunct teaching positions in academia, 'teaching college is no longer a middle-class job'.

Many faculty, staff, and students in academia come from working-class backgrounds, and as Lehmann (2009, 644) argues, 'Class identities do matter, particularly in social contexts, like university, in which the invisibility of class actually highlights its relevance'. The predominance of middle-class culture can present barriers for WCFG students and also faculty, as it creates a class–cultural mismatch for people from these backgrounds and implies that many WCFG individuals must adapt to middle-class culture (Hurst 2010; Jack 2014; Rice et al. 2017; Stephens et al. 2012). As we discuss below, these shifts in class–cultural identity can create ambivalence about the college experience (Banks-Santilli 2014). A common issue for WCFG people in academia is the importance of validation and forming a sense of belonging (Nora et al. 2011; Rendon 1994; Stebleton et al. 2014; Strayhorn 2012). With CBtC, we worked to resolve this cultural mismatch while celebrating the skills and diverse perspectives that WCFG people bring to campus. Rather than focusing solely on helping working-class people better navigate a middle-class system, we also worked to make space for and support working-class members of our community.

Faculty coming to academia from working-class backgrounds are likely to encounter difficulties on their way toward successful careers (Grimes & Morris 1997; Hurst & Nenga 2016; Warnock & Appel 2012). As Morris and Grimes explain (2007, 394): 'Since a large part of the content of working-class culture is antithetical to scholarly pursuit, having grown up in an environment that assumes the "naturalness" of working-class values presents a conflict for intellectuals from such backgrounds'. In this context, Wakeling (2010, 42) perceives that in higher education, 'very fine gradations of social distinction take on increased significance'.

As Morris and Grimes (2007, 376) conclude, 'The conflict is, for many, deep and aching, lingering long after they have become, objectively, members of the middle-class'. Many academics from WCFG backgrounds have shared their personal stories, reflecting on struggles and suggesting strategies for success (Dews & Law 1995; Ryan & Sackrey 1996; Warnock 2014, 2016). Ryan and Sackrey's book *Strangers in Paradise: Academics from the Working Class* illustrates how impostor syndrome and survivor guilt emerge in academics from working-class backgrounds from the contradictions of the capitalist system. These shared stories show that people from working-class backgrounds are not alone in these struggles: their stories are a source of support that nurture a sense of belonging for many readers. We made story-sharing a central part of CBtC events because of how stories foster validation and a sense of belonging among WCFG faculty and staff.

WCFG students bring important assets with them to campus, including tenacity, creativity, moral purpose, and unique cultural dispositions (Lehmann 2009; Yosso 2005). Their presence on campus and in the classroom enlivens the academic pursuits around them, and they contribute to the diversity of campus life (Casey 2005). Yosso (2005) argues that students of color, many of whom are WCFG students, bring forms of capital including knowledge and skills to the classroom. These unacknowledged contributions can strengthen students' abilities on campus and enrich campus culture for their peers.

As students from WCFG backgrounds struggle to make their way through college, many face challenges associated with their backgrounds that have little to do with academic ability (Banks-Santilli 2014; Hinz 2016; Hurst 2007, 2010; Petty 2014; Pyne & Means 2013; Stephens et al. 2012). Many first-generation students come from impoverished backgrounds (Young 2016b). Beyond class–cultural mismatch, WCFG students may struggle in navigating the 'hidden curriculum' (Anyon 1983; Soria 2015). They may experience what has been called survivor guilt (Piorkowski 1983), breakaway guilt (London 1989), or family achievement guilt (Covarrubias & Fryberg 2015) as they consider how their absence will impact life at home and how their educational experience will change their family relationships (Covarrubias et al. 2019). On campus they may experience imposterism, a sense of doubt about their achievements (Austin et al. 2009; Bernard et al. 2017; Warnock 2014). There may be little to support their sense of belonging, especially for students from racially diverse backgrounds, who may not find faculty with whom they identify (Baumeister & Leary 1995; Castellanos & Jones 2003; Strayhorn 2008, 2012). First-generation students are more likely than other students to take on indebtedness while in college (Furquim et al. 2017). These factors complicate the students' academic efforts and can also contribute to a sense of ambivalence toward college success (Banks-Santilli 2014).

As Lehmann (2009) finds, working-class students often construct moral value out of their class backgrounds. Lehmann (2013, 2) writes that success for working-class students often 'requires unique adaptive strategies, such as engaging in moral discourses about working-class values and ethics, including hard work, independence, and perseverance'. Hurst (2010) finds that successful working-class students take on one of three strategic roles in their path through college: loyalists maintain commitment to their working-class cultural roots; renegades embrace middle-class culture and goals; and double agents work to maintain a foothold in each world. Moving between these social-class–cultural worlds can be costly. Lehmann (2013, 9) finds that many successful working-class students report 'changing and usually conflicting relationships with parents and former friends'.

For these reasons, efforts to validate working-class students are pivotal (Rendon 1994). Espinoza (2011) argues that low-income minority students who attain academic success often rely on the academic guidance of at least one college-educated adult in their social network. Supporting WCFG students' sense of belonging is seen as essential (Baumeister & Leary 1995; Strayhorn 2008, 2012), and cultivating their voice is seen as a key aspect of supporting their success (Jehangir 2009). First-generation college students benefit from the support of faculty from similar backgrounds (Young 2016a). More broadly, class diversity on campus broadens awareness of social issues beyond the classroom; it enriches the educational experience for students and the work experience for faculty and staff. It is important to value class diversity while supporting the success of working-class students. Warnock (2014) highlights Casey's (2005) crucial point that 'the working-class student's difference, implicitly constituted as *lack*, is what college is designed to erase'. As a result, social-class inequalities are often ignored in campus diversity frameworks (Michaels 2007).

Students from working-class backgrounds bring skills and capacities to campus, and their perspectives diversify and enrich the classroom and campus experiences of all campus community members. Many efforts that support working-class students are actually efforts explicitly designed to help first-generation students, which means the working-class label gets subsumed under the banner of first-generation students (Engle et al. 2006; Saenz et al. 2007). The needs of WCFG students overlap substantially; efforts that support the success of one group often contribute to the success of the other. But as working-class identity gets subsumed under the first-generation label, the possibility lingers of continued cultural mismatch and persistent class antagonisms. Making efforts to support working-class students specifically on issues of social class can support their success while also making space for the working class in academia.

As Christopher (2005, 220) argues, 'we can transform higher education into something that works for, instead of against, the working class'. But doing so, Christopher (2005) contends, means that we must recognize that most of the public are working class. We must also foreground Brodsky's argument that public education 'belongs to the much broader realm of the public domain' and that public institutions were created to serve the 'great majority' who are 'the non-elite and the underprivileged' (quoted in Christopher 2005, 219). We organized CBtC not only to bring more attention to issues of class for students, faculty, and staff at our institution, but also to highlight the specific salience of these issues to public higher education institutions more broadly.

Aligning with Leondar-Wright's (2014) encouragement to build cross-class coalitions, we worked to foreground social class in our name (Class Beyond the Classroom) and in our efforts. We focused not so much on helping working-class students perform according to middle-class values, but on welcoming those from a working-class background and supporting their success on campus.

Programs in support of first-generation and working-class students

Many programs have emerged in support of first-generation and working-class college students. Some are student led and unique to one campus. These may be major, well-resourced initiatives on prominent campuses. Others are cross-campus programs that work to support WCFG students across all campuses. All of these programs work to support the success of WCFG students through a range of mechanisms: validating and normalizing their experiences, building communities of support, providing resources for learning and navigating the hidden curriculum, and building students' social and cultural capital. While the explicit purpose of these programs is to support the success of WCFG students, many have the additional function of supporting WCFG faculty and staff, by involving those who share their stories.

Many campus programs in support of WCFG college students have emerged from faculty, staff, and students sharing their stories and supporting each other. One important example is the First-Generation College Students @Michigan group at the University of Michigan. Formed in 2007, the student group is sponsored by the university's sociology department (Maize Pages n.d.). It maintains a website with information and resources for students, including videos of first-generation students offering advice (First Generation University of Michigan 2017), weekly meetings for participants, and a graduation ceremony organized for first-generation students and their families (Gearig 2015). Dwight Lang, a sociology lecturer at Michigan, first-generation college student, and WCSA member, has advised and written about this group (Lang 2015).

Whitman College hosts a First Generation/Working Class Club that organizes a mentoring program providing social and professional networking opportunities for first-year students

(Whitman College 2017). This club has also been involved with the on-campus Summer Bridge Program, and it maintains its own website (Whitman College First Generation/ Working Class Club 2017). At Georgetown University, four students who were members of the Georgetown Scholarship Program cofounded AL1GN, the Alliance for the Low-Income, First-Generation Narrative (Soza 2016). As its name suggests, it works to support members in constructing their own narratives while also addressing issues around 'first-generation' and 'low-income' labels (Young 2016b). At the University of Wisconsin–Madison, students have formed a group they call the Working Class Student Union (Wisconsin Involvement Network 2017; Working Class Student Union 2017).

A student-led initiative called 1vyG began as a student group at Brown University in 2015, specifically serving first-generation college students at Ivy League schools. Those efforts have developed into EdMobilizer, an organization led by alumni of several Ivy League schools, which hosts the 1vyG Conference and advocates for policies that support first-generation college or low-income students (EdMobilizer 2017).[1]

Faculty-led programs also support WCFG students. These are oriented more specifically to giving WCFG students opportunities to build relationships with mentors, who are faculty from WCFG backgrounds involved with these groups. In 2016 at University California-Irvine, faculty wore T-shirts that read '#Firstgen College Grad' during the campus's welcome week, and several faculty members shared their unique stories on the university's website (Rivenburg et al. 2016). A year later, Dr. Rebecca Covarrubias of University California-Santa Cruz is leading a system-wide effort to broaden the program, which is expecting more than 800 faculty across the state's higher education system to wear the shirts this year (Flaherty 2017). At the University of Washington Tacoma (UW-T) in Spring 2017, Dr. Tanya Valesquez moderated a student panel discussion, co-sponsored by UW-T's Office of Undergraduate Education's We are First Generation project (UW-T 2017), that highlighted experiences of first-generation students. At Oregon State, Dr. Allison Hurst has helped to organize efforts to support WCFG students, including a Celebrate First event in 2017 (OSU Division of Undergraduate Studies 2017). By validating and normalizing the experiences of WCFG students, efforts such as these, and ours with CBtC, have the latent function of supporting WCFG faculty and staff as well as the success of WCFG students.

Other programs in support of WCFG students extend across several campuses and are national in scope. Some are federally funded through the US Department of Education's TRIO Programs, which are designed to support people from disadvantaged backgrounds (US Department of Education 2017). A prominent example is the Ronald E. McNair Post-Baccalaureate Achievement Program. This TRIO program, currently funded at 151 institutions, prepares undergraduate students in research and other scholarly activities so that they can go on to doctoral studies (McNair Scholars Program 2017). Engle (2007) provides more detail on these and related programs.

NASPA, or the Student Affairs Administrators in Higher Education Foundation, recently announced its new Center for First-Generation Student Success, with goals of increasing research, scholarship, and practice supporting first-generation student success and encouraging expansion of the number of institutions with evidence-based programs supporting first-generation student success (NASPA 2017). Other national programs provide resources and support with a focus on sharing stories from successful WCFG students. For example, I'm First! is an online community founded by the Center for Student Opportunity, which has merged with Strive for College (Rubinoff 2016). It provides WCFG students and their mentors and advisors with information and support for navigating the college experience. The program's website offers diverse resources, and may be best known for its short videos in which successful WCFG students, including former

First Lady Michelle Obama, share their stories. Similarly, Firstgenerationstudent.com is a website and external resource that 'is devoted to helping first-generation college students navigate the college application process, from beginning to end and beyond'. This website, with participants from various locations in higher education, encourages current, potential, and former students to ask questions and share their stories.

Class Action is a nonprofit that works with organizations and institutions to end classism and extreme inequality by providing training and information for organizations and individuals (Class Action 2017). One of its growing programs is its annual First Generation College Student Summit (Fleming 2017). Class Action also works with Jane Van Galen through her First in Our Families digital storytelling project. This is a mobile, three-day workshop in which WCFG students learn to create digital stories to share their unique experiences (Van Galen 2017). The project has amassed and shared a diverse collection of stories from WCFG student perspectives.

These are some of the most interesting recent programs that work to support WCFG students. The priority for many is to make stories from WCFG faculty and mentors available to students as well as providing resources and other support to WCFG students. Many of these programs focus on first-generation rather than working-class student identity; while this makes these programs widely applicable for a diverse range of students, the identification of first-generation rather than working-class status as pivotal could further obscure how social-class mechanisms make college challenging for working-class students, especially those who are also among the first in their family to go to college.

Institutional context and organization of CBtC

We organized CBtC at BSU, a regional state comprehensive university originally founded as a normal school. *Bridgewater State University's Factbook 2015–2016* reports that BSU enrolled 9,608 undergraduate and 1,481 graduate students in fall 2015. Among undergraduates, 83% were enrolled full time, 96% were from Massachusetts, 41% were male, and 21% were students of color (Office of Institutional Research 2016a). The BSU *2015 Campus Climate Survey Final Report* revealed that about 59% of undergraduate respondents were first-generation college students, about 33% were low-income students, and 17% were students of color (Office of Institutional Research 2016b).[2]

In June 2014, CBtC organizer (and chapter co-author) Colby King attended the WCSA annual meeting at SUNY Stony Brook, where he learned from Dr. Debbie Warnock and other WCSA members about efforts to support WCFG college students. Realizing that many of his BSU colleagues come from these backgrounds, King brought these discussions back to BSU. He published an essay in the university's *Bridgewater Review* in which he reflected on his working-class background (King 2014). With support from the faculty union's then-president, he invited faculty and staff to meet to discuss support of first-generation and working-class students. King held meetings with interested participants that year, and with support from the faculty union he organized a preliminary panel discussion, 'Our Stories with Class Beyond the Classroom', with another faculty member and a student as panelists.

In fall 2015 the group planned another Our Stories program, which used a format described elsewhere (King, Griffith, & Murphy 2017). The dean of the College of Humanities and Social Sciences participated, sharing her story as a panel member alongside two faculty members and providing funding for the event. During fall 2015, administrative support helped solidify the group's efforts. The vice-president for student success and diversity provided guidance on organization and strategy, while a faculty associate in that office helped plan the event. An associate provost joined meetings and facilitated small-group discussion. The university president hosted a dinner meeting with lead organizers of CBtC. While administrative support was instrumental in the formation of CBtC, the group continued to function with only ad hoc funding for particular programs.

CBtC efforts for faculty and staff: Sharing stories and building institutional support

Since the group formed, CBtC participants have engaged in diverse activities, created campus programs, and shared their results at national conferences and in publications. CBtC's primary effort has been the Our Stories events, where participants share their stories with student attendees. Representing diverse institutional positions and intersectional identities, the panelists have related a range of stories on taking time off college, attending college without a regular place to sleep, having families that did not support their academic efforts, and so on. Panelists shared advice and suggestions for success, while student attendees participated in group discussions led by CBtC participants. King, Griffith and Murphy (2017) illustrate how these events validated students, increased their sense of belonging, helped build their social and cultural capitals, and encouraged informal mentoring. Members also drafted a mission statement, and two CBtC participants wrote an essay explaining how social and cultural capital are often critical for success, which was first published at the *Everyday Sociology* blog and was later revised and expanded for the *Bridgewater Review* (King & Griffith 2015a, 2015b).

CBtC participants secured BSU's Promoting Diversity Grant in spring 2016 and 2017, and they used it to host Class Action facilitators for events on classism for students, faculty, and staff. This grant also supported Jane Van Galen's visit to campus for a three-day digital storytelling workshop. In spring 2017, CBtC used funds from this grant to bring WCSA president and BSU alumnus Michele Fazio to campus for a series of events, including an Our Stories program in which she served as a panelist. CBtC participants also shared their efforts beyond campus, including at the 2016 WCSA annual meeting and the 2016 American Sociological Association's annual meeting.

CBtC efforts for students: The CBtC student group and the first-generation college student summit

Key to building a sustainable movement that addresses student needs is establishing and nurturing groups that let students accumulate cultural capital by learning how to identify, articulate, and advocate for their interests. Just as important for all group activities is building esprit de corps, or what in the case of WCFG students we might think of as class consciousness. WCFG college students often feel assailed in college—encouraged to cast off their class identity and acquire not only new skills but also a new cultural orientation that implicitly devalues their cultural and familial backgrounds (Casey 2005; Warnock 2014).

A key component of CBtC has been the effort to cultivate student involvement in group activities that are both inspiring and sustainable across generations of student participants and leaders. Because of the multiple, overlapping responsibilities borne by many students from these backgrounds, participation in extracurricular group activities is often difficult, but we have worked toward attracting and sustaining student participation.

In spring 2016, building on CBtC's Our Stories and other events, and the organizational work of assistant professor of sociology Danielle Kohfeldt and administrative assistant and BSU graduate student Casey Jo Dufresne, Ms. Dufresne and assistant professor of art history (and co-author of this chapter) Sean H. McPherson accompanied five BSU students to the fourth Annual First Generation College Student Summit at Williams College in Williamstown, Massachusetts. Ms. Dufresne organized a four-person panel that included BSU students Jonathan Resende-Barros, '17, and Riana Quinn, '18. The other students in attendance, Melanie Tummino, '18, Shannon Duchaine, '18, and Ismaris Ocasio, '16, shared the panelists' sense of empowerment and inspiration at meeting other students from similar backgrounds. All expressed excitement at participating in an event focused on issues relevant to their experiences and challenges in higher education. Ms. Ocasio is now a graduate student in the Social Justice Education program at the University of Massachusetts at Amherst, where she also serves as a resident director, while all but one of the student participants have continued their strong engagement with CBtC-related activities. All resolved to plan for full BSU participation in the next summit.

Although creating a viable student group had been a goal of CBtC for some time, concrete efforts were spearheaded in fall 2016 by Dr. McPherson, staff members Amy Couto and Ms. Dufresne, and several student participants in the 2016 summit, notably Riana Quinn and Melanie Tummino. On October 25, we held a student interest group meeting to introduce the work of CBtC to a wider audience and to brainstorm about practical aspects and broader priorities for a student group. The meeting attracted a small but diverse group of students. One of them, Ms. Lyndsey Boyle, has contributed extensively to the effort to shepherd the group's application for formal recognition through student governance channels.

In spring 2017, Dr. McPherson and Ms. Couto, currently Student Scholars Coordinator at BSU, accompanied a delegation of five BSU students to the 5th Annual First Generation College Student Summit at Tufts University in Medford, Massachusetts. This effort built on the CBtC student group's planning and the service of Dr. McPherson and Ms. Dufresne as members of the summit's planning committee. Dr. McPherson, Ms. Couto, Ms. Tummino, and Ms. Quinn presented on a panel entitled 'Study Abroad: New Horizons or False Promises'. Two other BSU students in attendance, Jennifer Ford, '17, and Lyndsey Boyle, '18, attended multiple panels. The panel discussion elicited intense audience engagement. Panelists discussed the complexity of cultural capital for students from diverse racial–ethnic and immigrant backgrounds, including immigrant parents' ambivalence toward their children's expressed desire to study in their parents' countries of origin. Students from working-class and financially insecure backgrounds unanimously emphasized how short-term study-abroad programs had broadened their horizons and expanded their conception of work and life possibilities.

At the close of the 2016–17 academic year, the CBtC student group changed their name to 'We Are First!' Under this revised title, and after creating a constitution, bylaws, and other prerequisites for BSU registration, the group has secured formal recognition by BSU's student government. In the coming academic year, we hope to build campus awareness of the group through outreach, including close coordination with CBtC programs and initiatives, planning for the 2018 summit at Mt. Holyoke College, and coordination with other student groups with intersecting interests in social justice and increased access to higher education.

Outcomes of CBtC: For students

Many of the important outcomes of CBtC's activities emerged from forming the student group and supporting those participants. The efforts to register the group on campus, and the opportunities for collaboration opened up by participation in the First Generation College Student Summit, have expanded students' understanding of the links between their backgrounds and challenges and the broader issues facing higher education. In particular, because of the widespread cognitive dissonance many first-generation students experience in higher education, it is important for them to grapple with how the 'ivory tower' of academia is often a microcosm of broader societal contexts of unequal access to cultural and economic capital. The unanimously positive comments by BSU delegates at the First Generation Summit mirror those of students who participate in CBtC events such as Our Stories and the digital storytelling project.

Recruiting a broader set of student participants remains a challenge: many students who might be most interested in participating are also juggling numerous off-campus responsibilities. Despite the modest number of core group members, the students are working to change the tenor of conversation on campus about class and higher education, not only to change the lived experience and academic outcomes of students from WCFG backgrounds, but also to advocate effectively for supporting student success in higher education.

Beyond the formation of the student group and the summit, other CBtC efforts have impacted students. More than 200 students attended Our Stories panel discussions. As CBtC participants have discussed elsewhere (King, Griffith & Murphy, 2017), this programming validated WCFG students, increased their sense of belonging, and encouraged the development of their social and cultural capitals. Nine BSU students used the three-day digital storytelling workshop to create their own digital stories, many now shared on the First in Our Families website (https://firstinourfamilies.org/category/bridgewater-state-university/). Importantly, while we share our stories and support students who join in our activities, we never put students in positions where they must publicly disclose their WCFG identity.

Outcomes of CBtC: For faculty and staff participants

We have also observed positive outcomes of CBtC activities for BSU faculty and staff, several of whom have informally expressed how their involvement has increased their sense of belonging and validation on campus. Many have noted and appreciated the institution's increased awareness and discussion of WCFG student issues; and many, through their efforts with CBtC, felt their stories were celebrated as valid and valuable contributions to our overall academic efforts.

We have worked to increase the validation and sense of belonging of WCFG faculty and staff by addressing classism and class–cultural mismatch on campus. Our efforts have helped many students, faculty, and staff feel they are not alone in their experiences. CBtC panelists shared vivid stories of their experiences as WCFG students, including returning to college after dropping out, dealing with housing and food insecurity, and contending with parents who were ambivalent about, or even hostile to, their college pursuits. Discussion leaders reported that many students identified with these shared stories because they helped them feel they were not alone in their experiences. Faculty and staff also gained an appreciation of their colleagues from WCFG backgrounds. We each made efforts to discuss how we see social class and its impact on our work and institution. We have noticed an increase in expressions of solidarity among CBtC faculty and staff participants. Several participants have expressed an interest in removing barriers to success for faculty and staff from WCFG backgrounds.

Our work was helped by the fact that BSU's full-time and part-time faculty are represented by the Massachusetts State College Association union. As D'Art and Turner (2005) emphasize, the degree of solidarity among academic workers is an interesting and important question, because individualist orientations among knowledge workers (including faculty) are often expected to eventually dilute solidarity among them. However, CBtC took shape when our university was re-examining its use of part-time labor. While not explicitly lobbying for improved working conditions or contract changes for any particular group of academic laborers associated with our organization (such as the alternative forms of collective action discussed by Pernicka and Lucking 2012), we believe our efforts contributed to intergroup solidarity between full-time and part-time faculty participants in CBtC.

Alongside full-time faculty, administrators, part-time faculty and staff all planned and organized activities and participated as panelists in Our Stories discussions. Because staff are represented by a separate union from faculty, we feel that our collaboration has encouraged solidarity among all people from WCFG backgrounds working in academia. CBtC activities have also nurtured the professional success of some of our most active participants. For example, Ms. Couto and Ms. Dufresne began their work with CBtC while working as administrative assistants at BSU. Ms. Couto gained experience through her work with CBtC, which she now applies in her position as Student Scholars Coordinator. In this role she is responsible for coordinating national fellowship advising, with a focus on recruiting and supporting WCFG and other underrepresented student populations and on increasing access to other high-impact practices such as the honors program, undergraduate research, and study abroad. Ms. Dufresne recently accepted a program director position at Amherst College, in which she works to support students from WCFG backgrounds.

Strategies and discussion

We hope our work with CBtC inspires similar efforts on other campuses, and we think that some strategies we adopted might be useful in those efforts. The group really began after several participants shared their stories of WCFG backgrounds with each other in informal social situations. As we identified these common interests, we worked to recruit and support a diverse group of people from a variety of positions across the institution who were willing to share their stories more formally with colleagues and students on campus. We have found that story-sharing, through the Our Stories program and other campus activities, validates students and normalizes their experiences—but these processes are especially powerful when the stories come from diverse individuals to whom students can relate.

Our open and inclusive approach to membership included a broad definition of WCFG background. If someone had a family member who had taken some college classes or earned an associate's degree, we still welcomed them to the group. We also welcomed anyone interested in supporting our efforts, regardless of class background. At a professional level, we recruited and involved people holding various positions across campus. Full- and part-time faculty and librarians are a core part of our group, but so are administrators and student-facing staff. Their involvement diversified the group's perspective, helping us accomplish different tasks. It is much easier to coordinate programming when you have the support of administrators and staff who are familiar with organizing similar activities on campus. More importantly, their unique institutional perspectives can shed light on where the group might best intervene to support WCFG students.

Of course, disclosing information about one's working-class background can be problematic, as it may invite skepticism about one's position in the institution and academia. We know, for example, that students are more likely to question the expertise of female faculty (Boring et al. 2016; Macnell et al. 2014). Especially for people from other marginalized backgrounds, it is important that the kind of sharing we practiced took place with the support of several colleagues representing diverse positions in the institution. The support of institutional leaders in positions of power and prestige is important in validating and fostering a sense of belonging.

We made specific choices along these lines, including having everyone share their stories at the start of many of our early meetings and having deans and part-time faculty in equal positions on the Our Stories panels. With a diverse group assembled, it was also critical in our group for people to acknowledge their privileged statuses in conjunction with their WCFG background and to model using those statuses to support other group members. For example, when Colby King moderated the Our Stories panel discussions, he shared that his status as a straight white male helped him navigate some challenges he faced in college. It was important then for participants to take on the ally role in supporting fellow CBtC participants (Mizock & Page 2016). With CBtC, we worked to leverage people's privileges to support participants.

Wakeling (2010, 46) notes that disciplinary diversity is often lacking among working-class academics sharing their story, with most voices from the humanities and social sciences. We sought to bring in voices from disciplines across colleges on campus. By supporting voices from a range of positions in the university and different intersectional identities, we aimed to show that their presence in our group was critical and that our voices on campus were valid and valuable.

Another important strategy for us was to explicitly contextualize the group's efforts in our institution's mission as a state comprehensive university. Connecting those efforts to the institutional mission can provide a strong rationale that supports the program's purpose and persuades observers that the group's activities are relevant to campus culture and student success. The specific mission of a state university built to provide access to college for all students was an important rationale for our activities. Connecting our efforts to the institution's mission, combined with administrative involvement and support, helped CBtC participants feel their efforts were valued. For this kind of service to be sustainable, potential participants must feel not only that they are supported in their activities, but also that their efforts will be recognized as a valuable contribution that—especially for faculty—will reflect well toward tenure and promotion.

We also found it was important for our efforts to underscore social class, in addition to first-generation college student status, as a specific factor in student, faculty, and staff success on campus. Recognizing that social-class–cultural mismatch can be a major dilemma on campus for students, faculty, and staff, we found it useful to talk about social class explicitly, because it allowed us to more easily address class–cultural mismatch and any ambivalence about college that students might feel. For us, this was the best way to alleviate class–cultural mismatch. As a state comprehensive university, we felt our efforts aligned with the institutional mission of broad access to higher education. With BSU's high proportion of WCFG students, supporting student success means supporting these students. Considering the institutional missions of state comprehensive universities and their high enrollment of WCFG students, we feel that these universities are well situated to serve as rallying points for faculty, staff, and students from WCFG backgrounds.

For CBtC participants, one of the most profound outcomes was the realization that we were not alone in our experiences. Connecting to others on campus who came from similar backgrounds or had parallel experiences helped us better navigate our work on campus. Each story that we shared, whether on a panel or in informal conversation, told others they were not alone in their experiences, that there were people on campus who would be happy to help them find their way in academia. By addressing the difficulties of navigating social class on campus together, we worked to support students, faculty, and staff in the classroom and beyond.

Acknowledgments

The authors thank those who have participated in Class Beyond the Classroom activities, especially the Our Stories panelists, including Christine Brandon, Janessa Carvalho, Dan Chase, Amy Couto, Casey Jo Dufresne, Michele Fazio, Miranda Giurleo, Robert Grantham, Jakari Griffith, Paula Krebs, Castagna Lacet, James Norman, Stephen Simms, Cynthia Svoboda, and Melinda Tarsi. We also thank BSU's Massachusetts State College Association faculty union, the College of Humanities and Social Sciences, and the Office of Student Success and Diversity for their support of CBtC. The authors were able to present on CBtC at the 2016 WCSA annual meeting with the support of a BSU Office of Teaching and Learning travel grant and support from the BSU Department of Art and Art History. We thank CBtC participants who helped organize the events and led small-group discussions, including Barbara Bond, Sabrina Gentlewarrior, Todd Harris, Danielle Kohfeldt, Paula Krebs, Meghan Murphy, Kacey O'Donnell, Brian Payne, Melinda Tarsi, Roben Torosyan, Cynthia Svoboda, Pamela Witcher, and Gay Yelle. We also thank all of the students who have participated in our activities. We thank Wendy Wright, Barbara Bond, and the editors for their helpful feedback on drafts of this manuscript. Colby King would like to extend an additional note of appreciation to Debbie Warnock for encouraging him to join the WCSA and inspiring him to work on these efforts.

Notes

1 Oriented as it is to Ivy League schools, it is interesting to note that EdMobilizer makes little mention of social class in their materials. They describe their mission as seeking to 'create equitable pathways to broaden college access and success for undocumented, first-generation college and/or low-income (UFLI) students to address financial, social, and academic disparities within HigherEd'. Lee's (2016) and Warnock and Hurst's (2016) research on first-generation college students at elite schools may be helpful in understanding this organization. Their research showed that WCFG college students often have uniquely fraught experiences as they navigate the campus culture of elite institutions. While participating in such groups may provide access to support and social networks, self-disclosing their WCFG background may also lead to stigmatization (Hurst & Warnock 2015; Warnock & Hurst 2016).

2 Among first-time, full-time freshmen at BSU, 28.8% of women and 41.9% of men were 19 or older, compared to 31% of women and 22.8% of men nationally. In a survey of fall 2015 first-time freshmen, 74.5% of BSU students said cost was 'very important' in their choice of college, substantially higher than the 59.4% nationwide rate (Office of Institutional Research 2016a).

References

Anyon, J. (1983) 'Social class and the hidden curriculum of work', in Giroux, H. and Purpel, D. (eds.) *The Hidden Curriculum and Moral Education*, Berkeley, McCutchan Publishing Corporation.

Austin, C.C., Clark, E.M., Ross, M.J. and Taylor, M.J. (2009) 'Impostorism as a mediator between survivor guilt and depression in a sample of African American college students', *College Student Journal*, 43, 4, pp. 1094–1109.

Ball, S.J. (2003) *Class Strategies and the Education Market: The Middle Classes and Social Advantage*, New York, Routledge.

Banks-Santilli, L. (2014) 'First-generation college students and their pursuit of the American dream', *Journal of Case Studies in Education*, 5, pp. 1–32.

Baumeister, R.F. and Leary, M.R. (1995) 'The need to belong: Desire for interpersonal attachments as a fundamental human motivation', *Psychological Bulletin*, 117, 3, pp. 497–592.

Bernard, D.L, Lige, Q.M., Willis, H.A., Sosoo, E.E. and Neblett, E.W. (2017) 'Impostor phenomenon and mental health: The influence of racial discrimination and gender', *Journal of Counseling Psychology*, 64, 2, pp. 155–166.

Boring, A., Ottoboni, K. and Stark, P. (2016) 'Student evaluations of teaching (mostly) do not measure teaching effectiveness', *ScienceOpen Research*. Available at: www.scienceopen.com/document?vid=818d8ec0-5908-47d8-86b4-5dc38f04b23e.

Casey, J. (2005) 'Diversity, discourse, and the working-class student', *Academe*, 91, 4, pp. 33–36.

Castellanos, J. and Jones, L. (2003) *The Majority in the Minority: Expanding the Representation of Latina/o Faculty, Administrators and Students in Higher Education*, Virginia, Stylus Publishing.

Chen, X. and Carroll, C.D. (2005) 'First-generation students in postsecondary education: A look at their college transcripts. postsecondary education descriptive analysis report', NCES 2005–171, Jessup, MD, US Department of Education.

Christopher, R. (2005) 'New working-class studies in higher education', in Russo, J. and Linkon, S.L. (eds.) *New Working-Class Studies*, Ithaca, Cornell University Press.

Class Action (2017) 'What We Do', available at: www.classism.org/about/what-we-do/.

Covarrubias, R. and Fryberg, S.A. (2015) 'Movin' on up (to college): First-generation college students' experiences with family achievement guilt', *Cultural Diversity and Ethnic Minority Psychology*, 21, 3, pp. 420–429.

Covarrubias, R., Valle, I., Laiduc, G. and Azmitia, M. (2019) '"You Never Become Fully Independent": Family Roles and Independence in First-Generation College Students', *Journal of Adolescent Research*, 34, 4, pp. 381–410.

D'Art, D. and Turner, T. (2005) 'Academic workers and union membership: An inevitable dilution of solidarity?' *Industrial Relations*, 44, 3, pp. 518–524.

Dews, C.L. and Law, C.L. (1995) *This Fine Place So Far from Home: Voice of Academics from the Working Class*, Philadelphia, Temple University Press.

EdMobilizer (2017) 'Equalizing Higher Education from Within', available at: www.edmobilizer.org/.

Engle, J. (2007) 'Postsecondary access and success for first-generation college students', *American Academic*, 3, pp. 25–48.

Engle, J, Bermeo, A. and O'Brien, C. (2006) *Straight from the Source: What Works for First-Generation College Students*, Washington, DC, Pell Institute for the Study of Opportunity in Higher Education.

Espinoza, R. (2011) *Pivotal Moments: How Educators Can Put All Students on the Path to College*, Cambridge, MA, Harvard Education Publishing Group.

First Generation University of Michigan (2017) 'We're the First Generation', available at: https://firstgen.studentlife.umich.edu/.

Flaherty, C. (2017) 'First-Gen Faculty: University of California plan forges connections between students and professors who were the first in their families to attend a four-year institution', *Inside Higher Ed*, available at: www.insidehighered.com/news/2017/06/02/university-california-plan-links-first-generation-students-similar-professors.

Fleming, N. (2017) '1st-generation collegians learn to navigate unfamiliar waters', *Boston Globe*, available at: www.bostonglobe.com/metro/2017/04/08/first-generation-college-students-learn-navigate-unfamiliar-waters/yTbvOvxPzaoCn7y4LhMq6J/story.html.

Furquim, F., Glasener, K.M., Oster, M., McCall, B.P. and DesJardins, S.L. (2017) 'Navigating the financial aid process: Borrowing outcomes among first-generation and non-first-generation students', *The ANNALS of the American Academy of Political and Social Science*, 671, 1, pp. 69–91.

Gearig, C. (2015) 'Faces of an invisible identity', *Michigan Daily*, available at: www.michigandaily.com/section/statement/first-generation-students.

Grimes, M.D. and Morris, J.M. (1997) *Caught in the Middle: Contradictions in the Lives of Sociologists from Working-Class Backgrounds*, Westport, Praeger.

Henderson, B.B. (2009) 'Introduction: The work of the people's university', *Teacher-Scholar: The Journal of the State Comprehensive University*, 1, 1, 2.

Hinz, S.E. (2016) 'Upwardly mobile: Attitudes toward the class transition among first-generation college students', *Journal of College Student Development*, 57, 3, pp. 285–299.

Hurst, A.L. (2007) 'Telling tales of oppression and dysfunction: Narratives of class-identity reformation', *Qualitative Sociology Review*, 3, 2, pp. 82–104.

Hurst, A.L. (2010) *The Burden of Academic Success: Loyalists, Renegades, and Double Agents*, Lanham, MD, Lexington.

Hurst, A.L. and Nenga, S.K. (eds.) (2016) *Working in Class: Recognizing how Social Class Shapes our Academic Work*, Lanham, MD, Rowman & Littlefield.

Hurst, A.L. and Warnock, D. (2015) 'Les Miracules: "The magical image of the permanent"—constructed narratives of self and mobility from working-class students at an elite college', in Lee, E. and LaDousa,

C. (eds.) *College Students' Experiences of Power and Marginality: Sharing Spaces and Negotiating Differences*, London, Routledge.

Jack, A.A. (2014) 'Culture shock revisited: The social and cultural contingencies to class marginality', *Sociological Forum*, 29, 2, pp. 453–475.

Jehangir, R.R. (2009) Cultivating voice: 'First-generation students seek full academic citizenship in multicultural learning communities', *Innovative Higher Education*, 34, 1, pp. 33–49.

Jehangir, R.R., Stebleton, M.J. and Deenanath, V. (2015) *An Exploration of Intersecting Identities of First-Generation, Low-Income Students* (Research Report No. 5), National Resource Center for The First-Year Experience and Students in Transition. Columbia, University of South Carolina.

King, C. (2014) 'Work to do', *Bridgewater Review*, 33, 2, pp. 12–14, available at: http://vc.bridgew.edu/cgi/viewcontent.cgi?article=1901&context=br_rev.

King, C. and Griffith, J. (2015a) 'Sports and socio-economic status: More than talent required', *Everyday Sociology Blog*, available at: www.everydaysociologyblog.com/2015/03/sports-and-socio-economic-status-more-than-talent-required.html.

King, C. and Griffith, J. (2015b) 'More than talent alone', *Bridgewater Review*, 34, 2, pp. 13–15, available at: http://vc.bridgew.edu/cgi/viewcontent.cgi?article=1930&context=br_rev.

King, C., Griffith, J. and Murphy, M. (2017) 'Story sharing for first-generation college students attending a regional comprehensive university: Campus outreach to validate students and develop forms of capital', *Teacher-Scholar: The Journal of the State Comprehensive University*, 8, 1, pp. 1–23.

Lang, D. (2015) 'Singing the first-generation blues', *Chronicle of Higher Education*, available at: www.chronicle.com/article/Singing-the-First-Generation/230143.

Lee, E.M. (2016) *Class and Campus Life: Managing and Experiencing Inequality at an Elite College*, Ithaca, NY, Cornell University Press.

Lehmann, W. (2009) 'Becoming middle class: How working-class university students draw and transgress moral class boundaries', *Sociology*, 43, 4, pp. 631–647.

Lehmann, W. (2013) 'Habitus transformation and hidden injuries: Successful working-class university students', *Sociology of Education*, 87, 1, pp. 1–15.

Leondar-Wright, B. (2014) *Missing Class*, Ithaca, NY, Cornell University Press.

London, H.B. (1989) 'Breaking away: A study of first-generation college students and their families', *American Journal of Education*, 97, 2, pp. 144–170.

Macnell, L, Driscoll, A. and Hunt, A.N. (2014) 'What's in a name: Exposing gender bias in student ratings of teaching', *Innovative Higher Education*, 40, 4, pp. 291–303.

Maize Pages (n.d.) 'First-generation college students @ Michigan', *University of Michigan*, available at: https://maizepages.umich.edu/organization/firstgens.

McNair Scholars Program (2017) 'About', available at: https://mcnairscholars.com/about/.

Michaels, W.B. (2007) *The Trouble with Diversity*, New York, Metropolitan Books.

Mizock, L. and Page, K.V. (2016) 'Evaluating the ally role: Contributions, limitations, and the activist position in counseling and psychology', *Journal for Social Action in Counseling and Psychology*, 8, 1, pp. 17–33.

Morris, J.M. and Grimes, M.D. (2007) 'Moving up from the working class', in Henslin, J.M. (ed.) *Down to Earth Sociology*, 14th ed., New York, Free Press.

NASPA (2017) 'Center for First-Generation Student Success', *NASPA Student Affairs Administrators in Higher Education*, available at: www.naspa.org/constituent-groups/groups/center-for-first-generation-student-success.

Nora, A., Urick, A. and Cerecer, P.D.Q. (2011) 'Validating students: A conceptualization and overview of its impact on student experiences and outcomes', *Enrollment Management Journal*, 5, 2, pp. 34–52.

Office of Institutional Research (2016a) *Bridgewater State University Factbook, 2015–2016*, Bridgewater State University, available at: http://vc.bridgew.edu/factbook/25.

Office of Institutional Research (2016b) *2015 Campus Climate Survey Final Report*, Bridgewater State University.

OSU Division of Undergraduate Studies (2017) 'Celebrating first-generation college students', *Oregon State University*, available at: http://undergraduate.oregonstate.edu/feature-story/celebrating-first-generation-college-students.

Pascarella, E.T., Pierson, C.T., Wolniak, C.G. and Terenzini, P. (2004) 'First-generation college students: Additional evidence on college experiences and outcomes', *Journal of Higher Education*, 75, 3, pp. 249–284.

Pernicka, S. and Lucking, S. (2012) 'How knowledge shapes collective action: Professionalism, market closure and bureaucracy in the fields of university and non-university research', *Journal of Industrial Relations*, 54, 5, pp. 579–595.

Petty, T. (2014) 'Motivating first-generation students to academic success and college completion', *College Student Journal*, 48, 2, pp. 257–264.

Piorkowski, G.K. (1983) 'Survivor guilt in the university setting', *Personnel & Guidance Journal*, 61, 10, pp. 620–622.

Pyne, K.B. and Means, D.R. (2013) 'Underrepresented and in/visible: A Hispanic first-generation student's narratives of college', *Journal of Diversity in Higher Education*, 6, 3, pp. 186–198.

Rendon, L. (1994) 'Validating culturally diverse students: Toward a new model of learning and student development', *Innovative Higher Education*, 19, 1, pp. 33–51.

Rice, A.J., Colbow, A.J., Gibbons, S., Cederberg, C., Sahker, E., Liu, W.M. and Wurster, K. (2017) 'The social class worldviews of first-generation college students', *Counselling Psychology Quarterly*, 30, 4, pp. 415–440.

Riederer, R. (2014) 'The teaching class: Teaching college is no longer a middle-class job, and everyone paying tuition should care', *Guernica*, available at: www.guernicamag.com/the-teaching-class.

Rivenburg, R, Wilson, J., Harriman, P. and UC Irvine (2016) 'Meet the mentors', *University California Irvine*, available at: www.universityofcalifornia.edu/news/meet-mentors.

Rubinoff, M. (2016) 'Center for Student Opportunity (CSO) announces merger with Strive for College', *I'm First!*, available at: www.imfirst.org/2016/05/cso-announces-merger-with-strive-for-college/.

Ryan, J. and Sackrey, C. (1996) *Strangers in Paradise: Academics from the Working Class*, 2nd ed., Lanham, MD, University Press of America.

Saenz, V.B., Hurtado, S., Barrera, D., Wolf, D. and Yeung, F. (2007) *First in My Family: A Profile of First-Generation College Students at Four-Year Institutions Since 1971*, Cooperative Institutional Research Program, Los Angeles, Higher Education Research Institution.

Soria, K.M. (2015) *Welcoming Blue-Collar Scholars into the Ivory Tower: Developing Class-Conscious Strategies for Students' Success*, Columbia, SC, National Resource Center for the First-Year Experience and Students in Transition.

Soza, C. (2016) 'GU alliance unites colleges', *The Hoya*, available at: www.thehoya.com/gu-alliance-unites-colleges/.

Stebleton, M.J., Soria, K.M. and Huesman, R.L., Jr. (2014) 'First-generation students' sense of belonging, mental health, and use of counseling services at public research universities', *Journal of College Counseling*, 17, 1, pp. 6–20.

Stephens, N.M., Fryberg, S.A., Markus, H.R., Johnson, C.S. and Covarrubias, R. (2012) 'Unseen disadvantage: How American universities' focus on independence undermines the academic performance of first-generation college students', *Journal of Personality and Social Psychology*, 102, 6, pp. 1178–1197.

Strayhorn, T.L. (2008) 'Fittin' in: Do diverse interactions with peers affect sense of belonging for black men at predominantly white institutions?' *NASPA Journal*, 45, 4, pp. 501–527.

Strayhorn, T.L. (2012) *College Students' Sense of Belonging: A Key to Educational Success for All Students*, New York, Routledge.

University of Washington-Tacoma (2017) 'First-generation students speak out—student panel!' available at: http://engage.washington.edu/site/MessageViewer?em_id=204795.0&dlv_id=195709#firsgen.

US Department of Education. (2017) 'TRIO Programs', available at: https://www2.ed.gov/about/offices/list/ope/trio/index.html.

Van Galen, J. (2017) 'About', *First in Our Families*, available at: https://firstinourfamilies.org/about/.

Wakeling, P. (2010) 'Is there such a thing as a working class academic?' in Taylor, Y. (ed.) *Class Intersections: Spaces, Selves, Knowledges*, New York, Routledge.

Warnock, D.M. (2014) 'On the other side of what tracks? The missing discussion of social class in the academy', *Rhizomes*, 27, available at: http://rhizomes.net/issue27/index.html.

Warnock, D.M. (2016) 'Paradise lost? Patterns and precarity in working-class academic narratives', *Journal of Working-Class Studies*, 1, 1, pp. 28–44.

Warnock, D.M. and Appel, S. (2012) 'Learning the unwritten rules: Working-class students in graduate school', *Innovative Higher Education*, 37, pp. 307–321, doi:10.1007/s10755-011-9204-x.

Warnock, D.M. and Hurst, A.L. (2016) '"The poor kids' table": Organizing around an invisible and stigmatized identity in flux', *Journal of Diversity in Higher Education*, 9, 3, pp. 261–276.

Whitman College (2017) 'First-generation/working-class students (FGWC)', available at: www.whitman.edu/student-life/student-clubs-and-organizations/first-generation-working-class-students.

Whitman College First Generation/Working Class Club (2017) 'Home', available at: https://fgwcwhitman.wordpress.com/.

Wisconsin Involvement Network (2017) 'Working-Class Student Union', available at: https://win.wisc.edu/organization/wcsu.

Working Class Student Union (2017) available at: www.facebook.com/wcsuuw/.

Yosso, T.J. (2005) 'Whose culture has capital? A critical race theory discussion of community cultural wealth', *Race Ethnicity and Education*, 8, 1, pp. 69–91.

Young, M.S. (2016a) 'Navigating campus together: First-generation faculty can steer first-generation college students toward success', *The Atlantic*, available at: www.theatlantic.com/education/archive/2016/05/how-first-generation-faculty-can-help-first-generation-students-succeed/481617/.

Young, M.S. (2016b) 'The cost of being first: Conflating "first-generation" and "low-income" students is inaccurate and isolating', *The Atlantic*, available at: www.theatlantic.com/education/archive/2016/10/the-cost-of-being-first/504155/.

6

Working-class student experiences

Toward a social class-sensitive pedagogy for K–12 schools, teachers, and teacher educators

Colleen H. Clements and Mark D. Vagle

Education has long been seen as a vehicle for upward mobility and 'climbing the social class ladder' in the U.S. The development and enactment of public education in the U.S., however, has a fraught history when it comes to the treatment of working-class and working-poor students, especially working-class students of color. In this chapter, we trace some of this history, situating it in relation to problematic colonial formation and traditions in the U.S. and analyzing the effects of this history on current educational policies and practices that affect working-class students. For instance, research has shown that school policies and norms tend to be based in middle-class notions of what education should be. In addition, an examination of the history of class and race in the U.S. helps teachers better understand aspects of their own identities with respect to class and race. Our goal, and the goal of this chapter, is to offer some suggestions for ways educators can employ a more social class-sensitive approach to pedagogy (Vagle & Jones 2012; Jones & Vagle 2013) and to make visible the problematic norms that are embedded in classrooms and curricula. The principles of social class-sensitive pedagogy engage educators in a more thoughtful, nuanced approach to working-class students, rather than offering easy 'solutions' which tend to frame working-class and working-poor students as 'the problem'.

Education in the U.S. has a long and complicated history and relationship with classism and racism. In order to examine how education and educational policy in the U.S. have developed in accordance with middle-class norms in ways that disadvantage working-class students, whether white students or students of color, some historical situating of this development is illuminating. Public schooling at its inception was primarily designed as a way to keep young, working-class students off the streets after child labor was outlawed in the early part of the 20th century (Kliebard 2004). Prior to the invention of compulsory public schooling, education was mainly reserved for the children of the wealthy and privileged, and it was delivered by way of private tutors, whose classrooms were in the homes of the mostly male, predominantly white students. The children of those 'less fortunate' in birth were often destined for work in factories and other similarly dangerous and physically demanding lines of work. This untenable situation came to an end when child labor was outlawed, and adults took over in the jobs previously held by children and adolescents (Kliebard 2004).

The question then became what to do with all these young, poor people. Leaving them unattended on the streets all day was cause for concern in the minds of the local authorities nationwide: so many young, idle hands were sure to result in increased levels of mischief and crime. The solution was both practical and aspirational, serving the function of getting the kids off the streets and simultaneously offering them tools for a more productive future: the establishment of public schools, where children who had once been laborers would instead become scholars (Kliebard 2004).

These schools were run very much like factories, in part because the factory environment was one with which many of the newly minted scholars were quite familiar, complete with loudly ringing bells to indicate the beginning and ending of a work period. The intent was not only to allow the students an easy and recognizable transition from their earlier work lives to these new, less familiar, but more academic, surroundings, but also to police the bodies of these young students. In spite of the fact that public schools were created for working-class and working-poor students, working-class students of color were not welcome, given the time in which public schools came into being and the segregation laws that existed in the U.S. at the time (Watkins 2001). In this way, one function of these schools was to reinforce segregation and to inspire the mostly white working-class students to 'better' themselves and strive to learn the required skills to 'pull themselves up by their bootstraps' and to use their education to become highly skilled workers, often in more intellectual fields, leading productive and happy middle-class lives and leaving their working-class roots behind in the process (Watkins 2001; Kliebard 2004).

While all of this may sound somewhat idealistic (if not problematic; and not unfamiliar), one of the many problems with this system was the way in which it conceived of working-class and working-poor students. This problem was rooted in the larger community, that tended to see people in poverty as the problem rather than seeing poverty itself as the problem that people were experiencing. This conception of people in poverty as the problem was seen in multiple arenas in that era, spurring the creation of the prison system, the hospital system, and the field of social work, as well as in education (Donzelot 1979; Rose 1990; Foucault 2008). In general, when it came to those in poverty, the authorities were interested in 'helping' them learn to be more like the middle class by adopting middle-class values (without regard for their actual material conditions) via 'helpful' white, female social workers and teachers; and when that failed to work, they locked them up, either in hospitals or prisons. In general, the desire was to get rid of the people in poverty – who were unpleasant reminders of the problem of poverty – rather than tackling the more entrenched issue of poverty itself.

Education in particular was seen as a hopeful solution to the problem of people experiencing poverty in that it would allow them to 'help themselves'. This is, it must be acknowledged, a goal that was rooted at least partially in a desire to be helpful. At issue, however, is the construction of working-class and working-poor students as 'the problem', a construction that still rings true today in education and in society at large.

Social class and racialized identity

In order to better understand the construction of social class identity in the U.S., it is helpful to look to its historical underpinnings. An examination of social class from a historical perspective illuminates the ways that class and race are bound together in the U.S. and continue to perpetuate injustices in multiple realms: the so-called 'achievement gap', police violence, and the school-to-prison pipeline, to name just a few. Understanding the division of labor during the founding of the U.S. reveals the significant role it played in this process. In the early years of U.S. history, much of the labor required for building the infrastructure of the country was performed by indentured servants and those considered 'nonwhite', primarily enslaved Black people in the colonial era (Roediger 1999). The citizen with full rights during this period was the landowning, Protestant, Anglo-Saxon white male, while all other categories of people were afforded less than full citizenship status (Roediger 1999; Thandeka 2007). The power of full citizenship was conferred solely on the elite class of white males, establishing the patriarchal order that is the base of the U.S. political economy.

This early social order of the white, male, land- and slave-owning elite was upset by the appearance of wave upon wave of immigrants as they arrived to the shores of the U.S. in the coming years and decades, starting in the colonial period and continuing through the 19th century (Roediger 1999). These new arrivals were often indentured servants, having won their passage to the U.S. on the promise of their labor once they arrived safely. These immigrants often mixed freely with the established labor class in the U.S., made up by this time primarily of (sometimes freed) slaves. As the ranks of these laborers grew and their tendency to intermingle freely extended over time, the established elite saw a potential threat to their power and decided it best to divide and conquer, lest this growing population use the strength of its numbers to challenge the status quo.

This division required devising a way to convince certain members of the laboring class to see themselves as inherently different from others in the same (or very similar) circumstances. The elite class made an appeal to the laborers with white skin, like their own, enticing them with the idea that one day, if they worked hard enough, they too may become part of the white, male elite of the dominant class (Roediger 1999; Thandeka 2007). Thus was born a central factor in the construction of racialized identity in the U.S., as the natural antecedent of this argument was that nonwhite members of this group could not similarly aspire to become part of the elite, nor were they to be trusted, mingled with, or otherwise considered legitimate members of the group, despite the earlier solidarity amongst workers that did not depend on skin color or the manufactured notion of different races based on skin tone.

In this way, racialized identity and social class are inextricably linked in U.S. culture. In order to strive to become part of the elite class, certain (white, male) members of the working class were told that through their labor and emulation of the white, male elite, they might have a chance to one day join the ranks of this elite class (Roediger 1999; Thandeka 2007). Thus, social class is not only an established hierarchy which one might strive to climb; it is also a process of becoming 'whiter', more upwardly mobile, and more separated from those in 'lower' classes. As such, social class is also a tool for creating and maintaining the divisions of race that are based on the false premise of some deeper difference related merely to the color of one's skin.

Although the above framing is a historical perspective on some of the ways that social class and racialized identity function, the argument can be made that the same forces are alive and well in contemporary U.S. culture in countless contexts, including (to name a few) the criminal justice system, housing policy, the realm of electoral politics, and (as is the focus of this chapter) education. In the academic field of critical whiteness studies (Roediger 1999; Leonardo 2002; Thandeka 2007; Lensmire 2014; Jupp, Berry, & Lensmire 2016), we have come to think of whiteness as a normalizing force in these contexts as well as in U.S. culture more broadly. This force is often invisible, especially to middle-class white people, as it is they who embody and enforce most of the cultural norms in the U.S.; but it is often painfully and wearyingly obvious to people of color. While one's social class position is also often invisible, the experience of social class is something everyone encounters, albeit often in very different ways; as such, class is an important element to be understood more fully as we strive to create a more just world and a more justice-oriented educational system as part of that process.

Popularized constructions of social class

It is important to think about the socially constructed nature of class, particularly in light of the tendency for some to essentialize the experiences and culture of the working class as problematic. In education, these essentializing narratives can result in teachers and administrators blaming working-class students and families for the lack of adequate resources they may face and assuming things about their lives that may not be true. The portrayal of working-class culture in the media can be influential in disrupting or reinforcing these narratives. Two recent examples of works that examine class come to mind: Nancy Isenberg's *White Trash: The 400-Year Untold History of Class in America* (2017) and J. D. Vance's *Hillbilly Elegy: A Memoir of a Family and Culture in Crisis* (2016). These books gained traction in part due to the 2016 presidential election and the media interest in the so-called 'white working class'. Isenberg's decidedly more academic and comprehensive work highlights the significance of understanding the historical construction of race and its relationship to social class. Vance, on the other hand, titled his book a memoir; in it he draws on his own experiences to make more sweeping and generalized claims about the culture of the working class and working poor in Kentucky and Ohio. Not only does he find much to be critical of in those communities, but his rendering of 'the culture' of working-class life, based solely on his experience as a straight, white male, erases the experiences of countless other working-class individuals. We have seen Vance's work taken up in the popular media and in other more localized settings to draw simplistic conclusions and make harsh judgments about the lives of working-class people while, at the same time, ignoring the influence and effects of the white, hetero-patriarchal capitalist system in the U.S. The reification of such damaging narratives is especially problematic given the political powers at play and the ways in which 'white, working-class folk' have been simultaneously and variously valorized for their work ethic and values, demonized for their lifestyles and values, and blamed for the results of the most recent presidential election when, in reality, some analyses suggest a more complicated story (e.g. Sasson 2016; Hurst 2017). In addition, it bears pointing out that in the construction of the notion of a 'white working class', we see that those old, false racial divisions are alive and well and that notions of class and race being put to work in troubling ways, much as they always have been in the U.S. Regardless of where one falls on the political spectrum in the U.S., a deeper understanding of the ways that class and race are intertwined will only help us make sense of the oft-mentioned, real or imagined, deeply entrenched divisions in our citizenry, which are reinforced by the either/or thinking that is predominant in discussions of race and class. The perpetuation of this false dichotomy stands in the way of true change for working-class students of all backgrounds.

Working-class bodies and school

Social class status, as we highlight above, is experienced in multiple ways. It is a way to sort bodies along a preestablished hierarchy. It can also be a process related to 'climbing' one's way up through that hierarchy. Additionally, it is used to confer identity on certain bodies (Vagle & Jones 2012; Jones & Vagle 2013). Each of these multiple ways of conceiving of social class is deeply embodied. In other words, the experience of becoming socially classed is one that we experience through our bodies, recognizing that our bodies can learn just as our minds do and that there is no hard line between learning that happens in our minds and in our bodies. When we identify with a particular social class, it is in no small part because our bodies feel comfortable in certain settings and less comfortable in others. The way we absorb our social class identities is very much through an embodied learning as we interact with the world around us.

Despite an emphasis on intellectual pursuits, schooling is very much about bodies as well (Jones & Vagle 2013; Coffee, Stutelberg, Clements, & Lensmire 2016). Teachers and students spend their days together, attending to their bodily needs throughout the day and experiencing the world through and in their bodies. While we may not often think of school in this way, it is the case that much of what happens in schools is about the bodies of students and teachers moving through spaces inside schools and, in the process, relating to one another and the surroundings of the school. Certain bodies find themselves more comfortable than others in traditional classrooms, given that those spaces are shaped mainly according to white, middle-class norms. For this reason, white, middle-class students tend to find their own values and experiences reflected back to them in their surroundings and in educational experiences. There tend to be few, if any, elements that white, middle-class students would find to be unfamiliar, whether it is the physical environment, the curriculum, or the teachers and administrators of the school.

The same cannot be said for working-class, or working-poor, students. Working-class and working-poor students are much less likely to see their own experiences reflected back to them in their school experience. The physical environment of the school and classroom, and the social relations in those spaces, may not match the surroundings in which they are most used to being (Massey 2005; Mitchell 2005; Henry 2014), and the curriculum is less likely to contain elements that they find familiar or that reinforce their knowledge and experience of the world. In fact, much of the curriculum and classroom practice may tend to do the opposite, calling into question their preexisting knowledge and sense-making of the world around them or even resulting in damaging attempts at discipline (Henry 2014). They may at times see their way of life being criticized and denigrated, sometimes overtly and sometimes implicitly (Vagle & Jones 2012; Jones & Vagle 2013). It is not uncommon for teachers to make well-meaning comments about the aspirations of their students, encouraging them to aim 'higher' than what are traditionally considered working-class jobs, often the very jobs their parents may be doing. This can cause students to experience a sense of shame regarding their families and home lives, particularly when opportunities have been systematically denied working-class individuals, notably working-class people of color (Ferguson 2001).

The sense of shame that many working-class students experience at school can result in a desire to perform a sort of 'class-passing', in which they attempt to remake their bodies into the idealized, middle-class norm toward which the school, and often the teachers, are pushing them. Again, we recognize that this is often done with the best of intentions, and working-class parents themselves sometimes hope for their children a different, seemingly more rewarding or less physically demanding line of work. None of this is inherently wrong. The damage comes from the often-inadvertent belittling of the lives and experiences of working-class students, which causes a sense of conflict in the bodies of working-class students, sometimes with the result that they do not feel they truly belong anywhere, alienated as they often are by the social relations embedded in these spaces (Massey 2005; Mitchell 2005).

This embodied class-passing can come in the form of dressing in a particular way, hiding parts of themselves from their peers and teachers, and striving to attain the outward physical attributes and accessories of middle-classness. This last example can be particularly dangerous for working-class students of color. In the workshops we have led (Other Side of Poverty in Schools; discussed later), many is the time a teacher has admitted to feelings of judgment toward a working-class family of color whose son or daughter may not have lunch money or money for a field trip, but brings a smartphone to school or has a fancy manicure or expensive athletic shoes. Often in these cases, the smartphone may be the only technology to which the family has access, and an aunt or grandparent is responsible for providing the phone, the manicure, or the shoes. But these affordances of thought are often not given to working-class families of color. Considering the way in which social class operates in the construction of racialized identity, it is 'easier' for white working-class students to class-pass without incurring the harsh judgments of teachers, but they too can suffer from similar instances of judgment and shaming.

Often, the teachers themselves have not given much thought to the role that social class plays in their own lives, much less in the lives of their students. Given that the majority of teachers in the U.S. are middle-class, white women (Meiners 2002; Coffee, Stutelberg, Clements, & Lensmire 2016), they have often had enjoyable educational experiences and have become teachers precisely because they had such a good time of it in school. In other words, their way of seeing the world is closely matched by the norms of school in the U.S., and as such they may never have been asked to look critically at the reinforcement of these norms in schools. There has been a necessary push in recent years for teachers to become more culturally competent and to take up the practices of critical pedagogy (Freire 1968[2000]), particularly in regard to building better relationships with their students of color. We contend one element that may assist in this endeavor is a close examination of social class, both in the teacher's own self-identity and in the lives and experiences of their students, in order to avoid the deficit thinking that allows teachers to 'shift the responsibility from themselves onto the students and their families' (Svec & Thomas 2016, 111). To this point, we advocate an approach to teaching that is termed 'social class-sensitive pedagogy', not in place of other forms of critical pedagogy but in tandem with them. This approach is aimed at helping teachers understand their own social class identities, recognizing social class as a force for normalization and creating hierarchies in schools and classrooms, and is intended as a way of acknowledging and valuing the experiences of working-class students in schools, classrooms, and curricula.

Social class and critical pedagogy

We contend, and research shows, that for education to be effective and meaningful, teachers would do best to follow the tenets of critical pedagogy (Freire 1968[2000]; Darder 2003). The goal of critical pedagogy is, at its heart, a move toward humanizing the relationship between teacher and student. That education should emphasize human connection may sound obvious and not necessary to put into words; but if we think about the history of education in the U.S., as well as educational practices in recent decades, we see that the pattern has not always been to prioritize shared humanity in education. For example, the historical underpinnings of schools echoing factory work is far from depicting an institution founded on valuing human relationships and caring interactions. In addition, the culture of high-stakes testing that has dominated schooling in more recent years is yet another example of the way in which factors other than promoting humanity can become central to the educational experience. Too often the protest that is heard from teachers is that the demands of schooling today get in the way of meaningful interactions with students. This is bad not only for students, but also for teachers; and for this reason, we contend that an emphasis on humanizing interactions in schools is imperative. Critical pedagogy provides one possible path toward humanizing educational practices.

Within the field of education, the emphasis on critical pedagogy has resulted in more recent moves toward cultural competence/relevance/sensitivity/responsiveness in teaching, generally known as culturally relevant pedagogy (Ladson-Billings 1995, 2014). The notion has undergone some evolution in terms of the way it is conceived, hence the complicated nomenclature. It began with the idea that teachers who may not share the same cultural background as their students would do well to become more familiar with their students' culture(s) and incorporate this cultural understanding into their teaching (cultural relevance). This notion was a step in the right direction, but in practice it was found that for some, a distance remained between teacher and student, creating obstacles to more meaningful connections in these relationships (Ladson-Billings 2008). This led to the shift toward cultural sensitivity (Thomas 1997), which encouraged an emotional connection between teacher and student, regardless of cultural differences. This conception, too, however, presented some difficulties in that emphasizing the emotional component of cultural difference relies on the notion of empathy. Empathy is often considered a positive element in trying to understand someone else's experience, but it can allow for one's assumptions about that person's experience to dominate the interactions, rather than learning about the other's actual lived experience. The evolution of these ideas culminated (so far) in the notion of cultural responsiveness and culturally sustaining pedagogy (Ladson-Billings 2014; Paris 2012), which suggest that the teacher must, first and foremost, learn from the student(s) about their experiences rather than drawing on outside knowledge (cultural relevance) or basing the relationship on the teacher's assumptions (cultural sensitivity). Finally, the notion of culturally sustaining pedagogy (Ladson-Billings 2014; Paris 2012) lends a subtle call for action and advocacy that teachers often discover once they have committed deeply to the work of humanizing education.

Social class-sensitive pedagogy (Vagle & Jones 2012; Jones & Vagle 2013) shares elements of both critical pedagogy and culturally sustaining pedagogy and can be practiced as a part of these approaches. Social class-sensitive pedagogy, like critical pedagogy, calls for a more humanizing way for teachers to interact with their students. Additionally, as 'a social, autobiographic, and pedagogical' practice (Vagle & Jones 2012), it shares with cultural responsiveness an emphasis on understanding the lived experience of social class, both in the teacher's life as well as in the student's, and attention to the resulting need for action. Jones and Vagle have laid out five principles for social class-sensitive pedagogy, designed to help teachers and administrators enact a more humanizing pedagogy with students, a part of which is examining their own relationship with and experience of social class (Vagle & Jones 2012; Jones & Vagle 2013). Let us look at each of the principles now.

'Five principles for change'

In their work *Living Contradictions and Working for Change: Toward a Theory of Social Class-Sensitive Pedagogy* (Jones & Vagle 2013), the authors drew on over a decade of their own research as well as an existing body of work related to issues of social class and education. One persistent issue of concern is the tendency for students and families experiencing poverty to be positioned as the problem rather than seeing poverty as an ongoing, systemic issue plaguing society. From this basis, the authors developed a set of principles for educators that seek to make apparent the mistakes and potential issues that may arise from the positioning of working-class and working-poor students and families as problems in need of remedy. These principles, listed and described below, move from the personal to the more structural, centering and valuing the stories of the lived experiences of both the educators and the students. The principles are not meant to be prescriptive or easy bromides for 'dealing' with students in poverty, but rather as a series of processes that lead to a shift in perspective and the development of a mindset that enables teachers to think in more complicated ways about issues of social class. They are as follows.

1. **Analyzing educators' and students' experiences of class within broad social and political contexts.** Personal experiences of social class are never really individual, but instead always tied to broader trends in social and economic policies, networks provided

by affiliations through social class and other groups, resources to which we have access, etc. This principle focuses on valuing individual experiences of social class and simultaneously points to the external forces that create those experiences, moving the focus away from individual children or families as 'problems' and toward a broader and deeper understanding of social class.

2. **Locating and disrupting social classed hierarchies in schools and communities.** Certain ways of talking and thinking in our society create hierarchies linking social class background to all sorts of things, including assumptions about intelligence, interests, talents, histories, possible futures, etc. Many of these hierarchies are created on false assumptions regarding what is most 'desirable' about life in general – assumptions based on materialism and classism that must be disrupted if a society is to hope for any kind of sustainable future.
3. **Integrating social class and marginalized perspectives into the curriculum**. Most children, youth, and adults in U.S. society have not had the opportunity to learn about working-class literature, issues important to working-class and working-poor people, economics with ethical aims, or the history of the U.S. 'economy', or to consider school curricula and current events from the perspectives of working-class people in the U.S. This is an imperative move for schools and classrooms so that all students can be reached and taught about issues that impact their daily lives.
4. **Perceiving classed bodies in moment-to-moment interactions with educators, students, and families.** Constantly recognizing how you are perceiving someone (a child, another adult) as a 'classed' person is important, as it allows you to stretch yourself and realize that the snapshot perception being created by you is only one of an infinite number of ways to perceive the person standing in front of you. Aiming for more complexity, nuance, and generosity in perceptivity is a crucial aspect of becoming more sensitive to how social class impacts one's perceptions and working against classist, hierarchical perceptivity.
5. **Changing broader school and classroom policies and practices to reflect an anti-classist and anti-poverty commitment.** Classroom and school policies can create explicit and implicit hierarchies based on social class that have detrimental influences over participation and achievement and can make families struggling economically suffer even more financial burden. Rethinking requests for money, supplies, materials, participation in fundraisers, etc. is just a first step in evaluating policies that systematically disadvantage children and families with humble material resources. Looking closely at communications, discipline practices, language use, materials used in the classroom (literature, videos, etc.), conferences, report cards, class assignments, extracurricular activities, and so on, can reveal classist practices that add to the financial burden of struggling families – the opposite of what most schools want to do. For example, some classrooms promote food drives as an activity for students. Students are encouraged to bring food from home for the drive. This practice, however, does not recognize that some students' families may themselves rely on a local food shelf to get their own food.

The development of these five principles has led to multiple avenues for educators and leaders to participate in social class-sensitive pedagogy. One such avenue that has been developed is daylong workshops on the Other Side of Poverty in Schools for educators and administrators. Those who attend one of these workshops also have the option of ongoing consultation for their institutions and administrations. Another example is the development of a college course on social class and pedagogy, designed for future teachers but offered across the college for anyone interested in bringing a deeper understanding of social class to their work.[1]

As authors of this work and colleagues engaged in social class-sensitive pedagogy, we have both taken part in the autobiographic element of this work, in which one considers one's own experience with social class. While some shared similarities in our experiences is one of the things that initially drew us to working together (e.g. our experiences of growing up working class and entering the academy), it is important to note the differences in our stories as well. We both self-identify as white and as having grown up in working-class families and communities, both in rural Minnesota, but with some significant differences. For one thing, our gender identities are different, which made for significant differences in our experiences of social class. In addition, the relative status of the work our parents did was also viewed differently in our respective communities, leading to other notable differences in our experiences. In other words, this work does not seek a unifying narrative of what it means to identify as working class, nor does it seek to subsume all other markers of difference. Quite the opposite is true. Rather, it asks us to be attuned to the actual lived experiences of those in the working class, without assumptions or judgment – or at least to learn to become aware of those moments when we assume things and make judgments about the experiences of others – and to think deeply about the intersectionalities (Carbado, Crenshaw, Mays, & Tomlinson 2013) of other markers of difference and the ways in which social class interacts with those identities.

When teachers engage in this work, as we have seen numerous times in the workshops and college courses on social class-sensitive pedagogy, it affords them what we have come to refer to as an 'entry point' for thinking about their own identities in more critical ways. This is especially true for those many white teachers who have not previously had the experience of critically examining their own lived experience and how it has been shaped by class and race. Often these topics can be seen as too foreign and controversial, better to be avoided under the guise of a common mantra among (especially future) teachers: 'I will see all my students as "the same", and I will never think that any of them is not capable of success'. While this common notion comes from a place of good intentions, its effect is akin to the problems of color-blindness, in which differences in experience are minimized in an attempt to treat everyone 'the same'. While we would never argue that the attitude that all students can succeed is a bad one to have, we are cautious to point out that while all students may have great potential, some have more challenges – not of their own making, but rather obstacles created by society and reinforced in many educational settings.

Conclusion

The work of teachers and education as a whole is multidimensional. There is a need to recognize that the educational system in the U.S. is constructed in such a way that it reinforces norms of middle-class whiteness, which can be damaging to students and families. While teachers and schools often have as a primary goal 'lifting' everyone to a comfortable, middle-class existence, the assumptions about working-class experience that are embedded in this goal can be problematic. For example, teachers often assume that working-class students lack the ability to reason that middle- and upper-middle-class students are assumed to possess, leading them to teach the curriculum to working-class students in a different way than they do with students from other backgrounds (Finn 2009). Social class-sensitive pedagogy gives educators and administrators the opportunity to think more deeply about the ways these norms are perpetuated and the effects they can have on students and families.

One major element of this work is for the teacher to think deeply about their own social class identity. This can help illuminate racialized experience, particularly for white teachers, who still make up the majority of teachers in the U.S. and who may not have had an opportunity to critically examine their own racialized identity. We contend that this examination puts white teachers in a better position to more fully recognize the roles that social class and racialized identity play in the lives of their students. This deeper apprehension of these forces enables teachers to engage more actively in critical and culturally sustaining pedagogy.

Working-class students and families of all cultural backgrounds will benefit from an educational system that recognizes and validates their experiences. Only by truly getting to know the students in one's classroom and the communities from which they come can teachers hope to help their students succeed. When they know something about the actual lived experiences of those students and their families, and they have done the work to see how their own experiences relate to and are informed by systems of power in the U.S., then we might hope for the sort of education that enables students not only to become successful, but to have their full humanity recognized. The recognition of the humanity of working-class students and their experiences is vital if we hope to engage all students in the civic project of democracy, in which we recognize our shared humanity both with those whose experiences we share as well as those with whom our experiences might differ.

Note

1 The course Social Class, Education and Pedagogy, offered at the University of Minnesota, is described as an examination of: 'Social, psychological, economic, political aspects of social class/poverty. Implications for education as social institution/classroom pedagogy. Social class in U.S., working-class literature for adults/children, labor histories, economic systems'. The curriculum was developed based on the work of Drs. Mark Vagle and Stephanie Jones, including the five principles detailed in this chapter, works of popular nonfiction and fiction that portray the working class and working poor in complex ways, and from an asset-based perspective. In addition, a workshop on the Other Side of Poverty in Schools is also available as professional development for teachers and administrators of schools. This workshop is similarly aimed at providing attendees with tools for thinking about poverty and working-class and working-poor students and families in complex and asset-based ways.

References

Carbado, D. W., Crenshaw, K. W., Mays, V. M. & Tomlinson, B. (2013) 'Intersectionality: Mapping the movements of a theory', *Du Bois Review: Social Science Research on Rac*, 10, 2, pp. 303–312.

Coffee, A. C., Stutelberg, E. B., Clements, C. H. & Lensmire, T. J. (2016) 'Control, waste, and danger in the lives of a white teacher and her students of color', in Hancock, S. & Warren, C. (eds.) *White Woman's Work: Examining the Intersectionality of Cultural Norms, Teaching, and Identity Formation in Urban Schools*, Charlotte, Information Age Publishing.

Darder, A. (2003) *The Critical Pedagogy Reader*, London, Psychology Press.

Donzelot, J. (1979) *The Policing of Families*, New York, Pantheon Books.

Ferguson, A. A. (2001) *Bad Boys: Public Schools in the Making of Black Masculinity*. Ann Arbor, University of Michigan Press.

Finn, P. J. (2009) *Literacy with an Attitude: Educating Working-Class Children in their Own Self-Interest*. Albany, State University of New York Press.

Foucault, M. (2008) *The Birth of Biopolitics: Lectures at the Collège de France*, trans. Burchell, G., Basingstoke, Palgrave MacMillan.

Freire, P. (1968/2000). *Pedagogy of the Oppressed*, London, Bloomsbury Publishing.

Henry, S. E. (2014). *Children's Bodies in Schools: Corporeal Performances of Social Class*, New York, Palgrave Macmillan.

Hurst, A. L. (2017) 'Have we been had? Why talking about the working-class vote for Trump hurts us', *LABORonline*. Available at www.lawcha.org/2017/06/20/talking-working-class-vote-trump-hurts-us/

Isenberg, N. (2017) *White Trash: The 400-Year Untold History of Class in America*, New York, Penguin.

Jones, S. & Vagle, M. D. (2013) 'Living contradictions and working for change: Toward a theory of social class-sensitive pedagogy', *Educational Researcher*, 42, 3, pp. 129–141.

Jupp, J. C., Berry, T. R. & Lensmire, T. J. (2016) 'Second-wave white teacher identity studies: A review of white teacher identity literatures from 2004 through 2014', *Review of Educational Research*, 86, 4, pp. 1151–1191.

Kliebard, H. M. (2004) *The Struggle for the American Curriculum, 1893–1958*, London, Psychology Press.

Ladson-Billings, G. (1995) 'Toward a theory of culturally relevant pedagogy', *American Educational Research Journal*, 32, 3, pp. 465–491.

Ladson-Billings, G. (2008) '"Yes, but how do we do it?": Practicing culturally relevant pedagogy', in Ayers, W., Ladson-Billings, G. & Michie, G. (eds.) *City Kids, City Schools: More Reports from the Front Row*, New York, New Press.

Ladson-Billings, G. (2014) 'Culturally relevant pedagogy 2.0: a.k.a. the remix', *Harvard Educational Review*, 84, 1, pp. 74–84.

Lensmire, T. J. (2014) 'White men's racial others', *Teachers College Record*, 116, 3, pp. 1–32.

Leonardo, Z. (2002) 'The souls of white folk: Critical pedagogy, whiteness studies, and globalization discourse', *Race Ethnicity and Education*, 5, 1, pp. 29–50.

Massey, D. (2005) *For Space*, London, Sage.

Meiners, E. R. (2002) 'Disengaging from the legacy of lady bountiful in teacher education classrooms', *Gender and Education*, 14, 1, pp. 85–94.

Mitchell, D. (2005) 'Working-class geographies', in Russo, J. & Linkon, S. L. (eds.) *New Working-Class Studies*, Ithaca, Cornell University Press.

Paris, D. (2012) 'Culturally sustaining pedagogy: A needed change in stance, terminology, and practice', *Educational Researcher*, 41, 3, pp. 93–97.

Roediger, D. R. (1999) *The Wages of Whiteness: Race and the Making of the American Working Class*, New York, Verso.

Rose, N. (1990) *Governing the Soul: The Shaping of the Private Self*, New York, Routledge.

Sasson, E. (2016) 'Blame Trump's victory on college-educated whites, not the working class', *New Republic*. Available at https://newrepublic.com/article/138754/blame-trumps-victory-college-educated-whites-not-working-class

Svec, M. & Thomas, P. L. (2016) 'The classroom crucible: Preparing teachers from privilege for students of poverty', in Hurst, A. & Nenga, S. (eds.) *Working in Class: Recognizing How Social Class Shapes Our Academic Work*, Lanham, Rowman and Littlefield.

Thandeka (2007) *Learning to Be White: Money, Race, and God in America*, New York: Continuum.

Thomas, E. (1997) 'Developing a culture-sensitive pedagogy: Tackling a problem of melding "global culture" within existing cultural contexts', *International Journal of Educational Development*, 17, 1, pp.13–26.

Vagle, M. D. & Jones, S. (2012) 'The precarious nature of social class sensitivity in literacy: A social, autobiographic, and pedagogical project', *Curriculum Inquiry*, 42, 3, pp. 318–339.

Vance, J. D. (2016) *Hillbilly Elegy: A Memoir of a Family and Culture in Crisis*, New York, Harper Collins.

Watkins, W. H. (2001) *The White Architects of Black Education: Ideology and Power in America, 1865–1954*, New York, Teachers College Press.

7

The pedagogy of class

Teaching working-class life and culture in the academy

Lisa A. Kirby

In 'Promises to keep: Working-class students and higher education', a chapter from Michael Zweig's edited collection *What's Class Got to Do With It?: American Society in the Twenty-First Century*, Michelle, M. Tokarczyk makes the point that

> higher education not only promises a chance for upward mobility. It also promises a fuller understanding of and interaction with one's self, community, and society. These are the promises we've made that we must keep, that we can keep, if only we acknowledge to whom we've made the promises.
>
> *(2004, 167)*

Renny Christopher writes in a similar manner in her chapter 'New working-class studies in higher education' from John Russo and Sherry Lee Linkon's 2005 *New Working-Class Studies*. Christopher points out that working-class studies requires a revision of both institutional narratives and classroom practices:

> we need to continue to transform the content of the curriculum by introducing a focus on the history, culture, and cultural productions of the working class. By so doing, we can transform higher education into something that works for, instead of against, the working class.
>
> *(2005, 220)*

These perspectives make clear the importance of making a space for the working class both in theory and practice.

Christopher and Tokarczyk offer a call to action: the academy can no longer marginalize working-class culture and experience and instead must find ways to place the working class at the center, both for the benefit of the institution and its students. Now, more than a decade after these chapters were published, it is necessary to consider the evolution of working-class studies and how the needs of working-class students are being met (or, perhaps, not met) in higher education. Has working-class studies, in fact, transformed the curriculum? Does higher education now work for, rather than against, the working class? Have we, as educators, kept our promises? This chapter, with an emphasis on practical pedagogical strategies and assignments, will explore the current state of working-class studies, its evolution in both content and pedagogy, and the promise it holds for transforming both the academy and students.

The evolution of working-class studies

In *What We Hold In Common: An Introduction to Working-Class Studies*, Janet Zandy issues an invitation: 'let us imagine what it would be like if the history and culture of working-class people were at the center of educational practices' (2001, xiii). How would our educational system differ if working-class life and culture were the norm rather than the exception, if the voices of the working class were at the center rather than on the margins? How would students benefit from a greater focus on social class, and how might this emphasis help change not only the academy but society in general? These are some of the questions that emerge as one considers the importance of teaching working-class studies. Providing the opportunity for our students to develop a class consciousness will allow them to more fully consider the complexities of social class, their own identities, and how these factors impact society. For working-class students, particularly, it will also provide them with context and opportunities for transformative education.

Working-class studies has existed for almost 25 years now, yet there is still much work that remains to be done, as social class is often missing from many conversations in higher education. It is interesting that in the trinity of race, class, and gender so often acclaimed in the academy, socioeconomic status is often an invisible and ignored entity. It is not unusual to see many college courses that focus on race and gender, yet social class is an issue that is rarely discussed. This is perhaps because Americans are so accustomed to thinking that we live in a 'classless' society or a society that supports class mobility through hard work and education. As Nancy Isenberg suggests, 'I think Americans like to believe that they support the idea of equality. We think that equality is something that can be earned' (2016). In a country where the American Dream reigns supreme, many Americans believe that through hard work, anything is achievable. The very notion of a working class, then, is often counter to this narrative of American success and exceptionalism.

In the academy, specifically, working-class experience has rarely been at the center of pedagogy and scholarship. This could be due, in part, to the fact that social class is often an 'invisible' part of identity, but it is more likely a result of the academy's privileging of certain types of experience. As Lawrence Hanley points out,

> revolutions in syllabi and curricula can come and go, as they have for the past century, so long as the University continues to reproduce class structures and relations by reproducing cultural capital-the cultural taste, languages, and knowledges that serve to distinguish the proper and the 'high' from the vulgar and the 'low'.
>
> *(2003, 28)*

While there have certainly been movements to broaden definitions of history, literature, and so forth, the fact remains that part of the reason working-class studies emerged was 'out of a frustration with contemporary multiculturalism's apparent silence on matters of class' (Hanley 2003, 28). For a long time, social class was not a consideration when discussing identity, even among those who sought to broaden definitions of diversity.

Perhaps another reason social class has been largely ignored is due to the fact that it was often not part of the conversation in identity politics. As Courtney B. Tablante and Susan T. Fiske point out, 'discussing social class is uncomfortable, even taboo in many circles. While administrators may try to augment socioeconomic diversity, students often try to pretend that campuses are classless' (2015, 184). In some ways, too, social class can be masked when at university in ways not previously possible in students' own communities. Going to college reflects a new start, away from home and family, and so an individual's social class may not be as apparent. Tablante and Fiske continue,

> at the same time that many colleges and universities are making a concerted effort to recruit students from varied socioeconomic backgrounds, social class topics are rarely reflected in psychology courses or in student groups. Even in social psychology, a field that excessively studies diversity, the vast majority of the traditional research has focused on race and gender. *(184)*

While Tablante and Fiske are discussing the field of psychology specifically, this also appears to be the case in many disciplines. Social class is often marginalized and rarely regarded.

My own experience in working-class studies began in 1996 as an undergraduate English major at Texas Christian University, enrolled in Gary Tate's inaugural Working-Class Literature course. When I signed up for Dr. Tate's class, I had little sense of what Working-Class Literature was—not necessarily surprising since social class has seldom been part of the conversation in the academy. As a student from a working-class background at a wealthy, privileged institution, this course opened up a new world for me. While I had loved much of the literature I had read in previous courses, in Dr. Tate's class, I read works by people who felt familiar to me, whose stories and voices were not unlike those of my own family. For the first time in my life, I began to think about my own social class and how it had impacted my decisions, education, and view of the world.

Undoubtedly, in the years since I took Dr. Tate's class, the discussion and consideration of social class has become less taboo than it once was. For example, many colleges and universities now use socioeconomic status as a factor when determining admission and financial aid. A report from the Jack Kent Cooke Foundation states, 'to date, eight states have instituted *new admissions preferences* for low-income and working-class students', considering factors that 'might put students at an academic disadvantage' such as 'concentrated neighborhood poverty' and being a 'first generation college goer' (Giancola and Kahlenberg 2016, 31). Whereas social class has long been masked and many students have been reluctant to admit their working-class status, using socioeconomic status as part of the admission criteria certainly has its advantages because 'such an approach would recognize that to overcome the burdens of poverty and nonetheless perform at a high level is itself an indicator of ability and perseverance' (Giancola and Kahlenberg 2016, 1). This recognizes that working-class and first-generation college students often have obstacles to overcome in addition to simply striving for academic success. In a 2014 speech, Michelle Obama, herself a first-generation college student, highlighted her own experiences as a 'hardworking, ambitious' high school student who lacked the resources she needed. That focus was meant as an attempt by the Obama administration to 'nudge along [. . .] the efforts of public and private universities to better recruit and graduate low-income, first-generation students' (Stratford 2013). These new admissions criteria are an important step in broadening higher education's definition of diversity and allowing more space for considerations of social class, and they speak to progress made in the last 10–15 years.

In addition to new admissions criteria, many scholars and teachers have made important strides in ending the marginalization of working-class students and focusing on issues of social class in both scholarship and pedagogy. Whether looking at seminal works—such as Janet Zandy's *What We Hold In Common* (2001), Alan Shepard, John McMillan, and Gary Tate's *Coming to*

Class: Pedagogy and the Social Class of Teachers (1998), Sherry Lee Linkon's *Teaching Working Class* (1999), and John Russo and Linkon's *New Working-Class Studies* (2005)—or more contemporary works—such as Allison L. Hurst and Sandi Kawecka Nenga's *Working in Class: Recognizing How Social Class Shapes Our Academic Work* (2016) and Dennis Deslippe, Eric Fure-Slocum, and John W. McKerley's *Civic Labors: Scholar Activism and Working-Class Studies* (2016)—it is clear working-class studies is evolving. It has emerged as an important inter-discipline that provides the opportunity to start new conversations about working-class life and culture.

Introducing working-class studies

Introducing working-class studies to students often opens with underlining the complexities of the field. To begin, it is important to explore the very phrase 'working class', a term that resists easy definition. As scholar Ira Shor states, the definition of working class is both 'elusive and common sense [...] and there is a fine line between the two' (Shor 2000). Here, Shor touches upon one of the central problems that is familiar to those in this field of study: how do we define the working class? The notion of what constitutes 'working class' has become a difficult idea to solidify. It varies according to each individual's work, economic status, education, family background, and a host of other factors. It is equally important to realize that social class extends beyond just economics. Coles and Zandy contend, 'working-class identity is, of course, much more than a matter of one's economic position; it is also a lived experience, a set of relationships, expectations, legacies, and entitlements (or the lack of them)' (2007, xx). As students begin to explore the working class, it is important they realize the complexity of working-class life and experience and that working-class studies is

> marked by its roots in ordinary people's experiences of particular places and historical moments [and ...] that the working class is not only a class that works—that produces goods and services; it is also a class that produces culture.
>
> *(Coles and Zandy 2007, xxiii)*

Moving beyond merely an economic narrative is one of the first steps in helping students consider the complexities of class.

Beyond these basic questions of definition, another complexity of teaching working-class studies is that this discipline often challenges ideas students have long been taught. When studying the working class, the idea of upward mobility and the American Dream are challenged by the fact that families often remain in the working class for generations. At the very heart of working-class existence is power or, perhaps more accurately, a lack of it. This demographic, 'because of its relative lack of economic and political power, is frequently out of work, as when decisions made in boardrooms result in the closing of a factory or the offshoring of a work center' (Coles and Zandy 2007, xxii). Yet, as a group, they often gain more power through 'solidarity' and group identity (Coles and Zandy 2007, xxii).

These are often difficult concepts for students to grasp because they have been taught to accept the notion of upward mobility and the American Dream; in fact, for many of them, it is why they are pursuing higher education. When asked to challenge the American Dream, many students are uncomfortable, and the discussions are often heated. Some students experience discomfort in critiquing an ideal that is so central to the American psyche, because, as Laura Hapke points out, a good number of working-class texts seek to 'challenge rather than celebrate upward mobility' and this idea of a shared notion of success is what most students have been taught to give credence to in capitalistic society (1995, 146). While Hapke speaks from the space of literary studies, the same is true of many disciplines. Providing students the opportunity to experience working-class culture, whether in the form of literature, historical documents, case studies, or even experiential or service learning, will allow for interrogation of class structures and a greater sense of class consciousness.

In the same vein, working-class studies, in its attempt to place value on working-class experience, reverses the paradigm of upward mobility in that it makes clear there is worth in working-class existence. As Hapke continues,

> perhaps the task of assigning fictive texts that pay compassionate attention to the factory worker ... involves too drastic a shift from the aesthetic to the humanistic or a relocation of the aesthetic in what Janet Zandy aptly terms the 'collective sensibility'.
>
> *(1995, 144)*

Working-class writings, in particular, often expose readers to ideas and situations that are almost uncomfortably realistic and personal. This can create discomfort both for students in the working class and those who are not. While reading these texts can provide invaluable insight into the working life, many non-working-class students often struggle to understand and appreciate the complexity of working-class culture. Some students of other classes cannot 'connect' with these works since the experiences are often so foreign to them. Others have misconceptions about working-class life, wondering why the working class 'chooses' to live the way they do. However, these points can lead to interesting discussions about working-class experience.

For students who themselves come from a working-class background, it can be difficult to read texts that portray their experience in such a realistic way. Even the use of personal experience can cause difficulties.

> [A]lthough the personal narratives of working-class students open up the site of conflict and allow the students to negotiate the borders between home, work, and classroom, this negotiation most often carries the expectation for the students to learn the codes of the institution and the language and way of thinking of particular disciplines.
>
> *(Marinara 1997, 4)*

Many working-class students may instead wish to mask their lives in an attempt to assimilate. Though their experiences might produce valuable writings and projects, they may not wish to be alienated or distinguished due to their socioeconomic status. Zandy points out that 'a working-class identity is an ambiguous gift. To develop that identity, to recognize its potential in a society where the working class is denied its own name, is to claim a responsibility that goes beyond the individual self' (1995a, 1). Many working-class students, consequently, are reluctant to express this identity and perhaps uncomfortable laying claim to such group identification in a classroom setting.

As such, working-class studies presents ideas and content that may dismantle many students' notions of the academy and culture. As Christopher points out, among many working-class studies scholars, there is a

> perception that the academic world is at best indifferent and at worst openly hostile to first-generation students, and that it demands that students from the working class deny their past, dissociate themselves from their families, and remake themselves in its own image in order to 'earn' a place within it.
>
> *(2005, 216)*

Part of what makes working-class studies so essential is that it disrupts these narratives and suggests that working-class students should embrace their identities and see the value in their experiences.

The working-class student

In these challenges to notions of both upward mobility and traditional 'academic' values, a tension also becomes apparent when we look at the place of the working-class student or first-generation college student in the academy. And perhaps nowhere is working-class studies more important than with this demographic. As Ira Shor points out in 'The working class goes to college', 'school [grades K–12] recreates a stratified society by socializing each new generation into its place in the established order' (1987, 2). Working-class students, in particular, are often at a disadvantage as they exist in a hierarchical system that strives to keep them in certain positions in the social order. Because of this power structure, working-class students are sometimes labeled in ways that are detrimental to their academic success, merely because they possess alternative discourses. Further, as Patrick J. Finn contends in *Literacy with an Attitude: Educating Working-Class Children in Their Own Self-Interest*, 'political, social, and economic forces have brought us to a place where the working class (and to a surprising degree, the middle class) gets domesticating education and functional literacy, and the rich get empowering education and powerful literacy' (1999, x). It seems that certain expectations are constructed for working-class students and their place in society that are perpetuated by educational structures. While Shor and Finn are addressing these specific instances of conflict in grades K–12, many of these issues become magnified as students reach university.

Many working-class or first-generation college students face difficulties as they make the transition into the academy. To begin, often, 'working-class students' needs are unmet because their presence in colleges and universities is largely ignored' (Tokarczyk 2004, 162). Many faculty and staff in higher education 'unconsciously embrace the American myth that everyone is middle class, that anyone who tries can succeed, and thus may be reluctant to acknowledge the impact of working-class status' (Tokarczyk 2004, 165). Moreover, the language and culture of the academy is difficult for many students, yet those of the middle and upper classes tend to learn them more quickly because they are already accustomed to the codes and habits necessary for achievement. By contrast, due to home environments, peer groups, and work settings, working-class students have often not been acclimated to these codes. Jane Nagle points out that these variances are due to many working-class students being 'influenced by the fact that their home literacy practices often reflected the parents' lack of success in accessing school literacy' (1999, 175). As such, a vicious cycle begins to emerge between generations of the working class in their attainment of the 'master' discourse and success in the academy. These students meet with difficulties in adjusting to the academic environment because of a disjuncture between their home, work, and school lives, as well as having to balance these different worlds. There are, then, many obstacles that working-class students encounter: 'some barriers are academic, involving college preparedness, many are institutional, resulting from policies and attitudes that are unfriendly to working-class students' (Tokarczyk 2004, 161). Whatever the challenge, the structure and culture of the academy is often counter to the success of these students.

Often, negotiating these borders creates even more difficulties, in part because students are asked to share their working-class experience in a language and environment very different from their home, work, and social communities. Working-class students sometimes have difficulty in aligning their personal and academic voices, because they are making use of unfamiliar discourse. As Lawrence MacKenzie asserts, many working-class students are the first in their families to attend college, and, as such, 'first-generation college attenders often start from a family and community base that gives them doubtful, neutral, or mixed messages with regard to college study and their chances of success in it' (1998, 96). Further, many working-class students feel a severe schism once they attend college. They feel torn between two worlds and an outsider in both. As Barbara Jensen suggests in *Reading Classes: On Culture and Classism in America*, working-class students often report feelings of 'anomie, imposter syndrome, and survivor's guilt' (2012, 162). The feeling of 'placelessness', the 'feeling that one has fooled people to be successful coupled with the fear that one "will be found out"' as well as worries about why they have succeeded where other friends and family members may have failed are common among working-class students and causes for academic difficulty (Jensen 2012, 162, 163). These can also lead to psychological problems, including 'chronic anxiety and fear' and 'a drop in self-esteem', that can be overwhelming (Jensen 2012, 165).

Because of these tensions, the emphasis on working-class studies in the academy is both complicated and important, not only for the scholarly opportunities but also for the ways in which this study can benefit working-class and first-generation college students. As those at the former Youngstown Center for Working-Class Studies made clear, 'class shapes the lives of individuals as well as the policies of our society. For individuals, class affects not only whether [one goes] to college, but also where [one goes] and how well prepared [one is] to succeed' ('What Is' n.d.). Identifying working-class students comes with its own complexities; however, many institutions use first-generation college student status as an indicator. According to the Department of Education, students with parents who lack any education beyond high school account for about 36 percent of all enrollment at post-secondary institutions, and many of those students are concentrated at two-year institutions (Schmidt 2010). These statistics show that we need to consider not just the financial complexities that attending college may have on these students, but the social and academic challenges as well. These are students who may work, have families, face transportation issues, and experience a variety of other obstacles to their education. It is important for institutions to recognize the demands and find ways to assist these students, and many universities are already making strides. The University of Illinois Urbana-Champaign, for example, recognizes that first-generation college students may have unique needs. The university's counseling center has set aside specific resources and recommendations for these students and their families (University of Illinois Urbana-Champaign 2007).

As faculty members, it also our responsibility to help these students steer through often unfamiliar waters. Faculty members can serve as important guides to academic culture. Jonathan Tyler Baker, a graduate student and first-generation college student, writes about his experience and the 'cultural shock' he experienced when moving from his Rust Belt town to university. He writes of how 'faculty members truly have an awesome responsibility. My professors gave me hope that a child from nowhere could go somewhere—and never have to leave his roots in doing so' (Baker 2017). I know I personally experienced this culture shock and was lucky to have professors to offer me guidance. I try to do the same for my own students today. I make sure to help my students learn more about on-campus resources like the writing center and counseling services. I spend time in my classes talking about 'college success' strategies, such as how to stay organized, read critically, and manage time effectively. I also share my own experiences as a working-class, first-generation college student with my own students, so they know they are not alone. When we make known and place value on working-class experience in the classroom, it reiterates the importance of this culture and can potentially help working-class students make a smoother transition into academic culture. Affording an opportunity for students, faculty, and administrators to consider and discuss class issues more fully can also provide opportunities to help our students make this move more successfully.

Students at many institutions seem to be taking the lead in these conversations. According to Libby Sander in *The Chronicle of Higher Education*, 'spurred by growing income disparities, the aftereffects of the recession, and debates over admissions policies that consider students' ability to pay, students on many campuses are trying to ignite frank—and sometimes uncomfortable—conversations about class' (2013). For instance, at my institution, Collin College, a two-year college in Texas, students approached me about starting a student organization to raise awareness about the working class. This student group has now been in existence for almost three years. As another example, at the University of Virginia, students are asking for financial literacy seminars, workshops, and conversations about class: 'many students are pushing their administrations for more support—stepped-up recruitment, more-egalitarian admissions policies, mentoring networks, resource guides—to help underprivileged students thrive' (Sander 2013). Moreover, many administrators are beginning to see the benefits of considering socioeconomic status: many are starting to 'make a greater effort to reach students from working-class and rural families. One of the goals is to bring more ideological diversity to campuses' (Mangan 2017). As educators, it is imperative to help these students navigate the academy, and a focus on the working class is one way to do this.

Integrating working-class studies

While it is clear that integrating working-class studies into the curriculum has benefits both in the academy and more broadly, many teachers are faced with the challenge of how to bring in this focus with an already full syllabus. There are a number of ways faculty can emphasize the working class. For those who wish to dig deep into the field, there are ways to focus entire courses on working-class studies while still meeting student learning outcomes. A quick survey of the field shows courses titled 'Working-Class Literature', 'Work in America', 'Sweatshop USA', 'American Work: A Narrative History', 'Class at Work in America', and 'Rhetorics of Social Class', to name just a few ('Working-class studies course syllabi'). In courses like these, working-class studies is front and center as teachers urge students to consider literature, history, sociology, and popular culture through the lens of social class. For instance, in my first-year composition courses, I have focused the curriculum on social class, and I provide students opportunities to explore issues of class and work while also developing their writing and rhetorical skills. Students engage with a variety of readings and films that help them consider work and class issues more fully. Whether reading about the conditions in which Amazon warehouse workers must toil, the rise of the 'gig' economy and Uber, or watching an episode of Morgan Spurlock's documentary series *30 Days* (2005–2008), that explores the viability of living on minimum wage, there are many ways students can begin to think about social class in new ways that they may encounter on a daily basis. They also write a number of essays about social class issues, including personal narratives, research-based arguments, and worker profiles. This approach has provided students the opportunity to polish their writing and rhetorical skills and to do so while exploring important social class issues and even their own family and class histories.

There are also ways to integrate social class into a course without it being the entire focus. Having students discuss working-class issues, write essays about social class or work, or consider sources through the lens of social class are just a few ways class studies can be brought into a course. For example, in my American literature survey course, I often teach *The Great Gatsby* (1925), certainly one of the most assigned novels in American literature. While we discuss those most common themes and symbols in the novel, such as the green light, the valley of ashes, and the setting of the 1920s, I spend a good deal of time discussing the working-class characters and how the novel interrogates and even indicts the American Dream. This exercise allows students to re-envision a text many are already familiar with in a way that privileges a focus on social class. The hope is that this emphasis on social class becomes an organic part of students' critical thinking and helps them become more aware of social class issues, both in the classroom and beyond.

While there are many approaches to teaching working-class studies, perhaps one of the most useful is to integrate the voices of actual working-class people through primary sources. Jane Van Galen, a professor of teacher education, begins her classes by assigning a variety of '"first person" readings [that] introduce [... the students] to the mothers, fathers, sons and daughters, teachers, physical spaces, dreams, and disappointments of poor and working-class people' (2010, 259). In her teacher education classes, Van Galen finds these '"first person" readings powerfully enable students to reframe what they'd assumed were their own very personal experiences as common experiences of class, even as they broaden their intellectual understanding of inequities in schools via the lived experiences of others' (2010, 259).

Melody M. Miyamoto Walters (2018), a professor of history, makes similar moves in her courses in American history by using primary sources to promote critical thinking. In her introductory course, Miyamoto Walters integrates drawings and journals from the girls working in the Lowell Mills to show the transition from family farms to a commercial economy, and slave narratives, such as *The Narrative of the Life of Frederick Douglass* (1843), to demonstrate the tensions between slavery and freedom from the varying perspectives of those who had freedom and those who did not. In American History II, Miyamoto Walters also helps students navigate class tensions and differences through the use of Hull House images and excerpts from Upton Sinclair's *The Jungle* (1900) and Andrew Carnegie's *The Gospel of Wealth* (1900). Throughout both courses, Miyamoto Walters seeks to help students work through class tensions and complexities in American history by asking them to think critically about primary sources through the lens of social class.

Grounding this critical thinking in real-world resources and experiences is important in integrating working-class studies, and this is exactly what Cathleen Brooks, a professor of Sociology, does with her students. Brooks has students choose a career and answer questions about it, such as projected growth, mean and median salaries, and job concentration, by using the Bureau of Labor Statistics website. She then has students 'talk about whether the job has prestige and power and how the salary (or hourly wage) might change ... class status', depending on geographic location, real estate prices, dependents, and so forth (2018). Brooks also begins class 'by asking students what they think of [words like] "poor" or "low-income neighborhood" and considering what those terms make them envision, how they make them feel, and who they might apply to' (2018). Brooks uses this exercise to 'represent the sociological concept of symbolic interaction: how do we learn the meaning of words and symbols' (Brooks 2018). Exploring and interrogating these concepts allows students to better understand the complexities of social class, meaning, and society.

Exploring working-class culture also provides working-class and first-generation college students an opportunity to explore their own family history and experience, and first-person narratives are a valuable way to allow these voices to be heard. Many faculty do this in their classes and integrate assignments that provide opportunities for working-class experience to be voiced. For instance, Martha Marinara (1997), who teaches composition, points out the importance of first-person narratives and how they can empower working-class student voices in her courses. Van Galen, a professor of teacher education, also asks students to write their own 'first-person narrative ... in which they recount a significant experience in school in which they sensed what they now recognize as class differences' (2010, 264). By putting these students' experiences at the center, Van Galen offers them the opportunity to 'write of the many obstacles they've faced, [while] they also craft narratives of agency and tenacity' (265). The assignment also allows these future teachers to 'interrogate the distinctive but unnamed social space within a trajectory of upward mobility that they occupy as college students and reflect on how that journey will impact their work as teachers' (255). In short, teaching working-class studies presents significant pedagogical moments that can ultimately help students, particularly working-class students, better navigate the academy and understand the world around them.

It is important to realize that teaching working-class studies is about both content and pedagogy. While making a place for working-class writers, historical events, and perspectives is important in terms of readings and assignments, it is also essential to provide a space where working-class students can feel comfortable and acclimate to academic conventions that may be unfamiliar. For many working-class students, critical thinking, collaboration, and open classroom discussion may be foreign concepts, since many working-class students have been taught to focus on 'minding the authority and denying much of their own world' (Schuster 2008, 165). As a result, many of their K–12 experiences 'have taught them to focus on the grade and the degree rather than on learning and individual development' (Schuster 2008, 164). However, many faculty are seeking to disrupt this narrative by placing at center not only working-class content but working-class students' experiences. Leslie A. Schuster, who teaches history, 'seeks to ground … the process and subject of the course in the student's own experiences, explicitly recognizing and valuing their sensibilities and knowledge, and creating an environment devoted to collaboration and discussion' (2008, 166). She does this in her introductory historical methods course by including a 'low-stakes' assignment early in the semester that requires both mandatory revisions and peer feedback (171). Likewise, Schuster's revision of her course also 'puts working people, through subjects like immigration and the 1929 depression, at the center' (169).

Conclusion

While there are certainly many ways to integrate social class into the classroom, no matter how a teacher chooses to do so, it is important that the relevance of this focus be at the center of the pedagogy, and it seems the discussion of social class could not be timelier. Though there is now evidence the working class did not vote for President Trump in the numbers previously thought (Carnes and Lupu 2017), what is true is that the working class is at the center of conversations that were not previously taking place. This, along with the popularity of such bestsellers as Nancy Isenberg's *White Trash: The 400-Year Untold Story of Class in America* (2017) and J. D. Vance's *Hillbilly Elegy: A Memoir of a Family and Culture in Crisis* (2016), make clear that social class is something Americans are discussing much more regularly. Moreover, for millennials in particular, these conversations need to take place. With concerns about high student loan debt and diminishing career opportunities, 'millennials in the US see themselves as less middle class and more working class than any other generation since records began three decades ago' (Malik, Barr, and Holpuch 2016). The economy and the world are changing for our students in complicated ways, and teaching social class allows them to interrogate and explore these complexities.

Taking all this into account, working-class studies, therefore, is an endeavor that requires a reconsideration of traditional notions of culture, innovative new pedagogical strategies, and often difficult questioning of our own societal and aesthetic values. Essentially, working-class studies encourages a larger worldview and places value on diverse experiences and, as such, needs to be an integral part of the classroom. There are many ways scholars and teachers can integrate class studies into their curricula, in both large and small ways, as a means for those voices to no longer be silenced.

Providing an opportunity for these voices to be heard is perhaps the most important part of teaching working-class studies. As Zandy makes clear, 'according to the book of success, a working-class identity is intended for disposal' (1995b, 1). Teaching working-class studies disallows the academy and society to 'dispose' of these identities and texts. Moreover, the study of the working class allows the opportunity to redefine and re-envision our notions of what constitutes this 'book of success' and how we might reconstruct our traditional notions of society, culture, and history in order to give voice and significance to the working class and their culture.

To conclude, it is important to reconsider the opening quote from Zandy: 'let us imagine what it would be like if the history and culture of working-class people were at the center of educational practices'. While working-class culture may not yet be at the center of the academy, progress has certainly been made in the years since Christopher and Tokarczyk's articles were written. Many institutions are now considering socioeconomic and first-generation college student status in admissions and working to provide these students with resources to help them acclimate to academic life. Working-class studies is now an important part of many courses and disciplines, not to mention the scholarship that has been produced in the field. However, with all this progress, there is still important work to be done, and the stakes are high, not just for the working class but for all of us. If the working class were at the center rather than on the margins, the academy would be a more accepting, diverse, and rich place. Providing students the opportunity to explore working-class studies allows them to understand that there is more than one version of American literature, history, and culture, so that they can subsequently develop both a greater understanding of and appreciation for the diversity of American experience. For working-class students, specifically, working-class studies can prove the academy is, in fact, working 'for' them by making clear their voices are heard and that promises can be kept.

References

Baker, J. T. (2017) 'Hope and care can bridge the gap', *The Chronicle of Higher Education*, February 26.

Brooks, C. (2018) E-mail interview with Cathleen Brooks, January 4, 2018.

Carnegie, A. (1900) *The Gospel of Wealth and other Timely Essays*, New York, Century Co.

Carnes, N. and Lupu, N. (2017) 'It's time to bust the myth: Most Trump voters were not working class', *The Washington Post*, June 5.

Christopher, R. (2005) 'New working-class studies in higher education', in Russo, J. and Linkon, S. L. (eds.) *New Working-Class Studies*, Ithaca, Cornell University Press.

Coles, N. and Zandy, J. (eds.) (2007) *American Working-Class Literature: An Anthology*, New York, Oxford University Press.

Deslippe, D., Fure-Slocum, E. and McKerley, J. W. (2016) *Civic Labors: Scholar Activism and Working-Class Studies*, Champaign, University of Illinois Press.

Douglass, F. (1843) *The Narrative of the Life of Frederick Douglass*, Garden City, NY, Dolphin.

Finn, P. J. (1999) *Literacy with an Attitude: Educating Working-Class Children in Their Own Self-Interest*, Albany, State University of New York Press.

Fitzgerald, F. Scott (1925) *The Great Gatsby*. New York: C. Scribner's Sons.

Giancola, J. and Kahlenberg, R. D. (2016) *True Merit: Ensuring Our Brightest Students Have Access to Our Best Colleges and Universities*, Jack Kent Cooke Foundation.

Hanley, L. (2003). 'Working-class cultural studies in the university', *Radical Teacher*, 68, pp. 26–31.

Hapke, L. (1995) 'A wealth of possibilities: Workers, texts, and reforming the English Department', *Women's Studies Quarterly*, 23, 1/2, pp. 142–154.

Hurst, A. and Nenga, S. K. (eds.) (2016) *Working in Class: Recognizing How Social Class Shapes Our Academic Work*, Lanham, Rowman and Littlefield.

Isenberg, N. (2016) Interview. *All things considered*. NPR, July 7, 5:33.

Isenberg, N. (2017) *White Trash: The 400-Year Untold History of Class in America*, New York, Penguin.

Jensen, B. (2012) *Reading Classes: On Culture and Classism in America*, Ithaca, Cornell University Press.

Linkon, S. L. (ed.) (1999) *Teaching Working Class*, Amherst, University of Massachusetts Press.

MacKenzie, L. (1998) 'A pedagogy of respect: Teaching as an ally of working-class college students', in Shepard, A., McMillan, J. and Tate, G. (eds.) *Coming to Class: Pedagogy and the Social Class of Teachers*, Portsmouth, Boynton/Cook.

Malik, S., Barr, C. and Holpuch, A. (2016) 'US millennials feel more working class than any other generation', *The Guardian*, March 15.

Mangan, K. (2017) 'Cultural divide', *The Chronicle of Higher Education*, February 26.

Marinara, M. (1997) 'When working-class students "do" the academy: How we negotiate with alternative literacies', *Journal of Basic Writing*, 16, 2, pp. 3–16.

Miyamoto Walters, M. M. (2018). E-mail interview with Melody M. Miyamoto-Walters, January 3, 2018.

Nagle, J. P. (1999) 'Histories of success and failure: Working class students' literacy experiences', *Journal of Adolescent and Adult Literacy*, 43, 2, pp. 172–185.

Russo, J. and Linkon, S. L. (eds.) (2005) *New Working-Class Studies*, Ithaca, Cornell University Press.

Sander, L. (2013) 'Students try to break taboo about social class on campus', *The Chronicle of Higher Education*, May 13.

Schmidt, P. (2010) 'In push for diversity, colleges pay attention to socioeconomic class', *Chronicle of Higher Education*, 57, 5, pp. B5–B7.

Schuster, L. A. (2008) 'Working-class students and historical inquiry: Transforming learning in the classroom', *The History Teacher*, 41, 2, pp. 163–178.

Shepard, A., McMillan, J. and Tate, G. (eds.) (1998) *Coming to Class: Pedagogy and the Social Class of Teachers*, Portsmouth, Boynton/Cook.

Shor, I. (1987) 'The working class goes to college', in *Critical Teaching and Everyday Life*, Chicago, University of Chicago Press.

Shor, I. (2000) Telephone interview, March 29.

Sinclair, U. (1900) *The Jungle*, New York, Double Day, Page.

Stratford, M. (2013) 'The Obamas' new focus', *Inside Higher Ed*, November 13.

Tablante, C. B. and Fiske, S. T. (2015) 'Teaching social class', *Teaching of Psychology*, 42, 2, pp. 184–190.

Tokarczyk, M. M. (2004) 'Promises to keep: Working class students and higher education', in Zweig, M. (ed.) *What's Class Got to Do With It? American Society in the Twenty-First Century*, Ithaca, Cornell University Press.

University of Illinois Urbana-Champaign (2014) 'First-generation college students', Counseling Center, viewed August 8, 2017, https://counselingcenter.illinois.edu/brochures/first-generation-college-students

Van Galen, J. A. (2010) 'Class, identity, and teacher education', *The Urban Review*, 42, 2, pp. 253–270.

Vance, J. D. (2016) *Hillbilly Elegy: A Memoir of a Family and Culture in Crisis*, New York, Harper.

'What is working-class studies?' (n.d.) Center for Working-Class Studies, Youngstown State University.

'Working-class studies course syllabi' (n.d.) Center for Working-Class Studies, Youngstown State University.

Zandy, J. (1995a) 'Editorial', *Women's Studies Quarterly*, 23, pp. 3–6.

Zandy, J. (ed.) (1995b) 'Introduction', in *Liberating Memory: Our Work and Our Working-Class Consciousness*, New Brunswick, Rutgers University Press.

Zandy, J. (ed.) (2001) *What We Hold In Common: An Introduction to Working-Class Studies*, New York, Feminist Press.

30 Days (2005–2008) Actor/producer M. Spurlock [Television series].

8

Being working class in the English classroom

Diane Reay

Introduction

As an English, working-class professor who has worked for the last 14 years as a professor at one of England's most elite universities, I was struck by an assertion made by one of the respondents in the Great British Class Survey (Savage 2015). A male professor commented that he would rather think of people for their inherent value rather than their class. But the problem is that the question of an individual's inherent value can never be disentangled from their class position in England. This differential valuing of the upper, middle and working classes not only infuses the educational system – it has shaped its structure, influenced its practices, and dictated the very different relationships different social classes have to the system since the inception of state education in 1870. In order to understand how this situation has persisted over the past 150 years, we need to examine the social and political values and motivations of our political elites. From the very beginning, the educational system was designed to provide an inferior education for the working classes, producing different educational opportunities appropriate to one's station in life. The upper and middle classes wanted to prevent any challenge to their own privileged positions, 'to inure them [the working classes] to habits of obedience' (Johnson 1976, 45).

Adam Smith epitomized this English middle- and upper-class viewpoint regarding working-class education in *The Wealth of Nations* when he argued that 'an instructed and intelligent people besides are always more decent and orderly than an ignorant one ... less apt to be misled into any wanton or unnecessary opposition to the measures of the government' (1785, 305). It is unsurprising, then, that despite an expectation that the working classes should have the same relationship to state education as the middle classes, they do not. As Andy Green (1990) shows, the history of English working-class education has been one of control and cultural domination. It would be hard to portray working-class experiences in education as generally fulfilling, as about 'bettering oneself' in the classic middle-class mode. The working-class experience of education has traditionally been one of educational failure, not success. Central to working-class relationships to English state schooling is that it is not their educational system. The system does not belong to them in the ways it does to the middle classes, and they have little sense of belonging within it. As Smith's quote makes clear, English education has always been about control and containment of the working classes, not their empowerment and emancipation.

As a consequence, aspects of education often appear pointless and irrelevant to working-class students, and there is extensive research documenting, in particular, white working-class boys' sense of futility in relation to official school-based learning (Willis 1977; Stahl 2015). In place of middle-class enthusiasm for school-based learning, there is more often a pragmatism and strong remnants of historically rooted attitudes to education that recognize at an important level that the educational system is not theirs, does not work in their interests, and considers them and their cultural knowledge as inferior.

This denigration of working-class knowledge has a long history that dates from the establishment of state schooling through to the present. There was a brief hiatus after the Second World War when there was a taste for the working classes and a collective sense of gratitude for the enormous contribution they had made to the war effort (Todd 2014). But it did not last long. Micky Flanagan, an English Comedian, in his Radio 4 programme on social class, discussed with his old school friends his experiences of being an East End working-class comprehensive school pupil in the 1970s. He joked that they had all left school with nothing, adding that he got to make an ashtray in the second year and then a bottle opener in the third year. Micky and his friends reminisced about Barry Hutton, who was the most ambitious kid in the class, because he wanted to be a van driver. Flanagan told how the whole class had erupted in laughter at Barry the dreamer, because no one in their school ever got to drive a van. What they did get to do was carry the stuff from the market to the van, but never actually drive the van. He concluded that for him and his friends, school and educational qualifications just seemed totally pointless.

The working classes have always got less of everything in education, including respect (Ferguson 2017). Yet, far too often the constant spectre of failure and the elusiveness of success that the working classes encounter daily in English schooling and the lack of recognition, both as successful learners and as valuable individuals, that they constantly have to deal with in the classroom are taken for granted, routinely accepted as simply 'the way things are'. As John Smyth and Robin Simmons outline in the introduction to their edited book *Education and Working-Class Youth* (2017), the last 20 years has seen a plethora of educational policies that have further diminished the low value of the working classes in English education. Whilst reducing the well-being of all children, they have had a particularly pernicious impact on the self-esteem of working-class children. Schools have been bombarded with a wide raft of policies designed to raise attainment, improve teaching, and increase accountability. These include the introduction of testing regimes and school league tables, a re-traditionalising and narrowing of the school curriculum, the growth of tracking throughout primary and secondary school years, and an increased focus on competition both within classrooms and between schools (Smyth and Simmons 2017). The damage such policies have had on the working class will be explored in this chapter through empirical case studies. The case studies included interviews with working-class young people about their experiences of being in the bottom sets as well as interviews with working-class young people who feel excluded and alienated by a national curriculum that denigrates and marginalizes working-class forms of knowledge.

Tracking and the invidious consequences of being in the bottom sets

In order to understand English working-class educational experiences in the 21st century, it is important to have an overview of recent educational policies. In particular, policies of testing and assessment, and educational choice have increased social divisions in education and resulted in a deterioration of working-class educational experiences. The sense of futility and worthlessness expressed by Mickey Flanagan and his friends about 1970s schooling is still evident in contemporary schooling. In my research in English schools over a period of 25 years, working-class children have frequently said that they feel stupid, rubbish, 'no good', or even that 'they count for nothing' in the school context. Classrooms are often places of routine everyday humiliations and slights for working-class children. And those working-class children who become disaffected with school developed strong resentments about mistreatment and what they saw as unfairness. Their words were often infused with a sense of the righteous indignation that once underpinned a strong working-class politics. In the absence of that righteous indignation more generally, there has been a re-emergence of a class cultural oppression characterized by a middle-class horror at the sight of poverty and the ridiculing of the white working-classes through portrayals of 'chav' culture (Jones 2011). Working-class children across race and gender frequently talk about feeling a powerful sense of injustice at the way they are seen and treated. Such factors are at the heart of the social divide in educational outcomes and are linked to the invidious divide between vocational and academic education in England.

Vocational education, which English children take up from age 14, has a long history of stigmatization – stereotyped and devalued as education desired by, and more suitable for, children of the working classes. As a result, in Britain, it has always approximated to what John Dewey called 'narrow technical trade education for specialized callings, carried on under the control of others' (1916, 325), a restricted, atheoretical type of apprenticeship. Unsurprisingly, attempts to upgrade vocational education have failed because the British middle classes have never countenanced it as appropriate education for their own children (Tomlinson 2005). Despite a great deal of rhetoric about high-status vocational routes, policies have always been directed at the lower-, and indeed lowest-, achieving young people (Wolf 2002). Any sort of equality between vocational and academic education would require a transformation in both what vocational education constitutes and who engages in it.

It is unsurprising then that vocational education in England is working-class education. A study that examined the degree of democratic participation among young people who had been educated in vocational streams in England, Denmark, and Germany (Hoskins et al. 2014) found that inequalities in democratic engagement are increased by allocating young people to different tracks on the basis of what is described as their ability. This was particularly noticeable in England, the country where vocational tracks had the lowest status. The English vocational students described the powerlessness they felt when it came to influencing wider political and social issues.

> There's nothing we can say about it because to them we're no one, we're a nobody. (Julie)
>
> I think that no matter what my point of view is, it's not going to change anything. (Sam)
>
> We're not looked at, us little people, we're not; I just wish something could be done about bad things, but nothing ever can because that's life. (Jane)
>
> *(Hoskins et al. 2014, 819)*

What is also striking is the sense of abjection, and feelings of worthlessness they display. The authors conclude that 'prior experiences of inequalities in the educational system', such as 'prior to placement in the vocational tracks … which included unfair treatment and selective processes at school … appear to be associated with lower levels of confidence and aspiration, in other words, low general self-efficacy' (820). Both the continued failure to develop vocational education that has equivalent value with academic education and the growing preoccupation with testing and assessment, have resulted in more and more tracking and setting in English schools and nurseries, with the latest research showing children being allocated to attainment groups from age 2 (Adams 2017).

My own research confirms Hoskins et al.'s findings on the damage inflicted by being placed in sets and tracks seen to be for those of low 'ability'. As part of a recent research study, I spent time interviewing and talking with bottom set students aged 12 to 14 in an English comprehensive school (Reay 2012). Their sense of abjection and failure was palpable.

> *Satvinder:* Right now, because I'm in the bottom set for everything, I don't like it, because I'm only doing the foundation paper, and I don't … I really don't want to do that. Because from Year 6 when I left, I went I'm going to put my head down and do my work, but I never did. And then it … like, every year I say it, but I never do it. […] I haven't even done it this year either. […] Yeah, I could have, like, gone to a better higher place, and then I could have done everything I was hoping to.
>
> *Diane:* And now?
>
> *Satvinder:* There is no hope.
>
> *Atik:* I think I failed proper badly in the tests and that's why I'm in a proper bad set now … I can just answer the questions really easy because there's like no really smart people and they behave quite bad as well and they influence me. … So I've just become rubbish.
>
> *Joe:* The behaviour's bad. You don't learn unless you're in the first set.
>
> *Shulah:* The behaviour, it gets worse in the bottom set when like teachers don't pay attention to you. And they pay attention to like the higher-ability students and like you get bored because there's nothing for you to do if you don't understand the work.

In all these quotes, low sets are clearly perceived to be places of educational failure and despair, where children are written off and have no hope of succeeding. This is not what any parent would want for their child or what any teacher should want for their students. Yet, over the past 25 years I have been researching in schools, children in bottom sets have regularly described themselves as stupid, useless and rubbish.

Even starker was the collective view of a group of white working-class boys in the bottom set, who felt that school had nothing to offer them.

> *Diane:* If you had a choice, what would you choose to learn?
>
> *Jason:* Nothing.
>
> *George:* Nothing.
>
> *Andy:* No idea.
>
> *Paul:* Definitely nothing!

Here we see how destructive the educational system is for those who struggle, swallowed up in a remorseless system of hierarchical ranking and a competitive counting culture. We can see the consequences for the individual in Jason's poignant advocacy for children like himself.

> Some kids they just can't do it – like they find the work too hard, or they can't concentrate because too much is going on for them. Then they are put like as rubbish learners and put in the bottom set, and no one cares about them even though they are the ones who need the most help. They should be getting the most help.

So far I have drawn on the voices of secondary school students, but there are growing practices of setting and streaming in primary schools. This is a working-class 6-year-old in a London primary school:

> They [the lions] think they are better than us. They think they are good at every single thing and the second group, Tigers, there are some people that think they are good and more important than us. And one of the boys in giraffes, he was horrible to me and he said, 'get lost, slow tortoise', but my group are monkeys and we are only second to bottom.

At a recent conference, a researcher spoke with a mixture of horror and disbelief as he recounted going into a primary classroom where there were four ability groups – flying squirrels, tree squirrels, ground squirrels, and a bottom set called marmots, because they are a type of squirrel that lives under the ground.

In addition to their feelings of futility, unfairness, and humiliation, what concerned me was that unlike the top sets – which were predominantly white and middle class – all the lower set students were working class and ethnically diverse. These young people may express a strong sense of individual failure, but they simultaneously share a collective class fate. The young people I met have little opportunity for finding self-fulfilment and realizing their potential through schooling. Schooling should be about establishing 'a community of learners', but setting and streaming on the basis of perceived ability destroys any sense of community. It also widens the class attainment gap as middle-class children in the top sets benefit, while working class children, disproportionately placed in lower sets and streams, are further disadvantaged (Parsons and Hallam 2014).

Working-class responses to the educational system are in large measure a reaction to the attitudes and actions of those with more power and agency to effect policies and practices within schooling. These include not only teachers but, more influentially, the middle-class majority, policymakers and politicians. In a research project investigating the extent to which children felt included in schooling, secondary school students were asked whether they felt that they had the confidence to act within schooling; whether they felt they belonged, as individuals and as groups, within the school community; and whether they felt they had the power to influence the procedures and practices which shaped their learning (Arnot and Reay 2007). The vast majority of the working-class students talked about a sense of powerlessness and educational worthlessness, and feelings that they were not really valued and respected within education. Educational processes in the classroom are rarely uniform and clearly do not affect all working-class students in the same ways, and indeed the roots and the consequences of alienation from schooling are differentiated by both ethnicity and gender. However, across lines of race and gender, all the working-class students in the study experienced varying degrees of alienation. But it was working-class boys, in particular, who expressed anger at the way they were treated.

> *Danny:* Some teachers are a bit snobby, sort of. And some teachers act as if the child is stupid. Because they've got a posh accent. Like they talk without 'innits' and 'mans', like they talk proper English. And they say, 'That isn't the way you talk' – like putting you down. Like I think telling you a different way is sort of good, but I think the way they do it isn't good, because they correct you and make you look stupid.
>
> *Martin:* Those teachers look down on you.

In both Danny and Martin's words we can see how educational processes are simultaneously classed processes in which relations of teaching and learning too often position working-class pupils as inadequate learners with inadequate cultural backgrounds, looked down on for their 'stupidity'. I suggest it is not insignificant that their teacher with 'the posh accent' who 'looks down on them' is a middle-class, white Oxbridge graduate just one year out of teacher training. Many of Danny and Martin's teachers were similarly young and inexperienced. As Danny told me in a later interview: 'Who is he to look down on me? He's just a kid'. Of course, schools benefit from a mix of new and experienced teachers, but Danny and Martin's inner city comprehensive had far more of the former than the latter when it would have benefitted from a mix of both.

Yet, as the extract below shows, black working-class girls can feel just as marginalized and alienated by schooling as the white working-class boys.

> *Sharmaine:* Sometimes we feel left out.
> *Sarah:* Because you know, teachers are not meant to have favourites.
> *Sharmaine:* You can have, but you can't show it, you know. That's unfair to the other people.
> *Sarah:* Because there's a whole class there and you want to pick that particular person, and you are nice to that one, and the rest you don't care about.
> *Alex:* But everyone has to be the same.
> *Sharmaine:* He needs to treat everyone equal.

Psychological research (Buss 2001) shows that performance and behaviour in an educational context can be profoundly influenced by the way we feel we are seen and judged by others. When we expect to be viewed as inferior our abilities seem to be diminished. And this sense of inferiority was particularly strong in the bottom sets.

Reduced to a number: The impact of excessive testing and assessment on learner identities

As the previous section showed, we can see in what both working-class boys and girls say across ethnic difference some of the hidden injuries of class (Sennett and Cobb 1972) that are enshrined and perpetuated through educational policies and practices. These injuries of class are particularly raw and vivid in relation to growing processes of assessment and testing in schools. England is now the most tested nation in the world (Woolcock 2008). I first became concerned about the effect of Standard Assessment Tests (SATs) in primary schools at the turn of the 21st century (Reay and Wiliam 1999). Below are some quotes from the 40 10- and 11-year-olds I interviewed. From visiting primary schools and observing in classrooms, I could see that the SATs were shifting children's identifications as learners; many, particularly the girls and the working-class children, were expressing lots of anxiety and a lack of confidence in themselves as learners.

> *Hannah:* I'm really scared about the SATs. Mrs O'Brien [a teacher at the school] came and talked to us about our spelling, and I'm no good at spelling and David [the class teacher] is giving us times tables tests every morning and I'm hopeless at times tables, so I'm frightened I'll do the SATs and I'll be a nothing.

Diane: I don't understand, Hannah. You can't be a nothing.

Hannah: Yes, you can 'cause you have to get a level like a level 4 or a level 5, and if you're no good at spellings and times tables, you don't get those levels and so you're a nothing.

Diane: I'm sure that's not right.

Hannah: Yes it is 'cause that's what Mrs O'Brien was saying.

This is a particularly stark example, but it exemplifies some of the ways in which children's identifications as learners were being constructed through the assessment process. For working-class Hannah, what constitutes academic success is correct spelling and knowing your times tables. She is an accomplished writer, a gifted dancer and artist, and good at problem-solving, yet none of those skills make her somebody in her own eyes. Instead she constructs herself as a failure, an academic non-person, by a metonymic shift in which she comes to see herself entirely in terms of the level to which her performance in the SATs is ascribed.

Hannah was far from alone. Nearly all the children indicated a sense of unease and feelings of discomfort about what SATs might reveal about themselves as learners. But it was working-class children, in particular, who seemed to be indicating far-reaching consequences in which good SATs results were linked to positive life prospects and, concomitantly, poor results meant future failures and hardships.

Sharon: I think I'll get a 2. Only Stuart will get a 6.

Diane: So if Stuart gets a 6, what will that say about him?

Sharon: He's heading for a good job and a good life, and it shows he's not gonna be living on the streets and stuff like that.

Diane: And if you get a level 2, what will that say about you?

Sharon: Um, I might not have a good life in front of me, and I might grow up and do something naughty or something like that.

Performance in SATs was about far more than simply getting a test right or wrong; it was conflated in the children's minds with future prospects. To perform badly is 'to ruin one's chances'.

Diane: You mean, you think that if you do badly in SATs, then you won't be able to do well or get good jobs?

Jackie: Yeah, 'cause that's what David's saying.

Diane: What is he saying?

Jackie: He's saying if we don't like, get good things, in our SATS, when we grow up we are not gonna get good jobs and…

Ricky: Be plumbers and road sweepers …

Tunde: But what if you wanted to do that?

Diane: Instead of what?

Ricky: Footballers, singers, vets, archaeologists. We ain't gonna be nothing like that if we don't get high levels.

Diane: And does that worry you about your future?

Jackie: Yeah.

Lewis: Yeah.

There has been increasing protest and opposition among teachers, and more recently, head teachers (National Union of Teachers (NUT) 2016), about the cruelties and costs of excessive testing and contemporary austerity education for students, but also the damaging impact of both on their own morale and well-being. One of the most powerful illustrations of the latter was an open letter written by a teacher to Nicky Morgan, at that time Secretary of Education, that was published in the *New Statesman* (Brown 2016). The teacher reflected that

> In some ways I don't feel like a teacher at all any more. I prepare children for tests and, if I'm honest, I do it quite well. It's not something I'm particularly proud of as it's not as if it provided my class with any transferable, real life skills during the process. They've not enjoyed it, I've not enjoyed it but we've done it: and one thing my children know how to do is answer test questions. They've written raps about how to answer test questions, they've practised test questions at home and test questions in school, they've had extra tuition to help them understand the test questions. They can do test questions – they just haven't had time to do anything else … worse than being a teacher in this system is being a child at the mercy of it.

In 2016 a NUT survey on primary assessment found that 97% of teachers agreed or strongly agreed that testing had a negative impact on children's access to a broad and balanced curriculum (NUT 2016). They also wrote of demoralization, demotivation and physical and mental distress. The following are just two of many quotes from the survey indicating the negative consequences for both children's well-being and their sense of themselves as learners.

> We have had a massive increase in social, emotional and mental health issues this year. It has been reported that teachers and schools are to blame for this, but we have not designed a curriculum and testing for which most of our children are not emotionally or developmentally ready. Our children are being set up to fail! Ministers don't seem to realise that there are children at the end of these tests. They are only concerned with measuring teacher accountability.
>
> Many of the children who previously enjoyed school now detest education. This is a crime and a shame because, in its incompetence, the Government is willingly and knowingly making children hate learning with a passion, rather than harbour an environment of life-long learning.
>
> *(NUT 2016, 3)*

However, although the excessive competition and testing impacts on all children and their well-being, the main costs are borne by working-class students. They are disproportionately found to have the lowest grades and to be in the bottom sets.

A curriculum that marginalizes working-class knowledge?

In English society, any critical engagement or creativity in formal schooling, especially for those in the later years of schooling, has increasingly become the preserve of the upper and middle classes. In the research project I conducted in 2012 on the educational experiences of working-class young people in a period of austerity, it was evident that learning out of school was seen as both more rewarding and relevant than school-based learning (Reay 2012). However, it is important to point out from the outset that these activities were very different in both variety and purpose from the often-expensive activities underpinned by an objective of concerted cultivation that the middle and upper classes were regularly engaged in (Lareau 2003). A small number of working-class young people, who often had damaged learner identities in school, had succeeded in creating supportive social networks through engaging in a range of out-of-school activities, mostly connected to sports. In the process, they had frequently acquired social and cultural capital as well as useful practical knowledge. This minority of working-class young people, who described taking part in a variety of out-of-school activities, conveyed a sense of passion, motivation and the critical engagement missing from their descriptions of school learning. So Ricky talks about 'his adventurous side', which is expressed not through school but in the many things he does outside of school: cricket, cycling, rugby, skating, fishing, and making things with his hands. Asked to describe his most exciting learning experiences, he told me:

> When I was about 9 or 10, I made a bicycle out of wood by myself, and then when I was 10, I built a cupboard for me mum. Well, me and my dad made a cupboard out of wood and stuff like that for over our stairs so we could put our towels and stuff in it. And that's when I was 10 and it is still up there now.

In the following extract, Shianne describes her latest outing with the Air Cadets. It is clear that among the excitement and fun involved there is also a great deal of learning taking place, academic as well as practical.

> I am in this thing called Air Cadets, so I went with them and er … we have to get all kitted up with helmets and gloves and parachute and stuff like that. And I was flying it, and you get to do, like, acrobats and tricks and flips and stuff like that. And I got to control the plane and then I got to do a flip with it. And then we did this thing where … you know in space they have no gravity … we did that in the cockpit of our plane, so there is no gravity, then I took my glove off and let it float about, and then everything was floating about. And then we went back to gravity and everything just come back down again. So it was fun, and then I had to land the plane as well.

When asked about school-based science, however, Shianne claimed 'I hate it – it's boring'. These young people, with damaged and tenuous learner identities in school, managed to nurture interests, talents and valued identities in their activities outside school.

A possible clue to this disjuncture between enjoyment and engagement in out-of-school activities and an instrumentalized accommodation to school-based learning lies in the very different language young people used to describe such experiences. Out-of-school activities are characterized by collaboration and collectivity. School, in contrast, was seen to be more about failure than success, a race to beat your friends that often felt to these young people like a 'no-win situation'. As Pritti pointed out, 'you feel bad if you do a lot better than your friends 'cos you've shown them up and they think you are a geek, and you feel bad if you do badly 'cos you've let yourself down'. Part of the systemic problem here, which became increasingly obvious as I spoke to more working-class students, was that the subjects and activities they enjoyed, and often excelled at, had little status and recognition within the current educational system. This suggests, as Jessica Gerrard (2013) has argued, that working-class educational activities occur through diverse forms that are not immediately identified by, let alone incorporated into, the formal educational system. Furthermore, this failure within education to respect and value working-class knowledge has resulted in the invidious divide between vocational and academic knowledge, discussed earlier.

Conclusion

In this chapter I have attempted to provide an overview of 'the current state of play' for the working classes in English education. The principles underpinning state-maintained education in England is 'equal opportunities for all', but the reality for working class children is very different. They remain Bourdieu and Champagne's (1999) 'outcasts on the inside' despite over 150 years of state education. Recent and contemporary policies of testing and assessment, setting and streaming, and increased competition have added to their marginalization rather than alleviating it. The two case studies I have drawn on – testing and assessment, and setting and streaming – reveal just how damaging neoliberal educational policies have been for the well-being of all children, but particularly those who are working class. They have also encouraged growing practices of polarization and segregation within state schooling, as advantaged parents invest time, energy and resources in ensuring their own children have sufficient support, either through private tuition or enrichment activities both in the home and outside it, to dominate the top sets and streams and occupy the position of 'best learners'. The latest Social Mobility Commission report (2017) laments the lack of social mobility in England. But in view of the current educational state of play, it is unsurprising that the working class are being left behind (Weale 2017).

We have never had social justice for the working classes in English education (Reay 2017). But now with our political right wing in retreat and disarray, and a new left-wing resurgence, there are, for the first time this century, opportunities for educational change. The Labour Party in England has laid out plans for a National Education Service that puts comprehensive schooling at the centre of the educational system, and it supports a broader and more balanced curriculum and the reinvention of local democratic control. It is also considering free higher education as well as free nursery provision. The last time we were in this situation, in the period after the Second World War, those opportunities were largely squandered. We must ensure this does not happen again, and fight for an educational system that works for the many and not just the few. However, this involves a struggle not just at the policy level but also in relation to knowledge and epistemology. This is why it is so important to develop and expand the field of working-class studies. Working-class studies as an academic field has been more successful in the US than the UK (Russo and Linkon 2005). Yet, at a time when the English working classes are increasingly portrayed as 'left behind' and a 'residuum', it is vitally important for complex and informed understandings of working-class experiences to counter stereotypical and oversimplified mainstream representations.

References

Adams, R. (2017) 'Children as young as two grouped by ability in English nurseries', *The Guardian,* 1 December. www.theguardian.com/education/2017/dec/01/children-two-grouped-ability-english-nurseries

Arnot, M, and Reay, D. (2007) 'A sociology of pedagogic voice: Power, inequality and transformation, *Discourse*, 28, 3, pp. 171–182.

Bourdieu, P. and Champagne, P. (1999) 'Outcasts on the inside', in Bourdieu, P. et al. (eds.) *Weight of the World: Social Suffering in Contemporary Society*, Cambridge, Polity Press.

Brown, Z. (2016) 'Dear Nicky Morgan', *The New Statesman*, 16 May.

Buss, A. H. (2001) *Psychological Dimensions of the Self*, Thousand Oaks, CA, Sage.

Dewey, J. (1916) *Democracy and Education*, New York, The Free Press.

Ferguson, D. (2017) 'The working classes get less of everything in education, including respect', *The Guardian*, 21 November. www.theguardian.com/education/2017/nov/21/english-class-system-shaped-in-schools

Gerrard, J. (2013) 'Class analysis and the emancipatory potential of education', *Educational Theory*, 13, 2, pp. 185–201.

Green, A. (1990) *Education and State Formation: The Rise of Education Systems in England, France and the USA*, Basingstoke, Macmillan.
Hoskins, B., Janmaat, J., Han, C. and Muijs, D. (2014) 'Inequalities in the education system and the reproduction of socioeconomic disparities in voting in England, Denmark and Germany: The influence of country context, tracking and self-efficacy on voting intentions of students age 16–18', *Compare*, 44, 5, pp. 801–825.
Johnson, R. (1976) 'Notes on the schooling of the English working class 1780–1850', in Dale, R., Esland, G., and MacDonald, M. (eds.) *Schooling and Capitalism: A Sociological Reader*, London, Routledge.
Jones, O. (2011) *Chavs: The Demonization of the Working Class*, London, Verso Books.
Lareau, A. (2003) *Unequal Childhoods*, Berkeley, University of California Press.
National Union of Teachers (NUT) (2016) *The Crisis in Primary Assessment: Report of an NUT Survey of Primary Teachers and Head Teachers*. www.teachers.org.uk/news-events/press.../crisis-primary-assessment-nut-survey
Parsons, S. and Hallam, S. (2014) 'The impact of streaming on attainment at age seven: Evidence from the Millennium Cohort Study', *Oxford Review of Education*, 40, 5, pp. 567–589.
Reay, D. (2012) '"We never get a fair chance": Working class experiences of education in the twenty-first century', in Atkinson, W., Roberts, S. and Savage, M. (eds.) *Class Inequality in Austerity Britain*, London, Palgrave MacMillan.
Reay, D. (2017) *Miseducation: Inequality, Education and the Working Classes*, Bristol, Policy Press.
Reay, D. and Wiliam, D. (1999) '"I'll be a nothing": Structure, agency and the construction of identity through assessment', *British Educational Research Journal*, 25, 3, pp. 343–354.
Russo, J. and Linkon, S. L. (eds.) (2005) *New Working-Class Studies*, Ithaca, Cornell University Press.
Savage, M. (2015) *Social Class in the 21st Century*, London, Penguin Books.
Sennett, R. and Cobb, J. (1972) *The Hidden Injuries of Class*, Cambridge, Cambridge University Press.
Smith, A. (1785) *An Inquiry into the Nature and Causes of the Wealth of Nations*, London, Liberty Press.
Smyth, J. and Simmons, R. (eds.) (2017) *Education and Working-Class Youth*, London, Palgrave Press.
Social Mobility Commission (2017) *Time for Change: An Assessment of Government Policies on Social Mobility 1997–2017*, London, Social Mobility Commission.
Stahl, G. (2015) *Identity, Neoliberalism and Aspiration: Educating White Working-Class Boys*, London, Routledge.
Todd, S. (2014) *The People: The Rise and Fall of the Working Class 1910–2010*, London, John Murray.
Tomlinson, S. (2005) *Education in a Post-Welfare Society*, 2nd edition, Maidenhead, Open University Press.
Weale, S. (2017) 'UK second only to Japan for young people's poor mental wellbeing', *The Guardian*, 8 February.
Willis, P. (1977) *Learning to Labour*, Farnborough, Saxon House.
Wolf, A. (2002) *Does Education Matter?* London, Penguin Books.
Woolcock, N. (2008) 'English children "are most tested in the world"', *The Times*, 8 February.

9

Getting schooled

Working-class students in higher education

Bettina Spencer

I spent this morning sitting at my computer tinkering with my syllabi for courses that begin in less than seven days. I have taught these courses before, but this semester will be different because I need to travel to my hometown during the first week of classes to be with my sister while she has a scheduled C-section. I 'need' to 'be with my sister'. These are the two points I waver on. I want to be there, just like I was for her previous children, but do I 'need' to be at the actual birth? Can I go a day later when I don't have classes to teach? Does my sister actually need me 'to be with' her or is my presence actually more of a burden? I ask my nephew, who is currently in college, the second college student in our family – 20 years after me, the first in the family – what days he will travel home to see the baby, and he texts back, 'the day of the birth lol', like I would even consider otherwise. And he is right; originally, I did not consider otherwise, but my calendar is filling up with deadlines, meetings, events, and it is so difficult to cancel classes during the first week of the semester. This is the constant push-pull I feel between my obligations as a professional-class professor and a member of a tightly knit working-class family that lives far away. Despite leaving home 20 years ago to go to college and then graduate school, despite conducting research in working-class studies, despite giving regular talks for first-generation college students and mentoring those students who come to me for advice, I still have not completely figured out how to balance my current independent life with the interdependent expectations of my family, although I am significantly better at it than I was as an undergraduate student experiencing this culture clash for the first time.

When students from working-class backgrounds enroll in college, they are, for the most part, moving in to primarily middle-class environments with middle- or professional-class peers and faculty, particularly if they enroll in elite universities (Christopher 2005). Because college faculty members are rarely from working-class backgrounds, these institutions tend to reinforce middle-class norms (Markus and Conner 2013). For working-class students, their experiences, stigmas, and cultural values as a working-class person often remain, and the new burden of being working class in an essentially non-working-class environment creates a unique set of barriers. For example, in addition to facing financial stressors, and learning how to navigate an entirely new system if they are the first in their family to go to college, working-class students also face psychological stressors that can detrimentally affect their college experience. Working-class students often feel as though their class background prevents them from completely 'fitting in' at college; yet, by going to college, they no longer 'fit' with their family and friends. In an essay about being a woman from a working-class background in the academy, Donna Langston (1993) writes about her reoccurring dreams involving an inability to 'feel at home' with either her working-class friends and family or her middle-class colleagues and environment. Working-class students often describe their pursuit of a college degree as a 'trade-off', in that they believe in the importance of receiving an education but feel like they are losing a part of their identity because of it (Markus and Connor 2013). This tension can create psychological demands that can detrimentally impact their educational experience, thereby reinforcing their feeling of not belonging.

Although these obstacles may seem insurmountable, working-class students can and do thrive in supportive environments. For example, educational research with first-generation students suggests that upwardly mobile working-class students can identify as both working and middle class without rejecting one or the other (Hinz 2016). That is, rather than feeling isolated or distant from their current or previous contexts, students from working-class backgrounds can become inter-cultural, which can thereby reduce or eliminate effects of psychological stressors.

This chapter reviews the psychological and physical demands that working-class students face when in higher education and how these demands can impact their academic performance and sense of belonging.[1] It concludes with intervention techniques to help reduce the negative effects that working-class[2] college students may experience.

Psychological demands

Psychologically, working-class students are more likely than their middle- and upper-class peers to experience depression, anxiety, avoidance, rejection sensitivity, and decreased life and academic satisfaction, amongst other psychological barriers to success (Jury et al. 2017). Ibrahim, Kelly, and Glazebrook (2013) surveyed undergraduate students across six different universities and found that low-socioeconomic status (SES) students reported significantly higher levels of depression than their high-SES counterparts. Overall, a low sense of control was negatively correlated with increased depression, which partially mediated the SES and depression relation. That is, low-SES students had a lower sense of control, which impacted, in some part, their level of depression. However, because this relation was only partially mediated by sense of control, this finding indicates that SES alone significantly contributed to depression. Similarly, students who reported experiencing classism on campus also reported significantly decreased life satisfaction and academic satisfaction as compared to students who did not experience classism (Allan, Garriott, and Keene 2016). Adding to the burden, first-generation college students have reported that they have fewer opportunities to talk about such experiences and emotions (Barry, Hudley, Kelly, and Cho 2009).

In a diary study, a wide range of undergraduate students, some with a concealable stigma such as being low-income, recorded their current mood, how they felt about themselves, what they were doing, and who they were with every time a watch alarm notified them to record (Frable, Platt, and Hoey 1998). On average, the low-income students reported feeling less good about themselves, more anxious, more depressed, and less socially confident than their high-income peers. Additionally, low-income students spent more time on academic activities and the least time in social activities, and they were significantly more likely to be alone. However, these participants did feel better and had less anxiety and depression when around similar others rather than around high-income students. That is, for the low-income students, being around other students with similar backgrounds eased the situation, whereas for high-income students, being around similar others did not change their emotional or psychological well-being in any significant way (Frable, Platt, and Hoey 1998).

Community is incredibly psychologically important to working-class students, more so than for middle-class students; and as such, feeling like one does not have a working-class community at school, or that one might be rejected from the middle-class school community because of class background, can be particularly painful. When working-class undergraduate students suspect that they are being rejected based on their social class (known as class-based rejection sensitivity), particularly if they believe that they do not have the potential to grow, they tend to blame themselves for academic setbacks and have an increased sense of hopelessness (Rheinschmidt and Mendoza-Denton 2014). Students are less likely to believe in growth potential when they do not see a clear connection between their effort and their achievement (Hong, Chiu, Dweck, Lin, and Wan 1999), which, for working-class students can be fairly common if they have put in a lot of effort to their academics but are still falling behind due to psychological stressors. Although a sense of community can buffer many of these negative effects, research in education and psychology has established that working-class students often report a sense of social isolation (Ostrove and Long 2007) and are less integrated in social networks than their upper-class peers (Rubin 2012). They often experience a cultural mismatch between their home environments and school environments (Stephens, Townsend, Markus, and Phillips 2012), which can lead to feeling disconnected from the school environment (Reay, Crozier, and Clayton 2010).

In order to fit in with a community where they are typically marginalized, low-SES college students may end up depleting their psychological resources, such as self-regulation, because their energy is being spent on being mindful that they present themselves appropriately in the particular environment. Johnson, Richeson, and Finkel (2011) conducted a series of four studies that tested how low-SES college students manage their self-presentation within an academic setting. Importantly, low-SES students were more depleted in self-regulation than high-SES students after talking about an academic topic. In the experimental context, this meant that low-SES students who discussed academic achievement were more likely to underperform on tasks that require concentration and self-control (such as the Stroop task). In an applied or real-world context, self-regulation in academic environments includes setting priorities and managing time. If a student struggles to set priorities and manage time while in college, they can easily fall behind on their coursework and perform poorly in their courses, thereby creating a cycle of depletion and underperformance. This cycle of struggling to 'keep up' while also feeling isolated, anxious, and depressed is a large psychological burden that working-class students must manage in addition to financial stressors and all the typical college stressors (e.g. disagreements with roommates, moving away from home, adapting to a new schedule, etc.) faced by their peers.

Physical demands

Of course, psychological demands create stress, and stress creates physical illness, so working-class students often experience physical illness during college. Working-class students may experience a disproportionate amount of financial, psychological, and academic stress as compared to their high-income peers and, as aforementioned, have reported that they have fewer opportunities to talk about their emotions and experiences (Barry, Hudley, Kelly, and Cho 2009). This is often because they feel like they cannot discuss their financial stress with their peers, or their academic stress with their family, and as such, the stressors can accumulate to the point of interfering with students' health, well-being, and academic performance.

Stephens, Townsend et al. (2012) argued that working-class students can experience a cultural mismatch between their family culture and school culture. There are two major cultural models for how people think about themselves in relation to others that are learned from their dominant cultural context: interdependent and independent. The interdependent model, which tends to be the model for people of color in America, working-class Americans, and the vast majority of the global South, emphasizes connections to other people, anticipating others' needs and feelings, and promoting the group above the self. The independent model, which tends to be the model of white people in America, high-income Americans, and Western Europeans, emphasizes uniqueness and being distinct from others, expressing one's emotions, and promoting the self over the group (Markus and Kitayama 1991). Given the history of the American educational system, most American colleges and universities promote and reinforce independent cultural norms. Indeed, a study of high-level administrators at a range of colleges and universities indicates that institutions *do* expect and promote independent cultural norms (Stephens, Fryberg, Markus, Johnson, and Covarrubias 2012).

Because working-class college students are often experiencing a mismatch between the interdependent culture in which they were raised and the independent culture in which they are studying, they may experience class-specific stressors. Nicole Stephens and colleagues (Stephens, Fryberg et al. 2012) manipulated the type of school culture that first-year students expected to experience, by exposing first-generation and continuing-generation students to college welcome letters that emphasized either interdependent or independent norms. For example, the interdependent letter focused on community, working with other students and with faculty, learning from others, and participating in collaborative research. By comparison, the independent letter focused on independent research, exploring personal interests, expressing one's own opinion, and creating one's own intellectual path. After reading one of the welcome letters, students gave a five-minute speech about their academic goals, which they were told would be recorded and evaluated. Throughout the session, students gave saliva samples at various time points – once before the speech stressor (baseline) and several times after the stressor. The saliva samples were analyzed for levels of cortisol, the main stress hormone, produced as part of the 'fight or flight' response. For the first-generation students, cortisol significantly increased from the baseline after reading the independence-focused letter, demonstrating increased stress. When first-generation students read the interdependence-focused letter, there were no differences in cortisol levels between first- and continuing-generation students. Continuing-generation students, regardless of condition, did not experience significant increases in cortisol. That is, the brief cultural mismatch that first-generation students experienced in the independent letter condition created physical stress, even in a fairly low-impact, short-term situation (Stephens, Townsend et al. 2012).

Considering that most colleges and universities do promote independent cultures in their advertising, their materials, their coursework, and their bureaucratic processes, it is safe to assume that first-generation students are continually bombarded with this mismatch and, therefore, experience the college environment as a chronic stressor. Chronic stressors are linked to several serious negative health outcomes including wearing down the immune system (Webster Marketon and Glaser 2008), contributing to heart disease (Krantz and McCeney 2002), and speeding the aging process (Choi, Fauce, and Effros 2008). Because physical and psychological health are so closely linked, working-class students can get caught in an unhealthy pattern of stress-induced illness, which leads to more psychological distress, not to mention increased absences, bills, and possible medical leave from school.

Academic performance

Taken together, the psychological and physical demands, as well as decreased sense of belonging or 'fit', can impact working-class students' academic performance. Aside from being especially prone to 'imposter syndrome' (Gardner and Holley 2011), the fear of being exposed as a 'fraud' despite being competent, working-class students often face real academic setbacks due to the tolls taken by the psychological and physical stresses they experience during college. Allan, Garriott, and Keene (2016) found that working-class students had decreased academic satisfaction and lower grade point averages (GPAs) than middle-class students, particularly when they perceived their institution to be classist. Concerns about classism, the institution, and professors and peers within the institution can further impact working-class students' academic performance. In a longitudinal study with undergraduate students, working-class students who viewed their characteristics as fixed (as opposed to having the ability to grow and change) and who were concerned about experiencing classism at matriculation had lower grades and worse test performance by the end of the semester. This pattern of results occurred whether the students truly believed that their characteristics were fixed or whether students were primed to think that their characteristics were fixed, which means that these beliefs can impact performance both naturally and after working-class students receive an explicit or implicit message that they are incapable of growth.

Sensitivity to the environment, perceptions, or experiences of classism, and anticipating class-based rejection, can increase vigilance, particularly when working-class students feel like they are being judged or evaluated. In an eye-tracking study, first-generation students, but not continuing-generation students, spent more time looking at their performance results on a computer in comparison to other students, while also underperforming on the actual computerized task (Jury, Smeding, and Darnon 2015). At the same time, high-achieving working-class students, who are close to achieving upward mobility, will try harder to avoid poor academic performance than middle-class students or low-achieving working-class students (Jury, Smeding, Court, and Darnon 2015). This may be because these students in particular are so close to achieving their goals that, without the safety net of their middle-class peers, they are more motivated to have high academic performance. Again, working-class students' belief that they can actually achieve upward mobility impacts how they navigate the college experience, which directly affects their academic performance. Because working-class students who do succeed academically are more likely to feel proud of their academic identity, as compared to their lower-performing peers, they will often invest a large amount of self-esteem in their 'good student' identity. Ironically, performing well academically can actually leave these students psychologically vulnerable. Whereas working-class students who underperform may disengage from their academic setting and begin to find self-esteem in other domains, working-class students who stay connected to the academic setting, and for whom academic success is a large part of their sense of self, can be the most negatively affected by class-based stereotyping in academic contexts.

According to the theory of stereotype threat, students who are stigmatized within a particular domain (academics, athletics, memory, etc.) but who strongly identify with and excel in the domain despite the stereotypes are the most susceptible to underperforming on standardized tests of that domain (Steele and Aronson 1995). It is the students who are stereotyped the most and who also care the most who can fail the worst in testing situations. It is these students who worry about confirming the stereotype associated with their ingroup and, thus, can become overwhelmed when taking a test, because they know that if they underperform, they will essentially confirm the stereotype. Stereotype threat has been well established for African Americans taking the verbal portion of the SAT (Steele and Aronson 1995), women taking standardized math tests (Spencer, Steele, and Quinn 1999), and a range of other groups within various settings where that particular group is stereotyped.

Low-SES people, of course, are often stereotyped as unintelligent and uninterested in learning (Brantlinger 2003), and low-SES students do, indeed, tend to score lower on standardized tests than high-SES students (College Board 2015). These stereotypes are reinforced by the testing agencies who have, in part, put this performance gap down to the belief that 'parents with college degrees may be more inclined to motivate their children' (Educational Testing Service 2009, 9). To test whether low-SES students' low standardized test scores may be due to stereotype threat, Spencer and Castano (2007) tested low- and high-SES college students on the verbal section of the Graduate Record Examinations (GRE) test. Half of the participants completed demographic measures including several questions about social class (parents' income and occupation) before taking the test, while the other half completed the demographic questions after taking the test. Therefore, half of the participants were primed to think of their social class before completing the GRE (which is how standardized tests are generally presented), whereas the other half were not primed and completed the test without any reminder of their class status. Results indicated that the low-SES students who were primed to think of their social class significantly underperformed compared to high-SES students in either condition, and the low-SES students in the 'no prime' condition. Interestingly, the low-SES students who were not primed to think about their social class before taking the test performed better than the high-SES students in the same condition. When the threat of being stereotyped was removed from the test-taking situation, the testing gap disappeared. When highly motivated working-class students are in a non-classist, supportive environment, they can thrive.

Intervention techniques

For all of the barriers that working-class students face in higher education, there are also interventions. The specific challenges working-class students encounter range from emotional to academic to physical, and as such, the intervention techniques are broad in scope and application. Because many of the challenges working-class students face include a diminished sense of fit or belonging, there have been several interventions aimed at helping working-class students see themselves as an important part of the college environment. Although many colleges now offer programs to assist underrepresented students, including first-generation students, these programs often focus on building academic skills (Inkelas, Daver, Vogt, and Leonard 2007), which does not address the range of obstacles detailed above. In order to address the distinct cultural mismatch that working-class students may feel in college, Stephens, Hamedani, and Destin (2014) developed a 'difference-education' intervention that highlighted how students' diverse backgrounds can help them transition in college. This builds off of previous research on multicultural education which emphasizes that different types of backgrounds matter and are important because once students understand that their background is valued, they feel more comfortable in the college environment and more adept at navigating the context (Gurin et al. 2013). In order to test this intervention strategy, incoming first-generation and continuing-generation college students were invited to participate in a student discussion panel about college adjustment one month prior to the beginning of the academic year. Half of these participants were randomly assigned to the difference-education panel, and the other half were assigned to a standard panel. Both panels were comprised of the same culturally diverse students, but in the difference-education panel they talked about their social-class backgrounds in reference to overcoming obstacles and adjusting, whereas in the standard panel the panelists talked about how they overcame obstacles, without referencing their backgrounds. After the panel, all participants completed a brief survey about what they learned, and at the end of the first year of college they completed a second survey that asked whether they had taken advantage of college resources during the year, recorded their end-of-year GPA, and administered several psychosocial measures of adjustment, including for academic engagement, stress, and anxiety. There was also a control group that completed the measures but was not exposed to one of the panels (Stephens, Hamedani, and Destin 2014).

Overall, first-generation students who had been exposed to the difference-education panel showed an increase in using college resources, which led to an increase in overall end-of-year GPA. This increase in GPA eliminated the SES-based performance gap between the first-generation students compared to the continuing-generation participants and the control participants. That is, the first-generation students exposed to the intervention had similar GPAs to average continuing-generation students and better GPAs than first-generation students who did not receive the intervention treatment. All participants in the difference-education panel (first-generation and continuing generation) showed an increase in the psychosocial outcomes; thus, everyone benefitted in some form from learning about their peers' diverse backgrounds. In a follow-up study two years later, the students who had previously participated in the study were asked to give an impromptu speech about transitioning to college, geared towards incoming students. During the speech, the students who had previously been in the difference-education panel talked about their backgrounds more frequently than those who were exposed to the standard panel, indicating that the difference-education students remembered and were influenced by the content of the original message that they heard two years earlier. Importantly, the first-generation students who initially participated in the difference-education panel also showed healthier balances of hormone secretion while experiencing a stressful situation (completing a difficult portion of the GRE), compared to first-generation students who did not receive the intervention but also the continuing-generation students who did receive the intervention (Stephens, Townsend, Hamedani, Destin, and Manzo 2015). This means that for first-generation students in particular, reflecting on one's background, after learning that one's background is valuable, can actually work as a buffer rather than a stressor or distractor. Because various colleges and universities may not have the student panelists necessary to conduct such an intervention each year, research on higher education administration suggests that faculty and academic advisors can be trained to serve this function by helping working-class students identify the source of their stress while also valuing and integrating their own class norms in an academic setting (Soria and Bultmann 2014)

Building on this, a more direct intervention for helping working-class students involves teaching them to see the personal relevance of course materials (Harackiewicz, Canning, Tibbetts, Priniski, and Hyde 2016) or to reflect on their own personal values (Tibbetts, Harackiewicz, Canning, Boston, Priniski, and Hyde 2016). After reflecting on their personal values in the context of a particular course, first-generation students ended up being less concerned about their own academic fit and increased their course grades by the end of the semester. However, when first-generation students did not have the opportunity to reflect on their personal values, they had increased concern about academic fit and lower course grades by the end of the semester.

At the institutional level, colleges and universities can make simple changes to their policies, procedures, and programs that will have a large impact. As previously mentioned, simple wording changes on admissions letters and materials can reinforce independent or interdependent norms, which in turn can negatively impact first-generation students (Stephens, Fyberg et al. 2012). When these materials use interdependent language ('collaborative research', 'community learning'), first-generation students not only have lowered cortisol levels, but also see academic tasks as less difficult. Continuing-generation students were not negatively impacted by interdependent language; thus, the performance gap was eliminated, with first-generation and continuing-generation students performing equally well when primed with interdependent norms. Additionally, slightly modifying the questions and topics at student panels for incoming students, to include discussion about the importance of the panelists' backgrounds, can create a long-lasting boost for everyone, particularly first-generation students. Research in education has demonstrated that retention rates for white working-class students increase when colleges create summer programs that provide academic advising and mentoring (Stuber 2011), as can having colleges and advisors establish relationships with parents to lessen the cultural divide (Lightweis 2014). At the individual level, faculty and staff can also make simple additions to their teaching or work that will have long-lasting positive effects. In advising sessions, professors and advisors can use more interdependent language and can also encourage students to reflect on their own personal values when choosing courses, majors, or career paths. In the classroom, professors can use ten minutes of the first day of class, after reviewing the syllabus, to have students write down how the course material is relevant to their own lives, thereby easily creating a stronger sense of 'fit' for students who may already be feeling like they do not belong.

Conclusion

Taken together, it is clear that working-class students face a unique set of barriers in higher education. Although access to resources and knowledge about college environments can be major obstacles, so too are the psychological and physical demands that impact working-class students in multiple ways. Throughout the psychological literature on working-class students, the most frequent themes are belonging and academic performance – the two constructs being closely related, with one impacting the other. For working-class students to succeed academically, they must have some sense of belonging; yet when they do underperform academically, that disrupts perceived belonging. As such, working-class students can get trapped in a cycle of isolation, depression, anxiety, avoidance, and underperformance. They receive implicit and explicit messages that they do not belong, even in the very materials that are meant to announce their admission and welcome them to college. Working-class students who do manage to stay invested in their academics and perform well become vulnerable to stereotype threat because so much of their self-esteem is invested in defying the stereotype.

But for each of these barriers, there are solutions. Working-class students have reduced anxiety and depression when they are around other working-class students. They have decreased stress and increased health when they are made to feel as though they belong. They perform as well or better than their continuing-generation peers when stereotypes are removed from the situation and their own personal values are reinforced. These intervention strategies can be easily implemented at multiple stages of an academic career, and the effects of the interventions are long-lasting. Although working-class students' class status may start to change once they enroll in college, they still in many ways culturally maintain their class identities, and as they move through academia, their voices contribute to the diverse perspectives that we value within higher education. It is this perspective that I brought to my students when I decided to cancel classes and go home for my sister's delivery. I told my students the truth; that I hated to cancel class, but that I did, indeed, need to be home with my family. I also told them that it is hard to balance family needs with personal needs, particularly when your family relies on you or when you are heavily interdependent with them, as is common in working-class families. I saw many students shake their heads in agreement, with a look of recognition on their faces,[3] and then I happily traveled home, sat next to my sister, and waited with the rest of my family for my new niece, Cecilia, to be born.

Notes

1 These studies were conducted at a range of four-year institutions, from regional campuses to elite universities. Two-year universities are not studied in these samples.

2 Because 'working class' can be hard to define, particularly in experimental studies, psychological research often uses other measures of class, such as income level and parents' education level, as proxies. As such, the following studies are presented with the original language and criterion that was used as a measurement of social class.

3 Although anecdotal, I believe that this small disclosure of personal information, and explicit acknowledgment of my working-class background, shaped the discussions in my courses in interesting ways as the semester progressed. Although I have always been up front about my background, I believe that addressing the class struggles that remain (as well as some that have lessened) during the first week of the semester encouraged my working-class students to be more open about their own social-class-related problems. Additionally, my students from more professional or capitalist class backgrounds became more curious about social class and seemed to have a better understanding of the impact of social class in college settings than they have had in previous years.

References

Allan, B. A., Garriott, P. O. and Keene, C. N. (2016) 'Outcomes of social class and classism in first and continuing-generation college students', *Journal of Counseling Psychology*, 63, 4, pp. 487–496.

Barry, L. M., Hudley, C., Kelly, M. and Cho, S. J. (2009) 'Differences in self-reported disclosure of college experiences by first-generation college student status', *Adolescence*, 44, 173, pp. 55–68.

Brantlinger, E. A. (2003) *Dividing Classes: How the Middle Class Negotiates and Rationalizes School Advantage*, New York, Routledge Falmer.

Choi, J., Fauce, S. R. and Effros, R. B. (2008) 'Reduced telomerase activity in human T lymphocytes exposed to cortisol', *Brain, Behavior, and Immunity*, 22, 4, pp. 600–605.

Christopher, R. (2005) 'New working-class studies in higher education', in Russo, J. and Linkon S. L. (eds.) *New Working-Class Studies*, Ithaca, Cornell University Press.

College Board (2015) *2015 College-Bound Seniors Total Group Profile Report*. Retrieved from https://securemedia.collegeboard.org/digitalServices/pdf/sat/total-group-2015.pdf

Educational Testing Service (2009) *Factors that Can Influence Performance on the GRE General Test, 2008–2009*. Retrieved from www.ets.org/Media/Tests/GRE/pdf/gre_0809_factors_2006-07.pdf

Frable, D. E. S., Platt, L. and Hoey, S. (1998) 'Concealable stigmas and positive self-perceptions: Feeling better around similar others', *Journal of Personality and Social Psychology*, 74, 4, pp. 909–922.

Gardner, S. K. and Holley, K. A. (2011) '"Those invisible barriers are real": The progress of first-generation students through doctoral education', *Equity & Excellence in Education*, 44, 1, pp. 77–92.

Gurin, P., Nagda, B. A. and Zuniga, X. (2013) *Dialogue across Difference: Practice, Theory, and Research on Intergroup Dialogue*, New York, Russell Sage.

Harackiewicz, J. M., Canning, E. A., Tibbetts, Y., Priniski, S. J. and Hyde, J. S. (2016) 'Closing achievement gaps with a utility-value intervention: Disentangling race and social class', *Journal of Personality and Social Psychology*, 111, 5, pp. 745–765.

Hinz, S. E. (2016) 'Upwardly mobile: Attitudes toward the class transition among first-generation students', *Journal of College Student Development*, 57, 3, pp. 285–299.

Hong, Y.-y., Chiu, C.-y., Dweck, C. S., Lin, D. M.-S. and Wan, W. (1999) 'Implicit theories, attributions, and coping: A meaning system approach', *Journal of Personality and Social Psychology*, 77, 3, pp. 588–599. https://doi.org/10.1037/0022-3514.77.3.588

Ibrahim, A. K., Kelly, S. J. and Glazebrook, C. (2013) 'Socioeconomic status and the risk of depression among UK higher education students', *Social Psychiatry and Epidemiology*, 48, pp. 1491–1501.

Inkelas, K. K., Daver, Z. E., Vogt, K. E. and Leonard, J. B. (2007) 'Living-learning programs and first-generation college students' academic and social transition to college', *Research in Higher Education*, 48, pp. 403–434.

Johnson, S. E., Richeson, J. A. and Finkel, E. J. (2011) 'Middle class and marginal? Socioeconomic status, stigma, and self-regulation at an elite university', *Journal of Personality and Social Psychology*, 100, 5, pp. 838–852.

Jury, M., Smeding, A., Court, M. and Darnon, C. (2015) 'When first-generation students succeed at university: On the link between social class, academic performance, and performance-avoidance goals', *Contemporary Educational Psychology*, 41, pp. 25–36.

Jury, M., Smeding, A. and Darnon, C. (2015) 'First-generation students' underperformance at university: The impact of the function of selection', *Frontiers in Psychology*, 6, Article 710.

Jury, M., Smeding, A., Stephens, N. M., Nelson, J. E., Aelenei, C. and Darnon, C. (2017) 'The experience of low-SES students in higher education: Psychological barriers to success and interventions to reduce social-class inequality', *Journal of Social Issues*, 73, 1, pp. 23–41.

Krantz, D. S. and McCeney, M. K. (2002) 'Effects of psychological and social factors on organic disease: A critical assessment of research on coronary heart disease', *Annual Review of Psychology*, 53, pp. 341–369.

Langston, D. (1993) 'Who am I now? The politics of class identity', in Tokarczyk, M. M. and Fay, E. A. (eds.) *Working-Class Women in the Academy*, Amherst, University of Massachusetts Press.

Lightweis, S. (2014) 'The challenges, persistence, and success of white, working-class, first-generation college students', *College Student Journal*, 48, 3, pp. 461–467.

Markus, H. R. and Conner, A. (2013) *Clash! 8 Cultural Conflicts that Make Us Who We Are*, New York, Hudson Street Press.

Markus, H. R. and Kitayama, S. (1991) 'Cultures and selves: A cycle of mutual constitution', *Perspectives on Psychological Science*, 5, 4, pp. 420–30.

Ostrove, J. M. and Long, S. M. (2007) 'Social class and belonging: Implications for college adjustment', *Review of Higher Education*, 30, 4, pp. 363–389.

Reay, D., Crozier, G. and Clayton, J. (2010) '"Fitting in" or "standing out": Working-class students in UK higher education', *British Educational Research Journal*, 36, 1, pp. 107–124.

Rheinschmidt, M. L. and Mendoza-Denton, R. (2014) 'Social class and academic achievement in college: The interplay of rejection sensitivity and entity beliefs', *Journal of Personality and Social Psychology*, 107, 1, pp. 101–121.

Rubin, M. (2012) 'Social class differences in social integration among students in higher education: A meta-analysis and recommendations for future research', *Journal of Diversity in Higher Education*, 5, 1, pp. 22–38.

Soria, K. and Bultmann, M. (2014) 'Supporting working-class students in higher education', *NACADA Journal*, 34, 2, pp. 51–62.

Spencer, B. and Castano, E. (2007) 'Social class is dead. Long live social class! Stereotype threat among low socioeconomic status individuals', *Social Justice Research*, 20, 4, pp. 418–432.

Spencer, S. J., Steele, C. M. and Quinn, D. (1999) 'Under suspicion of inability: Stereotype threat and women's math performance', *Journal of Experimental Social Psychology*, 35, pp. 4–28.

Steele, C. M. and Aronson, J. (1995) 'Stereotype threat and the intellectual test performance of African Americans', *Journal of Personality and Social Psychology*, 69, 5, pp. 797–811.

Stephens, N. M., Fryberg, S. A., Markus, H. R., Johnson, C. and Covarrubias, R. (2012) 'Unseen disadvantage: How American universities' focus on independence undermines the academic performance of first-generation college students', *Journal of Personality and Social Psychology*, 102, 6, pp. 1178–1197.

Stephens, N. M., Hamedani, M. G. and Destin, M. (2014) 'Closing the social-class achievement gap: A difference-education intervention improves first-generation students' academic performance and all students' college transition', *Psychological Science*, 25, 4, pp. 943–953.

Stephens, N. M., Townsend, S. S. M., Hamedani, M. G., Destin, M. and Manzo, V. (2015) 'A difference-education intervention equips first-generation college students to thrive in the face of stressful college situations', *Psychological Science*, 26, 10, pp. 1–11.

Stephens, N. M., Townsend, S. S., Markus, H. R. and Phillips, L. T. (2012) 'A cultural mismatch: Independent cultural norms produce greater increases in cortisol and more negative emotions among first-generation college students', *Journal of Experimental Social Psychology*, 48, 6, pp. 1389–1393.

Stuber, J. M. (2011) 'Integrated, marginal, and resilient: Race, class, and the diverse experiences of white first-generation college students', *International Journal of Qualitative Studies in Education*, 24, 1, pp. 117–136.

Tibbetts, Y., Harackiewicz, J. M., Canning, E. A., Boston, J. S., Priniski, S. J. and Hyde, J. S. (2016) 'Affirming independence: Exploring mechanisms underlying a values affirmation intervention for first-generation students', *Journal of Personality and Social Psychology*, 110, 5, pp. 635–659.

Webster Marketon, J. I. and Glaser, R. (2008) 'Stress hormones and immune function', *Cellular Immunology*, 252, 1–2, pp. 1672–1677.

10

Learning our place

Social reproduction in K–12 schooling

Deborah M. Warnock

This chapter focuses on social class inequalities in educational experiences and outcomes among K–12 students. Beginning with a discussion of relevant sociological theories, I summarize and synthesize historical and contemporary research on socioeconomic stratification in schooling. In this chapter I examine mechanisms and trends that sociologists have identified as integral to understanding the ways in which K–12 schooling has exacerbated social class inequalities rather than leveled them. The chapter is organized into sections that further explore each mechanism or trend, including segregation, cultural capital, the testing gap, and differential investment in education. Next I synthesize sociological studies of social mobility, including how students from working-class backgrounds employ strategies to navigate upward mobility. I also focus on how class inequalities in K–12 schooling contribute to disparities in access to higher education. Throughout the chapter I highlight studies which have examined the intersection of social class with other social identities, such as race and gender. Finally, I conclude with a note on future research directions for the study of social class in K–12 education.

Theoretical frameworks

While education is often touted as the pathway to success and the 'American Dream', the classed realities of the K–12 system do not often lend themselves to mobility, but instead to reproduction. Sorokin (1959) identifies this tension when he describes education not as an equalizing force in society, but as a sieve, meant to select some students while sorting others out of the opportunity structure. Collins (1971) further questions the purpose of education in his quest to explain the broad educational expansion that took place in the 20th century. Rather than being driven by technological changes and a commensurate increased demand for skills, Collins argues that as a greater percentage of people attain a given educational credential, it ceases to hold value. He finds more support for a Weberian conflict theory of education, which states that education serves as a mechanism to maintain inequality within a society, than for a functional theory, which argues that schooling delivers skills necessary for labor market success. Rather than dealing in skills, Collins argues that schools trade in status, with those who hold credentials seen as more properly socialized into a white-collar or managerial class than those who do not.

In *Schooling in Capitalist America*, economists Bowles and Gintis (1975) offer a Marxist critique of the function of education in modern American society. Through 'the correspondence principle' they argue that schools are organized similar to the exploitative and hierarchical capitalist labor market. Through a reliance on obedience, conformity, and uniformity in school lessons and structure, working-class pupils are taught to be workers. Rather than operate as an equalizing force in a class-structured society, Bowles and Gintis argue that work casts a 'long shadow' on education, which is used as a justifying force for inequality. Unhappy with your lot in life? Not making enough money to feed your family? You should have tried harder or gone further in school. In this way, the bourgeoisie use education as a tool to justify the exploitation of the proletariat in modern capitalist society.

Turner (1960) describes the mobility norms in American society, or the stories we tell ourselves to explain why certain people are socially mobile while others are not, as being a form of contest. Unlike in Europe where educational systems tend to sort pupils early and blatantly into separate classed tracks, success in America is a constant contest. You haven't won or lost yet – you could always go back to school or win the lottery tomorrow. Central to this system is the belief that all Americans are afforded equal educational opportunities and each student's success is based upon his or her merit, as measured by aptitude, hard work, or both. Contest mobility norms put all of the onus on the individual – where you end up depends entirely on you – and if you're not happy with it, the game is not over yet! You could still find a way, through education or other routes, to achieve the American Dream. In what follows I discuss the sociological mechanisms through which K–12 schooling maintains and exacerbates social class inequalities.

Segregation within and among schools

Research demonstrates that, contrary to contest mobility norms, not everyone has access to equal educational opportunities in this country. Schools are overwhelmingly segregated by social class. The average poor student attends a poor school. The curriculum and resources in schools varies by the socioeconomic composition of those schools. As demonstrated in Kozol's (1991) bestselling *Savage Inequalities*, poor students are educated in overcrowded classrooms in dilapidated buildings by less-qualified teachers and are less likely to have access to resources such as books and technology. Meanwhile, class-privileged students learn in well-maintained buildings and are taught critical thinking skills by competent teachers who have a variety of resources at hand.

Schools have remained segregated and are becoming increasingly so (Orfield, Kucsera, & Siegel-Hawley 2012). However, even among schools that serve a diverse student body, students are still likely to be segregated by class. In her work on tracking, Oakes (1985) details how schools sort students into different tracks by race, ethnicity, and social class background. Middle-class students are more likely to be assigned to college prep, advanced, or gifted classes, while working-class students are more likely to take vocational prep or remedial classes. When asked what they have learned, students in the advanced classes describe particular skills or aspects of the curriculum. However, students in the tech prep classes are more likely to say that they haven't learned anything. Evoking Bowles and Gintis' (1975) 'correspondence principle', in one school she observed, Oakes describes working-class students being required to clock in and clock out of the classroom. In addition to class disparities in opportunities to learn, research shows that teachers have lower expectations for students from working-class or low-income families (Rist 1977). Teachers are more likely to label these children as slow or deviant, which in turn becomes a self-fulfilling prophecy that alienates working-class children from the learning environment.

Cultural capital

Bourdieu (1977) argued that the educational system is central to the cultural and social reproduction of the social classes. Schools reflect and reward the values and tastes of the dominant class by privileging a dominant form of cultural capital. Cultural capital is 'institutionalized, i.e., widely shared, high status cultural signals (attitudes, preferences, formal knowledge, behaviors, goals and credentials) used for social and cultural exclusion' (Lamont & Lareau 1988, 156). Bourdieu argued that schools and other institutions use cultural capital as a tool for excluding the working class from opportunity while simultaneously outwardly subscribing to the ideals of meritocracy.

Using Bourdieu's concept of cultural capital as a theoretical framework, Annette Lareau (2003) and a team of researchers shadowed a diverse group of students and their families for many years, observing them not only in school but also at home, at play, running errands, and going to appointments and practices. She identified two class-based parenting approaches: accomplishment of natural growth and concerted cultivation. Working-class parents tend to allow their children more free time and independence in play, which tends to happen in informal neighborhood settings or with extended family members. They are less likely to have extended conversations with their children and are also less likely to directly question authority figures. This parenting style, accomplishment of natural growth, leads to an emerging sense of constraint, according to Lareau.

Middle-class parents, however, take a concerted cultivation approach, conversing frequently with their children and scheduling (and over-scheduling) their children's time in organized activities with same-aged peers. In their interactions with authority figures, such as teachers or doctors, middle-class parents demonstrate how to successfully navigate institutions and rules in order to obtain their desired goals. This concerted cultivation style leads to an emerging sense of entitlement.

While Lareau does not argue for the superiority of one approach over the other, she does allow that the concerted cultivation approach couples more effectively with contemporary expectations of parenting, or the dominant form of cultural capital, among middle-class institutions. Schools, for example, expect parents to be involved in their children's education in proactive and visible ways, and these expectations lead to certain parents and their students being labeled as more or less committed. These labels may then extend to evaluations of the child's academic potential, leading fewer working-class students to be identified as 'gifted' or academically talented (Card & Giuliano 2015).

Students themselves may learn to navigate interactions with school authority figures to their advantage, which may result in discipline gaps as well. In her study of elementary school children, Calarco (2014) finds that middle-class students, who are more likely to contest rules and the consequences of ignoring them, may be punished less often than working-class students, who are more likely to obey the teachers and accept punishment without complaint.

Lareau's work has been criticized as ignoring the structural for the cultural. For example, some have suggested that these are not different cultural parenting orientations, but instead relate to time and resources, or the lack thereof. Concerted cultivation, with its extensive parental involvement and high prices of scheduled activities, costs time and money. Therefore, Lareau's critics have argued that these approaches differ only in terms of access to these two resources. For example, Roksa and Potter (2011) compared class-stable mothers to those who had been upwardly or downwardly mobile over their lives. If parenting styles are cultural and socialized, one would think that the parenting style in which one was raised would most affect one's one approach. However, with the mobile mothers, Roksa and Potter found that class of destination mattered more than class of origin in predicting parenting style. Regardless of their class of origin, mothers who lived middle-class lives as adults were more likely to use a concerted cultivation style, whereas the parenting approach of mothers who lived working-class lives as adults more resembled accomplishment of natural growth. These findings suggest that adherence to costly parenting norms may rely less on culture and more on access to resources.

The achievement gap

Many scholars have debated the causes of the Black-white achievement gap (see Jencks & Phillips 1998); however, this gap has steadily closed over the past few decades. Meanwhile, the income achievement gap has grown significantly during this time, eclipsing the Black-white gap in the process (Reardon 2013). For example, the reading test score gap between high- and low-income families was over 40% larger in 2000 than it was in the 1970s. Test scores are but one measure of educational outcomes, but gaps in other measures have also grown. Students from high-income families have become increasingly likely to complete college, while the rate for students from low-income families has not grown significantly (Bailey & Dynarski 2011). For the 1979–1982 birth cohort, 54% of students from families in the top income quartile completed college, while only 9% of students from the bottom income quartile did so. The share of high-income students at the most selective colleges and universities has also grown (Reardon, Baker, & Klasik 2012).

One possible reason for income disparities in achievement is the summer learning gap. Multiple studies have shown that low-income students show comparable skill gains to middle- and high-income students during the school year. However, when students are tested at the beginning of the school year, low-income students show a loss in skills, whereas high-income students show gains. These findings relate back to Lareau's work on parenting approaches, in which middle-class parents have the resources and time to plan many learning enrichment activities over the summers. Lack of access to comparable activities may help to explain the growth in the income achievement gap.

However, Reardon (2013) also argues that rising income inequality and the concurrent decline in social mobility are to blame. In 1970 a family at the top of the income distribution earned five times as much as a family at the bottom. In 2010 the average high-income family earned 11 times as much as the average low-income family. This growing gap is reflected in the class disparities in access to educational resources and opportunities that families are able to provide to their children. Meanwhile, upward mobility rates in the last 40 years have stalled, and educational credentials have become more and more necessary for economic success (Reardon 2013). In addition, the growing reliance on test scores as measures of academic prowess have placed low-income students, whose parents are less likely to have the financial or cultural resources to assist their children in success, at a disadvantage.

Investment in education

Some popular conservative arguments suggest that working-class students and their families are less likely to find academic success because they either do not try or do not value education. For example, in his bestselling memoir *Hillbilly Elegy: A Memoir of Family and Culture in Crisis*, J. D. Vance (2016) relies on a cultural argument to explain his family's poverty. Specifically, he makes the case that descendants of the Scots-Irish in the Appalachian region of America have embraced an oppositional mindset that prohibits them from attaining upward mobility, instead encouraging community-wide social rot and resentment. Citing a lack of work ethic, deficient morals, drug addiction and abuse, and failure to take personal responsibility for one's actions, Vance blames the Appalachian poor for their own socioeconomic misfortune. Turning this argument on its head, some sociologists have argued that when working-class students do not try in school, it is because they understand that the deck is already stacked against them.

In Paul Willis' (1977) seminal book *Learning to Labor: How Working-Class Kids Get Working-Class Jobs*, he follows a group of working-class boys, or 'lads', attending high school in a British factory town, watching as they 'have a laff' at the expense of their teachers and more obedient peers. Willis argues that this oppositional attitude is actually a form of resistance. The lads have 'penetrated' through the veneer of education to understand that their performance in school has no bearing on their adult lives. Even if they were to excel in school, there are few opportunities to obtain a better-paying job. And if they were to go away to college, they would be, in a sense, betraying their own community. One lad's individual upward mobility will not raise an entire community or class of people. For this reason, Willis argues that the lads resist schooling in order to make their 'failure' appear to be a personal choice. In this way, they are striving for a sense of agency in a system that denies them equal opportunity, while simultaneously equating success with individual merit and not access to opportunity. Ironically, through their resistance, the lads are participating in their own social reproduction as they get low-paying, difficult jobs in the same factories where their parents worked. However, Willis suggests that this social reproduction was inevitable and that, through their oppositional attitudes and behaviors, the lads were attempting to undermine the system that serves to legitimate their 'failure'.

When working-class students do seek upward mobility through education, their pathways abound with obstacles. MacLeod (1987) followed two groups of boys who lived in the projects in a northeastern American city. One group, the 'Hallway Hangers', was a group of predominantly white boys who resembled Willis' 'lads' in their derisive attitude towards school. When asked where they saw themselves 20 years into the future, their pessimistic predictions included incarceration or death. The 'Brothers', meanwhile, a group of predominantly Black young men who resided in the same projects, were unflaggingly optimistic about the future. Unlike the Hallway Hangers, they saw education as a pathway out of poverty and worked hard in school. Their descriptions of their future lives included all of the trappings of the metaphoric American Dream: big house with a yard, nice car, good job, wife and kids, etc. The differing orientations of these two groups of boys appear to lend credence to cultural arguments of social mobility. If one is willing to try hard, one will succeed. And, yet, when MacLeod returned to the projects eight years later, he found that neither group of boys had seen much success. Just as they themselves predicted, some members of the Hallway Hangers were imprisoned, while others were selling drugs in the underground economy. Both groups of boys worked in the secondary labor market, in low-wage service jobs with high turnover. Only one of the Brothers had managed to land a unionized job as a postal carrier. In spite of their divergent attitudes, aspirations, and actions, the Brothers had not been much more successful than the Hallway Hangers. A study that initially appeared to serve as evidence against an economically determinist argument of social reproduction only ended up confirming the difficulty of upward mobility.

Social mobility

For working-class students who seek upward social mobility through education, the challenges they face along the way vary by race and ethnicity. In her study of upwardly mobile Mexican-American and white high school students, Bettie (2003) found that white working-class students articulated their feelings of discomfort and distance from their communities as individualized. Whites, who tend not to identify strongly with their own racial category (Perry 2002), also lacked a language around a collective class experience with which to articulate the feelings of loss and alienation that can accompany the process of upward mobility (Lubrano 2004). While this 'unarticulated class longing' may be painful, especially, perhaps, in an environment in which class differences are more salient, the association of whiteness with class privilege can also smooth the transition of whites across class boundaries by making it easier for them to 'pass' (Bettie 2003, 161–162).

Meanwhile, the Mexican-American girls in Bettie's study were 'more consciously aware of themselves as a community of people' with a shared history of oppression (Bettie 2003, 161). They tended to define their own trajectories of upward mobility in racialized terms, using the strategy of 'accommodation without assimilation' (Gibson 1988). Rather than view the middle class as a necessarily white domain, they expressed pride in their ethnic identities, and did not view their mobility as a form of assimilation to white culture. Simultaneously, these students had to remain vigilant and resist teachers' and counselors' tendencies to steer them to the vocational track. Whereas working-class white students more visibly fit in due to their race, Mexican-American girls are marked as different in college prep classes that tend to be populated by economically privileged and white students (Tyson 2011). Experiences of schooling and upward mobility through education are shaped not by race or class alone, but by how the two intersect.

Indeed, because schools are classed and raced places, in her study of low-income, native-born African-American and Latino youth, Carter (2005) found that students engage in different strategies that help them traverse cultural divides. She identified three types of students: the assimilationists, or 'cultural mainstreamers', the non-assimilationists, or 'noncompliant believers', and the code-switchers, or 'cultural straddlers'.

Cultural mainstreamers had the highest mean grade point averages (GPAs) and were the most optimistic about how education would affect their life chances; 100% of students in this group expected to attend college. However, in their quest to conform to the white, middle-class norms that dominate college-prep-track classes, they were also more likely to be teased by other Black and Latino students for 'acting white'. Because advanced classes tend to be populated with white and middle-class students, high-achieving students of color were more likely to count white students among their friend groups, which also put them at risk of being ostracized by their Black and Latino peers.

Noncompliant believers had the lowest mean GPAs and were least optimistic about schooling as a pathway for mobility, and only 55% expected to enroll in college. These students were critical of education and sought to remain true to their own ethno-racial style of dress, tastes, and interaction (Carter 2005). In addition, they were critical of co-ethnic peers, whom they viewed as adopting white and middle-class norms and values as their own.

Finally, cultural straddlers were those that sought to keep a foot planted in both worlds, staying true to their low-income backgrounds and ethno-racial identities while cultivating the dominant form of cultural capital that would help them to succeed in the white and middle-class schooling environment. Just as they sought to straddle cultural boundaries, this group found themselves in between mainstreamers and believers when it came to achievement metrics.

Still, Carter (2005) argued that the straddlers ultimately deployed the most successful strategy. By maintaining ties to their families, co-ethnic peers, and neighborhoods, they were able to draw on a support network intertwined with their own identities while simultaneously building capital and ties that would help them to succeed in a white and middle-class educational setting. For the mainstreamers who sought only to assimilate, they risked losing an important part of their identity in a gamble for upward mobility, which might not ultimately pay off. Finally, noncompliant believers maintained ties to their home community, but abandoned any possibility of upward mobility through schooling. Ultimately, Carter (2005) demonstrates not only that low-income youth of color face unique challenges in adapting to culturally distinct educational settings, but also that these youth employ diverse strategies to overcome these challenges.

Access to college

There is ample evidence to suggest that working-class youth do not have equal access to information about applying for and paying for college. Their parents are less likely to have attended college themselves and, therefore, lack the firsthand knowledge to help guide them through the process that middle-class parents often take for granted. They are more likely to attend overcrowded high schools that do not expect their students to enroll in four-year institutions upon graduation. Therefore, they struggle to obtain accurate information about the college application process from their families and schools.

Research has shown that parents are the most influential 'significant others' in affecting a student's educational expectations and preparedness behaviors (Hossler, Schmit, & Vesper 1999). Yet low-income families and parents without a college degree are less likely to report that they have information about paying for college and more likely to report that their children will need to work their way through college (Warnock 2016a). This lack of information affects students' educational expectations and preparedness behaviors in high school, determining whether or not they will even be eligible to apply to a four-year institution upon graduation (Warnock 2010). In her longitudinal study of Wisconsin college students, Goldrick-Rab (2016) demonstrates how this lack of information affects where students apply and attend college and whether or not they apply for financial aid (or even know about their eligibility).

The high schools working-class students attend do not effectively address this information gap. McDonough (1997) found that guidance counselors often steered working-class students toward community colleges. In his study of admissions at an elite liberal arts college, Stevens (2007) demonstrated that students attending working-class high schools are at a disadvantage compared with those at upper-middle-class high schools. He showed that admissions counselors develop relationships with 'feeder' schools and often engage in 'horse-trading' with the guidance counselors at these schools. Meanwhile, they see it as a waste of time and resources to visit high schools where they do not have a relationship with the counselor or which do not have a history of sending them students. Working-class students are less likely to receive extensive information about college from their guidance counselors and are less likely to have the chance to interact with college representatives.

Working-class students who are 'college-ready' are less likely to attend four-year institutions than their comparable middle-class peers (Hoxby & Avery 2012). High-achieving working-class students are less likely to attend selective institutions as well, a phenomenon known as 'undermatching' (Bastedo & Jaquette 2011). Research has shown that the selectivity of the college one attends predicts labor market success (Gaddis 2015), so the underrepresentation of working-class students on selective campuses puts them at a further disadvantage. However, it is important to note that working-class students may experience culture shock and find it difficult to integrate at selective institutions (Hurst & Warnock 2015; Lee 2016; Stuber 2011; Warnock & Hurst 2016). Drawing on Bourdieu (2004), Lee and Kramer (2013) find that working-class students on a predominantly wealthy campus may be more likely to experience a 'cleft habitus', in which they find themselves caught between their home communities and new college identity. It is important for researchers to identify the social and emotional consequences of upward mobility, which are often overlooked in the extant academic literature, which focuses primarily on economic measures of 'success'.

Moving forward

Particularly in an economic climate wherein income and wealth inequality gaps are constantly growing and research demonstrates that working-class students are still being denied equal access to quality education, the study of social class and education remains vital. Even more important are the contributions of working-class studies scholars, whose foundational grounding in the study of social class can bring a much-needed new perspective to extant literature. As Warnock (2016b) notes, working-class academics are more likely to bring a nuanced understanding of the functions of class to their scholarship, as their work is informed by their valuable lived experiences. Identifying and supporting working-class academics who are doing work on social class and education will be essential to continuing to build knowledge in the field.

Scholars continue to argue about how best to define and measure social class. While some use economic measures such as income and wealth, others are more inclined to consider one's level of education (Wright 2005). Still others examine the amount of autonomy one has in the workplace (Zweig 2011). Finally, some have framed it as a type of identity location, somewhat similar to race and gender (Warnock & Hurst 2016). What everyone seems to agree upon is how tricky class can be to measure, in part because of its fluid nature. One's social class may change over one's lifetime and, yet, research often seems to consider class as static. More studies that acknowledge both upward and downward forms of class mobility and how education contributes to these patterns would be useful. Roksa and Potter's study (2011) of upwardly and downwardly mobile mothers and how their mobility affected their approaches to their children's education, cited earlier in this chapter, is one helpful example. More recently, Streib (2020) examines trends in social mobility, identifying incomplete socialization processes that lead to downward outcomes. More studies should examine the ways in which class changes (and also does not) over time and how education either shapes or is shaped by these fluctuations.

In addition, more intersectional research examining how class interacts with other social locations, such as race and ethnicity and gender, is needed. As Fraser and Honneth (2003) have noted, class is but one stratifying identity position in modern society. Other status identities, such as race and gender, must be considered alongside class in order to best understand how inequality persists. Intersectionality theory posits that these identities are not experienced separately but simultaneously, in ways that intersect to determine and shape individual's social standpoints, experiences, and access to resources (Collins 2000). There is evidence to suggest that classed experiences vary by race (Bettie 2003; Warnock 2019) and by gender (DiMaggio 1982; Rivera & Tilcsik 2016), and researchers should seek to tease out these effects in students' experiences of education. Understanding how class inequalities function in society necessitates recognition of how race and gender operate in similar stratifying processes.

This chapter has focused on the ways in which class is socially reproduced through schooling. However, these findings differ from the dominant narrative which American citizens are taught from a young age, contesting mobility norms that suggest that hard work is all that is needed to succeed (Turner 1960). Some researchers, such as MacLeod (1987), who truly thought he had found an exception to economic determinism in 'the Brothers', suggest that educators disrupt that narrative. Specifically, he suggests that schools replace the teaching of achievement ideology with a way of motivating students that acknowledges rather than denies their social statuses. This paradigm shift would allow working-class students to feel pride in their families and communities, rather than stigmatizing them. This approach would validate students' identities rather than trying to change them and would teach about social justice as a way to motivate students with indignation.

One recent study suggests that teaching low-income students of color system-justifying beliefs about individual meritocracy undermines student self-esteem and contributes to delinquent behavior (Godfrey, Santos, & Burson 2017). In effect, marginalized youth who are indoctrinated with myths that belie the class and race discrimination rampant in American society engage in resistance behavior, much like Willis' lads. In this way, they also appear to contribute to their own social reproduction. One way to resist perpetuating the myth of meritocracy is for teachers to acknowledge that racism and classism do exist and to allow students space to be critical of American society and their status in it. Schooling should be used to empower working-class people rather than to justify their subjugation through its contribution to cultural and social reproduction.

References

Bailey, M. J. and Dynarski, S. M. (2011) 'Gains and Gaps', in Duncan, G. and Murnane, R. (eds.) *Whither Opportunity?* New York, Russell Sage Foundation.

Bastedo, M. N. and Jaquette, O. (2011) 'Running in Place', *Educational Evaluation and Policy Analysis*, 33, 3, pp. 318–339.

Bettie, J. (2003) *Women without Class*, Oakland, University of California Press.

Bourdieu, P. (1977) 'Cultural Reproduction and Social Reproduction', in Karabel, J. and Halsey, A. H. (eds.) *Power and Ideology in Education*, New York, Oxford University Press.

Bourdieu, P. (2004) *The Science of Science and Reflexivity*, Chicago, University of Chicago Press.

Bowles, S. and Gintis, H. (1975) *Schooling in Capitalist America*, New York, Basic Books.

Calarco, J. M. (2014) 'Coached for the Classroom', *American Sociological Review*, 79, 5, pp. 1015–1037.

Card, D. and Giuliano, L. (2015) *Can Universal Screening Increase the Representation of Low Income and Minority Students in Education?* Cambridge, National Bureau of Economic Research.

Carter, P. (2005) *Keepin' It Real*, Oxford, Oxford University Press.

Collins, P. H. (2000) *Black Feminist Thought: Knowledge, Consciousness, and the Politics of Empowerment*, 2nd ed., New York, Routledge.

Collins, R. (1971) 'Functional and Conflict Theories of Educational Stratification', *American Sociological Review*, 36, 6, pp. 1002–1019.

DiMaggio, P. (1982) 'Cultural Capital and School Success', *American Sociological Review*, 47, 2, pp. 189–201.

Fraser, N. and Honneth, A. (2003) *Redistribution or Recognition? A Political-Philosophical Exchange*, New York, Verso.

Gaddis, S. M. (2015) 'Discrimination in the Credential Society', *Social Forces*, 93, 4, pp. 1451–1479.

Gibson, M. A. (1988) *Accommodation without Assimilation*, Ithaca, Cornell University Press.

Godfrey, E. B., Santos, C. E. and Burson, E. (2017) 'For Better or Worse?', *Child Development*, 90, 1, pp. 180–195.

Goldrick-Rab, S. (2016) *Paying the Price*, Chicago, University of Chicago Press.

Hossler, D., Schmit, J. and Vesper, N. (1999) *Going to College*, Baltimore, Johns Hopkins University Press.

Hoxby, C. M. and Avery, C. (2012) *The Missing 'One-Offs'*, Cambridge, National Bureau of Economic Research.

Hurst, A. L. and Warnock, D. M. (2015) '*Les Miraculés:* "The Magical Image of the Permanent Miracle" – Constructed Narratives of Self and Mobility from Working-Class Students at an Elite College', in Lee, E. and LaDousa, C. (eds.) *Sharing Space, Negotiating Difference: Contemporary Ethnographies of Power and Marginality on Campus*, New York, Routledge.

Jencks, C. and Phillips, M. (1998) *The Black-White Test Score Gap*, Washington, Brookings Institution Press.

Kozol, J. (1991) *Savage Inequalities*, New York, Crown Publishers.

Lamont, M. and Lareau, A. (1988) 'Cultural Capital: Allusions, Gaps and Glissandos in Recent Theoretical Developments', *Sociological Theory*, 6, 2, pp. 153–168.

Lareau, A. (2003) *Unequal Childhoods: Class, Race, and Family Life*, Oakland, University of California Press.

Lee, E. M. (2016) *Class and Campus Life*, Ithaca, Cornell University Press.

Lee, E. M. and Kramer, R. (2013) 'Out with the Old, In with the New?' *Sociology of Education*, 86, 1, pp. 18–35.

Lubrano, A. (2004) *Limbo*, Hoboken, John Wiley & Sons.

MacLeod, J. (1987) *Ain't No Makin' It*, Boulder, Westview Press.

McDonough, P. M. (1997) *Choosing Colleges*, Albany, State University of New York Press.

Oakes, J. (1985) *Keeping Track*, New Haven, Yale University Press.

Orfield, G., Kucsera, J. and Siegel-Hawley, G. (2012) E Pluribus *Separation*, Los Angeles, The Civil Rights Project.

Perry, P. (2002) *Shades of White*, Durham, Duke University Press.

Reardon, S. F. (2013) 'Widening Income Achievement Gap', *Educational Leadership*, 70, 8, pp. 10–16.

Reardon, S. F., Baker, R. and Klasik, D. (2012) *Race, Income, and Enrollment Patterns in Highly Selective Colleges, 1982–2004*, Center for Education Policy Analysis, Stanford, Stanford University.

Rist, R. C. (1977) 'On Understanding the Processes of Schooling', in Karabel, J. and Halsey, A. H. (eds.) *Power and Ideology in Education*, New York, Oxford University Press.

Rivera, L. A. and Tilcsik, A. (2016) 'Class Advantage, Commitment Penalty', *American Sociological Review*, 81, 6, pp. 1097–1131.

Roksa, J. and Potter, D. (2011) 'Parenting and Academic Achievement', *Sociology of Education*, 84, 4, pp. 299–321.

Sorokin, P. (1959) *Social and Cultural Mobility*, New York, Free Press.

Stevens, M. L. (2007) *Creating a Class*, Cambridge, Harvard University Press.

Streib, J. (2020) *Privilege Lost: Downward Mobility in the New Gilded Age*, Oxford, Oxford University Press.

Stuber, J. M. (2011) *Inside the College Gates*, Lanham, Lexington Books.

Turner, R. (1960) 'Modes of Social Ascent through Education', *American Sociological Review*, 25, 6, pp. 855–867.

Tyson, K. (2011) *Integration Interrupted*, Oxford, Oxford University Press.

Vance, J. D. (2016) *Hillbilly Elegy: A Memoir of Family and Culture in Crisis*, New York, HarperCollins.

Warnock, D. M. (2010) *When Does Money Matter?* PhD thesis, Seattle, University of Washington.

Warnock, D. M. (2016a) 'Inequalities at the Outset', *Journal of College Student Development*, 57, 5, pp. 503–521.

Warnock, D. M. (2016b) 'Paradise Lost?', *The Journal of Working-Class Studies*, 1, 1, 28–44.

Warnock, D. M. (2019) 'Race-Based Assumptions of Social Class Identity and their Consequences at a Predominantly White (and Wealthy) Institution', in Brunn-Bevel, R. J., Byrd, W. C. and Ovink, S. (eds.) *Intersectionality and Higher Education*, New Brunswick, Rutgers University Press.

Warnock, D. M. and Hurst, A. L. (2016) '"The Poor Kids' Table": Organizing around an Invisible and Stigmatized Identity in Flux', *Journal of Diversity in Higher Education*, 9, 3, pp. 261–276.

Willis, P. (1977) *Learning to Labor: How Working-Class Kids Get Working-Class Jobs*, New York, Columbia University Press.

Wright, E. O. (2005) *Approaches to Class Analysis*, Cambridge, Cambridge University Press.

Zweig, M. (2011) *The Working-Class Majority: America's Best Kept Secret*, 2nd ed., Ithaca, Cornell University Press.

Part III

Work and community

Section introduction

Work and community

Tim Strangleman

Work and community are central to working-class life. In many ways, this is an obvious statement. But work and communities are not fixed; they constantly change and evolve. In turn, working-class life changes too. Working-class studies as a field emerged out of a concern for working class employment and communities at a moment of flux. Let's take a moment to look back at the beginning of the field. If the 1990s was our starting point, work, and I mean here paid employment, was in crisis in multiple ways. The biggest issue here was in the catastrophic loss of traditional manual working-class jobs, a process that had begun in the 1970s but stepped up apace during the 1980s. This was the classic era of deindustrialisation, the sometimes deliberate, sometimes accidental stripping out of productive capacity and the export of jobs to developing nations elsewhere in the world (Bluestone and Harrison 1982). In the wake of deindustrialisation, new forms of work began to emerge, or to become more important. Often these would be in the service sector involving so-called emotional labour (Hochschild 1983). Some writers, especially in the 1990s, began to consider the 'end of work'. This was the idea that work could no longer provide the kind of meanings, attachments and social structures that it had in the past (see Strangleman 2007). The crisis in work had big implications for working-class people.

If the immediate crisis in work was one of the main catalysts for working-class studies, the field has always had a tendency to look back at how employment *had* structured working-class life and community in the past. The reasons for this backward reflection are interesting and complex. Working-class studies emerged from the end of the period of Fordism. This phrase captures a number of different aspects of economy and society in the post-war era. Across the developed world in the wake of the Second World War, working-class people experienced thirty years of rising standards of living and material worth. This is variously described as the 'long boom', or the 'Glorious Thirty'. This pattern was replicated across the industrial world, and while it may have privileged certain categories of workers, this benign rising economic tide lifted all the boats (Piketty 2014; Rosanvallon 2013). This period was an exceptional one, or as labour historian Jefferson Cowie (2016) has described it, 'the great exception', an era out with the normal experience of capitalism. It was, though, perhaps a time when ideas about working-class life and culture began to be firmed up, and this was largely around the ideas of the stability of working-class work in that same period.

Many of the early writings in the field of working-class studies turn on a reflection on types of work born out of the long boom. They focus on vibrant culture and communities shaped by post-war work, where individual and collective workers felt a strong sense of ownership in their work, a greater understanding of the collective power they had in the places of employment, and this was underpinned by the confidence of rising real wages and living standards (see, for example, Bruno 1999). As Jack Metzgar notes of his steelworker father's generation who experienced the period: 'No regular guy in the history of the world had seen the material conditions of his life improve more dramatically. And he knew that it had not just happened, as if by magic' (2000, 6).

What developed out of this was a focus on work and community *before* and *after* the fall, with the fall being plant closure and job loss. What was being marked was a strong vibrant working-class culture now subject to far more challenging times. In part this focus reflected a generational perspective. Many of those who were initially attracted to the field had themselves grown up in working-class neighbourhoods and carried out working-class work, even if they had eventually 'escaped' it, usually by way of education.

In the early days of the field there was a tendency to record work in some of the staple industries such as coal, steel, shipbuilding and car plants. Timing was all important here. By the mid-1990s, it was obvious that this productive capacity was being lost permanently rather than it being a temporary phenomenon. Working-class studies therefore developed out of a desire to set the record straight in terms of working-class life in its heyday, and in its decline, arguing that being working class was a positive identity, rather than a deficit culture to be escaped from.

It is important to stand back a little here to reflect on the obvious danger for the field: the romanticising of its subject matter, an exercise in unreflective nostalgia or a sentimental reflex to the loss of a traditional working-class life. This is certainly an issue and one that has been levelled if not at the field as such, then at those seeking to find value in working-class life more generally. In Cowie and Heathcott's introductory essay in *Beyond the Ruins: The Meanings of Deindustrialisation*, they coin the phrase 'smokestack nostalgia'.

> The time is right to widen the scope of the discussion beyond prototypical plant shutdowns, the immediate politics of employment policy, the tales of victimization, or the swell of industrial nostalgia. Rather, our goal is to rethink the chronology, memory, spatial relations, culture and politics of what we have come to call 'deindustrialization'.
>
> *(Cowie and Heathcott 2003, 1–2)*

They go on to point out the imperative of having to 'strip industrial work of its broad-shouldered, social-relist patina and see it for what it really was: tough work that people did because it paid well and it was located in their communities' (Cowie and Heathcott 2003, 15).

Cowie and Heathcote are surely right to remind their readers of the dangers of romanticising the past and those who inhabited it. Indeed, we could go further and reflect on issues of race, gender and sexuality discrimination within and beyond working-class communities. As a number of studies of factory towns and industrial closure note, tradition industry was frequently underpinned by, and in some cases defined through, the prism of race and ethnic tensions (Cowie 1999; Fine 2004; Honey 1999; McIvor 2013; Virdee 2014). Likewise, I'll never forget a talk given at one of the early Youngstown conferences by a female master electrician who gave a wonderfully moving autobiographical account of struggling to gain her status in the face of almost total misogyny from her male peers. I don't think anyone who sat through that paper could ever again think of the working class as anything but complex!

Equally, there is a danger too of seeing working-class community as static entities preserved in aspic. As one of the contributors here, Kate Dudley, noted in her earlier book, *End of the Line: Lost Jobs, New Lives in Postindustrial America*, we run the risk of exoticising working-class communities like endangered tribes:

> This form of lament is not limited to anthropological writings about non-Western societies caught in the grip of brutalizing 'development' and 'modernising' programs. The rhetorical bells toll just as dolorously in the newly emerging ethnography of deindustrialization. As titles like *Rusted Dreams* or *The Magic City* suggest, American industrial workers are also subject to the kind of historicizing and romanticizing imagery that characterizes nostalgic treatments of more distant but nonetheless passing ways of life.
>
> *(1994, 179)*

This criticism is important and valuable in that the field has, early on, had to recognize the complexity of working-class life. Working-class studies was never, and is not now, an uncritical celebration of all things working class in the arenas of work, community, or any other space. It is a field that finds value in working-class life in all its diversity while also recognising that it is messy, contradictory and compromised in all sorts of ways.

Notwithstanding the valuable critique offered by the charge of 'smokestack nostalgia', it is important that we recognize the positive narratives of work given by deindustrialized workers. Many of these tropes of deindustrialisation critically juxtapose the 'good jobs' of the past versus the 'poor jobs' of the now. While it is essential to interrogate these claims of value, it is equally vital to recognize what was valued about those types of jobs: security, availability, provision of health care and other benefits and, above all, relative stability (see K'Meyer and Hart 2011; Strangleman 2012). Tom Juravich captures the quality of working life in a quote from a laid off machinist:

> My godmother's brother was a foreman over here for years. My next door neighbour when I was little, little kid worked there … my oldest boy is named after a toolmaker that I worked for when I first got here. My godchild, who I gave away last summer at her wedding, was one of the guys I worked with's daughter, and he passed away at a young age … and I gave her away. And it goes on and on and on. I mean, the girl in the office in personnel, she and I went through kindergarten and through all of school together. In this plant, everybody had those interactions. These weren't just people you worked with. They were sometimes your relatives, they were mostly your friends.
>
> *(Boden, quoted in Juravich 2009, 152)*

Boden's quote speaks to a whole different way in which people engage and position themselves in terms of work; it shows the way people see themselves, formally at least, as being embedded in their work. We see here and in many of the other oral histories from deindustrialized workers the interpenetration of economic, social and cultural lives. What these insights reveal about deindustrialisation is how the process inspires complex reflection on industrial work and its meanings. We can see the consideration of loss, of nostalgia, and of critique, as the industrial past is continually subject to forms of emphasis, erasure and contestation (see, for example, Mah 2012; Walley 2013).

This generational aspect to working-class studies is important in other ways. While many of the founding figures in the field cut their teeth in the 1960s and 1970s, many of us that came after them represent a bridging generation between that older generation and younger people coming to working-class studies. The editors of this volume all recognize the value in looking at class and work as evolving out of that period of the long boom, but equally are very aware of the huge differences between work then and now and the potential futures it may hold.

The challenge for working-class studies going forward is precisely to bridge the gap between the experience of class in the past with the lived reality of today and tomorrow. New forms of work are emerging rapidly, and it is important that we listen to those caught up in that process. In recent years the field has paid close attention to the notion of precarity, popularized by UK economist Guy Standing (2011). Standing's work gives a new name to the type of insecurity felt at the bottom of the labour market, but with a sociological eye for the corrosive effects such work formation has on class solidarities. Precarity is part of a longer-term trend of increasing individualisation in workplaces and society more generally (see, for example, Lane 2011; Strangleman 2007).

More recently still, new features have been identified in the transformation of work including the 'gig economy', the 'platform economy', the 'sharing economy' and so on (see Howcroft and Bergvall-Kåreborn 2019; Srnicek 2017). Often these forms of work radically disrupt structures of control – legislative, legal, labour standards, etc. They collectively break down established ways of viewing the relationship between capital and labour, often by spuriously reclassifying workers as self-employed. Another major change related to the 'new' economy is the rise of new forms of technology such as advanced robotics, artificial intelligence, large data sets coupled to machine learning and machine reading (Brynjolfsson and McAfee 2014; Ford 2015). It is always vital to put claims of novelty in historical perspective. Fears of the impact of new technology have been with us since the dawn of the industrial age and the working class itself. While many of the arguments being made about work futures may seem hyperbolic, there is a real sense of paradigm shift occurring in how capitalist work is organized locally and internationally. One major aspect of this change is how capitalism is aggressively accelerated, with our notions of time, generated in the past, starting to break down. How does one start to compare a working-class life lived out in a fixed community with a stable if low-paid job across decades with that of someone working in the gig economy whose experience of work is measured in seconds, minutes and swipes? What is the basis on which those new workers can build a working-class identity? (See Snyder 2016). Guy Standing (2011) is quite pessimistic about the political potential of the precariat; he argues that their highly differentiated characteristics mediate against shared solidarities based on the types of short-term, gig-based work. This makes working-class studies all the more vital in being able to understand how class works, even in the most impoverished settings.

The chapters in this section offer some answers to these questions even as they examine work and labour in the past. Each of the chapters highlight work in the past as offering a model for organising and building even in the context of loss and destruction. In Arthur McIvor's chapter, we see the way health and safety, occupational accidents and industrial disease has been a major feature of working-class life. McIvor highlights the long-standing battles for safer workplaces and how former industrial workers and their families still have to manage the half-life of industrial health issues. Kate Dudley's contribution looks at the impact of industrial loss on one North American city, Gardner, Massachusetts. Dudley examines industrial loss playing out in deindustrialized spaces and how former workers and their families are caught up in the ongoing opioid crisis. Dudley shows how this crisis is itself a by-product of the lack of any sense of optimism and hope about the future. Geoff Bright examines how class and the industrial past resurface through what he calls 'ghostly hauntings'. Bright's chapter illustrates beautifully the power of working-class studies to open up spaces of potential and hope. Through his 'ghost labs' Bright and his colleagues have created a new language for discussing the past, present and future of working-class community. Korte and Chen place contemporary working-class employment now in historical context, offering an account of the impact of the deteriorating conditions many workers now find themselves in. Finally, Canadian oral historian Steven High reflects on his extensive research into deindustrialized communities to think about what has been lost through closure and its aftermath. He examines how communities have thought about work and how that has changed through the often-brutal closure process.

Together these chapters allow us to see that working-class culture in and through the workplaces of the past was often constructed against the odds and in the face of great challenges. The good wages and conditions that were a feature of the long boom era were not gifted to ordinary people, but demanded and won. As Jack Metzgar noted, the good conditions of the long boom 'had to be fought for … people had died for it and suffered for it, and, most of all, endured for it' (2000, 6–7).

In all of the negative accounts of the consequences of the new economy there is still great hope. There is the hope offered by gig workers organising, by environmental campaigns and the work necessarily created to tackle global warming. There is the hope offered by those arguing for citizen's income or universal basic income and more widespread acknowledgement of social justice issues. But perhaps the past of work can also help to frame our future understanding. If we take seriously the charge of smokestack nostalgia, we must acknowledge the profound cost paid by working-class people and communities in terms of pollution, industrial accidents and disease and the ongoing price paid by communities struggling with opioid and alcohol addictions. Working-class work in the future *should*, even *has* to, be different.

References

Bluestone, B. and Harrison, B. (1982) *The Deindustrialization of America: Plant Closings, Community Abandonment, and the Dismantling of Basic Industry*, New York, Basic Books.

Bruno, R. (1999) *Steelworker Alley: How Class Works in Youngstown*, Ithaca, Cornell University Press.

Brynjolfsson, E. and McAfee, A. (2014) *The Second Machine Age: Work, Progress, and Prosperity in a Time of Brilliant Technologies*, New York, Norton.

Cowie, J. (1999) *Capital Moves: RCA's 70-Year Quest for Cheap Labor*, Ithaca, Cornell University Press.

Cowie, J. (2016) *The Great Exception: The New Deal and the Limits of American Politics*, Princeton, Princeton University Press.

Cowie, J. and Heathcott, J. (eds.) (2003) *Beyond the Ruins: The Meanings of Deindustrialisation*, Ithaca, Cornell University Press.

Dudley, K. (1994) *The End of the Line: Lost Jobs, New Lives in Postindustrial America*, Chicago, Chicago University Press.

Fine, L. (2004) *The Story of Reo Joe: Work, Kin, and Community in Autotown, USA*, Philadelphia, Temple University Press.

Ford, M. (2015) *The Rise of the Robots: Technology and the Threat of Mass Unemployment*, London, Oneworld.

Hochschild, A. (1983) *The Managed Heart: Commercialisation of Human Feeling*, London, University of California Press.

Honey, M. K. (1999) *Black Workers Remember: An Oral History of Segregation, Unionism, and the Freedom Struggle*, Berkley, California University Press.

Howcroft, D. and Bergvall-Kåreborn, B. (2019) 'A typology of crowdwork platforms', *Work, Employment and Society*, 33, 1, pp. 21–38.

Juravich, T. (2009) *At the Altar of the Bottom Line: The Degradation of Work in the 21st Century*, Amherst, University of Massachusetts Press.

K'Meyer, T. and Hart, J. (2011) *I Saw It Coming: Worker Narratives of Plant Closing and Job Loss*, Basingstoke, Palgrave.

Lane, C. (2011) *A Company of One: Insecurity, Independence, and the New World of White-Collar Unemployment*, Ithaca, Cornell University Press.

McIvor, A. (2013) *Working Lives: Work in Britain Since 1945*, Basingstoke, Palgrave.

Mah, A. (2012) *Industrial Ruination, Community, and Place: Landscapes and Legacies of Urban Decline*, Toronto, Toronto University Press.

Metzgar, J. (2000) *Striking Steel: Solidarity Remembered*, Philadelphia, Temple University Press.
Piketty, T. (2014) *Capital in the Twenty-First Century*, Cambridge, MA, Harvard University Press.
Rosanvallon, P. (2013) *The Society of Equals*, Cambridge, MA, Harvard University Press.
Snyder, B. (2016) *The Disrupted Workplace: Time and the Moral Order of Flexible Capitalism*, Oxford, Oxford University Press.
Srnicek, N. (2017) *Platform Capitalism*, London, Polity Press.
Standing, G. (2011) *The Precariat: The New Dangerous Class*, London, Bloomsbury.
Strangleman, T. (2007) 'The nostalgia for permanence at work? The end of work and its commentators', *Sociological Review*, 55, 1, pp. 81–103.
Strangleman, T. (2012) 'Work identity in crisis? Rethinking the problem of attachment and loss at work', *Sociology*, 46, 3, pp. 411–425.
Virdee, S. (2014) *Racism, Class and the Racialized Outsider*, Basingstoke, Palgrave.
Walley, C. (2013) *Exit Zero: Family and Class in Postindustrial Chicago*, Chicago, Chicago University Press.

11

Deindustrialization and its consequences

Steven High

> I heard about the closure on television on the six o'clock news. Then a couple of weeks later they phoned me up and said, 'You got a 35-year pin that we have here. We'd like to give it to you.' I said 'okay.' He said, 'Meet us at the front gate.' You know, everything was closed, so the fellow, our superintendent at the time, he gave me the 35-year pin. You can picture a chain-link fence; he handed it to me through the fence. 'Here is your 35-year pin.

This story was told to me in Lackawanna, New York, back in 1998. I had been invited by the local chapter of the Steelworkers Organization of Active Retirees to do a 'group interview' with former Republic and Lackawanna steel workers. The 'group' was not the 10 or 12 people that I had been expecting, but a hundred or more. What was I to do? Each one of these men and women had a story to tell. So, I circulated from table to table, the best that I could, recording their stories. They spoke of their multigenerational connection to the mill, as they followed their grandfathers, fathers, uncles, older brothers, cousins, and sometimes mothers and sisters into the mill. The work was hard but the money was good. Their work was invested in moral meaning. Many then spoke of the devastating effects of the mill closures, as the impact rippled outward through their lives and those of their families as well as the local community. It was an act of violence, tearing through the social fabric of the area (Walley 2013, 1). Incomprehension, anger, grief, sadness, resentment, and sometimes shame surfaced in these brief mutual encounters. But it was the outrage at the injustice of it all that was most apparent. Emotions are not trivial, they are invariably about something (Sayer 2005, 36).

Of all the stories shared with me that day, and since, it is the story of the 35-year pin that has stuck with me. It is a powerful moral critique of an economic and political system that has failed industrial workers. In *The Moral Significance of Class*, Andrew Sayer speaks of the structural humiliation of plant closings and of the 'moral-rage' that it produces (Sayer 2005, 226). It is a powerful read, helping me realize the extent to which emotions are part of the story being told. Even when interviewed years, sometimes decades, later, many industrial workers had yet to 'get the anger out of their gut' (Dudley 1994, 158). Their plants may have closed, but they are still living with its social, economic, and political consequences. Sometimes 'memory' does not begin to capture the depth of feeling, rawness of emotion, and immediacy revealed in oral history interviews. Anger and resentment run deep within deindustrialized areas.

Deindustrialization first emerged as an explanatory framework in the 1970s and 1980s. Those who initially took up the idea sought to explain what was happening around them and to measure it (Blackaby 1978; Raines et al. 1982; Martin and Rowthorn 1986; Rodwin and Sazanami 1989). You did not have to go far to see signs of industrial ruination. The United States lost almost eight million manufacturing jobs between 1979 and 2010. Textiles and apparel was one of the most battered sectors. In 1973, there were 2.4 million textile and apparel workers in the United States. By 2012, there were only 383,600 left (Minchin 2013, 1). Sometimes this collapse in industrial employment came suddenly, as happened in the automotive sector. Between 1978 and 1982, 300,000 auto jobs were lost in the United States – 85,000 of them in Detroit (Dicken 1986, 314). The scale of this body count is staggering, as are its far-reaching consequences.

Other countries did just as poorly. The United Kingdom saw total manufacturing employment drop from 6.8 million in 1979 to just 2.5 million by 2010. In British coal mining, the number of active pits fell from 822 in 1957 (employing 704,000) to 241 in 1975 (245,000) and 17 in 1994 (8,518) (McIvor 2017, 27). The last deep mine in the United Kingdom closed in 2015. Across Europe, meanwhile, steel industry employment fell by half a million workers between 1974 and 1992 (Smith 1998, 157, 186). Economic decline, like growth, is spatially uneven. Older industrial regions such as Lorraine, France, and the Ruhr district of Germany bore the brunt of these job losses. As historian Jackie Clarke observed, 'labels such as "industrial region" or "mining town" may seem self-evident, but even these are identities in process' (2017, 112).

At the same time, the deindustrialization thesis was also a political 'tool, a rallying cry' against those who close mines, mills, and factories (B. Laxer 1973, 9). In Canada, the concept was first proposed in 1973 by left-nationalists who blamed plant closures on foreign ownership and the protectionist policies of President Richard Nixon. 'Nixonomics means de-industrialization', declared Jim Laxer (1973, 145). With the 1982 publication of *The Deindustrialization of America: Plant Closings, Community Abandonment and the Dismantling of Basic Industry*, economists Barry Bluestone and Bennett Harrison popularized the term. For them, deindustrialization did not just happen, but was made to happen. Corporations sought to cut corners by moving production to low-wage areas farther and farther afield. It was not inevitable. Commissioned as it was by a coalition of labor and community groups, Bluestone and Harrison's research was both a contributor to and a product of political resistance to plant closings – casting it as a 'fundamental struggle between capital and community' (Bluestone and Harrison 1982, 19).

Out of this economic and political crucible, an interdisciplinary field of politically engaged research – which I loosely call 'deindustrialization studies' – has taken root. There have been big international conferences, special themed issues of journals (Altena and van der Linden 2002; High, 2007; Daumalin and Mioche 2013; Strangleman, Rhodes and Linkon 2013; Foster and Sandberg 2014), and edited volumes (Cowie and Heathcott 2003; High, MacKinnon and Perchard 2017; Orange 2015). Historiographical essays have also appeared, providing a sociological or historical reading of the field (Strangleman and Rhodes 2014; High, 2013).[1] Important monographs have likewise been produced. Most focus on a single locality or region, with only a few reaching across national borders in order to make wider comparisons or connections (High 2003; Mah 2012; Neumann 2016). One of the most influential studies of this kind was Jefferson Cowie's (1999) *Capital Moves: RCA's 70-Year Quest for Cheap-Labor*, which followed RCA as it shifted radio and television manufacturing from one American city to another before moving the jobs to Ciudad Juarez, Mexico. In doing so, Cowie points to a troubling dilemma for trade unionists: each capital shift was partly the result of rising local demands for higher wages and increased benefits. It is a recurring cycle.

Despite its growing geographic and temporal reach, the historiographic ground zero remains the US Rust Belt – that great swathe of deindustrializing America from St. Louis and Milwaukee in the west to Philadelphia and Lowell in the east. Many Rust Belt towns and cities now have their own biographer of urban decline (Cumbler 1989; Dandaneau 1996; Serrin 1993; O'Hara 2010). Youngstown, Ohio, has many (Lynd 1982; Linkon and Russo 2002; Safford 2009). Concentrated as they are in the inner-city areas of industrial cities, racial minorities were particularly hard hit (Squires 1994, 20–21). Thomas Sugrue, for example, showed the degree to which race was bound up with deindustrialization: 'Detroit's post-war urban crisis emerged as the consequence of two of the most important, interrelated, and unresolved problems in American history: that capitalism generates economic inequality and that African Americans have disproportionately borne the impact of that inequality' (2014, 5; see also Hinshaw and Modell 1996).

From its movement origins in the anti-shutdown campaigns of the 1970s and 1980s, the study of deindustrialization in the new millennium has shifted from plant closings and the body count of jobs lost to its wider cultural meaning, memory and representation. Many have turned to oral history and photography to reveal the human face of the unfolding tragedy. Two of the most compelling studies of this kind are Daniel James' (2000) *Dona Maria's Story: Life History, Memory and Political Identity*, which explores the meaning of deindustrialization in Berisso, Argentina, as understood by one labor activist, and Alessandro Portelli's (2012) majestic *They Say in Harlan County*, that explores the legacies of coal mining, labor struggle, and deindustrialization in Kentucky. That said, we are now seeing a return to political economy as well as the long-term social, health, and environmental consequences for working-class communities. Brexit, Trump, and the rise of right-wing populism in deindustrialized areas are reinforcing this trend, sparking a renewed interest in working-class studies more generally (Frank 2017). It is too early, however, to know if this represents the beginnings of a return to class analysis in our universities. It is no coincidence that the mainstream study of class fell out of favor precisely when post-industrialism was sweeping aside industrial workers and their institutions. I see this as being part of a wider political and cultural erasure of working people. The rest of this chapter will consider two areas of sustained scholarly engagement within deindustrialization studies: political resistance and cultural persistence or erasure.

The sources and limits of resistance

Resistance to plant closings comes in many forms. In my own interviews with displaced workers, I have encountered many acts of spontaneous resistance during plant closings. These range from proliferating 'sick days' and slowed production during the notice period to verbally abusing managers. While none admitted to small acts of sabotage or theft, we know that this happens. Jackie Clarke, for example, has highlighted various examples in France, including the threatened dumping of highly flammable acid from a closing textile mill into the environment (Clarke 2011). Resistance is also collective. Where they can, unions negotiate close-out agreements with their employers. But effects bargaining has its limits, especially when soon-to-be unemployed workers have no political leverage. Union acquiescence is thus bought relatively cheaply with a six-month extension of health benefits (a key concern in the United States), increased severance payments, or small bonuses, all conditional on workers meeting their production and safety targets. Plant closing agreements thus have the effect of quieting the workforce to ensure an 'orderly' close out.

One of the most heated debates in the field relates to the sources and limits of successful resistance. Let me offer two examples. In *Industrial Sunset: The Making of North America's Rust Belt, 1969–1984*, I argued that the militancy of Canadian trade unions successfully slowed the rate of deindustrialization in Canada during the 1970s and early 1980s. Wrapping themselves in the maple leaf flag, Canadian unionists were able to politicize plant closings at a time of heightened nationalist anxiety – pushing governments to legislate a variety of things including the regulation of foreign investment (High 2003). For a time, foreign-owned companies closing plants in Canada paid a political price for their actions. Another historian, Dimitry Anastakis, later argued that I placed too much emphasis on pressure from below, crediting instead forward-thinking civil servants who negotiated managed trade agreements. The 1963 Auto Pact, for example, included stringent Canadian content requirements for the Big 3 automakers with regards to auto parts and a requirement to make as many cars as they sold in Canada and (Anastakis 2007, 2013). What we agree on is the public bailout of Chrysler in 1979–1980. Whereas the US government only signed on the condition that US autoworkers accepted steep wage concessions, the Canadian government required that the company instead reinvest in its Canadian production facilities. These differing responses speak volumes about the politics of the day in each country. With free trade, and the end of the Auto Pact, the Big 3 automakers are now free to shift production at will. The result has been lost jobs and closed plants.

The second debate centres on whether or not localities can realistically take on capital and win. A number of researchers have argued that local labor community coalitions can make a difference (Nissen 1995). Others have pointed to place-based remedies and regional economic management (McKee 2008; Manuel 2015; Wilson 2009; Portz 1990). One of the most emphatic cases for local agency is made in *Rust Belt Resistance: How a Small Community Took on Big Oil and Won* by Perry Bush, who takes issue with those (like myself) who argue that local communities are no match for global capital: 'By the late 1990s, a scholarly consensus held that the mobility of international capital in the new age of globalization had placed local municipalities, and the public officials who led them, in a position of inescapable dependency' (Bush 2012, 95). While Bush recognizes the 'imbalance of forces' (141), he argues that corporate decisions are not immutable and absolute: after all Lima, Ohio, took on British Petroleum and won. He credits the town's activist mayor for saving the local refinery. Indeed, local communities 'have a variety of tools and resources at their disposal for exerting agency over their common lives and futures' (237). While I agree that firm local leadership can make *a* difference, the 'tools' and 'resources' available to local municipalities are limited to say the least. Even in Lima, we learn on the book's final page that most of the town's *other* factories closed down.

Other researchers have pointed to employee or community ownership as a viable way to save mills and factories from closing. The number of Employee Stock Ownership Plans in the United States jumped from 300 in 1974 to 7,000 in the early 1990s (Squires 1994, 23). A few of these, like McLouth Steel downriver from Detroit and Wierton Steel in West Virginia, involved large-scale industrial operations. Both mills have since closed. Unfortunately, the results were no better in Connecticut. In *Banded Together: Economic Democratization in the Brass Valley*, Jeremy Brecher (2011) tells the story of the Naugatuck ('Brass') Valley Project's energetic response to deindustrialization. The project's early success at Seymour Manufacturing, reopened under an employee stock ownership plan, was widely heralded at the time.

Employee ownership and community ownership have proven somewhat more successful in Canada, thanks to the backing of provincial governments. The paper mill in Temiskaming, Quebec, for example, was saved in 1972 after the community used fishing boats to blockade the river and stop the departing company's spring river run (when they floated logs downriver). Backed into the corner by local activism, with the full support of the Quebec government, Canadian International Paper was forced to sell the mill to employees and local managers, who then formed Tembec – a highly successful forestry company. Six other paper mills across Quebec, Ontario and Manitoba were 'saved' in the 1990s, but only the one in Kapuskasing, Ontario, is still operating. Time and again, workers agreed to sell back their shares in their mill to corporate interests, who later closed the mill. Generally, trade unions were ambivalent, or outright hostile, to these schemes.

Clearly, then, political resistance has largely failed to prevent mines, mills, or factories from closing. With few exceptions, the best that industrial workers could hope for is managed or slowed decline and a softened economic blow. There are many reasons for this failure. Increasingly, workers' moral critique of plant closings failed to resonate with middle-class people. Another reason is the political containment of deindustrialization. As James Rhodes suggests, those economically left-behind by deindustrialization are imaginatively contained to 'areas of relegation' such as the Rust Belt (Rhodes 2012, 686). 'One of the great ironies of differential regional deindustrialization', noted historian Christopher H. Johnson, 'which is the standard form of capitalist "crisis", is that it hardly leads to revolution, but rather engenders quiescence, the internalization of despair' (Johnson 1995, 258–259). Now, with Brexit, Trump, and the rise of the populist right and the insurgent left, we have an unstable political situation where angry working-class voters have succeeded in disrupting the status quo and raising fundamental concerns about the global neoliberal order and the class politics of liberalism itself. Michael Zweig (2017) notes that the 2016 US presidential vote saw a significant shift in voting in union households, especially in the so-called 'Rust Belt 5' (Iowa, Wisconsin, Michigan, Ohio, and Pennsylvania), that flipped from Obama to Trump. Whereas Obama beat Romney by 23 per cent in union households in 2012, Trump beat Clinton in these same households by 9 per cent.[2] Indeed, 66 per cent of Americans without a college degree voted for Trump. The Democrats, it seems, have a growing class problem as well as a racial one.

Deindustrialization makes visible a 'deep cultural antagonism' that has long divided industrial societies (Dudley 1994, xxv). In her study of Kenosha, Wisconsin, for example, anthropologist Kathryn Marie Dudley found that in 'America's new image of itself as a postindustrial society, individuals still employed in basic manufacturing industries look like global benchwarmers in the competitive markets of the modern world' (1994, 161). Accordingly, industrial workers are 'portrayed as a vanishing breed, the contemporary representatives of a dying way of life' (177). A similar story has unfolded in the UK, where white working-class people are dismissed by middle-class liberals and conservatives as 'left behinds, the remnants of an old world that had been trampled on by the inevitable march of history' (Jones 2011, 71).

Cultural persistence versus erasure

Fundamentally, deindustrialization is a process of physical and social ruination as well as part of a wider political project that leaves working-class communities impoverished and demoralized. Not only is the social world of the factory floor destroyed, so too is the wider economic and social structure that validates working-class lives. Forced forgetting is an integral part of the deindustrialization process as mills and factories are demolished, their production records shredded, working-class institutions crushed, and areas recontextualized as something new. In a post-industrial era, industrial workers are usually assigned to the past, not the present, and are thereby rendered invisible to others (Clarke 2011, 446). The class cleansing of our cities begins with mill and factory closings and ends with their post-industrial occupation and gentrification; this two-step process represents a double erasure. Gritty has become cool, as old industrial neighborhoods in Brooklyn, New York, and other cities are converted into high-end condominiums and restaurants or art spaces (Zukin 2010). Even the Rust Belt has become chic in some circles, valued for its aura of verité or authenticity.

Yet, as always, there is resistance even in the face of historical erasure. A number of the displaced workers that I interviewed over the years salvaged a box here or a file there from their dying mills. Hubert Gervais, a paper mill worker, told me how the plant manager denied him permission to transfer a box of the employee newsletters to the local museum. He said it was the company's property. Overhearing this exchange, someone else in the office told Hubert to drive up to the loading dock at a predetermined time, when the historical contraband was handed over (High 2010). These newsletters are now in the local museum. Public archives are peppered with salvage stories like this one, but much more is being lost.

While 'economic obliteration incurs a cultural and social cost', in the memorable words of historian John Kirk (2007, 25), class subjectivities built up over generations are not so easily vanquished. To explain this persistence, British labor historians have leaned heavily on Raymond Williams' notion of 'structure of feelings' to show how the culture of industrialism remains in place long after jobs are gone. Cultural survival was at the core of a special issue of *International Labor and Working Class History* on 'Crumbling cultures of deindustrialization'.

Historian Kirk Savage has noted that the 'deindustrialized landscape, like a ruined battlefield that heals over, is ripe for commemoration' (2003, 237). With deindustrialization, 'the urge to reaffirm or celebrate the industrial past seems to grow stronger' (237). There has been a lot of that in recent decades with the proliferation of industrial heritage memorials, museums and historic sites as well as songs, poetry, novels, photography books, film and other cultural representations of lost industry. It also extends to urban development, as historic industrial buildings are transformed into condominiums, art galleries or other post-industrial spaces of consumption. Tim Strangleman, James Rhodes and Sherry Linkon argue that these cultural representations can provocatively 'disrupt power' and force society to 'ponder the meaning and role of work and industrial society' (2013, 15). Indeed, we can discern a 'broader questioning of what it means and how it feels to live in a deindustrializing society' (20).

The after-lives of industrial sites, or the 'half-life' (Linkon 2013) of deindustrialization, have been the subject of much discussion and debate within deindustrialization studies. To be sure, industrial heritage is one way for governments to visibly respond to the loss of industry. Claims that industrial heritage projects provide economic lifelines for struggling communities are overstated, however, as the immediate economic benefits have proven to be limited at best (Edwards and Llurdes 1996; Overton 2007). But there is also a promise of cultural stabilization, as 'historic' mine and mill towns become sites of industrial heritage (Wallace 1987, 10). In recent years, a growing number of deindustrialized sites have been declared World Heritage Sites or have joined the growing network of industrial heritage trails. The Zollverein mining and coke complex in Essen, Germany – Europe's cultural capital for 2010 – with its Ferris wheel taking visitors into the remains of the coke ovens is a case in point. So too is the former steel mill in nearby Duisberg, which has been converted into a landscape adventure park where visitors can climb, slide, dive and play in the ruins of the industrial age. We must ask ourselves about the class politics of these transformed industrial environments. What, precisely, are we preserving and why?

It is for this reason, then, that Australian historian Lucy Taksa has raised important political questions about the 'culture-based approach' to urban revitalization, going so far as to suggest that labor history and public history are incompatible (2009). In these sites, as in others, the history of work and working-class struggle is rendered invisible as a 'redundant industrial landscape' is transformed 'into a marketable historical commodity' (Taksa 2003, 394).

We certainly see this consumptive pattern in the former textile mill town of Lowell, Massachusetts – since 1978 the home to the Lowell National Historic Park. Anthropologist Cathy Stanton raises critical questions about the ability of industrial sites 'to question and perhaps challenge the dominant forces in our lives' (2006, 39). Stanton takes aim, specifically, at the historic site's segregation of the past from the present. At Lowell, we hear about past exploitation in the textile industry, but not the fact that these issues remain current in the world today. Failure to make this link serves to depoliticize site interpretation, as visitors leave thankful that they didn't live 'back then'.

Even so, not all industrial heritage projects are alike. After Le Creusot, France, lost its major employer in the early 1970s, it saw the birth of the first industrial 'ecomuseum'. Unlike industrial archaeology, it was focused on people and not dead material objects. Part of a wider rethinking of the museum's place in a changing world, the ecomuseum sought to validate working-class heritage by transforming local residents into historical interpreters of their own past. This memory work was a far more political approach than the state-run 'living history' museums of North America; history was not so much re-enacted as reanimated to restore life (Orange 2015; Chauliac and Raggi 2010). By 1988, there were 25 ecomuseums in France with a scattering of others elsewhere in the world (High 2017a; Cousin 2000; Debary 2002; Jaumain 2000; Poulard 2007). That said, it is important to heed Australian historian Seamus O'Hanlon's warning that a town's industrial era not be treated as the authentic urban self and everything that has happened since as only loss (O'Hanlon 2017, 234).

Historians Jefferson Cowie and Joseph Heathcott warned us against smokestack nostalgia in their 2002 appeal to widen the scope of discussion beyond 'tales of victimization' and the 'swell of industrial nostalgia' (Cowie and Heathcott 2003, 1–2; Strangleman, 2013). While nostalgia, best understood as a 'longing for a lost home' (Boym 2001, xiv) is often treated as pejorative, others have suggested that it can serve a 'radical' purpose: 'reinfusing lost histories with credibility, substance, and emotional resonance' (Glazer 2005, 7). Still, there are dangers in locating a golden age in the past. In her study of a Rotterdam neighborhood, which had experienced deindustrialization and subsequent immigration, for example, Talja Blokland (2001) found that recalling the industrial past risked overlooking the multicultural present. Conversely, in a devastating article, Leon Fink questioned the glowing recollections of the industrial past being memorialized in the former textile mill town of Coolomee, North Carolina, as they didn't acknowledge Jim Crow racism.[3] Others point to the mixed legacies of industrialism itself: environmental pollution, industrial disease, broken bodies and gender inequality. These political concerns can even extend to those no longer present. I recently made this point in regard to 'mill colonialism' in my home region of Northern Ontario, as the process of industrialization was bound up in wider processes of indigenous dispossession and exclusion (High 2017b). How we remember the industrial past is therefore a matter of some debate.

Conclusion

We live with the consequences of deindustrialization long after the mines, mills and factories fall silent. Working lives are ruptured, communities slowly eviscerated. More research needs to be done on how people live in and with industrial ruination. Historian Arthur McIvor has called on deindustrialization scholars to examine the embodied effects of deindustrialization, engaging with issues of health and environment especially. Growing economic disparity, precarious work, lower levels of unionization, the rise of the carceral state and gentrification are all tied up in the deindustrial knot. The political aftershocks of deindustrialization continue to be felt – but why now? How does racism play into the politics of deindustrialization? What has culture-led redevelopment meant to working-class communities? All of these questions are central to working-class studies, as we are reminded again and again – to our dismay – that the half-life of deindustrialization is not only protracted but politically devastating.

However, the deindustrialization scholarship needs to reach beyond the towns of single industry where nothing has filled the economic or cultural vacuum and consider the wider post-industrial transformation of our major cities and resource peripheries. I agree with anthropologist Cathy Stanton when she cautions us to resist the notion that there is a linear progression from industrialization to deindustrialization and finally to post-industrialism (Stanton 2017, 158). Areas often deindustrialize and industrialize concurrently, as jobs shift from one economic sector to another. Industrial labor is still part of our present. But we also need to scale up our analysis and engage with wider transnational and interregional patterns and flows. The state and capital need to be an integral part of our analysis if we are to go beyond effects-based analysis. Now, more than ever, a lament for the losses incurred by working people is not enough. We need to understand the wider repercussions of these losses and find real-world alternatives to the false hope provided by a resurgent populist right. For me, at least, the story of the 35-year pin passing through the chain-linked fence raises profound questions about deindustrialization as a socio-economic and cultural process as well as its far-reaching political consequences.

Notes

1 For a reflection on how the work of E. P. Thompson and others on industrialization might help us understand deindustrialization, see Strangleman (2016).

2 For more on why some working-class voters vote Republican, see Prasad, Hoffman, and Bezila (2016). For the UK, see McKenzie (2017).

3 For another perspective, see Wedgwood (2011).

References

Altena, B, and van der Linden, M. (eds.) (2002) 'De-industrialization: Social, Cultural, and Political Aspects', *International Review of Social History*, Supplement 10, 47.

Anastakis, D. (2007) 'Industrial Sunrise? The Chrysler Bailout, the State, and the Re-Industrialization of the Canadian Automotive Sector, 1975–1986', *Urban History Review*, 35, 2: 37–50.

Anastakis, D. (2013) *Autonomous State: The Struggle for a Canadian Car Industry from OPEC to Free Trade*, Toronto, University of Toronto Press.

Blackaby, F. (ed.) (1978) *De-Industrialisation*, London, Heinemann Educational Books.

Bluestone, B. and Harrison, B. (1982) *The Deindustrialization of America: Plant Closings, Community Abandonment and the Dismantling of Basic Industry*, New York, Basic Books.

Blokland, T. (2001) 'Bricks, Mortar, Memories: Neighbourhood and Networks in Collective Acts of Remembering', *International Journal of Urban and Regional Research*, 25, 2, 268–283.

Boym, S. (2001) *The Future of Nostalgia*, New York, Basic Books.

Brecher, J. (2011) *Banded Together: Economic Democratization in the Brass Valley*, Chicago, University of Illinois.

Bush, P. (2012) *Rust Belt Resistance: How a Small Community Took on Big Oil and Won*, Kent, Ohio, Kent State University Press.

Chauliac, M. and Raggi, P. (eds.) (2010) *Le dir pour le fer*, Aumetz, Éditions Serpenoise.

Clarke, J. (2011) 'Closing Moulinex: Thoughts on the Visibility and Invisibility of Industrial Labour in Contemporary France', *Modern & Contemporary France*, 19, 4, 443–458.

Clarke, J. (2017) 'Afterlives of a Factory: Memory, Place and Space in Alencon', in High, S., MacKinnon, L. and Perchard, A. (eds.) *The Deindustrialized World: Confronting Ruination in Post-Industrial Places*, Vancouver, University of British Columbia Press.

Cousin, S. (2000) 'Un Brin de Culture, Une Once d'économie: écomusée et economusée', *Publics et Musées*, 17, 1, 116–121.

Cowie, J. (1999) *Capital Moves: RCA's 70-Year Quest for Cheap-Labor*, Ithaca, Cornell University Press.

Cowie, J, and Heathcott, J. (eds.) (2003) *Beyond the Ruins: The Meanings of Deindustrialization*, Ithaca, Cornell University Press.

Cumbler, J. (1989) *A Social History of Economic Decline: Business, Politics, and Work in Trenton*, New Brunswick, NJ, Rutgers University Press.

Dandaneau, S. P. (1996) *A Town Abandoned: Flint, Michigan, Confronts Deindustrialization*, Albany, SUNY Press.

Daumalin, X, and Mioche, P. (eds.) (2013) 'La désindustrialisation au regard de l'histoire', *Rives Méditerrane éennes*, 3, 46, 5–9.

Debary, O. (2002) *La fin du Creusot ou L'art d'accommoder les restes*, Paris, Éditions du CTHS.

Dicken, P. (1986) *Global Shift: Industrial Change in a Turbulent World*, London, Harper and Row.

Dudley, K. M. (1994) *The End of the Line: Lost Jobs, New Lives in Postindustrial America*, Chicago, University of Chicago Press.

Edwards, J. A. and Llurdes, J. C. (1996) 'Mines and Quarries: Industrial Heritage Tourism', *Annals of Tourism Research*, 23, 341–363.

Foster, J, and Sandberg, L. A. (2014) 'Post-Industrial Urban Greenspace', *Local Environment*, 19, 10, 1043–1048.

Frank, T. (2017) *Listen, Liberal: Or, What Ever Happened to the Party of the People?* New York, Picador.

Glazer, P. (2005) *Radical Nostalgia: Spanish Civil War Commemoration in America*, Rochester, NY: University of Rochester Press.

High, S. (2003) *Industrial Sunset: The Making of North America's Rust Belt, 1969–1984*, Toronto, University of Toronto Press.

High, S. (2007) 'Introduction: The Politics and Memory of Deindustrialization in Canada', *Urban History Review*, 35, 2, 2–13.

High, S. (2010) 'Placing the Displaced Worker: Narrating Place in Deindustrializing Sturgeon Falls, Ontario', in Opp, J. and Walsh, J. (eds.) *Placing Memory and Remembering Place in Canada*, Vancouver, UBC Press.

High, S. (2013) 'Beyond Aesthetics: Visibility and Invisibility in the Aftermath of Deindustrialization', *International Labor and Working Class History*, 84, 140–153.

High, S. (2017a) 'Brownfield Public History: Arts and Heritage in the Aftermath of Deindustrialization', in Gardner, J. and Hamilton, P. (eds.) *Oxford Handbook of Public History*. New York, Oxford University Press.

High, S. (2017b) 'Deindustrialization on the Industrial Frontier: The Rise and Fall of Mill Colonialism in Northern Ontario', in High, S., MacKinnon, L. and Perchard, A. (eds.) *The Deindustrialized World: Confronting Ruination in Postindustrial Places*, Vancouver, University of British Columbia Press.

High, S., Mackinnon, L. and Perchard, A. (eds.) (2017) *The Deindustrialized World: Confronting Ruination in Post-Industrial Places*, Vancouver, University of British Columbia Press.

Hinshaw, J, and Modell, J. (1996) 'Perceiving Racism: Homestead from Depression to Deindustrialization', *Pennsylvania History*, 63, 1, 17–52.

James, D. (2000) *Dona Maria's Story: Life History, Memory and Political Identity*, Durham, Duke University Press.

Jaumain, S. (2000) *Les musées en movement: Nouvelles conceptions, nouveaux publics*, Bruxelles, Éditions de l'Université de Bruxelles.

Johnson, C. H. (1995) *The Life and Death of Industrial Languedoc, 1700–1920*, New York, Oxford University Press.

Jones, O. (2011) *Chavs: The Demonization of the Working Class*, London, Verso.

Kirk, J. (2007) *Class, Culture and Social Change: On the Trail of the Working Class*, London, Palgrave Macmillan.

Laxer, B. (1973) 'Foreword', in Laxer, R. M. (ed.) *(Canada) Ltd.: The Political Economy of Dependency*, Toronto, McClelland and Stewart.

Laxer, J. (1973) 'Canadian Manufacturing and US Trade Policy', in Laxer, R. M. (ed.) *(Canada) Ltd.: The Political Economy of Dependency*, Toronto, McClelland and Stewart.

Linkon, S. L. (2013) 'Narrating Past and Future: Deindustrialized Landscapes as Resources', *International Labor and Working Class History*, 84, 38–54.

Linkon, S. L. and Russo, J. (2002) *Steeltown USA: Work & Memory in Youngstown*, Lawrence, University Press of Kansas.

Lynd, S. (1982) *Fight Against Shutdowns: Youngstown's Steel Mill Closings*, New York, Singlejacket Books.

McIvor, A. (2017) 'Deindustrialization Embodied: Work, Health, and Disability in the United Kingdom since the Mid-Twentieth Century', in High, S., MacKinnon, L. and Perchard, A. (eds.) *The Deindustrialized World: Confronting Ruination in Post-Industrial Places*, Vancouver, University of British Columbia Press.

McKee, G. A. (2008) *The Problem of Jobs: Liberalism, Race, and Deindustrialization in Philadelphia*, Chicago, Chicago University Press.

McKenzie, L. (2017) '"It's Not Ideal": Reconsidering "Anger" and "Apathy" in the Brexit Vote among an Invisible Working Class', *Competition & Change*, 21, 3, 199–210.

Mah, A. (2012) *Industrial Ruination, Community, and Place: Landscape and Legacies of Urban Decline*, Toronto, University of Toronto Press.

Manuel, J. T. (2015) *Taconite Dreams: The Struggle to Sustain Mining on Minnesota's Iron Range, 1915–2000*, Minneapolis, University of Minnesota Press.

Martin, R. and Rowthorn, B (eds.) (1986) *The Geography of De-Industrialisation*, London, Macmillan.

Minchin, T. (2013) *Empty Mills: The Fight Against Imports and the Decline of the US Textile Industry*, Lanham, Rowman and Littlefield.

Neumann, T. (2016) *Remaking the Rust Belt: The Postindustrial Transformation of North America*, Philadelphia, University of Pennsylvania Press.

Nissen, B. (1995) *Fighting for Jobs: Case Studies of Labor-Community Coalitions Confronting Plant Closings*, Albany, SUNY Press.

O'Hanlon, S. (2017) 'Selling "Lifestyle": Postindustrial Urbanism and the Marketing of Inner City Apartments in Melbourne, Australia, 1990–2005', in High, S., MacKinnon, L. and Perchard, A. (eds.) *The Deindustrialized World: Confronting Ruination in Post-Industrial Places*, Vancouver, University of British Columbia Press.

O'Hara, S. P. (2010) *Gary, the Most American of All American Cities*, Bloomington, Indiana University Press.

Orange, H. (ed.) (2015) *Reanimating Industrial Spaces: Conducting Memory Work in Post-Industrial Societies*, Walnut Creek, CA, Left Coast Press.

Overton, J. (2007) '"A Future in the Past?" Tourism Development, Outport Archaeology and the Politics of Deindustrialization in Newfoundland and Labrador in the 1990s', *Urban History Review*, 35, 2, 60–74.

Portelli, A. (2012) *They Say in Harlan County*, New York, Oxford University Press.

Portz, J. (1990) *The Politics of Plant Closings*, Lawrence, University of Kansas.

Poulard, F. (2007) 'Les écomusées: Participation des habitants et prise en compte des publics', *Ethnologie française*, 111, 3, 551–557.

Prasad, M., Hoffman, S. G. and Bezila, K. (2016) 'Walking the Line: The White Working Class and the Economic Consequences of Morality', *Politics & Society*, 44, 2, 281–304.

Raines, J. C., Berson, L. E. and Gracie, D. (1982) *Community and Capital in Conflict: Plant Closings and Job Loss*, Philadelphia, Temple University Press.

Rhodes, J. (2012) 'Stigmatization, Space and Boundaries in De-Industrial Burnley', *Ethnic and Racial Studies*, 35, 4, 684–703.

Rodwin, L. and Sazanami, H. (eds.) (1989) *Deindustrialization and Regional Economic Transformation: The Experience of the United States*, Boston, Unwin Hyman.

Safford, S. (2009) *Why the Garden Club Couldn't Save Youngstown*, Cambridge, Harvard University Press.

Savage, K. (2003) 'Monuments of a Lost Cause: The Postindustrial Campaign to Commemorate Steel', in Cowie, J. and Heathcott, J. (eds.) *Beyond the Ruins: The Meaning of Deindustrialization*, Ithaca, Cornell University Press.

Sayer, A. (2005) *The Moral Significance of Class*, Cambridge, Cambridge University Press.

Serrin, W. (1993) *Homestead: The Glory and Tragedy of an American Steel Town*, New York, Random House.

Smith, W. R. (1998) *The Left's Dirty Job: The Politics of Industrial Restructuring in France and Spain*, Toronto, University of Toronto Press.

Squires, G. D. (1994) *Capital and Communities in Black and White: The Intersections of Race, Class, and Uneven Development*, Albany, SUNY Press.

Stanton, C. (2006) *The Lowell Experiment: Public History in a Postindustrial City*, Amherst, University of Massachusetts Press.

Stanton, C. (2017) 'Keeping "the Industrial": New Solidarities in Postindustrial Places', in High, S., MacKinnon, L. and Perchard, A. (eds.) *The Deindustrialized World: Confronting Ruination in Post-Industrial Places*, Vancouver, University of British Columbia Press.

Strangleman, T. (2013) '"Smokestack Nostalgia", "Ruin Porn", or Working-Class Obituary: The Role and Meaning of Deindustrial Representation', *International Labor and Working Class History*, 84, 39–83.

Strangleman, T. (2016) 'Deindustrialisation and the Historical Sociological Imagination: Making Sense of Work and Industrial Change', *Sociology*, 51, 2, 466–482.

Strangleman, T. and Rhodes, J. (2014) 'The "New" Sociology of Deindustrialization? Understanding Industrial Change', *Sociology Compass*, 8, 4, 411–421.

Strangleman, T., Rhodes, J. and Linkon, S. (2013) 'Introduction to Crumbling Cultures', *International Labor and Working Class History*, 84, 7–22.

Sugrue, T. (2014) *The Origins of the Urban Crisis: Race and Inequality in Postwar Detroit*, Princeton, Princeton University Press.

Taksa, L. (2003) '"Hauling an Infinite Freight of Mental Imagery": Finding Labour's Heritage at the Swindon Railway Workshops' STEAM Museum', *Labour History Review*, 68, 3, 391–410.

Taksa, L. (2009) 'Labor History and Public History in Australia: Allies or Uneasy Bedfellows?', *International Labor and Working-Class History*, 76, 82–104.

Wallace, M. (1987) 'Industrial Museums and the History of Deindustrialization', *Public Historian*, 9, 1, 9–19.

Walley, C. J. (2013) *Exit Zero: Family and Class in Postindustrial Chicago*, Chicago, University of Chicago Press.

Wedgwood, T. (2011) 'A Working Town Empowered: Retelling Textile History at Cooleemee, North Carolina', in Smith, L., Shackel, P. A. and Campbell, G. (eds.) *Heritage, Labour and the Working Classes*, London, Routledge.

Wilson, G. (2009) *Communities Left Behind: The Area Redevelopment Administration, 1945–1965*, Knoxville, University of Tennessee Press.

Zukin, S. (2010) *Naked City: The Death and Life of Authentic Urban Places*, New York, Oxford University Press.

Zweig, M. (2017) 'White Working-Class Voters and the Future of Progressive Politics', *New Labor Forum*, 26, 2, 28–36.

12

Economic dislocation and trauma

Patrick Korte and Victor Tan Chen

What has become of the blue-collar worker? Over the past half-century, neoliberal restructuring has challenged the optimistic view of the post-World War II era that the market economy could provide socioeconomic stability through an enduring labour-capital pact. Indeed, dislocation and trauma have become integral to what it means to live as a worker today. In the U.S., a middle tier of jobs – well-paid manual jobs and lower-level office jobs – has been hollowed out, even as positions on the labour market's upper and lower tiers have proliferated (Kalleberg 2011; Temin 2017). As polarization has intensified and job opportunities have shifted to the service and logistics sectors, the white male factory worker of the mid-twentieth century has become outdated as a symbol of the working class, arguably replaced by the Walmart employee: paid meagre wages with minimal benefits, perhaps uninsured and involuntarily part time, often a woman or person of colour.

This uprooting of segments of America's working class from their traditional sites of labour has had significant social and political consequences. The factory was once the hub around which working-class life was constituted, and the foundation on which working-class organizations built political power (Georgakas and Surkin 1998). Yet the neoliberal counter-offensive against the 'rank-and-file rebellion' of blue-collar workers in the 1960s and 1970s decomposed and deterritorialized this particular form of U.S. working-class life – only to reassemble it in new forms, in new locations, and with new workers (Moody 2017). This has radically transformed what it means to work in today's economy – and, for many, what it means not to work.

Understanding these changes and their consequences demands a broader analysis than scholars working in disciplinary silos can typically provide. Research on employer–employee or union–management relations – or even the divide between the employed and unemployed – may miss large segments of the working class who no longer fit into these conventional categories. A focus merely on market mechanisms or policy regimes may come at the cost of understanding the interplay between economic, political, social, and cultural factors in determining those conditions. Here, the multidisciplinary and integrative approach of working-class studies can be helpful in understanding the multidimensional and intertwined nature of the trends shaping working-class life.

This chapter examines the causes and consequences of economic dislocation for America's working class. In using the term 'working class', we acknowledge the complexity of the concept and its changing historical meanings: from the all-encompassing proletarian subject forcibly integrated into the circuits of capital to its narrower popular usage to describe workers with relatively less income and less access to schooling. With the term 'dislocation', we mean to cover not only a person's separation from paid work, but also the larger implications in the sundering of social ties and upheaval in communities haemorrhaging jobs.

The state of today's working class can be seen as a return to the normal relations of capital and labour – with a post-war period of relatively muted economic inequalities in the richest nations being a brief detour set in motion by global wars and economic crisis (Cowie 2017; Piketty 2014). Building upon an analysis of surplus population and the growth of precarious work, we argue that today's labour market is characterized by a growing *division of non-labour*, as workers increasingly find themselves not in discrete categories of employed and unemployed, but existing somewhere along a spectrum of greater or lesser access to formal, remunerative, and reliable work. In other words, a degree of dislocation has become endemic to modern economic life.

In the second section, we examine the forms of trauma that dislocated workers suffer as a result of these economic transformations. Here, we define 'trauma' as experiences of harm and shock across multiple dimensions: financial, psychological, and social. We end the chapter with some forward-looking thoughts on how dislocation and trauma for the working class may intensify or diminish across the possible scenarios of technological innovation, policy choices, and political organizing.

The growing danger of dislocation

Over the span of the post-war period, the urban working class in the Global North saw their well-paid factory jobs disappear as companies ramped up the use of industrial robots and moved production outside the urban core (Bluestone and Harrison 1982; Wilson 2010). In the U.S., factories relocated at first to the suburbs and less union-friendly regions, but eventually the political will to protect domestic markets weakened, too, as capital, spurred by the perpetual-motion machine of profit, lobbied for its expansion overseas. In recent years, these trends of labour automation and creative dislocation have accelerated, and even higher-wage office jobs have been uprooted by outsourcing or swept aside by technological advances (Cleaver 2017). So far, though, less-advantaged workers and communities have experienced the brunt of these shocks. For them, the service economy offers 'non-routine', rooted jobs that cannot be as easily automated or transplanted but typically pay paltry wages (Albanesi et al. 2013). Employment in logistics networks has grown – there is still a need to distribute the products made elsewhere or by machine – but the wages and working conditions in warehouses run by Amazon and its retail rivals tend to be poor, and other key logistics workers, such as truck drivers, appear vulnerable to further automation and rationalization (Korte 2018).

However, this skills mismatch between existing workers and available positions cannot fully explain the widening gap in outcomes between the top 1 per cent of earners and the rest of society, given enormous increases in inequalities among the college-educated as well (Hacker and Pierson 2010). In the U.S., seemingly inexorable trends toward skill-biased technological change occurred within a context of policy choices to cut taxes on the wealthy and remove constraints on capital. This shifting balance of power in favour of employers can also be seen in the rise of precarity: unpredictable and insecure jobs, often performed by a contingent workforce stripped of employee status and its corresponding protections (Kalleberg 2018; Ravenelle 2019; Smith 2010). The lowest-paid workers are disproportionately stuck in the worst of these arrangements, such as temporary and on-call work (Katz and Krueger 2016).

It is important to note that precariousness has been central to the experience of work throughout history, even if organized worker power briefly interrupted this state during the twentieth century to establish a new paradigm of relatively protected and long-term employment (Doody et al. 2016). Indeed, what we today call the 'precariat' is better understood as part of a larger surplus population that the market economy creates through the unemployment and underemployment of differentiated strata of workers. At risk of falling into this category, workers are unable to bargain up their wages. In short, endemic joblessness is a feature, not a bug, of capitalist production. According to Marx, the surplus population is comprised of several groups. One is the *stagnant* population of 'highly disposable' workers with 'extremely irregular employment' – in short, the precariat. Another is the *pauperized* population at the very bottom, which encompasses not just 'vagabonds, criminals, prostitutes' and other stigmatized groups, but also 'demoralized' and 'ragged' individuals unable to work – 'chiefly people who succumb to their incapacity for adaptation, an incapacity which results from the division of labour' (Marx 1977, 796–797).

This last group is of particular concern today. Over the last half-century, large numbers of workers (first men and African Americans, but increasingly women and whites) have been falling out of – or not entering – the labour force; similar shifts have occurred in Europe and Japan to a lesser extent. The labour force has shrunk in part because more people are retired and more young people are pursuing higher degrees. What is shocking, however, is the growing numbers of Americans ages 25 to 54 who have been exiting, or never entering, the labour market in recent decades – to the point that the percentage of 'prime-age' men not in the labour force is now roughly the same as it was during the late years of the Great Depression (Eberstadt 2016). Working-class men are leading this drift away from work. At the other extreme, however, college-educated professionals and managers embrace a macho culture of overwork (Schulz 2012). The end result is an inequality of industriousness/idleness to complement the economy's inequalities of income and wealth: a labour market polarized between one group either jobless or scrambling for time on the clock and another hoarding work hours – voluntarily or not (Schor 1993).

Today, the dominance of a post-Fordist, post-Keynesian regime of neoliberal governance has created a superfluous working class, which 'can be thrown into the wilderness or recruited back into jobs according to the state of orders' (Biel 2000, 171). That said, certain segments of the working class are seen as more superfluous than others. Unemployment rates are higher for African Americans and Hispanics, partly due to a relative lack of skills, but also due to discrimination in hiring (Lang et al. 2012; Quillian et al. 2017). Here, it is important to note how the African American working class has served as a 'canary in the coal mine', with the early waves of drug proliferation and deindustrialization that their communities endured prefiguring what was to come for other segments of the working class (Guinier and Torres 2003). We can take this comparison further. Historian Thomas Sugrue argues that the destruction of African American working-class power and community set in motion a process of 'deproletarianization', as young Black men 'gave up on work' (2005, 262). One might argue that the same process is happening today to the working class more widely. The idea of de-proletarianization, however, implies that these individuals have, through the loss of work, experienced a loss of their class status, which is unclear. We believe it is more useful to think of this dislocation not in terms of how the identity of the working class has changed, but rather what, exactly, they have been deprived of: their labour.

Under the economy's growing division of non-labour, we argue, individuals are categorized not according to a dichotomy of employed and unemployed, but by their degree of disengagement from the orthodox model of formal, regulated, long-term employment. This concept speaks to processes of technological, political, and social differentiation – innovations in capital's use of creative dislocation – that make it easier to segment the surplus population into a multitude of groups, thereby reflecting capitalism's inherent tendency to produce inequality as a means of increasing profit. Importantly, the division of non-labour is not just about some people having more work and others less; it is also about qualitatively different characteristics that disconnect and distance individuals from the once-standard paradigm of secure employment. Just as workers are more or less employable (Smith 2010), for instance, they are more or less 'deportable' – to draw from Nicholas de Genova's (2002, 437) terminology for a status of 'enforced and protracted vulnerability' imposed on undocumented workers. Likewise, they are more or less constrained by their incarceration status – whether they are engaged in the denigrated work of prison labour or face later difficulties becoming employed due to criminal records (Pager 2007; Western and Pettit 2010).

Here, we can see how different degrees of legal protection and cultural stigma affect the ability of workers to assert their power when dealing with management. For example, within the single category of immigrant labour, subcategories include undocumented workers, guest workers, and refugees, each with vulnerabilities of distinct kinds and severities. Workers in the underground economy, the most precarious economy of all, differ by degrees of legal and cultural exposure, too: from off-the-books labour to drug dealing and theft, all income-generating opportunities that lure workers away from low-wage work – but at the cost of their engagement with formal markets.

Traumas of dislocation

For many, work is a source of personal fulfilment and a marker of social as well as moral status. Beyond its income-generating role, it provides a range of benefits: concrete goals, self-esteem, interpersonal contact, life motivation, a framework for daily behaviour, and opportunities to use talents and skills. Joblessness has been linked to higher rates of depression, anxiety, heart disease, and other physiological and psychological problems, which may, in turn, shorten lifespans (for a review, see Brand 2015). A job loss is typically followed by a decline in subjective well-being that is greater than the drop in income would predict – one comparable to other major crises such as divorce – and that persists to some extent even if the person finds another job (Clark et al. 2001; Young 2012). Meanwhile, spells without work tend to increase the likelihood of future bouts of joblessness and worsen the quality of later jobs – thereby raising the risk of longer-run cycles of downward mobility (Gangl 2006).

The eroded financial underpinnings of households in general – thanks to rising debt and the shifting of risks relating to health care and retirement from employers to workers – mean that the dangers of dislocation have grown even for professional-managerial workers (Cooper 2014; Hacker 2008). Nevertheless, the low-wage and no-wage strata of the working class often endure the worst of the insults and injuries of non-labour, given their lack of financial, human, social, and cultural capital. The economists Anne Case and Angus Deaton (2017) explicitly connect working-class trauma to a complex intersection of inequalities – what they dub 'cumulative disadvantage' – weighing down on these vulnerable communities. In their view, a perfect storm of readily accessible opioids, fraying social institutions, and fading economic prospects has brought about surges in drug overdoses, liver disease, suicides, and other physical and mental health problems, particularly among less-educated populations. Interestingly, the data from recent decades do not show similarly sharp upticks in suicides and drug poisonings – so-called deaths of despair – among non-whites, which may be because they went through similar crises earlier or are more hopeful given real economic progress made across generations (Graham et al. 2017; Pierce and Schott 2016).

Growing competition and uncertainty within the labour market have broadened the experience of dislocation-related trauma. Workers who are not yet displaced, but perceive themselves to be either at risk of being laid off or underemployed, experience higher rates of depression and anxiety, and rising rates of unemployment are associated with declining happiness even among the employed (Burgard et al. 2012; Dooley et al. 2000; Frey and Stutzer 2002). Today's workers tend to believe it will be difficult to find another job that pays wages and benefits similar to their current one, and trepidation about job loss and deteriorating finances is particularly high among working-class individuals (Jacobs and Newman 2008; Stettner and Wenger 2003). This suggests that the extent to which the existence of a surplus population makes workers insecure in their own economic position is determined not just by the size of the 'unemployed' population, but also by workers' subjective appraisals of the risk of losing their jobs, as well as their perception of other trends in the division of non-labour. In this sense, being a 'precarious' worker is not just about believing one's current job will end in the near future; it is a more generalized anxiety about the stability and security of one's work. Today, even workers who are more advantaged are not immune from such doubts.

It is well established that job losses worsen family tensions and outcomes for children in these households (Charles and Stephens 2004; Johnson et al. 2012; Page et al. 2009). But there is also growing evidence that the prodigious scale of economic dislocation among the working class has contributed to the transformation of its family structures over recent decades. While Northern societies as a whole have moved away from marriage and become more accepting of childbirth outside marriage, there is now a considerable, and growing, gap between the family-formation patterns of working-class individuals and those of the college-educated (Chen 2017b). In 1990, Americans without a bachelor's degree were more likely to be married by the age of 30 than those with a degree. By 2008, that trend had reversed. Today, working-class women are also much less likely than their college-educated peers to give birth to their children while married (Cherlin 2014). Again, African Americans – who experienced sharp drops in marriage and childbirth within marriage before other groups did – have served as a miner's canary. Falling employment and wages in deindustrialized communities downgraded men's desirability as partners, while surges in incarceration physically removed many men from the marriage market (Wilson 2010). In recent years, researchers have examined the declining 'marriageability' of working-class men more broadly. One study found that in parts of the country with greater income inequality – where middle-skill jobs have dwindled away – women were more likely to have children out of wedlock (Cherlin et al. 2016). Another concluded that in areas where local manufacturing was hit hard by competition from Chinese imports, women were less likely to marry, and the share of kids born outside of marriage, and living within poverty, grew (Autor et al. 2017).

When joblessness and other forms of non-labour expand within a locality, the isolated and personal experience of dislocation becomes a collective and public crisis, visible in rising rates of crime, the closure of stores, banks, and other businesses dependent on a well-paid workforce and the loss of local populations (and the taxes they pay) to areas with more jobs (Dudley 1994). Gentrification has stimulated many urban economies, but the resulting boom in real estate has pushed out working-class families unable to afford the rent (Newman and Chen 2007). As downtown areas cast off the last vestiges of working-class life in favour of start-up companies, hip breweries, and chic boutiques, poverty and joblessness have moved into the 'hinterlands' that surround the metropolitan core (Berube 2016; Neel 2018).

While earlier research found that unemployed workers tend to be disconnected from community life, more recent studies have suggested that they are now little different from the employed in their rates of volunteering and other civic participation; rather, it is those out of the labour force who are disengaged (Brand and Burgard 2008; Rotolo and Wilson 2003; Wiertz and Lim 2019). This may speak to how unemployment is becoming normalized in today's market economy and how its consequences of social stigma and exclusion are shifting to those out of the labour force – a very rare status among American men until recent decades (Clark 2010). That said, as joblessness of various kinds and degrees continues to spread throughout the economy, even the act of dropping out of the labour market may become less psychologically costly.

Although globalization and automation are often taken to be implacable forces, outcomes for the working class have diverged considerably in countries that have experienced these same trends – suggesting that judicious social policy can ameliorate the traumas of dislocation (Chen 2015; Sharone 2013; Zuberi 2006). For example, rates of working-class labour force participation are considerably higher in Germany and Japan, which have long-established traditions of vocational training for young people not bound for college (Newman and Winston 2016). Likewise, the absence of a strong social safety net in the U.S. makes it harder to sustain relationships put under strain by a job loss, especially for working-class families heavily dependent on a second income (Chen 2015).

Yet in America's individualistic culture, the judgment of the unemployed and underemployed – often cast as parasites who live off the benefit-cheque largesse of taxpayers – is particularly strong (Chen 2015; Newman 1988). This stigma has varied over historical periods (Katz 1989; Schlozman and Verba 1979), but nowadays it appears to have more of a class component, with society idealizing higher education and a 'culture of the mind' (Dudley 1994). The resulting denigration of manual labour means the loss of a sense of working-class pride, along with the rise of a Social Darwinian perspective that those who are losing their jobs in the changing economy deserve their fates (Sennett and Cobb 1973). At the same time, today's thriving culture of entrepreneurship romanticizes the self-reliant free agent or 'company of one', encouraging workers to embrace precarity and a perpetual state of overwork and see themselves as 'personal brands' always in need of self-marketing and self-improvement (Boltanski and Chiapello 2005; Doody et al. 2016; Lane 2011; Vallas and Cummins 2015). These ideological lenses of self-initiative and self-blame that workers see through can exacerbate the trauma they experience after economic trends disorient and displace them. Furthermore, as non-labour becomes a more commonly experienced condition, its perennial state of anxiety and risk seeps into other aspects of people's lives. Lower-placed individuals find it harder to participate in modern consumer culture and thereby become integrated members of society. To cope with their various dimensions of disconnection from well-paid work, they may resort to debt or even illegal activities as supplements to their incomes. This growing burden of financial and legal liability, however, pushes individuals deeper into their position of powerlessness, placing further pressures on them to accept less from employers.

The broader division of non-labour, in turn, focuses workers' attention myopically on their position within the labour market's hierarchy. This reinforces the social distance that separates them from more marginalized groups, deepening the sorts of internecine conflict that often benefit employers. The obvious example would be undocumented workers competing with the native-born. But innovations in creating and structuring precarious work have generated other divisions: inmate firefighters, for instance, can take on jobs that unionized firefighters might otherwise do. Relegated to narrow niche groups separated by degrees of privilege – and often contemptuous of each other – individuals within this surplus population become further alienated from one another; fractured politically, they come to see their immiseration as an individual problem. Their experience of non-labour becomes a lonelier one.

Conclusion

What can be done to halt or ameliorate the modern economy's increasingly frequent dislocations of mass unemployment and precarious underemployment, which, as we have argued, are fundamental to the workings of capitalism? If full automation is within the range of possibility, the resulting upheaval in the labour market could become catastrophic. The pacing of change will be critical – slower transitions may allow older workers to plan for their obsolescence – and to that end, governments could levy taxes to make adopting new technologies costlier for capitalists (Atkinson 2015). But this would just be a stopgap measure. A more muscular government response, of New Deal vintage, would be the creation of a multitude of new jobs in the public sector. Another idea, championed by libertarian Silicon Valley entrepreneurs and left economists alike, is to establish a universal basic income, eliminating the need for paid work. If such aggressive policies to reshape the market economy and social safety net are implemented, the automation of human labour need not lead to nightmarish inequality. In fact, it may allow for the utopian future that the economist John Maynard Keynes envisioned a century earlier: a world where the 'economic problem' will have been largely resolved and 'man will be faced with his permanent problems' of wisely using the time that 'science and compound interest' – and, we might add, smart robots – 'will have won for him' (2009, 198). In such a 'post-work' world, there would be no need for compulsory labour – and no need to dwell piously on the work lives of others (Aronowitz and Cutler 1998; Srnicek and Williams 2015).

Like many utopias, however, this vision of an egalitarian future is at risk of falling into old patterns of exploitation. If Northern societies fully automate, would they ramp up resource and labour extraction from the South, which already builds the hardware that underpins the North's consumer wonderland? How would a full-automation society deal with issues of resource scarcity in the midst of climate change? As the 'robotization' of everyday life progresses, what will that mean for the affective and cognitive labour of caregiving and other forms of social reproduction that are so essential to human flourishing (Federici 2012)?

Of course, fears of automation leading to mass joblessness and massive inequality may be overblown. Throughout history, disruptive technological innovation has increased the net number of jobs available. Furthermore, given that 'good' white-collar positions are increasingly being automated – and artificial intelligence by its very nature would threaten many more of these jobs – it is conceivable that the 'skill bias' of technological change will diminish over time, actually reducing levels of inequality.

Regardless whether full automation is ultimately achievable, labour organizing will remain critical for the foreseeable future. To address the changing nature of worker dislocation and trauma, however, it will need to adopt new forms. Those out of the labour force are largely excluded from traditional unions, for example, and the difficulties in organizing contingent workers speak to the problems that the division of non-labour poses for consolidating worker power. The cultural and political divides that often emerge between higher- and lower-placed groups also make it harder to achieve broad-based solidarity.

In recent decades, activists have developed innovative approaches to organizing workers, some better suited to the intensifying division of non-labour. So-called Alt-Labour groups tend to eschew collective bargaining in favour of a larger toolkit of advocacy – from demonstrations and community organizing to lawsuits and media pressure targeted at corporate brands. In the U.S., these efforts have thrived among marginalized groups (such as immigrant workers served by worker centres and legal-justice groups) and garnered national attention through social media-backed movements by fast-food workers and others to raise minimum wages.

Many of these campaigns rely heavily on funding from labour unions, and it is unclear whether they can sustain themselves without the institutional resources that unions have traditionally provided. Yet they offer hope that new strategies adapted to the evolving economy can work. Likewise, although worker advocacy and student activism have become harder as sites of production and learning have been scattered across real and virtual space, such fragmentation has also created opportunities for organizing (Cleaver 2017; Korte 2018). In rapidly growing working-class-dominated sectors like logistics operations, 'landlocked' jobs enmeshed in global supply chains offer labour activists a variety of strategic pressure points (Moody 2017). And some activists – among Spain's Indignados and Occupy Wall Street, for example – have embraced a larger struggle over the costs of public utilities, transportation, housing, groceries, schooling, disaster relief, and the other essential needs of communities cut loose from the most remunerative sectors of the economy. These wide-ranging campaigns suggest that the total war that the modern economy wages on today's workers will beget more integrated and expansive forms of resistance, including new capacities to reappropriate indirect forms of social cooperation and networked communication (Negri 1989) and pursue collectivist-democratic forms of organizing like worker cooperatives (Chen and Chen 2021). While these are not 'worker movements' in the traditional, narrow sense, they are well-adapted to today's division of non-labour, finding ways to reach those hard to organize by conventional means.

As economic dislocation spreads, the social movements emerging to combat it will likely ride broader cultural shifts. This ideological renewal will be especially critical in the U.S., given how much a cult of meritocratic morality and a culture of personal judgment push Americans to reject collective solutions in favour of individual blame. In response, Chen (2017a) argues for a morality of grace – a perspective of radical acceptance and non-judgment – that will open up more political space for egalitarian policies. Such a viewpoint, he argues, can connect with people who take issue with the market economy's mantra of material and social advancement. And as a new technology of meritocracy makes the evaluation of workers ever more encompassing, and a growing division of non-labour makes them ever more isolated, it may also appeal to those increasingly being cast aside by economic trends.

A movement to bring about cultural change is no substitute for organizing on behalf of political and economic change. But each builds on the other. As theorists such as Herbert Marcuse (1964) have argued, a society without rampant economic dislocation and trauma will only take root through careful cultivation: local and global efforts to learn new values and new ways of life, as well as the gradual building of countervailing institutions to sustain them. Much like the labour unions of an earlier era evangelized an egalitarian creed that seeped into the larger consciousness, those who wish to remake today's post-industrial economy need a movement and a faith – ones adapted to the evolving nature of today's global working class.

Acknowledgments

The authors would like to thank the editors and Katherine K. Chen for their thoughtful feedback on earlier drafts.

References

Albanesi, S., Gregory, V., Patterson, C. and Sahin, A. (2013) *Is Job Polarization Holding Back the Labor Market?* New York, Federal Reserve Bank of New York.

Aronowitz, S. and Cutler, J. (1998) *Post-Work: The Wages of Cybernation*, New York, Routledge.

Atkinson, A.B . (2015) *Inequality: What Can Be Done?* Cambridge, Harvard University Press.

Autor, D., Dorn, D. and Hanson, G. (2017) *When Work Disappears: Manufacturing Decline and the Falling Marriage-Market Value of Men*, Cambridge, NBER.

Berube, A. (2016) *American's Male Employment Crisis Is Both Urban and Rural*, Washington, Brookings Institution.

Biel, R. (2000) *The New Imperialism: Crisis and Contradictions in North/South Relations*, London, Zed Books.

Bluestone, B. and Harrison, B. (1982) *The Deindustrialization of America: Plant Closings, Community Abandonment, and the Dismantling of Basic Industry*, New York, Basic Books.

Boltanski, L. and Chiapello, E. (2005) *The New Spirit of Capitalism*, Brooklyn, Verso.

Brand, J. E. (2015) 'The Far-Reaching Impact of Job Loss and Unemployment', *Annual Review of Sociology*, 41, pp. 359–375.

Brand, J. E. and Burgard, S. A. (2008) 'Job Displacement and Social Participation over the Life Course: Findings for a Cohort of Joiners', *Social Forces*, 87, 1, pp. 211–242.

Burgard, S., Kalousova, L. and Seefeldt, K. (2012) *Perceived Job Insecurity and Health: The Michigan Recession and Recovery Study*, Population Studies Center Research Report No. 12–750, Ann Arbor, University of Michigan.

Case, A. and Deaton, A. (2017) 'Mortality and Morbidity in the 21st Century', *BPEA Conference Drafts*, 23–24 March.
Charles, K. K. and Stephens, M., Jr. (2004) 'Job Displacement, Disability, and Divorce', *Journal of Labor Economics*, 22, 2, pp. 489–522.
Chen, V. T. (2015) *Cut Loose: Jobless and Hopeless in an Unfair Economy*, Oakland, University of California Press.
Chen, V. T. (2017a) 'An Economy of Grace', *Religions*, 8, 3, pp. 1–13.
Chen, V. T. (2017b) 'America, Home of the Transactional Marriage', *The Atlantic*, 20 August.
Chen, K. K. and Chen, V. T. (eds.) (2021). *Organizational Imaginaries: Tempering Capitalism and Tending to Communities through Cooperatives and Collectivist Democracy*, Bingley, UK, Emerald.
Cherlin, A. J. (2014) *Labor's Love Lost: The Rise and Fall of the Working-Class Family in America*, New York, Russell Sage.
Cherlin, A. J., Ribar, D. C. and Yasutake, S. (2016) 'Nonmarital First Births, Marriage, and Income Inequality', *American Sociological Review*, 81, 4, pp. 749–770.
Clark, A. E. (2010) 'Boon or Bane? Others' Unemployment, Well-Being and Job Insecurity', *Labour Economics*, 17, 1, pp. 52–61.
Clark, A. E., Georgellis, Y. and Sanfey, P. (2001) 'Scarring: The Psychological Impact of Past Unemployment', *Economica*, 68, 270, pp. 221–41.
Cleaver, H. (2017) *Rupturing the Dialectic: The Struggle Against Work, Money, and Financialization*, Oakland, AK Press.
Cooper, M. (2014) *Cut Adrift: Families in Insecure Times*, Berkeley, University of California Press.
Cowie, J. (2017) *The Great Exception: The New Deal and the Limits of American Politics*, Princeton, Princeton University Press.
De Genova, N. (2002) 'Migrant "Illegality" and Deportability in Everyday Life', *Annual Review of Anthropology*, 31, pp. 419–447.
Doody, S., Chen, V. T. and Goldstein, J. (2016) 'Varieties of Entrepreneurial Capitalism: The Culture of Entrepreneurship and Structural Inequalities of Work and Business Creation', *Sociology Compass*, 10, 10, pp. 858–876.
Dooley, D., Prause, J. and Ham-Rowbottom, K. A. (2000) 'Underemployment and Depression: Longitudinal Relationships', *Journal of Health and Social Behavior*, 41, 4, pp. 421–436.
Dudley, K. M. (1994) *The End of the Line: Lost Jobs, New Lives in Postindustrial America*, Chicago, University of Chicago Press.
Eberstadt. N. (2016) *Men without Work: America's Invisible Crisis*, West Conshohocken, Templeton.
Federici, S. (2012) *Revolution at Point Zero: Housework, Reproduction, and Feminist Struggle*, Oakland, PM Press.
Frey, B. S. and Stutzer, A. (2002) *Happiness and Economics: How the Economy and Institutions Affect Well-Being*, Princeton, Princeton University Press.
Gangl, M. (2006) 'Scar Effects of Unemployment: An Assessment of Institutional Complementarities', *American Sociological Review*, 71, 6, pp. 986–1013
Georgakas, D. and Surkin, V. (1998) *Detroit: I Do Mind Dying, A Study in Urban Revolution*, Boston, South End Press.
Graham, C., Pinto, S. and Juneau, J. (2017) *The Geography of Desperation in America*, Washington, Brookings Institution.
Guinier, L. and Torres, G. (2003) *The Miner's Canary: Enlisting Race, Resisting Power, Transforming Democracy*, Cambridge, Harvard University Press.
Hacker, J. S. (2008) *The Great Risk Shift: The New Economic Insecurity and the Decline of the American Dream*, New York, Oxford University Press.
Hacker, J. S. and Pierson, P. (2010) *Winner-Take-All Politics: How Washington Made the Rich Richer – and Turned Its Back on the Middle Class*, New York, Simon & Schuster.
Jacobs, E. and Newman, K. S. (2008) 'Rising Angst? Change and Stability in Perceptions of Economic Insecurity', in Newman, K. S. (ed.) *Laid Off, Laid Low: Political and Economic Consequences of Employment Insecurity*, New York, Columbia University Press.
Johnson, R. C., Kalil, A. and Dunifon, R. E. (2012) 'Employment Patterns of Less-Skilled Workers: Links to how Children's Behavior and Academic Progress', *Demography*, 49, 2, pp. 747–772.
Kalleberg, A. L. (2011) *Good Jobs, Bad Jobs: The Rise of Polarized and Precarious Employment Systems in the United States, 1970s to 2000s*, New York, Russell Sage.
Kalleberg, A. L. (2018) *Precarious Lives: Job Insecurity and Well-Being in Rich Democracies*, Cambridge, Polity Press.
Katz, L. F. and Krueger, A. B. (2016) *The Rise and Nature of Alternative Work Arrangements in the United States, 1995–2015*, Cambridge, NBER.

Katz, M. B. (1989) *The Undeserving Poor: From the War on Poverty to the War on Welfare*, New York, Pantheon.
Keynes, J. M. (2009) *Essays in Persuasion*, New York, Classic House.
Korte, P. E. (2018) 'Blast the Chain of Logistics! Investigating Global Class Recomposition', presentation at VCU Sociological Research Symposium, Richmond, May 2, 2018.
Lane, C. M. (2011) *A Company of One: Insecurity, Independence, and the New World of White-Collar Unemployment*, Ithaca, ILR.
Lang, K., Lehmann, J. and Yeon, K. (2012) 'Racial Discrimination in the Labor Market: Theory and Empirics', *Journal of Economic Literature*, 50, 4, pp. 959–1006.
Marcuse, H. (1964) *One-Dimensional Man: Studies in the Ideology of Advanced Industrial Society*, Boston, Beacon.
Marx, K. (1977) *Capital: A Critique of Political Economy, Volume One*, New York, Vintage.
Moody, K. (2017) *On New Terrain: How Capital is Reshaping the Battleground of Class War*, Chicago, Haymarket.
Neel, P. A. (2018) *Hinterland: America's New Landscape of Class and Conflict*, London, Reaktion.
Negri, A. (1989) *The Politics of Subversion: A Manifesto for the Twenty-First Century*, Cambridge, Polity.
Newman, K. S. (1988) *Falling from Grace: The Experience of Downward Mobility in the American Middle Class*, New York, Free Press.
Newman, K. S. and Chen, V. T. (2007) *The Missing Class: Portraits of the Near Poor in America*, Boston, Beacon.
Newman, K. S. and Winston, H. (2016) *Reskilling America: Learning to Labor in the Twenty-First Century*, New York, Metropolitan.
Page, M., Stevens, A. H. and Lindo, J. (2009) 'Parental Income Shocks and Outcomes of Disadvantaged Youth in the United States', in Gruber, J. (ed.) *The Problems of Disadvantaged Youth: An Economic Perspective*, Chicago, University of Chicago Press.
Pager, D. (2007) *Marked: Race, Crime, and Finding Work in an Era of Mass Incarceration*, Chicago, University of Chicago Press.
Pierce, J. R. and Schott, P. K. (2016) *Trade Liberation and Mortality: Evidence from U.S. Counties*, Cambridge, NBER.
Piketty, T. (2014) *Capital in the Twenty-First Century*, Cambridge, Harvard University Press.
Quillian, L., Pager, D., Hexel, O. and Midtbøen, A. H. (2017) 'Meta-Analysis of Field Experiments Shows No Change in Racial Discrimination in Hiring over Time', *PNAS*, 114, 41, pp. 10870–10875.
Ravenelle, A. J. (2019) *Hustle and Gig: Struggling and Surviving in the Sharing Economy*, Oakland, University of California Press.
Rotolo, T. and Wilson, J. (2003) 'Work Histories and Voluntary Association Memberships', *Sociological Forum*, 18, 4, pp. 603–619.
Schlozman, K. L. and Verba, S. (1979) *Injury to Insult: Unemployment, Class, and Political Response*, Cambridge, Harvard University Press.
Schor, J. (1993) *The Overworked American: The Unexpected Decline of Leisure*, New York, Basic.
Schulz, J. (2012) 'Talk of work: Transatlantic Divergences in Justifications for Hard Work among French, Norwegian, and American Professionals', *Theory and Society*, 41, 6, pp. 603–634.
Sennett, R. and Cobb, J. (1973) *The Hidden Injuries of Class*, New York, Norton.
Sharone, O. (2013) *Flawed System/Flawed Self: Job Searching and Unemployment Experiences*, Chicago, University of Chicago Press.
Smith, V. (2010). 'Enhancing Employability: Human, Cultural, and Social Capital in an Era of Turbulent Unpredictability', *Human Relations*, 63, 2, pp. 279–303.
Srnicek, N. and Williams, A. (2015) *Inventing the Future: Postcapitalism and a World without Work*, Brooklyn, Verso.
Stettner, A. and Wenger, J. (2003) *The Broad Reach of Long-Term Unemployment*, Washington, Economic Policy Institute.
Sugrue, T. J. (2005) *The Origins of the Urban Crisis: Race and Inequality in Postwar Detroit*, Princeton, Princeton University Press.
Temin, P. (2017) *The Vanishing Middle Class: Prejudice and Power in a Dual Economy*, Cambridge, MIT Press.
Vallas, S. P. and Cummins, E. R. (2015) 'Personal Branding and Identity Norms in the Popular Business Press: Enterprise Culture in an Age of Precarity', *Organization Studies*, 36, 3, pp. 293–319.
Western, B. and Pettit, B. (2010) 'Incarceration and Social Inequality', *Daedalus*, 139, 3, pp. 8–19.
Wiertz, D. and Lim, C. (2019). 'The Civic Footprints of Labor Market Participation: Longitudinal Evidence from the United States, 2002–2015', *Social Forces*, 97, 4, pp. 1757–1784.
Wilson, W. J. (2010) *More than Just Race: Being Black and Poor in the Inner City*, New York, Norton.
Young, C. (2012) 'Losing a Job: The Nonpecuniary Cost of Unemployment in the United States', *Social Forces*, 91, 2, pp. 609–634.
Zuberi, D. (2006) *Differences that Matter: Social Policy and the Working Poor in the United States and Canada*, Ithaca, Cornell University Press.

13

Working-class studies, oral history and industrial illness

Arthur McIvor

Social class was and continues to be a key determinant of health and well-being: materialist interpretations that emphasize the importance of economic power relations have real traction in explaining patterns of mortality and morbidity in industrial and post-industrial societies. Health sociologist Clare Bambra, for example, has recently argued that 'Paid work, or lack of it, is the most important determinant of population health and health inequalities in advanced market democracies' (Bambra 2012, ix). My argument, however, is that to really comprehend what is happening here, we need to understand work-health cultures – that is, the way that workers experienced, understood, reacted to and narrated such power relationships in their homes and workplaces. What did ill health, disability and death signify and mean to individuals, to families, and to working-class communities? What impact did it have? And how did workers react to risk and manage illness, mobilize and organize around these issues? It is the contention here that for the period within living memory these sorts of questions can be elucidated by an oral history approach, developing a dialogue with those directly affected. We need to listen (and to listen closely) to workers' voices to connect better to their worlds. Recently, oral historians Michelle Winslow and Graham Smith commented: 'It is a mark of the contribution of oral history to the history of medicine that studies located within living memory are open to criticism if they fail to include oral history' (2011, 372). A similar case might be made for working-class studies.

Oral history, working-class studies and illness

Oral history is a method of reconstructing the recent past through tapping into people's memories, usually these days using an electronic solid state recorder directly in new interviews and/or consulting the vast archives of existing recordings housed in public record offices, sound libraries and museums. Oral interviewing as a research methodology has been applied to the field of Working-Class Studies since oral history began, emerging as it did from socialist- and feminist-inspired work – for example, from Paul Thompson (2017) and Elizabeth Roberts (1984) in the UK. Illness featured in such early studies, though was not a primary focus. Subsequently historians deploying an oral history interviewing methodology have drilled down and focused more on health cultures. One example would be Lucinda McCray Beier's 2008 monograph *For Their Own Good: The Transformation of English Working Class Health Culture, 1880*–1970, which explored changing working-class attitudes to health and illness in England from 1880 to1970. Based on oral history interviews with 239 people from north-west England undertaken in the 1970s and 1980s, McCray Beier's work shows the potential of oral history to inform us about everyday health cultures, behavior and responses to disease and disability in working-class communities; how people understood and managed their illnesses and, later, engaged with state services (the NHS).

Other work has shifted the focus to the patient – and here oral testimony is especially vital, providing a counter-narrative to hegemonic medical models (Bornat et al. 1999). An oral history approach essentially enables a *refocused* history centred on peoples' lives, on emotions, on personal experience and on narrators' voices. It informs us about how big processes such as industrialization and deindustrialization impacted upon working-class lives and on bodies. In her work on disability in Alberta, Canada, Claudia Malacrida has argued persuasively that oral history enables people to 'bear witness'.

> These narratives provide a politicized reading of relations of power, offering the patient an opportunity to bear witness to harms suffered, and drawing on the perspectives of subordinated individuals to expose the workings of power and domination within the medical encounter.
>
> *(Malacrida 2015, 322)*

And much of the best work is gendered, enriching, for example, our understanding of health cultures and the agency, interventions and roles working-class women played as 'guardians' of family health, care and well-being (McCray Beier 2008, 9). This was a core element of unpaid domestic labor. Working-class femininity, gender relations and the body have been a key focus in the pioneering work of, for example, Ann Oakley (1984), Jocelyn Cornwall (1990), Jan Walmsley and Dorothy Atkinson (2000) and Joanna Bornat (2000). These writers have drawn heavily upon oral interviews to critically examine issues around sexuality, ageing, health, disease, disability and illness in working-class communities (see also Fisher 2006).

An oral history methodology is capable, then, of enriching our understanding of encounters between the environment (work, home, family) and the body. It enables us to locate those affected by illness within the specific sociocultural spaces they occupied at that time. Whilst oral interview material requires critical and sensitive treatment (necessitating reflective evaluation of how memories are constructed and the past recalled), these personal narratives provide a wide range of insights into ill health.

Take, for example, the way that employment facilitates health (by providing purpose, identity and income) but also makes people ill. The history of occupational health and safety has been dominated by studies that have focused on the role of the state, policymaking (e.g. on Factory Acts and compensation systems) and corporate irresponsibility and neglect, in some notable cases forensically exposing the prior knowledge of hazards, neglect and abuse that resulted in disasters – like the chemical leak at Bhopal – and epidemics of industrial disease – such as 'black lung' (coal workers' pneumoconiosis) and asbestos-related diseases. A range of interpretations exist within what is a hotly contested terrain, with those at one end of the spectrum making a case for corporate irresponsibility (economic violence, corporate killing) and those at the other defending industry, shifting the blame elsewhere, and castigating left-orientated historians and other researchers for inappropriate use of hindsight and failing to contextualize occupational illness in the period and the prevailing state of knowledge and existing work-health cultures in the past. The historiography of asbestos illustrates this contested terrain very well (see, for example Bartrip 2001; Tweedale 2001; McCulloch and Tweedale 2008). Company records, court files, and state papers and enquiries were amongst the core source materials for such studies. With some exceptions, the debates tended to pass over or neglect the lived experience of disability and disease and to gloss over the agency of victims and their individual and collective responses.

The shift in research toward the personal and to discourses, influenced firstly by socialist and feminist ideas, then by postmodernism, changed this landscape. The history of work was an early focus of oral historians, but a clutch of more recent studies focus directly on work-health cultures, the lived experience of disability and illness and how people directly affected articulated their stories and shaped their narratives. By providing a view from the workplace, we gain valuable insights into the limited effectiveness of regulatory frameworks whilst also getting a sense of the complexity of work-health and body cultures, the interplay of identities (such as gender, race and class), and the agency of workers negotiating paths through hazardous, exhausting, dusty, dirty and toxic work environments. A growing number of studies have turned to oral evidence to elucidate work and occupational health. These include Bloor (2002), Perchard (2013), Walker (2011), McIvor (2015; 2017a) and Johnston and McIvor (2000; 2004), which focus on the UK; High (2018) and Storey (2017) on injured workers in Canada; Portelli (2010) on coal miners in Harlan County, USA; and Mukherjee (2010) on Bhopal, India. Economic violence and damaged bodies are recurring motifs in these studies.

These investigations have taken place and have been influenced by concurrent developments in the discipline of oral history. Partly in response to criticisms about the unreliability of memory, oral history has morphed from what has been termed 'reconstructive' oral history – typically where testimony was uncritically accepted at face value – toward more 'interpretative' approaches. The latter was influenced by the postmodernist turn and by the influential work of Italian oral historians, notably Luisa Passerini (1987) and Alessandro Portelli (1991). What emerged was a phase of introspection in the discipline, and the outcome was a more theoretically informed and methodologically rigorous oral history. Ideas were borrowed from a wide range of social science and other disciplines (including sociology, anthropology, psychology and linguistics) and tested against the empirical evidence. Memory studies analysed the working of memory, basically confirming the fundamental reliability of long-term memory whilst the subjective nature of the evidence – formerly criticized as a weakness – became recognized as a strength. Silences in life stories and misremembering were identified as being significant in their own right and judged to be full of meaning. Inter-subjectivities also became a focus. Testimonies were observed to be composed and shaped both by the interviewers' subjectivities (such as gender and class) and in a dialogue with the interviewee as well as by the prevailing wider media and culture – what has become known as 'the cultural circuit' (Thomson 1994; Summerfield 1998). The present thus impinges upon the past in oral interviews. It was established that repetitions, metaphors and anecdotes in oral testimonies have significance and that personal storytelling is subject to prevailing narrative structures and 'rules' within particular societies and cultures. In recalling their past in an interview context, narrators are filtering and sieving memories, constructing and composing their stories, and mixing factual evidence with their own interpretations as they try to make sense of their lives in an active, dialogic and reflexive process of remembering. Lynn Abrams recent book *Oral History Theory* (2010) provides perhaps the best guide through such developments in the oral history discipline (see also Summerfield 2019).

Oral history scholarship and methodologies have thus become more sophisticated and have contributed to widening understanding of working-class health cultures. The unique nature of oral evidence is now widely accepted and its veracity recognized. Oral historians are now much more reflexively critical of their material and acknowledge the influence their own subjectivities have upon the interview and how informants position themselves in the narrative, frequently using the encounter as a way of projecting a sense of self. Oral historians have postulated that *what* is remembered and *how* it is recalled is significant in its own right. The 'new oral history' influenced by postmodernist ideas has challenged and been fused onto the radical tradition of oral history, driven by a desire to give marginalized people a voice and a place, with an equality and democratizing agenda for history.

Work-health cultures, risk and the body

The contribution that oral history can make to the study of illness can be illustrated with reference to occupational health. Eye-witness testimonies lay bare the realities of irresponsible and abusive power relationships – economic violence – at the point of production and the limited resources that workers could bring to bear upon their situation (McIvor 2015). The space in which workers toiled and the environment in which bodies were located was frequently vividly recalled in interviews, with dust, death, illness and disability as recurring motifs. Asbestos workers in the UK (and elsewhere) recalled asbestos dust suspended like a 'fog' or falling like 'snow' in their post-war workplaces and of *playing* with the material – for example making 'monkey dung' (asbestos cement paste), 'wigs' and 'snowballs' (Johnston and McIvor 2000). Information was withheld from workers, or only selective and sometimes misleading information about hazards was leaked out – such as the erroneous claim that white asbestos (Chrysotile) was benign (Johnston and McIvor 2015). Whilst workers often had some intuitive and lay knowledge, they were not informed of the *extent* of the dangers to their health. They recalled feeling pressured to work with toxic and carcinogenic raw materials or in dusty work environments at the coal face, to 'cut corners', ignore safety regulations and maximize productivity. An unskilled machine operator who worked at the Turner and Newall Clydebank (Scotland) asbestos factory in the 1960s commented, 'I knew it was dangerous before I went in there 'cause there was people complaining, but when you have two of a family to bring up it was better than walking the streets. I never was idle in my life' (Scottish Oral History Centre–hereafter SOHC – interview, 1 June 1999, SOHC/016/A26). In the same interview his wife recalled, 'He was frightened to walk out of the job because he was married with a family and he just could not afford to do it'. Motifs of danger and fear, the work ethic and family are evident here. Connections between disempowerment and illness are suggested and affirmed, not least in what happened to Owen and Margaret Lilly, who both subsequently died respectively of asbestosis and mesothelioma. These workers were victims of a Fordist culture that exalted hard graft and the maximization of production and earnings at all costs, including serious cumulative damage to the body.

Occupational disease epidemics have to be understood, however, within a cultural framework – a milieu that facilitated the tolerance and persistence of abusive economic violence. There was a profound acculturation to undertaking dangerous and unhealthy work, a high-risk threshold, and a fiercely independent working-class culture where 'outside interference' could be resented and it was frowned upon for men to complain or 'make a fuss' about their health. A dominant (or hegemonic) mode of 'hard man' masculinity was forged in heavy industry workplaces in the UK and elsewhere (Johnston and McIvor 2004). Stakhanovite grafting was exalted within working-class communities, where the 'top producers' and highest earners were lauded and praised. Those who sought to protect themselves beyond acceptable workplace norms could be pilloried as lesser men and their sexuality questioned – as 'jessies' or 'sissies' (homosexuals) – and subjected to peer pressure to take risks, to compete, to conform and to maximize earnings. This was what was expected of men in the performance of their 'provider' role as 'breadwinners', which lay at the very core of working-class masculinities.

This high-risk threshold culture and 'macho' behavior was invariably condoned by employers and management, but to a surprising degree was also accepted as an integral, immutable part of working-class life. Male workers were socialized into this as kids and youths. Such risks were part of the fabric of manual working lives and rarely questioned. Heavy manual work forged masculinities and men developed a complex relationship with dangerous, health-threatening manual work. High has discussed how working men understood danger and contained it by identifying 'danger spots', regarding risk as 'localised'; hence they could remember the workplace as relatively safe in their 'accident stories' (High 2018, 102–122). Whilst attuned to hazards via accumulated lay knowledge on the job, working men were also capable of embracing the very processes that consumed their bodies in order to fulfil manly roles (Connell 2000; Johnston and McIvor 2004). You had to be seen to be grafting – as a 'worker' not a 'waster' (Wight 1994) – and as acting like a *real* man. This 'cultural disposition', as Portelli (2010, 139) puts it, contributed to the endemic bodily damage in mining communities caused by managerial economic violence.

Exposure to risk at work was not just confined to male workers, though the existence of a patriarchal dangerous work 'taboo' insulated most women from the highly hazardous and unhealthy industrial jobs. Some evidence suggests working-class women in some jobs embraced a high risk threshold and a willingness to put wage maximization before the protection of their bodies. Abendstern et al. (2005) have argued this case for textile weaving in the UK. Recent research has also shown how a sense of patriotic duty in wartime also shifted attitudes toward work-related dangers and potential damage to health, inducing male and female workers on the home front to accept higher risks (Pattinson et al. 2017). The workers' trade unions might have challenged this, during hostilities and in peacetime, but also at times tolerated it and legitimized it – as, for example in their support for the system of extra payments (sometimes referred to as 'danger money') for working in dust and some trade unions' endorsement of asbestos (even long after the dangers of it were well known). This is an area of considerable debate in the British literature and merits more attention. Trade unions were, on balance, undoubtedly important ameliorative interlocutors responsible for protecting workers' bodies and improving health. Still, there was a tension between, on the one hand, protecting the body and conserving labor power and, on the other, maintaining jobs, taking risks and pushing bodies to the limit to maximize production, earn fatter wage packets and fulfil managerial and (in wartime) national expectations.

The Scottish Oral History Centre (established in 1995) has undertaken under its auspices a series of interview-based projects that explore the historical meanings of work and the ways that work interacted with the body, notably in the heavy industry sectors. Some of the interviews we did with metal workers, construction workers, dockers and coal miners fizzed with bitterness and anger over needless illness, disability and fatalities; in others, the tone was quiet stoicism and fatalistic acceptance of damaged bodies. Discovery of and confirmation that employers were aware of the risks long before workers were told were repeated narratives in the oral testimonies, as was the perception that what had happened was preventable killing and disabling of workers predicated upon prior knowledge of the toxic and deadly nature of the raw materials being mined, processed or handled. 'We were murdered' was a common enough refrain amongst interviewed workers exposed to asbestos. Clearly, however, evidence and knowledge that has accumulated since exposure has influenced the way people remember and recount illnesses and trauma – and we do need to be aware of the pitfalls of hindsight and potential distortion and 'contamination' of oral accounts influenced by the 'cultural circuit' (Summerfield 2019, 118–122; 127). Memories were framed with reference to the media and trade union exposures of coal workers' pneumoconiosis, bronchitis and the deadly risks of working with asbestos, influenced by awareness of a changing compensation culture and incremental knowledge accumulation since the personal experiences being recalled – sometimes 30, 40 or more years previous. Such critical reflection does not invalidate the oral evidence, but does need to be taken account of in our interpretation of the material.

Living with illness, disability and death

Illness caused pain, sapped energies and affected identities and undermined lifestyles. What we now term 'social exclusion' was a common enough outcome of serious illness and disability. Industrial injuries and chronic disease in traditional 'heavy' industries like coal mining, iron and steel manufacture, shipbuilding, heavy chemicals, asbestos manufacture and the like were capable of destroying lives – leaving a legacy of disability, premature death, and deep psychological distress somewhat akin to other post-traumatic stress disorders. As a 64-year-old Scottish electrician with mesothelioma reflected, 'Until now I thought trauma was a fad imported from America and reserved for the middle classes. I am now wiser' (interview, 15 March 1999, SOHC/016/A13). Oral interviewing methodologies enable this experience to be explored and elucidated – to get behind the sterile body counts to the human dimension, the lived reality. Oral testimonies of those suffering from asbestos-related diseases, pneumoconiosis and bronchitis, for example illuminate a hidden world of private grief, sadness, anger, frustration, disappointment, pain and suffering. Ill men's lives shifted from the workplace to the feminized space of the home. They spoke movingly of restricted social and physical activities (such as walking, sports and dancing). They told of relative economic deprivation associated with income reduction, of the trauma associated with medical diagnosis, and of living and coping strategies as people struggled to adapt and survive with the news they were going to die from an incurable cancer. Social exclusion of varying degrees was the outcome, though this could be mitigated in some close-knit working-class communities (such as the coal mining villages). Relatively few workers in the twentieth century got any meaningful financial compensation for such damage to their bodies

Speaking to those directly implicated enables a *refocused* history revealing much about the emotional journey involved in the transition from fit and able worker to disabled and dependent, with all that represented for gendered identities. Such conversations take us deep into a personal (and often hidden) domain, informing us about how illness was managed and the impacts on the individual, the family and the community. What is being recalled is frequently an intimate, personal story of damage, loss, pain, adjustment – and of mutating identities through the illness journey. For working-class men, this could involve degrees of emasculation linked to being unable to perform traditional male breadwinner roles and other physical activities associated with masculinity. Male workers experienced loss of independence and dwindling financial resources, making it difficult to sustain a consumption pattern commensurate with male identities, such as heavy drinking and smoking. This threatened a loss of work identity and the package of intrinsic and extrinsic rewards that were associated with work (such as camaraderie, pride in the job, self-esteem). And such disruptions and destabilization could lead to tensions within the family.

Working-class men also appear to have responded less directly to health education and hazards-awareness campaigns than did women, and were generally more reluctant to admit they had a health problem and seek medical intervention. And when ill, they could refuse to allow help or admit they needed help. A wife whose husband died of mesothelioma reflected after his death that 'he never made a fuss … I was the one that used to see him sitting on the edge of the bed with his arms around himself rocking back and forward in pain' (interview, 22 March 1999, SOHC/016/A20). A 61-year-old shipyard engineering worker with mesothelioma commented: 'A lot of it's my own problem. Too macho to be shouting out when I should be, you know, when I'm in pain … "just stop this bloody pain will you"' (Clayson 2008, 140).

In their oral testimonies, those affected narrated how this was lived in the everyday and how this *felt* to them. A Glasgow sheet metal worker reflected, 'I've had no social life since about 1980. Eh, people unfortunately don't want to know you when you're ill' (interview, 1 May 1999,

SOHC 016/A9). Another bluntly commented on his inability to socialize and enjoy activities like dancing: 'I'm buggered' (interview, 22 December 1998, SOHC 016/A2). Emotions might be controlled by many men, except in private moments.

> He took my hand and said: 'I'm not going to see xxx as a bride'. Then we went up to bed together and we just cuddled and we both cried. And it's the one and only time that I saw my husband crying.
>
> *(Interview, 22 March 1999, SOHC/016/A20)*

This interviewee told of how her husband insisted on driving the car out of the drive, 'and then we would pull in and stop and I would take over'. 'Men eh', she pondered, 'don't like to give in'. Of course, coping capacities and strategies ranged widely, but oral testimonies consistently refer to the psychosocial distress and disruption to lives, commensurate to trauma, experienced by many such illness victims.

From adversity to advocacy: Building an occupational disease movement

Those affected by illness were not just passive, inert victims but active and vocal agents in these processes that were consuming their bodies. In regions with a radical, socialist tradition, like Glasgow and many of the UK coalfields, levels of protest and resistance were high, and powerful injured and diseased workers' movements emerged. A sense of injustice could be channelled into activity through mobilizations with advocacy groups, alliances with sympathetic doctors, physicians and environmental health activists, and campaigning for more effective preventative measures, fairer compensation and better palliative care. An oral interviewing approach enables the dynamics of such resistance, advocacy and mobilization within working-class communities around illness to be elucidated. For example, whilst national, industry-wide strikes on occupational health and safety issues were virtually unknown in the UK, in oral history interviews, a hidden, subterranean history of struggle at plant level and even work-group walkouts (and *threats* of industrial action) when health was jeopardized has been revealed (McIvor 2017b).

And there was significant collective mobilization around health issues. The first known asbestos victims' advocacy group in the world (the Society for the Prevention of Asbestosis and Industrial Diseases) was established in London in 1978 by Nancy Tait, the wife of a Post Office worker who had died of mesothelioma. Tait was a tireless advocate for victims' rights and an outspoken campaigner against the asbestos industry lobby until her death in 2009. Now (2020) at least 35 such asbestos-related disease victims' groups exist across the globe, and the global Ban Asbestos Network, headed by the tireless campaigner Laurie Kazan-Allen, coordinates the anti-asbestos campaign.

The role of trade unions on health, illness and disability, explored recently by Vicky Long (2011), has been neglected and merits more attention. There is some evidence that the unions in Britain were investigating illness more extensively from the 1930s, including marshalling alternative epidemiology to challenge medical orthodoxies around workers' chronic diseases (including silicosis, pneumoconiosis and tuberculosis). The appointment of the first full-time Medical Advisor to the Trades Union Congress in 1933 (Thomas Legge) marked something of a turning point.

In coal mining, the trade unions spearheaded the injured and diseased workers' movement, campaigning to improve safety underground, to prevent illness in the pits and to establish coal mining-related diseases as linked to occupation (and hence subject to compensation). The mobilizing capacity of injury, illness, harm and a burning sense of injustice has been apparent across the globe, evident, for example in the oral history-based work of Robert Storey (2017) on the injured workers movement in Canada and in recent work on tuberculosis as an occupational disease (McIvor 2012). One area that remains particularly neglected and merits more attention is the role of trade unions as advocates of improved mental health. The UK Trades Union Congress was an active player, for example in identifying and campaigning on the late-twentieth-century stress at work epidemic. Nonetheless one constituent trade union general secretary noted in an oral interview that a 'blind spot' for the National Union of Mineworkers was mental illness (Nicky Wilson, oral interview, 28 April 2014; SOHC Archive).

Blighted lives: Deindustrialization, job loss and illness

Whilst work could be toxic and dangerous, job loss and unemployment were also capable of causing illness in working-class communities. A series of path-breaking studies – particularly focusing on North America and Britain – have deployed an oral-history-based methodology to reconstruct the impact that deindustrialization and unemployment have had on workers' identities, health and sense of well-being. The work of Steven High (2003, 2018) and Tim Strangleman (2004) are amongst those studies that stand out here. Still, there is scope within deindustrialization studies for a sharper focus upon the body, illness and disability (McIvor 2017a). The research agenda here might embrace how deindustrialization added to stressors – through work intensification, the pressure of mass unemployment and 'cutting corners' with health and safety, endangering and undermining further the health of those 'survivor' workers trying to hold down their industrial jobs during rationalizations and contraction.

Given the power of the work ethic in working-class communities (Wight 1994), identity disintegration is frequently central to unemployed workers' 'scrap heap' stories. Job loss resulted in a range of illnesses and adverse health impacts, from anxiety-induced depression to heart problems to suicide. Deindustrialising communities sought consolation in drink and drugs – heroin use, for example shot up in deindustrialising working-class communities, including ex-coal mining villages, as did dependency on antidepressant pills (Perchard 2013, 80). And oral interviews in some working-class communities suggest that people were very aware of the illness caused by loss of work and directly attributed this to the neoliberal political onslaught on labor in the 1980s and 1990s (Mackenzie et al. 2015). This health-eroding crisis of identity was a recurring motif in oral history collections of interviewed ex-heavy industry workers, evident, for example in the work of Walkerdine and Jimenez (2012) on Welsh steelworkers. Deindustrialising regions in post-socialist countries registered similar patterns, as David Kideckel's oral-history-based work on Romanian chemical workers and coal miners indicates. 'Stress about the present and uncertainty about the future is written in their bodies in anger, resignation and ill-health' (Kideckel 2008, 235). But there was a complex relationship between job loss and health. In their testimonies, redundant manual workers express both a dominant narrative depicting tangible negative consequences imprinted on their bodies and a less evident but persistent underlying story of liberation and escape from alienating, physically exhausting, stressful, dangerous and toxic work environments. K'Meyer and Hart's (2009) oral-history-based investigation of deindustrialization in the USA captures this brilliantly. As one worker made redundant from International Harvester, Kentucky, USA, commented: 'I was overjoyed, I was sad, I was hurt' (K'Meyer and Hart 2009, 97). In British coal miners' oral narratives, there was definitely a deep sense that pit closures and job losses induced illness, but also that there could be health benefits escaping from dangerous and polluted work environments.

Concluding comments: What does oral history contribute?

The argument advanced here is that an oral history methodology can add other important dimensions and insights on the history of illness in working-class communities. This is one approach in what Tim Strangleman has referred to as a 'social industrial archaeology, the seeking out of intangible aspects of culture' (2017, 479) and one that could fruitfully be deployed more systematically in working-class studies of illness as we move forward. It provides a different focus through the lens of those affected. This is discussed here with reference to some of the literature and some of my own work in the field on occupational illness. Workers' own narratives inform us of their own understandings of how work affected them and of their often sensitive awareness of how processes such as deindustrialization, plant closures and neoliberalism directly affected their bodies, increasing illness and disability levels in their working-class communities and hence widening health inequalities. Oral interviews provide workers, patients and survivors perspectives on economic violence, enabling the latter to be understood within the prevailing and mutating cultures of the time and place. In the 'heavy' industry workers' interviews we have conducted at the Scottish Oral History Centre, what stands out is the frequency of stories about bodies – fit and honed bodies; diseased, disabled and injured bodies; dead bodies. This is paralleled in other recent oral-history-based work such as that of Portelli (2010) on Harlan County, USA, and Selway (2016) on accidents in the South Wales coal mines.

In interpreting such oral evidence, narrative analysis is important, as researchers such as Kleinman (1988) and Reissman (2008) have noted in relation to illness and disability. However, we can become too preoccupied with language, narrative and intersubjectivity. In their moving and earnest articulation of their illness experiences in oral interviews, workers are bearing witness and revealing something of themselves and much about their bodies, including how they were affected – directly and indirectly – by the productionist ethos and cultural norms of their workplaces. 'Each of us has only one body', Carol Wolkowitz has noted, 'and it feels the pinch' (2006, 117). Much remains to be done, and there are whole swathes of working-class experience of illness that still require investigation and which would benefit from an oral history approach. For example, we know little about the shop floor, grass-roots environmental health movement that Mackinnon has investigated in his work on steel communities in Nova Scotia, Canada (Mackinnon 2017). Mental health merits more attention – and here Ali Haggett's nuanced oral-history-based study of the neuroses of housewives comes to mind (Haggett 2012). The modern-day epidemic of work-related stress might also fruitfully be the subject of a systematic oral-history-based investigation, as would a series of ailments evident within working-class communities, such as alcohol and drug dependency, tuberculosis, bronchitis, obesity and diabetes. And the lived experience of disabled people in working-class communities is still also woefully neglected. Whether interest lies in the narrative discourse or lived experience, oral testimony is revealing at many levels. Developing a dialogue through oral interviews with those directly involved and affected, and those who shaped advocacy and the building of injured and diseased workers' movements, deserves to be utilized more widely within studies of health, disability and illness in working-class communities.

References

Abendstern, M., Hallett, C. E. and Wade, L. (2005) 'Flouting the Law: Women and the Hazards of Cleaning Moving Machinery in the Cotton Industry, 1930–1970', *Oral History*, 33, 2, pp. 69–78.

Abrams, L. (2010) *Oral History Theory*, London, Routledge.

Bambra, C. (2012) *Work, Worklessness and the Political Economy of Health*, Oxford, Oxford University Press.

Bartrip, P. (2001) *The Way from Dusty Death*, London, Athlone Press.

Bloor, M. (2002) 'No Longer Dying for a Living', *Sociology* 36, 1 (2002), pp. 89–105.

Bornat, J., Perks, R., Thompson, P. and Walmsley, J. (eds.) (1999) *Oral History, Health and Welfare,* London, Routledge.

Clayson, H. (2008) 'The Experience of Mesothelioma in Northern England', MD thesis, University of Sheffield.

Connell, R.W. (2000) *The Men and the Boys*, Cambridge, Polity Press.

Cornwall, J. (1990) *Hard Earned Lives: Accounts of Health and Illness from East London*, London, Tavistock.

Fisher, K. (2006) *Birth Control, Sex and Marriage in Britain, 1914–1960*, Oxford, Oxford University Press.

Haggett, A. (2012) *Desperate Housewives: Neuroses and the Domestic Environment 1945–1970*, Abingdon, Routledge.

High, S. (2003) *Industrial Sunset: The Making of North America's Rust Belt, 1969–1984*, Toronto, University of Toronto Press.

High, S. (2018) *One Job Town: Work, Belonging, and Betrayal in Northern Ontario,* Toronto, University of Toronto Press.

Johnston, R. and McIvor, A. (2000) *Lethal Work: A History of the Asbestos Tragedy in Scotland,* East Linton, Scotland, Tuckwell Press.

Johnston, R. and McIvor, A. (2004) 'Dangerous Work, Hard Men and Broken Bodies: Masculinity in the Clydeside Heavy Industries, c1930-1970s', *Labour History Review*, 69, 2, pp. 135–152.

Johnston, R. and McIvor, A. (2015) 'Urban information flows: workers' and employers' knowledge of the asbestos hazard in Clydeside, 1950-1970s', in Fischer-Nebmaier, W., Berg, M.P. and Christou, A. (eds.) *Narrating the City: Histories, Space and the Everyday*, New York, Berghahn, pp. 199–218.

Kideckel, D. A. (2008) *Getting By in Post Socialist Romania: Labor, the Body and Working-Class Culture,* Bloomington, Indiana University Press.

Kleinman, A. (1988) *The Illness Narratives: Suffering, Healing and the Human Condition*, New York, Basic Books.

K'Meyer, T. E. and Hart, J. L. (2009) *I Saw it Coming: Worker Narratives of Plant Closings and Job Loss,* New York, Palgrave Macmillan

Long, V. (2011) *The Rise and Fall of the Healthy Factory*, Basingstoke, Palgrave.

Mackenzie, M., Collins, C., Connolly, J., Doyle, M. and McCartney, G. (2015) 'Working-class discourses of politics, policy and health: "I don't smoke; I don't drink. The only thing wrong with me is my health"', *Policy & Politics*, pp. 1–19.

Mackinnon, L. (2017) 'Environmental Justice and Workers' Health: Fighting for Compensation at the Sydney Coke Ovens, 1986–90', in High, S. (ed.) *Beyond Testimony and Trauma: Oral History in the Aftermath of Mass Violence*, Vancouver, University of British Columbia Press, pp. 68–86.

Malacrida, C. (2015) 'Contested Memories: Efforts of the Powerful to Silence Former Inmates Histories of Life in an Institution for "Mental Defectives"', in Llewellyn, K.R., Freund, A. and Reilly, N. (eds.), *The Canadian Oral History Reader*, Montreal, McGill-Queens University Press, pp. 318–334.

McCray Beier, L. (2008) *For Their Own Good: The Transformation of English Working Class Health Culture, 1880–1970*, Ohio, Ohio State University Press.

McCulloch, J. and Tweedale, G. (2008) *Defending the Indefensible: The Global Asbestos Industry and Its Fight for Survival,* Oxford, Oxford University Press.

McIvor, A. (2012) 'Germs at work: Establishing tuberculosis as an *occupational* disease in Britain, c1900-1951', *Social History of Medicine*, 25, 4, pp. 812–829.

McIvor, A. (2015) 'Economic violence, occupational disability and death: oral narratives of the impact of asbestos-related disease in Britain', in High, S. (ed.) *Beyond Testimony and Trauma: Oral History in the Aftermath of Mass Violence*, Vancouver, University of British Columbia Press, pp. 257–284.

McIvor, A. (2017a) 'Deindustrialisation Embodied: Work, Health and Disability in the United Kingdom since the Mid-Twentieth Century', in High, S., Mackinnon, L. and Perchard, A. (eds.) *The Deindustrialized World: Confronting Ruination in Postindustrial Places*, Vancouver, University of British Columbia Press, pp. 25–45.

McIvor, A. (2017b) 'Was Occupational Health and Safety a Strike Issue? Workers, Unions and the Body in Twentieth Century Scotland', *Journal of Irish and Scottish Studies*, vol 8.2., pp. 5–33.

Mukherjee, S. (2010) *Surviving Bhopal*, New York, Palgrave.

Oakley, A. (1984) *The Captured Womb: A History of the Medical Care of Pregnant Women*, Oxford, Blackwell.

Passerini, L. (1987) *Fascism in Popular Memory*, Cambridge, Cambridge University Press.

Pattinson, J., McIvor, A. and Robb, L. (2017) *Men in Reserve: British Civilian Masculinities in the Second World War,* Manchester, Manchester University Press.

Perchard, A. (2013) '"Broken Men" and "Thatcher's Children": Memory and Legacy in Scotland's Coalfields', *International Labor and Working-Class History,* 84, pp. 78–98.

Portelli, A. (1991) *The Death of Luigi Trastulli and Other Stories: Form and Meaning in Oral History,* Albany, SUNY Press.

Portelli, A. (2010) *They Say in Harlan County: An Oral History,* New York, Oxford University Press.

Riessman, C. H. (2008) *Narrative Methods for the Human Sciences,* London, Sage.

Roberts, E. (1984) *A Woman's Place: An Oral History of Working-Class Women 1890–1940,* Oxford, Basil Blackwell.

Selway, D. (2016) 'Death Underground: Mining Accidents and Memory in South Wales, 1913–74', *Labour History Review,* 81, 3, pp. 187–210.

Strangleman, T. (2004) *Work Identity at the End of the Line: Privatisation and Culture Change in the UK Rail Industry,* Basingstoke, Palgrave Macmillan.

Strangleman, T. (2017) 'Deindustrialisation and the Historical Sociological Imagination: Making Sense of Work and Industrial Change', *Sociology,* 51, 2, pp. 466–482.

Storey, R. (2017) 'Beyond the Body Count? Injured Workers in the Aftermath of Deindustrialisation', in High, S., Mackinnon, L. and Perchard, A. (eds.) *The Deindustrialized World: Confronting Ruination in Postindustrial Places,* Vancouver, University of British Columbia Press, pp. 46–67.

Summerfield, P. (1998) *Reconstructing Women's Wartime Lives,* Manchester, Manchester University Press.

Summerfield, P. (2019) *Histories of the Self: Personal Narratives and Historical Practice,* Abingdon, Routledge.

Thompson, P. with Bornat, J. (2017) *The Voice of the Past,* (4th ed.), Oxford, Oxford University Press.

Thomson, A. (1994) *Anzac Memories: Living with the Legend,* Melbourne, Oxford University Press.

Tweedale, G. (2001) *Magic Mineral to Killer Dust,* Oxford, Oxford University Press.

Walker, D. (2011) '"Danger was Something You Were Brought up wi": Workers' Narratives on Occupational Health and Safety in the Workplace', *Scottish Labour History,* 46, pp. 54–70.

Walkerdine, V. and Jimenez, L. (2012) *Gender, Work and Community after Deindustrialisation,* Basingstoke, Palgrave Macmillan.

Walmsley, J. and Atkinson, D. (2000) 'Oral History and the History of Learning Disability', in Bornat, J., Perks, R., Thompson, P. and Walmsley, J. (eds.) *Oral History, Health and Welfare,* London, Routledge, pp. 181–204.

Wight, D. (1994) *Workers not Wasters: Masculinity, Social Status and Respectability in Central Scotland,* Edinburgh, Edinburgh University Press.

Winslow, M. and Smith, G. (2011) 'Ethical Challenges in the Oral History of Medicine', in Ritchie, D.A. (ed.) *The Oxford Handbook of Oral History,* Oxford, Oxford University Press, pp. 372–392.

Wolkowitz, C. (2006) *Bodies at Work,* London, Sage.

14

Precarity's affects

The trauma of deindustrialization

Kathryn Marie Dudley

Its future uncertain, Gardner, Massachusetts, still calls itself Chair City. Since the early 1800s, this mill town linked hardwood forests to railway distribution points in Boston, Philadelphia, and New York, making it a prime location for New England's burgeoning furniture industry. At its zenith, the city's factories turned out four million chairs a year. This claim to fame has bestowed upon posterity the ladder-back chair motif that adorns municipal signage and looms large as public sculpture, epitomized by a series of giant wooden chairs built between 1905 and 1976, each boasting to be the biggest chair in the world. As deindustrialization ravaged the Midwest and Atlantic seaboard during the 1980s and 1990s, Gardner survived, thanks in good part to the skilled workforce at Nichols and Stone, best known for its upscale Windsor chairs. Yet in 2000, when Congress expanded trade relations with China, opening the floodgates to low-cost imports from outsourced firms, the competition proved insurmountable. Nichols and Stone closed in 2008, the nation's oldest furniture maker at the time.

A decade later, Gardner sits in the crosshairs of a regional suicide epidemic. Accompanied by the same toxic brew of alcohol and opioid addiction now afflicting the white working class nationwide, the unprecedented rise in deaths and injuries caused by self-harm has mobilized community health services to target working-age adults who are unemployed, chronically underemployed, or prematurely retired (see Case and Deaton 2015, 2017; Classen and Dunn 2012; Cherlin 2016; Cutler et al. 2006; Pierce and Schott 2016; Quinones 2015; Fernandes 2016).[1] Through its public awareness campaign, the Montachusett Suicide Prevention Task Force broadcasts radio announcements and distributes brochures about the 'warning signs of suicide' encouraging people to seek treatment for depression and attend the local hospital's support groups for 'families in crisis' and 'survivors of suicide loss'. Given Gardner's recent history, the medicalization of social suffering is striking for what it leaves out. Few doubt that industrial decline, downward mobility, and job insecurity have contributed to this health emergency. But what, exactly, is the relationship between economic distress, whiteness, and so-called 'diseases of despair'? Commentators yearn to hold something or someone accountable, whether it is the deleterious effects of global capitalism or the self-defeating pathologies of working-class culture. To those beset by precarity's affects, however, dreams of social justice, like participatory democracy itself, have become increasingly beside the point.

The betrayed aspirations of America's working class are not simply a response to disrupted economies and expectations. Nor are they merely ephemeral products of aggrieved psyches. Like monster chairs, the traumatic affects of deindustrialization are monumentalized in landscapes that exert ongoing effects. In Gardner, head-tilting factories and warehouses still stretch for blocks—up and down narrow, steeply raked, diagonally intersecting streets—erupting from concrete sidewalks like geological formations. Several landmark buildings have been demolished to make way for parking lots and convenience stores; others have been converted into condominiums and senior assisted-living centres. Yet many remain standing as commercial property for which there is no alternative use or market demand. A newcomer such as myself might be excused for assuming that the ubiquitous signs affixed to many of these buildings—a red square crossed with a white 'X'—are the trademark of an enterprising real estate company or graffiti artist. But locals know the truth. Marking structurally unsound buildings that have been emptied of value, these fire safety warnings tell first responders not to enter: there is nothing inside to save.

When scholars of the working class refer to the 'hollowing out' of urban, rural, and suburban regions of the United States, they usually wish to index the dismantling of a historically unique demographic and political coalition, not the abandonment of communities, built environments, and regional ecologies. Focus is on the fate of blue-collar workers who lack educational credentials, especially the white, male heads of hetero-normative households favoured by the New Deal's post-war compact between labour and management in basic manufacturing industries. It is the precipitous loss of status, respect, and national belonging for members of this once prosperous population that drives nostalgia for its past way of life, despite its well-documented racism, sexism, and xenophobia (see Anderson 2016; Cherlin 2014; Cowie 2010; Dudley 1994, 2000; Gest 2016; Isenberg 2017; Walley 2013).[2] No explanation of the political backlash dramatized by Brexit and Donald Trump's 2016 victory enjoys greater currency than this twice-told tale of working-class politics of resentment. So linked in the popular imaginary are boarded up shops on Main Street and the reactionary politics of disenfranchised whites that demographic maps showing correlations between Trump voters, economically distressed counties, and 'deaths of despair' appear self-explanatory (see Monnat 2016b; Case and Deaton 2015).[3] Where else does impotent rage about lost glory days go, this line of thought proposes, except into addiction, suicide, and election of a demagogue?

In this chapter, I argue that other histories of post-industrial ruination must be told. It is not enough for working-class studies to observe that economic insecurity repeatedly triggers paranoid, racialized, and patriarchal modes of redress, although that is undeniably part of the story. Nor is it sufficient to summon radical 'empathy' as the principal conduit through which understandings of political difference can be negotiated, although that too is necessary (Hochschild 2016).[4] Attunement to the lived experience of global capitalism today involves recognizing that deindustrialization—and its world-destroying effects—is traumatic. This trauma lies not solely, nor even primarily, in the precipitating event—in what happens in the instant when we realize that our collective life, as we have known it, can no longer be lived. This trauma resides in the lost futurity that attends the anticipation and repetition of the mind-numbing awareness that our well-being does not matter to the systems of power upon which we depend (see Dudley 2000).[5] Appreciating what it takes to survive amidst working-class precarity requires tracking the affective histories of social and material landscapes that have been hollowed of economic value.

Loss of futurity

Flowers cut from colourful construction paper dance across the plate-glass windows on either side of the entrance to the Chair City Community Workshop. Were it not for this sign of life within, I might have mistaken the small storefront space for yet another vacant shop nestled into a desolate stretch of Gardner's business district. But as the lights come on, dispelling the gloom of an overcast sky in April, I am drawn to the creative vision and sense of possibility that this place holds for the Workshop's founding director, Tracie Pouliot. Having grown up near Gardner as the daughter of a Nichols and Stone employee, Pouliot has applied her talents and training in printmaking and community art to the challenge of commemorating what furniture making meant to her hometown and helping it recover from this loss. The year after Nichols and Stone closed, she began interviewing workers and, with seed grants from several funding sources, is producing, in concert with community volunteers, handcrafted books of each oral history.

'Making books—learning how to set type, operate the press, sew binding, or carve and ink the woodblock prints to illustrate them—it brings people together', Pouliot explains.

> It's an opportunity to socialize, sure, but also to be doing something, making something together, like they did in the factory. That's one of the biggest things they say they miss. We try to create a space for something like that to happen here.

Image 14.1 Fire safety warning telling firefighters that there is nothing in the building to save
Source: Ben Savoie 2017

For six years, during summers at home while in college and graduate school, Pouliot worked as a seasonal floater at Nichols and Stone. When she speaks of shop floor camaraderie, it is with a feeling born of intimacy, intensified by the awareness of how others' longer terms of service dwarfed her own.

Aligned across the wall adjacent to the printing press are captivating photographs of the furniture factory and workers at stations in various departments. Pouliot points to one portrait and says, 'That's Guy Savoie'. The balding man sports a shy smile and looks to be around 50 years old. I do not recognize his name, although I feel I should. Was his oral history among the completed books she has just given me? 'Yes', she nods, her eyes finding mine. 'He committed suicide the year after I interviewed him'.

I was invited to Gardner as a consultant on Pouliot's Healing Our Communities project, which culminated in a public event on deindustrialization and suicide prevention staged at the local history museum later that year. What had been a relatively abstract proposition suddenly became personal. I would eventually meet Savoie's mother, sister, and brother, and through these encounters gain a sense of the person he was and how his death reverberated through a tightly knit network of former Nichols and Stone employees. But in this moment of affective transmission, as I connect Savoie's otherworldly gaze with Pouliot's resolve to bear witness to the loss of a once viable way of life, I am mindful of the multiple temporalities of our work. Standing in the shadow of dreams cut short by discontinuities between the past and present, we both, in our own ways, hope to recuperate a sense of futurity for those caught in deindustrialization's wake.

Holding a Chair City Community Workshop book in your hands awakens an intuitive tactility. The texture of the thick, craft milled paper, thread binding, and raised ink of the typeface and woodcut prints gives you the feeling that you can absorb the text's meaning by touch. Put another way, opening these books opens you to an artisanal aesthetics of grief, a haptic desire to soothe the pain of ruptured worlds and foreclosed futures by making present again, in a materially sensuous way, something of what was lost (Dudley 2014).[6] Like the heirloom furniture cherished by former factory workers in Gardner, these books, and the life stories they tell, are artefacts that promise to outlast their makers and survive in a world that is inhospitable, and sometimes unlivable, to those who value how they were made. Read in this spirit, Chair City's oral histories invite us to consider the possibility that suicidality, far from being an aberrant response to deindustrialization, is the affective atmosphere through which precarity is known and embodied.

> 'I worked at Nichols and Stone until the very end' Guy Savoie tells Pouliot in an interview conducted at her parents' home in 2009. 'It was an empty feeling when it closed. Everyone was gone. You just felt it in your bones, your whole body. Then you had to deal with it. It was sad. It still is. It's too bad it had to go this way. There were rumors for about a year that it would happen, and you could see it would happen just by the amount of work that was coming in and going out. The orders weren't there anymore. You could feel the end coming. People were talking. 'Cause now you've got to figure out, where am I going to go next and try to make the same salary? You have to start over again after 35 years. It can be mind-boggling, and it's hard.'
>
> *(Savoie 2015)*

The spectre of 'starting over again' hangs over Savoie's account of economic dislocation as a palpable dread. He repeats the phrase several times throughout his interview, at one point applying it to the town as a whole.

> The closing has affected the area because at one time you had over 200 people working there, and they have to start all over again. Even going back last year Gardner lost H&R, a gun shop. They lost over 200 people within a few months right after we lost ours, so right there you're talking 500 people in a matter of six months to a year. What do you do, how do you replace it? You just don't. And then the town hurts from there. Taxes, too—which the city needs—are gone. Everybody hurts 'cause then nobody buys anything, nobody shops. People move out. The town gets smaller. It's a ghost town.
>
> *(Savoie 2015)*

There is a Sisyphean quality to this kind of beginning again. What feels irreplaceable is not just the progress made toward a distant horizon or the energy invested in assembling a life worth living, but the optimism it takes to believe that your labour will pay off in the end. Confidence in the future is not a feeling you can sustain alone. When 'everybody hurts'—when 'the town hurts'—the social safety net that might otherwise rekindle hope or arrest a free fall becomes frayed, leaving precious little in its place save for the memory of what once was or might have been (see Cowie and Heathcott 2003; High 2003; High and Lewis 2007; Linkon and Russo 2002; Mah 2012; Strangleman et al. 2013; Taft 2016; Vaccaro et al. 2016).[7] In this context, the prospect of starting over can feel overwhelming: the odds are stacked against you and people like you, and this is not new—you have been in this situation before. The 'mindboggling' aspect of getting on with your life is not only that the way forward is fraught with risk; it's that the humiliating sensation of getting nowhere, of having no future, is happening *again*. To 'feel the end coming', as Savoie and his co-workers viscerally could—months, even years, before the shutdown—is to brace for a social abandonment they have already been exposed to, in myriad ways, countless times before.

Post-industrial society, heralded as America's future with millenarian zeal since the 1970s, has always denied futurity to those who fail to heed its dictates. Its insidious message, that economic ruin awaits anyone without advanced education, masquerades as an empowering doctrine of self-reliance, even as it holds victims of free trade agreements and corporate imperialism responsible for their own fate (Bell 1976; see Bluestone and Harrison 1984 for a critique). Working-class studies may have inured us to the brutality of neoliberalism by highlighting the (almost always white, male, heteronormative) forms of agency that operate to resist the structural logic of capitalism, particularly when they prove futile in the end (see Willis 1981).[8] But we must not be deterred from naming precarity's affects for what they are: the ongoing effects of politically orchestrated economic violence in which power operates through regimes of whiteness, masculinity, and heteronormativity to repeatedly revisit the trauma of dispossession on vulnerable populations whose labour is deemed expendable. Under these conditions, we must look more closely at 'ghost towns' and see them not merely as what remains of a devastated past, but as landscapes that are actively produced in the present by expropriations of futurity that are registered well before, and long after, the first plant closes.

Precarity and grievability

'You get your hopes up because things would pick up a little bit and then the next thing you know they're just dropping down again', Barbara Suchocki (2017) recalls in her Chair City oral history, lapsing into a conditional present tense.

> We'd get the scan sheet and it started out this thick and then it would get thinner and thinner and thinner and the next thing you know you got two pages of orders. 'This isn't

> good. This is the whole week's stuff?' 'Yep'. You could just see it dwindling away. Right after 9/11, the orders just went bye-bye.

Suchocki's association of the terrorist attack on the World Trade Center with the crash in market demand for high-quality furniture elides the economic effects of the nation's 2000 trade pact with China, which were also beginning to be felt at that time (see Autor et al. 2013; Autor et al. 2014; Pierce and Schott 2016). But '9/11' as an event and, more importantly, as an affective atmosphere, stands out for Suchocki as a portent of the social suffering to which her own community would be subjected in the years to come. When the death toll in lower Manhattan was announced, she attests, a moment of silence was observed on the shop floor.

> We all just stood around holding hands and everybody was crying, just thinking of all them people that died. But that shows you how strong we were as a family and how we watched out for each other. You know, when people pass away it spreads through the shop like that. If something happens upstairs, five minutes later it's downstairs. We had one woman, she ended up taking her fingers off. And it took two seconds for that to get through the whole shop. Everybody knows each other, so it's like, is she alright? Most of the time, people go into shock right away when they got hurt that bad; they don't even realize how bad they got hurt until later. She had no idea what she did to herself. She was working on a planer and they were putting boards in. And they always shot 'em in quick, you know, piecework. She could have lost her whole arm. And the guy on the other side of course didn't know what was goin' on, and he sees fingers and crap comin' through. I'm surprised he didn't pass out, because, you know, you work with somebody that many years, and to see her get hurt that bad. Then you get guys working on the lathes, and they get the tips of their fingers taken off, and people screwing drills through their hand. You just never know what's going to happen day to day in that place.
>
> *(Suchocki 2017)*

When I initially selected this quote for discussion, I was tempted to replace Suchocki's grisly description of her co-worker's accident with an ellipsis and focus my analysis on how she frames the event as something this woman 'did to herself', struck as I was by the image she conjures of someone who 'ends up taking her fingers off'. To be sure, a fantasy of personal responsibility for one's own fate operates in this narrative to organize what is otherwise a chaotic scene of unpredictable hazards. But my desire to trace the figure of individual agency came with an initial discomfort, and lack of curiosity about, the materiality of 'getting hurt' in an industrial system where the imperatives of profit and productivity incentivize speed and dissociation from the vulnerabilities of the body. To dwell on the 'fingers and crap' is to appreciate that, for Suchocki, the 'surprise' of her other co-worker's presence of mind, her amazement that he *didn't* 'pass out', is as much a part of the scene as the 'shock' of those who don't realize the extent of their injuries until later. This wish, for a mindful witnessing that registers the pain of mangled limbs and lives—for a community that 'watches out' for its own as if they were kin—holds out hope that Gardner, too, can someday face its losses and mourn its dead.

Yet for such a reckoning to happen, as Judith Butler might say, the life worlds lost must be recognized as 'grievable'. Butler (2006, 2009) develops the concept of grievability to account for why some casualties of war, and not others, are publicly mourned. In her writings post 9/11, she urges us to consider the relationship between the violence of an endless war on terrorism and the lack of grief permitted for lives lost by enemy combatants, civilian populations, and prisoners in indefinite detention. 'Is the prohibition on grieving the continuation of the violence itself?'

she asks rhetorically, ultimately arguing that the 'derealization' of loss, suffering, and death is the psychic means by which dehumanization occurs. Consciously acknowledging and experiencing grief, in Butler's analysis, is the only way to break war's traumatic cycle of victimization and violence. Only when we apprehend the shared precariousness of all life—that our lives are 'always in some sense in the hands of the other'—can we be held by a 'social network of hands' that endows our life with a value that is grievable when lost. Her formulation of trauma is consistent with other work in contemporary affect studies that emphasizes the embodied experience of a precarious existence (see Berlant 2011; Eng and Kazanjian 2003; Muehlebach 2013; Muehlebach and Shoshan 2012; Stevenson 2014; Stewart 2005, 2012; Stoller 2013; Tsing 2017).

Suchocki's invocation of collective grief in response to lives lost on 9/11 enacts a parallel insistence on the precariousness of factory work, on its vulnerability to consumer markets, government policies, and physical dangers on a daily basis. But the grievability of her work culture, and its distinctive forms of life and labour, remains an open question. Suchocki is sure that word of harm to one would travel to all within seconds on the shop floor. Yet uncertainty remains about whether anyone outside the factory or Gardner knows or cares about what happened, and is still happening, to its workforce. In such moments of doubt, when the recurrent shock of being dispossessed of bodily integrity, economic stability, and national belonging makes it hard to identify the source of social suffering, the fantasy of individual agency and self-sufficiency creeps in, fuelling the notion that fingers can be removed at will and that such sacrifices are required to stay in the game and have a shot at a better life, let alone the good one.

Over 19½ years at Nichols and Stone, Suchocki came up through the ranks to become its first female supervisor, managing 30 employees in the finishing department at the time of the shutdown. Among her duties was serving on the company's first-aid team, a responsibility she took to heart, as it drew upon, and amplified, her desire to anticipate misfortune and proactively avert it.

> I was always prepared. My first aid kit always had everything in it. No matter what it was. I was ready for major stuff and little stuff. Everything. I was always stocked. Probably about three years before Nichols and Stone closed I took some night courses at Monty Tech [Montachusett Regional Vocational Technical School]. I took phlebotomy and MA [Medical Assistant] courses, 'cause I knew something was coming and I wanted to start thinking about my future. I'm a survivor. I'm always looking ahead. I don't wait for things to happen. I make things happen. 'Cause I don't like to be left out in the field there sayin' 'oh what am I going to do now?' I'm going to better myself. I'm going to keep my life going smoothly.
>
> *(Suchocki 2017)*

Being 'a survivor', Suchocki attests, requires 'thinking about your future' and taking steps toward realizing it in the present. Staking a claim to futurity, in this formulation, involves hewing to neoliberal prescriptions for overcoming adversity that place the onus of survival on individuals and their capacity to persevere against the odds. To be 'left out in the field' not knowing what to do or how to 'better' oneself is presented as the result of failing to prepare for shocking 'things that happen' well before they actually do. Yet the cost of this ideological premium on 'self-care' becomes apparent in the context of a community that has been left to fend for itself. You may act courageously, as Suchocki did by becoming a registered medical assistant. But resolute individualism is no guarantee of 'keeping your life going smoothly'. Moreover, should you wind up exactly where you feared—forced to 'wait for things to happen'—you will have no one to blame but yourself and no moral framework within which to grieve what has been lost. As Suchocki reports to Pouliot,

> I'm still looking for a job. There's nothing out there but I'm waiting. I've had a few interviews and it just seems to be people are better than me, because I'm just starting out and they're taking people who are more experienced. I'm trying to be patient.
>
> *(Suchocki 2017)*

Conclusion

The field of working-class studies has long harboured the suspicion that the affective terrain of blue-collar life is traumatic and even definitive of what 'class' itself is, whether experienced as 'worlds of pain' or inequality's 'hidden injuries'. What stands out in this literature are the myriad ways that working people sacrifice individual forms of futurity in order to pursue collective ones, in their families and in their communities, and the toll taken when the value of their sacrifice is minimized, often by those who benefit the most (see Sennett and Cobb 1973; Rubin 1976; Walley 2013; Walkerdine and Jiminez 2012). What has yet to be reckoned with, however, is the sacrifice of futurity that is demanded of not only of individuals, but entire communities and regions of the country. When we filter out the grisly remainders and ghostly reminders of the traumatic effects of deindustrialization, whether in our scholarship or daily lives, we become complicit in devaluing the collective labour required to sustain the social cohesion and temporal continuity that makes life worth living. Under regimes of care that attribute suicide, addiction, and obesity to a lack of education, individual willpower, or willingness to seek medical treatment, disparities in mortality rates will always be presented as the moral and cultural failings of particular 'classes' of people. Class, in this popular imaginary, becomes a marker not just of socioeconomic vulnerability but intergenerational pathology and maladaptive socialization (see Murray 2013).[9]

Yet a hazy line separates the kinds of sacrifice and truncated futurity that are 'self-inflicted' from those that are, as a matter of public policy and corporate priorities, levied on working-class communities. When a 'whole town hurts', as Guy Savoie put it, what is the cause of those injuries? From whence does the violence come that strikes suddenly, like a low-flying plane out of the blue, leaving whole sectors of the workforce unemployed and in shock? And what kind of ruination is it when the infrastructural ecology that has served a region for well over a century is so hollowed of resources that it becomes unsafe even for those whose mission is to assist survivors? Unless we can acknowledge that our society routinely sacrifices the livelihoods of workers whose labour has been devalued and rendered redundant, we will be in no position to appreciate what we have lost, let alone honour it with our grief. And herein lies the trauma of deindustrialization. To the extent that the losses inflicted on abandoned communities are figured as the inevitable result of forces beyond social control or punishment deserved for individual failures and poor decision-making, the blows will continue to come in a repetitious cycle of violence that cares not whether the injury is delivered at the hands of victimizers or victims themselves.

As scholars of precarity's affects, we must develop a concept of class that does not reproduce the traumatic effects of deindustrialization. By this I mean we must recognize, and also be willing to disrupt, the atmospheric suicidality that attends popular as well as academic accounts of working-class demise. Rather than trade in political iconography that depicts scenes of social suffering as an epidemic of pathological behaviour, we can move toward a reading of 'classed' embodiment that emphasizes its proximity to historically situated modes of futurity. We can insist, along with former furniture workers in Gardner, that there is enduring value to making material goods of high quality and that out of the ruins of twentieth-century capitalism, skilled labour may take new forms and be socially revalued. Doing so will necessitate vigilance against the reflexive ways that traumatic repetition induces us to reaffirm—in ourselves and in others—the very regimes of futurity that foreclose alternative possibilities.

In 2008, the Stickley Company acquired Nichols and Stone's intellectual property rights and other assets. As plant manager with 31 years of service, Denis Boucher was on the transition team that moved production of Nichols and Stone's furniture lines to Stickley's flagship plant in Manlius, New York, and facilities in Vietnam. Boucher was among the last to leave the Gardner factory, and in his interview with Pouliot at a local café, he speaks with emotion about his final day.

> [My last day was] tough, it was after the auction had already come. I was there after all the employees were gone. It was a handful of us left cleaning up the place as best we could, after the auction was done we saw people just come in there tearing the place apart. They want this machine, cut this off here, cut that off there. Throwing junk. These people just coming in and tearing it apart. No regard, it was becoming a real mess. And when you see 'em doing it [you think], 'Hey wait!'! But there's nothing you can do, they bought it, it's theirs. They're dismantling the company everybody worked so long to build.
>
> *(Boucher 2016)*

Community abandonment is an extractive process that accumulates capital for some at the expense of others. So naturalized is this facet of political economy that it's difficult to imagine things could be otherwise, that corporate interests need not dictate the disposition of public property or the dispossession of the common good. Indeed, to maintain that a 'company' is an entity that 'everybody'—not just owners of capital—'worked so long to build' is to invoke an alternative moral economy, one in which working-class labour has a value that is grievable if lost. But Boucher hesitates. He wants to say, 'Hey wait!'—he wishes to halt the destruction—but psychically repeating the traumatic acts of those 'with no regard', he 'cuts off' his own call for justice, certain that nothing can be done to alter this course of events. Yet in the space of his hesitation, we can hear an unstated possibility. It is the hope held out by an artisanal aesthetics of grief—that by collectively revaluing embodied labour's tactile power, dignity and futurity can be restored to working-class lives and the communities that hold them dear.

Notes

1 See also Massachusetts Department of Public Health (2017), Monnat (2016a), and University of Massachusetts Memorial Health Care Alliance (2015). Note, however, that the current focus on white mortality rates tends to overlook longstanding racial health disparities as well as entrenched racialized drug policy and criminal policing (Hart 2017; Netherland and Hansen (2017); Wailoo 2014).

2 Carr and Kefalas (2010) explicitly invoke the concept of 'hollowing' to refer to the 'brain drain' of educated residents in rural America, but the notion of 'hollowing out the middle' quintiles of the national income distribution has been a persistent trope in the sociology of the post-World War II middle class regardless of geographic region.

3 In the immediate aftermath of the 2016 presidential election, Monnat (2016b) produced striking demographic evidence that linked support for Trump to rising mortality rates due to 'deaths of despair', a term that has come to reference the findings of Case and Deaton (2015). The taken-for-granted quality of this correlation, however, draws on a well-established history of theorizing and anticipating white working class 'politics of resentment'. See, for example, Cramer (2016), Frank (1996), Hochschild (2016), Kimmel (2013), and Lash (1991).

4 As Hochschild (2016) argues in her ethnography of Tea Party adherents living in a polluted Louisiana bayou, support for petrochemical industries and lax governmental regulation stems from 'emotional interests' that far outweigh the receding dream of good jobs, upward mobility, and a life-sustaining environment. Hochschild, true to dominant liberal narratives, highlights the fury and resentment that conservatives direct against women, racialized others, and endangered species—political agents perceived to be unfairly 'cutting ahead' of them as they wait patiently in line to receive a just reward for their hard work and self-sacrifice. Rather than dismissing these feelings as irrational, she urges us to scale the 'empathy wall', asserting that only by listening to this 'deep story' and appreciating the pain it encapsulates can we hope to find common cause and reunite a divided electorate.

5 In *Debt and Dispossession* (Dudley 2000), I track the experience of traumatic repetition in the social suffering caused by widespread farm foreclosures in the 1980s. The punitive force of ritualized forms of status degradation that are epitomized by, but by no means limited to, lender-initiated farm auctions intimately and mercilessly drives home the point that capitalism operates to the benefit of some at the expense of others.

6 In my ethnography of North American guitar makers, I explore the affective power that performing a pre- and early-industrial craft tradition has for white working- and middle-class men and women (Dudley 2014). Although I don't explicitly formulate the concept of an 'artisanal aesthetics of grief' in that book, all the elements of it, and its relationship to precarity, futurity, and national belonging, are there, I argue, in the 'tone of things', that elusive sonic quality that artisanal luthiers aspire to achieve in their instruments.

7 In his pioneering ethnographic studies of disaster and trauma, Erikson (1978, 1994) makes the point that it is injury to the social fabric, not just to individuals, that impedes a community's efforts to recover some semblance of the way of life it lost.

8 Ever since Willis's (1981) influential proposition that working-class lads develop an oppositional culture in school that effectively funnels them into factory labor, a social reproduction theory of class has infused sociological accounts of how working-class masculinity and anti-intellectualism backfires in the face of deindustrialization and the rise of 'service' and 'knowledge' economies. While this thesis has also been extended to the black poor and working class—see, for example, Wilson (1987)—far too little attention has been paid to how such mobilizations of the culture concept uncomfortably revive the racialized 'culture of poverty' thesis associated with Lewis (1959, 1966), eliding significant differences in how various forms of 'deviance' are embodied and socially experienced. It is no coincidence that Vance's memoir, *Hillbilly Elegy: A Memoir of a Family and Culture in Crisis* (2016), has become conservatives' go-to text for explaining the rise of Trump, as it deftly recycles heroic narratives of white working-class masculinity as a once proud assertion of social nobility, however 'dysfunctional' it may be in this day and age.

9 Murray (2013) is a prime example of the conservative right's updating of the 'culture of poverty' thesis to apply to the supposed collapse of moral values among working-class whites, but he is not alone in promulgating this burlesque racialization of whiteness. The liberal left, too, has a meritocratic version of deviance, readily apparent in recent press coverage of rising white mortality rates, which advances the belief that a 'lack of a college education has become a public-health crisis' (Brown and Fischer, 2017). In such media representations, we find the human—albeit dehumanizing—equivalent of 'smokestack nostalgia' and 'ruin porn'. On the latter, where the material landscapes and artifacts of abandoned communities are aestheticized as cultural commodities, see High (2013) and Strangleman (2013).

References

Anderson, C. (2016) *White Rage: The Unspoken Truth of Our Racial Divide*, New York, Bloomsbury.

Autor, D. H., Dorn, D. and Hanson, G. H. (2013) 'The China Syndrome: Local Labor market Effects of Import Competition in the United States', *Economic Review*, 103, 6, 2121–2168.

Autor, D. H., Dorn, D., Hanson, G. H. and Song, J. (2014) 'Trade Adjustment: Worker Level Evidence', *Quarterly Journal of Economics*, 129, 4, 1799–1860.

Bell, D. (1976) *The Coming of Post-Industrial Society: A Venture in Social Forecasting*, New York, Basic Books.

Berlant, L. (2011) *Cruel Optimism*, Durham, Duke University Press.

Bluestone, B. and Harrison, B. (1984) *The Deindustrialization of America*, New York, Basic Books.

Boucher, D. (2016) *Denis Boucher: Plant Manager, Nichols & Stone Employee for 31 Years, Gardner*, The Chair City Community Workshop.

Brown, S. and Fischer, K. (2017) 'A Dying Town', *The Chronicle of Higher Education*, Dec. 19.

Butler, J. (2006) *Precarious Life: The Powers of Mourning and Violence*, London, Verso.
Butler, J. (2009) *Frames of War: When is Life Grievable?* London, Verso.
Carr, P. and Kefalas, M. J. (2010) *Hollowing Out the Middle: The Rural Brain Drain and What It Means for America*, Boston, Beacon Press.
Case, A. and Deaton, A. (2015) 'Rising Morbidity and Mortality in Midlife among White Non-Hispanic Americans in the 21st Century', *Proceedings of the National Academy of Sciences*, 112, 49, 15078–15083.
Case, A. and Deaton, A. (2017) 'Mortality and Morbidity in the 21st Century', *Brookings Panel on Economic Activity*, 1–63.
Cherlin, A. (2014) *Labor's Love Lost: The Rise and Fall of the Working Class Family in America*, New York, Russell Sage Foundation.
Cherlin, A. (2016) 'Why are White Death Rates Rising?', *The New York Times*, Feb. 22.
Classen, T. J. and Dunn, R. A. (2012) 'The Effect of Job Loss and Unemployment Duration on Suicide Risk in the United States: A New Look Using Mass-Layoffs and Unemployment Duration', *Health Economics*, 21, 3, 338–350.
Cowie, J. (2010) *Stayin' Alive: The 1970s and the Last Days of the Working Class*, New York, The New Press.
Cowie, J. and Heathcott, J. (2003) 'The Meanings of Deindustrialization', in Cowie, J. and Lewis, J. (eds.) *Beyond the Ruins: The Meanings of Deindustrialization*, Ithaca, Cornell University Press.
Cramer, K. (2016) *The Politics of Resentment: Rural Consciousness in Wisconsin and the Rise of Scott Walker*, Chicago, University of Chicago Press.
Cutler, D. M., Deaton, A. and Lleras-Muny. A. (2006) 'The Determinants of Mortality', *Journal of Economic Perspectives*, 20, 3, 97–120.
Dudley, K. (1994) *The End of the Line: Lost Jobs, New Lives in Postindustrial America*, Chicago, University of Chicago Press.
Dudley, K. (2000) *Debt and Dispossession: Farm Loss in America's Heartland*, Chicago, University of Chicago Press.
Dudley, K. (2014) *Guitar Makers: The Endurance of Artisanal Values in North America*, Chicago, University of Chicago Press.
Eng, D. L. and Kazajian, D. (eds.) (2003) *Loss: The Politics of Mourning*, Berkeley, University of California Press.
Erikson, K. (1978) *Everything in Its Path: Destruction of Community in the Buffalo Creek Flood*, New York, Simon & Schuster.
Erikson, K. (1994) *A New Species of Trouble: Explorations in Disaster, Trauma, and Community*, New York, W. W. Norton and Co.
Fernandes, D. (2016) 'As Jobs Left the US, Suicides Rose', *The Boston Globe*, Dec. 26.
Frank, T. (1996) *What's the Matter With Kansas? How Conservatives Won the Heart of America*, New York, Henry Holt & Co.
Gest, J. (2016) *The New Minority: White Working Class Politics in an Age of Immigration and Inequality*, Oxford, Oxford University Press.
Hart, C. (2017) 'The Real Opioid Emergency', *The New York Times*, Aug. 18.
High, S. (2003) *Industrial Sunset: The Making of North America's Rust Belt, 1969–1984*, Toronto, Toronto University Press.
High, S. (2013) 'Beyond Aesthetics: Visibility and Invisibility in the Aftermath of Deindustrialization', *International Labor and Working-Class Studies*, 84, 140–153.
High, S. and Lewis, D. W. (2007) *Corporate Wasteland: The Landscape and Memory of Deindustrialization*, Ithaca, Cornell University Press.
Hochschild, A. (2016) *Strangers in Their Own Land: Anger and Mourning on the American Right*, New York, The New Press.
Isenberg, N. (2017) *White Trash: The 400-Year Old Untold History of Class in America*, New York, Penguin Books.
Kimmel, M. (2013) *Angry White Men: American Masculinity at the End of an Era*, New York, Nation Books.
Lash, C. (1991) *The True and Only Heaven: Progress and Its Critics*, New York, W. W. Norton & Co.
Lewis, O. (1959) *Five Families: Mexican Case Studies in the Culture of Poverty*, New York, Basic Books.
Lewis, O. (1966) *La Vida: A Puerto Rican Family in the Culture of Poverty—San Juan and New York*, New York, Random House.
Linkon, S. L. and Russo, J. (2002) *Steeltown USA: Work and Memory in Youngstown*, Lawrence, University Press of Kansas.
Mah, A. (2012) *Industrial Ruination, Community, and Place: Landscapes and Legacies of Urban Decline*, Toronto, University of Toronto Press.

Massachusetts Department of Public Health. (2017) *Suicides in Massachusetts 2014.*
Monnat, S. (2016a) 'Drugs, Death, and Despair in New England', *Communities & Banking*, Fall, 22–25.
Monnat, S. (2016b) 'Deaths of Despair and Support for Trump in the 2016 Presidential Election', *Department of Agricultural Economics, Sociology, and Education Research Brief*, State College, Pennsylvania State University, Dec. 4.
Muehlebach, A. (2013) 'On Precariousness and the Ethical Imagination: The Year 2012 in Sociocultural Anthropology', *American Anthropologist*, 115, 2, 297–311.
Muehlebach, A. and Shoshan, N. (2012) 'Post-Fordist Affect', *Anthropological Quarterly*, 85, 2, 317–343.
Murray, C. (2013) Coming Apart: The State of White America, 1960-2010. New York, Random House.
Netherland, J. and Hasen, H. (2017) 'White Opioids: Pharmaceutical Race and the War on Drugs that Wasn't', *Biosocieties*, 12, 2, 217–238.
Pierce, J. R. and Schott, P. K. (2016) *Trade Liberalization and Mortality: Evidence from US Counties*, National Bureau of Economic Research, Working Paper No. 22849, November.
Quinones, S. (2015) *Dreamland: The True Tale of America's Opiate Epidemic*, New York, Bloomsbury Press.
Rubin, L. (1976) *Worlds of Pain: Life in the Working-Class Family*, New York, Basic Books.
Savoie, G. (2015) *Guy Savoie: CNC Operator, Nichols & Stone Employee for 35 Years*, Gardner, The Chair City Community Workshop.
Sennett, R. and Cobb, J. (1973) *The Hidden Injuries of Class*, New York, W. W. Norton & Co.
Stevenson, L. (2014) *Life Beside Itself: Imagining Care in the Canadian Artic*, Berkeley, University of California Press.
Stewart, K. (2005) 'Trauma Time: A Still Life', in Rosenberg, D. and Harding, S. (eds.) *Histories of the Future*, Durham, Duke University Press.
Stewart, K. (2012) 'Precarity's Forms', *Cultural Anthropology*, 27, 3, 518–525.
Stoller, A. L. (2013) '"The Rot Remains": From Ruins to Ruination', in Stoller, A. L. (ed.) *Imperial Debris: On Ruins and Ruination*, Durham, Duke University Press.
Strangleman, T. (2013) '"Smokestack Nostalgia," "Ruin Porn" or Working-Class Obituary: The Role and Meaning of Deindustrial Representation', *International Labor and Working-Class* History, 84, 23–37.
Strangleman, T., Rhodes, J. and Linkon, S. (2013) 'Introduction to Crumbling Cultures: Deindustrialization, Class, and Memory', *International Labor and Working-Class History*, 84, 7–22.
Suchocki, B. (2017) *Barbara Suchocki: Table & Case Finishing Department Supervisor, Nichols & Stone Employee for 19½ Years*, Gardner, The Chair City Community Workshop.
Taft, C. (2016) *From Steel to Slots: Casino Capitalism in the Postindustrial City*, Cambridge, Harvard University Press.
Tsing, A. (2017) *The Mushroom at the End of the World: On the Possibility of Life in Capitalist Ruins*, Princeton, Princeton University Press.
University of Massachusetts Memorial Health Care Alliance. (2015) *Community Health Assessment of North Central Massachusetts*, May.
Vaccaro, I., Harper, K. and Murray, S. (eds.) (2016) *The Anthropology of Postindustrialism: Ethnographies of Disconnection*, New York, Routledge.
Vance, J. D. (2016) *Hillbilly Elegy: A Memoir of a Family and Culture in Crisis*, New York, HarperCollins.
Wailoo, K. (2014) *Pain: A Political History*, Baltimore, Johns Hopkins University Press.
Walkerdine, V. and Jimenez, L. (2012) *Gender, Work, and Community After De-Industrialization*, New York, Palgrave Macmillan.
Walley, C. (2013) *Exit Zero: Family and Class in Postindustrial Chicago*, Chicago, University of Chicago Press.
Willis, P. (1981) *Learning to Labour: How Working Class Kids Get Working Class Jobs*, New York, Columbia University Press.
Wilson, W. J. (1987) *The Truly Disadvantaged: The Inner City, the Underclass, and Public Policy*, Chicago, University of Chicago Press.

15

Feeling, re-imagined in common[1]

Working with social haunting in the English coalfields

Geoff Bright

Introduction

In this chapter, I discuss a body of research[2] that focuses on the entanglement of affect[3] and imagination[4] in working-class experience (see Bright 2012a, 2012b, 2016, 2018) and how it has played out in the UK at key moments of a thirty-year period of deindustrialisation. As an adjunct to telling that still developing story of a 'social haunting' – which focuses primarily, but not exclusively, on ethnographic and co-produced arts-based work I've done in the English coalfields – I'll explain in passing why '*New* Working-Class Studies' is the only field in which I have felt free to articulate such an account of the *felt/imagined* dimension of working-class life, and how that sense of freedom is related to the 'newness' (as I read it) originally claimed for the field (Russo and Linkon 2005; Linkon and Russo 2016). In explaining that, I'll effectively be hinting at a larger argument; namely, that attunement to the affective/imaginative register of class (and haunting, as an expression of it) is important to the field of Working-Class Studies. It is essential prior to any new 'assembly' (Hardt and Negri 2017) of political forces; will help our organisations and networks in the necessary task of protecting (we) activists against the constant affective repetitions and imaginative depletions of 'burnout'; and is vital in developing a class account of affect-laden political phenomena such as the rise of Trump in the US or the Brexit vote in the 2016 UK European Union Referendum.

As I write, colleagues and I are near to completing the third of three related UK Arts and Humanities Research Council Connected Communities (AHRCCC) projects that have steadily refined a co-produced inquiry into what – following Avery Gordon (2008) – we have called a 'social haunting' of deindustrialised communities in England. Our current project, Song Lines: Creating Living Knowledge through Working with Social Haunting, is pointed firmly at the UK Brexit context and responds to our two key community partners, Unite Community and the Co-operative College. Both are alarmed at divisive political discourses about a north/south UK fracture along lines of class and ethnicity in which the coalfields are profiled in a way that is negatively at odds with their history and traditions,[5] and they are keen to develop a strategic response to Brexit. Song Lines builds on two earlier investigations, the first of which worked on the South Yorkshire coalfield and in the former textile production area of Rochdale in Lancashire during 2015, the second of which was based mainly in the North Staffordshire coalfield during 2016. Song Lines itself, while working again in some of the same areas, has extended the inquiry to the Durham coalfield in the north-east of England during 2017.

Background

All three projects grew out of ethnographic research that I carried out between 2000 and 2013, after I'd already had a good proportion of a working lifetime in the UK coalfields of Derbyshire and South Yorkshire, initially as a steel union and railway trade union activist heavily involved in the 1984–85 miners' strike and, from the 1990s on, as a community activist/educator. My doctoral study focused on pit village youngsters from coal-mining family backgrounds who were being excluded from school for 'behavioural difficulties' and concluded that, twenty-five years after its end, the 1984–85 strike and its aftermath of rapid deindustrialisation were far from being matters merely of historical interest. Indeed, the conflicted nature of coalfield deindustrialisation remained as an unspoken affective context in which the swathe of school exclusions that I witnessed could be read as part of a 'kind of haunting', as my research participants often described it.

The miners' strike will soon be thirty-five years past, and the coal industry has now completely gone. Coal has been definitively repositioned from industrialisation's priceless 'black diamond' to the bête noir of the Anthropocene, but the feelings generated by coal's conflicted past endure. More than a dozen years after I began that initial research, similar affective/imaginative intensities continue to circulate through the absent presences of the coal industry, flowing now here and coalescing now there, in a complex material entanglement of historical, geographical, economic and psychosocial elements. The spontaneous 'Thatcher funerals' that celebrated the death of former UK Prime Minister Margaret Thatcher in 2013 had their root in those revenant energies (see Bright 2016) as did the widespread Brexit vote across the coalfields.

A social haunting

Essentially, the projects I've brought together in the last three years have tried to operationalise the insights into social haunting first elaborated in Avery Gordon's *Ghostly Matters: Haunting and the Sociological Imagination* (2008, first published in 1997) but with a greater emphasis on an approach that addresses the complexities of what Beverley Skeggs has called 'person value and autonomist working-class value practices' (Skeggs 2011; and see Bright 2016). I don't think this is any significant departure from Gordon (who is close to our work, as it happens), but rather a development. Gordon's own inquiry began from a focus on complexity, asserting 'that life is complicated is … perhaps the most important theoretical statement of our time' (Gordon, 2008, 3). Presciently acknowledging a debt to a Marxism more 'magical' than orthodox, Gordon called for attention to two particular complexities that had been notoriously poorly addressed in the orthodox canon. These were: complexity of *power* and complexity of *personhood*. Our work, an attempt to implement a form of community inquiry highlighting those specific complexities as they have informed the composition of working-class value practices through the period of UK deindustrialisation, is basically a response to that call.

A social haunting, Gordon tells us, is made evident in social settings when 'disturbed feelings cannot be put away'. It is an entangling reminder of lingering trouble relating to 'social violence done in the past' and a notification 'that what's been concealed is very much alive and present [and showing] up without any sign of leaving'. As such, it 'alters the experience of being in time, the way we separate the past, the present, and the future' (Gordon 2008, xvi). Social ghosts, while strongly felt, are, however, not easily known. Indeed, a social haunting is 'often barely visible or highly symbolised' (Gordon 2008, 50) It resides at the

> 'cusp of semantic availability' (in Raymond Williams' term) as a 'practical consciousness that is always more than a handling of fixed forms and units' [and] describes just those 'experiences to which the fixed forms do not speak at all, which they do not recognize'.
>
> *(Gordon 2008, 200, citing Williams 1977)*

Other work has, to be fair, probed similar territory in the overlap between memory studies' focus on collective/social memory (Fentress and Wickham 1992; Olick et al. 2011) and emotional geographies of place and culture (Smith et al. 2009). Some of the most recent research has focused on the Left too (Bonnett 2010) and on activism (Brown and Pickerill 2009) as well as specifically on post coal-mining settings (Perchard 2013). So the idea that the past acts in the present through historical geographies of gender, class and race is thus reasonably well developed.

Nevertheless, in calling for 'a method of knowledge production … that [can] represent the damage and the *haunting of the historical alternatives*' (Gordon 2008, xvii, my emphasis), Gordon's notion of a social haunting still breaks new ground. The important point is that a *social* haunting, in Gordon's perspective, is a generative 'sociopolitical-psychological state' (2008, xvi). That is, it alerts us not to a therapeutic problematic related to individualised trauma (which, in fact, may well be present to a greater or lesser degree) but to an immanent collective practice addressing how the past 'could have been and *can be* otherwise' (Gordon 2008, 57, my emphasis). A social haunting is, thus, a call to political action. It is 'precisely the domain of turmoil and trouble, that moment … when *something else, something different from before*, seems like it must be done' (Gordon 2008, xvi, my emphasis).

If our work can claim any lasting originality, it is in developing the laboratory space of the 'Ghost Lab' as a germination chamber for that 'something different from before' that needs to be done.

The Ghost Labs

Fundamentally, a Ghost Lab is a participatory *process* space: a semi-improvised, horizontal, community/activist/arts workshop 'event space' (Massumi 2015) – if I can be excused the ugly locution – which aims to collectively re-imagine 'what the ghosts might want from us' (Back 2011, 3). Its only real defining feature is a commitment to let the ghosts speak, come what may. It is co-produced through a group of academics, artists and activists, whose primary commitment is to establish and maintain that process as an open, acceptant and non-judgemental encounter. In nudging the encounter along in a rudimentary way, the Ghost Lab is facilitated, but loosely and with an improvisational sense, and a repertoire of playful arts devices are used to approach affective/imaginary materials that are hidden in plain sight in the life of our partner communities. The arts devices employed have commonly included what we've called 'ghost hunting'; co-operative and individual creative writing; comic strip production; and – most frequently – 'community Tarot readings'.[6]

The Ghost Lab is a *laboratory* space in that the process it sets up is experimentally productive rather than pedagogic or organisational in focus – though pedagogy and organisation may well be outcomes. It is pretty much the case that anything can happen, in a DIY sort of way. The fundamental working hunch is that whatever *does* happen will allow atomised feelings/imaginings to be re-articulated out of the blind field of a haunting and into the range of a collective, agentic re-imagination *in common*. It is a site, therefore, that is at least proto-political and, at best, one where 'commonwealth', in Hardt and Negri's (2009) use of the term, can be actively created. With an eye on the 'new material' turn in arts practice (Barrett and Bolt 2013) and the growth of affective methodologies (Knudsen and Stage 2016), the Ghost Lab design finds inspiration in a promiscuous cohabitation of affect theory (Clough 2007), dialogic arts practice (Kester 2004), 'redemptive' memory work (McLaren and Tadeau da Silva 1993); transversal group practice (Guattari 2015) and autonomist militant research (Shukaitis and Graeber 2007). Ethnography and autoethnography are core to the approach, as is a base ethic of *each being alongside all* in affirmation, celebration and a 'properly political form of love' (see Berlant 2011; Hardt and Negri 2009). Any particular Ghost Lab might, from moment to moment, incorporate aspects of asset-based community work, multisensory mapping and narrative performance. The Ghost Lab is, then, intentionally something of a ragbag of a space – but a playfully relaxed, benevolently productive and purposefully 'steely' (Gordon 2008, 57) ragbag, nevertheless. And it is at home, as I said at the outset, in Working-Class Studies. Let us take a moment, now, to have a look at why.

Why New Working-Class Studies?

Russo and Linkon's 2005 edited collection *New Working-Class Studies* pretty much delineated the field of Working-Class Studies, and its founding ambitions have recently been revisited and re-endorsed with a few lightly changed emphases (Linkon and Russo 2016). In the introduction to the 2005 collection, the editors asked the question 'What's new about New Working-Class Studies?' and drew the following conclusions:

> a clear focus on the lived experience and voices of working-class people; critical engagement with the complex interactions that link class with race, gender, ethnicity, and place; attention to how class is shaped by place and how the local is connected to the global. Rather than embracing any single view of class, [New Working-Class Studies] is committed to ongoing debates about what class is and how it works … is multi-disciplinary as well as inter-disciplinary; it provides a site for conversation and opportunities for collaboration among scholars, artists, activists, and workers.
>
> *(Russo and Linkon 2005, 14)*

Given the dozen or so years that separate that publication and the recent one – a period in which globalisation, crisis and a generalised precaritisation of life and labour have energised right-wing populist appeals to working-class communities around nation and race (see Streeck 2017) – this was a remarkably prescient plea to address the complexity of class in general, and the composition of the working class in particular, as a prime concern. The thematic of complexity that we found in Gordon's work is clearly visible in the genealogy of Working-Class Studies. Similarly, Working-Class Studies' 'innovative [approach] in the way it integrates multiple disciplines and uses different kinds of materials' to emphasise 'the centrality of cultural representations' (Russo and Linkon 2005, 1) was also noteworthy, anticipating as it did models of co-created 'living knowledge' (Facer and Enright 2016) developed in the intervening period and now influencing research councils such as our funders, the UK AHRCCC.

So, we are in tune here, as we are with Working-Class Studies' central focus on class (coal-mining communities have been paradigmatic of 'working-class community' within sociology), its commitment to joining knowledge production and activism (the focus of our relationship with Unite Community) and the recognition of the need to understand precarity (Bright 2016). Perhaps the most important aspect of Working-Class Studies for the work we're doing, though, is the emphatic openness to multidisciplinary (or, strictly, '*post*-disciplinary') inquiry, as this gives us room to deploy a new vocabulary that has emerged from anthropology. This latter point, when wedded to the other characteristics of Working-Class Studies to which I've drawn attention, is critically important in making our home in the field a comfortable one.

The projects

Focusing on the two activist networks of Unite Community and the Co-operative College, our first, 2015, project – Working with Social Haunting: Past- and Present-making in Two 'Communities of Value' (WwSH) – took up Walkerdine and Studdert's call for an 'amplification and extension of work on communal being-ness' within AHRCCC-funded research. It adopted their conceptualisation of community as a lived process of 'linkages, actions, speech, affect, practices, grounded in communal interaction' (Walkerdine and Studdert, n.d., 7) but emphasised community being-ness as produced through conscious *and* unconscious means that are often not initially obvious to community members themselves. WwSH ran for a year out of the South Yorkshire Community branch of the large general trade union Unite (based out of the National Union of Mineworkers headquarters in the former coal-mining town of Barnsley) and Co-op facilities including the headquarters of the College and the Rochdale Pioneers Museum.

Our initial aim was to establish a novel form of co-produced research exploring how particular affective and imaginative aspects of communal being-ness were operating at a moment of change for our partner communities. Certain discernible forces of feeling were influencing how each of the two organisations sought to re-imagine themselves, and both were negotiating strategic change within a context that was shaped in various ways by affective historical identities focused around specific sites, historical experiences and foundational sets of values. Thatcher's death in 2013 and the thirtieth anniversary of the 1984–85 miners' strike in 2014 had re-energised coalfield activism, and a narrative of the strike as *the* default model of militancy and commitment had become dominant among Unite Community activists. At the same time, a financial scandal in the corporate structure of the Co-operative movement had prompted reflection about the role of co-operative values among individuals. Our activities set out to explore how the past was immanent within the present in a multiplicity of forms – as affective practice, narratives, values, artefacts, industrial remains, buildings and sites – and brought together a team from the following fields: performance ethnography; creative writing; architecture and urban planning; comics studies; archaeology and heritage studies; sonic art and composition; and radio documentary.

Our second project, Opening the 'Unclosed Space': Multiplying Ghost Labs as Intergenerational Utopian Practice (OUS), grew out of WwSH in response to a 2016 AHRCCC funding call around the theme of Community Futures and Utopia. Our project maintained the element of arts-based methods and community radio and extended the geographical scope of the work by collaborating intergenerationally with the established WwSH partnership, but this time supplemented by our Staffordshire coalfield theatre partner, New Vic Theatre Borderlines, and an autonomist youth group in East London. The project was delivered in two phases, the first of which involved the project team working with Borderlines at the New Vic theatre in Newcastle under Lyme, Staffordshire, in a coalfield community outreach process that we called 'Utopia Ghost-hunting', which eventuated in a community theatre performance entitled 'The Unquiet'. The second phase took the Ghost Lab model to the National Festival of Utopia at Somerset House in London, running open Ghost Labs on each of the two days. In a shift of theoretical emphasis from WwSH, this project gave particular attention to Ernst Bloch's (1995) work by posing community futures as an always present not-yet of contested communal pasts. Poetry and comic strip workshops were once again the core of the Ghost Labs.

The current project, Song Lines, has had wider national and international ambitions. It uses the core technique of 'Community Tarot' readings and the vehicle of community radio to reach new participants in the UK and to link to other national and international audiences in the Basque Country, Slovenia, Hungary, Malawi, Indonesia and the US. The Community Tarot, devised by our partner New Vic Theatre Borderlines, has become our most commonly employed arts-based method. Designed around individual 'readings' from of a pack of cards produced from images and words collected from our partner communities, it offers a simple, playful, but richly productive device with which to bring to light contradictory and troubling aspects of contested pasts and re-imaginable futures as they emerge at individual level. Then, as individual readings are collected together and scaled up as *community readings*, a kind of living cultural lexicon of community imagination is assembled as themes emerge for sustained reflection, creative work, and action.

Again, this has been a project of two phases, delivered over a year. In phase one, the Community Tarot technique was rolled out by means of Ghost Labs held in six new communities. In the second phase, the creative materials generated through those Community Tarot readings have been used to stimulate the creation of a set of contemporary 'video ballads' that have been specially written in the tradition of dissenting song and recorded by our newest project partners, folk musicians Ribbon Road. These video ballads have then been used to initiate 'song lines' of living knowledge from the originating communities outwards, through a community radio documentary and a series of public engagement and dissemination outlets – such as the Durham Miners' Gala – that have had local, regional, national and international reach. These have included pop-up theatre, devised again by New Vic Theatre Borderlines, and, most notably, *interactive* audience features of community radio. The established project team has been joined this time by an artists' network in the north-east of England and community broadcast media specialists Sheffield Live and the World Association of Community Radio Broadcasters.

So, what really happens in the Ghost Labs? A roof fall, Boundary Road, and a 'dark saviour'

In this section, I want to examine what actually happens in the Ghost Labs when the various arts-based approaches are used. First, however, it is important to note that the individuals participating over the three projects have varied in terms of gender, age and ethnicity. Across the whole series of twenty or so 'official'[7] Ghost Labs, participants have come from groups of Unite Community members; active co-operators; a community arts group; asylum seekers; young people's groups; and British Asian women. Some Ghost Labs have been made up of retired people (in the north-east, for example) or diverse young people under the age of 20 (London). The British Asian women's group was obviously a single ethnicity and gender group, and the London youth group were also mainly young women. Equally, involvement in activism (the original focus of the work) has varied. The very first South Yorkshire Ghost Labs were made up of Unite Community members who were mainly engaged activists (indeed, two of them eventually became formal 'co-investigators' in research council terms). The London youth group was also specifically autonomist. The other groups involved have had a much wider spread. OUS, for example, had a participant base that extended right across a spectrum from activists to the general public, and Song Lines has deliberately sought a wider geographical variation and ethnic diversity of participants.

In terms of 'feel', too, the Labs have varied. Sometimes, as contingencies have determined, the ambience has been that of an arts or community workshop, sometimes much more intimate than that. In terms of content, there has been neither a 'curriculum' nor preset learning outcomes.

Most commonly, a Ghost Lab begins with a circle discussion prompted by 'haunted objects' that people have brought along, and things develop from there to talking, writing together as a group, cartooning or being involved in a 'reading' from the community Tarot pack. The intention has been to work in a 'long form' that allows the sessions to breathe. At a given moment, everyone might be riveted to the voice of a single person. At another, they'll be talking wildly over each other as re-inhabited feelings find expression. Things will fly off at a tangent, then meander and repeat a while. Exchanges are by turn heart-rending (there are frequently tears), stomach-churning and uproariously funny. Jokes are cracked. Stories – of place, change, conflict, growing and ageing, trauma, lightness, love, loss, cherished hobbies, risks taken, joys enjoyed, death – are ubiquitous, and the rhythm is one of intensifying and diminishing intensities. Given my limited space, let me share just three vignettes selected from the scores of equally vivid examples on which I could draw.

The first is an account of an underground 'roof fall' at a coalface six miles out and 500 metres deep under the North Sea off the east Durham coast. It was given by D, a former coal miner who 'after workin' in rehab an' that' now runs an agricultural and outdoor education project for young people. D's story was part of his response to his 'haunted object': his colliery identity tag (or 'pit check' as they were known). D began by evoking the strangeness of the underground colliery environment, describing how a permanent wind (caused by the unidirectional flow of mechanical ventilation) is always present and, depending on your position, is 'either in your face or behind yer. It *never* changes'. D was working in a 'forty-two inches deep coal seam with a post stone roof … a very hard stone', and he describes how, when the coal was cut and the face 'retreated', the roof supports were meant to 'just drop' in a predictable way; but

> post stone just stands for a very long time and we kept coming back, and coming back, an' it got to about 500 metres still standing, standin' behind you, and your light couldn't get to where you started from … and we could see this fault comin' in the roof like a pencil line on a piece o' paper. You're watchin' it and it's just comin' further and further doon the face as you're retreatin' the coal, and then once it got the other end, this whole roof, about 550 metres by then, it just dropped – *schfff!* – and the weight and volume of stone just pushed all the air off the coalface. An' it just stopped the wind. Everything just stagnant for a while. And then after a while you could feel the wind startin' to come back. And that terrified the life out o' us. The noise of it, and the feel of the air.

The second vignette is from one of the 2016 Barnsley Ghost Labs, where T, a voluntary mental health activist, a member of the Socialist Party and one of the most energetically committed members of the South Yorkshire branch of Unite Community, was part of a comic strip workshop. T shared his scenario sketch for a comic strip that he called 'Boundary Road'. Running diagonally across his sheet of paper, Boundary Road intersected one particular urban parliamentary constituency in the city of Sheffield. In this constituency, the Labour Party has long been historically dominant, and the particular locality on which T focused his drawing is, according to him, always approached complacently as if its politics, and thereby any local campaigning, is uniform and can always be relied upon. T's Boundary Road (a real road with a different name) had been imaginatively renamed, he told us, because it is *really* a boundary between two divergent class-based political geographies: one – on one side of the road – around the university and its community of students and academics; another – on the other side of the road – the home to a very diverse and precarious inner city working-class population. The naming, and open acknowledgement of the separation between these two geographies, T insisted, was vital to understanding unacknowledged subterranean tensions underlying the local politics of the area.

Boundary Road, he said, was a kind of fault line – an insight that has since come to pass in a bitter conflict between local citizens and the Labour-led city council around the issue of extensive tree felling contracted out to the private sector by the council.

The third vignette is from a Ghost Lab that was offered for the East London autonomist youth group with whom we were working on the first day of the 2016 Utopia Festival, the day after the EU Referendum and the day on which the narrow Brexit result was declared. The Lab was a development of previous ones in that it combined three of the devices we had developed. A three-card Community Tarot reading was facilitated jointly by our in-residence poet, Andrew McMillan, and our theatre partners from New Vic Borderlines, while verbatim comic strip was used as a form of representation (a professional comic strip artist was also part of our team). The young people in attendance, a diverse and politicised metropolitan group, were very agitated about the Referendum result and talked of being 'robbed of our future'. One young woman drew her three cards: *Sleep*, *Summer*, and a card showing the untitled image of a petrol service station. She immediately repositioned the cards to make a narrative that expressed her experience and nominated *Sleep* as her 'present' card, saying, 'I was kind of confused because I thought this represents me *now*. I'm really tired'. *Summer*, she decided, was her 'past' card: 'But for the past, I've done it as last summer. And sleep, I don't really get any sleep'. The petrol station was her 'future' card: 'like a place you go to stop off and just get a breather sort of thing, and it's, sort of, like a – gateway – of having some sleep'. From this stimulus, she wrote the following poem without any assistance.

> An exhausted way
> Out of the city
> Pretending to find happiness
> With only a road away
> Two, three streets of
> Love a day
> But not a sound
> Or sleep could make me happy –
> Summer light to cause a future
> But a dark night
> To cause a saviour

An anticipatory poetics of forces and intensities

These vignettes might at first glance seem slight, though I now think of them, rather, as 'compressions'. If we set them in a context of a social haunting, however, they speak resonantly out of the 'blind field', as Gordon (2008) called it. Recently, Valerie Walkerdine (2016) has emphasised how *affective histories* of communities make themselves present through small, anecdotal details in conversations and interviews that, taken together, constitute a space of community self-determination. It is this kind of territory that these stories occupy. In the three vignettes, there are commonalities across very different times and contexts. In all three, we see powerful and unpredictable forces; fault lines that are geological, geographical and political; an anticipatory sense of warning; precision of imagination; a feel for agency in materials that are other than human and both organic and inorganic; and an acute sense of the precarity – in Butler's (2004) sense as well as Standing's (2011) – of events and their outcomes. Further, all of these features suddenly take on a much deeper relief when the unspoken context of what remains hidden – Brexit – is factored in. Our projects went looking for the particularities of class composition in the deindustrialised areas of the north of England, fully expecting to bump firmly into Brexit at a moment when the referendum decision was being read nationally as the most significant working-class political choice of a generation. Yet there was barely a single direct mention of it. Rather, affective particularities lived out at individual, family and community levels – anger, loss, humiliation, powerlessness, betrayal, shame, nostalgia, fear and a jeopardised attachment to place – were everywhere. They poured out at the slightest stimulus of a cherished object, a path to work that now goes nowhere, a misrecognised urban architecture, a random arrangement of three cards. Yet underneath all of that, a recalcitrant, obstreperous, self-reliant, vivacious solidarity evidently remained, holding its extraordinarily creative capacities in readiness and waiting.

As I took part in and witnessed many startling moments like those in the vignettes, I felt compelled to try and identify the *mechanics* of what was happening in the Ghost Labs. If only we could isolate the active elements and maybe write a manual for union branches and community partners floundering in their attempts to understand the erratic forces at play. Steadily, though, it became clear that we were dealing not with a mechanics, but a *poetics* – a poetics, indeed, that seemed to 'shimmer' (Seigworth and Gregg, 2010) out of the Ghost Labs as a surprise, an excess, rather than as any technically reproducible 'output'. I should have expected this really, as the firm direction of my own ethnographic work had been increasingly towards forces of affect and imagination and to anthropologist Kathleen Stewart's "ficto-critical" approach, which brings us back to the point about the fruitfulness of anthropology made above.

Stewart has characterised her ethnographic project as a

> slow, and sometimes sudden, accretion of ways of attending to the charged atmospheres of everyday life. How they accrue, endure, fade or snap. How they build as a refrain, literally scoring over the labor of living out whatever's happening.
>
> *(Stewart 2010, 2)*

Drawing, like Gordon, on a literature that sees (as we do) a crux point in Raymond Williams' (1977) work on structures of feeling, Stewart calls for an attunement to 'ordinary affects' that 'come into view as habit of shock, resonance or impact' (Stewart, 2007, 1), that 'work not through "meanings" per se, but rather in the way that they pick up density and texture as they move through bodies, dreams, dramas, and social worldings of all kinds' (3).

In our experience, narrative is the most prominent mode through which the forces and intensities of a haunting is 'socially worlded'. Another anthropologist, Peter Collins, has recently addressed the challenge that haunting brings to anthropology and, as we have, has zeroed in on imagination and affect as key. Reminding us that '[g]hostly presence reaches beyond the allegorical and metaphorical' (2015, 113), Collins notes that 'the relationship between imagination and haunting is complex [and is] an imaginative process, that is itself inherently social and generative of relationships … that has been largely overlooked' (112). Hauntings, he asserts unambiguously, 'can only be understood … in relation to narrative' (99), and, what is more, 'the narrative gaps, spaces, lacunae' that are characteristic of them – as they are of the life of the Ghost Labs – 'are completed or repaired, most often by the prompting of ghosts' (111).

Feeling, held in common: A utopian grace?

In conclusion, it now strikes me very clearly that the Ghost Labs' distinguishing feature is precisely their capacity to enable a poetics of forces and intensities, of 'ordinary affects', to flourish and move towards the repair and completion (that Collins identifies) through collective reconfiguration. The language – of flows and of pause and acceleration; of accruals and fractures;

of embodied dreaming; of densities, textures and, notably, of the refrain of forces and intensities – is the Ghost Labs' natural register, just as the Lab's laboratory space is the natural locus of these forces' collective 'worlding'. Basically, ghosts are made *material* here by being transformed 'from the apparitional through the concerted efforts of participants', such as, in our vignettes, D, T, and the young woman from East London, 'who are familiar with their haunting presence' (Collins 2015, 111). Feeling, initially held privately – and *this* is the crux – is made available for re-imagination in common and, being thus *made* common, is thence forward *held in common* as a collective bond, collectively carried in a uniquely working-class counter-value practice of relationality (Skeggs 2011).

These are still preliminary thoughts, and our account is developing steadily as we begin to mine the vast amount of Ghost Lab materials – audio, video, arts products, blog postings, responses to songs and broadcasts – that we have in our archive. There remains, too, a clear need to develop Ghost Labs that are both deep and longitudinal, as we have been limited to one-off sessions thus far. It is only with commitment to a local setting for, say, three months at a minimum that the potential for meaningful links to activist campaigns and sustained inquiry becomes realisable. So while we are ambitious, we remain realistic. The funding implications are very considerable. Nevertheless, as Principal Investigator of the projects completed so far, I would still contest that the promise of our approach to the affective/imaginative dimension of class is already clearly a rich and necessary one. As categories of class are flattened ever more in the contracted affective yah-boo rhetorics of contemporary social media, the capacity of our work to model an independent class practice that works the complex affective register of 'broken, polemical voices' (Rancière 2011, 12), rather than received political abstractions, is potentially very valuable. It is through those voices (and nowhere else, in my view), that the Ghost Labs might quietly instantiate the Benjaminian 'profane illumination' that 'things could have been and can be otherwise'; that is, in Gordon's words (2008, 57), the 'utopian grace' of a social haunting and, for me, the real beginning of our doing our collective 'something else, different before, that [still] needs to be done'.

Notes

1 I've borrowed Zandy's notion of holding 'in common' (see Zandy 2001).
2 For a host of materials relating to all our related projects, see our comprehensive website at socialhaunting.com.
3 Throughout this account I'm thinking of affect as 'an impingement or extrusion of a momentary or sometimes more sustained state of relation *as well as* the passage … of forces or intensities … that pass body to body' (Seigworth and Gregg 2010, 1).
4 I'm thinking of imagination, here, as a 'space of indeterminacy amid social and cultural life' (Rapport 2015, 7).
5 The English and Welsh coalfields generally voted around 60/40 in favour of Brexit.
6 For pictorial examples of these devices in operation, see socialhaunting.com.
7 A series of Ghost Labs grew out of the funded project and took place in Doncaster, Sheffield and Stockport.

References

Back, L. (2011) 'Haunted Futures: A Response to Avery Gordon', *borderlands*, 10, 2, pp. 1–9.
Barrett, E. and Bolt, B. (eds.) (2013) *Carnal Knowledge: Towards a 'New Materialism' through the Arts*, London, I.B. Tauris.
Berlant, L. (2011) 'A Properly Political Love: Three Approaches in Ten Pages', *Cultural Anthropology*, 26, 4, pp. 683–691.

Bloch, E. (1995) *The Principle of Hope*, Cambridge MA, MIT Press.

Bonnett, A. (2010) *Left in the Past: Radicalism and the Politics of Nostalgia*, New York, Continuum.

Bright, N. G. (2012a) '"Sticking Together!" Policy Activism from within a Former UK Coal-Mining Community', *Journal of Education Administration and History*, 44, 3, pp. 221–236.

Bright, N. G. (2012b) 'A Practice of Concrete Utopia? Informal Youth Support and the Possibility of "Redemptive Remembering" in a UK Coal-Mining Area', *Power and Education*, 4, 3, pp. 315–326.

Bright, N. G. (2016) '"The Lady is Not Returning!" Educational Precarity and a Social Haunting in the UK Coalfields', *Ethnography and Education*, 11, 2, pp. 142–157.

Bright, N. G. (2018) '"A Chance to Talk Like This": Gender, Education, and Social Haunting in a UK Coalfield', Smyth, J. and Simons, R. (eds.) *Education and Working-Class Youth*, London and New York, Palgrave Macmillan.

Brown, G. and Pickerill, J. (2009) 'Space for Emotion in the Spaces of Activism', *Emotion, Space and Society*, 2, pp. 24–35.

Butler, J. (2004) *Precarious Life: The Powers of Mourning and Violence*, London, Verso.

Clough, P.T. (2007) *The Affective Turn: Theorising the Social*, Durham and London, Duke University Press.

Collins, P. (2015) 'From Anthropology of the Imagination to the Anthropological Imagination', in Harris, M. and Rapport, N. (eds) *Reflection on Imagination: Human Capacity and Method*, London and New York, Routledge.

Facer, K. and Enright, B. (2016) *Creating Living Knowledge*, Bristol, University of Bristol and AHRC Connected Communities Programme.

Fentress, J. and Wickham, C. (1992) *Social Memory*, Oxford, Blackwell.

Gordon, A. (2008) *Ghostly Matters: Haunting and the Sociological Imagination* (2nd ed.) Minneapolis, University of Minnesota Press.

Guattari, F. (2015) 'Transversality', *Psychoanalysis and Transversality: Texts and Interviews 1955–1971*, Semiotext(e), Cambridge MA, MIT Press.

Hardt, M. and Negri, A. (2009) *Commonwealth*, Cambridge MA, Harvard University Press.

Hardt, M. and Negri, A. (2017) *Assembly*, Cambridge MA, Harvard University Press.

Kester, G. (2004) Dialogic Aesthetics, in *Conversation Pieces: Community and Communication in Modern Art*, Berkeley: University of California Press.

Knudsen, B and Stage, C. (eds) (2016) *Affective Methodologies: Developing Cultural Research Strategies for the Study of Affect*, New York, Springer.

Linkon, S. L. and Russo, J. (2016) 'Twenty Years of Working-Class Studies: Tensions, Values and Core Questions', *Journal of Working-Class Studies*, 1, 1, pp. 4–13.

Massumi, B. (2015) *The Politics of Affect*, Cambridge, Polity.

McLaren, P. and Tadeau da Silva, T. (1993) 'Decentring Pedagogy – Critical Literacy, Resistance and the Politics of Memory', in McLaren, P. and Leonard, P (eds) *Paulo Freire – A Critical Encounter*, Routledge, London.

Olick, J., Vinitsky-Seroussi, V. and Levy, D. (eds) (2011) *The Collective Memory Reader*, Oxford, OUP.

Perchard, A. (2013) '"Broken Men" and "Thatcher's Children": Memory and Legacy in Scotland's Coalfields', *International Labor and Working-Class History*, 84, pp. 78–98.

Rancière, J. (2011) *Staging the People: The Proletarian and his Double* [trans. D. Fernbach]. London and New York: Verso.

Rapport, N. (2015) '"Imagination is in the Barest Reality": On the Universal Human Imagining of the World', in Harris, M. and Rapport, N. (eds) *Reflections on Imagination: Human Capacity and Ethnographic Method*, London and New York, Routledge.

Russo J. and Linkon S. (2005) 'Introduction: What's new about New Working-Class Studies?', in Russo, J. and Linkon, S. (eds) *New Working-Class Studies*, Ithaca, Cornell University Press.

Seigworth, G. J. and Gregg, M. (2010) 'An Inventory of Shimmers', in Seigworth, G. J., Gregory, J. and Gregg, M. (eds) *The Affect Theory Reader*, Durham NC and London, Duke University Press.

Shukaitis, S. and Graeber, D. (eds) (2007) *Constituent Imagination: Militant Investigations, Collective Theorization*, Oakland, AK Press.

Skeggs, B. (2011) 'Imagining Personhood Differently: Person Value and Autonomist Working-Class Value Practices', *Sociological Review*, 59, 3, pp. 496–513.

Smith, M, Davidson, D, Cameron, L. and Bondi, L. (eds) (2009) *Emotion, Place and Culture*, London and New York, Routledge.

Standing, G. (2011) *The Precariat: The New Dangerous Class*, London, Bloomsbury.

Stewart, K. (2007) *Ordinary Affects*, Durham NC and London, Duke University Press.

Stewart, K. (2010) 'Atmospheric Attunements by Kathleen Stewart', *Rubric*, Issue 1.
Streeck, W. (2017) 'Return of the Repressed', *New Left Review*, 104.
Walkerdine, V. (2016) 'Affective History, Working Class Communities and Self-Determination', *Sociological Review*, 64, 4, pp. 699–714.
Walkerdine, V. and Studdert, D. (n.d.) *Connected Communities: Concepts and Meanings of Community in the Social Sciences*, AHRCCC.
Williams, R. (1977) *Marxism and Literature*, Oxford: Oxford University Press.
Zandy, J. (2001) *What We Hold In Common: An Introduction to Working-Class Studies*, New York, The Feminist Press at CUNY.

Part IV
Working-class cultures

Section introduction

Working-class cultures

Tim Strangleman

In this section we look at working-class culture – how it has been thought about generally and specifically in the field of working-class studies. Working-class culture has been the object of study for decades, reaching back to the nineteenth century and the birth of the social sciences, most notably sociology. It is often viewed as a deficit culture, the absence of material things such as money and property, or immaterial disadvantage – education, manners, or the appreciation of high culture, etc. Over the years, there has been a growing appreciation of a more rounded working-class culture, one that is richer and deserving of fuller attention. Often times this attention was paid by historians rather than social scientists. An important jumping-off point for this discussion, therefore, is the work of cultural historians such as E. P. Thompson and Raymond Williams. It was Thompson's 1963 volume *The Making of the English Working Class* that was to influence a whole wave of sociologists and social historians to take working-class life seriously as a dynamic, independent, and vibrant way of being. Thompson's basic thesis was that the English working class was present at its own birth, in that the culture of pre-industrial ordinary common people was a set of customs held in common which allowed the newly emerging proletariat to make sense of themselves as industrial workers subject to capitalist organisations. Thompson argued there was a strong moral basis to this culture which facilitated a critique of the new social order opening up before them.

Around the same time that Thompson was writing, there was an expansion in social history and cultural studies which took seriously working-class life and culture. Authors like Richard Hoggart (1957) and Raymond Williams (1973) produced seminal texts that understood working-class life from within; both authors having strong roots in working-class communities in inner city Leeds and rural Wales, respectively. Later, their work was developed by the Birmingham Centre for Contemporary Cultural Studies, founded in 1964 by Hoggart (see Webster 2004). These events coincided with an expansion in interest in the 'history from below' movement, a great attention to issues of gender, feminism, class and race. Academically this bore fruit with the founding of the History Workshop movement and the Oral History Society (see Samuel 1991).

In 1972, the US saw the publication of the seminal *The Hidden Injuries of Class* by Richard Sennett and Johnathan Cobb (1972). This was and remains an important text for sociologists interested in how class works, the contradictions in working-class identity, and the pride and shame associated with blue-collar life. I remember vividly reading *Hidden Injuries* as an undergraduate and being stunned by how sociologists writing two decades before and over 3,000 miles across the Atlantic could write a book that spoke so clearly to my own experience of class.

In both the US and the UK, this interest in class was stimulated by the rising standards of living in the era of the long boom between the late 1940s and the mid-1970s. It reflected a growing self-confidence among working-class individuals and communities coupled with a growing economic power formed by three decades of rising standards of living and full employment underpinned by increased unionisation. The working class mattered to society. However, by the mid-1970s these benign circumstances were beginning to change dramatically, with layoffs, closures, static or falling real wages, and deindustrialisation ripping the heart out of industries and the communities in which they were located. The established certainties about class began to look shaky (see, for example, Hobsbawm 1978).

Working-class studies, and especially interest in class cultures, was also born out of a crisis in the study of class itself. In the 1980s and 1990s it became fashionable to talk of 'classless societies' or as class as a 'zombie category,' ideas and concepts that were effectively dead but kept alive nonetheless (see Beck and Beck Gernsheim 2001). This itself reflected the abolition of many of the traditional industrial jobs, higher standards of living and education.

Paralleling the emergence of working-class studies primarily in the US, there was a resurgence in the study of class in the UK. This was a reaction against what was seen as an overly narrow account of what counted as class analysis; at the time a largely quantitative exercise in understanding class as static categories inferred through labour market position. In reaction to this limited view of class, a set of British sociologists sought to reinvigorate class analysis qualitatively, looking at issues of culture, often downplaying, or even ignoring, work and workplaces altogether (see, for example, Crompton et al. 2000; Savage 2000). Instead of economic life, greater attention was paid to education, consumption patterns and issues of representation.

Many of those involved in this move embraced the ideas and concepts of French sociologist Pierre Bourdieu – most notably his ideas of habitus, field and various forms of 'capitals' (economic, symbolic, cultural and social). Derived from both Marxian and Weberian understandings of class, Bourdieu wanted to show how class was formed, played out and reproduced in real settings (see Bourdieu 1984). This Bordieuan influence on the writing of scholars of class can be seen in the work of Beverley Skeggs (1997; 2003), Tony Bennett (Bennett et al. 2009), Mike Savage (2000), Steph Lawler (2008) and Andrew Sayer (2005) amongst many others. It is interesting that many of these authors have engaged to some extent with working-class studies over the last two decades but perhaps do not feel rooted in the field.

What perhaps is missing from these Bordieu-inspired accounts is the ethnographic eye that many rooted in working-class studies possess. Here I think it is useful to expand on Sennett and Cobb's notion of the *Hidden Injuries of Class* by thinking more expansively about the hidden rewards of class too. One of the reasons people are attracted to the field of working-class studies is that it allows people to be proud and critical of their roots. They recognize the really important positive aspects of class cultures such as close communities, a sense of people looking out for one another and, above all, humour. Taken together, it is the simultaneous recognition of both the rewards and injuries that mark out the field.

The influence of Bourdieu's ideas have had more limited impact on working-class studies than we might have expected. Perhaps this reflects the limited number of sociologists involved in the field in its early days. Bourdieu certainly had his followers in the US in class studies; the work of Michele Lamont (1992, 2000) and Annette Lareau (2003) attest to this influence. We can also see the potential power and reach of Bourdieu's ideas in the chapters that follow by Betsy Leondar-Wright and Jessi Streib.

So the question is, then, what is the point of working-class studies in terms of looking at class cultures? If sociologists and others look at class, what does our field do that others don't? First, working-class studies' strength is in its inter- and multi-disciplinary approach. The field draws upon sociology alongside other social sciences, as well as arts and humanities disciplines. This approach allows a dynamic and deeper account of the variety and contradictions in working-class life. Secondly, as highlighted elsewhere in this volume, working-class studies' signature theme is the way it often draws on autobiographical reflections on class from working-class people. This brings a distinctive and critically sympathetic perspective to class analysis. Finally, I think a working-class studies approach rejects the perspective that working-class culture is a deficit culture, something to be lifted out of, changed or 'improved.' Elements of this approach can be seen in some of the important texts published by some of the leading figures in the field, such as Metzgar's (2001) *Striking Steel: Solidarity Remembered*, Torlina's (2011) *Working Class: Challenging the Myths about Blue-Collar Labor*, Jensen's (2012) *Reading Classes: On Culture and Classism in America*, and Leondar-Wright's (2014) *Missing Class: Strengthening Social Movement Groups by Seeing Class Cultures*. Each, in their very different ways, shows how class works in distinct settings – the workplace, around the family kitchen table, in front of the TV and in activist settings. What is noteworthy here is how these authors and their books pivot and leverage off each other; they both are shaped by the field and, in turn, shape the field themselves. It might help to return to the tension between *rewards* and *injuries* of class. The value that working-class studies adds in any discussion of class culture is this sense of real value in working-class culture while being fully aware of the limitation, contradictions and problems that such a culture represents.

This section explores working-class life and culture through five related chapters. Jack Metzgar makes an argument for a genuine working-class culture and uses his own autobiographical reflections on both class and the field of working-class studies. This is an excellent example of the kind of critical reflective autobiographical writing which is a hallmark of the field. Barbara Jensen examines working-class culture and in particular how increasing precarity among younger working-class people is having devastating psychosocial consequences. Jensen's chapter draws on her own biography to understand the direr straits of a younger generation of working class people having to face extreme labour market insecurity with far fewer of the support structures of older forms of working-class culture that previous generations enjoyed. Betsy Leondar-Wright's essay looks at different class cultures in the context of activist groups. She offers important insights into how dialogue between working-class and middle-class activists might be better achieved. Leondar-Wright's chapter is an excellent example of how class works, from top down and bottom up – the injuries and rewards. Jessi Streib's chapter presents a general account of the differences between working-class cultures and lifestyles and those of the middle class. Streib draws on Bourdieu to examine different types of class capitals that working and middle-class cultures draw on. Sarah Attfield looks at working-class culture and how it is (mis) represented in Australian media of various types. What is fascinating about Attfield's account is the striking similarities between working-class representation and misrepresentation in Australia and those tropes in the UK, the US and elsewhere.

So what does working-class studies and its focus of class cultures add and what might we take from it for building the field in the future? On a personal note as a historical sociologist, I welcome the way increasing numbers of sociologists from the US, the UK, Europe and elsewhere are coming to the field. This is important. As this introduction has shown, there is a long-standing lineage of writing on class sympathetic to working-class culture. Without writers such as E. P. Thompson, Richard Hoggart, Raymond William and Stuart Hall many of us would never have made it to working-class studies in the first place. Now that trickle of sociology has greatly expanded, it will be interesting to see how more mainstream sociological theories, methods and concepts cross over and cross-pollinate working-class studies. Likewise, it is important that the approaches and insights of working-class studies scholars and activists are recognised and picked up by sociology, other disciplines and the media. It has been interesting to see the way mainstream media and academia claim we know nothing about the ignored and left-behind communities in the wake of Brexit and Trump.

Arguably the most important agenda for the field in terms of class cultures is to understand how they adapt and evolve over time. Much of the writing on class cultures and those rewards that I've talked about is rooted in very different types of communities than those working-class people now live in. Working-class culture has had to face five decades of job loss and deindustrialisation, plant closures and shutdowns. This has put a tremendous stress on individuals, families and communities. Many formerly prosperous working-class communities now face multilayered and complex social, economic and health challenges. The sense of stability that rooted communities once enjoyed is precarious at best. The task of working-class studies is to understand, chart and attempt to help working-class people in their future.

References

Beck, U. and Beck-Gernsheim, E. (2001) *Individualization: Institutionalised Individualism and its Social and Political Consequences*, London, Sage.

Bennett, T., Savage, M., Silva, E., Warde, A., Gayo-Cal, M. and Wright, D. (2009) *Culture, Class, Distinction*, London, Routledge.

Bourdieu, P. (1984) *Distinction: A Social Critique of the Judgment of Taste*, Cambridge, MA, Harvard University Press.

Crompton, R., Devine, F., Savage, M. and Scott, J. (eds.) (2000) *Renewing Class Analysis*, Oxford, Blackwell.

Hobsbawm, E. (1978) 'The Forward March of Labour Halted?' *Marxism Today*, September, pp. 279–286.

Hoggart, R. (1957) *The Uses of Literacy*, London, Penguin.

Jensen, B. (2012) *Reading Classes: On Culture and Classism in America*, Ithaca, Cornell University Press.

Lamont, M. (1992) *Money, Morals, and Manners: The Culture of the French and American Upper-Middle-Class*, Chicago, University of Chicago Press.

Lamont, M. (2000) *The Dignity of Working Men: Morality and the Boundaries of Race, Class, and Immigration*, Cambridge, MA, Harvard University Press.

Lareau, A. (2003) *Unequal Childhoods: Class, Race, and Family Life*, Berkeley, University of California Press.

Lawler, S. (2008) *Identity: Sociological Perspectives*, Cambridge, Polity.

Leondar-Wright, B. (2014) *Missing Class: Strengthening Social Movement Groups by Seeing Class Cultures*, Ithaca, Cornell University Press.

Metzgar, J. (2001) *Striking Steel: Solidarity Remembered*, Philadelphia, Temple University Press.

Samuel, R. (1991) *History Workshop: A Collectanea 1967–1991*, London, History Workshop 25.

Savage, M. (2000) *Class Analysis and Social Transformation*, Buckingham, Open University Press.

Sayer, A. (2005) *The Moral Significance of Class*, Cambridge, Cambridge University Press.

Sennett, R. and Cobb, J. (1972) *The Hidden Injuries of Class*, London, Norton.

Skeggs, B. (1997) *Formations of Class and Gender: Becoming Respectable*, London, Sage.

Skeggs, B. (2003) *Class, Self, Culture*, London, Routledge.

Thompson, E. P. (1963) *The Making of the English Working Class*, London, Penguin.

Torlina, J. (2011) *Working Class: Challenging the Myths about Blue-Collar Labor*, Boulder, Lynne Rienner Publishing.

Webster, F. (2004) 'Cultural Studies and Sociology at, and After, the Closure of the Birmingham School,' *Cultural Studies*, 18, 6, pp. 847–862.

Williams, R. (1973) *The Country and the City*, Oxford, Oxford University Press.

16

There is a genuine working-class culture

Jack Metzgar

> Nothing epic. Just the small heroics of getting through the day when the day doesn't give a shit.
>
> Philip Levine

> If I'm not what the white man thinks I am, then he has to find out what *he* is.
>
> James Baldwin

In the summer of 1999 I attended my first Working-Class Studies conference in Youngstown, Ohio. I had just finished *Striking Steel: Solidarity Remembered*, and a tangential part of that book articulated what I saw as core differences between professional middle-class and working-class cultures. For the conference, I planned to read a 12-minute passage from the book describing how weird and unproductive it felt to displaced steelworkers to be taught to write resumes in the 1980s. To account for this phenomenon, I boldly explained that in contrast to middle-class culture, 'working-class culture emphasizes being and *belonging*, not achieving and *becoming*' (Metzgar 2000, 203).

I was nervous about reading this passage because I had never heard anybody articulate the idea that there were distinct class cultures, let alone sum up their differences in a sentence. What's more, my favorite sociology book at the time, *Habits of the Heart: Individualism and Commitment in American Life*, firmly declared that for the past century 'the middle class … has so dominated our culture that neither a genuinely upper-class nor a genuinely working-class culture has fully appeared. Everyone in the United States thinks largely in middle-class categories, even when they are inappropriate' (Bellah et al. 1996, xliii). Though I knew this was wrong, *Habits* is such a rich appreciation and critique of middle-class Americanism by a team of five authors who seemed to know everything that it seemed preposterous that I could be so firmly right and they so terribly wrong.

At the conference, however, counseling psychologist Barbara Jensen delivered a paper including references to the exciting potentials of middle-class *becoming* and the warm advantages of working-class *belonging* (Jensen 1997, 2012). What's more, in the question-and-answer period, a room of some 30 people argued with Jensen about this or that, but they all seemed to assume that becoming and belonging marked core differences between the class cultures. Through a wave of vertigo, I went from 'how could I be the only one who knows this?' to 'geez, everybody here knows this, and I have nothing to say.'

Maybe you have to be an academic to realize what an existential panic this can put people like us in. But that panic passed quickly into a sense of both relief and excitement. I realized what a burden I had been carrying around trying to think through on my own what I saw as an impenetrable middle-class misunderstanding of working-class people and, therefore, of themselves/ourselves *and* of our society and its social, political, and economic prospects. I quickly made friends with Jensen and her cohort of mostly female academics, and for four days soaked up stories about how fucked-up the middle class was contrasted with warm though often troubled remembrances of working-class pasts. I learned about 'imposter syndrome,' 'survivor guilt,' and 'code switching' – common phenomena among people who cross over from working-class families of origin to professional middle-class jobs, especially in academia. I had known lots of middle-class people from working-class backgrounds, of course, but what was distinctive about this group was their fiercely stated preference for working-class ways and their ability to articulate what they liked and disliked about each way of life. Many of them loved their jobs but felt stressed and uncomfortable around their colleagues while also no longer feeling quite at home with their parents, siblings, and old friends. I found myself sharing stories I could tell briefly and easily, because I didn't have to explain context and insist on nuance; instead I got knowing looks, nodding heads, and 'yes, but' responses. I was joining a conversation they had begun a few years before, so there was an intellectual seriousness to their discussion that went beyond a support-group experience. But for me it was something like therapeutic.

I discovered, however, that others from working-class backgrounds were less positive about their culture of origin, especially if they were from hard-living or poverty-class families, including both those who were and were not comfortable in their current middle-class environments. They had made great efforts to wean themselves from that culture and were eager to help others do the same; but they were not interested in defending or preserving a culture they did not see as separable from poor living standards and bad working conditions. Other crossovers didn't like our 'essentializing' or 'stereotyping' the two class cultures, which seemed to them to ride roughshod over the complex individuals they knew in each class. Often these were folks who identified themselves as 'working-class academics,' proudly 'coming out' on their campuses as committed to working-class ways (especially an egalitarian anti-status ethic) and actively resisting the impulse to code-switch or to see themselves as imposters in a professional middle-class world. Working-class academics also saw aspects of working-class culture as positive, but they tended toward the specific aspects of lifestyle, tastes, and manners of speaking rather than the kind of more universal characteristics Jensen had asserted. Meanwhile, those from middle-class backgrounds often express frustration with our 'navel-gazing' penchant for autobiographical thinking, and they fear that 'romanticizing' the working class and its ways might undermine the broader project of transforming workers' living standards and working conditions.

What many of us from working-class origins share at these conferences, however, is an ability to relax and just be our complete selves. Since midlife I haven't felt alienated from either middle-class or working-class worlds, fancying that I can move back and forth with relative ease, being a little working class in middle-class environments and a lot middle class in working-class ones. But the emotional power of that first encounter – a feeling of finally being at home that had me uncontrollably weeping when I had my first quiet moment at the end of that 1999 conference – suggests that I had been more alienated than I realized. Others have told me about similar experiences, including people now in their twenties and thirties. Swapping poignant stories about our first encounters with Working-Class Studies is now a standard part of evening socializing at these conferences.

This experience of class cultural clash and of how deeply it is felt has been thoroughly documented over the past 30 years. Anthologies like *Strangers in Paradise: Academics from the Working Class* and *This Fine Place So Far From Home: Voices of Academics from the Working Class*, and *Working-Class Women in the Academy: Laborers in the Knowledge Factory* have gathered poignant accounts of how difficult and complicated college can be for students from working-class families (Ryan and Sackrey 1984; Dews and Law 1995; Tokarczyk and Fay 1993). Class culture differences are widely recognized today in academia, with many universities paying increasing attention to the specific problems of first-in-family (or first-generation) college students, including criticism of how middle-class biases exacerbate the obstacles these working-class students typically face (Hurst and Nenga 2016).

Cultures cannot clash unless there are more than one of them and their differences are substantial. But that does not mean that the clashing cultures are both 'genuine' and of roughly equal value. Working-class culture could be, as often envisioned, merely a *deficit culture* – one characterized by the absence of mainstream values, skills, and ways of thinking and doing, a culture that is best understood as deficient in the kinds of things necessary to be a fully developed human being. A deficit culture is not genuine, in the sense that it is just a backward version of the mainstream, a culturally lagging receptacle of another culture that it is gradually, perhaps all-too-slowly, adopting. Or working-class culture might be a *dominated culture* – one shaped, indeed deformed, by the material, social, and psychological conditions of its domination. A dominated culture is not genuine either. Since it is merely a result of its domination and exploitation by others, it does not fashion its own way of doing and seeing things but is instead a series of programmed responses to stimuli in somebody else's Skinner's Box. Finally, working-class culture might be a *residual culture* – one destined to fade away (Williams 1973/1980). A residual culture is genuine and may once have been (and, for some, still be) valuable, but it no longer suits the current time.

My argument is that working-class culture is genuine in the sense that it has an internal coherence that is separate and distinct from middle-class culture; has positive value both in itself and for American society; and vitally contributes to the shaping of middle-class life and culture even as it forms itself within and around that dominant culture. Working-class culture does indeed have some deficits, some of which I have spent my life as a teacher trying to fill, and it has been formed in conditions of domination. But professional middle-class culture has some deficits too; and is not without its conditions of domination either, even if not as severe and if weighted more toward the social psychological than the economic and material. Finally, I suggest that the working class's deep culture – as distinct from lifestyles, tastes, and changing norms – is not merely residual but is shared by the majority of Americans of all ethnicities and colors, including many standard-issue middle-class professionals as they reach midlife. Working-class culture embodies what some labor historians have called a 'making do' (Martin 2015) or a 'getting-through-the-day' (Arnold 2014, 224) culture and what Barbara Jensen calls 'a roomier sense of now' (2012, 60). It is more reactive than proactive and, thus, can benefit from exposure to the more ambitious and aspirational character of middle-class professionalism. But its greater agility within the force of circumstance and its narrowing of life to the immediacy of being and belonging have a lot to offer in filling those empty spaces in middle-class life with its relentless pursuit of status and achievement. If the working class is not what we think it is, then we middle-class professionals may have a valuable opportunity to get a better sense of who we are.

Class blindness and the one right way of middle-class life

Habits of the Heart is unique in declaring outright that there is no genuine working-class culture. But it was merely being explicit about what is still conventional scholarly practice more than three decades later: casting arguments about American society as a whole by focusing on its 'main element,' the ubiquitous but nevertheless elite middle-class – meaning people with a college education, a professional or managerial occupation, and a healthy family income. Today this practice can seem quaint amidst the array of sociological studies of ethnic/racial, gender, and, to a lesser extent, class differences. But that habit of mind that thinks it's okay to take the professional middle-class part as if it were the whole of American culture and society is still the predominant one among the education-communications wing of the professional middle class. It's a combination of a relatively superficial but widely accepted intellectual convention supported by a deep class insularity and prejudice.

The claim that there is only one genuine culture in the US was made in *Habits*' original preface, and it was neither developed nor supported there or later in the book. We are not told what the authors think constitutes a genuine culture. Nor are we told why they think middle-class culture is genuine and working-class culture is not. The bald statement in the preface is merely a dismissive gesture that allows them to conflate 'middle class' with 'American' for the rest of the book.

This is common practice. Books like *American Manhood: Transformations in Masculinity from the Revolution to the Modern Era* (Rotundo 1993) and *American Cool: Constructing a Twentieth-Century Emotional Style* (Stearns 1994), for example, make similar claims, often admitting a certain narrowness in their prefaces but then proceeding to treat their version of middle-class culture as synonymous with American culture. Peter Stearns, for example, not only admits a middle-class narrowness in his introduction to *American Cool*, he further lets the cat out of the bag by granting that '[l]ike many studies of the middle class, it is biased toward evidence from Protestants in the North and West' (1994, 4). Likewise, Claude Fischer's *Made in America: A Social History of American Culture and Character* grants in his first chapter that his sense of a singular American culture 'originated among Northeastern Protestants and then spread and gained power over time' (2010, 12).

I can see why authors and publishers would not want more descriptive, but unwieldy titles like 'American middle-class Protestant manhood in the north and west,' but this is more than a matter of deceptive marketing. The practice of excluding working-class and other cultures from the discussion and of assuming 'people like us' are the singular norm is what Benjamin DeMott (1990) has called 'middle-class imperialism.' It is not direct economic or political domination, but it supports that domination. It also is unlikely conscious and intentional, since it is hard for any culture *not* to take itself as the norm, to experience its ways as appropriate and natural, and to assume that the way it understands things is the correct way. It is convenient to assume that other cultures are best understood simply by what they lack in comparison with the dominant, mainstream one. But what if that understanding is simply false? What if working-class culture has a coherent, but different set of values and norms that fit into and around the dominant mainstream culture? If that were true, then the mainstream culture, though dominant, would be subject to a series of mistakes and illusions about the society it culturally dominates. It would also be likely to misunderstand itself as a culture.

The professional middle class in America *is* culturally dominant, even though we are economically subordinate to a ruling class and somewhat less politically subordinate but in a more complicated way. But the concept of a 'dominant culture' presumes that there are other cultures different from the dominant one – Protestants in Italy, for example, or Slovaks in the former

Czechoslovakia, Kurds in Iraq, or new and recent immigrants in all countries. A dominant culture cannot be understood by excluding reference to the ones it dominates, how and why it predominates, and how it influences – and is influenced by – other cultures.

Claude Fischer's *Made in America* marshals a wonderful combination of statistics, survey research, and insightful historical interpretation to demonstrate that across the 19th and 20th centuries '[i]ncreasing proportions of women, youth, ethnic minorities, and the working class adopted [middle-class] culture, even after sometimes resisting it' (2010, 12). Fischer is undoubtedly right that today 'the American middle class lives and promulgates the distinctive and dominant character of the society' and that across the twentieth century 'more and more Americans joined the mainstream culture' (2010, 12). But 'increasing proportions' and 'more and more,' like 'dominant,' don't mean that middle-class professionalism is the one and only culture, or the only valuable one. Nor does it mean that, even after all the increasing proportions, it is the culture that is lived and promulgated by the majority of Americans. It just means that it is dominant.

A dominant culture does not need to dominate. It can be predominant, the preferred culture, first among equals, if you will. But when it construes itself as the one and only right way, it cannot help but dominate other cultures and the people who live within those cultures, whether it consciously intends to or not. Black Studies and Women's Studies as academic fields have decisively shown how narrow-minded and harmful construing white maleness as the norm has been. Likewise, those whose regional cultures differ from northeastern Protestantism often resent how their differences are routinely seen as mere backwardness. Indeed, Colin Woodard (2011) has cogently argued that there are no less than 11 'American nations' with not just different regional cultures but 'rival' ones.

When you consider how diverse we actually are by race, ethnicity, gender, sexuality, religion, region, and life stage, it can make your head spin. And spinning heads naturally desire some mainstream unity among this potentially explosive diversity. To a large extent, a rough unity can be productively provided by middle-class professionalism, but only if we don't lose sight of our middle-ness, our ability to see and live our positioning between a ruling class (whether you call it capitalist, owning class, or an oligarchy of wealth) and a working class that have genuinely different ways of living a life. Superficial conventions that allow and, indeed, encourage us to talk among ourselves, to mistake our part for the whole, let alone to dismiss other classes as uninteresting, backward, and not genuine blind us to fundamental realities of the society we are trying to understand. *Habits of the Heart*'s more fundamental intellectual flaw derives from this simple but blinding convention. The convention allows a rather spectacular lack of curiosity about working-class life and how it must be distinct from middle-class ways – just logically, without any empirical investigation, let alone daily experience of working-class people.

Habits poignantly bemoans a narrowing of middle-class life as now centered on a *career* rather than a *calling*. Once upon a time, 'to enter a profession meant to take up a definite function in a community and to operate within the civic and civil order of that community.' A calling was less individualistic, less focused on developing one's self, and more focused on fulfilling a social role that functioned to benefit one's community and a broader social good. A career, by contrast,

> was no longer oriented to any face-to-face community but to impersonal standards of excellence, operating in the context of a national occupational system. Rather than embedding one in a community, following a profession came to mean, quite literally, 'to move *up* and away.' The goal was no longer the fulfillment of a commonly understood form of life but the attainment of 'success,' and … whatever 'success' one had obtained, one could always obtain more.
>
> *(Bellah et al. 1996, 119–120)*

For the authors of *Habits*, this constant urging to self-improvement, to achieving higher and higher levels of success, led to 'unprecedented psychic demands,' (119) resulting in a 'therapeutic culture' that has come to define the dominant middle-class and, thus, American culture. They called for a more civic form of professionalism, restoring a sense of calling and a greater sense of social vision and mission.

This is still a powerful critique of 'American life,' that has engaged subsequent generations of social scientists and other thinkers.[1] But how could it not occur to these authors that there are lots of people, probably an overwhelming majority, who do not have careers and have never thought of their lives that way – people who have 'just a job,' neither a calling nor a career, but merely a way to *earn a living*? How could these people not have a culture, a way of living a life, that is very different from one built around a career?

Let me start with that relatively uncommon group of people who hate their jobs and are willing to tell you that even if you haven't asked. People like Joan C. Williams' father-in-law who dropped out of school in the eighth grade to help support his family and eventually 'got a good, steady [factory] job he truly hated … for 38 years' (Williams 2017, 1). I've always admired people like this. Most people who hate their jobs find ways to tolerate them. They enjoy the workplace social life of the people they work with. Or they value the work they do even though they don't like doing it. Or they find ways to create little spaces within their work that they like living in. And, above all, they avoid calling attention to how much they hate their jobs, especially to others but also to themselves; 'it's not so bad' or 'it could be worse,' they tell me. On the other hand, those who can flat out say 'I hate what I do every day' and keep it in front of them have a special strength of will that may not be good for their mental health, but is an extreme form of the dignity and self-respect working-class people win with the unadulterated grit of sticking with a bad job, 'taking it,' and 'hanging in there.' Their job complaining is often a backhanded form of bragging. My boss is worse than your boss, my job is dirtier, scarier, or more tedious than yours, what I do is worthless, and all the people I work with are assholes, but I get up every day and get the job done. I've witnessed these my-job-is-worse-than-your-job competitions dozens of times in working-class settings – albeit mostly among men with some alcohol in them, but also less dramatically among sober working-class women. I have yet to witness, and cannot imagine, a middle-class professional describing their job as so bad they deserve respect, even a round of applause, for simply enduring it.

Many working-class people don't hate their jobs, of course. Even though, like the job haters, they take pride in showing up every day and doing a good job, they genuinely enjoy enough aspects of their work to keep them 'satisfied' at the level job surveys ask about.[2] Many have intrinsically interesting and satisfying work – from skilled building trades workers at the high end of wages (when there is work) to personal care workers at the low end. But even this varies a lot across a work life as supervisors vary from great to awful, as work is deskilled or sped up, and as the aches, pains, and injuries of aging accumulate to make lifting or standing all day more difficult and painful. Still, they *take it*.

If you have a *career*, it makes sense to view life as a journey, one where you constantly strive to see what you can achieve and who you can yet become. But if you have a *job*, especially one that pays decently, it makes more sense to see life as a daily cycle of punishment and reward, of their time and my time, of necessity and freedom, of earning a living and living. People with jobs invest much less of their selves in their jobs than people with careers. As a result, what they do to earn a living has less of a hold on them than people with careers from which they are never quite free. I've been part of hundreds of conversations where people debate the relative merits of 'leaving the job behind when I walk out the door' versus 'being engaged with it more or less all the time.' As a middle-class professional with no fixed workday, I could see how much freer people with jobs were when not working than I was or could ever be, even though I was so much freer at work. I've always felt as though they were more present in the present than I was, as my mind could never quite empty itself of the schedule of tasks ahead of me. I cannot remember a time when I did not appreciate their way even as I realized I could never live that way.

How could having a job rather than a career not result in and require a different kind of culture, a different set of predispositions and expectations, norms and values, and ways of living a life? This different culture could not simply be the absence of dispositions required to have a career, norms and values that could eventually be handed down like second-hand clothes to cultural laggards. The culture needs to be different to accommodate different circumstances. Nor could this different culture be merely residual, a leftover from the past that will eventually disappear, so long as our economy still produces more jobs than careers, which it does and will go on doing (Metzgar 2014). And who is more dominated? Those of us who invest so much of ourselves in our careers that inevitably tie us into larger systems of command and control or those who keep the biggest part of themselves free of those systems?

Middle-class observers, even the newer class-aware generation of sociologists, often assume that professional middle-class careers are objectively better not just as jobs but as ways of life, and that's why even the most empathetic observers – from Paul Willis (1977) to Julie Bettie (2014) – focus on the irony and tragedy of working-class young people reproducing their class positions with the cultural choices they make within educational and societal systems in which they are 'unpreferred,' at best. The best of these sociologists, like Willis and Bettie, appreciate the immediate logic of working-class anti-school cultures among young people, but they see only the long-term hardship, the absence of broader choices, a future without becoming that seems only negative and unfortunate in reproducing a system of inequality. The presumption that careers are always and everywhere better than jobs blinds them to the preservation of self and the choice for a simple integrity that often lies at the core of working-class young people's rejection of middle-class ways. An aspiration to get a good job, defined as one that is decently paid and steady, can seem like no aspiration at all unless you see it as an affirmative choice to avoid the selling of one's soul that seems to them involved in pursuing a career, careers that are highly structured by others and that can dig deep into yourself and into your relationships with friends and family.

As an exercise, let's say you could get the same pay and benefits for being either an advertising executive or a personal care worker. Would it be irrational to choose the latter because you thought advertising was mostly a form of lying to people, whereas you found everyday satisfaction in helping people who need help (as one of my middle-aged nephews does)? That, of course, is not the way it works. These are not the kinds of choices anybody actually has. But what about the choice between being an operations manager getting $84,000 a year versus a union-protected but highly monitored UPS delivery driver getting $71,000.[3] As an operations manager, 'you can't be your own man,' 'you're simply a tool of upper management,' 'you're cut off from the people you work with,' 'you no longer own yourself.' Might not the sense of independence you get from simply being bossed, being scheduled and monitored by others, but not having responsibility to enforce and reproduce the system, not being responsible to force, cajole, and intimidate others – might not that be worth $13,000 less? I have talked with scores of people who think so, including some UPS drivers, and it has never occurred to me to argue with them.

Advertising executives and operations managers may take offense at this way of stereotyping them and their jobs, but such perceptions and evaluations of middle- and upper-class people are widespread among the working class, as documented in numerous social science investigations (Lamont 2000; Bettie 2014; Stephens et al. 2012; Stephens et al. 2014; Piff et al. 2012b). Working-class people with jobs could be too simplistic or outright wrong in their assessment of middle-class professionals and the way our careers can twist us into inauthenticity in our interpersonal relations. But that does not mean that there is nothing in these assessments but 'class envy' and the 'healing of class injuries' (Bettie 2014, 125–127) or a merely 'reactive identity' (Cherlin 2014, 111–113) that compensates for the shame they are thought to feel for not being successful. Instead, it may be an affirmative choice for simple integrity, either because they value integrity more than we do or because they are cynical about the more complex integrity we middle-class professionals think we can achieve, especially when we're young. In my judgement, their cynicism about complex integrity is usually too sweeping, but it's not like there's no evidence for their view. I have known and read about advertising executives, operations managers, and even sociologists who were either a little or a lot twisted by careerism. Indeed, a 2012 study in the *Proceedings of the National Academy of Sciences* found that 'higher social class predicts increased unethical behavior' (Piff et al. 2012a). As in gymnastics, we middle-class professionals should get some points for attempting the more complex, but we should at least be aware that there is more than one right way to live a life, that there are advantages and disadvantages to any culture, even ours, and that there may be profoundly legitimate reasons for folks to choose a different culture than the one we know and love.

Today the disadvantages of choosing eight hours for work, eight hours for sleep, and eight hours for what you will instead of a career are larger and stronger, and getting more so. Because I graduated from high school smack in the middle of 30 years of rising wages and expanding opportunities, I was especially aware of the value of a choice for simple integrity and preservation of self, because we talked about it as working-class teens and young adults and because my working-adult students often brought that discussion into my classrooms in later years. In current conditions I can't be sure that the choice between a job culture and a career culture is still as palpable and affirmative as it was for my generation. Logically, it would seem unlikely as steady jobs with decent wages and benefits are so much less readily available now. But I still see working adults with sturdy job cultures all around me. I think they often exaggerate how terribly corrupting having a career can be, but I still often witness the same ingenuity in living a job life even as the work is less steady and not paid as well as it used to be.

Of one thing I'm sure: careers are not as readily available today as most middle-class professionals think, and forcing, cajoling, and scaring all young people into college tracks and college is a fool's errand. Barely more than one in five US jobs today require at least a bachelor's degree, the document required for entry into most careers. And while that proportion is growing, there will only be one of four such jobs 20 years from now (Metzgar 2014). By this measure, the vast majority will still have jobs, not careers. For them, a 'taking it' job culture that frees up the rest of life for what you will makes a lot of sense if, and only if, we can get back to the kind of steadily increasing wages and decreasing work time the US had for the 30 years after World War II when unions were strong and productivity gains were shared with workers.

But as conditions in the working class are steadily eroding, dramatically increased by periodic economic collapses like those in the early 1980s and late 2000s, the professional middle class is not untouched. Those deteriorating conditions are coming our way, and some have already arrived, as we can see with the rise of contingent academic labor and other forms of short-term contract work for even the most highly skilled professionals (Kusnet 2008; Weil 2014). And it's not just economics. As the gap continues to widen between their and our life conditions and life chances, our fear of falling intensifies as the fall becomes steeper and scarier, if not for us then for our children and grandchildren (Ehrenreich 1990). As more of us are forced into defensive crouches, middle-class professionalism can turn into its opposite – less and less about achieving and becoming and more and more about preserving our privileges so we can pass them on to our progeny. My guess is that jobs and careers – the waged and the salaried – stand and fall together, not all at the same time, but like erosion followed by an avalanche.

It is an act of generosity that so many of our professional big thinkers seek to share our cultural capital with the poor and working classes by using that great equalizer, education at all levels, to help them and especially their children become more like us (Putnam 2015; Cherlin 2014; Reeves 2017). Despite this generous impulse, however, such approaches cannot work, for two big reasons. First, there are not and will not be enough jobs requiring our kinds of social and cultural capital, not enough professional jobs with possibilities for careers. Most of the work that needs done in our society – cleaning, cooking, caring, clerking, moving and making things, selling, waiting, and guarding (Bureau 2016) – does not require much education, and people who do that work generally do it simply to earn a living. What they most need is not our cultural capital, but steady work, much more income, and increasing amounts of free time for what you will. Secondly, they have their own cultural capital and, though open to and often hungry for education, they have a strong tendency to resent and resist the kinds of cultural capital we're trying to sell them. Sometimes this resistance is irrational and unproductive, especially from a professional perspective that tends to see the potential of only one individual at a time, but mostly it is based on a strong attachment to the culture they already have, a realistic appreciation of how it works in their lives, what they value more than we seem to, and a gut-level wish not to be like us.

If free wage labor has divided itself, or been divided, into jobs and careers with distinct class cultures, as I have come to believe, then it would be important to recognize that. If middle-class professionals go on treating working people as if they are just underdeveloped versions of ourselves, it will just continue to piss them off, often mixed with dangerous levels of ethnic, racial, and nativist resentments as economic conditions get worse. But if we realize how much we depend on them and how much they depend on cultural dispositions different from ours, we might just recognize how much a job culture of being and belonging might offer us, especially in midlife as most of us run out of potential to achieve and become. We might also come to political accommodations that would enable us, together, to mount the kind of strong countervailing force to our ruling class that would provide the economic base for both class cultures to flourish once again.

Notes

1 Like *Habits*, Rakesh Khurana traces a declension narrative from management as a professional calling to a merely utilitarian career (Khurana 2007). Jennifer Silva (2013) finds working-class young people adopting a hand-me-down version of the middle-class mainstream's therapeutic culture, as *Habits* would expect. Claude Fischer, on the other hand, is more positive than *Habits* about middle-class individualism, which he says affirms the importance of community while insisting on 'the freedom to choose one's community': 'What is most notable about America is not radical individualism, the principle of going it alone, but voluntarism, the principle that individuals choose with whom they go' (Fischer 2010, 98).

2 Harris Interactive does a large national workplace survey, which it considers proprietary information, but Career Vision's headline summary of Harris, at https://careervision.org/job-satisfaction-statistics/, reports that only 45 percent of American workers are satisfied with their jobs.

3 Pay Scale has average UPS wages and salaries at www.payscale.com/research/US/Employer=United_Parcel_Service_(UPS)%2C_Inc./Salary.

References

Arnold, A. (2014) *Fueling the Gilded Age: Railroads, Miners, and Disorder in Pennsylvania Coal County*, New York, New York University Press.

Bellah, R., Madsen, R., Sullivan, W., Swidler, A. and Tipton, S. (1996) *Habits of the Heart: Individualism and Commitment in American Life*, Berkeley, University of California Press.

Bettie, J. (2014) *Women without Class: Girls, Race, and Identity*, Berkeley, University of California Press.

Bureau of Labor Statistics (2016) 'Occupations with the Most Job Growth, 2014 and Projected 2024' at www.bls.gov/emp/ep_table_104.htm.

Cherlin, A. (2014) *Labor's Love Lost: The Rise and Fall of the Working-Class Family in America*, New York, Russell Sage Foundation.

DeMott, B. (1990) *The Imperial Middle: Why Americans Can't Think Straight About Class*, New Haven, Yale University Press.

Dews, C. L. and Law, C. (eds.) (1995) *This Fine Place So Far from Home: Voices of Academics from the Working Class*, Philadelphia, Temple University Press.

Ehrenreich, B. (1990) *Fear of Falling: The Inner Life of the Middle Class*, New York, HarperCollins.

Fischer, C. (2010) *Made in America: A Social History of American Culture and Character*, Chicago, University of Chicago Press.

Hurst, A. and Nenga, S. (eds.) (2016) *Working in Class: Recognizing How Social Class Shapes Our Academic Work*, New York, Rowman & Littlefield.

Jensen, B. (1997) 'Becoming Versus Belonging: Psychology, Speech, and Social Class,' paper presented at Youngstown State University Working-Class Studies Conference, available on *Class Matters* website at www.classmatters.org/2004_04/becoming_vs_belonging.php.

Jensen, B. (2012) *Reading Classes: On Culture and Classism in America*, Ithaca, Cornell University Press.

Khurana, R. (2007) *From Higher Aims to Hired Hands: The Social Transformation of American Business Schools and the Unfulfilled Promise of Management as a Profession*, Princeton, Princeton University Press.

Kusnet, D. (2008) *Love the Work, Hate the Job: Why America's Best Workers Are Unhappier Than Ever*, Hoboken, NJ, Wiley & Sons.

Lamont, M. (2000) *The Dignity of Working Men: Morality and the Boundaries of Race, Class, and Immigration*, New York, Russell Sage Foundation.

Martin, L. (2015) *Smokestacks in the Hills: Rural-Industrial Workers in West Virginia*, Urbana, University of Illinois Press.

Metzgar, J. (2000) *Striking Steel: Solidarity Remembered*, Philadelphia, Temple University Press.

Metzgar, J. (2014) 'Our Overeducated Workforce: Who Benefits?' at *Working-Class Perspectives* blog, https://workingclassstudies.wordpress.com/2014/09/29/our-overeducated-workforce-who-benefits/

Piff, P., Stancato, D., Cote, S., Mendoza-Denton, R. and Keltner, D. (2012a) 'Higher Social Class Predicts Increased Unethical Behavior,' *Proceedings of the National Academy of Sciences*, 109, 11, pp. 4086–4091.

Piff, P., Stancato, D., Martinez, A., Kraus, M. and Keltner, D. (2012b) 'Class, Chaos, and the Construction of Community,' *Journal of Personality and Social Psychology*, 103, 6, pp. 949–962.

Putnam, R. (2015) *Our Kids: The American Dream in Crisis*, New York, Simon & Schuster.

Reeves, R. (2017) *Dream Hoarders: How the American Upper Middle Class Is Leaving Everyone Else in the Dust, Why that Is a Problem, and What to Do about It*, Washington, DC, Brookings Institution Press.

Rotundo, E. A. (1993) *American Manhood: Transformations in Masculinity from the Revolution to the Modern Era*, New York, Basic Books.

Ryan, J. and Sackrey, C. (eds.) (1984) *Strangers in Paradise: Academics from the Working Class*, Boston, South End Press.

Silva, J. (2013) *Coming Up Short: Working-Class Adulthood in an Age of Uncertainty*, Oxford, Oxford University Press.

Stearns, P. (1994) *American Cool: Constructing a Twentieth-Century Emotional Style*, New York, New York University Press.

Stephens, N., Cameron, J. and Townsend, S. (2014) 'Lower Social Class Does Not (Always) Mean Greater Interdependence: Women in Poverty Have Fewer Social Resources than Working-Class Women,' *Journal of Cross-Cultural Psychology*, 45, 7, pp. 1061–1073.

Stephens, N., Fryberg, S. and Markus, H. (2012) 'It's Your Choice: How the Middle-Class Model of Independence Disadvantages Working-Class Americans' in Fiske, S. and Markus, H. (eds.) *Facing Social Class: How Societal Rank Influences Interaction*, New York, Russell Sage Foundation.

Tokarczyk, M. and Fay, E. (eds.) (1993) *Working-Class Women in the Academy: Laborers in the Knowledge Factory*, Amherst, University of Massachusetts Press.

Weil, D. (2014) *The Fissured Workplace: Why Work Became So Bad for So Many and What Can Be Done to Improve It*, Cambridge, Harvard University Press.

Williams, J. (2017) *White Working Class: Overcoming Class Cluelessness in America*, Boston, Harvard Business Review Press.

Williams, R. (1973/1980) 'Base and Superstructure in Marxist Cultural Theory,' *Problems in Materialism and Culture*, London, Verso.

Willis, P. (1977) *Learning to Labor: How Working-Class Kids Get Working-Class Jobs*, New York, Columbia University Press.

Woodard, C. (2011) *American Nations: A History of Eleven Rival Regional Cultures of North America*, New York, Viking.

17

Class, culture, and inequality

Jessi Streib

Unlike in Working-Class Studies, many people are uneasy about the idea that each class has a culture. As individuals, we like to think of ourselves as untouched by forces outside of our control. We take credit for our thoughts, tastes, and styles rather than attributing them to our social class. Many academics, too, are uncomfortable with the idea that class shapes culture. Some object to the idea because class is just one of the many social forces we encounter, intersecting with our many other identities. Others balk at the idea that classes have cultures, because individual people don't always know how to identify their social class. If people misrecognize their own class position, how can they share a culture? There is one last objection as well – perhaps the most important one. If classes have cultures, won't people who want to preserve the status quo say that it's the working-class's fault that they don't enter the middle-class? If there are cultural differences between the classes, maybe culture is to blame for inequality.

The denial of class cultures belies our experiences. The working-class student who attends a university dominated by middle- and upper-class students often undergoes culture shock. Few things feel familiar – how people talk, what they talk about, how people spend their time, or how they approach college. Similarly, the middle-class young adult who stumbles into a working-class bar won't take long to figure out that something's different. People order different drinks, talk in different tenors, and TVs broadcast different shows. Likewise, when we enter someone's home, we can often recognize that the furniture and decorations reveal the occupants' social class – something we know because we understand that tastes reflect class position. Of course, in each of these situations, the word "class" might never be used, our perceptions also intersect with our own and others' multiple identities, and the cultural indicators of class that we observe – the type of clothes people wear, the type of beer they drink, and the brand of furniture in their homes – are not the primary cause of social class inequality. Yet class cultures are there – shaping not just each group's style but also how others treat and judge them.

This chapter articulates what many of us know deep down and what Working-Class Studies emphasizes – that classes do have cultures. Our thoughts and feelings are not entirely our own but are shaped by the class into which we were born. Our class position gives us similar perspectives to others in our class, even people who differ from us in other important ways and even if we can't name our social class. However, just because there are class cultures does not mean that people at the bottom of the class hierarchy have the wrong worldviews, tastes, and values to make it to the top. Far from it. Rather, class cultures work in the reverse way. They give people at the top the license to discriminate against those at the bottom, all while feeling that their own culture is superior. Part of what Working-Class Studies does is to identify the content of these cultures and reveal how culture is used as a weapon to maintain some people's class position at the expense of others. Despite many of us thinking we are untouched by class, class cultures are real and, as Working-Class Studies scholars know all too well, so are their consequences.

What is a class culture?

Working-Class Studies scholars do not agree about the definition of culture, but many of us do agree on some starting points. Culture helps people make sense of the world and includes things like tastes (what we like and dislike), worldviews (ideas that orientate us toward the world), dispositions (habitual tendencies), and linguistic styles (how we talk) (Bourdieu 1984). To say that each class has a culture is to say that people in different classes tend to have distinct tastes, worldviews, dispositions, and linguistic styles. These distinctions are not complete – there is overlap in culture across classes – nor does culture align perfectly with people's class position. Rather, *on average*, class corresponds to how people make sense of the world.

Where do class cultures come from?

According to Bourdieu (1980, 1984), we learn our class-specific sets of tastes, dispositions, worldviews, and linguistic styles from growing up in a particular social class. Our families, as members of particular classes, teach us how to interact in the world in class-specific ways. We later enter schools that reinforce this message, then workplaces that do the same. As families, schools, and workplaces teach class-specific lessons, we become people who are shaped by our class. We become people, for example, who hang back around authority figures or approach them, who use direct language or more roundabout talk, and who want to stay in our hometowns or leave them.

Many scholars have documented the ways this occurs. Middle-class and working-class parents, on average, use different parenting styles. Middle-class parents tend to use a parenting style that sociologist Annette Lareau (2003) calls *concerted cultivation*. Parents using this style assume that their children need constant guidance and stimulation to grow into high-functioning adults. As such, they talk to their children constantly, fill their time with many adult-led activities, and teach their children how to navigate institutions. Working-class parents, on the other hand, tend to take an approach she calls *the accomplishment of natural growth*. Parents who subscribe to this style believe that children will grow up to be successful adults without endless parental interventions. Parents provide the necessities then let children decide how to use their own time. These different parenting styles produce children who think in different ways. Middle-class children, raised through concerted cultivation, come to see the need to be constantly involved in activities, to ask institutions to cater to their own needs, and to develop a sense of entitlement. Working-class children, raised through the accomplishment of natural growth, learn to go with the flow, craft their own activities, and develop a sense of constraint, especially within institutions.

In a related take on how parenting practices shape class cultures, the anthropologist Adrie Kusserow (2004) found that middle-class parents raise their children in a style of *soft individualism*. In this approach, parents consider children to be fragile. Parents then cater to their children's personal needs, offer their children constant encouragement, and nurture their children's autonomy and creativity. Working-class parents, on the other hand, tend to use a style of *hard individualism*. They believe that children are and should be tough. Parents tease and discipline their children, encourage them to abide by others' rules, and foster their children's conformity. They want to make sure their children can make it in what they see as a harsh world.

Of course, there is a reason why parents of different classes raise their children in different ways. Parents themselves live in different social worlds. Middle-class parents tend to live in environments that are safe and stable, allowing them to make plans about how to use their time, achieve their goals, and focus on their own autonomy. The jobs they hold require them to "use their words" often and allow them to change workplace rules as they see fit (Kohn 1969; Kusserow 2004; Streib 2015). Working-class parents, instead, tend to live in neighborhoods that are less safe and lead lives that are less predictable. Toughness and adaptability to external constraints helps them get by. And, in working-class parents' jobs, learning to fit oneself into the workplace structure, conform to bosses' demands, and follow rules are critical for keeping their jobs (Kohn 1969; Kusserow 2004; Metzgar 2000). Parents then teach their children the skills their children need to succeed in their environment. In doing so, they teach their children to have different dispositions and worldviews.

Schools play a role in fostering these different cultures too. Schools in working-class communities tend to focus on following rules and conforming to teachers' demands (Anyon 1981; Golann 2015). Schools in middle- and upper-class communities tend to focus more on teaching children to find solutions on their own and to generate their own ideas (Anyon 1981; Nunn 2014). Even within the same school, tracking often separates working-class and middle-class children and instills in them different dispositions (Bettie 2003; Oakes 2005). To the extent that working-class children become working-class workers and middle-class children become middle-class workers, this cycle then repeats itself. At these jobs, messages about what is important are reinforced, and parents then pass these ideas down to their children.

How cultures vary by class

How else do cultures vary by class? They vary in terms of tastes, worldviews, dispositions, and language styles.

Tastes. From food to sports to music, working-class and middle-class people tend to have different tastes. There are two different ways that tastes are organized, and social scientists still debate which is most accurate. In the first, the middle-class is likely to *distance themselves from necessity*, whereas the working-class is likely to *make a virtue of necessity*. In other words, the middle class holds tastes that show they are not working class, and the working class like what they can afford (Bourdieu 1984). In this way, the middle class is likely to enjoy salad and lobster – foods that are low-calorie, unfilling in small doses, expensive, and impractical for people who want to quell hunger on a budget. The working class, instead, tend to have a taste for foods like hotdogs, sloppy joes, and potatoes – foods that are filling and cheap (Bourdieu 1978, 1984). Similarly, the middle class tends to prefer sports that show their distance from necessity, such as golf, which requires use of expensive equipment, considerable space, and time, whereas the working class more often enjoys boxing, a sport that takes less equipment, space, and time (Bourdieu 1978). Likewise, the middle class is more likely to prefer opera – a type of music that is less accessible, as it is not broadcast from as many radio stations, whereas the working class is more likely to enjoy country music, due in part to its easy access (Lizardo and Skiles 2016).

Other social scientists find that tastes revolve around a different axis: the omnivore/univore axis. In this model, the middle class are cultural omnivores. Their tastes revolve around variety; they like all kinds of foods, sports, music, and styles, except for those that working-class people like. The working class, by contrast, are univores. They tend to like one type of food, sport, or music far more than others (Peterson and Kern 1996). For example, middle-class people tend to say they enjoy classical, jazz, oldies, pop, and rock music, but they are unlikely to say that they enjoy hip hop and heavy metal – genres they know to be associated with the working class (Lizardo and Skiles 2016). Working-class people, instead, are likely to say they prefer only one or two genres – just, say, heavy metal or country music (Bryson 1996). Similarly, middle-class people attend more sporting events in general than working-class people, but they tend to stay away from sports they perceive as working class, such as car racing. Working-class individuals, by contrast, tend to attend just one or two types of sporting events (Wilson 2002). Whether snobs or omnivores, those who make a virtue of necessity or univores, our tastes are not freely decided but are byproducts of our social class.

Worldviews. One key way that worldviews vary by social class is the extent to which individuals are individualistically or collectively oriented. Middle-class people tend to take an individualistic focus – to prioritize their own achievement, well-being, and needs (Lareau 2003; Stephens et al. 2012). They learn this from a young age. Middle-class children often experience a child-centered parenting style where children's individual needs are put first (Hays 1996; Lareau 2003). Parents pour great resources into middle-class children's achievement and happiness, crafting activities around their interests and convincing institutions to cater to their children's needs (Lareau 2003). Middle-class children learn that the goal is for them to stand out – to excel through achievements in academics, athletics, art, or music. By contrast, working-class families tend to instill in their children a more collective ethos. Parents are more likely to stress the good of the family rather than the individual, and children are likely to spend more time with family and less in achievement-related activities outside the home (Lareau 2003; Kusserow 2004). Working-class children tend to grow up not wanting to stand out, but to fit in to the group (Stephens, Markus, and Townsend 2007; Willis 1977). Working-Class Studies scholar Barbara Jensen (2012) puts this difference in a provocative way: middle-class children learn to focus on *becoming* while working-class children learn to focus on *belonging*.

As adults, these different orientations play out in many ways – from trivial to important. Based on a series of laboratory experiences, psychologists found that when asked to pick a prize, middle-class college students are more likely to choose the unique prize, whereas working-class college students pick the prize others commonly chose (Stephens, Markus, and Townsend 2007). Middle-class students are more likely to be upset if a friend chooses a car like their own – their car is a symbol of their identity and they wanted to stand out. Working-class students tend to be pleased if their friend acquires the same care they have – if the car makes them happy, it might make their friend happy too (Stephens, Markus, and Townsend 2007). In talking about their expressions of love, middle-class adults deride Hallmark cards as unoriginal; working-class adults see the cards as a heartfelt way to express feelings (Illouz 1997). More importantly, dozens of experiments have shown that middle- and working-class people tend to understand and treat people differently. Middle-class individuals tend to be less accurate than working-class people at reading others' emotions (Kraus, Côté, and Keltner 2010), less generous (James and Sharpe 2007; Piff et al. 2010), less compassionate (Stellar et al. 2011), less likely to take others' opinions into account when making decisions (Na et al. 2016), and more likely to break rules that favor themselves (Piff, Stancato, Côté et al. 2012). In addition, middle-class young adults tend to perform at higher rates when given messages about finding passions and expressing themselves – all individualistic messages – whereas working-class students perform better when exposed to messages about helping the community (Stephens et al. 2012). These differences likely reflect that people with more resources – middle-class people – do not need to be as attuned to or as helpful to others to meet their own needs, whereas people with fewer resources – working-class people – tend to need to understand and rely on others more to get by.

Dispositions. People who grow up in the working class and middle class tend to develop different ideas about how to approach situations. Studies based on interviews with people raised in different social classes have found that working-class people, who tend to grow up with fewer resources and less predictable lives, typically take a laissez-faire approach to their daily lives (Streib 2015). That is, they tend to go with the flow and take things as they come. People who grew up in the middle class, by contrast, tend to take a *managerial* approach. Having grown up with more resources and more predictable lives, they typically prefer to organize, plan, and oversee situations. As explained above, this divide maps onto parenting practices, with working-class parents preferring to let their children grow and middle-class parents preferring to manage their children's lives (Lareau 2003). It also extends to other domains. It relates to how individuals think about work (to take opportunities as they come or to plan a career trajectory), housework (to let the division of labor unfold or to plan it), leisure (to go with the flow in regard to free time or to organize activities), and even emotions (to express emotions as they are felt or to carefully mange the expression of them) (Streib 2015). The wide range of domains that are shaped by our social class highlights that class is always shaping our lives, whether we know it or not.

Language. Linguistic styles also vary by social class. Middle-class parents tend to say more words to their children compared to working-class children (Hart and Risley 1995; Heath 1983). Working-class parents also tend to give more orders ("Go to bed now"), while middle-class parents give more options ("Do you want to go to bed now or in five minutes?") and to negotiate more with their children over rules and routines (Lareau 2003; Kusserow 2004). Working-class adults also tend to speak in a more direct and concrete fashion, saying what they mean, whereas middle-class people tend to use more indirect and abstract speech (Bernstein 1974; Kusserow 2004; Leondar-Wright 2014). Moreover, working-class people tend to include more emotion in their language, whereas middle-class people are taught to hide their emotional language through rationalized and intellectualized speech (Walkerdine et al. 2001).

Why class cultures matter

Many people like to think that we celebrate our differences and respect that some people have different tastes, dispositions, worldviews, and language styles. It's a nice idea, but Working-Class Studies scholars find that most people aren't good at living up to it. The reason why class cultures matter is that they offer the middle and upper classes an advantage. Their own culture is widely viewed as superior, and they use that supposed superiority to discriminate against the working class.

There is evidence all around us that middle-class culture is generally viewed as superior to working-class culture. People talk of wanting to be "classy" – wanting to display the tastes and styles of people in higher classes. The word "isn't" is standard and the word "ain't" is considered wrong, even though we all know what both words mean and we all know that it ain't working-class people who most often say "isn't." On Facebook, 45 times more people talk about *The Atlantic*, a "middle-class" magazine, than *The National Enquirer*, a "working-class" magazine, even though 3 times as many people subscribe to the latter (Stephens-Davidowitz 2017). We hear about people who try to appreciate golf and opera; we don't hear about many people striving to appreciate NASCAR or country music. In many countries, class cultures are not only widely seen as different (when they are acknowledged at all); one is widely viewed as better than the other.

Many middle-class people use the supposed superiority of their culture to exclude working-class people. Middle-class people often accuse working-class people of being too loud, emotional, and tactless, then seek to avoid them (Bettie 2003; Lawler 2005; Walkerdine et al. 2001).

They look down on and disassociate with people they view as enjoying mass-produced goods, reality television, and uncultured vacations (Holt 1998; Illouz 1997; Skeggs et al. 2008), and they try to set themselves apart by emphasizing their own cultural sophistication (Lamont 2000). Such distinctions are based on arbitrary criteria about what is sophisticated and desirable, but they nevertheless have consequences. When middle-class people exclude working-class people from their lives, they also exclude them from their resources (Bourdieu 1984). They then don't share tips about how to get ahead in school or tell each other which employers are hiring. Increasingly, middle-class adults are also refusing to marry working-class adults – not sharing their wealth and connections with people from another class (Mare 2016).

Institutions also enforce this hierarchy and thereby provide different opportunities for different people. In preschools, teachers treat middle-class linguistic styles as normal. They reward students who "use their words," negotiate, and demand help. These children then receive more attention and help than working-class children, who are more likely to wait to talk until spoken to and to defer to authority rather than negotiate (Streib 2011). In preschool, 4-year-olds who express soft individualism are viewed by teachers as smart and creative, whereas students who express hard individualism are viewed as less intelligent troublemakers (Kusserow 2004). In elementary school, teachers view children who participate in many organized extracurricular activities as smarter than those who don't (Dumais et al. 2012). In high school, teachers view middle-class girls' interactional style and language style as superior to that of working-class girls, and then see middle-class girls as better students (Bettie 2003). In college, professors view the writing style of middle-class students as intelligent and the writing style of working-class students as unsophisticated (Bourdieu 1989; Linkon 1999; McMillian et al. 1998). Out of college, elite firms are more likely to hire graduates involved in expensive extracurricular activities like squash, crew, and orchestra than graduates who worked for pay or participated in more accessible clubs (Rivera 2015; Rivera and Tilcsik 2016). And, of course, selective colleges' preference for students involved in a variety of extracurricular activities tilts the playing field toward the middle class (Stevens 2007).

The middle-class's exclusion of working-class people from their networks and institutions maintains inequality. Working-class people struggle to get ahead as middle-class people and institutions judge their tastes, worldviews, dispositions, and language styles as not only different but worse (Bettie 2003; Bourdieu 1984, 1989). Middle-class individuals, for their part, do not typically understand that part of their economic success stems from being raised in the culture that is more rewarded by schools and employers. They think that the world is fairer than it is, and many take great credit for their own success (Hunt and Bullock 2016; Kluegel and Smith 1986).

Some might still say that it's the working class's fault for not getting ahead, even if it's the middle class who does the excluding. They would say that if the working class really wanted to earn more or get more education, they could assimilate into the middle class. There are several problems with this argument. For one, the evidence shows that it's not easy to change class cultures (Bourdieu 1984; Karp 1986; Streib 2015). As outsiders to other classes, we don't always have the information about what culture other classes reward, and even when we do, it's not easy to change. Changing your language style, dispositions, worldviews, and tastes is like changing your accent. Over time and with a lot of work, you can make progress, but it may never seem natural, and insiders will always know that you weren't born where they were. Change just isn't that easy.

Perhaps more importantly, blaming working-class people's culture for not allowing them to get ahead only makes sense under a series of faulty assumptions. Cultural commentators tend to start from the assumption that the working class has fewer resources than the middle class *because* of their culture. They then skew their vision to reflect their conclusion, focusing only on the positive aspects of middle-class culture and the negative aspects of working-class culture. Doing so sets themselves up to believe that the working class is responsible for its class position and the middle class is deserving of theirs (Murray 2013; Vance 2016). Of course, this overlooks all the ways that working-class culture – if recognized by middle-class people – could be beneficial to their mobility. Care about integrity? Working-class people say they care more about it than do middle-class people, and the evidence suggests that they are more honest too (Lamont 2000; Piff, Stancato, Martinez et al. 2012). Care about having strong group dynamics? Working-class people tend to have experiences that make them better at working in teams (Brienza and Grossman 2017; Piff et al. 2010; Snibbe and Markus 2005). Think it's good to have someone who can stay calm in the midst of change or who is skilled at forseeing structural barriers? Working-class people often outshine middle-class people on these tasks as well (Chiraag et al. 2015; Kraus et al. 2012). In other words, working-class culture is full of traits that could be associated with getting ahead if only people with power recognized, valued, and sought them out. The argument that working-class people's culture is what locks them in a lower class only works by systematically ignoring the parts of working-class culture that would seem to help their mobility – a shaky premise for an argument.

Along the same lines, commentators tend to ignore that many differences in class cultures are arbitrary. That is, can we really argue that having two forks on the table is better than one, or that wine is better than whiskey? And, even if one is better than the other, are the differences so important as to exclude another group because of it? It surely seems that people who exclude others based on these criteria are more interested in shoring up their own advantages than keeping out people who are, in some way or another, actually undeserving.

Finally, the assumption that the working-class's culture causes them to stay in their class is based on an untenable assertion: that just because there are cultural differences, they *cause* class differences. In reality, some differences are not consequential for groups' class position, and other differences reflect rather than cause inequality. Give people different resources and they'll end up with different tastes and practices. Allow people to grow up with more similar resources and they'll likely have more similar cultures.

Lingering questions about class and culture

There is still room for studies of class and culture to expand and for Working-Class Studies to grow. As the world changes, we're left with many questions. For example, many places have witnessed rising inequality, social class segregation, and animosity between the classes (Autor 2014; Pew Charitable Trusts 2009; Reardon and Bischoff 2011). At the same time, the social safety net fluctuates over time, the economy loses some types of jobs and adds others, and new ideas of gender change what economic activities are viewed as appropriate for men and women. As these changes take place, the content of class cultures will likely change too. We need to keep studying what working-class and middle-class cultures consist of and how new similarities and differences among the classes emerge.

In addition, Working-Class Studies scholarship needs to become more attentive to how local environments shape class cultures. How does working-class culture in one part of a country differ from working-class culture in another part? And how do each differ from class cultures in other countries? And, more importantly, what conditions create similarities and differences across places? Understanding the extent to which class cultures vary across place can reveal important insights about whether there are universal responses to living with limited resources or if each class culture develops in response to the particularities of each place.

Future Working-Class Studies scholars can also study how changes in the *evaluations* of class cultures take place. That is, can segments of the middle class learn to revise their standards of merit, to recognize some differences as arbitrary, and to see the value of parts of working-class culture? And, if some individuals can do this, can schools and workplaces introduce programs to reduce the extent to which their employees discriminate by class? And what distinguishes the institutions that are interested and successful at making these changes from the institutions that are not?

Finally, having one's culture stigmatized can have important implications for mental health (Sennett and Cobb 1972). We need to know more about how some working-class people resist and push back against societal forces that position their culture as inferior, and why other working-class people instead internalize that middle-class ways are better than their own. We also need to understand if the cultural aspects of living in an unequal society have implications for physical health. The stress of living among middle-class people who judge working-class people for their language, tastes, and worldviews may lead to real health disparities. Just how class gets "under the skin" and into our bodies requires further study.

As Working-Class Studies moves forward, we'll have the opportunity to answer these questions. Doing so will continue to require a comparative approach – of how working-class culture compares to the culture of other classes – as well as sustained attention to the variation in working-class culture across time, place, and subgroups. For now, we can say that it's time to get past the common idea that classes do not have cultures. They do, and the judgements those in power make about them matter for who gets and stays ahead.

References

Anyon, J. (1981). 'Social Class and School Knowledge,' *Curriculum Inquiry* 11, 1, pp. 3–42.

Autor, D. (2014) 'Skills, Education, and the Rise of Earnings Inequality Among the "Other 99 Percent,"' *Science* 344, pp. 843–851.

Bernstein, B. (1974) *Class, Codes and Control, Volume 3: Towards a Theory of Educational Transmissions*, New York, Routledge.

Bettie, J. (2003) *Women Without Class: Girls, Race, and Identity*, Berkeley, University of California Press.

Bourdieu, P. (1978) 'Sport and Social Class,' *Social Science Information* 17, 6, pp. 819–840.

Bourdieu, P. (1980) *The Logic of Practice*, Cambridge, MA, Polity Press.

Bourdieu, P. (1984) *Distinction: A Social Critique of the Judgment of Taste,* Cambridge, MA, Harvard University Press.

Bourdieu, P. (1989) *The State Nobility*, Palo Alto, Stanford University Press.

Brienza, J., and Grossman, I. (2017) 'Social Class and Wise Reasoning about Interpersonal Conflicts across Regions, Persons and Situations,' *Proceedings of the Royal Society* B, pp. 284–292.

Bryson, B. (1996) 'Anything but Heavy Metal: Symbolic Exclusion and Musical Dislikes,' *American Sociological Review* 61, 5, pp. 884–899.

Chiraag M., Griskevicius, V., Simpson, J., Sung, S., and Young, E. (2015) 'Cognitive Adaptations to Stressful Environments: When Childhood Adversity Enhances Adult Executive Function,' *Journal of Personality and Social Psychology* 109, 4, pp. 604–621.

Dumais, S., Kessinger, R., III, and Ghosh, B. (2012) 'Concerted Cultivation and Teachers' Evaluations of Students: Exploring the Intersection of Race and Parents' Educational Attainment,' *Sociological Perspectives* 55, 1, pp. 17–42.

Golann, J. (2015) 'The Paradox of Success at a No-Excuses School,' *Sociology of Education* 88, 2, pp. 103–119.

Hart, B., and Risley, T. (1995) *Meaningful Differences in the Everyday Experiences of Young American Children*, Baltimore, Paul H. Brookes Publishing Co.

Hays, S. (1996) *The Cultural Contradictions of Motherhood*, New Haven, Yale University Press.

Heath, S.B. (1983) *Ways with Words: Language, Life, and Work in Communities and Classrooms*, New York, Cambridge University Press.

Holt, D. (1998) 'Does Cultural Capital Structure American Consumption?' *Journal of Consumer Research* 25, 1, pp. 1–25.

Hunt, M. and Bullock, H. (2016) Ideologies and Beliefs about Poverty,' Brady, D., and Burton, L. (eds.), *Oxford Handbook of Poverty and Society*, New York, Oxford University Press.

Illouz, E. (1997) *Consuming the Romantic Utopia: Love and the Cultural Contradictions of Capitalism*, Berkeley, University of California Press.

James, R., III, and Sharpe, R. (2007) 'The Nature and Causes of the U-Shaped Charitable Giving Profile,' *Nonprofit and Voluntary Sector Quarterly* 36, pp. 218–238.

Jensen, B. (2012) *Reading Classes: On Culture and Classism in America*, Ithica, ILR Press.

Karp, D. (1986) '"You Can Take the Boy Out of Dorchester, But You Can't Take Dorchester Out of the Boy": Toward a Social Psychology of Mobility,' *Symbolic Interactionism* 9, 1, pp. 19–36.

Kluegel, J., and Smith, E. (1986) *Beliefs About Inequality: Americans' Views of What Is and What Ought to Be*, New York, Routledge.

Kohn, M. (1969). *Class and Conformity: A Study in Values*, Homewood, IL, Dorsey Press.

Kraus, M., Côté, S., and Keltner, D. (2010) 'Social Class, Contextualism, and Empathic Accuracy,' *Psychological Science* 21, 11, pp. 1716–1723.

Kraus, M., Piff, P., Mendoza-Denton, R., Rheinschmidt, M., and Keltner, D. (2012) 'Social Class, Solipsism, and Contextualism: How the Rich are Different from the Poor,' *Psychological Review* 112, 3, pp. 546–572.

Kusserow, A. (2004) *American Individualisms: Child Rearing and Social Class*, New York, Palgrave MacMillan.

Lamont, M. (2000) *The Dignity of Working Men: Morality and the Boundaries of Race, Class, and Immigration*, Cambridge, MA, Harvard University Press.

Lareau, A. (2003) *Unequal Childhoods: Class, Race, and Family Life*, Berkeley, University of California Press.

Lawler, S. (2005) 'Disgusted Subjects: The Making of Middle-Class Identities,' *The Sociological Review* 53, 3, pp. 429–446.

Leondar-Wright, B. (2014) *Missing Class: Strengthening Social Movement Groups by Seeing Class Cultures*, Ithaca, Cornell University Press.

Linkon, S. (1999) *Teaching Working Class*, Amherst, University of Massachusetts Press.

Lizardo, O., and Skiles, S. (2016) 'Cultural Objects as Prisms: Perceived Audience Composition of Musical Genres as a Resource for Symbolic Exclusion,' *Socius* 2, pp. 1–17.

Mare, R. (2016) 'Educational Homogamy in Two Gilded Ages: Evidence from Inter-Generational Social Mobility Data,' *The ANNALS of the American Academy of Political and Social Science* 663, 1, pp. 117–139.

McMillian, J., Shepard, A., and Tate, G. (1998) *Coming to Class: Pedagogy and the Social Class of Teachers*, Portsmouth, NH, Heinemann.

Metzgar, J. (2000) *Striking Steel: Solidarity Remembered*, Philadelphia, Temple University Press.

Murray, C. (2013) *Coming Apart: The State of White America, 1960–2000*, New York, Crown Forum.

Oakes, J. (2005) *Keeping Track: How Schools Structure Inequality*, New Haven, Yale University Press.

Na, J., McDonough, I., Chan, M., and Park, D. (2016) 'Social-Class Differences in Consumer Choices: Working-Class Individuals Are More Sensitive to Choices of Others than Middle-Class Individuals,' *Personality and Social Psychology Bulletin* 42, 4, pp. 430–443.

Nunn, L. (2014) *Defining School Success: The Role of School and Culture*, New Brunswick, Rutgers University Press.

Peterson, R., and Kern, R. (1996) 'Changing Highbrow Taste: From Snob to Omnivore,' *American Sociological Review* 61, 5, 900–907.

Pew Charitable Trusts. (2009) Findings from a National Survey & Focus Groups on Economic Mobility, Washington DC. www.pewtrusts.org/~/media/legacy/uploadedfiles/wwwpewtrustsorg/reports/economic_mobility/emp20200920survey20on20economic20mobility20for20print2031209pdf.pdf

Piff, P., Kraus, M., Keltner, D., Côté, S., and Cheng, B.H. (2010) 'Having Less, Giving More: The Influence of Social Class on Prosocial Behavior,' *Journal of Personality and Social Psychology* 99, 5, pp. 771–784.

Piff, P., Stancato, D., Côté, S., Mendoza-Denton, R., and Keltner, D. (2012) 'Higher Social Class Predicts Increased Unethical Behavior,' *Proceedings of the National Academy of Sciences* 109, 11, pp. 4086–4091.

Piff, P., Stancato, D., Martinez, A., Kraus, M., and Keltner, D. (2012) 'Class, Chaos, and the Construction of Community,' *Journal of Personality and Social Psychology* 103, 6, pp. 949–962.

Reardon, S., and Bischoff, K. (2011) 'Income Inequality and Income Segregation,' *American Journal of Sociology* 116, 4, pp. 1092–1153.

Rivera, L. (2015) *Pedigree: How Elite Students Get Elite Jobs*, Princeton, Princeton University Press.

Rivera, L., and Tilcsik, A. (2016) 'Class Advantage, Commitment Penalty: The Gendered Effect of Social Class Signals in an Elite Labor Market,' *American Sociological Review* 81, 6, pp. 1097–1131.

Sennett, R., and Cobb, J. (1972) *The Hidden Injuries of Class*, New York, W.W. Norton & Company.

Skeggs, B., Thumim, N., and Wood, H. (2008) '"Oh Goodness, I *Am* Watching Reality TV": How Methods Make Class in Audience Research,' *European Journal of Cultural Studies* 11, 1, pp. 5–24.

Snibbe, A., and Markus, H.R. (2005) 'You Can't Always Get What You Want: Educational Attainment, Agency, and Choice,' *Journal of Personality and Social Psychology* 88, pp. 703–720.
Stellar, J., Manzo, V., Kraus, M., and Keltner, D. (2011) 'Class and Compassion: Socioeconomic Factors Predict Responses to Suffering,' *Emotion* 12, 3, pp. 449–459.
Stephens, N., Fryberg, S., Markus, H.R., Johnson, C., and Covarrubias, R. (2012) 'Unseen Disadvantage: How American Universities' Focus on Independence Undermines the Academic Performance of First-Generation College Students,' *Journal of Personality and Social Psychology* 102, 6, pp. 1178–1197.
Stephens, N., Markus, H.R., and Townsend, S. (2007) 'Choice as an Act of Meaning: The Case of Social Class,' *Journal of Personality and Social Psychology* 93, 5, pp. 814–830.
Stephens-Davidowitz, S. (2017) *Everybody Lies: Big Data, New Data, and What the Internet Can Tell Us About Who We Really Are*, New York, HarperCollins.
Stevens, M. (2007) *Creating a Class: College Admissions and the Education of Elites*, Cambridge, Harvard University Press.
Streib, J. (2011) 'Class Reproduction by Four Year Olds,' *Qualitative Sociology* 34, 2, pp. 337–352.
Streib, J. (2015) *The Power of the Past: Understanding Cross-Class Marriages*, New York, Oxford University Press.
Vance, J.D. (2016) *Hillbilly Elegy: A Memoir of a Family and Culture in Crisis*, New York, Harper.
Walkerdine, V., Lucey, H., and Melody, J. (2001) *Growing Up Girl: Psychosocial Explorations of Gender and Class*, New York, New York University Press.
Willis, P. (1977) *Learning to Labor: How Working-Class Kids Get Working-Class Jobs*, New York, Columbia University Press.
Wilson, T. (2002) 'The Paradox of Social Class and Sports Involvement: The Roles of Cultural and Economic Capital,' *International Review for the Sociology of Sport* 37, 1, pp. 5–16.

18

Post-traumatic lives

Precarious employment and invisible injury

Barbara Jensen

'I'll kill myself if I have to do this for the rest of my life', Lucy threatened. She had tears of despair and frustration running down her cheeks, spilling onto her Nine Inch Nails t-shirt. She wiped them angrily away, disgusted with herself for 'giving in' to her despair. Lucy is a very bright and poor young woman. In the alternative high school where I counsel teenagers two days a week, she became part of a group of young intellectuals. People respected her sensitivity, her creative writing, her piercing critiques of society. She came to replace shame with pride for the African American part of herself and to develop the beginnings of an original and courageous theory of the particulars of mixed-race Americans. Two years later she was spending her time applying her considerable intelligence to the creative task of how to commit suicide without hurting people who love her.

She spends her days ringing up items on a cash register in a drug store. At first she tried to engage her customers with her witty conversations. 'I don't even exist to them! I might as well be some idiot that can't do anything but run a stupid cash register!' Recently, she was put on job probation by the manager. She had quizzed then debated with a man who had come in to buy film. Why had he had 'Dr.' printed on his checks, she wanted to know.

'I have a doctorate in American Studies', he said. 'I'm proud of that'.

'Don't you think other people work hard, too, even if they never get any degrees awarded to them?! Don't you think that as an African American poor woman I know more than you about American experience?' Lucy retorted.

'As a matter of fact, I don't', he replied curtly. 'And I'd like my film, please'.

It degenerated from there.

Lucy visited me in the late 1990s, two years after her triumphant graduation from high school, and told me this story. As I was the school's counsellor, she had seen me often. Lucy had survived sexual abuse as a child and the death of her mother at an early age. Classmates had bullied her during primary school for being mixed race, and a resentful older sister bullied her at home. Lucy was a tough cookie with a soft heart and a quick mind, but haunted by depression and post-traumatic stress disorder (PTSD). She was determined to be resilient. Every session ended with some version of, 'I'm not letting these fools get me down. No way!' I wrote about her then, after a promising high school experience, to illustrate the difference in life trajectories for working- and middle-class teenagers. At that point, Lucy still thought of herself as part of a group of radical intellectuals, who had by then already begun their college careers via support from their middle-class parents. Lucy delayed school to work full time to support herself.

This chapter is about harmful psychological effects of working-class work and social status. Lucy's experience mirrors the decline in opportunity for working-class people in the U.S. It also illustrates the psychological injuries of working-class work, particularly in the age of precarious employment. Though I have praised qualities of working-class cultures (Jensen 1998, 2004, 2012), this chapter compares the human consequences of precarious employment with the psychology of learned helplessness, cognitive dissonance, and class-prejudice on working-class strivers like Lucy. Cultures are dynamic and they change over time. New working-class studies arose in the midst of this decline and continues to map new terrain as an amalgam of labor studies, literature studies, political theory, feminism, economics, art, theatre, music, and more. Defined as the study of 'lived experience', working-class studies strives to hear the voices of those disenfranchised by social and economic class. When working-class studies first began in the early nineties, my contribution was to show working-class inner (and outer) life included crucial cultural differences from the professional middle class. A cultural approach has expanded since that time, perhaps ironically, as the working-class lives (and culture) I once described have changed dramatically in the 20 plus years of new working-class studies. In this historical moment, working-class work (and life) is increasingly infused with instability and economic hardship.

When work hurts

Lucy embodied some of the best qualities working-class culture gives: guts; straight talk; the merging of complex ideas with life stories; her kindness toward others; her passion to repair the world. I was somewhat like her in my high school: an organic, working-class intellectual; eager to blossom into a life of the mind, but in a very different historical moment (1960s and 1970s). As a psychologist, I write about inner life, but I would miss the forest for the trees if I ignored the simple fact that Lucy hated her work life and was miserable doing it. Bright and ambitious, she spent her days ringing up drug store items on a cash register, fetching cigarettes and boxes of film.

In 1986, when I wrote my thesis on counselling working-class people, I found a pervasive attitude of negativity toward working-class clients. Curious why everything I liked about working-class life seemed invisible, I set out to show healthy, humane aspects of working-class psychology and cultures. I treasure the working-class people and culture I came from: the stories, humor, loyalty, teamwork, music and much more. But if working-class life has a culture(s) of its own, then it is a colonized culture. There is the uncle who could never walk right after that work accident, the neighbor who lost a whole finger at work, the crippling arthritis Auntie has from spending 40 to 50 hours a week on her feet for 45 years. These are the ruins and scars left behind by the conquerors.

In the 1970s and 1980s, I was examining cultural differences and prejudice, when income from good working-class jobs still overlapped with middle-class, white-collar jobs in the U.S. Working-class work was still a mixture of well-paid, unionized work (nearly 40% unionized, particularly white men) and unstable, low-control/high-demand work (women of all colors, black and brown men) (Lerner 1986; Benach et al. 2014). In a classed society, working-class people – of all ethnicities and colors – are colonized people by definition: it is their job in life to do the dirty or menial work for the higher classes.

In this sense, class itself is the enemy of equality, but within a well-regulated state that values equal opportunity, a lower social status can be (was) greatly mitigated for at least a large segment of the population. A hundred years of labor organizing and collective bargaining won the

American working class high enough wages to turn formerly dangerous, dirty factory work into good jobs. With union representation came higher wages, health care, retirement pensions, sick pay, seniority, vacation pay, and federal regulations to curb toxic exposure and other work-related dangers (mainly for white men). America was thriving. A majority of Americans were able then to be raised in stable working-class neighborhoods where people took pride in their (still dirty and difficult) work and enjoyed rich lives outside the workplace. The 2014 *Annual Review of Public Health*, on precarious employment, reported that this period of American history was characterized by the 'standard employment contract', which meant permanent, full-time, and year-round employment with generous benefits. In addition, there was the right to collective representation, legal restraints against arbitrary firing, minimum wages, nonwage benefits, and pensions for retirement years (Benach et al. 2014, 231).

This life became less and less possible in the last two decades of the 20th century as deregulation and tax cuts for the wealthy transferred a 70% increase in wealth to the upper quintile of our population, while the bottom three quintiles started falling. The 21st century has only escalated this trend, and inequality has gotten much greater (Zweig 2012). As the percentage of unionization fell, so did the standards and safety provisions put in place for workers in manual and skilled labor. Over time, wages dropped dramatically. To better view these changes, I turn to sociologist Lillian Rubin (1976, 1994) on working-class families. She concluded life had become considerably worse for working-class families in those decades. Both parents had to work full time; unable to afford child care, many couples worked opposite shifts. Partners barely saw each other, and this left marriages and family life to decay. As Rubin put it: 'Nothing exemplifies the change in the twenty years since I last studied working class families more than the fear of "being on the street"' (1994, 114).

Things have only deteriorated since 1994. Ten years later, British epidemiologist Michael Marmot (2004) documented the effect of social class – and class inequality in particular – on physical health. He found that lower-status jobs increased the risk of heart disease, lung cancer, stroke and other serious medical conditions. Filtering out other variables, Marmot found that higher-status, higher-paid people were much healthier than lower-status, poorly-paid people. Marmot measures status by relative amounts of personal power and control over one's work life. In my counselling and community work over the last four decades, I have also seen that improvements in levels of power and control in the workplace lead to self-confidence, initiative, and a greater sense of personal power in one's non-working life. But this is not the current trend.

By 2017, Sweet and Meiksins found that working-class people either barely get by, or they simply do not. Forty years of decline in wages, worker control, and available jobs has devastated the American working class. Millions of jobs have gone missing. Millions of Americans have lost their homes. Millions have lost much or all of their retirement accounts. Families have unravelled. Suicides have skyrocketed as has obesity, hypertension, cancer, heart disease, alcoholism, drug abuse, and more (Case and Deaton, 2017). American global-capitalists have hired illegal workers in the U.S. to circumvent hard-won labor laws. These capitalists vilify these same employees of color to get elected! Their corporations move manufacturing wherever labor is cheapest, showing no loyalty to American workers that helped build their empires; they ship miserable working conditions around the globe. Meanwhile, American workers are replacing well-paying, productive, unionized jobs with stocking shelves at Walmart and Target (Sweet and Meiskins 2017, 66). These changes have nearly erased those protections and benefits that only lasted about 35 years of American history.

Precarious employment is the trend. It involves short-term work contracts, arbitrary firing and hiring, compulsory overtime (without overtime pay); little or no health care; part-time employment (to get around having to offer benefits), toxic exposures and a rollback of worker safety measures (Standing 2011, 2016). And all this for wages so low one can live in poverty even with multiple jobs. Again, the 2014 *Annual Review of Public Health* found exactly what Lucy discovered in her life.

> [P]recarious jobs may limit workers' control over their professional and personal lives, leading to psychosocial stress. ... [This is then] related to experiences of job insecurity, feelings of betrayal and injustice ... feelings of powerlessness and being out of control, lack of future opportunities, or denial of a[n] [occupational] identity, which is an essential social role.
>
> *(Benach et al. 2014, 241–242)*

On-the-job training in learned helplessness

In the toxic inequality of the 21st century, Lucy lost her job and couldn't find one that would give her the flexibility to attend college. She started attending the University of Minnesota a couple times, then dropped out to earn a living – just enough to leave her with debt she couldn't pay. She found meaning in music and a community centered in a local cafe. By the time Lucy was in her thirties, she fell into a desperate, anxious depression and then street drugs and petty crime, issues she had successfully avoided in school while excelling academically. She had learned helplessness: first in her childhood, as a victim of abuse, then as a young adult unable to follow her dream of college and career. As Lucy's story shows, researchers have found that mental health is the most rapidly deteriorating effect of precarious employment (Benach et al. 2014, 239).

To this counselling psychologist and working-class studies scholar, descriptions of the effects of precarious employment bear striking similarity to the psychological phenomena called learned helplessness, common in people mistreated in situations where they have no control. Learned helplessness theory provides a deeper glimpse into invisible injuries in working-class psychology. I draw briefly on the work of two men, pioneer Martin Seligman and Mario Mikulincer, who takes a different approach from Seligman's. Both contend that learned helplessness consists of three interlocked elements: an environment where crucial goals are beyond one's control; the psychological act of giving up; and then the ongoing belief that nothing they do can change things (Seligman 1992, xvii).

How does this relate to work life? As psychologist Michael Lerner pointed out, low-control/high-demand work is the kind that most often leads to a losing a sense of personal control, and to a pervasive sense of powerlessness in general. This then engenders self-blame and self-hatred (1986). Lerner said that therapy 'does not eliminate the need to deal with Real Powerlessness, as manifested in the lack of control that working people have at the workplace' (1986, 49). Lucy didn't come to see me when she was at her worst, but I can't imagine what I could have done to help her. As a psychotherapist, it is painfully clear to me that powerlessness in the workplace cannot be changed by individual therapy, or 'self-helped' away. Repeated exposure to situations that are low control/high demand, where real powerlessness is experienced, leads to learned helplessness. Precarious workers risk much higher exposure to low-control/high-demand jobs with forced speed-ups, working while sick, rigid and arbitrary schedules, and much more. As if that weren't enough – due to their unpredictable work schedules, the need for multiple jobs to get by, and often single-parenting – these workers can experience a crushing social isolation, even when not at work. All of these conditions lead to deteriorating mental and psychosocial health (Benach et al. 2014, 241–242).

Let me be clear, working class people are not delicate or frail. They are tough and resilient, and, generally, the last people to admit they have been victimized. But there is only so much a person can withstand, particularly without social support. By the time Lucy finally collapsed in a psychiatric ward, she could not see any future for herself. She has been on a series of antidepressants ever since. I thought about her as I read research on the effect of long-term deprivation in early life and learning helplessness. Researchers found that the more deprived of basic needs (like safety) one's life has been, the more easily learned helplessness takes hold later in life. They underlined inadequate emotional and motivational experiences in daily life and found that such a personal history, combined with current helplessness, quickly produced a psychological sense of incompetence and ineffectiveness, which then led to a generalized sense of helplessness, a loss of control over one's ability to create desirable outcomes, and a general 'sense of resignation and utter powerlessness' (Mal et al. 1989, 194). This work has obvious ramifications for understanding depressed and highly anxious people. My own clinical work has often been with victims of family and spousal abuse, where depression and PTSD – difficult to treat and repair – are common.

While Seligman described symptoms of major depression, Mikulincer focused on pathological anxiety like PTSD, generalized anxiety disorder, and the emergence of multiple clinical phobias. Both researchers observed that there is a 'turning inward' after the loss of control. Often intense emotions and thoughts distract people from anything outside their heads. Learned helplessness then leads people to avoid situations (or thoughts) that remind them of their powerlessness. A negative spiral keeps such people from engaging in activities that might challenge helplessness. That feeling can generalize to other areas of life that are then also avoided and so on down the rabbit hole of depression.

I see this kind of dynamic often in counselling. People looking for work who get rejected over and over will stop looking. Likewise, people who lose multiple jobs through no fault of their own (arbitrary lay-offs, absences for a sick child) can feel helpless and stop looking. Lucy finally gave up on higher education, though I have never seen anyone so motivated. 'Together, these two emotions [depression and anxiety] *reflect the person's strong concern with an irrevocable loss* and its implications for his or her well-being' (Mikulincer 1994, 256–257, emphasis mine). In plain language, they give up. In the misery of precarious employment, how many learn to regard loss of control and meaning in work, even in their own lives, as 'irrevocable loss'? Giving up may be a relief after a race so cluttered with obstacles, never fully run. Depression can be a relief after chronic anxiety; though it can also kill you.

Though I helped to establish working-class studies as a field, and stressing cultural aspects of class experience in particular, the culture I once both treasured and left has changed dramatically due to the rise of precarious employment and the erasure of leisure time.

> 'Leisure', snorts Peter Pittman, a twenty-eight-year-old African American father of two, married for six years. 'With both of us working like we do, there's no time for anything'. Tina Mulvaney, a thirty-five-year-old white mother of two teenagers says this of her life: 'It's hard, very hard; there's no time to live or anything'.
>
> *(Rubin 1994, 96–97)*

We have had four decades of job losses due to run-away shops. Americans experience uncontrollable helplessness on the couch with no work, or they replace former jobs with the low-paid/high-demand jobs described above for half of what their fathers and grandfathers (in adjusted dollars) made just decades ago. Is it any surprise that meanness and verbal abuse of strangers has sharply risen in digital America? Is it surprising that some taunt more privileged people as useless, delicate 'snowflakes'?

In 2017, 23 years after Rubin wrote the above examples, Case and Deaton documented that white working-class people were the fastest-rising group for suicide and a host of other clinical mental, physical, and chemical dependency disorders. They specifically documented 'deaths by despair: drugs, alcohol or suicide' (Case and Deaton 2017, 408). In 1990, the 50–54 age group had a much lower rate of deaths by despair in the U.S. than their counterparts in Germany or France or Sweden (and even less than in the U.K.). Case and Deaton (2017) found that by 2014 deaths by despair had skyrocketed in the U.S., soaring high above any other nation in the developed world, while in Germany and France they had dramatically declined. In 2015 they exposed the opioid overdose crisis that was killing white working-class men in numbers never seen before (Case and Deaton 2015). By 2017 they redefined that crisis as just one part of a much larger trend of 'deaths by despair' among all Americans in that age group and linked it to economic despair. When people repeatedly find themselves out of control over the conditions of their work or their ability to find work, learned helplessness can overwhelm the will to live.

Not all working-class people experience all, or any, of these responses due to their work or the conditions of it. When work involves difficult skills that produce something that inspires pride, and thus a sense of competence and confidence, learned helplessness does not occur. I liked my work in food service (I was young and full of energy). As a waitress, then a cook, I loved the social bouncing and banter that accompanied bringing people eggs and bacon; the intricate and intimate dance of a dozen workers all quickly doing their jobs together in a small space. Jeff Torlina (2011) documented that in working-class jobs with higher status, wages, and, especially, control over their work (skilled trades for example), workers preferred their working-class jobs to middle-class ones. When Marmot filtered his social epidemiology for skilled and so-called unskilled labor, he also found workers in the trades fared far better than the majority of other working-class workers in pay, control, and power on the job, and thus in both mental and physical health (2004, 2015). What's more, as we will see, steady employment with higher pay and good benefits, even in low-control/high-demand jobs, can significantly offset learning helplessness.

But as Seligman has pointed out, 'a major consequence of experience with uncontrollable events is motivational: uncontrollable events undermine the motivation to initiate voluntary responses that control other events' (1992, 37). What was lively and vital becomes passive and numb. The once energetic young woman or man who couldn't wait to get off work to 'rock and roll' devolves into a tired, defeated lump, old at 40, who can't muster up the energy to do anything but stare at the TV. The rapid-fire programming noisily anesthetizes the weary souls who collapse in front of it at the end of the day. 'Helplessness is a disaster for organisms capable of learning that they are helpless' (Seligman 1992, 43–44). As precarious employment increasingly becomes the new normal, the conclusions of the *Annual Review of Public Health* become increasingly relevant: 'The cumulative vulnerability of some groups of workers, combining precarious employment conditions with harmful physical and psychosocial working conditions needs to be [seen as] a main public health concern' (Benach et al. 2014, 243).

Cognitive dissonance

Lillian Rubin spoke eloquently on the effects of unemployment and underemployment in middle-aged and older American men in particular.

> For American men—men who have been nurtured and nourished in the belief that they're masters of their own fate—it's almost impossible to bear such feelings of helplessness. So they find themselves in a cruel double bind. If they convince themselves that their situation

> is beyond their control, there's nothing left but resignation and despair. To fight their way out of the hopelessness that follows, they begin to blame themselves. But this only leaves them, as one man said, 'kicking myself around the block'—kicks that, paradoxically, allow them to feel less helpless and out of control, while they also send them deeper into depression, since now it's no one's fault but their own.
>
> *(Rubin 1994, 110–111)*

As we approach the third decade of the 21st century, we find a collective loss of hope for meaningful work and equal status in the 'American Dream'. This loss is a dissonant one. Working-class people know the deck is stacked against them, but they may still feel like a failure, a loser. Cognitive dissonance research also gives us a glimpse into the inner life of the working class. With reference to working-class life, Lillian Rubin concludes that people would rather blame themselves than feel completely helpless, but this puts them in a 'cruel double bind' (1994, 110–111). They blame themselves, and yet they know they never had a chance. In cognitive dissonance theory, contradictory beliefs create a painful internal clash of values, and people resort to all kinds of strange conclusions and self-defeating behavior to reduce the psychological strain.

The classic experiment in cognitive dissonance, 'Cognitive consequences of forced compliance' by Festinger and Carlsmith (1959; see also Festinger 1957), had subjects perform monotonous tasks, then lie to a new experimental subject, saying the tasks were fun. One group was paid $1 to lie to new subjects, and another group was paid $20. Afterwards, when asked how they felt about the task, the people who were paid only $1 to lie reported they enjoyed the (monotonous) task, while those paid $20 did not (nor did controls who had only done the task but not lied to other subjects).

In other words, with enough cognitive dissonance, people will try to justify bad things happening to them rather than admit their time or effort was worthless. A sense of one's human dignity trumps the perception that one is merely a pawn in a behavioral game of chess (Sennett and Cobb 1972). People lie to themselves to reduce the pain of dissonance. I first noticed this with victims of family sexual abuse. As children, they chose to blame themselves rather than face the helplessness of uncontrollable abuse. While researching Nazi Germany for my community psychology course, cognitive dissonance theory helped me understand how Christian Germans gave up Jewish Germans in their own neighborhoods to the Nazis for (supposed) deportation. The greater the dissonance of values, the harder people will work to justify what they have done.

Not surprisingly, collective action seems the best option for changing the lot of working-class people, and historically this has been the most effective. Learned helplessness and cognitive dissonance, of course, make belief in collective action more difficult, as they blame individuals rather than encourage them to resist impossible conditions. In the absence of real opportunities, they can also lead to unproductive cycles of vengeful resentment and self-blame, aggressive anger, and passive depression. But when workers share their stories together and realize they are not alone, cognitive dissonance can also produce insights that lead to new paths forward. Unfortunately, psychotherapeutic approaches offer little to help in this regard, centered as they are on individual experience.

The invisible ism: Classism

Beyond the fact of spending many hours a week doing difficult, dangerous, and monotonous work, there is considerable prejudice one must face for being the one who has to do it! The belief that people who service cars or run cash registers are lesser human beings, ones who lack the desire and ability for meaningful work, is a dehumanizing and cruel myth. Currently, it is used to create an immensely unequal workforce where some peoples' work includes veterinary care for their pets while other working Americans can't even get health care for their sick kids. Marmot stressed that it is the level of inequality (pay and status) within a population (a company, a town, a nation) that causes a dangerous, life-threatening status effect (2004, 2015).

Back in the late 1990s, in the meeting that began this chapter, Lucy was already well on her way to internalizing the classism she would need to be a success in the professional middle class. Of her upwardly mobile manager, she reported: 'He can't even spell, Barb! He can barely even write'. So who is he to tell her anything?

Other workers, trying to comfort her, only incensed her. 'They act like I'm one of them! This one woman lives in a trailer court and her husband used to beat her! And she's feeling sorry for me!' The tears began again; her voice got small and frightened. She repeated, 'She thinks I'm one of them!' dissolving into sobs. 'Is this it?' she cried as I remembered the night of her high school graduation … the shining promise in her face of a meaningful and interesting life ahead.

Like Lucy, my own upward mobility was primarily intellectual, and I was part of an alternative counterculture, so I could pass as middle class with jeans, t-shirts, and Standard English. But I corrected my mother's 'bad' English. I reviled her plastic flowers and orange-plaid, polyester couch. Like Lucy, I was a young anti-capitalist without a clue how thoroughly classist I was myself.

Class says you are the people that will do the manual labor that often is mind-numbing and/or dangerous. Classism says you will do it because it is all you deserve; other people are smarter, or they worked harder and deserve more freedom and dignity than you do. Classism says most of us have similar starting points but only the most hard-working, the best and brightest, make it to the top. Classism says that if you have not achieved society's prizes, it is because you are a lesser person. That is the American achievement myth, undergirded by our (wishful) valuing of egalitarianism and equal opportunity. As Lucy found out, it is a lie. The erasure of working-class experience, including its cultural integrity and the full humanity of every person within it, is classism. As ugly as racism, classism justifies the increasingly opulent lifestyles of the Somebodies in the burgeoning upper class, as well as alleviating the guilt of American 'dream hoarders' in the professional middle class (Reeves 2017).

Avoidable human suffering: Repair the world

At the end of the day, we are talking about very real human suffering on a massive scale. Work conditions that cause poor mental and physical health, with cascading negative effects on families and communities, is entirely avoidable. What does it mean when corporate power brokers force public policy that actually causes measurable mental distress, powerlessness, fatal physical illnesses, and even psychiatric disorders and suicide in ordinary American people (and others around the globe)? As the world of work inflicts generalized learned helplessness on workers, we have a shocking, large-scale community mental health crisis.

As a counselling psychologist, it is my job to help individuals with mental illness. How on earth can I do that when their work lives are causing such problems? I grasp that my clients are lonely and isolated and don't know where they belong. But therapy can't possibly do what a good life can. As a working-class-studies scholar, I find that, in this historical moment, we are witnessing a vicious, asymmetrical battle between so-called winners and losers. We are subject to a real-life game of class warfare that is almost entirely rigged. The world of work is stripping away the humanity of anyone not deemed a winner. In terms of working-class studies, I have to say, it seems almost frivolous to talk about cultural differences in this context, with working-class life decaying so profoundly. Working-class studies should develop cultural understandings in tandem with examining conditions in the world of work and the economy, and find ways to publicize the dramatic and community-wide psychological consequences of the so-called 'gig' economy. We also need to account for new cultural and psychological strategies that have arisen; that is, activism as a form of resilience in the lives of young people over the last 15 years.

Our current state of affairs is by design. A massive transfer of wealth from the vast majority of Americans to the upper class was engineered by the upper class, disproportionately represented in all three branches of government. The winners in America have spent trillions on political propaganda convincing workers that government is the problem and they should all try to be millionaires. In the meantime, they should settle for $7.25 an hour. But we have seen precarious employment before! America once had sweatshops, child labor, poverty-stricken tenements, forced overtime, ten-hour days, and horrible, dangerous working conditions. As a nation we changed that. That fight led to the standard employment contract that meant millions and millions reached for the American Dream, a home and a radical increase in leisure time and happiness for the majority (but not all) Americans.

On social media I found out recently that Lucy, nearing age 40, was thrilled to find an upscale retail job with benefits. It was a good working-class job. Increasingly, working-class people serve and enable the very comfortable lives of the professional class and the ridiculously posh lifestyles of the new upper class. A surprising 57% of U.S. young people identify as working class (Malik et al. 2016). They value community-mindedness over individuality. I worked six and a half years at a residential psychiatric facility and then in an alternative public high school for 24; I found that healthy community helped people as much as (or more) than counselling. People need other people to heal. In 2016, Bernie Sanders' winning of 22 states without one corporate penny was an astonishing reversal in American politics. In 2020, he won the first three state primary elections before the other candidates coalesced against him. He floated, as did Obama, on the shoulders of the millennials, who are tired of 'compromise' that leaves rich people even richer and treats average workers badly. More recently, freshman congresswoman Alexandra Ocasio-Corez has proposed a 70% tax on American's making more than $10 million per year.

Americans could have their government help them rather than trick and rob them. In 2017, the top 10% of our population owned 77% of all wealth in America (Bruenig 2017). That leaves 23% to be divided by the bottom 90% of the population.

This wealth could have been shared more evenly across our nation, as it was after the Great Depression (the last time a callous upper class crashed our economy with speculation and greed). We could be much happier than we are. We could repair our world.

References

Benach, J., Vives, A., Amable, M., Vanroelen, C., Tarafa, G., and Muntaner, C. (2014) 'Precarious Employment: Understanding an Emerging Social Determinant of Health', Annual Review of Public Health 2014, 35, 229–253.

Bruenig, M. (2017) 'New Fed Data: Top 10% Now Own 77% Of The Wealth', *Peoples Policy Project*: http://peoplespolicyproject.org/2017/09/27/new-fed-data-the-top-10-now-own-77-of-the-wealth/. [Based on Federal Reserve's 2016 Survey of Consumer Finances: https://www.federalreserve.gov/econres/scfindex.html.]

Case, A., and Deaton, A. (2015) 'Rising Morbidity and Mortality in Midlife among White Non-Hispanic Americans in the 21st Century', *Proceedings of the National Academy of Sciences of the United States of America*, 112, 49, pp. 15078–15083.

Case, A., and Deaton, A. (2017) 'Mortality and Morbidity in the 21st Century', *Brookings Papers on Economic Activity*, pp. 397–476.

Festinger, L. A. (1957) *Theory of Cognitive Dissonance*, Evanston, IL, Row, Peterson.

Festinger, L, and Carlsmith, J. M. (1959) 'Cognitive Consequences of Forced Compliance', *Journal of Abnormal and Social Psychology*, 58, 203–211.
Jensen, B. (1998) 'The Silent Psychology', *Women's Studies Quarterly*, 26, 1–2, pp. 202–215.
Jensen, B. (2004) 'Across the Great Divide: Crossing Classes and Clashing Cultures', in Zweig, M. (ed.) *What's Class Got To Do With It?* Ithaca, Cornell University Press.
Jensen, B. (2012) Reading *Classes: On Culture and Classism in America*, Ithaca, Cornell University Press.
Lerner, M. (1986) *Surplus Powerlessness*, Highlands, NJ, Humanities Press.
Mal, S., Jain, U., and Yadav, K. S. (1989) 'Effects of Prolonged Deprivation on Learned Helplessness', *Journal of Social Psychology*, 130, pp. 191–197.
Malik, S., Barr, C., and Holpuch, A. (2016) 'US Millennials Feel more Working Class than Any Other Generation', *The Guardian*, March 15.
Marmot, M. (2004) *The Status Syndrome: How Social Standing Affects Our Health and Longevity*, New York, Times Books.
Marmot, M. (2015) *The Health Gap: The Challenge of an Unequal World*, London, Bloomsbury.
Mikulincer, M. (1994) *Human Learned Helplessness*, New York, Plenum Press.
Reeves, R. (2017) *Dream Hoarders*, Washington DC, Brookings Institution Press.
Rubin, L. (1976) *Worlds of Pain*, New York, Basic Books.
Rubin, L. (1994) *Families on the Faultline*, New York, Harper Perennial.
Seligman, M. (1992) *Helplessness: On Development, Depression and Death*, New York, W. H. Freeman.
Sennett, R., and Cobb, J. (1972) *The Hidden Injuries of Class*, New York, Random House.
Standing, G. (2011) *The Precariat: The New Dangerous Class*, London, Bloomsbury Academic.
Standing, G. (2016) *The Corruption of Capitalism: Why Rentiers Thrive and Work Does Not Pay*, London, Biteback.
Sweet, S., and Meiksins, P. (2017) *Changing Contours of Work: Jobs and Opportunity in the New Economy*, London, Sage.
Torlina, J. (2011) *Working Class: Challenging Myths About Blue-Collar Labor*, Boulder, Lynne Rienner.
Zweig, M. (2012) *The Working Class Majority: America's Best Kept Secret*, 2nd ed. Ithaca, Cornell University Press.

19

Activist class cultures

Betsy Leondar-Wright

In these dangerous times, we need stronger progressive social movements, and building them depends in part on understanding class culture differences among activists. Just as there are cultural differences among people of different races and nationalities—distinct ways of talking, acting and thinking—there are also cultural differences among people who vary by education level, occupation, neighborhood and finances. Within the field of working-class studies, class cultures have been a focus primarily in the field of education, such as the culture shock of first-generation college students. But social movement organizations are another field where it's important to develop the cultural competence to see the specific strengths and limitations of all classes' cultures. Very little research has been done on how class plays out in activist groups, even though they are settings where strangers meet and need to collaborate and are, thus, ideal for observing how class cultures encounter each other and clash or mesh.

Besides adding to our understanding of how class cultures work, studying them in activist groups has many practical applications for enabling progressive voluntary groups to reach their missions. Here's one example of how simply seeing a specific class culture difference could help some activists become more effective. Every activist group, whatever its cause, worries about how to recruit new people. When more than 60 diverse progressive activists were asked by a researcher how they would get more people involved, there was a class difference in their answers. The most common answer from working-class and poor activists was food: serve better food, or advertise the food. In other words, entice people in the door and then get them more involved once they are there.[1] On the other hand, when college-educated activists with professional-middle-class (PMC) parents were asked the same question, surprisingly, *none* of them mentioned food. Instead, their most common answers focused on the ideas underlying the group's work, whether to add appealing new issues or shift the ideological tone.

This contrast reflects not just a difference in class cultures—habits and assumptions imbued by class backgrounds—but also different movement traditions with classed roots, in which activism is seen differently. Shared food is more common in labor-sponsored coalitions' and community organizing groups' meetings (which typically have a working-class majority attending) and less common in anarchist groups' meetings and in progressive protest groups associated with non-profit organizations, in which college graduates from PMC backgrounds predominate. As always, class culture differences play out in specific ways depending on the context (called the 'field' by class cultural theorist Pierre Bourdieu (1984)).

There are two reasons that such class culture differences matter to activists. First, cross-class coalitions involve learning to work together. Second, drawing on the strengths of all class cultures improves how social justice efforts are carried out. Using the food example, several majority PMC activist groups in the same study sat around at two small meetings at 6.30 p.m., with not a calorie in the room, asking 'Where is everybody?' Knowing that community organizing meetings typically included food would have suggested new solutions.

The food example is just one of many activist class culture differences found in a study of 25 varied progressive groups in five states in the US (Leondar-Wright 2014). Just as class culture differences have been found in families (Lareau 2003; Streib 2015), higher education (Hurst 2012; Lee 2016) and workplaces (Metzgar 2000; Torlina 2011), they also show up in grassroots progressive organizations (Croteau 1995; Stout 1996; Reed 1999; Rose 2000; Cummings 2003). These working-class studies scholars have taken a sharp departure from past demeaning and stereotyped portrayals of working-class and poor people (Greenbaum 2015) and now look respectfully at the cultures of less-privileged communities, without romanticizing.

To understand the class cultural dynamics of an activist group requires understanding both the individual members' class predispositions (called 'habitus' by Bourdieu (1984) and others) and movement traditions, discussed in the next two sections. First the influence of childhood class experiences will be applied to approaches to activism and, in particular, to differences in vocabulary and speech styles. Then the following section will briefly describe the movement traditions active in the US today, with the classed roots and class makeup of each. These individual and organizational dimensions of class cultures will then be applied to a major area of class difference, understandings of leadership. Just as Lareau (2003) applied Bourdieu's theories to a field, childrearing, that has great practical relevance for education practices, this article attempts to connect general class culture theory with specific examples that meet the needs of those building cross-class coalitions.

Activists' class predispositions

Rooted and unrooted paths to activism

People of different classes tend to come to activism by different paths. College-educated professionals are more likely to choose a cause first and then seek a group to act on it. Typically expected to uproot themselves from their hometowns and families by going away to college and then moving for careers, PMC adults have a predisposition to see themselves as lone individuals making choices for themselves. Frequently they form their activist identities in opposition to the more mainstream views and lifestyles of their families of origin, neighbors and colleagues; thus, they are more likely to be attracted to the distinct lingo, group process, clothing style and lifestyle of a counterculture movement (Breines 1989; Epstein 1991; Brooks 2001).

By contrast, lifelong working-class people (defined as the second generation without a college degree and without a professional/managerial occupation) tend to have more rooted lives, more often staying in their hometowns as adults or moving or migrating along with other family members (Jensen 2012). They are more likely to join an activist group through preexisting affiliations, such as sharing a neighborhood or workplace, or being invited by an extended family member. In labor and community groups, members tend to retain similar ways of talking, acting and dressing as non-activists in the same workplace or community.

In particular, those that Howell (1972) described as settled-living working-class people—those with stable, skilled and/or unionized jobs that pay well enough to allow for homeownership, cars and free time—are more likely than PMC or very poor people to center their lives around extended family ties and involvements with religious congregations, sports teams, clubs, friendship circles and other collective affiliations. Organizational experience and skills may be carried over into activist involvements. Thus settled-living working-class activists tend to be more rooted; PMC activists tend to be more unrooted.

This rooted/unrooted difference contributed to the animosity in the 1990s between labor and environmental groups over cutting old-growth trees in the northwest. Rose (2000) reports that union members suspected out-of-town environmentalists of being spies for the timber companies. Most of the union members had grown up in the area, and many were second- or third-generation timber workers. They saw themselves as fighting for their jobs and their way of life. The motivations of someone coming from out of town to defend the trees were unfathomable and, therefore, suspicious. The bridge people between the two groups, who successfully built a labor/environmental coalition to press for more sustainable timbering methods, better for long-term jobs *and* for forests, had to build trust first by talking with people on all sides and enabling them to understand these cultural differences.

Class speech codes

A major area of class cultural difference is language, and understanding class speech codes is crucial for building cross-class coalitions. College-educated professionals, regardless of their race, region or generation, tend to speak the American Standard dialect used by newscasters, and to speak more abstractly than working-class people do (Bernstein 1971; Heath 1983). Working-class speech styles are as diverse as the US working class, including African American Vernacular English, southern redneck style and Spanglish; but in all cases, working-class speech is more colorful and concrete. Aphorisms may come from cultural heritage: a low-income Caribbean immigrant said, 'Back home they say "you want good, your nose has to run.". Or colorful metaphors may be newly coined: 'I'm a pebble in their shoe,' said a working-class court-observer of domestic violence cases.

Abstract speech styles are learned in college, but also in PMC families and communities. College-educated activists use many abstract nouns; compared to working-class activists, they use the following terms many times more often per 10,000 spoken words: network, outreach, perspective, context, activism and strategy, as well as ideological terms such as socialism, anarchism and nonviolence. (Fortunately for cross-class communication, not all general terms are so class-skewed; words used at equal rates by all classes include goal, story, recruit, community, conflict and decision.) Ironically, the abstract terms used less often by working-class activists include the word 'class' (in the sense of social class) and the rallying cry of the labor movement, solidarity (Leondar-Wright 2013).

Activist author Linda Stout, who grew up in poverty, mentions one of these terms when she describes her first time working with middle-class activists.

> I remember getting frustrated with words like 'strategies and tactics' … I came to terms with the language problem by translating what I was taught into my own language. For 'strategy,' I thought, oh, this is what I call a 'plan.' I realized that I had different words for the same concepts and that, in fact, some of the things I was doing as a community organizer, and which felt to me like just common sense, were being taught as complicated concepts.
>
> *(Stout 1996, 119–120)*

In transcripts of meetings and interviews, the correlation between class identity and abstract/concrete language showed up thousands of times. In one striking example, note how differently two middle-aged African American activists in the same organization answered the same question by the same interviewer:

> *Interviewer:* What are the goals of your group?
> *Upper-middle-class man:* One, we want to end the war, two is to become a multi-racial, multi-class, multi-ethnic peace movement for social and economic justice.

> *Interviewer:* What are the goals of your group?
> *Working-class woman:* We don't want to see the war in Iraq; we want to see that come to an end. We don't want to see the recruiters harassing the kids in the high school, which they do.

Note that the second interviewee drew a vivid picture of a conflict, including setting and actors, in her last sentence of only 17 words, while the first interviewee packed a remarkably compact political philosophy and vision in his single sentence. Both are admirable communicators, but in class-contrasting ways.

Some PMC activists put paramount importance on a single abstract term that encapsulates their analysis (such as 'sustainability,' 'white supremacy,' 'patriarchy' or 'capitalism'). To promote such a term, the best method of communication is to bring it alive through stories about impact on individuals, full of sensory details and colorful analogies. The dry rhetoric common in academia and ideology-heavy sectarian groups lacks the leavening of working-class speech codes. For audiences of any class, persuasion involves connecting with listeners' emotions as well as their minds, with their personal experiences as well as their big-picture worldviews; thus, a mix of the two class speech codes will be the most persuasive. Class-bilingual code-switchers tend to be more successful activists, which is an example of how awareness of class culture differences strengthens social justice work.

Class and disempowerment

Another area where class background plays out in activism is in self-confidence about making a difference. For all classes, lack of belief that social movements can actually bring about change is a major obstacle to activism. But since the fields of politics and media are professional-dominated, alienation from them and skepticism about changing them are stronger in working-class and poor communities. Croteau (1995) interviewed working-class non-activists about why they didn't get involved in middle-class-led social movements. His findings show that it wasn't primarily disagreement with the cause, lack of knowledge, lack of time or logistical obstacles that kept his working-class informants from becoming activists. The main reason for their lack of involvement was 'the absence of efficacy,' a sense that activism wouldn't do any good.

The exceptions tend to be when the lessons and culture of prior movements have been passed down. Some rank-and-file labor activists grew up in union families, and some immigrant organizing has been led by working-class people who were dissenters in their countries of origin, such as Salvadorans active in the FMLN (Farabundo Martí National Liberation Front) or Mexicans affiliated with the Zapatistas. But most working-class people in the US have no such movement influences and, unlike many college graduates, typically have had few chances to learn about social movements in school.

Reluctance to confront unjust authorities stems in part from the working-class childrearing practices documented by Lareau (2003). Most upper-middle-class parents coach their children to be assertive with teachers and doctors, but most working-class parents coach deference to authority. The upper-middle-class predisposition to speak up can ease the transition to activism, in particular to tactics that involve contact with target power holders, such as lobbying and public confrontation. While working-class life experience does produce some formidable powerhouses, there are also multiply-marginalized people (such as low-income, low-literacy immigrant women of color) for whom empowerment can be a long process. Social movement organizations with large disempowered constituencies face the challenge of how to build up the skills of speaking in public, understanding issues and participating in organizations. These skills are usually taken for granted in PMC-majority groups, leading to less emphasis on leadership development.

As in other fields, there is classism in social movement organizations. Stout (1996) writes about peace activists discouraging her from public speaking because of her working-class Southern accent, and not considering her for leadership roles. Many activists of all classes value the assertiveness gained from upper-middle-class upbringing as a leadership trait, and they regard specialized movement lingo as more politically correct than working-class expressiveness. Rather than options being weighed by their strategic impact, PMC activists' norms often prevail, in particular in PMC-dominated movement traditions, as the next section will describe.

Four classed movement traditions

Walking into different activist spaces can feel like entering different worlds. Are meetings run by facilitators or by chairs, by rotation or always by the same person? Are picket lines the most habitual public actions, or marches, or blockades? Are conflicts among members quelled by calls to solidarity, by calls to civility or by anti-oppression workshops? Do activists wear matching t-shirts, black clothes and piercings, or business-casual outfits? Nothing is universal in progressive groups except for the determination to make a change in society. It is not only individual class predispositions that lead to these differences in activist groups, but also movement traditions.

Each movement tradition has distinct organizational forms and tastes in tactics (Jasper 1997), some very distinct from mainstream culture and others integrated into the local culture (Lofland 1995). Movement traditions have historical classed roots, related to the class of those who founded them, even if many generations ago. Since some organizations within each tradition have succeeded at their goals, clearly there are strengths to each way of operating.

The four biggest traditions in the US today are briefly profiled below, two with working-class roots and two with PMC roots. To prevent class culture clashes that impede cross-class coalition-building, not only individual class culture differences but also the norms of these traditions must be understood. As Bourdieu (1984) said, it's in the interaction of field and habitus that class culture distinctions are put into practice.

Labor and community organizing are two century-old U.S. working-class traditions. While both have mixed-class memberships today, they are still the traditions where most working-class-majority groups are found. The Fight for $15 minimum wage campaigns and the two biggest networks of interfaith coalitions, PICO, and the Industrial Areas Foundation, are contemporary examples of these traditions.

Labor leaders are most often college-educated professionals (from a variety of class backgrounds); lifelong working-class people risen from the rank and file are only rarely in charge.

While small and mostly or all volunteer, grassroots community groups are more likely to have homegrown working-class or poverty-class activists in leadership roles; in the larger federations, college-educated professionals tend to be hired as staff. Nevertheless, the norms of the majority of members still influence the class cultures of the groups.

The core principle of the labor movement and community organizing groups has been solidarity among people personally affected by similar hardships and their allies (Flacks 1988). In line with the working-class ethic of belonging, membership comes from a preexisting affiliation with a workplace, occupation or neighborhood, as noted above. Ideological agreement is not usually a requirement for involvement.

By contrast, shared ideologies and political values are central to movement traditions where college-educated activists from PMC backgrounds predominate. College students are a natural constituency for activism. Full-time students with no dependents and flexible schedules have the necessary biographical availability where activism can flourish (McAdam 1988). The norm that activism means long conversations into the night about ideology, process and strategy grows out of the residential four-year college experience, which is then carried over into the two predominantly PMC movement traditions, anarchism and progressive protest groups affiliated with nonprofits. Most groups in these traditions have crystallized around an issue or ideology, attracting members who agree with the premise of the group.

Class and race composition varies within these two college-educated-majority traditions. Anarchist groups (such as Food Not Bombs and some of the Occupy encampments) are the most likely to include the class trajectory of voluntarily downwardly mobile (VDM) from an upper-middle-class background. Mass mobilizations of young people of color organized by Black Lives Matter and United We Dream have been led predominantly by straddlers (Lubrano 2004), or first-generation college graduates (Milkman et al. 2014). And there is historical continuity from the so-called new social movements of the 1970s and 1980s—feminist, environmental and anti-militarist protest groups—to the Women's Marches and climate change organizing today, which have white, PMC majorities.

The interplay of these four movement traditions with class culture predispositions is reflected in every aspect of an activist group's style and operations. One especially striking area is contrasting attitudes towards leadership, an area essential for compromise in building successful cross-class coalitions.

Approaches to leadership in classed movement traditions

Very different paradigms of leadership can be found in different movement traditions and class predispositions. But the contrast among activists doesn't fall in the traditional polarity between directive versus participative modes (Likert 1961; Heller 1973). Top-down command-and-control leadership isn't a feasible option when involvement is voluntary. Since the 1960s, it has been almost universally understood that social movement organizations grow and succeed by developing the active participation of voluntary activists.

But how can participation be activated? Understandings of leadership roles in recruitment vary by activists' class and by movement tradition, along a continuum: pro-leader attitudes correlate with working-class people and traditions and anti-leader attitudes with more-privileged people and traditions. When varied activists were asked 'Who are the leaders of your group?' most answers fell into this pattern. Anti-leadership responses were heard only from college-educated people, most often from young, white, VDM activists in the anarchist tradition. For example, Leon, a VDM white protester at a 2008 political convention, answered, 'I hate the word "leaders." I see it come up over and over, informal hierarchies.'

Straightforward, upbeat replies were most often heard from working-class activists in labor-sponsored or community organizing groups. For example, a white working-class woman in a local anti-poverty group, Nicole, thought the question about leaders was a simple one.

> *Interviewer:* And who do you see as the leaders of the group?
> *Nicole:* Fred.

As the conversation continued, note how Nicole linked Fred's strong leadership style with his empowering effect on members.

> *Interviewer:* And how is he as a leader?
> *Nicole:* I think he does a great job. He's very organized. He knows how to recruit people to get them to where he needs them.

Other studies have also discovered this correlation between class and attitudes towards hierarchy. Lichterman's (1996) ethnographic observation of four California environmental groups found that organizational styles varied by participants' education level. He contrasted two Green Party-related groups, with average education of more than four years of college, with two local anti-toxics groups, one mostly black and one mostly white, with an average education of slightly more than high school. He calls the PMC groups' style 'personalist' and the working-class/lower-middle-class anti-toxic groups' style 'communitarian.' In the personalist groups, egalitarian participatory process was an end in itself. Any unequal power or formal leadership violated group norms; there was an expectation and insistence on vocal participation by all. Lichterman's informants told him, 'All members are leaders.' One of these groups had as many projects as it had active members, as each person had started their own project. In the solidaristic groups, traditional hierarchical roles were not seen as contradictory to the group's mission. Many members were happy to let someone else lead; there was more deference to expertise and experience and more tutelage of new members. It was more permissible to hang back quietly or be a worker bee, and a gradual process of empowerment was a collective responsibility. Sometimes the groups had too few roles for non-leaders; there was a risk of accommodating leaders too much or not holding them accountable.

To working-class and poor people in the labor and community organizing traditions, commitment to the group is often equated with loyalty to the leaders. In the face of conflict, loyal working-class members sometimes circle the wagons and defend a leader. But when a leader is perceived as violating members' trust or working against the community's interests, a common response is to quit the group.

Except for occasional annoyance at pretentious-seeming, elaborate parliamentary procedure, opinions on group process rarely come up in interviews with working-class community or labor activists. For example, Laverne, a middle-aged black veteran of many grassroots campaigns in her urban neighborhood, answered questions about group process with brief, vague answers, but became passionate when discussing her past community activities and their leaders. She said about one group, 'Oh my goodness, they kept us hopping! [Well-known bla ck male leader] was a very good teacher!' After repeatedly probing for group process opinions and finding none, the interviewer finally asked her directly.

> *Interviewer:* Some people are really opinionated about how decisions get made, by a vote or who's facilitating and how that's done ... what about you?

Laverne: Well, as long I'm able to take part in the meetings, I'm not really too upset about who's facilitating the meeting. As long as it comes to a good conclusion.
Interviewer: You don't care how you get there.
Laverne: Exactly. As long as it's not too drastic.

This combination of admiration of empowering leaders with disinterest in internal methods of running the group was common among working-class interviewees.

In the two PMC-majority movement traditions, on the other hand, group process is often a passionate preoccupation. Many feel that organizational structure should reflect the values of the group, prefiguring its vision of how a better society should run. Members often contrast their groups' participatory process with corporate and other mainstream institutional ways.

Sometimes norms from non-activist nonprofits are carried over into PMC-majority social movement organizations, in particular if the group is a nonprofit corporation itself. Group bylaws may define board and staff roles, for example, and may require a quorum. But even in these cases, the prefigurative ideal of 'be the change you want to see' often comes out in meeting process.

Structured consensus decision-making (in which verbal consent must be obtained by all members present through a series of steps before a decision can be finalized) is found only in majority-college-educated groups with strong prefigurative ideals. In the 1970s and 1980s, such egalitarian group processes were most often referred to as 'feminist process.' The ideal of making space for each voice to be heard, drawn from consciousness-raising groups, was emphasized during the second-wave feminist movement, more so in cultural feminism than in socialist feminism (Taylor and Whittier 1995). Never uncontroversial, the nonhierarchical all-voices organizational forms were critiqued in the widely circulated and influential article 'The tyranny of structurelessness' (Freeman 1972).

Today the same group processes are most often called 'horizontal.' Anarchist activists sometimes refer to them as 'anarchist process.' In the Occupy movement of 2011–13, an elaborate consensus decision-making process was one of the few core points that all participants had to agree with (Milkman et al. 2014).

It may seem backwards that meeting efficiency would be a working-class norm given that in social and family life, the class differences tend to run the other way (Jensen 2012; Streib 2015). But meeting process is an exception. Working-class activists do tend to have a looser style of hanging out, but it is expressed at bars or kitchen tables after meetings, not during meetings, where brevity is valued and where stylized speech rules can be uncomfortable.

Similarly, the correlation between class and attitudes towards leadership can seem counterintuitive. Don't most working-class employees develop an aversion to hierarchy from their experience of being closely supervised at work? Yes, but the pleasurable involvements where they find respite from workplace constraints often have strong leaders as well. Many working-class people, in particular older residents of stable working-class communities, have voluntary memberships in religious congregations, sports teams and fraternal orders that are rule-based, with designated roles, procedures and hierarchy.

These contrasting attitudes towards hierarchical roles of activists of different classes can be found in religious denominations. In Baptist, African Methodist Episcopal, Catholic, evangelical and Pentecostal churches, it would be disrespectful to call clergy by their first name. But informal, peer-like relationships with clergy are more common in the predominantly white PMC denominations that produce the most progressive activists, such as Unitarian Universalist, Reconstructionist Jewish, United Church of Christ, and Quaker congregations. Similarly, there are no umpires in yoga. To hear a loud, authoritative 'you're out!' would be jarring to many PMC and upper-middle-class people, raised to be autonomous professionals or managers in charge.

These contrasting attitudes towards leadership lead to three different strategies for activating the inactive, each more common in a certain movement tradition and among activists of a certain class.

Holding back from domination. For VDM and lower-professional activists in the anarchist tradition and in the more countercultural wing of the progressive protest tradition, 'leader' means dominator, and so the strategy for member activation is self-monitoring and allowing others more room to speak. Sometimes this strategy works to draw out less-active members, but sometimes it fails. An ineffective example of this strategy was seen in one unusually quiet meeting of a globalization group. Concerned that most members were inactive, two male, college-educated core members left long pauses, which one of them later described as 'stepping back and not taking up so much space.' To perform a non-dominating, egalitarian role, they eschewed any active steps to encourage quiet members' involvement. But in that meeting the strategy backfired, as the less-active members also sat there silently and did not volunteer for any tasks. Clearly holding back isn't always a sufficient solution to the problem of inactive members.

Facilitating stylized group processes. For college-educated professional activists, primarily in the progressive protest tradition and in the more structured anarchist groups, 'leader' means manager of others' participation, through designing and running processes that require everyone to speak in a particular way. Go-arounds are the most common of these processes—not the simple introductions ubiquitous in all movement traditions, but questions requiring a newly coined response, such as: 'What's a highlight of your summer?' or 'What's your top-priority goal?' Other common ones are small-group report-backs written on flip-chart paper, rotating facilitation, and consensus decision-making. Often these techniques do succeed in enabling all voices to be heard.

But those who dissent from or do not cooperate with such stylized processes tend to be lifelong working-class and poor people (Cornell 2011). One white working-class member of a peace group put it this way:

> I come out of the union movement, but the way small groups, you know, and this writing things on a paper and putting them all up, I don't happen to think that any of that is very useful … I feel that that practice, although it tries to present itself as being very democratic, and it really strives for everyone to participate, but the reality is if a small number of people develop a very complex agenda and really control what happens, my view is that, in fact that's less democratic than something that's more spontaneous.

Working-class people new to activism may be more comfortable with a natural back-and-forth conversational style, in contrast with PMC people, who may have been fondly quizzed and asked to do freestanding speech performances in childhood (Lareau 2003). To overcome reluctance, structured process advocates often suggest training in consensus and meeting facilitation, which can solve the problem of unfamiliarity with the process; but since the workshops themselves tend to use stylized process, they don't resolve the deeper class cultural difference in speech styles.

Trustworthy championing of member interests. In the working-class majority movement traditions, 'leader' means trusted champion. The method of activating the inactive that is preferred by working-class activists, and practiced by their typically college-educated leaders, is strong chairing, one-on-one conversations with members and fostering loyalty via concrete aid to members.

In this strategy, the forcefulness of a leader is closely tied with member empowerment, not at odds with it. Members of labor and community groups speak admiringly of their leaders for going to bat for them with politicians and bosses and other authorities. Leaders' powerful effectiveness in the wider world seems to be an antidote to the lack of efficacy that so often prevents working-class activism. For example, a white working-class man in a labor-sponsored coalition praised the organization's president by saying, 'He's been around. He knows how to argue. He knows how to fight. He knows when to make his point, when to shut up … he's very effective as a political leader.'

Black women leaders have been those most celebrated as practitioners of this strategy (Leondar-Wright and Gamson 2010); for example, civil rights leader Ella Baker (Belenky et al. 1997; Ransby 2005). In talking about their own empowerment process, formerly apolitical recruits speak in glowing terms about how the leader mentored them step by step, affirming a powerful role in the development of new activists. While college-educated activists in PMC movement traditions are monitoring who takes up how much airspace, alert to domination, working-class activists are monitoring who is acting for or against the interests of the community, alert to trustworthiness.

Since there are successful organizations within each movement tradition, it's clear that there's no single best model of leadership. The class difference in predominant models reflects, to some extent, the challenges of organizing different constituencies, whether it's herding personalist, ideology-driven cats or developing efficacy and skills among disempowered grassroots recruits. The cultural competence to understand these different concepts of leadership, and to choose the strategy most likely to be effective in a given situation, requires an understanding of class cultures and movement traditions.

Conclusion

The understanding that activist class culture differences stem from the interaction of movement traditions with individual activists' class predispositions expands the field of working-class studies into new territory. The growing emphasis on class cultures within the discipline should not be limited to workplace, family and education, but can illuminate voluntary associations as well. More research is needed to look for the class culture traits described in this chapter in religious congregations, amateur sports teams and community service activities, as well as in social movement organizations in additional countries and movements.

More research is also needed into the specific class culture traits of activists in different regions, ethnic groups and generations, and into the varied mechanisms of organizational classism among groups and movement traditions. The rich literature on cases of successful cross-class coalitions (Anner 1999; Rose 2000; Reynolds 2004) could be analyzed to find the factors they share.

Currently, progressive social movements are riddled with class bias, and weakened by it. Class inclusiveness requires class consciousness and class identities, which are too scarce in the US today. The nonprofit Class Action (n.d.) creates opportunities for people in educational, nonprofit and activist settings to look at their own class backgrounds, engage in cross-class dialogue and lay the groundwork for action against classism. Without a cultural lens, this work can't be done well.

Culture matters. Of course, differences between working-class and middle-class activist groups can also arise from different self-interests, related to their different structural positions; they can arise from different types and amounts of resources, such as money and institutional affiliations.

But culture has a greater degree of autonomy and greater longevity than most assume; cultures continue after situations change. More awareness of class cultures will make possible more cross-class alliances with working-class leadership, invigorated by more working-class cultural strengths.

Note

1 All examples and quotes are from Leondar-Wright (2014) unless noted. Methodological note: The author's fieldwork involved two years of observation by three researchers of 34 meetings of 25 varied social movement organizations in eight cities in five US states; 362 surveys to establish members' class background and current class through an index of several indicators; and 61 interviews of members of varied classes. The analysis used mixed methods, with qualitative coding of over a thousand pages of transcripts and statistical analysis on the association of class with cultural traits.

References

Anner, J. (1999) *Beyond Identity Politics: Emerging Social Justice Movements in Communities of Color*, Boston, South End Press.

Belenky, M, Bond, L. and Weinstock, J. (1997) *A Tradition That Has No Name: Women's Ways of Leading*, New York, Basic Books.

Bernstein, B. (1971) *Class, Codes and Control*, Volume 1, New York, Routledge & Kegan Paul.

Bourdieu, P. (1984) *Distinction: A Social Critique of the Judgement of Taste*, Cambridge, MA, Harvard University Press.

Breines, W. (1989) *Community and Organization in the New Left, 1962–1968: The Great Refusal*, 3rd ed., New Brunswick, NJ, Rutgers University Press.

Brooks, D. (2001) *Bobos in Paradise: The New Upper Class and How They Got There*, New York, Simon and Schuster.

Class Action (n.d.) www.classism.org, retrieved January 25, 2019.

Cornell, A. (2011) *Oppose and Propose! Lessons from Movement for a New Society*, Oakland, AK Press.

Croteau, D. (1995) *Politics and the Class Divide: Working People and the Middle-Class Left*, Philadelphia, Temple University Press.

Cummings, C. (2003) *Class Lessons*, PhD dissertation, Department of Sociology, University of Massachusetts, Boston.

Epstein, B. (1991) *Political Protest and Cultural Revolution*, Berkeley, University of California Press.

Flacks, R. (1988) *Making History: The Radical Tradition in American Life*, New York, Columbia University Press.

Freeman, J. (1972) 'The Tyranny of Structurelessness,' *The Second Wave*, 2, 1. Retrieved August 26, 2017, www.jofreeman.com/joreen/tyranny.htm.

Greenbaum, S. (2015) *Blaming the Poor: The Long Shadow of the Moynihan Report on Cruel Images About Poverty*, New Brunswick, Rutgers University Press.

Heath, S. B. (1983) *Ways with Words: Language, Life, and Work in Communities and Classrooms*, Cambridge, Cambridge University Press.

Heller, F. A. (1973) 'Leadership, Decision Making and Contingency Theory,' *Industrial Relations*, 12, 2, 183–199.

Howell, J. T. (1972) *Hard Living on Clay Street*, New York, Anchor Books.

Hurst, A. (2012) *College and the Working Class*, New York, Springer.

Jasper, J. (1997) *The Art of Moral Protest: Culture, Biography, and Creativity in Social Movements*, Chicago, University of Chicago Press.

Jensen, B. (2012) *Reading Classes: On Culture and Classism in America*, Ithaca, Cornell University Press.

Lareau, A. (2003) *Unequal Childhoods: Class, Race, and Family Life*, Berkeley, University of California Press.

Lee, E. (2016) *Class and Campus Life: Managing and Experiencing Inequality at an Elite College*, Ithaca, Cornell University Press.

Leondar-Wright, B. (2013) 'Pretense, Put-Downs and Missing Identities in Activists' Class Talk,' *Humanity & Society*, 37, 3, 225–247.

Leondar-Wright, B. (2014) *Missing Class: Strengthening Social Movement Groups by Seeing Class Cultures*, Ithaca, Cornell University Press.

Leondar-Wright, B. and Gamson, W. A. (2010) 'Social Movements,' *Political and Civic Leadership: A Reference Handbook*, Los Angeles, Sage Publications.

Lichterman, P. (1996) *The Search for Political Community: American Activists Reinventing Commitment*, Cambridge, Cambridge University Press.

Likert, R. (1961) *New Patterns of Management*, New York, McGraw-Hill.

Lofland, J. (1995) 'Charting Degrees of Movement Culture: Tasks of the Cultural Cartographer,' in Johnston, H. and Klandermans, B., (eds.) *Social Movements and Culture*, Minneapolis, University of Minnesota Press.

Lubrano, A. (2004) *Limbo: Blue-Collar Roots, White-Collar Dreams*, Hoboken, NJ, John Wiley & Sons.

Mayer, B. (2008) *Blue-Green Coalitions: Fighting for Safe Workplaces and Healthy Communities*, Ithaca, Cornell University Press.

McAdam, D. (1988) *Freedom Summer*, New York, Oxford University Press.

Metzgar, J. (2000) *Striking Steel: Solidarity Remembered*, Philadelphia, Temple University Press.

Milkman, R., Luce, S. and Lewis, P. (2014) 'Occupy Wall Street,' in Goodwin, J. and Jasper, J. M. (eds.) *The Social Movements Reader*, New York, John Wiley and Sons.

Ransby, B. (2005) *Ella Baker and the Black Freedom Movement: A Radical Democratic Vision*, Chapel Hill, NC, University of North Carolina Press.

Reed, A., Jr. (1999) *Stirrings in the Jug: Black Politics in the Post-Segregation Era*, Minneapolis, University of Minnesota Press.

Reynolds, D. (2004) *Partnering for Change: Unions and Community Groups Build Coalitions for Economic Justice*, New York, M.E. Sharpe.

Rose, F. (2000) *Coalitions across the Class Divide: Lessons from the Labor, Peace, and Environmental Movements*, Ithaca, Cornell University Press.

Stout, L. (1996) *Bridging the Class Divide and Other Lessons for Grassroots Organizing*, Boston, Beacon Press.

Strieb, J. (2015) *The Power of the Past*, New York, Oxford University Press.

Taylor, V. and Whittier, N. (1995) 'Analytical Approaches to Social Movement Culture: The Culture of the Women's Movement,' in Johnston, H. and Klandermans, B. (eds.) *Social Movements and Culture*, Minneapolis, MN, University of Minnesota Press.

Torlina, J. (2011) *Working Class: Challenging Myths About Blue-Collar Labor*, Boulder, Lynne Rienner Publishers.

20

The Australian working class in popular culture

Sarah Attfield

It is never easy to discuss class in Australia because the nation presents itself as the land of the 'fair go' – egalitarian (Leigh 2013, 3), a country where snobbery is not tolerated. In Australia you can call the Prime Minister 'mate' and have a beer with your boss. The image of the 'battler' is celebrated and is a favourite go-to slogan for Australian politicians who build campaigns based on their support for the typical 'Aussie Battler'. This resistance to snobbery (and refusal to defer to authority) arguably has its origins in the defiance against authority found among the convicts of the penal colony and in Indigenous people who resisted the invasion. But what does this all mean? If the existence of 'ordinary' people is acknowledged, why is it that the mention of class leads to the denial of a class system, and 'working class' is considered an outmoded term?

Scholars have noted that class as a topic of discussion and debate has waned since the 1980s (Barnes and Cahill 2012, 47). While a number of pieces did appear in the early 2000s to the mid-2000s, there have been very few since (see Greig et al. 2003; Hindess and Sawer 2004; Kuhn 2005; and McGregor 2001). This is where working-class studies is useful. The field provides a way to discuss class and working-class life that counters these denials or the attempts to define class away. A working-class studies approach can examine how class is being constructed and reveal what kinds of understandings of class are contributing to the national imaginary. In this chapter I will focus on some forms of Australian popular culture and consider how working-class life is being represented. I'll be asking whether these representations provide a nuanced picture of working-class experience or whether Australian popular culture reinforces class stereotypes, or renders the working-class invisible.

Historical context

To understand contemporary representations of class in Australia, a detour into history is required. The founding myth of Australia suggests that anyone who came to Australia (the 'Lucky Country'[1]) had equal opportunities, unencumbered by the class system of Britain that highly restricted class mobility (Greig et al. 2003, 160). There are stories of entrepreneurial ex-convicts who set up businesses and became wealthy. Free settlers also came, but the majority of those who set off to farm or search for precious metals already came with some resources. It is not difficult to challenge this idea of egalitarian Australia (Leigh 2013, 4). The British colonisers planted their class system firmly in Australia (Buckley and Wheelwright 1994, 1). The working-classes of Australia were made up of the ex-convicts who worked as labourers, the descendants of convicts who worked as farm labourers or as factory hands, the Indigenous people who worked for rations for wealthy landowners or wealthy families in the cities (Haskins and Scrimgeour 2015, 89),[2] migrants from Asia and Europe and the Pacific Islanders who were either kidnapped or tricked into boarding ships for Australia to end up as slave labourers in the sugar cane fields (Speedy 2015, 344).

The hard-working, white, Australian man – the 'bush man' (Greig et al. 2003, 174) – epitomised this myth. The bush man valued his mates and was always loyal (Page 2002, 193). He worked hard in the harsh conditions of the Australian bush and never complained (Ward c1966, 2). This sense of 'toughness' is an enduring element of the myth of Australian masculinity. Australian men (those who are white, straight and Anglo-Celtic) have been portrayed as hardy, strong, unafraid, stoic (except when angry), always on the lookout for their mates, larrikins (ready to joke around) and drinkers, and as refusing to defer to their 'betters' (Hudson and Bolton 1997, 1). This image of the Australian man has its origins in the ANZAC[3] myth – the nation-building appropriation of the World War One soldier – a heroic man who always looked after his mates and treated everyone as an equal (Williams 1995, 109), the brave soldier who, once removed from the trenches, continued to show his mettle in the shearers' shed or the factory floor – an all-round 'good bloke'.

But of course, any national myth is built on exclusions. The men who are not included in the ANZAC myth are the Indigenous men, the queer men, the men from ethnic minorities and so on. And women are absent completely (Page 2002, 195). What is also often missing is the white bush man's link with the violence of European invasion – the massacres of Indigenous people and the theft of Indigenous land. As Woollacott (2009) states, 'frontier men celebrated their own and each other's toughness, endurance and bravery – descriptions in which the use of violence could be implicit but was glossed over' (11,10). And the mateship forged in the trenches of World War One was also predicated on violence – a soldier would look out for his mates in the act of killing the enemy in what Page (2002, 198) describes as 'military solidarity'. The bush man and the ANZAC have featured heavily in literature and popular culture. Many of Australia's most iconic literary works such as the poetry of A. B. (Banjo) Paterson and Henry Lawson included rural workers such as 'drovers' and 'shearers'. Popular songs also immortalised the bushman – a rogue, but a loveable one.

This history reveals a major contradiction of Australian culture – while the rural worker and the humble soldier have been awarded legendary status, class systems are rarely acknowledged and the existence of the working class is disputed. Further contradictions abound – while the majority of Australians have working-class backgrounds, there are rarely overt representations of working-class life in mainstream popular culture (outside of sport). And the world of 'high art' is dominated by the middle classes.

Whitman (2013, 52) suggests that white working-class masculinity is at the 'centre of narratives concerning what it means to be an Australian'. Developing this idea further, Whitman argues that this 'cultural ideal' of heterosexual, white, working-class masculinity can be seen in media representations in advertising that use white working-class men to sell products and services and encourages middle-class men to adopt working-class characteristics (Whitman 2013, 52). I'd agree that certain products and services are sold in this way, but they belong to a specific category of products that are often associated with working-class culture, such as beer (not craft or micro-brewery beer), sport (and sport betting), utility vehicles and some fast food. Most other advertisements use middle-class characters – it would be highly unlikely, for example, that advertisements for products associated with middle-class consumers, such as wine, would feature obvious working-class characters, unless used ironically. There is a sense of snobbery in Whitman's argument – she claims that 'anti-elitism' and 'anti-intellectualism' (2013, 60) is another staple of white working-class masculinity that has become part of this 'cultural tool' used to legitimate the working-class masculinity of Australian identity (2013, 52). But this demonstrates a lack of understanding of working-class culture. Anti-intellectualism is not common among working-class people, who are inclined to value education and the notion of being 'smart'. Anti-elitism is more likely, though not directed at the targets that Whitman implies (creative professionals and academics), but at the 'bosses' and politicians who seem out of touch with working-class life. The sort of anti-elitism and anti-intellectualism that she points to is expressed by dominant right-wing male figures in the mainstream media – the 'shock jocks' (talkback radio hosts) and their TV talk show host equivalents, who rail against the left and social justice activists.

It should be noted here, that the Australian working class is diverse. Often, it seems that 'working class' refers to white people. This is not the case. People of colour make up a large proportion of the Australian working class. Australia has a history of immigration, and many immigrants arriving since British invasion have been people of colour (or people not considered 'white' at the time of their arrival, such as Italians and Greeks). The majority of Indigenous people in Australia are working class (Grieg et al. 2003, 129) due to the inequality experienced by Indigenous communities. In this chapter, I refer specifically to 'white working-class' people at times; otherwise, the assumption should be that working-class people are from a variety of racial and ethnic backgrounds.

Popular culture

Popular culture gives us somewhere to look for representations of working-class experience, and it is a good place to search because of the importance of popular culture in people's everyday lives. Outside of the scholarly studies of class by labour historians, political economists and sociologists, people are experiencing the lived reality of class every day and, at the same time, consuming popular culture. So what can popular culture tell us about how class works in Australia? Sport is a quite complex area, popular music offers some examples of cultural products that demonstrate how class and other categories of identification (such as race), intersect, but film and television provide slightly more straightforward examples of representation, or absence.

The official 'national imaginary' of Australia always includes sport. And, according to Moore (2000, 58), sport has 'expressed and shaped the working-class experience'. Rugby league (NRL) and Australian Rules football (AFL) are the two most popular football 'codes'. Rugby league is unashamedly working class (Moore 2000, 58), linked to the union movement and arguably formed as a challenge to the class hierarchies within sports such as rugby union, which were played by private school boys (Moore 2000, 60). Rugby League players are almost always from working-class families, and the culture is almost stereotypically working class. Footy players tend to be big drinkers. Fans consume beer and meat pies at the matches. The matches are shown in big suburban pubs. There was a dedicated television show called *The Footy Show* (1994–2019) that revelled in its self-consciously working-class culture. The presenters of the show were mostly ex-players, and presented themselves as unsophisticated and as 'ordinary' (mostly) 'blokes'. The show is what might be described as sport combined with 'light' entertainment, and due to the backgrounds of the presenters, the players and the majority of fans, it was a very working-class space.

Australian popular music has often been a site of working-class expression, with stories of working-class life featuring in country songs, rock and rap. Bennett (2001, 1) states that popular music has always functioned at a 'collective level', reflecting and shaping contemporary issues. If this is the case, then it makes sense that working-class experience would also be reflected in popular music. This collective consciousness has also been identified by Shepherd (1990, 136), who describes working-class music as rooted in shared experiences that are concrete, rather than abstract. Some iconic Australian songs have had working-class themes, such as Jimmy Barnes' 'Working class man', released in 1985. Indigenous artists have recorded songs about hardship, racism and colonisation using country, rock and reggae genres. Bands such as The Warumpi Band, Us Mob and No Fixed Address created anthems about their experiences that were sung by both Indigenous and non-Indigenous fans (Dunbar-Hall and Gibson 2004, 47). Australian hip hop has represented working-class life. The pioneers of Australian hip hop were 1990s artists such as Def Wish Cast from the multicultural working-class suburbs of Sydney – these groups localised the genre, rapping with Australian accents and writing lyrics about their lives as working-class and ethnic minority Australians (Mitchell 2007). According to Dunbar-Hall and Gibson (2004, 122), rap music is also very popular among young Indigenous Australians, who identify with its 'ethos of solidarity and loyalty' (122). Indigenous duo A. B. Original released a song in 2016, 'January 26th', calling for a change to the date of Australia's national day (Australia Day), currently celebrated on 26 January. This date marks the anniversary of the landing of the First Fleet in 1788, a day that is called Invasion Day by most Indigenous Australians. In their song and the accompanying video clip, the group uses imagery from working-class Australia to support their message. Australia Day is mostly embraced by white working-class Australians, who host barbeques at the beach or in their homes and mark the day with drinking and displays of nationalism (such as flag waving). In order to win support for a date change from legislators, activists need to win over the white working class and convince them that their celebration is based on a violent history.

Film

Zaniello (2005) suggests that film is an excellent medium for understanding how class works (and the history of working-class experience), because film texts demonstrate how class and working-class history is both 'open or suppressed', in that films reveal 'erasure' and 'disclosure' of class (152). Williamson et al. (2001, 100) argue that working-class characters have often appeared in film, but the majority of these portrayals have been stereotypical or exist to make a specific point about class, which they argue can result in a lack of interest in a character (104). Although Williamson et al.'s and Zaniello's studies are focused on Hollywood and British film, their ideas can be applied to Australian film, and it's possible to consider which images of working-class life have been dominant and where and when they have been present.

Representation is important because it shapes views about people. According to Stuart Hall (1997, 1), representation is 'one of the central practices which produce culture'. Culture is important because it is 'concerned with the production and exchange of meanings … between the members of a society or group' (Hall 1997, 2). Hall goes on to say that cultural meanings 'organise and regulate social practices, influence our conduct and consequently have real, practical effects' (1997, 4). Therefore, what we see in cultural products and practices can have a very real impact on how we behave. If we only ever see a certain group of people represented in a negative way, we will think of them in negative terms and be less inclined to accept them as our equals. Those of us from these groups can be disempowered by negative representations and even internalise these depictions. Hall states that meaning is produced in mass media (as well as in other places) and 'helps to set the rules, norms and conventions by which social life is ordered and governed' (1997, 4).

I would suggest that there are a number of tropes used in Australian film to portray working-class people – most noticeably, the figure of the white, violent man, and the 'bogan'. Bogan is a derogatory short-hand term used to describe working-class people in Australia who are perceived as having no taste (Gibson 2013, 62). Bogans are uncouth, uneducated, unsophisticated and the object of ridicule. The term is similar to 'white trash' in the US and 'chav' in the UK, although less ethnically specific as 'white trash'.

Australia has a long history of films focusing on working-class life, and since the beginning of the Australian film industry there have been many iconic films made about working-class people. A very early example is *The Sentimental Bloke* made in 1919 and based on a famous poem of the same name by C. J. Dennis, about a working-class man in Sydney (called 'The Bloke'), who is released from jail (he had been a petty criminal) and decides to stay on the straight and narrow in order to pursue the woman of his dreams (Shirley and Adams 1989, 54). It's a wonderful film – a lot of it is filmed on location in the streets of Sydney and provides a glimpse into what was then a very working-class city centre, before the area became gentrified and sought after for its harbour views. The Bloke is trying to avoid crime, but he still manages to get involved in fights with other working-class men and the police. The working-class men in the film are tough, heavy drinking, crude and often ready for a fight. The bloke is depicted as a bit 'soppy' due to his interest in a girl, but the film is overall a sympathetic representation of working-class inner-city life (Morgan 2011, 323).

There has been a continuing focus on white male violence in Australian films about working-class life. This leads me to pose a number of questions. Why are film-makers representing white working-class men as violent towards each other and/or violent towards women and minorities? What are the limitations of these kinds of representations? Do they paint an overly negative picture of white working-class men in Australia, or are they revealing a reality that needs to be addressed? What is the effect of the absence of female working-class characters (except as victims of violent men)?

There seems to be a particular preoccupation in contemporary Australian film with stories that are based on crimes committed by white working-class men. It could be suggested that this interest in criminality can be traced back to colonial Australia. Early colonial literature often featured stories of the convicts – some acknowledged as criminals, others as political prisoners or wrongfully accused. One of Australia's most iconic figures is a criminal: Ned Kelly, the leader of the Kelly Gang (a group of bushrangers who robbed banks), who was famously caught after a shoot-out with police and then hanged. Kelly's legendary status centres around his early life as the son of an Irish convict who died in prison. There have been numerous cinematic representations of Kelly and his gang since the beginnings of Australian cinema; the world's first feature film, made in Australia in 1906, is Charles Tait's *The Story of the Kelly Gang.* Basu et al. (2013, 2) suggest that Kelly represents 'the whiteness, hyper-heterosexual masculinity, and violence of "Australianness"'.

Some contemporary examples include films such as Geoffrey Wright's 1992 *Romper Stomper.* This is a bleak film that explores racism in a working-class suburb of Melbourne, using what O'Brien (2013) describes as an 'embodied mode of address' (67) and 'robust muscularity' (68). Russel Crowe stars as Hando, a neo-Nazi skinhead who heads a gang that terrorises ethnic minorities, particularly Vietnamese Australians (Butterss 1998, 41). The gang is brutal and terrifying and their violence is also directed at women (both in their gang and outside). They are the epitome of violent white masculinity, and while the film is ultimately an anti-racism film (Butterss 1998, 42), it does potentially confirm a stereotype of white working-class men as racist. This is not to suggest that racism is not a problem in working-class communities, but films like *Romper Stomper* depict people of colour and women as victims only and present a view of working-class people as exclusively white.

Australian scholars have examined masculine violence and considered the flip side of mateship that manifests in gang loyalty and celebrations of violence (particularly against women). Connell (1995, 111) suggests that hegemonic forms of masculinity play out in working-class communities as desires to exert dominance over those considered less powerful. While Connell doesn't articulate this in her work necessarily, there is an assumption here that working-class means white. Connell (1995, 55) points to working-class men who are racist and violent towards ethnic minorities, gay men and women, and sees this as the men taking out their resentment and powerlessness on those they perceive as weaker, rather than 'punching up', by engaging in collective action and challenging those in power (Curthoys and Markus 1978, xv). This definitely comes through in some Australian working-class films – there is often a sense that the violent men are resentful due to their own powerlessness, and while films like *Romper Stomper* do attempt to engage with racism, the majority of the violent men in Australian films commit violent acts on women, children or gay men (Butterss 1998, 41). This can also be seen in some of the films that base their stories on true crime. Of note, are *The Boys* (Rowan Woods 1998), *Blackrock* (Steve Vidler 1997) and *Snowtown* (Justin Kurzel 2011). Sexual violence, particularly when perpetrated by a group of men, features quite often in film about white working-class men. According to Heller-Nicholas (2013), these depictions are used to illustrate how 'the loyalty' associated with the Australian notion of male 'mateship' can come with a 'horrific cost' in the shape of sexual violence – a form of violence that has long history in colonised Australia (109).

In *The Boys*, *Blackrock* and *Snowtown*, there is an emphasis on the consumption of alcohol and drugs and other 'bodily pleasures' – a potential rejection of society and respectability and a focus on hedonistic pursuits (Butterss 1998, 40). The working-class men in these films rape, torture and murder both women and gay men. They commit these crimes together, but there is no sense of working-class community outside of these terrible acts, and their victims are provided with no agency (Holland and O'Sullivan 1999, 80). Working-class neighbourhoods in these films are dysfunctional. There is no hope for any of the characters; they are trapped in their circumstances (O'Brien 2013, 70). This presents a picture of working-class people as pitted against each other and offers no insight into working-class community or collective action. Working-class people are dangerous and to be feared.

As a counter to these depictions are some films made by Indigenous film-makers and women that are also centred on working-class communities. Films employing 'Indigenous realism' (Woodhead 2011, 38) – such as Ivan Sen's 2011 *Toomelah*, set in a disadvantaged Indigenous rural neighbourhood – also include male violence. But the violence in Sen's film, and those of many other Indigenous film-makers is the result of the continuing trauma experienced by Indigenous people due to invasion and colonisation (Woodhead 2011, 40). The violence is mainly directed at other Indigenous men, rather than women or children. In some Indigenous films, the violence is perpetrated by white people against Indigenous people, but this violence is committed by white people of all classes and is not confined to white working-class people. According to Collins (2010), the generally positive reception from the pubic for films that engage with the violence and legacy of colonialism 'suggests that cinematic events that address Indigenous–settler relations do have the capacity to galvanize public attention' (65). There are many other Indigenous film-makers whose work displays the intersections of class, race and gender. As well as Ivan Sen's body of work, there are also powerful films by Warwick Thornton, Catriona McKenzie and Rachel Perkins (among others). Indigenous films reveal structural inequalities created and reinforced by class and racism.

Female directors such as Anna Kokkinos have also set films in working-class communities. Kokkinos' 2009 film *Blessed* is an adaptation of a stage play written collaboratively between working-class and non-working-class writers (Tsiolkas 2005, 6). The film is a powerful representation of the injuries of class and centres on the stories of a number of working-class children and their mothers over the course of one night. This film gives agency to the working-class characters and contains many nuanced female characters. And there are ethnic minorities represented too. It is a very bleak film overall though, and extremely sad. While the representations of the impact of class are very real and there is less focus on white violent masculinity, there is still little sense of community on display.

Although there are some exceptions, Australian working-class films that fall outside of this violent white male category tend to be comedy films or 'quirky' films made by middle-class film-makers about working-class people. Classic Australian films, such as Rob Sitch's 1997 *The Castle*, depict working-class people as simple but kind-hearted. The family in *The Castle* (the Kerrigans) discover that their home has been earmarked for demolition (in order to expand the adjacent airport). They fight the decision with the help of a solicitor and a sympathetic barrister. While portrayed as sympathetic characters, fighting for equality (Milner 2009, 160), the family are buffoons. Their lack of cultural capital is regularly mocked. They like kitsch objects and have unsophisticated eating habits. It is assumed that the audience knows why the Kerrigans' tastes are to be laughed at. Middle-class audiences are aware that 'rissoles' are not sophisticated, and they also are aware that the Kerrigans' desire to live next to a runway is ridiculous. The comedy comes from the perceived incongruity of the Kerrigans' love for trashy things and the audiences' understanding of 'good' taste, in what has been described as 'suburban camp' (Lloyd 2002, 127). The Kerrigans are sympathetic 'bogans' – rather than being objects of scorn, they deserve the patronising sympathy of middle-class viewers (Gibson 2013, 65).

While the majority of films about working-class life tend to offer images of working-class people as either violent or simple, there are some that provide a more sympathetic representation. This is the case in Clayton Jacobson's 2006 mockumentary, *Kenny*. The central character of this film, Kenny, is a plumber who works for a company that fits portable toilets at festivals and other events. We follow Kenny through his work days as he encounters plumbing issues and philosophises on life and people's behaviour. Kenny takes pride in his work, and he is represented as a likeable, intelligent and complex character. The film is a comedy, but the joke is not on Kenny; it is on the people he encounters who either don't appreciate his work or who behave badly around him (such as the middle-class attendees at the events). Milner (2009,154) suggests that the character of Kenny epitomises the Australian figure of the 'battler', which was recognisable to audiences.

Overall, the representation of working-class Australians on film is quite limited. While some of the films about violent white men are realist and convincing, there is very little depiction of working-class people outside of this small grouping. Indigenous films provide nuanced representation of Indigenous experience, which overlaps with issues of class, but few non-Indigenous films feature working-class women or working-class people from ethnic minority backgrounds.

Television

The importance of television as a cultural tool should not be underestimated. Television is not just about entertainment but is also a source of education and socialisation. Television is one of the main sites for the creation and reinforcement of cultural memory and what O'Regan (1993, 81) describes as 'a common cultural and political core'. The consumption of television has been high in Australia, and Turner (2000) suggests that in Australia, television consumption takes up more leisure time than any other activities (3). A sense of national imaginary is still disseminated via television programmes and events, and it continues to be an important aspect of the Australian public sphere (Cunningham 2000, 29).

According to Skeggs and Wood (2011, 1), it is not possible to separate class from television, because of the emphasis in television on representing 'everyday lives and ordinary people'. Television is also popular with working-class viewers who often occupy the position of 'subordinated groups in capitalism' (Fiske 1989, 73). But when looking at working-class representation in the medium, it becomes necessary to separate television shows into genres. Working-class people do appear on TV, but are usually restricted to reality TV and game shows. There is very little working-class representation in Australian television drama or comedy (Speed 2006, 408). It is interesting to consider this in light of the ways in which drama, in particular, is valued as 'quality' TV in comparison to reality TV and game shows (Bonner 2003). Contemporary Australian TV dramas are dominated by stories about professionals, mostly doctors and lawyers. In reality TV, it is possible to watch people at work, although most of the shows involve law enforcement of one kind or another. There are fly-on-the-wall documentaries about Gold Coast cops, Random Breath Test units, Kalgoorlie cops, Northern Territory cops and highway patrols, as well as border security (mostly set in Australian airports) and some shows that feature outback truck drivers. Hospital-based fly-on-the wall documentaries include working-class patients, and there are working-class contestants on game shows, talent shows and some cooking competition shows (in cooking shows, working-class contestants are usually presented as the 'underdogs'). Working-class people are 'spectacularly visible' (Skeggs and Wood 2011, 1) across reality TV even when there is no explicit class commentary included. There are fewer of the shows in Australia that portray working-class behaviours as 'pathological abjectness' (Skeggs and Wood 2011, 2) – a mode of representation that has been common in US and UK reality TV. An exception is *Struggle Street*, which aired in Australia in 2015 and featured poor working-class people from a Sydney suburb. There was a focus on dysfunction – the subjects were battling addictions, family breakdowns and chronic unemployment (Simic 2016, 171). A sensationalist voice-over narration provided little context for the situations of the subjects, and the show was an example of 'poverty porn' (Simic 2016, 172), made by and for middle-class audiences.

The lack of working-class characters on Australian TV (outside of reality TV, game shows and sports) is problematic. It suggests that the lives of working-class people are not interesting enough to be dramatised, and it renders working-class people invisible despite the working-class majority in Australia. Working-class characters do occur, but often as patients or criminals. There are some working-class characters in Australian comedy shows, but they often exist as stereotypes and are subject to mockery, such as the titular characters in the early 2000s sitcom *Kath and Kim* (Gibson 2013, 65), or the grotesque caricatures in *Housos* (2011–2013), set on a public housing estate. Slightly better is the sitcom *Upper Middle Bogan* (2013–present), which centres on an upper-class woman who discovers that her birth parents are working class (Campbell 2014, 37); while still employing some stereotypes, the show critiques the snobbery of the upper-class characters. A soap opera called *The Heights,* first broadcast in 2019, has challenged some of these stereotypes though with its sympathetic and quite nuanced depiction of residents of a public housing estate in Western Australia (Attfield 2019, para. 5).

The exception to this mostly narrow representation occurs in Indigenous dramas. A recent wave of television shows written and directed by Indigenous Australians offers more representation of working-class life (both Indigenous and non-Indigenous). In the Indigenous shows, characters are working-class blue- and white-collar workers living in public housing and working-class neighbourhoods. A note here on Indigenous representation – Marcia Langton (1993, 24) points to a 'dense history of racist, distorted and often offensive representations of Indigenous people' and identifies a need for Indigenous people to make self-representations to create an anti-colonial cultural critique in order to 'undermine the colonial hegemony' (8). Self-representations can change the way that non-Indigenous people understand Indigenous people, because most of what is known is based on representations. According to Langton (1993), when Indigenous people are in control of representations, the 'subject speaks back and the dominant culture is informed by Indigenous Cultural Practices, particularly practices of resistance' (36). For Langton, Indigenous representations should be as diverse as Indigenous culture. Aileen Moreton-Robinson (2004) suggests that historically, Indigenous people have been 'placed outside discursive regimes of power and knowledge' (83). Indigenous people have often been (and still are) the subjects of investigation (such as in anthropology and ethnography), but have not often been considered by non-Indigenous people as providers of knowledge. Indigenous writers, directors and producers are therefore challenging the discursive regimes and the coloniser's gaze.

The ground-breaking TV series *Redfern Now*, which first aired on ABC TV in Australia in 2012, tells the stories of Indigenous characters living in the inner-city suburb of Redfern (Collins 2013, 216) – traditionally an Indigenous working-class community. The representations of Indigenous characters are nuanced and realistic, and while not all characters are working class, the show reveals the intersections between race, class, gender and sexuality. Other shows (also aired on the ABC) such as family drama *The Gods of Wheat Street* (2014), science-fiction drama *Cleverman* (2016–present) and comedies *Black Comedy* (2014–present) and *8MMM Aboriginal Radio* (2015) also illustrate these intersections in interesting ways.

Conclusion

Popular culture is an important place to look for working-class representation and working-class expression. It is possible that nuanced representations can shift attitudes towards working-class people and open up conversations about class and the ways in which class structures create and reinforce inequality. With inequality growing in Australia, the timing is important. As politicians deny or downplay the existence of inequality, the persuasiveness of popular culture becomes even more important. As asserted in the introduction, the field of working-class studies plays an important role. Through critical analysis of cultural texts, products and practices, scholars working in the field are able to bring to light the ways in which class works and advocate for change and improvements to working-class life. Revealing the limitations of current representations opens up conversations about how working-class life should be presented and can encourage more nuanced representations to be made. It's possible that films and television shows to come will offer a more positive and empowering depiction of working-class life without shying away from the realities of inequality and discrimination.

Notes

1 In 1964 Australian author Donald Horne wrote *The Lucky Country*. While Horne intended this description of Australia to be ironic, the term is most often used favourably.
2 Indigenous rural workers on the many sheep and cattle stations expected to work for rations rather than wages. Indigenous rural children were taken from their families, sent to 'missions' to receive a 'white' education and then taken to far away cities to work as indentured domestic servants.
3 ANZAC stands for Australian and New Zealand Army Corps – originally those who fought during the Gallipoli campaign of 1915.

References

Attfield, S. (2019) 'The Heights – At Last, a Credible Australian Working-Class Soap', *The Conversation*, March 6, viewed September 2 2020, https://theconversation.com/the-heights-at-last-a-credible-australian-working-class-soap-112961

Barnes, T. and Cahill, D. (2012) 'Marxism and Class Analysis in Australia', *Journal of Australian Political Economy*, 70, pp. 47–69.

Basu, L., Erll, A. and Nunning, A. (2013) *Ned Kelly as Memory Dispositif: Media, Time, Power, and the Development of Australian Identities*, Berlin, De Gruyter.

Bennett, A. (2001) *Cultures of Popular Music*, Buckingham, Open University Press.

Bonner, F. (2003) *Ordinary Television: Analysing Popular TV*, London, Sage Publications.

Buckley, K. and Wheelwright, T. (1994) *No Paradise for Workers: Capitalism and the Common People in Australia*, Melbourne, Oxford University Press.

Butterss, P. (1998) 'When Being a Man Is All You've Got: Masculinity in *Romper Stomper, Idiot Box, Blackrock* and *The Boys*', *Metro Magazine: Media & Education Magazine*, 117, pp. 40–46.

Campbell, M. (2014) 'Opposite Ends of the Freeway: Upper Middle Bogan and the Mobility of Class Distinction', *Metro Magazine: Media & Education Magazine*, 181, pp. 36–40.

Collins, F. (2010) 'After the Apology: Reframing Violence and Suffering in *First Australians, Australia* and *Samson and Delilah, Continuum*, 24, 1, pp. 65–77.

Collins, F. (2013) 'Blackfella Films: Decolonizing urban Aboriginality in *Redfern Now*', *Studies in Australasian Cinema*, 7, 2–3, pp. 215–225.

Connell, R. W. (1995) *Masculinities*, California, University of California Press.

Cunningham, S. (2000) 'History, Contexts, Politics, Policy', in Turner, G. and Cunningham, S. (eds.) *The Australian TV Book*, St Leonards, Allen and Unwin.

Curthoys, A. and Markus, A. (1978) (eds.) *Who are our Enemies? Racism and the Australian Working Class*, Neutral Bay, Hale and Iremonger.

Dunbar-Hall, P. and Gibson, C. (2004) *Deadly Sounds, Deadly Places: Contemporary Aboriginal Music in Australia*, Randwick NSW, University of New South Wales Press.

Fiske, J. (1989) 'Everyday Quizzes, Everyday Life' in Tulloch, J. and Turner, G. (eds.) *Australian Television: Programs, Pleasures and Politics*, Sydney, Allen and Unwin.

Gibson, C. (2013) 'Welcome to Bogan-Ville: Reframing Class and Place through Humour', *Journal of Australian Studies*, 37, 1, pp. 62–75.

Greig, A., Lewins, F. and White, K. (2003) *Inequality in Australia*, Cambridge, Cambridge University Press.

Hall, S. (1997). *Representation: Cultural Representations and Signifying Practices*, London, Sage.

Haskins, V. and Scrimgeour, A. (2015) '"Strike Strike, We Strike": Making Aboriginal Domestic Labor Visible in the Pilbara Pastoral Workers' Strike, Western Australia, 1946–1952', *International Labor and Working-Class History*, 88, pp. 87–108.

Heller-Nicholas, A. (2013) 'The Dark Side of Mateship: Rape and Silence in *Blackrock*', *Screen Education*, 68, pp. 109–114.

Hindess, B. and Sawer, M. (2004) *Us and Them: Anti-Elitism in Australia*, Perth, API Network.

Holland, F. and O'Sullivan, J. (1999) '"Lethal Larrikins": Cinematic Subversions of Mythical Masculinities in *Blackrock* and *The Boys*', *Antipodes*, December, pp. 79–84.

Horne, D. (1964) *The Lucky Country*, Ringwood, Penguin.

Hudson, W. and Bolton, G. (eds.) (1997) *Creating Australia: Changing Australian History*, St Leonards, Allen and Unwin.

Kuhn, R. (2005) *Class and Struggle in Australia*, Sydney, Pearson Education Australia.

Langton, M. (1993) *'Well, I Heard It on the Radio and I Saw It on the Television' ...: An Essay for the Australian Film Commission on the Politics and Aesthetics of Filmmaking by and about Aboriginal People and Things*, Melbourne, Custom Book Centre.

Leigh, A. (2013) *Battlers and Billionaires: The Story of Inequality in Australia*, Collingwood, Schwartz Publishing.

Lloyd, J. (2002) '*The Castle*: A Cinema of Dislocation', *Australian Screen Education*, 30, pp. 125–130.

McGregor, C. (2001) *Class in Australia*, Ringwood, Penguin.

Milner, L. (2009) 'Kenny: The evolution of the Battler Figure in Howard's Australia', *Journal of Australian Studies*, 33, 2, pp. 153–164.

Mitchell, T. (2007) 'The Reography of Reason: Australian Hip Hop as Experimental History and Pedagogy', *Altitude* 8.

Moore, A. (2000) 'Opera of the Proletariat: Rugby League, the Labour Movement and Working-Class Culture in NSW and Queensland', *Labour History*, 79, pp. 57–70.

Moreton- Robinson, A. (2004) *Whitening Race: Essays in Social and Cultural Criticism*, Canberra, Aboriginal Studies Press.

Morgan, S. (2011) 'Woolloomooloo or Wapping? Critical responses to *The Sentimental Bloke* in 1920s London and the Normalization of the Inner-City Working Class', *Studies in Australasian Cinema*, 5, 3, pp. 321–332.

O'Brien, G. (2013) 'Getting under your Skin: Revisiting "Romper Stomper" and "Snowtown" through Embodied Film Theory', *Metro Magazine: Media & Education Magazine*, 178, pp. 64–71.
O'Regan, T. (1993) *Australian Television Culture*, St Leonards, Allen and Unwin.
Page, J. (2002) 'Is Mateship a Virtue?', *Australian Journal of Social Issues*, 37, 2, pp. 193–200.
Simic, Z. (2016) '*Struggle Street* ... Poverty Porn?', in Arrow, M., Baker, J. and Monagle, C. (eds.) *Small Screens: Essays on Contemporary Australian Television*, Clayton, Monash University Publishing.
Shepherd, J. (1990) *Music as Social Text*, Cambridge, Polity Press.
Shirley, G. and Adams, B. (1989) *Australian Cinema: The First Eighty Years*, Sydney, Currency Press.
Skeggs, B. and Wood, H. (eds.) (2011) *Reality Television and Class*, Basingstoke, Palgrave Macmillan.
Speed, L. (2006) 'When the Sun Sets over Suburbia: Class and Subculture in Bruce Beresford's Puberty Blues', *Continuum: Journal of Media & Cultural Studies*, 20, 3, pp. 407–418.
Speedy, K. (2015) 'The Sutton Case: The First Franco-Australian Foray into Blackbirding', *Journal of Pacific History*, 50, 3, pp. 344–364.
Tsiolkas, C. (2005) 'Still Lives: Who's Afraid of the Working Class? A Play Commissioned in 1998 to Celebrate the Tenth Anniversary of Melbourne Workers Theatre', *Australian Author*, 37, 2, pp. 6–7.
Turner, G. (2000) 'Studying Television', in Turner, G. and Cunningham, S. (eds) *The Australian TV Book*, St Leonards, Allen and Unwin.
Ward, R. (2003, c1966) *The Australian Legend*, Melbourne, Oxford University Press.
Whitman, K. (2013) 'The "Aussie Battler" and the Hegemony of Centralising Working-Class Masculinity in Australia, *Australian Feminist Studies*, 28, 75, pp. 50–64.
Williams, J. (1995) *Quarantined Culture: Australian Reactions to Modernism 1913–1939*, Cambridge, Cambridge University Press.
Williamson, J., Beynon, H. and Rowbotham, S. (2001) 'Changing Images', in Rowbotham, S. and Beynon, H. (eds.) *Looking at Class: Film, Television and the Working Class in Britain*, London, Rivers Oram Press.
Woodhead, J. (2011) 'A Remote Possibility? The Uncomfortable Realities of "Toomelah"', *Metro Magazine: Media & Education Magazine*, 170, pp. 38–40.
Woollacott, A. (2009) 'Frontier Violence and Settler Manhood', *History Australia*, 6, 1, pp. 11.1–11.15.
Zaniello, T. (2005) 'Filming Class', in Linkon, S. and Russo, J. (eds.) *New Working-Class Studies*, Ithaca, Cornell University Press.

Filmography

Black Comedy, Directors Beck Cole et al., 2014.
Blackrock, Director Steven Vidler, 1997.
Blessed, Director Anna Kokkinos, 2009.
Cleverman, Directors, Wayne Blair and Leah Purcell, 2016–2017.
Housos, Director Paul Fenech, 2011–2013.
Kath and Kim, Director Ted Emery, 2002–2007.
Kenny, Director Clayton Jacobson, 2006.
Redfern Now, Directors Rachel Perkins et al., 2012–2015.
Romper Stomper, Director Geoffrey Wright, 1992.
Snowtown, Director Justin Kurzel, 2011.
Struggle Street, Producer Marc Radomsky, 2015.
The Boys, Director Rowan Woods, 1998.
The Castle, Director Rob Sitch, 1997.
The Gods of Wheat Street, Directors Wayne Blair et al., 2014.
The Heights, Directors Karl Zwicky et al., 2019–present.
The Sentimental Bloke, Director Raymond Longford, 1919.
The Story of the Kelly Gang, Director Charles Tait, 1906.
Toomelah, Director Ivan Sen, 2011.
Upper Middle Bogan, Directors Wayne Hope and Tony Martin, 2013.
8MMM Aboriginal Radio, Director Dena Curtis, 2015.

Discography

January 26th, A. B. Original, Adam Briggs and Daniel Rankine, 2016.
Working Class Man, Jimmy Barnes, 1985.

Part V
Representations

Section introduction

Representations of the working class

Michelle M. Tokarczyk

When we refer to representations of the working class, we refer both to works composed by those outside of the working class that reflect these classes' conceptions, and often stereotypes of working-class people, as well as those composed by and about people from the working class. The latter category is the thrust of much representation in literature, art, and music that working-class scholars study and working-class people appreciate as a rendition of their experience. However, working-class scholars are not only interested in work that speaks to the working class and accurately represents their lives for other classes, although these concerns are paramount. Popular visual media – films, television shows, and Netflix series, for example – have a powerful hold on the contemporary imagination. Developed nations are often segregated by classes, so people will formulate many of their images of the working classes on the basis of popular media representations. Hence, it is extremely important for working-class scholars to analyze popular media as well as forms that speak to a narrower audience.

The project of building working-class studies in general and the study of representations in particular followed a trajectory similar to that in women's studies. Initially, scholars knew that more working-class texts existed than their peers would acknowledge. In literature, for example they knew that American working-class texts included far more than the novels of John Steinbeck and Stephen Crane. So the work of recovery began, and texts such as Pietro di Donato's *Christ in Concrete* (1939/1993) and Anzia Yezierska's *Bread Givers* (1994) came to signify the immigrant working-class experience. Yezierska's novel was actually rediscovered by feminist historian Alice Kessler-Harris, but that does not reduce the importance of working-class scholars recognizing it as a text that represented the situation of the working-classes in early twentieth-century America. Janet Zandy, one of the pioneers in the study of working-class representations, helped to solidify the field with her anthologies. In 1990, she published *Calling Home: Working-Class Women's Writings*. This text includes the works of established writers such as Dorothy Allison, Audre Lorde, and Tillie Olsen as well as work by less-recognised writers such as Sue Doro and Donna Langston. The anthology takes a broad view of literature and includes reportage, speeches, and songs as well as more traditional literary genres. Each of the text's three sections begins with a collage of photographs, many donated from family collections. Zandy's first anthology thus provided a model for what working-class scholarship would look like: it would be interdisciplinary and cross-disciplinary, and it would look at those at the margins of the discipline to dismantle privilege and critique the canon scholars were forming. Later, Janet Zandy and Nicholas Coles compiled an exhaustive anthology, *American Working-Class Literature* (Coles and Zandy 2007). This text organises its material historically and traces American working-class writing to the earliest days of colonization and the formation of the republic. The editors include numerous spirituals, union songs, and other protest songs, thus making popular representations of working-class life performed by working-class people available to a readership of students and scholars. Again, the placement of songs popular with working-class people with texts by numerous recognized authors, such as Herman Melville and Tillie Olsen, validates these songs as a form of cultural production.

In addition to recovering and re-presenting working-class texts, scholars needed to find a way to explain how they recognized working-class texts. As important, they needed to develop criteria for judging working-class texts; as many working-class scholars have noted, neither the themes nor the form of bourgeois literature was often appropriate for working-class texts. In her seminal 'In the skin of a worker; or, what makes a text working class?' Zandy (2004b) theorizes how one can recognize a working-class text and, by extension, a working-class artist. (I am using 'artist' as an inclusive term for those who create representations.) She argues that a working-class text represents the lived experience of class by representing it from inside ('in the skin') the working-class perspective rather than from a voyeuristic outside experience. Unlike some contemporary American discourse around class, Zandy notes, working-class writing is not de facto white writing. It depicts a consciousness of class oppression and the suffering resulting from injustice and affecting working people across races. While working-class texts might represent particular persons' struggles, the texts are not concerned with private psychological crises as much as they are with the collective fate of the working class. It is important to note that Zandy believes a person needn't be from the working class to represent it; those from higher classes will need to put in incredible work and develop empathy for working-class experiences, but if they do so they can accurately and movingly represent this class.

Renny Christopher and Carolyn Whitson, in 'Toward a theory of working-class literature' (1999), take up the question of audience and argue that working-class and middle-class literature have substantive differences; for one, working-class literature implicitly demands action from the reader. Paul Lauter's (2005) 'Under construction: Working-class writing.' included in John Russo and Sherry Lee Linkon's *New Working-Class Studies*, examines the conditions that produce working-class writing as well as the relationship of representations with their audiences, stressing that working-class writing and the study of working-class literature are continually evolving, being constructed and reconstructed. Working-class studies scholarship is acutely aware of the fluidity of class compositions and representations.

Working-class studies scholars have noted that the Depression Era (1929–1942) was the heyday of class consciousness and working-class representation. It spawned writers such as John Steinbeck, Muriel Rukeyser, and Clifford Odets, songs such as 'Brother can you spare a dime?' (1932), and visual artists such as Diego Rivera and Dorothea Lange. A few influential critical works on Depression literature were written shortly before the dawn of new working-class studies. Barbara Foley's *Radical Representations: Politics & Form in U.S. Proletarian Fiction, 1929–1941* (1993) analyzed the proletarian novel in this period and argued that the genre's success was limited not because it was too radical or too prescriptive, as was often asserted, but rather because it was not radical enough. Paula Rabinowitz, in *Labor and Desire: Women's Revolutionary Fiction in Depression America* (1991), examines the work of women writers voicing feminist concerns in an era which was thought to be a quiet one for women's issues. *Writing Red: An Anthology of American Women Writers, 1930–1940* (1993), edited by Charlotte Nekola, Paula Rabinowitz, and

Toni Morrison, does the recuperative work of foregrounding working-class women's writing, a step that was essential for Rabinowtiz's own scholarship. Constance Coiner likewise promoted the recovery and analysis of proletarian women writers. Her article 'U.S. working-class women's fiction: Notes toward an overview' (1995b) is widely cited, and her *Better Red: The Writing and Resistance of Tillie Olsen and Meridel LeSueur* (1995a), the first book-length study of these authors, is an interdisciplinary interpretation of the writers' works as well as their negotiations with feminism, politics, and motherhood. Texts such as Foley's, Rabinowtiz's, and Coiner's demonstrate increasing interest in representations of the working class.

What We Hold in Common: An Introduction to Working-Class Studies (1991), Zandy's edited anthology, includes autobiographical and pedagogical pieces as well as literary theory and criticism. Her essay on poems about the Triangle Shirtwaist Factory Fire written by several contemporary American poets probes at the centrality of this tragedy to working-class poets' imaginations. Her text *Hands: Physical Labor, Class, and Cultural Work* (2004a), in which 'In the skin of a worker' appears, begins with the question 'How much are two hands worth?' An organically interdisciplinary book, *Hands* examines the representations of disposable workers in Audre Lorde's and Muriel Rukeyser's work, the prison-industrial complex, and the paintings of Ralph Fasanella, a self-taught painter and chronicler of New York urban life.

New Working-Class Studies (2005), edited by John Russo and Sherry Lee Linkon, is composed of essays written by scholars across disciplines who consider themselves practitioners of new working-class studies. This anthology features scholars from numerous disciplines who apply an intersectional and interdisciplinary analysis of class. Paul Lauter's 'Under construction: Working-class writing' examines the conditions that produce working-class writing as well as its relationship with its working-class audience. In his 'Work poetry and working-class poetry' (2005), Jim Daniels, a widely recognized poet, examines how working-class poetry attempts to construct a literary home for a constituency that has been displaced in canonical work. Tom Zaniello's 'Filming class' (2005) tackles the contradictory nature of film as both photographically accurate and ideologically problematic because ideology suppresses or reshapes content. Rachel Lee Rubin's (2005) '"Working man's Ph.D.": The music of working-class studies' begins with the question of what insight we might gain from examining how music is a primary means through which working-class people comfort and define themselves. She also asks what the study of class adds to the study of popular music. As there are few scholarly articles on working-class film or music, Zaniello's and Rubin's are groundbreaking.

My anthology *Critical Approaches to American Working-Class Literature* (2011) was compiled to expand the kinds of work analyzed by working-class studies scholars as well as the critical apparatus they used. It includes pieces such as Paula Rabinowtiz's '"between the outhouse and the garbage dump": Locating collapse in depression literature' and Phoebe S. Jackson's 'Cultural geographies and local economies.' that examine the physical spaces of working-class lives. Renny Christopher, in 'Work is a war, or all their lives they dug their graves.' analyzes how several working-class texts across genres unflinchingly depict workplace hazards and injuries that are rarely recognized. In one of the rare treatments of theatre, Maria F. Brandt's 'The man in the family' unpacks the performance of gender in 1930s protest theatre.

A History of British Working Class Literature (2017), a collection of essays on said topic edited by John Goodridge and Bridget Keegan, places the birth of working-class literature at around 1700, corresponding with the advent of the Industrial Revolution. Like other working-class scholars, these editors grapple with questions of definition. They propose defining working-class literature as having been 'produced by individuals who have not enjoyed social, economic and educational advantages' (Goodridge and Keegan 2017, 1). Yet they also make use of the OED definition that states the working class works for wages and comes from families that are typically considered as part of the lowest class in terms of economic and social status. The editors take as their starting point that writing among the laboring classes was recognized since the early eighteenth century, but was represented as either an act of isolated natural genius or the results of efforts of self-improvement among blighted individuals.

Goodridge and Keaton include numerous genres of and approaches to working-class literature. Florence S. Boos' 'At the margins of print: Life narratives of Victorian working class women' examines the ever popular genre of life writing among the working class during a period when class oppression was made visible in the novels of Charles Dickens. While most of the essays are about traditional literary genres, there is one about serial fiction and one about newspapers. Rod Hermeston's 'Tensions, transformations, and local identity: The evolving meanings of nineteenth-century Tyneside dialect songs' examines northeast music hall culture. *A History of British Working Class Literature* demonstrates both the similarities and departures (notably around questions of intersectionality) on questions about and approaches to working-class literature on both sides of the Atlantic.

Nicholas Coles and Paul Lauter's *A History of American Working-Class Literature* was also published in 2017. This anthology's scope is historical, ranging from critical work on texts from the colonial period and early African-American culture to Sherry Lee Linkon's study of the literature of deindustrialization. Theoretical essays such as Paul Lauter's 'Why work? Early American theories and practices' and Sara Appel's essay on applying an intersectional analysis to literary and media texts are also included. Amy Brady's 'The workers' theatre of the twentieth century' begins by noting that workers' theatre began in around 1910, rather than in the Depression era with which it is so strongly associated. In examining some of the theatre tropes into the twenty-first century, Brady demonstrates how workers' theatre's commitment to educating and inspiring audiences was subversive of Western theatre practices.

The contributors to *The Routledge International Handbook of Working-Class Studies* have broadened the scope of their investigations from the national to the international and expanded the genres they investigate. As important, the contributors often analyze texts in different media genres, thus demonstrating the pliability of theories of working-class texts as well as the ways that these texts interact with multiple audiences.

The publication of Sonali Perera's *No Country: Working-Class Writing in the Age of Globalization* (2014) marked a move away from European-dominated analyses of class, shifting the focus of class analysis to the Global South and, in the process of doing so, finding new ways of interrogating Western working-class texts. Perera revises questions as to what constitutes working-class literature and interrogates her own project with the words 'What does it mean to invoke working-class writing as a mode of internationalism in an age of comparative advantage and outsourcing?' (2014, 4). Her critical study includes Muk Raj Anand from India, Mahasweta Devi from Bangladesh, Ambalavaner Sivanandan from Sri Lanka, Bessie Smith from South Africa as well as Tillie Olsen.

Issues that Perera addresses such as exile and decoloniality are taken up Christine Schlote in 'Writing Dubai: Indian labour migrants and taxi topographies,' which examines the representation of South Asian migrant labor in this petro state. In a pioneering essay 'Petrofiction: The oil encounter and the novel.' Amitav Ghosh argues that literary representations of the workers in petro states are imaginatively sterile. Schlote challenges this assessment through her readings of Shamlal Puri's novel *Dubai Dreams: The Road to Riches* (2010) and Ali F. Mostafa's film *City of Life* (2009). Schlote focuses on the forms and conventions in these representations, and finds in them an alternative narrative to what Ghosh termed the 'muteness of the Oil encounter.'

Tom Zaniello focuses on the global precariat, specifically the vast majority of them who have migrated to urban centers for work and have inspired filmmakers to bear witness to these people's struggles. "The cinema of the precariat" references early texts on the subject such as Andrew Ross's *Nice Work If You Can Get It* (2009) and Guy Standing's *The Precariat: The New Dangerous Class* (2011), then focuses on both traditional documentaries and online innovative forms that represent a pervasive yet often hidden component of the global economy.

Documentaries provide particularly complex sites for the study of representations of the working class. These works are created, sometimes by upper classes, with certain interpretations in mind; yet the many visual cues inherent in visual media as well as the ease with which a viewing audience can share interpretations serve to layer and complicate meanings. Carol Quirke explores such issues in 'The "body of labor" in U.S. postwar documentary photography: A working-class studies perspective.' In 1946, *Fortune* featured a spread of pictures of workers by the recognized photographer Walker Evans titled 'Labor anonymous.' Quirke explores the tensions between the editors' reading of these photos as depicting workers' value to the nation and the post-World-War II ideology that still kept workers on the margins.

While scholars of working-class art often stress the importance of this genre's bearing witness to working-class life, Janet Zandy begins with the premise articulated in a speech by labor activist Rose Schneiderman: 'The worker must have bread, but she must have roses too' (Eisenstein 1983, 32). The quest for beauty, Zandy, like Schneiderman, argues, is as essential to the working classes as it is to the upper classes. Yet we are hampered in understanding this impetus for beauty by an incomplete cataloging of working-class art and a lack of understanding as to how working-class art is perceived by and interacts with the mainstream art establishment of grants, museums, and the like. Working-class art often falls into the category of outsider art: art that is created by those without formal training and on the margins of the art establishment. 'Mapping working-class art' begins with Denis Wood's argument that maps are working instruments of particular and often masked interests and uses the metaphor of mapping to analyze how workers are presented aesthetically (Wood and Fels 1992; Wood 2010).

While Schlote expands the evolving canon of working-class representations, Ben Clarke, in '"Things that are left out": Working-class writing and the idea of literature.' critiques the ways that the literary establishment (the canon, publishers' lists, and syllabi) marginalize or even exclude working-class writing. As a category, class is viewed as archaic; working-class writing itself is interpreted as didactic and formally stilted. Building on Zandy's call for a new criteria by which to judge working-class literature, Clarke proposes a new critical engagement with working-class texts. In what he calls women's sensational writing, especially abolitionist and feminist narratives, he sees a model for intervention in the ideologically driven literary criteria that often exclude political texts. His essay examines prominent works such as D.H. Lawrence's *Sons and Lovers* (1913[BIB-023/1997][1997]) and Pat Barker's *Union Street* (1982), but focuses on novels, short stories, and nonfiction of less recognized mid-twentieth-century authors. The inclusion of such marginal voices in a critical reconsideration, Clarke argues, complicates our understanding of working-class writing as well as of literature itself.

Striving to particularize working-class motifs and trace their historical significance and adaptation, Simon Lee, in 'Lit-grit: The gritty and the grim in British working-class cultural production.' examines representations of gritty spaces as a constituent part of the realist novel. After tracing the development of this genre in romantic and sentimental novels, Lee surveys working-class novels, drama, and films of the twentieth and twenty-first centuries to examine the ways that the amplifications of gritty spaces in cultural representations function as a vehicle for exploring the relationship between aesthetics and ethics. Finally, Lee advances criteria for evaluating representations of gritty spaces in working-class literature and highlights concerns about the ideologies behind representations of the working class.

While many gritty spaces are easily identified as working class, some must be named, because our biases impede us from recognizing the classed nature of spaces such as prisons. Prisons are sites of labor: inmate work. Yet according to the International Labor Organization, between 2000–2011 wages in United States' prisons ranged between $0.23 and $1.15 an hour. Moreover many inmates have not been convicted of crimes; they could not afford bail and are awaiting trial in jails. Nathaniel Heggins Bryant's chapter argues for the need to introduce critical prison studies into working-class studies, especially in an American context. He begins to do so by critiquing the punitive philosophies behind penal labor from the early days of capitalism to the current prison-industrial complex. He then examines contemporary prison-oriented narratives, such as *Orange is the New Black* (2013–2019), as texts that risk fetishizing prison experiences but concurrently perform important intellectual work in representing occluded spaces.

Consumerism is particularly intertwined with one of the most influential twentieth- and twenty-first-century mediums: television. Television, financed by advertisements, revolutionized the way that people entertained themselves and paved the way for extensive representations of class as well as its commodification. The quintessential television series representing the working class was *The Honeymooners* (1955–1956). Set in mid 1950s Brooklyn, this half-hour weekly sitcom focused on the life of Ralph Kramden, a New York City bus driver, his wife Alice, his friend Ed Norton, a sewer worker, and his wife Trixie. Unlike most television households at the time and to date, Ralph's apartment was small and modestly furnished. Some of the plots involve Ralph's schemes to cheaply obtain goods or make money outside of his job. No television series depicting the working class achieved the popularity of *The Honeymooners* until *Roseanne* aired in 1988 and ran until 1997. This sitcom represented a working-class family: the wife Roseanne and her spouse Dan work at a number of blue-collar jobs, frequently experiencing job loss and economic struggle.

Sociologist Beverly Skeggs and American Studies scholar Hamilton Taylor agree that representations of the working class on television tend to reinforce gender stereotypes. Jennifer Forsberg finds these scholars' analyses perceptive, but notes that they have not focused on post-recession reality television. In 'Marketing millennial women: Embodied class performativity on American television,' Forsberg analyzes reality television shows and sitcoms about working-class identity among millennials. She argues that these programs represent working-class status as a lifestyle choice divorced from economic constraints and systems of oppression. Her examination reveals a neglected triangulation of gender, class, and work and a representation of twenty-first-century female bodies. Ultimately, Forsberg adds to the discussion of how class identity is made visible to television audiences and how they in turn legitimate existing class structures.

Representations of the working class by working-class artists or allies of the working class communicate how working-class people see themselves. They express the reality of workers' lives by, in Zandy's words, getting inside the skin of working-class people. While working-class texts (including music, art, media, etc.) represent suffering caused by class oppression, they also celebrate working-class culture and working-class perseverance. In media as diverse as novels and hip hop, working-class people represent themselves. To understand the complexity and variety of working-class life, we scholars must examine its multiple representations.

References

Appel, S. (2017) 'A Turn of the Sphere: The Place of Class in Intersectional Analysis.' in Coles, N. and Lauter, P. (eds.) *A History of American Working-Class Literature*, Cambridge and New York, Cambridge University Press.

Barker, P. (1982) *Union Street*, London, Virago Press.

Boos, F. S. (2017) 'At the Margins of Print: Life Narratives of Victorian Working Class Women.' in Goodridge, J. and Keegan, B. (eds.) *A History of British Working Class Literature*, Cambridge and New York, Cambridge University Press.

Brady, A. (2017) 'The Workers' Theatre of the Twentieth Century.' in Coles, N. and Lauter, P. (eds.) (2017) *A History of American Working-Class Literature*, Cambridge and New York, Cambridge University Press.

Brandt, M. F. (2011) '"The Man in the Family": Staging Gender in Waiting for Lefty and American Protest Theatre.' in Tokarczyk, M. (ed.) *Critical Approaches to American Working-Class Literature*, New York & Oxon, UK, Routledge.

'Brother, Can You Spare a Dime?' lyricist Yip Harburg and composer Jay Gorney. 1932.

Christopher, R. (2011) '"Work is a War, Or All Their Lives They Dug Their Graves,"' in Tokarczyk, M. (ed.) *Critical Approaches to American Working-Class Literature*, New York & Oxon, UK, Routledge.

Christopher, R. and Whitson, C. (1999) 'Toward a Theory of Working-Class Literature.' *Thought & Action*, 15, pp.71–81.

City of Life, Director Ali F. Mostafa, 2009.

Coiner, C. (1995a) *Better Red: The Writing and Resistance of Tillie Olsen and Meridel LeSueur*, Oxford and New York, Oxford University Press.

Coiner, C. (1995b) 'U.S. Working-Class Women's Fiction: Notes Toward an Overview.' *Women's Studies Quarterly*, 23, 1–2, Spring/Summer, pp. 248–267.

Coles, N. and Lauter, P. (eds.) (2017) *A History of American Working-Class Literature*, Cambridge and New York, Cambridge University Press.

Coles, N. and Zandy, J. (eds.) (2007) *American Working-Class Literature*, New York and Oxford, Oxford University Press.

Daniels, J. (2005) 'Work Poetry and Working-Class Poetry,' in Russo, J. and Linkon, S. L. (eds.) *New Working-Class Studies*, Ithaca, Cornell University Press.

Di Donato, P. (1939, 1993) *Christ in Concrete*, New York, New American Library.

Eisenstein, S. (1983) *Give Us Bread but Give Us Roses: Working Women's Consciousness in the U.S., 1890 to the First World War*, London & Kegan, Routledge Press.

Foley, B. (1993) *Radical Representations: Politics & Form in U.S. Proletarian Fiction, 1929–1941*, Durham &London, Duke University Press.

Goodridge, J. and Keegan, B. (eds.) (2017) *A History of British Working Class Literature*, Cambridge and New York, Cambridge University Press.

Hermeston, R. (2017) 'Tensions, Transformations, and Local Identity: The Evolving Meanings of Nineteenth-Century Tyneside Dialect Songs.' in Goodridge, J. and Keegan, B. (eds.) *A History of British Working Class Literature*, Cambridge and New York, Cambridge University Press.

The Honeymooners, Director Frank Satenstein, 1955–1956.

Jackson, P. S. (2011) 'Cultural Geographies and Local Economies: The Lesson from Egypt, Maine.' in Tokarczyk, M. (ed.) *Critical Approaches to American Working-Class Literature*, New York & Oxon, Routledge.

Lauter, P. (2005) 'Under Construction: Working-Class Writing,' in Russo, J. and Linkon, S. L. (eds.) *New Working-Class Studies*, Ithaca, Cornell University Press.

Lauter, P. (2017) 'Why Work? Early American Theories and Practices.' in Coles, N. and Lauter, P. *A History of American Working-Class Literature*, Cambridge and New York, Cambridge University Press.

Lawrence, D. H. (1913, Rpt. 1997) *Sons and Lovers*, Hertfordshire, UK, Wordsworth Publishing.

Nekola, C., Rabinowitz, P. and Morrison, T. (eds.) (1993) *Writing Red: An Anthology of American Women Writers, 1930–1940*, New York, The Feminist Press.

Orange is the New Black, Created by Jenji Kohan, 2013–2019.

Perera, S. (2014) *No Country: Working-Class Writing in the Age of Globalization*, New York, Columbia University Press.

Puri, S. (2010) *Dubai Dreams: The Road to Riches*, London, Crownbird Publishers.

Rabinowitz, P. (1991) *Labor and Desire: Women's Revolutionary Fiction in Depression America*, Chapel Hill, University of North Carolina Press.

Rabinowitz, P. (2011) '"between the outhouse and the garbage dump": Locating Collapse in Depression Literature.' in Tokarczyk, M. (ed.) *Critical Approaches to American Working-Class Literature*, New York & Oxon, UK, Routledge.

Roseanne, ABC, 1988–1997; 2017.

Ross, A. (2009) *Nice Work if You Can Get It*, New York, New York University Press.

Rubin, R. L. (2005) 'Working Man's Ph.D.: The Music of Working-Class Studies.' in Russo, J. and Linkon, S. L. (eds.) *New Working-Class Studies*, Ithaca, Cornell University Press.

Russo, J. and Linkon, S. L. (eds.) (2005) *New Working-Class Studies*, Ithaca, Cornell University Press.
Standing, G. (2011) *The Precariat: The New Dangerous Class*, London and New York, Bloomsbury Publishing.
Tokarczyk, M. M. (ed.) (2011) *Critical Approaches to American Working-Class Literature*, New York and Oxon, Routledge.
Wood, D. (2010) *Rethinking the Power of Maps*, New York, Guilford Press.
Wood, D. and Fels, J. (1992, rev. ed.) *The Power of Maps*, New York, Guilford Press.
Yezierska, A. (1994, 4th ed.) *Bread Givers*, New York, Persea Press.
Zandy, J. (1990) *Calling Home: Working-Class Women's Writings*, New Brunswick, NJ, Rutgers University Press.
Zandy, J. (1991) *What We Hold In Common: An Introduction to Working-Class Studies*, New York, The Feminist Press.
Zandy, J. (2004a) *Hands: Physical Labor, Class, and Cultural Work*, New Brunswick, NJ and London, Rutgers University Press.
Zandy, J. (2004b) 'In the Skin of a Worker; or, What Makes a Text Working Class?.' in Zandy, J. *Hands: Physical Labor, Class, and Cultural Work*, New Brunswick, NJ and London, Rutgers University Press.
Zaniello, T. (2005) 'Filming Class,' in Russo, J. and Linkon, S. L. (eds.) *New Working-Class Studies*, Ithaca, Cornell University Press.

21

Writing Dubai

Indian labour migrants and taxi topographies

Christiane Schlote

Introduction

The billboard of a Dubai real estate development company shows a seemingly endless line of workers, mostly clad in blue overalls and industrial helmets, standing in desert sand and disappearing in the distance.[1] The panel reads: 'To the ones who make it happen.' However, when turning to the reality of Dubai's migrant workers, this apparent acknowledgement that Dubai's 'economic miracle' has been built 'on the indentured labour of millions of Asian workers' (Hunt 2011) is revealed to be no more than a marketing ploy. In 2000, four million Indian, three million Bangladeshi and almost a million Pakistani labour migrants worked legally in the Gulf states, earning $200–400 a month (South Asia: A Special Report 2008).[2] Observing that recruitment agencies charge 'from £1,000 to £3,000 for the visa processing fee' and 'companies routinely confiscate' workers' passports, 'charging exorbitant "processing fees" if they want them back,' Nick Hunt calls the workers' condition 'essentially a three-way con, perpetrated between the recruitment agents, the companies and the UAE government.' Because they are deprived of 'legal rights, trapped in debt and desperate to send money home,' most workers 'have no choice but to stay and work, despite the demeaning conditions' (Hunt 2011).

Social science studies such as Barbara Ehrenreich and Arlie Hochschild's *Global Woman: Nannies, Maids, and Sex Workers in the New Economy* (2004), Toby Shelley's *Exploited: Migrant Labour in the New Global Economy* (2007) and *Global Cities At Work: New Migrant Divisions of Labour* (2009) by Jane Wills et al. have addressed the conditions of migrant workers in various contexts. Given that the 'flows of strategic resources such as oil and of migrant workers across national boundaries are among the most conspicuous phenomena' (Khalaf and Alkobaisi 1999, 273) and that 'the deadly trinity of oil, war and dictatorship' also 'presents the greatest challenge to humanity at the start of the new millennium' (Bacher 2000, 17), the lack of literary responses to what Amitav Ghosh has termed 'the Oil Encounter' (2002, 75) is striking. Arguing that the twentieth-century equivalent of the spice trade is the oil industry, in his pioneering essay 'Petrofiction: The Oil Encounter and the Novel' (first published in 1992), Ghosh claims that despite its dramatic nature, any literary engagement with the oil encounter has remained 'imaginatively sterile' (2002, 76).[3] This article explores the themes, forms and conventions of literary and filmic responses to petro-migrants in Dubai, with a particular focus on Shamlal Puri's *Dubai Dreams: The Rough Road to Riches* (2010), which portrays the lives of a group of Indian taxi drivers in Dubai,[4] and Ali F. Mostafa's film *City of Life* (2009). On the one hand, these literary and filmic responses to the lives of petro-migrants provide alternative narratives to the 'muteness of the Oil Encounter,' as identified by Ghosh (2002). On the other hand, they also exemplify the need for critically examining the hitherto neglected nexus between postcolonial and working-class literature. As Nicola Wilson observes in regard to British working-class writing:

> Twentieth-century British working-class writing has often been studied as a separatist white discourse, isolated from the colonial and postcolonial .... Though the work of first and second generation Asian, African and Caribbean writers is rarely considered in terms of the literary history of working-class writing, a too rigid separation of these fields perpetuates discussions of working-class writing under the implicit terms of whiteness, while also potentially ignoring what colonial and postcolonial writers have to say about class. This has limited our understandings of working-class writing.
>
> *(2015, 12)*

Literary representations of the oil encounter have been scarce in the Gulf states. One notable exception is Abdelrahman Munif's monumental five-part cycle of novels, *Cities of Salt* (1984–1989), which charts the 'psychological dislocation ... mark[ing] the impact of the discovery of oil ... on the individual, social, cultural and environmental life of ... Saudi Arabia' (Badawi 1992, 150).[5] This scarcity may partly be explained by the fact that a modern national literature has only begun to evolve in the United Arab Emirates and the Sultanate of Oman since the early 1970s (Ramsay 2006, 211). According to Ghosh, this is mainly due to the fact that, 'the history of oil is a matter of embarrassment verging on the unspeakable' (2002, 75). The muteness of the history of oil has been ensured 'through regimes of strict corporate secrecy' and 'by the physical and demographic separation of oil installations and their workers from the indigenous population' (Ghosh 2002, 77). Given that, as Jennifer Wenzel put it, institutionally and 'perhaps, at least to some extent, ideologically as well' (quoted in Potter 2017, 382), North America can be seen as the fossil fuel industry's centre, it is not surprising that writers and filmmakers in the Americas have addressed the oil encounter in various media and genres, from Upton Sinclair's *Oil!* (1927/2007) and Gustavo Luis Carrera's *La Novela del petróleo en Venezuela* (1972) to oil thrillers such as Stephen Gaghan's *Syriana* (2005) and Paul Thomas Anderson's *There Will Be Blood* (2007).[6]

The pioneering studies in the fields of petrofiction, petrocultures and energy humanities mainly focus on the analysis of nationally and regionally specific cultural texts such as Stephanie LeMenager's *Living Oil: Petroleum Culture in the American Century* (2013), in which she traces the story of petroleum and how it 'has come to play a foundational role in the American imagination' (4). In his essay '"The black and cruel demon" and its transformations of space: Toward a comparative study of the world literature of oil and place' (2012), Michael K. Walonen suggests 'a productive way of discursively situating texts from disparate cultural and linguistic traditions in terms of their responses to a common global and globalizing situation' (58), and he examines how world literature texts such as Hermann Melville's *Moby Dick* (1851), Upton Sinclair's *Oil!* (1927) and Patrick Chamoiseau's *Texaco* (1992) portray 'the pursuit of oil and the riches derived therefrom, particularly the manner in which this pursuit drastically alters place' (2012, 57–58). Whereas the editors of *Subterranean Estates: Life Worlds of Oil and Gas* (2015), Hannah Appel, Arthur Mason and Michael Watts, highlight the complex network of the global oil industry by examining the industry's sites of extraction, production, marketing and consumption across different regions, including the Russian Urals, Nigeria's Niger Delta, Ecuador and the Gulf of Mexico, Sheena Wilson, Adam Carlson and Imre Szeman's *Petrocultures: Oil, Politics, Culture* (2017), on the one hand, explores 'the claims and assumptions that shape and guide how we think and talk about fossil fuels' (4). On the other hand, this comprehensive collection, ranging from essays on rigs, platforms and pipelines and analyses of American petro-imaginaries to contributions about petro-matters, oil theory and petro-scape aesthetics, further maps out 'the social and political challenges' of our current energy transition (4).

Shamlal Puri's *Dubai Dreams* can be situated within this international body of petrofiction as well as within a variety of South Asian cultural texts (in English and in South Asian languages) concerned with South Asian migrant workers in the Gulf states. These South Asian texts include Benyamin's *Goat Days* (2012; published in Malayalam as *Aadujeevitham*, 2008), about a young Malayali labour migrant in Saudi Arabia, and Jacquelin Singh's children's book *The Case of the Shady Sheikh and Other Stories* (1993). In *Goat Days*, which Ben East (2013) has called 'a modern-day slave tale.' which is '[t]ragically … also based on a true story,' Benny Daniel, who publishes under his pen name, Benyamin, portrays 'the hollowing alienation of the Gulf Malayali like no other book ever had: the loneliness, servitude and despair of Najeeb in a goat pen in the vast barrenness of a Saudi desert … written in a sparse, psalm-like style' (Harikrishnan 2015). Singh's children's book depicts 'an Indian labor contractor and a Gulf sheikh who take money from poor men, promising passports, visas, and work permits for the Gulf' (Leonard 2002, 213). For Karen Leonard, the fact that these themes are even addressed in children's literature is only appropriate, given that 'some of the most highly publicised South Asian workers in the Gulf states are children, young boys from Bangladesh, India, and Pakistan who are used as jockeys in camel racing' (2003, 129).

Starting with a brief overview of South Asian migrant labourers' migration to and presence in the Gulf states, in the following, I will first address South Asian (and other) labour migrants' glaring absence from cultural texts. This aspect is also highly relevant for the general study of (working) class in literature and culture. As Ronald Paul ascertains:

> In his collection of essays entitled *The Bone Won't Break: On Theatre and Hope in Hard Times*, the … playwright John McGrath (1935–2002) points to the systematic social, political and economic marginalization and cultural misrepresentation of working-class people everywhere, a strategy that seeks to keep them from realizing their own collective interests, organization and power.
>
> *(2016, 149)*

For McGrath, radical and alternative group theatre could provide the means to 'combat this constant process of denigration of the working class' (Paul 2016, 149). In regard to the representation of labour migrants within the context of the oil encounter, I will explore questions of genre and Puri's use of literary journalism, in particular. The subsequent comparison between *Dubai Dreams* and Ali F. Mostafa's Emirati film *City of Life* (2009) further demonstrates the importance of medium and genre(s). In my final analysis of representations of labour migrants within a dystopian Dubai, I will especially concentrate on Puri's and Mostafa's use of spatial metaphors and on taxis as interclass encounter zones.

Making labour migration visible

According to Andrew Gardner, historically the South Asian presence in the Gulf is characterised by three overlapping periods. While the first period was marked by South Asian merchants' trade, the second period was dominated by the 'British presence in the region,' which resulted in a more constant connection between the Gulf states and the Indian subcontinent. The third period, beginning in the 1960s, signalled the development of the oil industry and was accompanied by modernisation programmes and increased infrastructures. During this last period, the number of South Asian migrants to the Gulf increased rapidly. Also, the previous movement of skilled migrant workers gave way to the migration of unskilled workers, who Gardner has called 'the transnational proletariat' (2010, 26–28). Andrzej Kapiszewski explains that the Gulf states' growing preference for an Asian workforce (instead of non-local Arab workers) has not only been due to the fact that 'Asians were less expensive to employ, easier to lay-off … and used to leaving their families at home,' but also because 'many Asians were Muslims too' (2006, 7).

Like labour migrants in general, Dubai's 'transnational proletariat' has been largely absent from cultural representations. As Ghosh states, 'the hundreds of thousands of Bengali-speaking people who live and work in the oil kingdoms scarcely ever merit literary attention – or any kind of interest, for that matter' (2002, 78). Furthermore, although 'the "Gulf phenomenon" has been the single development that has made possible the Kerala of today … it is conspicuously absent both in the popular notions that produce the idea of Kerala as a region and in the academic/critical engagements with it' (Radhakrishnan 2009, 218).[7] Over the last century, documentary photography and photojournalism, in particular, have been used to enlarge 'our conception of what human beings do to each other' (Linfield 2010, 38), which also includes capturing the plight of migrant workers in Dubai. Photo essays such as Florian Buettner and Christoph Woehrle's 'The slaves of Dubai' (2010) and Matilde Gattoni's 'Sonapur – Dubai's city of gold' (2011), Connie Samaras's photos of workers in Dubai and Ben Anderson's documentary for BBC One's *Panorama, Slumdogs and Millionaires* (2009), all visualise Mike Davis's suggestion that 'Dubai … has achieved the state of the art in the disenfranchisement of labor' (2005). As Davis declares:

> Trade unions, strikes, and agitators are illegal … while the building boom is carried on the shoulders of an army of poorly paid Pakistanis and Indians working twelve-hour shifts, six and half days a week, in the blast-furnace desert heat. … In addition to being super-exploited, Dubai's helots are also expected to be generally invisible.
>
> *(2005)*

Rahman Badalov observes that the spectacle of 'blazing oil gushers make[s] marvelous cinematographic material … the thick oil stream bursting forth like a fiery monster' (1997). The bodily presence of oil workers and petro-migrants, however, has often been seen as an expendable element in representations of the oil encounter. Almost without commentary and in alienated shots, Werner Herzog's film *Lessons of Darkness* (1992), for example, shows the seemingly surreal landscape of the Kuwaiti oil fires after the first Gulf War. Significantly, the very few human presences (e.g. the firefighters) in the film are described as 'creatures.'[8] Here, *Lessons of Darkness* can be seen to comply with Western literatures' mode of representation, where, instead 'of full representations of the life of the people, literary tradition has typically only offered servants, mere appendages of their master' (Robbins 1986, x). According to Linda Dittmar, the fact that workers and labour migration have hardly been represented in literature may be attributed to the marginalisation of class in favour of 'other group positionalities' within discourses of identity politics and a general 'preference for middle- and upper-class protagonists and perspectives' (1995, 39). The absence of migrant workers is one problematic aspect in representations of the oil encounter. Formally, the question of its appropriate genre is dominant.

Image 21.1 Dubai Gold Souq
Source: photo by Christiane Schlote

The oil encounter and genre

Ghosh suggests that 'we do not yet possess the form that can give the Oil Encounter a literary expression' (2002, 79). According to Ghosh, this is mainly due to the fact that the world of the oil encounter is multilingual, 'displaced, heterogeneous, and international' (2002, 79). It 'poses a radical challenge not merely to the practice of writing as we know it, but to much of modern culture: to such notions as the idea of distinguishable and distant civilizations' (Ghosh 2002, 79). In her analysis of Ghosh's *The Circle of Reason* (1986), Claire Chambers nonetheless observes that Ghosh's 'heterogeneous use of genre' allows for an adequate portrayal of the complexity of the oil encounter. In *The Circle of Reason*, marked by 'transnational settings and polyglot language,' Ghosh mixes the detective novel, the *Bildungsroman*, the picaresque novel and the Hindu epic (Chambers 2006a, 33–34, 47). Like Ghosh, many writers of petrofiction (e.g. Hanan Al-Shaykh, Daniel, Ghassan Kanafani, Munif, Puri) are familiar with migration and displacement. The multilingual and international world of the oil encounter is also less alien to them, since they have often experienced living and working in Gulf states first hand. On his blog (http://shamlalpuri.blogspot.de/), London-based Puri, who grew up in Tanzania, describes himself as an 'author, journalist, photographer, broadcaster' who has worked in East Africa, Britain and the Middle East. As far as genre is concerned, Puri partly follows Munif, who, in *Cities of Salt*, alternates 'between fiction and nonfiction' (Nixon 2011, 77).[9] The last volume of Munif's trilogy, *Desert of*

Darkness, includes 'prose quotations from classical Arabic sources as well as extracts from allegedly foreign journalists' diaries and correspondents' accounts of the general situation and catastrophic changes in the Kingdom of Muiran' (Badawi 1992, 154). In a similar vein, regarding his inspiration for *Dubai Dreams*, Puri explains that during his stay in Dubai he 'came across many friendly taxi drivers. … I have recounted a majority of these stories in this book. … I turned to the Gulf News, Khaleej Times, The National, GulfToday and The Ypress to piece some major events concerning taxi drivers' (2010, 6).

Although reviewers have classified *Dubai Dreams* as a novel, works such as Munif's trilogy have also often been received as sociological rather than literary. John Updike, for example, flouted *Cities of Salt*'s 'single insistent sociological point' (quoted in McLarney 2009, 196). In the case of Anglophone Arab and South Asian writing and its marketing, in particular, reviews and cover blurbs often resort to familiar and ambiguous (partly Orientalist) phrases. *Cities of Salt*, for example, is reviewed as 'seeing carved shutters thrown open or an embroidered veil drawn back' (McLarney 2009, 195). The back cover of *Dubai Dreams* informs readers that it 'lifts the lid off the lives of blue-collar workers in the Middle East.' As the marketing strategies of *Cities of Salt* and *Dubai Dreams* suggest, 'Indo Chic' and 'Arab Chic' function not just as 'a polyvalent cultural sign but as a highly mobile capital good' (Huggan 2001, 67). According to Graham Huggan, the overwhelming popularity of (South Asian) diasporic writers in the West is partly linked to the 'hegemony of the multinational publishing companies' (2001, 78) and to a desire 'to rejuvenate a humdrum domestic culture' (74). Puri's choice of genres for the episodic portrayal of the taxi drivers' hard life in Dubai in thirty-six chapters, most of which begin like a newspaper article (e.g. 'Maqbool Ahmed, a thirty-five-year-old … Muslim from Secundrabad,' 2010, 31), can be understood within the traditions of literary journalism as well as within the conventions of the urban novel.

Puri's choice of functional chapter titles (e.g. 'Simple Binu comes to Dubai,' 'Dirhams or dollars') is indicative of his interest in the mundane daily life of the taxi drivers and reminiscent of the contributions of the New New Journalism, 'the literature of the every day,' which drills 'down into the bedrock of ordinary experience' (Boynton 2005). The deceptive simplicity of Puri's titles also points towards the larger issues addressed in *Dubai Dreams*, which have long been the mainstay of the New New Journalism: 'How does a fast-growing society of immigrants construct a national identity? How does a country built by capitalism consider questions of economic justice? How does a nation of different faiths live together?' (Boynton 2005) The urban novel remains the preferred genre for exploring socio-economic and cultural transformations on a larger scale. It lends itself particularly well to the literary inscription of Dubai as a city, which tries to compensate for its 'relatively small oil-wealth' by 'promoting spectacle … for super-rich tourists' and by investing 'in the trappings – if not the reality – of a major node of knowledge in the global network' (Malecki and Ewers 2007, 475). In the wake of post-industrial transformations, the genre of the urban novel has undergone significant changes and, consequently, its analysis also requires different critical frameworks (e.g. transnationalism, consumerism, etc.) than those applied to the analysis of earlier urban fiction (see Keunen and Eeckhout 2000). Puri depicts Dubai's transnational and multilingual character and its reliance on a foreign workforce through a cast of multilingual and international protagonists, ranging from mainly Indian taxi drivers, Lebanese and Iraqi restaurant owners and Egyptian shopkeepers to Russian prostitutes, Filipino maids, Pakistani bankers and African con men. George Mutada Jr, a young refugee and 'illegal immigrant' from Liberia (Puri 2010, 41), who deals with counterfeit dollar bills, is one of them. Mutada is also exemplary of the implications of the novel's subtitle, *The Rough Road to Riches*.

According to Ellen McLarney, Kanafani's and Munif's work is marked by what – borrowing Raymond Williams's term – she calls 'retrospective radicalism' (2009, 194). This political principle critically contrasts contemporary capitalism with a more humane pre-capitalist world (McLarney 2009, 194). Puri, however, focuses unequivocally on the taxi drivers' current personal and professional hardships. Emirati locals, international business people, Western expatriates and tourists are relegated to the sidelines. In *Cities of Salt*, migrant workers are mainly absent, with the exception of stereotypical characters and 'faceless crowds' (Ghosh 2002, 88). By contrast, twenty-two of the chapters in *Dubai Dreams* start with the (mainly full) names of the novel's main protagonists: Uday Chacko, a 30-year old ambitious Keralite 'with a master's degree in philosophy and religion,' which gave him 'no passport to riches, not even a decent job' (Puri 2010, 9), the newly married Punjabi Hazara Singh, Maqbool Ahmed, 21-year-old Binu Menon from Kerala and 26-year-old Gabriel Matthew (Gabby), who first worked as a taxi driver in Jeddah, before moving from restrictive Saudi Arabia to Dubai.

In a NDTV news report on 'The hidden side of Dubai,' Anchal Vohra observes that the regional and national identities of the mainly Indian, Pakistani and Bangladeshi workers are 'subsumed in the sameness of their story' (Vohra 2009). To a certain extent, the same applies to Puri's protagonists concerning their common precarious status (e.g. no clearly defined rights, no trade unions, dependence on individual/institutional sponsors; Khalaf and Alkobaisi 1999, 294) and their 'not being in control' of their lives, which Guy Standing has identified as one of the key characteristics of the precariat (2009, 112).[10] Their lack of control is also expressed on a personal level, since they have to live in 'enforced bachelorhood' (Puri 2010, 28), which is reminiscent of the bachelor societies of Chinese migrants in North America at the turn of the

Image 21.2 Al Fahidi Street, Dubai
Source: photo by Christiane Schlote

twentieth century, a period when Chinese women were not allowed to immigrate and interracial marriages were illegal. However, Puri counterbalances their occupational identity ('We, the taxi drivers of Dubai'; Puri 2010, 50) with an emphasis on their very individual biographies, migration trajectories, likes and dislikes and (albeit limited) different choices (e.g. at the end of the novel, Uday and Gabby accept the offer of their landlord, Daswani, to participate in his plan to rob a jewellery store). Their heterogeneity reflects Lise Vogel's important observation that workers were never 'a monolithic mass sharing a single consciousness' and that an individual's consciousness 'does not conform in any simple way to the usual categories of political analysis' (Vogel quoted in Hapke 2001, 9). Similarly, the Frassanito Network stresses that, in view of 'the composition of contemporary living labour (from illegalised migrant janitors to temp-working computer freaks) … nobody should simplify precarisation into a new identity' (2005, 61).

In contrast to petrofiction texts by writers such as Al-Shaykh and Abdul-Wali, who also explore migrants' countries of origin, those left behind by the taxi drivers are hardly mentioned, except for the occasional reference to families in India awaiting their monthly remittance, a wife who left her husband in his absence or the death of a relative. The only retrospective elements are the drivers' rare (partly nostalgic) memories of their Indian homes. Before his shift, Uday's 'thoughts returned to India. The whiff of fresh fish arriving in the local market … overpowering him' (Puri 2010, 48). As if any detailed reminiscence of their families back home were to upset the migrants' precarious status and daily routine, the monotony of the taxi drivers' lives – waiting for passengers, navigating Dubai's highways, living in shared accommodation – is also reflected in the novel's pace. Uday describes the migrant workers' life as 'working, eating, sleeping and working again' (Puri 2010, 7). This monotony is further manifested in the taxi drivers' recurring vexations (exploitative employers, stingy passengers, greedy landlords, etc.) and sites (Dubai Airport, Dubai Internet City, Dubai Marina, etc.) and reinforced through Puri's employment of reiterative symbols (e.g. overbearing heat, currencies, etc.). Because of its sole focus on the taxi drivers' drab yet strenuous work, *Dubai Dreams* also brings to mind Michael Denning's argument that work 'itself resists representation,' since the 'labor to render the repetitive manual tasks of shop and home can prove as boring as the tasks themselves, not because of the writer's failure but because of the reader's resistance' (1997, 244).

Urban imaginaries: *Dubai Dreams* and *City of Life*

A comparison of *Dubai Dreams* with *City of Life* (2009), a film by the Emirati film-maker, writer and director Ali F. Mostafa, shows how the life and work of labour migrants can be represented in thematically and formally innovative ways. Similar to *Dubai Dreams*, *City of Life* is set in Dubai, features multi-ethnic characters (the film also has an international cast of actors) and portrays these in an episodic slice-of-life manner. Basu (played by Bollywood star Sonu Sood), an Indian taxi driver, is one of the film's main characters. Due to his resemblance to a Bollywood star called Peter Patel, Basu comes close to his dream of becoming an actor by getting the chance to perform as Patel's impersonator in a Bollywood bar. The Emirati characters include the well-off twenty-something Faisal and his poorer friend Khalfan, who are both shown as James Dean-like figures in their often reckless search for meaning and excitement, ranging from car racing to street fights. *City of Life* further includes two young flight attendants, the Romanian Natalie and the Russian Olga, who also seek their fortune in Dubai, involving the slick British advertising executive Guy Berger.[11] The often negative portrayal of British characters in *Dubai Dreams* and in *City of Life* can be read as critical references to Dubai's past as a British protectorate (1892–1971) and to India's colonial history. In *Dubai Dreams*, Uday tells Maqbool over the phone that his customer is 'No one important! Just one of the people who ruled us in India for 200 years'

(Puri 2010, 15). In *City of Life*, Basu (who is from Gujarat) takes a taxi driven by a Kashmiri taxi driver and asks him whether he could possibly adjust a twenty euro note (as he does not carry any Dirhams with him). But the Kashmiri driver is unwilling to do so, telling Basu that both of their countries have adjusted long enough.

In contrast to *Dubai Dreams*, where there is only indirect code-switching (e.g. 'Uday replied in Hindi'; Puri 2010, 15), *City of Life* is multilingual (Arabic, Hindi, Urdu and English). The film further features a trendy soundtrack including the work of local and international musicians. Puri mainly employs culinary markers to emphasise Dubai's transnationalism and transculturation and to highlight the influence Indian (and other) migrant workers have had on Dubai and on Emirati culture. As Neha Vora observes, 'Emiratis have been greatly impacted by Indian languages, food, dress, and popular media' (2013, 72). Puri and Mostafa adapt the conventions of the urban novel and the urban film, respectively, to 'write Dubai.' Mostafa (2010) emphasises that the film's storyline 'isn't the Emirati versus non-Emirati, locals versus expatriates,' but how all characters struggle to 'cope, to find true happiness' and 'how Dubai's fast pace life can also make you feel isolated.'

On the one hand, Puri clearly foregrounds the taxi drivers' urban experiences within Dubai's class topographies. On the other hand, Puri and Mostafa use similar narrative strategies, motifs and metaphors, including multi-perspective narration, sites of transportation and spatial metaphors. According to Ed Lake (2009), a film 'with many plot strands is a difficult genre to get right.' and Fionnuala Halligan (2009) has criticised *City of Life*'s 'thin characterisations and TV mini-series themes,' as well as the characters' 'soap-style dilemmas.' But the multi-perspective narration in *Dubai Dreams* and *City of Life*, where chapters and film episodes, respectively, are arranged like snapshots, equivalent to catching glimpses of people passing by in the city, reflects Dubai's trademark characteristics, such as velocity, rapid change and segregation. Mostafa explains that when the characters meet, they do not 'intrude on each other's story,' which is meant to be 'a reflection of the lack of real intermingling and interaction between different groups of people in Dubai' (2010). Although Puri's Indian taxi drivers support each other, their solidarity is often limited to regional in-groups. As Uday states: 'You are a fellow Malayalee so I will help you but if you were a Pakistani I would have never helped' (Puri 2010, 85). There are rare occasions when the taxi drivers are not shown as passive victims but as political agents. At one point, for example, they organise a strike that draws in 1,000 drivers 'from the several nationalities and taxi franchise companies' (Puri 2010, 205). But even then transregional and transnational solidarity remains an illusion, since the alleged 'members of a Pakistani trade union' (Puri 2010, 208), who offer their expertise, turn out to be 'a gang of scammers' (211) who pick the other drivers' pockets during the strike.

The fact that Dubai International Airport operates as a main setting, together with the importance of taxis and cars, in both *Dubai Dreams* and *City of Life* reflects the frantic and fleeting nature of human encounters in Dubai as well as the city's car-dominated topography. According to David Kendall, 'highways and roads ... spatially dominate and connect architectural zones within the city-state' (2012, 46). When lives do collide in *City of Life*, they do so literally and brutally. The extended car crash scene in *City of Life*, apparently modelled on Paul Haggis's *Crash* (Lake 2009), turns out to be one of the defining moments in the film, when the 'film's storylines wrap around each other in a multicultural pileup' (Hoad 2009). Although in *Dubai Dreams* car crashes are mainly narrated and referred to by the taxi drivers, without the drivers' direct involvement, they are clearly seen as one of their most dangerous work hazards (in addition to Dubai's impending financial crash).[12] At one point, one of the protagonists of *Dubai Dreams* is directly involved in a crash. This is described in the chapter 'Postcard millionaire' and refers to a major car crash on the Dubai-Abu Dhabi Highway on 11 March 2008, which is, in fact, based on a real car crash in Dubai on the same date. The crash leads to a 'horrific 200-vehicle pile up' and Gabby is

Image 21.3 Sheikh Zayed Road, Dubai
Source: photo by Christiane Schlote

'one of the 347 people hurt' (Puri 2010, 134–135). These accidents also already foreshadow the taxi drivers' fate at the end of the novel.

According to Sarah Sharma, a taxi can be seen as 'an intimate zone of human encounter, and … a communicative space between driver and fare for politicised discursive exchange, confession, and the sharing of knowledge about the local and the global' (2008, 457). Proceeding from this reading, in *Dubai Dreams*, the taxi as an intimate space enables encounters between the taxi drivers and their (mainly affluent) Emirati, Southeast Asian and Western passengers.[13] In his episodic 'taxi novel,' *Taxi* (2008), Khaled Al Khamissi argues that 'taxi drivers … really are one of the barometers of the unruly Egyptian street' (11). In a similar vein, Puri uses the taxi drivers' stories to map Dubai's transnationalism from below, which is manifested, for example, in the drivers' multilingualism (Maqbool speaks 'Hindi, Urdu, English, and … a smattering of Telugu'; Puri 2010, 32) and their status as able navigators of Dubai. Occasionally, their profession even provides them with the opportunity to re-tell Dubai's official history. On a tour through Dubai, for example, Maqbool tells a tourist: 'It is we the Indians, Pakistanis, Bangladeshis, Filipinos and Sri Lankans, among others, who built this city brick by brick through our sweat and blood' (Puri 2010, 197). The taxi can also be read as an indicator of globalisation on a material and on a representational level. Maqbool has always dreamt 'of driving a taxi in New York after watching those Hollywood block busters [sic] in the cinema halls' (Puri 2010, 34).[14] At one point, an American couple compliment him that New York cab drivers 'are very rough compared to you! You give an excellent service' (Puri 2010, 36–37). Whether in filmic intertexts, such as Jack Rosenthal's

Image 21.4 Arabian Tea House, Dubai
Source: photo by Christiane Schlote

Mister Burgess' Tour (1979) and Jim Jarmusch's *Night on Earth* (1991), or as tourist icons (included, e.g. in wooden play sets of London and New York), London's black taxicabs and New York's yellow cabs have themselves become urban landmarks.[15]

Dystopian Dubai

Whereas cars and taxis signify the characters' transient existence in Dubai and the mobility needed to pursue their (partly utopian) dreams of economic, social and personal advancement, Puri and Mostafa, respectively, employ spatial metaphors for the portrayal of Dubai's more static class and gender topographies. In addition, Dubai's image as a city of stark contrasts is explored through a kind of 'social chiaroscuro.' In reference to Edgar Degas's painting *Au Café* (c. 1876), Richard Armstrong has defined 'social chiaroscuro' as 'a strange exchange between light and dark, black and white, hope and despair' (2011). This kind of interplay is already apparent in *Dubai Dreams*'s and *City of Life*'s respective iconography. The cover of the Har-Anand Publications/Crownbird Publishers edition of *Dubai Dreams* shows a passing bright taxi with (presumedly) Dubai's darker skyline in the background.[16] One of the posters for *City of Life* also depicts Dubai's skyline in the background, yet illuminated in an alienated way and with the figure of an old Filipino cardboard collector and his bike in the left corner, whom Mostafa has identified as 'his favourite and probably most important character in the film' (2010). In fact, *City of Life* begins with the cardboard collector and Dubai is first seen from his perspective on the bike.

Mostafa has acknowledged that *City of Life* 'is a very big commercial for Dubai,' but he also maintains that it depicts Dubai as 'a real city … showing the rich, the super-rich, the middle-class, the poor and the dead poor' (Hoad 2009). The film's portrayal of its main characters (often shown in private spaces such as Natalia and Olga's flat, Berger's luxurious villa, etc.) mirrors the shift in urban fiction (and in extension in urban film) from a more socio-historical perspective to a focus on individual and psychological experiences of the city (see Keunen and Eeckhout 2000). Given Dubai's strong spatial segregation (Vora 2013, 73), Puri is primarily concerned with the sites of the division of labour and the taxi drivers' isolation, alienation and exploitation. His preference for realistic narration also manifests itself in his use of 'real' topographical signifiers (street names, landmarks, etc.). When picking up affluent passengers, the taxi drivers are regularly confronted with the stark (spatial) division between well-educated expatriates and lower-class migrants ('Arabian Ranches is the paradise of peace …, where only the mega rich lived. … [T]he ordinary workers are confined to the suburbs of Deira and Bur Dubai'; Puri 2010, 54). Sonapur, 'a crowded and rundown camp for Asian labourers … the golden place in Hindi, once a burial ground … now a collection of tenements housing more than 150,000 workers, mostly Indians and Pakistanis' (Dagher 2006), is the most infamous example of Dubai's migrant topographies and features regularly in news reports. Even Puri's taxi drivers usually avoid the route to 'Sonapur the Middle East's Soweto' with its 'open sewers … and the stench from the large pools of stagnant sewage' (Puri 2010, 254–255). *Dubai Dreams* shows that while middle-class Indians may describe Dubai as home and 'the westernmost city of India,' the experience of unskilled South Asian labour migrants is radically different (Kanna 2007).

According to Bart Keunen and Bart Eeckhout (2000), postmodern writers have been less concerned with classic urban motifs (such as, e.g., the arrival in the city), sociocultural transformations and conflicts in the material city than with the city's semiotics and with the performative aspects of urbanity. Dubai's image as 'a Middle-Eastern Shangri-La … a Disneyland for the ultra affluent living here' (Puri 2010, 8) is, indeed, highly appealing for most of the protagonists in *City of Life*. The movie's exuberant nightclub and pool party scenes correspond to forms of spectacle and self-fashioning that are ubiquitous in contemporary urban film and fiction. Mostafa captures these phenomena effectively in the film's multi-genre mix, comprised of drama, romance and action thriller. In contrast, *Dubai Dreams* is reminiscent of the pessimistic tone of earlier urban writing, in which the city was mainly experienced as alienating and threatening. Recent urban fiction has also emphasised cities' potential to provide increased freedom and opportunities for its (particularly female) citizens. But freedom and opportunities are hardly available to Puri's taxi drivers. On the contrary, throughout *Dubai Dreams* the people, institutions and even the money the drivers rely on are exposed as fake – from the fake tears and identity of Maqbool's second wife to fake trade unionists and fake dollars. In the end, for most of the taxi drivers, their dreams of earning enough dirhams to build up an existence in their homelands end in overall tragedy.[17]

Instead of returning to their families as wealthy men, their dead bodies are repatriated to India. Whereas Binu dies of diabetes, Gabby's and Maqbool's deaths are particularly gruesome and cruelly indicative of the drivers' general hopelessness. Gabby is caught and imprisoned after the robbery of a jewellery shop. In prison, he is so desperate that he swallows rat poison and razor blades and dies in his cell. Maqbool first sells his kidney to repay the debt accumulated by his second wife, who has returned to Mumbai after having taken advantage of him. In an act of utter despair, Maqbool commits suicide in a way which transforms the taxi, which assured his livelihood, into a means of self-destruction. He ties a rope to a lamp post, sits in the driver's seat and ties 'the other end of the rope around his neck.' Maqbool then 'close[s] his eyes, pray[s] for forgiveness and dr[ives] off at full speed' (Puri 2010, 331).[18] These desperate and drastic acts stand in stark contrast to the life of the characters in *City of Life*, who, despite the occasional setback, nonetheless thrive on the promises of Dubai as an urban utopia. *Dubai Dreams*, however, shows the need for a renewed attention to the reality of the material city, to its sites of the international division of labour and especially to its prime actors. It emphasises that analyses of these subjects have by no means been exhausted, but that they remain urgent and most important concerns within the context of diasporic and migrant urban fiction.

On a broader scale, as two very different narratives about Dubai, both *Dubai Dreams* and *City of Life* can be further read as highlighting the following three aspects of interdisciplinarity, intersectionality and genre/s, which are also particularly pertinent for the significance of literary and cultural representations in regard to working-class studies. First, just as Elleke Boehmer has called the British empire 'at least in part, a textual exercise,' which 'in its heyday was conceived and maintained in an array of writings' in a form of 'colonization by way of text' (2005, 14), Lawrence Driscoll has argued that 'the contemporary British novel, assisted by "class blind" post-ideological literary theories, both articulates and silences questions of class, thereby enabling and sustaining … the ideological notion of a "classless" … British … culture' (2009, 1). The power (and limits) of representations can thus be linked to Michael Denning's call to 'overcome false dichotomies between "textual" and "real" politics' (Reed 2014, 174) and to David Roediger's observation that 'the possibilities of interaction between working-class history and literature have perhaps never been better' and that even if 'a certain methodological conservatism walls off labor history from literature, the emergence of working-class studies as an interdisciplinary field largely pioneered by scholars of culture and class offers great opportunities to transcend parochialism' (2005, 36–38).

Second, and drawing on the tenets of intersectional theory, in that '[s]ituated gaze, situated knowledge and situated imagination … construct how we see the world' (Yuval-Davis 2011, 4), texts such as *Dubai Dreams* and *City of Life* emphasise the need for a more nuanced intersectionality approach, as outlined, for example, by Nira Yuval-Davis. In her use of intersectionality, Yuval-Davis pays particular attention to the following three aspects: first, Leslie McCall's differentiation between 'inter-categorical' (i.e. 'the way the intersection of different social categories, such as race, gender, class … affects particular social behaviours or the distribution of resources') and 'intra-categorical' approaches, which focus less on the 'relationships among various social categories' and more on the 'meaning and boundaries of the categories themselves'; second, the relationships between the different intersectional categories; and, third, the limits of the intersectional approach (Yuval-Davis 2011, 6). As Yuval-Davis explains: 'I consider as crucial the analytical differentiation between different facets of social analysis – that of people's positioning along socio-economic grids of power; that of people's experiential and identificatory perspectives of where they belong; and that of their normative value systems' (2011, 7). Referring back to the social locations (whether concerning class, nation, gender, etc.) of the labour migrants in *Dubai Dreams*, here, it is vital to remember Yuval-Davis's important caveat that these locations do not only 'tend to carry with them particular weights in the grids of power relations,' but also 'tend to be different in different historical contexts and are also often fluid and contested' (2011, 12–13).

Third, in addition to the analytical potential of interdisciplinary and intersectional approaches and concerning its significance for working-class studies, texts such as *Dubai Dreams* also indicate the need for a reconceptualisation of the genre of working-class literature as strictly 'writing by authors of working-class origin' (Perera 2014, 5), as demonstrated, for instance, by Sonali Perera in her study *No Country: Working-Class Writing in the Age of Globalization* (2014): 'I argue … for reconceiving working-class literature based on shared ideologies of form and comparative ideologies of socialist ethics. Working-class writings from different parts of the globe share more points of connection than are acknowledged by most literary histories' (2014, 5).[19] By linking 'traditions of literary radicalism from the 1930s to the feminist recovery projects of the 1970s, to the anticolonial and postcolonial fiction of the 1960s decolonization movements, and … contemporary counterglobalist struggles,' Perera charts 'the discursive unity of working-class writing across the global North-South divide' (Perera 2014, 5–6). Apart from assuming a globally comparative perspective to working-class writing, texts such as *Dubai Dreams* also remind critics of 'the complicity between a dominant aesthetic form and social domination' (Goldstone 2010, 616) and a renewed attention to what William Dow has called 'the legacy of literary journalism, whose cultural interventions and inscriptions of class must be more clearly recognized' (2009, 15–16). In this way, reading *Dubai Dreams* alongside *City of Life* not only allows for a more complex understanding of Dubai's 'economic miracle' and 'the ones who make it happen,' but also complicates and disturbs conventional globalisation narratives (Hunt 2011).

Notes

1 This chapter is derived from an article published in *South Asian Diaspora* on 13 September 2013, available online: www.tandfonline.com/10.1080/19438192.2013.828500.

2 As David Commins explains, naming 'the body of water between Iran and Arabia either the Persian Gulf or the Arabian Gulf is rooted in convention' (2012, ix). In this article, the use of 'Gulf states' refers to the Gulf Cooperation Council, which was established in 1981 as a 'collective security body' and which includes the following countries: Saudi Arabia, Kuwait, Bahrain, Qatar, Oman and the United Arab Emirates (Commins 2012, 234). 'Indians and Pakistanis make up nearly 45 percent of the UAE's population of about four million. Emiratis account for only 20 percent' (Dagher 2006).

3 Ghosh himself has addressed the oil encounter in *The Circle of Reason* (1986) and *In an Antique Land* (1992). For an analysis of his petrofiction, see Chambers (2006a, 2006b).

4 Dubai is one of the seven emirates of the nation-state the United Arab Emirates (also including Abu Dhabi, Sharjah, Ajman, Ras al-Khaimah, Umm al-Quwain and Fujairah; Khondker 2011, 428).

5 Arab petrofiction includes Ghassan Kasafani's *Men in the Sun* (1963), Hanan Al-Shaykh's *I Sweep the Sun of Rooftops* (1998), Nawal El Sadaawi's *Love in the Kingdom of Oil* (2001), Mohammad Abdul-Wali's *They Die Strangers* (2001), Yousef Al-Mohaimeed's *Wolves of the Crescent Moon* (2007) and Mohamed El-Bisatie's *Drumbeat* (2010).

6 Terminologically, Julia Elena Rial uses the term 'petro-narrativa' (2003) and Raúl Cazal uses the term 'novela del petróleo' (2012). Other works from South America and the Caribbean include Miguel Otero Silva's *Oficina N° 1* (1961), Carlos Fuentes's *La cabeza de la hidra* (1978), Héctor Aguilar Camín's *Morir en el golfo* (1985), Patrick Chamoiseau's *Texaco* (1998) and Laura Restrepo's *La Novia Oscura: Novela* (1999). North American fiction and film about the oil industry also include Mary King's *Quincie Bolliver* (1941), *Dallas* (1978–1991, 2012), *Dynasty* (1981–1991), James Keache's *The Stars Fell on Henrietta* (1995), Cole Thompson's *Chocolate Lizards* (1999), Lisa Moore's *February* (2009), Gus Van Sant's *Promised Land* (2012), Omar Madha's *Burn Up* (2008) and Gary Nunally's *The Gambit* (2006). Also, with respect to Nigeria, among others, Wole Soyinka's play *Opera Wonyosi* (1979) and Tanure Ojaide's novel *The Activist* (2006) both address the exploitation of the Niger Delta. Works including John McGrath's *The Cheviot, the Stag and the Black Black Oil* (1973) and Bill Forsyth's *Local Hero* (1983) and Scottish crime fiction such as Ann Cleeves's *Red Bones* (2010) and Ian Rankin's *Black and Blue* (2011) explore the oil encounter in the North Sea.

7 Ironically, while much of Kerala's male population has migrated to the Gulf states, Bengali migrants 'call Kerala their "Dubai"' and fill a 'massive labour gap' in Kerala (Menon 2011).

8 In contrast, Marc Wolfensberger's documentary, *Oil Rocks: City Above the Sea* (2009), is a detailed portrayal of the daily life of oil workers on an oil platform in the Caspian Sea. Azerbaijani cinema, while mainly used as a 'communist propaganda machine' during the Soviet period, also foregrounded oil workers as 'Soviet heroic labor' (Badalov 1997). Representations of the oil encounter in Azerbaijan include the Lumière Brothers' *Oil Wells of Baku: Close View* (1896), Boris Svetlov's *In the Realm of Oil and Millions* (1913), V. B. Pumpiyanski's *Symphony of Oil* (1933), Yusif Vazir Chamanzaminli's *Ali and Nino* (1937) and the Bond film *The World Is Not Enough* (1999).

9 Kamal's film *Gaddama* (2011) about a Kerala-born maid in Saudi Arabia is also based on a real story by K. U. Iqbal, published in the Malayalam literary magazine *Bhashaposhini*.

10 One of the projects of the non-profit Mideast Youth, Migrant Rights, is devoted to the plight of migrant and expatriate workers in the Middle East (see www.migrant-rights.org/about/).
11 Interestingly, *Dubai Dreams* also includes 'a British man who had set up a new advertising agency in the Media Zone' (Puri 2010, 153). Also, in *City of Life*, Natalia describes Berger with the same phrase that is used in *Dubai Dreams* to describe the Lebanese businessman Fadhi: 'He could sell desert sand to the Arabs' (Puri 2010, 96).
12 References include Uday witnessing a 'grisly crash in which both occupants in the car' are killed, Binu's involvement in an accident scam and Uday's warning that 'there are maniacs on the road' (Puri 2010, 54, 64, 102).
13 For a similar use of public space, see Tabish Khair's *The Bus Stopped* (2004), which depicts the stories of a variety of passengers travelling on a bus through India.
14 The Har-Anand Publications/Crownbird Publishers edition (2010) does include a number of typos.
15 See also Joshua Z. Weinstein's documentary *Drivers Wanted* (2012).
16 Given that a gendered perspective of South Asian labour migration to the Gulf is mainly absent in the novel, the small image of a woman's head (with a headscarf) on the cover is surprising. For a discussion of two of the very few works addressing the life of women migrant workers – in this case, foreign-born maids in Lebanon – Hoda Barakat's *Harith al-miyah* (1998) and Danielle Arbid's *Maarek Hob* (2004), see Dyer (2010). For a study of female Indian migration to the Gulf, see Percot (2006).
17 Light-hearted and satirical portrayals of the oil encounter and South Asian migration to the Gulf are rare and include Gary Shteyngart's *Absurdistan* (2006), Paul Carter's *Don't Tell Mom I Work on the Rigs She Thinks I'm a Piano Player in a Whorehouse* (2007), Sathyan Anthikkad and Sreenivasan's satirical comedy *Nadodikattu* (1987) and Soman Priyadarshan Nair's romantic comedy *Oru Marubhoomikkatha* (2011).
18 According to Stephen Jones, local 'papers are occasionally peppered with stories of Indian workers walking out in front of speeding cars in order for their families to claim a life insurance payment that often exceeds what they could offer through normal working means' (2008).
19 See also Paul Lauter's tellingly titled essay 'Under construction: Working-class writing' (2005).

References

Abdul-Wali, M. (2001) *They Die Strangers*, Austin, The University of Texas at Austin.

Al Khamissi, K. (2008) *Taxi*, Laverstock, Aflame Books.

Al-Shaykh, H. (1998) *I Sweep the Sun of Rooftops*, New York, Random House.

Appel, H., Mason, A. and Watts, M. (eds) (2015), *Subterranean Estates: Life Worlds of Oil and Gas*, Ithaca, NY and London, Cornell University Press.

Armstrong, R. (2011) *After Hours*. Accessed 20 April 2012. http://home.comcast.net/~flickhead/AuCafeDegas.html

Bacher, J. C. (2000) *Petrotyranny*, Toronto, Dundern Press.

Badalov, R. (1997) 'Oil, Revolution & Cinema.' *Azerbaijan International*, 5, 3, pp. 57–64. Accessed 14 April 2011. www.azer.com/aiweb/categories/magazine/53_folder/53_articles/53_revolution.html

Badawi, M. M. (1992) 'Two Novelists from Iraq: Jabrā and Munīf.' *Journal of Arabic Literature*, 23, 2, pp. 140–154.

Benyamin (2012) *Goat Days*, Gurugram, Penguin Books.

Boehmer, E. (2005) *Colonial and Postcolonial Literature: Migrant* Metaphors, Oxford, Oxford University Press.

Boynton, R. S. (2005) 'The Roots of the New New Journalism.' *The Chronicle of Higher Education*, 4 March. Accessed 20 February 2008. www.robertboynton.com/articleDisplay.php?article_id=1515

Buettner, F. and Woehrle, C. (2010), 'The Slaves of Dubai.' *Witness*. Accessed 20 April 2012. https://visionproject.org/images/img_magazine/pdfs/slaves_of_dubia.pdf

Carrera, G. L. (1972) *La Novela del petróleo en Venezuela*, Caracas, Servicios venezolanos de publicidad.

Cazal, R. (2012) 'El petróleo también impregnò la literature,' *Correo del Orinoco*, 3, 2 September. Accessed 2 December 2012. www.avn.info.ve/contenido/petr%C3%B3leo-tambi%C3%A9n-impregn%C3%B3-literatura

Chambers, C. (2006a) 'Representations of the Oil Encounter in Amitav Ghosh's *The Circle of Reason*.' *The Journal of Commonwealth Literature*, 41, 1, pp. 33–50.

Chambers, C. (2006b) 'Anthropology as Cultural Translation: Amitav Ghosh's *In an Antique Land*, *Postcolonial Text*, 2, 3, pp. 1–19.

City of Life, Director Ali F. Mostafa, 2009.

Commins, D. (2012) *The Gulf States: A Modern History*, London, I. B. Tauris.

Dagher, S. (2006) 'Sonapur Camp – Dubai's Dark Side.' *Middle East Online*. Accessed 14 April 2013. www.middle-east-online.com/english/?id=16217

Davis, M. (2005) 'Sinister Paradise: Does the Road to the Future end at Dubai?' Accessed 10 May 2010. www.commondreams.org/views05/0714-31.htm

Denning, M. (1997) *The Cultural Front: The Laboring of American Culture in the Twentieth* Century, London, Verso.

Dittmar, L. (1995) 'All that Hollywood Allows: Film and the Working Class.' *Radical Teacher*, 46, pp. 38–45.

Dow, W. (2009) *Narrating Class in American* Fiction, Houndmills, Palgrave Macmillan.

Driscoll, L. (2009) *Evading Class in Contemporary British* Literature, Houndmills, Palgrave Macmillan.

Drivers Wanted, Director Joshua Z. Weinstein, 2012.

Dyer, R. (2010) 'Representations of the Migrant Domestic Worker in Hoda Barakat's *Harith Al-Miya* and Danielle Arbid's *Maarek Hob*,' *College Literature*, 37, 1, pp. 11–37.

East, B. (2013) 'Goat Days is a Carefully Tended Tale.' *The National*. Accessed 18 March 2018. https://www.thenational.ae/arts-culture/books/goat-days-is-a-carefully-tended-tale-1.278248

Ehrenreich, B., and Hochschild, A. (2004) *Global Woman: Nannies, Maids, and Sex Workers in the New* Economy, New York, Henry Holt.

Frassanito Network (2005) 'Precarious, Precarisation, Precariat? Impacts, Traps and Challenges of a Complex Term and Its Relationship to Migration.' *Mute*, 2, pp. 60–63.

Gardner, A. M. (2010) *City of Strangers. Gulf Migration and the Indian Community in* Bahrain, Ithaca, NY, Cornell University Press.

Gattoni, M. (2011) 'Sonapur – Dubai's City of Gold.' *IPA*. Accessed 20 April 2012. https://invisiblephotographer.asia/2011/09/15/photoessay-sonapurdubai-matildegattoni/

Ghosh, A. (1986) *The Circle of Reason*, New York, Viking Penguin Press.

Ghosh, A. (1992) *In an Antique Land*, New York, Vintage Books.

Ghosh, A. (2002) 'Petrofiction. The Oil Encounter and the Novel,' in Ghosh, A. (ed.) *The Imam and the Indian*, Delhi, Ravi Dayal Publisher.

Goldstone, A. (2010) 'Servants, Aestheticism, and the "Dominance of Form,"' *ELH*, 77, 3, pp. 615–643.

Halligan, F. (2009) 'City of Life.' Accessed 19 April 2013. www.screendaily.com/reviews/city-of-life/5009079.article

Hapke, L. (2001) *Labor's Text: The Worker in American* Fiction, Piscataway, NJ, Rutgers University Press.

Harikrishnan, C. (2015) 'The Prodigal Son Returned: Author Benyamin on his Return to India.' *The Indian Express*. Accessed 18 March 2018. http://indianexpress.com/article/lifestyle/books/the-prodigal-son-returned-author-benny-daniel-on-his-return-to-india/

Hoad, P. (2009) 'The Responsibility is Insane.' Accessed 20 April 2013. www.guardian.co.uk/film/2009/apr/10/film-dubai

Huggan, G. (2001) *The Postcolonial Exotic: Marketing the Margins*, London, Routledge.

Hunt, N. (2011) 'From the Front Line: Dubai's Labour trap.' Accessed 29 November 2012. www.december18.net/article/front-line-dubai%E2%80%99s-labour-trap

Jones, S. (2008) 'Ill-Treated Cabbies Threaten to Bring Dubai to Grinding Halt.' *The Epoch Times*. Accessed 14 April 2013. www.theepochtimes.com/news/8-7-2/72798.html

Kanna, A. (2007) 'Diversity and Struggle in the Arabian Gulf.' *samar*, 27. Accessed 5 November 2012. http://samarmagazine.org/archive/articles/245

Kapiszewski, A. (2006) 'Arab versus Asian Migrant Workers in the GCC Countries.' Accessed 5 November 2012. www.un.org/esa/population/meetings/EGM_Ittmig_Arab/P02_Kapiszewski.pdf

Kendall, D. (2012) 'Always Let the Road Decide: South Asian Labourers along the Highways of Dubai, UAE: A Photographic Essay.' *South Asian Diaspora*, 4, 1, pp. 45–55.

Keunen, B. and Eeckhout, B. (2000) 'Whatever Happened to the Urban Novel?' Accessed 8 August 2010. www.nottingham.ac.uk/3cities/barts.htm

Khalaf, S. and Alkobaisi, S. (1999) 'Migrants' Strategies of Coping and Patterns of Accommodation in the Oil-Rich Gulf Societies: Evidence from the UAE.' *British Journal for Middle Eastern Studies*, 26, 2, pp. 271–298.

Khondker, H. H. (2011) 'Review: *Dubai: Gilded Cage.*' *Contemporary Sociology: A Journal of Reviews*, 40, 4, pp. 428–429.

Lake, E. (2009) 'City of Life.' Accessed 19 April 2013. www.thenational.ae/arts-culture/city-of-life

Lauter, P. (2005) 'Under Construction: Working-Class Writing,' in Russo, J. and Linkon, S. L. (eds) *New Working-Class Studies*, Ithaca, NY, Cornell University Press.

LeMenager, S. (2013) *Living Oil: Petroleum Culture in the American* Century, Oxford, Oxford University Press.

Leonard, K. (2002) 'South Asian Women in the Gulf: Families and Futures Reconfigured,' in Sarker, S. and De, E. N. (eds) *Trans-Status Subjects: Gender in the Globalization of South and Southeast Asia*, Durham and London, Duke University Press.

Leonard, K. (2003) 'South Asian Workers in the Gulf: Jockeying for Places,' in Perry, R. and Maurer, B. (eds) *Globalization under Construction: Governmentality, Law, and Identity*, Minneapolis, University of Minnesota Press.

Linfield, S. (2010) *The Cruel Radiance: Photography and Political* Violence, Chicago, IL, University of Chicago Press.

Malecki, E. and Ewers, M. C. (2007) 'Labour Migration to the World Cities: With a Research Agenda for the Arab Gulf.' *Progress in Human Geography*, 31, 4, pp. 467–484.

McLarney, E. (2009) 'Empire of the Machine: Oil in the Arabic Novel.' *Boundary*, 2, 36, pp. 177–198.

Menon, S. (2011) 'Kerala, a "Dubai" for Bengali Migrants.' *Business Standard*. Accessed 5 November 2012. http://business-standard.com/india/news/kerala039dubai039-for-bengali-migrants/443970/

Mister Burgess' Tour, Director Jack Rosenthal, 1979.

Mostafa, A. F. (2010) 'Review: City of Life.' Accessed 20 April 2013. www.theculturist.com/home/review-city-of-life-by-ali-f-mostafa.html

Munif, A. (1984–1989) *Cities of* Salt, New York, Vintage Books.

Night on Earth, Director Jim Jarmusch, 1991.

Nixon, R. (2011) *Slow Violence and the Environmentalism of the Poor*, Cambridge, MA, Harvard University Press.

Panorama, *Slumdogs and Millionaires*, Director Ben Anderson, 2009.

Paul, R. (2016) 'Representing the Working Class: Two Plays by John McGrath.' *Socialism and Democracy*, 30, 1, pp. 149–172.

Percot, M. (2006) 'Indian Nurses in the Gulf: Two Generations of Female Migration.' *South Asia Research*, 26, 1, pp. 41–62.

Perera, S. (2014) *No Country: Working-Class Writing in the Age of Globalization, New* York, Columbia University Press.

Potter, L. (2017) 'Postcolonial Resources, Pedagogical Resistance: An Energy-Driven Interview with Professor Jennifer Wenzel.' *Journal of Postcolonial Writing*, 53, 3, pp. 380–392.

Puri, S. (2010) *Dubai Dreams: The Rough Road to Riches*, New Delhi, Har-Anand Publications.

Radhakrishnan, R. (2009) 'The Gulf in the Imagination: Migration, Malayalam Cinema and Regional Identity.' *Contributions to Indian Sociology*, 43, 2, pp. 217–245.

Ramsay, G. (2006) 'Global Heroes and Local Characters in Short Stories from the United Arab Emirates and the Sultanate of Oman.' *Middle Eastern Literature*, 9, 2, pp. 211–216.

Reed, T. V. (2014) *Robert Cantwell and the Literary Left: A Northwest Writer Reworks American Fiction*, Seattle, WA, University of Washington Press.

Rial, J. E. (2003) 'Petro-Narrativas Latinoamericanas.' *Hispanista*, IV, 13. Accessed 2 December 2012. www.hispanista.com.br/revista/artigo113esp.htm

Robbins, B. (1986) *The Servant's Hand. English Fiction from Below*, New York, Columbia University Press.

Roediger, D. (2005) '"More than Two Things": The State of the Art of Labor History,' in Russo, J. and Linkon, S. L. (eds) *New Working-Class Studies*, Ithaca, NY, Cornell University Press.

Sharma, S. (2008) 'Taxis as Media: A Temporal Materialist Reading of the Taxi-Cab.' *Social Identities*, 14, 4, pp. 457–464.

Shelley, T. (2007) *Exploited: Migrant Labour in the New Global Economy*, New York, Zed Books.

Sinclair, U. (2007) *Oil!*, New York, Penguin Books.

Singh, J. (1993) *The Case of the Shady Sheikh and Other Stories*, Penguin, New Delhi.

'South Asia: A Special Report' (2008) Migration News, 15, 4. Accessed April, 2013. http://migration.ucdavis.edu/mn/more.php?id=3446_0_3_0

Standing, G. (2009) *Work After Globalization. Building Occupational Citizenship*, Cheltenham, Edward Elgar Publishing.

Syriana, Director Stephen Gaghan, 2005.

There Will Be Blood, Director Paul Thomas Anderson, 2007.

Vohra, A. (2009) 'The Hidden Side of Dubai.' Accessed 18 April 2013. www.ndtv.com/news/blogs/the_unadulterated_thoughts/the_hidden_side_of_dubai.php and www.youtube.com/watch?v=KRPdIZ3dexU

Vora, N. (2013) *Impossible Citizens: Dubai's Indian Diaspora*, Durham, NC, Duke University Press.

Walonen, M. K. (2012) '"The Black and Cruel Demon" and Its Transformations of Space: Toward a Comparative Study of the World Literature of Oil and Place.' *Interdisciplinary Literary Studies*, 14, 1, pp. 56–78.
Wills, J., Datta, K., Evans, Y., Herbert, J., May, J. and McIllwaine, C. (2009) *Global Cities at Work: New Migrant Divisions of Labour*, London, Pluto Press.
Wilson, N. (2015) *Home in British Working-Class Fiction*, Abingdon, Routledge.
Wilson, S., Carlson, A., and Szeman, I. (eds) (2017) *Petrocultures: Oil, Politics, Culture*, Montreal, Québec, McGill-Queen's University Press.
Yuval-Davis, N. (2011) *The Politics of Belonging: Intersectional Contestations*, London, Sage Publications.

22
The cinema of the precariat

Tom Zaniello

The precariat is the vast global workforce whose unstable relationship with their employers makes most of them liable for termination or furlough at any time. As Max Weber observed, 'It is the dark urge for personal freedom, which drives the workers to work in a foreign land' (Zimmerman 2013, 174). Their untenable status often forces them to migrate to a 'foreign land,' conflating their 'dark urge for personal freedom'—to be free of harsh employers or dictatorial regimes—and their desperate need for employment.

Wherever these workers migrate they are beset with tenuous employment situations such as zero-hour contracts (United Kingdom), casual employment (Australia), low-hour contracts (Iceland), mini jobs (Germany), subcontracted labor (India), non-hukou migration (China), and underemployment (USA), rather than a union or any other kind of work contract. In fact, the vast majority of workers, underpaid and underemployed, have no contract of any kind. There is almost a one-to-one correlation between the shrinking unionized share of any country's workforce and the corresponding expansion of the world-wide precariat.

Andrew Ross's *Nice Work If You Can Get It: Life and Labor in Precarious Times* (2009) and Guy Standing's *The Precariat: The New Dangerous Class* (2011) argued that the precariat is in itself not a new phenomenon, but that its incredible growth crowds out the traditional proletariat. Filmmakers have documented and dramatized this transition in immigrant communities, corporate farms, airport complexes, tech corridors, favelas, big-box stores, Export Processing Zones, street markets, and even garbage cities, all of which determine the new reality of the precariat.

In Standing's class analysis *Meet the Precariat* (2017), the *proletariat* is the 'old' working class, traditionally unionized and employed full time. The *precariat*, whose essence is 'existential insecurity,' are dismissible at will, with no benefits much less a contract. Beyond the ability to do physical labor, a worker's qualifications and a job's profile do not often match. Just above the proletariat are the *salariat*, who have secure employment with pensions, paid holidays, and medical leave, and the *proficiens*, who are typically college grads with the specialized training of experts. Below the precariat are the *unemployed* or *lumpen precariat*, who are neither working nor actively seeking work (Standing 2017).

Although Standing's class analysis has been critiqued (Bremen, J. 2013) and more research on the viability of the term may follow, the term *precariat* will need—as *globalization* before it—a conceptual framework as well as a social cartography (Zaniello 2007; Caquard and Bryne 2009). In one trend-setting instance in the US, for example, the relationship of existing union workers and new part-time, sometimes temporary, workers has already resulted in two-tier union membership, as in the Teamsters for the United Parcel Service and the United Auto Workers for auto manufacturers (Uchitelle 2013).

The cinema of the precariat would require an extensive guidebook, but, here, five significant moments will be scrutinized. The first section concentrates on American migrant workers, the precariat that received the earliest national attention. Surveys of three major groups of the precariat follow: mass Chinese internal labor migration in the context of international immigration; workers in waste, garbage, and other toxic zones; and the class of workers created by the Wal-Martization of American labor. And finally a trend: the precariat in virtual space.

The first cinema of the precariat: American migrant labor

Although migrant workers in America had already made their dramatic appearance as Oakies in John Steinbeck's *The Grapes of Wrath* (1939), one of the most famous labor films of all time, this segment of the precariat did not reach popular attention until the unprecedented TV broadcast of Edward R. Murrow's *Harvest of Shame* in 1960. This documentary classic of early investigative journalism was followed by two major cycles of now little-known but quite compelling film sequels from 1960 to 1998, almost exclusively for broadcast TV, capturing the changes in the identity and management of migrant workers.

Murrow, only twenty years after John Steinbeck portrayed the fictional Joads, stands in front of a field extending endlessly into the distance, the iconic shot that opens the film. Murrow introduces his subject with what we now realize perfectly defines the 1950s precariat as the 'forgotten people, the underprotected people, the undereducated, the underclothed, the underfed.' They service the 'best fed nation on earth,' but in the opening interview with Mrs. Dobie, a white women with nine children, all of whom except the baby work alongside her in the fields, she says she can only afford one gallon of milk a week. Mrs. Dobie longs for a house of their own—'we plan to buy one'—but when pressed, doubts that it will ever happen.

To make his point that the two to three million workers doing this work are black as well as white, we see an interview with Jerome, a nine-year-old black boy who has to stay in their shack because he stepped on a nail and also because he has to take care of his baby sister, who is right next to a mattress with a rat-chewed hole in the middle. His mother earns a dollar a day for ten hours of work.

Most Americans, stuffed with their feast on Thanksgiving the day before, saw Murrow's film as a poke in America's eye. It was hardly typical of mainstream media at this time. Murrow's nerve becomes obvious when we realize that a somewhat similar documentary on migrant workers just ten years earlier, *Poverty in the Valley of Plenty* (1948), had been successfully sued for libel by the Di Giorgio Fruit Corporation (founded by an Italian immigrant, Giuseppe Di Giorgio) and copies were ordered to be destroyed by the courts. This short documentary was a project co-sponsored by sympathetic Hollywood filmmakers and the AFL-CIO's National Farm Labor Union, in part led by Ernesto Galarza, the underappreciated pre-Cesar Chavez activist who later wrote a best-selling autobiography, *Barrio Boy* (1971).

With the union-centered *Poverty in the Land of Plenty* only as a dim memory, later TV documentaries followed Murrow's style, that gravitated toward muck-raking rather than simple reporting, even if it used the strong voiceover narration by a star or celebrity reporter. By the end of the decade, however, the exploited labor seemed to be primarily African-American. *What Harvest for the Reaper?* (1968), directed by Morton Silverstein for the NET (National Educational

Television) Journal, focused on just one of Murrow's original targets, a labor camp in Cutchogue, Long Island, whose farm owners seemed to Silverstein 'to be the modern equivalent of the slave masters of old' (Rosenthal 1971, 107).

That same year another daring broadcast documentary, Martin Carr's *Hunger in America* (1968), asserted that 'hunger is hard to recognize in America.' An opening shot shows a doctor attending to a tiny baby: 'This baby is dying of starvation. He was an American. Now he is dead.' Although the child's ethnicity was not specified, CBS Reports had sent Kuralt and others to focus on poverty among Mexican-Americans, Navajos, southern blacks, and white Virginia tenant farmers, the latter occupying the estates of Senator Everett Dirksen and the popular TV entertainer Arthur Godfrey. Two years later, NBC's *Migrants* (1970) sent Chet Huntley out in the field to document how Coca-Cola and its subsidiaries (Snowcrop, Hi C, Minute Maid, and Tropicana) exploited Florida farm workers. There were rumors that NBC's sponsor, Coca-Cola, tried to block the show; in any case, it was shown, in the end, without a single commercial.

The second film cycle generated by Murrow's *Harvest of Shame* mainly foregrounded Latino migrant workers. In fact one of the documentaries, Hector Galan's *New Harvest, Old Shame* (1990) on Frontline, demonstrated that 'little has changed' in thirty years for the Latino migrant workers who travel from Florida to New Jersey for their picking opportunities.

Five years later, Maurice Murad's *Legacy of Shame* (1995) emphasized that laws were finally in place to protect migrant workers but 'now the problem isn't the laws, it's their enforcement.' Rather chronicles both the highs—the Farm Labor Organizing Committee—and the lows—crew leaders and owners virtually treating their workers like indentured servants. *Children of the Harvest* (1998), an NBC Dateline film, concentrated on gross violations of child labor laws, although families who feel they must send their children out to work in order for all of them to survive are treated circumspectly. The film ends with one farmer, disciplined by Heinz for using child labor, predicting that when children are kept out of the fields, Heinz will go out of the pickle business.

The paradox of Chinese 'internal' migration

No continent is now without *cross-border* migratory labor streams, but China's peculiar problem, the result of its rapid industrialization, virtually forced the *internal* migration of rural workers into new factory compounds and crowded dormitory cities. Paradoxically the internal migration began to have many of the characteristics of cross-border migration, because for many years these migrants lost their *hukou* or household registration (guaranteeing medical access, pensions, and other advantages of the old communist model). When potential rural migrants refused to leave the cities, the central government (by 2010) began to at least consider modifying the rules for *hukou* (Hsiao-Hung, 2012, xvi).

The edge cities and other satellite factory towns drove its export goods industry, employing at least 130 million migrant workers, many of them traveling thousands of miles to work, returning home only once a year for Chinese New Year. Lixin Fan's documentary *Last Train Home* (2009) focuses on a single family from Sichuan Province: the parents have been making the incredibly crowded train journeys back home after fifteen years in a garment factory in Guangdong Province. They stay in a single 'room' with a flimsy half curtain for a 'door.' Their children and one set of grandparents remain behind; with a continuous litany of 'study hard' commands from all her elders, sixteen-year-old Lin is fed up and leaves school for her own garment factory, causing great dismay for her parents. When she uses a vulgar epithet at a family meetup, she and her father literally come to blows.

Lixin Fan's film is filled with breathtaking detail: tens of thousands of migrants besieging and, yes, even rioting, to board trains home; those very trains, crowded beyond belief, pass over trestles that are engineering marvels in spectacular landscapes. After the fight, young Lin turns to the camera: 'You want to film the real me? This is the real me.' By the end of the film, the Chinese economic miracle begins to recede: a credit line appears—'2008 World Finance Crisis'—and we see a shot of an entirely vacated factory floor where family members once worked.

The documentary *The Iron Ministry* (2014) follows workers on the trains themselves. The camera leaves the confines of the train only to record the countryside through which the train travels or at the occasional stop at a market town along the route for passengers to purchase fruits, vegetables, and cuts of meat, butchered between the cars. These long journeys reminded one reviewer (Scott 2015) of the post-apocalyptic film *Snowpiercer*, 2013), in which the entire surviving population of the world has been spread out in an unimaginably long train, with individual train cars designated for either the surviving workers or the Machiavellian elite.

One spin-off of the failure of the mass internal migration in China is that the dispossessed workers finally turn to illegal immigration to countries like Great Britain, where they make up a substantial proportion of the foreign-born precariat. Their exploitation has been documented by the investigative (and undercover) reporter Hsaio-Hung Pai in her journalism and books as well as in two collaborations with filmmaker Nick Broomfield, who made his reputation for cheeky exposés of the rich and famous, including *Tracking Down Maggie* (1994), in which he interviews Margaret Thatcher's former suburban neighbor who uses the Iron Lady's discarded loo as a planter in her living room. Hsaio-Hung Pai went undercover as a maid and cook in Chinese brothels (usually disguised as massage parlors) with a miniature concealed camera in the nose-piece of her eyeglasses. Broomfield's documentary, *Sex: My British Job* (2013), validated her exposé of exploited undocumented immigrants, especially women, literally prisoners of loan sharks and 'snakeheads' (smugglers). Broomfield's first feature film, *Ghosts* (2006), was based on her research into the Morecambe Bay cockle-gatherers tragedy, where twenty-three Chinese workers were swept to their deaths by the tricky currents in the UK's largest intertidal mudflats off the Lancashire coast, having received no directions and no supervision about this dangerous location.

Waste and recycling in the First and Third Worlds

The poor or the dispossessed who provide cheap labor for the metropolis have often lived in shantytowns in segregated zones because of official (e.g. apartheid in South Africa) or unofficial (e.g. the massive migration of Chinese peasants out of the countryside) pressures. The closing years of the 20th century brought an explosion of shantytowns and a new phenomenon of the 21st century—the garbage city. No longer would the laboring poor visit garbage dumps to scavenge food to eat and goods to sell—they would settle and create shantytowns on site. These garbage cities, where recyclers and other desperate scavengers live year round, are typified by Guatemala City's largest dump, possibly the largest in the world, detailed in the documentary *Recycled Life* (2006) and Shanghai's unnamed dump, larger than Central Park, surveyed in *Shanghai Journal: At the Dump* (2006), where peasants earn more than their previous precariat jobs as farmers or day laborers.

On-site footage can nevertheless seem global: when a new dump truck arrives, it is besieged by hundreds of scavengers even before the truck finishes disgorging its load. Garbage cities and dumps are simultaneously eyesores and essential depots, but the central authorities of the world's cities will do almost anything to hide these essential service centers. In Buenos Aires in the 1990s, as even the usual jobs of the proletariat began to collapse, former factory and domestic workers joined the precariat to became *cartoneras* or recyclers. They were dependent on a daily train, exclusively for their smelly job of transporting items from the city's garbage piles to the recycling center. All the seats have been ripped out of the train to make more room for the *cartoneras*, interviewed in the documentary *The White Train* (2002), named after their distinctive train.

Other waste and recycling sites may even be more dangerous. One of the lowest caste assignments in India is the cleaning of urban latrines by the Dalits or Untouchables, according to the documentary *The Worst Job in the World* (2007), but especially dangerous recycling is shown in the film *eDump* (2007), chronicling the work handling toxic by-products of the computer age that takes place in the villages of Guiyu in Guangdong Province, China, site of the world's largest recycling workforce, with 60,000 workers.

Two other vastly different waste and recycling phenomena, one First World, the other Third, have been captured extensively for the cinema of the precariat: the Zabbaleen caste of waste and recycling workers in Cairo and the nonresident workers of the Willet's Point enclave in New York City.

Mike Davis, in *Planet of Slums* (2006), points to child labor as the key to understanding waste and recycling in Cairo and other Egyptian cities, where thousands of street children collect and resell cigarette butts because of the expense of fresh packs of cigarettes. Children involved in more extensive e-waste and recycling are the ultimate precariat, as in the Zabbaleen, the primary caste of recyclers, an occupation they have been literally born into. The Zabbaleen recycle about 80% of the waste of the city of Cairo, population seventeen million. They are Coptic Christians, migrants from Asyut in Upper Egypt, a sect by most definitions but a tribe of garbage collectors by the one that now seems to fit. Unlike Muslins, the Copts eat pork, making them especially suited to this task: they raised pigs who devoured the organic trash while they dutifully recycled the paper, plastics, glass, and metal for money. The pigs stand on the street corners of Coptic Cairo like the reliable organic recycling machines they are.

Three documentaries capture the daily life of these unusual recyclers. In *Marina of the Zabbaleen* (2008), seven-year-old Marina is tracked as she goes about her daily tasks of collecting garbage. In *Garbage Dreams* (2009), the nightmare for the 30,000 Zabballeen comes in the form of professional contractors who the city see as a modernization trend. In *We Are the Zabbaleen* (2013), the portrait of the Zabbaleen as an independent, resilient, and innovative culture is apparent, as witnessed by their reaction to the 2009 epidemic of H1N1 swine flu. The Ministry of Agriculture panicked during the epidemic and ordered the slaughter of *all* Egyptian pigs, including of course the massively efficient Zabbaleen animals. The garbage that grew to great piles of awfulness turned out to be a political weapon against the government. Thus the revenge of the precariat helped fuel the revolution of 2011, because the Zabbaleen simply let the organic waste gather throughout the city—a stinking mess, in short, and a health menace all its own. They eventually got new pigs. And probably, inadvertently, helped to topple Hosea Mubarak's government.

In the terminal world of New York City's Willets Point metal, auto parts and other electronic waste, in particular, make up another specialty of the precariat in The Iron Triangle, as it is nicknamed: all transactions are cash, immigration papers are invisible, and available work, however precarious, seemed never-ending. Even savvy New Yorkers had trouble comprehending Willets Point in Queens, a seventy-five-acre, unpaved, semi-flooded enclave of 250 parts shops, auto repair businesses, chop shops (dismantling cars acquired legally or illegally for parts), and related businesses, employing upwards of 2,000 people, with a resident population—the estimate varies—from one to three people (total!) who lived in 'apartments' and an uncounted number of people living in their cars or vans. It's safe to say that a Third World resident would find its essence of continuous hustle for customers familiar: there are men who, for tips and a commission, 'steer' customers to the right shop. If you have a broken mirror, for example, you simply hold it out of your car window and a denizen leads you to the right parts and/or repair shop.

Willets Point is bounded by the Mets' Shea Stadium and two expressways, Grand Central and Van Wyck. For pedestrians, it's a few steps from a subway stop; upscale visitors could land at nearby La Guardia Airport. Although former Mayor Bloomberg's Economic Development Corporation relied on the Census of 2000—there was then supposedly only one recorded resident in Willets Point—the daily working population there has been without basic city services for so long that it has begun to resemble the sets from the post-apocalyptic *Escape from New York* (1981): workers swarm around derelict vehicles laboring to bring them back to life or in some instances take them apart for the resale of the parts. The streets fill with water after a storm, and the less said about sanitation the better, for there are no sewers. It was city planner Robert Moses' dream in the 1960s to tear it down, but only in 2016 under Mayor de Blasio did demolition begin in earnest. Three billion dollars to go, plus 5,500 condos and coops and 2.7 million feet of retail and office space, it will obviously require a different kind of precariat—at the very least, underpaid workers in the service industries.

Willets Point Beyond the Curbline (2007) is the rare documentary that takes the point of view of the small-business owners in Willets Point, talking up the virtues of their role in providing their service for working people and employing the precariat. The somewhat more successful workers of the precariat, likely to be displaced, are portrayed in the feature *Willets Point* (2009), that explores a Latino couple who try to survive on the husband's job as a mechanic and the wife's job as a salesperson for a wine jobber.

The first feature that was filmed and set in Willets Point was *Chop Shop* (2007), dramatizing what a twelve-year-old street kid has to do to survive, beginning with sales of sundry snacks aboard the subway until he lands a job in an auto shop that specializes in dismantling suspiciously acquired cars and allows him to live on the premises. The feature-length documentary *Foreign Parts* (2011) begins its very traditional cinema vérité exploration of four regulars of the Willets Point precariat with a sequence of a worker cutting loose the engine block from the bottom of a pickup truck, spewing engine fluids and radiator liquid like cut veins: in the background we see the façade of Citi Field, the new Home of the New York Mets baseball team, probably another reason why city developers need, very badly, for Willets Point to go. The gentrification of this neighborhood will never be completed if these seventy-five acres remain a living museum of the discombobulated.

The only real resident of Willets Point in the documentary is Joe Ardizzone, who trusts no one in the official world: 'They'll tell me I own $10 in taxes and then collect $20.' Touching but more than a little pathetic are a couple, Luis and Sara Zapain (who is the life of the party) and Julia (one name only), who live in their cars, technically leaving Joe as the only 'resident' in Willets Point (Nir 2013). Then comes Mayor Bloomberg with a plan: take over all the private property by eminent domain, raze the entire district, and create appropriate office and residential opportunities that will complement Citi Field. When Willets Point goes—and it will—not only do many members of the precariat and proletariat lose their jobs, but the part of New York City that most resembles the Global Shantytown will also disappear.

The Wal-Martization of the precariat

Before the precariat even had its current name, the widespread exploitation of Wal-Mart workers in big-box store sales and the virtually forced migration of millions of Chinese workers to new industrial cities to make the goods Wal-Mart sold epitomized how globalization has reordered the working world. On the surface, Wal-Mart was *the* all-American store. Rarely outdone by competitors, Wal-Mart's blockbuster and holiday sales, giant American flags flying over the store, and over-friendly staff resonated with patriotism. The fact of the matter is that virtually all of Wal-Mart's goods were made in massive Chinese factories, whose workers were often migrants from the cities, driven to those factories by the end of the traditional Chinese 'iron rice bowl' of state-supported factories and free health and other public services.

The best current wage for American Wal-Mart workers is just under $14/hour, although the number of hours they work can vary radically from 10 to 38 a week, the epitomé of the situation for the underemployed precariat. Wal-Mart is the leading corporate target of lawsuits, especially on their refusal to pay overtime, locking in workers overnight, not paying them for working off the clock, and a myriad of racial and sexual acts of discrimination. Not surprisingly, their employee turnover is in the 50% range. Virtually no Wal-Mart store in North America is unionized; only China and Germany have unionized Wal-Mart workers. Until stopped by a law suit, Wal-Mart routinely took out 'dead peasant' insurance for as many as 350,000 workers with itself as beneficiary in case of death.

Wal-Mart has generated three feature films and more than fifteen documentaries, a remarkable number for a single big-box store chain. Only one of the feature films is an unabashed sentimental letter to Wal-Mart—*Where the Heart Is* (2000). A homeless woman, stupendously pregnant, played in all unlikely bliss by Natalie Portman, secretly lives at night in a Wal-Mart store where her baby, America, is born. The store doesn't have her arrested but relishes the publicity for the Wal-Mart Baby, showers her with money, gifts, and a job. She even gets married in the store. This is Wal-Mart as it wishes to be perceived: proudly American, a community center for all, especially the marginally unsuccessful.

The other feature films have more of an edge, even a satirical punch. In *I Heart Huckabees* (2004), a corporate rascal and an environmentalist doofus battle for the soul of a store named Huckabees, whose slogan is 'One Store, One World.' Both men share coincidentally the same Freudian therapists who make anxious fools of them. No workers are in this film, no anti-union campaigns, and no actual big-box store either: in brief, it is a bad anxiety dream of how the precariat is controlled. *Chain* (2004), the other feature, is quite unconventional, with a documentary feel, tracking two characters with some of the same illusions about Wal-Mart: Amanda holds down two low-wage precariat jobs at Wal-Mart and a seedy motel, but most of the time she obsessively films big-box store malls as if they were postmodern art, while her corporate counterpart, Tamiko, is compiling a report predicting doom for the future of these stores.

The documentaries are of three types, depending on their explicit political and economic targets. The films establish the corporate goal of disempowering working-class sufficiency and even militancy, especially of women, in effect creating the precariat many studies have prophesized for years (see Ehrenreich 2001; Featherstone 2004; and Hoopes 2006). Their anti-union campaigns are notorious and almost always successful, despite the efforts of a relatively strong union, the United Food and Commercial Workers, to organize at their stores, as their own documentary, *Wal-Mart's War on Workers* (2002) demonstrates. Barbara Ehrenreich's *Nickle and Dimed: On (Not) Getting By in America* (2001) covered similar ground, showing how impossible it was to live on the kind of wages Wal-Mart paid; *Wage Slaves: On Not Getting By in America* (2002), was based on Ehrenreich's personal immersion in the precariat.

Two important top-down documentaries offered radical approaches: *The Corporation* (2003) diagnosed the psychopathology of Wal-Mart as if it were in need of therapy to improve. A BBC TV series, *Outrageous Fortunes* (2004), set out 'in search of the truth behind the biggest brands in the world and the families that control them.' The heirs of Sam Walton, the founder of Wal-Mart, were at the time of filming worth $20 billion each.

Radical critiques of Wal-Mart's hidden agenda dominate a number of other documentaries. *The Hidden Face of Globalization* (2003) from the activist National Labor Committee demonstrated the exploitation by Wal-Mart of Third World women workers, while the more established Frontline, in *Is Wal-Mart Good for America?* (2004), showcased Wal-Mart's obsessive competitiveness that comes at the price of relying on cheap Chinese production lines. Bill Moyers, in *Off the Clock* (2002), also critiqued Wal-Mart's payoffs to worker plaintiffs, while *Store Wars: When Wal-Mart Comes to Town* (2001), *Talking to the Wall* (2003), and *Wal-Mart: The High Cost of Low Price* (2005) all offered community activists' efforts to resist Wal-Mart's expansion into neighborhoods where strong small businesses and property values would be undermined by Wal-Mart's ambitious expansion program.

Wal-Mart has not been without defenders, although only two documentaries could be called outright positive views of the company, but even *Why Wal-Mart Works* (2005) tries to explain away why some Wal-Mart workers need Medicaid to survive. *This is Nowhere: RV Camping at Wal-Mart* (2002) offers the company a good public relations campaign because some Wal-Marts allow its parking lots to be used as RV parks.

Wal-Mart continues to draw very critical cinematic coverage. Although the NBC series *Superstore* (2016–2017), was at first set at a Kmart, the policies of Super Cloud 9 mimic Wal-Mart closely as well, with no maternity leave, no health insurance, no overtime, and extremely limited bathroom and lunch breaks. The series focuses on managerial staff, although at least one 'associate,' as workers in these stores tend to be called, is an undocumented immigrant and another—like Natalie Portman's character in *Where the Heart Is*—gives birth in the store.

The precariat in virtual space

The rise in the perception of the precariat has paralleled the rise of virtual gaming as cinema. Raffi Khatchadourian argued in *The New Yorker* in 2015 that 'the video-game industry now rivals Hollywood,' generating almost $90 billion in sales. Furthermore the 'marketing budgets for [top-of-the-line] games have become comparable to those of blockbuster films' (Khatchadourian 2015).

Some of the new generation of political or activist game-makers have chosen to focus on the social and economic facets of their characters' lives. Some are topical, such as *Fort McMoney* (2013), on the exploitation of the Ft. McMurray, Canada, oil sands—a release that the *New York Times* reviewer cited as 'where film meets video game' (Goldberg 2013); while *Disaffected!* (2006) takes up the cause of precarious workers in retail sales, using the mise en scene of a Kinko's store. *Kentucky Route Zero* (2012–2016) is a magic-realist tale of a truck driver following a mysterious road through Kentucky's iconic caves, mines, horse farms, and whiskey distilleries. *Virtual City* (now expanded as *Virtual City Playground* 2011) offers players not only the opportunity to create a 'sim' (simulated) city but to build jobs and manage industry by balancing 'Time, Income, Environment, Population, and Happiness.'

Disaffected! and *The McDonald's Game* (later version, *Burger Tycoon*) were classified by Ian Bogusi, a games developer, as 'anti-advergames,' since they target corporations who underemploy vast numbers of the precariat and were unspooling more and more of a corporate presence in video games (Terdiman 2006). The animation in *Burger Tycoon* is not sophisticated, but neither is the text: a manager pays off a 'health officer' with $200 a month so that the corporation can slaughter sick cows, genetically modified and grown with 'aggressive pesticides.' 'Organized workers' are treated as corporate enemies. Only when the game's 'consumers are happy again,' can the player 'deactivate' the activists. 'When anti-globalization movements rail against our brand,' the game generates 'an influential politician [who] can repress demonstrations and neutralize workers who instigate uprisings and revolts.' Although animated film in world cinema has for a number of generations reached an adult audience, the overly simplistic *Burger Tycoon* would probably fit a niche of activists' children best.

Games like *Kentucky Route Zero* have a deep cinematic texture created by self-conscious film-obsessed game-makers. Only *Fort McMoney* has been filmed as a *documentary* with real people and actual locales. Viewers click on a 'character' to learn his or her backstory, go to a low-rent trailer park, and pursue the easy but elusive cash promised by a boom town.

The player can control the plot of the PC mod, or modifiable game, *The Stanley Parable* (2013). This remarkably successful interactive game had sales of one million downloads in 2013, its first year. It adopted the most literary of cinematic conventions—the untrustworthy narrator. Furthermore, as the subjective 'camera' tracks down the hallways of an office building with endless corridors of alienating sameness, the narrator challenges the decisions made by the player as the latter tries to solve Stanley's problem. For Stanley is Employee 427, a desk worker whose coworkers have abandoned their desks and so far as he knows have abandoned him as well. The precariat can be very lonely in virtual space.

Stanley is a data cruncher, but we never learn exactly what he crunches or for whom. One day his screen and—for all intents and purposes—his life goes blank. As he makes his way through his office building, the player is cajoled by the narrator's voice, who we learn from gaming sources is the successful professional British voiceover actor Kevin Brighting, self-described in his promotional adverts as having a 'British rich warm authoritative voice.' The player soon realizes he is punching a keyboard like Stanley and that the player is in effect a Stanley! In this meta world the narrator can even turn the 'film' off or make the player start over again. In almost every instance a player's choice of a keystroke elicits the narrator's remark or a change in the action or both.

Papers, Please (2013), a puzzler game, also had a huge following of players, leading *The New Yorker* game reviewer Simon Parkin to call it one of the best video games of 2013: 'Grim yet affecting, it's a game that may change your attitude the next time you're in line at the airport.' The designer calls it 'a dystopian document thriller' (Parkin 2013).

What it should also do is help players understand why so many of the migrant workers of the precariat avoid border checkpoints. Like *The Stanley Parable*, the player becomes the lead character, an immigration inspector who uses his keyboard to process immigrants at the border of an imaginary Eastern European or former Soviet Bloc country that has regained control of a border town after a six-year war with its adjacent state. The inspector works piece rate: the more people he processes, the more he earns.

Of course, he faces both difficult and dubious, even morally compelling, decisions in these confrontations with animated figures. The player inspects the immigrant's documents and can even request fingerprints or a full body scan, leading to an arrest if smuggling or terrorism or other criminal behavior is suspected. The applicant can even resort to bribes. As soon as the player stamps the papers allowing or denying access, he is informed of any mistakes he has made in his analysis, getting his pay docked if he makes too many.

The cinematic features of the game are more obvious at the checkpoint: other countries cause problems, terrorists attack, and immigrants from certain countries become automatically banned. In the ultimate challenge to the inspector's lowly job, a secret anti-government organization begins sending its members across the border to win over the inspector to their revolutionary side.

Like many R-rated films, this game attracted censors. Apple at first wanted to modify the body-scanning images—too risqué, it seems—but in the end settled on a 'nudity option' that players could choose, perhaps the ultimate cinematic accolade: censorship.

A precarious conclusion

The *history* of the precariat has been told in its cinema, but its *future* is uncertain. We know with some certainty that before there was the term 'precariat,' there was a precariat. In a book published in 1997 based on many firsthand accounts of what it means to be a 'temp slave,' Jeff (Keffo) Kelly wrote: 'Temp workers are not only used for cheap labor, they are used to keep full timers in line. Temps are used to make full timers think twice about raising questions about work conditions' (1997, xiii). Of course, this role of the precariat as potential strikebreakers has remained constant for generations, an irony of their lowly position: not holding a regular job makes any job attractive.

References

Bremen, J. (2013) 'A Bogus Concept,' *New Left Review*, 84, November–December. Available at: https://newleftreview.org/II/84/jan-breman-a-bogus-concept [Accessed 26 July 2017].

Caquard, S., and Bryne, A. (2009) 'Mapping Globalization: A Conversation between a Filmmaker and a Cartographer,' *The Cartographic Journal*, November. Available at: www.tandfonline.com/doi/abs/10.1179/000870409X12554350947340 [Accessed 24 July 2017].

Davis, M. (2006) *Planet of Slums*, London, Verso.

Ehrenreich, B. (2001) *Nickel and Dimed: On (Not) Getting By in America*, New York, Henry Holt

Featherstone, L. (2004) *Selling A Women Short: The |Landmark Battle for Workers' Rights at Wal-Mart*, New York, Basic Books.

Galarza, E. (1971) *Barrio Boy*, South Bend, University of Notre Dame Press.

Goldberg, H. (2013) 'Were Film Meets Video Game,' *New York Times*, 26 November. Available at: www.nytimes.com/2013/11/27/arts/video-games/where-film-marries-video-game.html [Accessed 26 July 2017].

Hoopes, J. (2006) 'Growth through Knowledge: Wal-Mart, High Technology, and the Ever Less Visible Hand of the Manager,' in Lichtenstein, N. (ed.) *The Face of Twenty-First Century Capitalism*, New York, Basic Books.

Hsiao-Hung, P. (2012) *Scattered Sand: The Story of China's Rural Migrants*, London, Verso Books.

Kelly, J. (1997) (ed.) *Best of Temp Slave*, Madison, Garrett County Press.

Khatchadourian, R. (2015) 'The Galaxy-Sized Video Game,' *The New Yorker*, 18 May. Available at: www.newyorker.com/magazine/2015/05/18/world-without-end-raffi-khatchadourian [Accessed 24 July 2017].

Nir, S. (2013) 'The End of Willets Point,' *New York Times*, 22 November. Available at: www.nytimes.com/2013/11/24/nyregion/the-end-of-willets-point.html [Accessed 24 July 2017].

Parkin, S. (2013) 'The Best Video Games of 2013,' *New Yorker*, 13 December. Available at: www.newyorker.com/tech/elements/the-best-video-games-of-2013 [Accessed 26 July 2017].

Rosenthal, A. (1971) *The New Documentary in Action*, Berkeley, University of California Press.

Ross, A. (2009) *Nice Work If You Can Get It: Life and Labor in Precarious Times*, New York, New York University Press.

Scott, A. (2015) 'Review: *The Iron Ministry* Uses Train Passengers to Tell China's Story,' *New York Times*, 20 August. Available at: www.nytimes.com/2015/08/21/movies/review-the-iron-ministry-uses-train-passengers-to-tell-chinas-story.html [Accessed 26 July 2017].

Standing, G. (2011) *The Precariat: The New Dangerous Class*, London, Bloomsbury Press.

Standing, G. (2017) *Meet the Precariat, the New Global Class Fueling the Rise of Populism*, World Economic Forum. Available at: www.weforum.org/agenda/2016/11/precariat-global-class-rise-of-populism [Accessed 7 July 2017].

Steinbeck, J. (1939) *The Grapes of Wrath*, New York, Viking Press.

Terdiman, D. (2006) 'Games that Stick It to "The Man,"' *La Molleindustria*, 2 January. Available at: www.molleindustria.org/node/149 [Accessed 26 July 2017].

Uchitelle, L. (2013) 'How Two-Tier Union Contracts Became Labor's Undoing,' *The Nation*, 6 February. Available at www.thenation.com/article/how-two-tier-union-contracts-became-labors-undoing [Accessed 24 July 2017].

Zaniello, T. (2007) *The Cinema of Globalization: A Guide to Film about the New Economic Order*. Ithaca: ILR/Cornell University Press.

Zimmerman, A. (2013) 'German Sociology and Empire: From International Colonization to Overseas Colonization and Back Again,' in Steinmetz, G. (ed.) *Sociology and Empire: Colonial Studies and the Imperial Entanglement of a Discipline*. Durham, Duke University Press.

Films and television

Chain, Director Jem Cohen, 2004.
Children of the Harvest, Produced by NBC Dateline, 1998.
Chop Shop, Director Ramin Bahrani, 2007.
The Corporation, Directors Mark Achbar and Jennifer Abbott, 2003.
Disaffected, Produced by Persuasive GamesDirector, 2006.
eDump, Director Michael Zhao, 2007.
Escape from New York, Director John Carpenter, 1981.
Foreign Parts, Directors Verena Paravel and J. Sniadecki, 2011.
Fort McMoney, Produced by DOXA and National Film Board of Canada, 2013.
Garbage Dreams, Director Mai Iskander, 2009.
Ghosts, Director Nick Broomfield, 2006.
The Grapes of Wrath, Director John Ford, 1940.
Harvest of Shame, Produced by Edward R. Murrow, 1960.
The Hidden Face of Globalization, Produced by Crowing Rooster Arts, 2003.
Hunger in America, Director Martin Carr, 1968.
I Heart Huckabees, Director David O. Russell, 2004.
The Iron Ministry, Director J. P. Sniadecki, 2014.
Is Wal-Mart Good for America?, Director Rick Young, 2004.
Kentucky Route Zero, Produced by Jaske Elliott and Tamas Kemenczy, 2012–2016.
Last Train Home, Director Lixin Fan, 2009.
Legacy of Shame, Director Maurice Murad, 1995.
Marina of the Zabbaleen, Director Engl Wassef, 2008.
Migrants, Director Martin Carr, 1970.
New Harvest, Old Shame, Director Hector Galan, 1990.
Off the Clock, Produced by Bill Moyers and Andrea Fleischer, 2002.
Outrageous Fortunes, Produced by BBC Three, 2004.
Papers, Please, Produced by Lucas Pope, 2013.
Poverty in the Valley of Plenty, Produced by National Farm Labor Union, 1948.
Recycled Life, Director Lesie Iwerks, 2006.
Sex: My British Job, Director Nick Broomfield, 2013.
Shanghai Journal: At the Dump, Produced by New York Times, 2006.
Snowpiercer, Director Boon Jung-ho, 2013.
The Stanley Parable, Produced by Davey Wreden and William Pugh, 2013.
Store Wars: When Wal-Mart Comes to Town, Director Micha X. Peled, 2001.
Superstore, NBC, 2016–2017.
Talking to the Wall, Director Steve Alves, 2003.
This is Nowhere: RV Camping at Wal-Mart, Directors Doug Hawes-Davis and John Lilburn, 2002.
Tracking Down Maggie, Director Nick Broomfield, 1994.
Virtual City Playground, Produced by G5 Games, 2011.
Wage Slaves: On Not Getting By in America, Produced by Bill Kurtis, Erik J. Nelson, and Amy Briamonte, 2002.
Wal-Mart: The High Cost of Low Price, Director Robert Greenwald, 2005.
Wal-Mart's War on Workers, Produced by United Food and Commercial Workers, 2002.
We Are the Zabbaleen, 2013.

What Harvest for the Reaper?, Director Morton Silverstein, 1968.
Where the Heart Is, Director Matt Williams, 2000.
The White Train, Directors Sheila Perez Gimenez, Nahue Garcia, and Ramira Garcia, 2002.
Why Wal-Mart Works: And Why That Drives Some People Crazy, Director Ron Galloway, 2005.
Willets Point, Director T. J. Collins, 2009.
Willets Point Beyond the Curbline, Produced by Willets Point Industry and Reality Association, 2007.
The Worst Job in the World: The Bhangis of India, Directors Jens Pedersen and Kuljit Bhamra, 2007.

23

The 'body of labor' in U.S. postwar documentary photography

A working-class studies perspective

Carol Quirke

In November 1946, as the United States experienced unprecedented labor turmoil, *Fortune* magazine published a photo spread entitled 'Labor Anonymous' (Evans 1946). Henry Luce, the nation's top magazine publisher, had made *Fortune*, with its modernist design and exceptional art and photography, his paean to capitalism (Doss 2001). Its editors sent nationally recognized documentary photographer Walker Evans to Detroit, the 'arsenal of democracy,' for the spread (Evans 1946, 152–153). Evans photographed self-possessed individuals as they walked by his lens. A few men with crumpled overalls shuffled home after a long shift, women in bright uniforms rushed past to their restaurant jobs, and others ambled by. *Fortune*'s editors employed nineteenth-century physiognomic metaphors to describe Evans's workers: some were 'peasant-like,' others 'patrician.' But workers' heterogeneity made them, according to *Fortune*, 'in the mass, the most resourceful and versatile body of labor in the world.' Affirming workers' efficiency and productivity, *Fortune* argued that labor contributed to the nation's victory in World War II (Evans 1946; Campany and Thompson 2015). The nation's top business magazine embraced American workers en masse, literally blending them into the whole of American life, while effacing their particularity and demands.

The working class had long been a preoccupation for photographers. Such interest flourished in the Great Depression, a result of economic devastation, New Deal commissions, and radical leftist efforts, such as New York's Photo League. 'The documentary,' which appeared to extol labor and the 'common man,' was named in the late 1930s and solidified as a practice and aesthetic, coincident with populist film, proletarian literature, and public murals.[1] Simultaneously, Luce's splashy photo magazine *Life* promoted photojournalism's development; it too was preoccupied with labor (Quirke 2012).

In conventional chronologies, the documentary aesthetic lost its public salience as the postwar compact resolved the 'labor question' by accommodating unionization and securing workers' economic stability (Guimond 1991; Bezner 1999; Lichtenstein 2003, 99–100, 1982; Metzgar 2000). In this chronology, workers, now woven into the fabric of American life, attracted photographers' interest less, akin to abstract expressionism supplanting social realism. In the 'new documentary,' photographers pursued individual expression; social concern was passé. Art institutions such as the Museum of Modern Art (MOMA) promoted apolitical visions (Phillips

1989). Simultaneously, profit-driven photojournals purveyed a burnished vision of the United States, and the federal government repressed radical photographers' critique of U.S. social relations. Hence Evans's anonymous workers, stripped of identifying context, coincide with the documentary's decline in standard art historical periodization; industrial workers no longer appeared as 'the Other' in the political or representational spheres.

This chapter challenges the accepted chronology, demonstrating photographers' continued documentary representation of workers. Evans had photographed Detroit workers as two million workers were striking in major industrial sectors such as steel, coal, and meat-packing. *Life*, *Collier's* and *Fortune*, mass-market magazines, covered labor in text and image as it made headlines. Corporations, using welfare-capitalist strategies to diminish labor discord and constrain labor's newfound economic and political power, portrayed their workforce in documentary-style photographs in employee magazines (Plattner 1983). Artists themselves remained curious about class dynamics and workers' lives, from the politically engaged Sid Grossman, Vivian Cherry, Walter Rosenblum, Max Yavno, and Ralph Steiner to the less obviously political, such as Irving Penn, Danny Lyon, and Eve Arnold. Labor historians and working-class studies scholars have explored the work of Milton Rogovin, Hansel Mieth, and Earl Dotter, but this chapter suggests we should cast our net more widely (Herzog 2006; Zandy 2013, 2004).

This interdisciplinary working-class studies analysis puts workers to the fore. They are subjects who are represented before the camera lens and agents, working behind the lens, whose photographs comment on class relations. The analysis centers on three postwar photographers who engaged with the working class: Arthur Leipzig, Dan Weiner, and Robert Frank. Their photography exemplifies overlapping fields—documentary, photojournalism, and art photography—and it circulated in multiple venues: employee magazines, mass-market magazines, galleries, and art books (Hapke 2002). This study draws on U.S. history, art history, visual culture, and media studies, and uses archival research, oral history, and textual and visual analysis (Linkon and Russo 2012). Guiding questions include: How are workers represented? How do photographers understand their photographic interventions? Why do corporations, media corporations, and photographers take an interest in labor? How are the documentary and photojournalism aesthetic of 'the real' exploited in workers' postwar representation?

One of the chapter's aims is recuperative. As Janet Zandy argues in *Coming Home: Working-Class Women's Anthology*, working-class 'lives are obscured and erased; their work is barely visible' in the academy, and 'their writing is not read in literature classes' (1990, 5; Lauter 1996).[2] Additionally, photographic representations, critical 'as sources for understanding working-class experience,' are often neglected by historians and labor historians, especially in the postwar era (Linkon and Russo 2005, 2, 11–12). In contrast, this analysis privileges the political stakes of workers' representation.

Recuperating Leipzig, Weiner, and Franks's *oeuvre* tracks how class travels outside the factory. As Eric Schocket writes about literature,

> An anti-essentialist approach to class and representation sees the problem of classed representation as itself historically contingent. The modes through which writers have engaged the working class and the poor reflect an ongoing perceptual struggle that is part of class relations.
>
> *(2006, xi, 7)*

(See also Schocket 2002; Denning 1997.) This analysis meditates on the problem of workers' representation, not to judge photographers' accuracy, but to chart photographers and their sponsors' motives and attempts to shape U.S class relations. Class happens in strikes, in sociality, and also within photographs published in the news and in employee magazines, and exhibited in art institutions.

By identifying labor's continued presence within the documentary tradition, the chapter also engages crucial debates about the politics of documentary photography. For much of the twentieth century, observers believed documentary photography's visual record exposed social problems, particularly economic inequalities, motivating social change. Jacob Riis's New York City tenement photographs are seen as initiating the tradition in the United States.[3] His 1888 *New York Sun* article 'Flashes from the slums' suggested documentary's rationale, 'showing ... misery and vice' to 'call attention to the needs of the situation and suggest the direction to which much good might be done.' Elsewhere he argued that letting 'in the light where it was so much needed' would effect change (1890, 129). Similarly, Lewis Hine, famous for his industrial and child labor photos, thought 'social photography [a] lever for social uplift' (1980, 111). Reformers must persuade with photographs, much as business advertised. The term 'documentary' only came into common usage in the late 1930s, though later practitioners acknowledge Riis and Hine's impact upon their photographic projects. An undergirding assumption of the documentary was the image's truthfulness, what essayist and novelist James Agee called 'the cruel radiance of what is' (in Agee and Evans 1960, 11). Photography shows what sits before the camera eye, seemingly without mediation, central to the documentary's power.

But documentary photographs employ rhetoric, not just detail. Critic Beaumont Newhall writes that the documentary photographer's 'aim is to persuade and to convince' (1964, 137). Documentary photographs, he adds, 'inform us' and 'move us' ; the photos are 'vivid human documents' because of their truthfulness *and* their expressive, aesthetic qualities (1964, 137). Depression-era photographer Dorothea Lange rejected 'invention,' but she also called her photographs 'ammunition'; they advocated change (Farm Security Administration correspondence 1937; see also Meltzer 1978) . Additionally, the struggles of working people and the poor and an embrace of society's marginalized were documentary's primary subjects for decades (Stott 1973, 8–9, 30; Coles 1997, 109). Scholars accepted this dual charge for documentary well into the postwar era.

But in the 1970s, scholars and practitioners questioned documentary's purpose. In a seminal 1974 *Artforum* essay, photographer-critic Allan Sekula, examining Hine's work, claimed documentary photographers granted the downtrodden 'a bogus Subjecthood,' allying their photography with a 'bourgeois esthetic discourse' (21, 20). A decade later, artist and theorist Martha Rosler characterized much of the documentary tradition as 'victim photography' (1989, 316). For these critics, photographs contained evidence of the real, but their ideological thrust sustained the status quo (1989, 316). Influenced by such arguments and by poststructuralism, a generation of scholars penned harsh assessments of Riis, Lange, Hine and other documentarians (Stein 1983; Curtis 1989). Critics argue photographers exploit 'human decay' to build their careers; documentary viewers affirm their class status by looking down on others; and the documentary offers a meager or nonexistent challenge to grave inequalities (Rosler 1989, 308).[4]

The careers of Leipzig, Weiner, and Frank demonstrate that working Americans remained a critical subject through the 1950s; their sensitive portrayals rebut the documentary critique. An oral history I conducted with Leipzig and Mimi Leipzig, his wife and business agent, provoked this investigation, and offers the deepest exploration of a photographer's aims and work. But the inclusion of the two other photographers suggests further study is required to adequately understand the relationship between postwar documentary imagery and working-class lives.

Leipzig came to the camera by accident—literally. He dropped out of high school in the Depression, in his words:

> with no idea in the world of what I wanted to do … I did all kinds of odd jobs. I worked throughout the country; I worked for my uncle in Texas at his plate glass factory. I came back to New York with my arm in a cast.
>
> *(Leipzig 2010, 2011)*[5]

Leipzig had severed veins and nerves when his arm broke a sheet of glass. Disability and odd jobs, including a stint in the fur industry, sustained him. Then a friend suggested he learn photography at the Photo League. Still adrift, Leipzig received a scholarship—'a big thing' he said—from the League's school director, Sid Grossman.

In offering Leipzig a scholarship, the Photo League enacted one of its primary purposes: teaching workers photography so they could represent their lives and struggles. The League originated from the Communist Party-connected Film and Photo League, part of an international movement of workers' camera clubs, though not all members were communists or fellow travelers. Photo League members enjoyed classes in lighting and composition, and attended lectures from famous photographers like Lange, Margaret Bourke-White, Manuel Alvaro Bravo, and Paul Strand. League members trained unionists to take visually arresting and politically powerful photographs, and it lent out cameras to those who could not afford them. The League held regular exhibitions, and it designed photographic surveys of working-class communities. Aaron Siskind's *Harlem Document* is famous, but the League also organized one in the working poor neighborhoods of Pitt Street and Chelsea in Manhattan. Members collectively sought to interpret workers' lives (Klein and Evans 2011; Tucker 1994; Bezner 1999, 73–75).[6] Photo Leaguers were cognizant, even then, of a critique of the documentary that saw it as patronizing or as intended to meet the emotional needs of an assumed middle-class audience. The organization's newsletter, *Photo Notes*, rejected such claims: 'We aren't tourists because these are our mothers' (1948, 7).

The League led Leipzig to a career in photography. After serving as their lab tech, he ran League classes and contests. Lessons with Paul Strand and Grossman taught him to be a rigorous editor. He soon found a staff position at *PM*, a populist response to Luce's *Life* magazine. Founded by Ralph Ingersoll, former *Time Life* editor, *PM* was a visually compelling, advertisement-free New York City newspaper. *Life*'s 'all-seeing eye with a brain' revolutionized photojournalism and was central to twentieth-century culture's increased visuality, but *Time Life*'s anti-labor politics incensed Ingersoll (Advertisement 1940, 78–79). *PM* followed labor sympathetically and it represented working New Yorkers' lives (Milkman 1997). The publication's photo director, modernist Ralph Steiner, employed photographers with unique aesthetics, such as Arthur Felig (Weegee) and Lisette Model. In 1943 Leipzig became *PM*'s assignment dispatcher, then was a staff photographer until 1946. Leipzig appreciated *PM* for nurturing photographers' vision by giving them the freedom to develop their 'twist' on stories. In 1946 Leipzig moved to International News Photos, a Hearst syndicate, but was fired eight months later when he refused editors' demands to photograph only white schoolchildren in Harlem.

As he worked on commission for newspapers, global nonprofits, and corporations from 1947 onward, Leipzig's work retained the look of the populist documentary. Two of his corporate commissions that complicate an analysis of postwar documentary photography and class are explored here. The Singer Sewing Machine Company sent Leipzig to Quebec in 1952 to photograph the lumberjacks whose felled timber became sewing machine cabinets. Articles praising

Image 23.1 Arthur Leipzig, 'Portrait of Axel Christiansen, 1955'
Source: copyright Arthur Leipzig Estate

managers and discussing dollar-stretching suggests a readership of line employees for the quarterly *Singer Light*. And in 1955 U.S. Rubber had Leipzig document New Bedford fishermen using rubber products for its monthly employee publication, *Us*, 'published for all the people of U.S. Rubber' (see Image 23.1). In these commissions Leipzig dignified laborers in their work and domestic lives, presenting them as both heroic and ordinary. Corporations' appropriation of the documentary style suggests cooptation of the aesthetic (Tagg 1993; Barthes 1977) but this position overlooks Leipzig's political commitments and tensions in the corporate narratives—the employee magazines' photo stories could not contain the power of the images to provoke identification with, or questions about, working Americans.

The *Singer Light* story, 'Lumberjack in Singer's Canadian forests' (1953) comprises a day in the life of the subject. Daniél Dumouchel began with a full-page shot of Dumouchel directing work horses 'snak[ing]' logs across the frozen ground to their collection point (Image 23.2). Leipzig's vantage, just slightly above his subject, lets viewers participate in lumberjack Dumouchel's labors (*Singer Light*, 1953). Leipzig shows loggers headed to work in the company train, their work clothing, and their labors: the scoring and sawing of timber and its placement in ice storage until spring. Another page showed men at evening's rest, eating, playing checkers, and joking around at camp. The final page detailed Dumouchel's domestic life (Image 23.3). The father of five feeds livestock, enjoys his new five-room home, and attends Sunday afternoon hockey games with his wife. This narrative formula suggests a story relayed in its entirety, one running from sunrise to sunset, Monday to Sunday. Readers need not ask more about Dumouchel.

Daniél Dumouchel

Image 23.2 Arthur Leipzig, 'Daniél Dumouchel, 1953'
Source: copyright Arthur Leipzig Estate

Leipzig's 'The fishing industry' (1955) photo essay for *Us* is more dramatic. His trip on the *Joan and Ursula* coincided with an intense Atlantic 'Nor'easter.' *Us*'s cover displays the boat's mate, Axel Christianson, who wears mackintosh and cap; his face and glasses are studded with droplets, a maritime seer. In a second photo accompanying the story, Christianson is warmed by wool jackets and cap, his leg up in relaxed mastery, as he calmly wipes his spectacles (Image 23.4). He regards the 'brewing storm' with a pensive expression. Leipzig presents Christianson's stoicism in the face of the voyage's limited catches and harsh storm, a laborer conditioned to nature's vagaries but still in charge. *Us* published dynamic photos of engineer Frenchy Maillet as he plunges his spear into a tuna, moving it from the net into the hold (Image 23.5). And it printed slice-of-life portraits, such as the one of Cyril O'Leary who takes a drag from a cigarette. The men concentrate as they repair nets in the storm-tossed seas or chip ice off the riggings. Leipzig's photos of the ice-laden ship against the storm-stirred waters convey a sense of vertigo even today. He communicates workers' peril and their commitment, which could be ascribed to workers' valor and skill, or loyalty to their employer (Image 23.6).

Leipzig identified how labor is collective and relational, requiring workers' full involvement. When logging in the Northwoods, the men engage with their work and with one another; they appear self-directed, not controlled by their managers. At home, they are part of a circle of domestic activity including its labors. Mass-circulation periodicals such as *Life* typically ignored or naturalized such labors as woman's gendered responsibility. Leipzig instead recognized women's cooking and cleaning for the company camp and home as critical (Quirke 2012). Leipzig conferred dignity on the workers; his portrayal was not worshipful but matter-of-fact.

Leipzig's low-angle portraits and dynamic point of view on the Atlantic fishing tip exalt labor, however, and the men in the storm are breathtaking in the drama they evoke. The composition

After Sunday morning chores, Daniël walks a half mile to the village general store in Ripon for some "roll-your-own" tobacco.

Veneer cores hauled from the Singer plant in Thurso are fuel for the kitchen stove.

Daniël and his wife, Ireine, moved into a five-room house from a three-room apartment that they occupied with their three children until two weeks ago.

Mrs. Dumouchel prepares chicken for dinner while the babysitter for the afternoon amuses Marcelle, 5, and the 14-months-old twins — John and Peter.

Feeding the rabbits, pigs and chickens in the barn behind the house is a leisurely Sunday morning chore.

Three long and four short rings for the Dumouchels on the party line they share with 35 others. Shopping and "visiting" are done during the week by telephone.

Daniël and his wife start on the 27-mile trip to Thurso to see a Sunday afternoon hockey game and to visit friends while a baby-sitter cares for the children.

• 12 •

Image 23.3 Arthur Leipzig, 'Dumouchel family, 1953'
Source: copyright Arthur Leipzig Estate

draws from a tradition of marine paintings by Rembrandt, Jonathon Singleton Copley, and Winslow Homer. In these canvases, man is minute, his vulnerability absolute. Leipzig's photos, sublime or slice-of-life, join other midcentury populist visual culture that celebrated the working man.

Image 23.4 Arthur Leipzig, 'Portrait of Axel Christiansen, inside the *Joan and Ursula*, 1955'
Source: copyright Arthur Leipzig Estate

These photographs' dissemination in corporate communications appears to sustain contemporary critics' argument that the documentary lacked political punch or even hindered change. The photos did not promote government programs, as with New Deal photographs; nor did they indict class inequalities, as with Photo League or *PM* photographs. On the contrary, in *Singer Light*'s story, contented men worked outdoors in zero degree weather in 'light but warm clothing.' Captions assured readers of workers' comfort and described loggers' shorter work shifts and commodious cabins. Photographs of Dumouchel's family and home suggested that Singer's workforce enjoyed America's postwar affluence. The Singer Corporation thus appropriated the documentary aesthetic to demonstrate their altruism toward workers.

Us more ingeniously assimilated the documentary style while publicizing its rubber products and promoting a managerial worldview. Its article, 'The fishing industry' (1955) sympathized with fishermen's difficulties such as foreign competition, steep investment for equipment, and the job's danger. Simultaneously, the article extolled progress. Packing technology (via U.S. Rubber conveyor belts) and radar promised greater productivity. Fishing would alleviate world hunger, even though overfishing had already forced New Bedford fisherman into deeper seas. Finally, the photo essay explained the corporation's role in aiding the 'men who go down to the sea in ships.' For *Us*, 'Rubber keeps them dry. Sometimes it keeps them alive.'

Image 23.5 Arthur Leipzig, 'Work Portrait of Frenchy Maillet, 1955'
Source: copyright Arthur Leipzig Estate

Us's photo essay linked U.S. Rubber with working Americans' needs and fears about security, engaging readers' sympathies (Image 23.7). *Us* editors even included Leipzig's anxious diary of being stuck on ship during the Nor'easter. He described the crew's calm despite their peril and their awareness of comrades lost on the seas. Corporate photography typically had a 'managerial eye' that organized production processes from managers' standpoint, akin to nineteenth-century efficiency engineer Frederick Taylor's dream of managers taking the knowledge from under the workingman's hat (Montgomery 1987, 218–219). Disciplined coordination, prioritized by the managers, not labor, came to the fore. Such photos are often mundane. They suggest an antiseptic production process, orchestrated through managers' technocratic plans (Nye 1988; Brown 2005). But *Us*'s 'The fishing industry' proffered instead an adventure tale composed of Leipzig's images and eyewitness account.

Both photo essays represented heroic labor fighting elemental battles seemingly outside of time, in subzero temperatures in Quebec forests or far off the Atlantic Coast. In Leipzig's photographs, no manager supervises the loggers' or fishermen's work; they were not on an assembly line or timed. Workers controlled their labors and their fates, in the face of the Nor'easter, literally.[7] These were not industrial laborers, though their activities were directed by industry. Instead, the corporate publication ennobled the labor of those seemingly outside Taylorist constraints, which Singer and U.S. Rubber employed with their assembly-line workforce in factories in New Jersey, South Carolina, Connecticut, and Wisconsin. In these photo essays the companies purveyed increasingly obsolete forms of un-alienated labor. Workers have

Image 23.6 Arthur Leipzig, '*Joan and Ursula* Crew during Nor'easter, 1955'
Source: copyright Arthur Leipzig Estate

cut timber and fished the seas for millennia. The company magazines harnessed Leipzig's documentary photographs to a fable about labor without corporate strictures. Simultaneously and paradoxically, U.S. corporations' reach was everywhere. They established camps on civilization's margins, and their products protected fishermen in the middle of the Atlantic Ocean.

In adopting the documentary aesthetic, with a half-century connection to social reform, companies asserted their continued paternalism toward workers in the face of a union movement that for the first time in U.S. history was powerful enough to insist on workers' rights and securities. The corporations spoke to their workforce, relying on photo narratives about the labor of others, seemingly unlike them, to suggest the corporations' benevolence and good citizenship. The documentary tradition seems bent to the dictates of capital.

WINTER STORM ON THE ATLANTIC

The log of an "Us" photographer

by Arthur Leipzig

"they realize on what slim threads their lives hang . . ."

Image 23.7 Arthur Leipzig, 'Winter Storm on the Atlantic, 1955'
Source: copyright Arthur Leipzig Estate

And yet, what of the man who took these photographs? An artwork's meaning is not limited to its author's understanding of it, and yet neglecting this consideration privileges theory over history and negates the consciousness of its maker. Consider the photographer as worker. Leipzig began his career at *PM* and the Photo League, which the U.S. government, under Harry Truman, extinguished through the Attorney General's List of Subversive Organizations, a precursor to McCarthyism. Photographers lost jobs and commissions because of their connections to the League. Leipzig never dwelt on lost commissions, but his political commitments to racial and class equality jeopardized his family's economic stability (Saretzky 2000; Frankel 1993; Bezner 1999). Freelancing also makes for a precarious livelihood, particularly when supporting a family. Leipzig's agent, Mimi Leipzig, a 'shill' in her words, utilized her networking skills and exploited gendered expectations when 'engage[ing]' editors to promote her husband's work. She described a film scene where an editor examines a photographer's portfolio over lunch, then tosses the photographs on the floor. Mimi Leipzig said, 'Can you imagine? We used to collect bottles to get money to go into the city.' Economically vulnerable photographers were at editors' whims. Unless one had the status of Walker Evans or Margaret Bourke-White, maintaining oneself through commissions was difficult. Why would Leipzig subvert political commitments he had already dearly paid for?

Additionally, the photographer's conception of his or her political and aesthetic motives is relevant. Leipzig noted that for Photo League members, 'commercial work' offered a 'chance to pay your bills,' whereas 'straight photography without a client' was 'not very good for immediacy.' But art historian Bonnie Yochelson (1989) observes that Leipzig transformed many commercial jobs into long-term photographic explorations. Ultimately, he rejected labels: 'The attitude about what's commercial, what's fine art, what is documentary, and so on is a strange one.' His primary concern with the photograph was, 'does it work?'[8] In Leipzig's fifty-year career, his photographs insisted on the dignity of his subjects, whether street urchins, workers, or the rural poor in the United States or abroad.

Arthur and Mimi Leipzig's lived realities challenge critical theory. Like many midcentury documentarians, Leipzig worked at the edge. Documentarians sought acknowledgment and sustenance for themselves and their families. But like Leipzig, many also explored labor and insisted on workers' full humanity in the face of democratic-capitalism's failure to do so, economically, politically, and representationally. Leipzig's photos do not signal a political program, but they do assert an egalitarian vision that is a prerequisite for a more egalitarian politics.

Why did corporations appropriate this aesthetic in the 1940s and 1950s?[9] Might their use of the documentary speak to populism's power, much as Michael Denning has argued for a 'cultural front' emerging from the 1930s that remade U.S. culture and society to include workers (Denning 1997)? What did employees see when they viewed a coatless Daniel Dumouchel logging in Quebec or New Bedford fisherman confronting possible death on the job? Because Leipzig takes us into their lives, viewers are more apt to remember workers' courage than their U.S. Rubber mackintoshes and boots or corporate benevolence.

Many other internationally recognized photographers explored workers' lives, and this chapter now turns to two of them, Dan Weiner and Robert Frank. Their interest in the dimensions of class has largely been neglected.[10] Weiner, a fellow Photo League member, was the child of working-poor New York City immigrants. Like Leipzig, Weiner encountered Hine's and Lange's engaged documentary photography at the League. He contributed to its 'East Side document,' which rooted community life in the dynamics of a larger society. Weiner then freelanced for corporate clients and magazines such as *Fortune* and *Collier's*. He traveled extensively, to Russia, to South Africa, collaborating with novelist Alan Paton for a photo-text on apartheid, and to Montgomery for the 1955 bus boycott. Weiner also turned his camera on America's growing consumer culture, suburbia, and the managerial class.

Scholars have paid less attention to Weiner's photographs of blue-collar workers and the marginalized. He often employed irony, and several portraits of executives placed them in relationship to the blue-collar employees they depended upon, reversing media narratives that promoted corporate elite as responsible for the nation's economic prowess. In 1952, in the midst of the postwar construction boom, Weiner portrayed a dapper young executive, Willard Garvey, head of Wichita, Kansas's Builders, Inc. Garvey's hands are ambiguously clasped in front of his chest, perhaps in prayer or perhaps the gesture of a champion (Image 23.8). His serious expression reflects a traditional portrait, as does Garvey's gaze, which ignores the viewer. He stands against the wood exterior of a Builders Inc. home. The window aperture, a frame, makes visible two carpenters who literally frame the house. The composition created an inverted triangle, where the Builders Inc. CEO, 'the head,' as the caption said, lays at the bottom point of the triangle, and at the top, the triangle's base, are the carpenters. Weiner's composition emphasized the photograph as representation, as the squares of the house exterior, window, and home's interior framing are all frames. The photograph contends that the building boom was not solely the product of businessmen like Garvey, but also of workers' conscious labor, much as Lewis Hine reminded readers of labor's necessity in his *Men at Work*, about Empire State Building construction workers: 'Cities do not build themselves, machines cannot make machines, unless back of them all are the brains and toil of men' (Hine 1977).

Weiner's 1955 photograph of a Campbell's Soup warehouse adds additional irony. *Fortune*'s mission was conveying corporate strength and managerial expertise. But the two executives in the central position of the photograph are dwarfed by hundreds of pallets of soup. A forklift operator moves several pallets perilously over the executives' heads. As with much corporate

Image 23.8 Dan Weiner, 'Willard Garvey, Head of Builders, Inc., Wichita, Kansas,' 1952
Source: appeared in *Fortune*; Copyright John Broderick

photography, this photograph is highly organized. We know that the forklift will not drop the soup, yet the photograph demands viewers appreciate labor and management's interdependency and the power that workers enjoy.

Weiner also showed workers at leisure, often as they shopped, referencing the consumerism that lay at the heart of the postwar economy's promise. Weiner explored working urbanites, buying in all kinds of settings from elite perfumers to the remnants of New York's peddler-pushcart district. A photograph of a Brooklyn family buying furniture for their home delights in its ambiguity (Image 23.9). Unlike the families portrayed in advertisements, this family seems ill at ease. The father sits at the table as the head of house. But his head is bowed, his expression ambivalent. His son stands beside him, and the woman, probably wife and mother, regards her husband anxiously. The family occupies a consumption stage set, with a Danish table, Eames's Eiffel chair, and modern light fixtures and ceramics. This photo communicated the complex decision-making, in all likelihood driven by budgetary constraints, that working consumers faced. As curator William Ewing writes in *America Worked: The 1950s Photographs of Dan Weiner*, Weiner saw 'behind the façade of the American dream and reveal[ed] its frayed edges and split

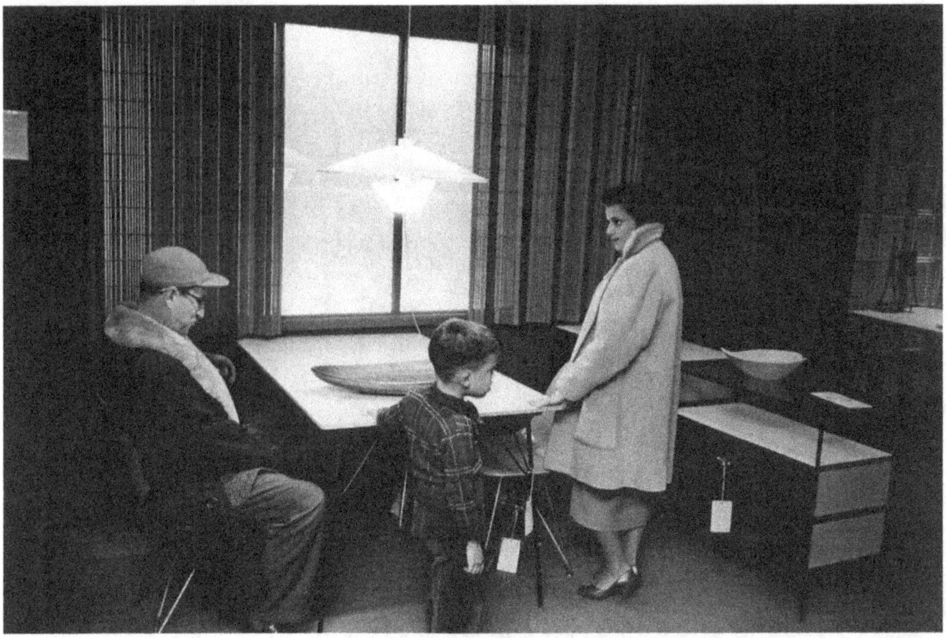

Image 23.9 Dan Weiner, 'Family Shopping for Modern Furniture, Brooklyn, Department Store,' 1952

Source: appeared in *Fortune*; copyright John Broderick

seams, that not all Americans of that era … cruised in shark-finned convertibles or relaxed on "colonial" sofas in split-level "rec rooms"' (Ewing 1989, 14).

Weiner found magazine photo stories overly formulaic, but he embraced their mass audiences over an insular art world. He focused on 'photographing human relations' and believed his photographs' immediacy would gain resonance over time (Capa, 1968). Retrospectively, Weiner offers insight to the postwar era's new consumer and labor relations, as it circulated in photography in a growing, increasingly visual, mass culture.

Unlike Leipzig and Weiner, the art world celebrated Swiss immigrant Robert Frank for shifting the trajectory of the documentary away from concern with social injustice toward personal expression. He too worked for magazines like *Fortune*. In art historian Jonathon Green's words, Frank substituted the 'the public document for private vision' (Green 1984, 85). Frank's *The Americans* (2008), a Guggenheim grant-funded photo book, offered eighty-seven images of a disaffected nation. On Frank's year-long automobile tour of the United States, he sought the quotidian, 'a parking lot, a supermarket, a highway … backyards' (Green 1984, 82). His photographs did not monumentalize or sentimentalize; they were cool and off beat. Green claimed he depicted 'the invisible America of the fifties,' a 'hidden country' of 'strangers in America's midst' (84). If embraced by critics, Frank was initially savaged by mainstream press, who saw his view of the United States as perverse, mendacious, and spiteful, 'an attack on America' (Green 1984, 85).[11] Oddly, commentators argue Frank's view of postwar America was personal, even while acknowledging his critique of U.S. politics, consumerism, and racism. Frank's exploration of workers' lives, particularly service workers, has been overlooked.

Frank's images of labor explored how gender and race inflected U.S. class relations. His 'Men's Room, Railway Station, Memphis, Tennessee' showed a middle-aged, African-American shoe shiner hovering over a white businessman's shoes. If hairlines serve as evidence, the worker was older than his client. The businessman, enthroned on the shoe-shiner's platform, sat higher than the urinals surrounding him. A broom and a hat stood as lone witnesses to this labor. Frank sequenced this image between a photo of a Chicago political convention, where tense men argued with one another, and one of soignée New Yorkers at an outdoor cocktail party. The jarring juxtaposition between the crowded spaces of white elites politicking and reveling and the behind-the-scenes view of the worker in the men's room pushes the reader to consider the social relations resulting in the alienated work space of the men's room.

'Charleston, South Carolina' more pointedly testifies to America's class and race relations. Nearly one in five of Frank's *Americans* images explored African-American life, a subject disdained by U.S. mass media. In Frank's photograph, a black middle-aged woman in a crisp white uniform holds a white baby. The child, with plump cheeks and pursed lips, appears privileged. They stand on the street, against a wall; there are no domestic trappings. The worker's expression seems alternately persistent and resigned; her brow is untroubled, but her lips are compressed. Unlike many images of mother and child, such as Dorothea Lange's 'Migrant Mother,' there is little feeling between the two figures. The child appears self-sufficient; the nanny contained. Frank condenses in two figures the nature of service labor as it intersects with class and race. Mary Ellen Mark called it the 'quintessential photographic statement about race and class' (cited in *Photo Booth* 2017). The subjects were bound in a socioeconomic relationship where needs are paid for and provided, and yet the emotional cost of such care cannot be calculated, either to the child or the woman-provider. In *The Americans* Frank sequenced this nurse or nanny between photographs of New York City transvestites self-consciously mugging for the camera and a Hollywood diner decorated with Santa Claus. Frank's photos can be read as a comment on the masks required in traversing or laboring across class and race lines; he casts a gimlet eye on the gendered and raced relations of work (Frank 2008).

The documentary did not languish in the postwar era; documentary photographs appeared in mass-market magazines, corporate communications, even art books. Indeed, documentary-style photography formed the backbone of MOMA's 1955 *Family of Man* exhibition, seen by nine million visitors as the exhibition traveled across the United States and then to thirty nations (MOMA, 1955). Half a million people bought the exhibition catalog. *The Family of Man*, a bestseller for nearly all of 1955, is still in print (*New York Times* 1956, 15). Over a tenth of the catalog addressed work: industrial and agricultural labor, and men and women's work, including domestic labor. Leipzig and Frank both published photos in it, though not about labor. This crowd-pleasing exhibition ignored U.S. racism, imperialism, and the Cold War, and assumed a universal human experience that blunted regional, racial, gender, and class disparities. But *The Family of Man*'s appeal establishes the documentary's endurance and practitioners' persistent focus on labor. Understanding how class works in the postwar era requires that scholars recognize this and not rely on a traditional art historical chronology that erases labor—though they should reflect upon that erasure. Moreover, scholars should map map labor's visual representation over time to evaluate how such images shape public understanding of workers and their demands.

Documentary photography was less yoked to explicit demands for social change, but it was not politically neutral. Artists' insistence on representing workers as fully conscious, engaged beings retained a linkage to the earlier documentary tradition. For Leipzig, Weiner, and Frank, workers were no anonymous mass, nor alien other; the photographers navigated new socio-political realities in the United States, exploring new concerns—consumerism, the growth and travails of service work, and the complexities of a heterogeneous workforce. Further research is required to address the effects of such imagery upon workers or workers' reception of such representations.

Hence, a working-class studies analysis of postwar photography enriches our understanding of the photographic tradition in the twentieth century's second half, and it challenges the critique of the documentary pervading scholarship since the 1970s. *Fortune* sought anonymous labor, and corporations commissioned a classless view of America that promoted a harmony of interests. Instead, documentary photographers probed the contours of workers' lives; their labor, their domestic lives, and their interior being. When Leipzig and Weiner depicted labor off the assembly line or outside the Taylorist order, they provoked questions about labor's alienation. Leipzig challenged a traditional corporate photography style that emphasized managerial prowess by probing the lives of fully conscious workers; Weiner destabilized the concept of managerial control by identifying workers' power, and Frank insisted that grave class and race inequalities eroded U.S. social relations. Documentary photographs of labor did cultural work, shaping ideas about class relations and workers' lives. From the vantage of today's neoliberal world, where images predominate and few are of workers, where few call for change, and fewer still challenge class inequalities, this working-class studies reassessment of the documentary's chronology and motives rebuts the medium's characterization as apolitical, conservative, or cynical. The commissions and projects of Leipzig, Weiner, and Frank indicate that a reckoning of postwar class relations circulated within the heart of capitalism.

* Special thanks to Mimi and Judy Leipzig for their generosity in sharing Arthur Leipzig's photographs for this published essay. The Leipzig estate retains the copyright to these images.

Thanks to Marcella Bencivenni, Dan Wishnoff, Evelyn Burg, Nancy Berke, Linda Grasso, Nina Bannett-Fox, and Phyllis vanSlyck for their careful readings of earlier versions of this chapter, and the book's editors, Michele Fazio, Tim Strangleman, and Christie Launius, for sharpening the chapter's argument.

Notes

1 This chapter primarily explores white male laborers' representation. A rich and growing literature investigates the racing and gendering of midcentury visual culture; scholarship on class lags. Within photojournals and employee magazines, white men typically, if inadequately, represented the working class (Melosh 1991; Enstad 1999).
2 *Aperture*'s Spring 2017 'American destiny' issue offers a superb exception.
3 This origins story is more complex. (Hales 2006, 342–345).
4 Those rebutting the documentary critique focus on its neglecting of the aesthetic dimensions of documentary photographs, and engage less with the aesthetic's production and history (Linfield 2010, 3–31; Levi Strauss 2003, 3–11).
5 Unless otherwise noted, Leipzig quotations are from oral history transcripts (interviewed by the author, January 2010 and July 27, 2011, Sea Cliff, New York).
6 Middle-class and elite amateurs flocked to camera clubs in the late nineteenth century; by the mid twentieth century, clubs developed mass audiences (Quirke 2018, 98).
7 These industries were, however, increasingly rationalized (Evolution of a Logger Superintendent, 1921).
8 This quote comes from an unpublished interview conducted by the author.
9 John Tagg argues the photograph's meaning inheres in its use.
10 Recent exhibitions hint at a redress to such neglect. See 'Small Trades,' *Vogue*, July 1951 in *Irving Penn Centennial* (2017) [Exhibition] Metropolitan Museum of Art, New York City, April 24–July 30, 2017; Eve Arnold's work in *Magnum Manifesto* (2017) [Exhibition] International Center for Photography, New York City, 26 May–3 September 2017; and *Danny Lyon: Message to the Future* (2016) [Exhibition] Whitney Museum of American Art, New York City, 17 June–25 September 2016.
11 Penn, Diane Arbus, Gary Winograd, and Lee Friedlander would be other art 'stars,' ostensibly rejecting political content in their work. For another extended analysis of this phenomenon, see James Guimond, *American Photography and the American Dream*, (1991, 233–244), and Lili Corbus Bezner's monograph, *Photography and Politics in America: From the New Deal into the Cold War*, cited above.

References

Advertisement. (March 25, 1940). Life, 8, 13, pp. 78–79.
Agee, J. and Evans, W. (1988) *Let Us Now Praise Famous Men*, 5th ed, New York, Houghton Mifflin.
Barthes, R. (1977) *Image—Music—Text*, Stephen Heath (ed.) New York, Farrar, Strauss, Giroux.
Bezner, L. (1999) *Photography and Politics in America: From the New Deal into the Cold War*, Baltimore, Johns Hopkins University Press.
Brown, E. (2005) *The Corporate Eye: Photography and the Rationalization of American Commercial Culture*, Baltimore, Johns Hopkins University Press.
Campany, D. and Thompson, J. (2015) *Walker Evans: Labor Anonymous*, New York: D.A.P./Koenigm.
Capa, C. (1968) *The Concerned Photographer*, New York, Grossman Publishers.
Center for Working-Class Studies. 'About.' Available at http://cwcs.ysu.edu/about/.
Coles, R. (1997) *Doing Documentary Work*, New York, Oxford University Press.
Curtis, J. (1989) *Mind's Eye, Mind's Truth: FSA Photography Reconsidered*, Philadelphia, Temple University Press.
Denning, M. (1997) *The Cultural Front: The Laboring of American Culture in the Twentieth Century*, New York, Verso.
Doss, E. (2001) *Looking at* Life *Magazine*, Washington D.C., Smithsonian Press.
Enstad, N. (1999) *Ladies of Labor, Girls of Adventure: Working Women, Popular Culture, and Labor Politics at the Turn of the Twentieth Century*, New York, Columbia University Press.
Evans, W. (November 1946) 'Labor Anonymous,' *Fortune*, pp. 152–153.
Evolution of a Logger Superintendent. (1921) *American Lumberman.*
Ewing, W. (1989) *America Worked: The 1950s Photographs of Dan Weiner*, New York, Harry Abrahms.
Museum of Modern Art. (1955) 'Family of Man Press Release,' available at www.moma.org/documents/moma_press-release_325967.pdf.
'The Fishing Industry.' (1955) *Us*, pp. 4–13.
Frank, R. (2008) *The Americans*, Germany, Steidl.
Frankel, G. (1993) Interview for American Archives of Art, Smithsonian Institute, by Merry Forresta, available at www.aaa.si.edu/collections/interviews/oral-history-interview-godfrey-frankel-12004.
Green, J. (1984) *A Critical History of American Photography*, New York, Harry Abrahms.
Guimond, J. (1991) *American Photography and the American Dream*, Chapel Hill, University of North Carolina Press.
Hales, P. B. (2006) *Silver Cities: Photographing American Urbanism, 1839–1939*, Albuquerque, University of New Mexico Press.
Hapke, L. (2002) 'Marxism and American Exceptionalism,' *Rethinking Marxism*, 14, 3, 32–35.
Herzog, M. (2006) *Milton Rogovin: The Making of a Social Documentary Photographer*, Tuscon, Center for Creative Photography.
Hine, L. (1977) *Men at Work*, 2nd ed., New York, Dover.
Hine, L. (1980) 'Social Photography; How the Camera May Help in the Social Uplift,' in Trachtenberg, A. (ed.) *Classic Essays on Photography*, New Haven, Leete Island Books.
Klein, M. and Evans, C. (2011) *The Radical Camera: New York's Photo League*, New Haven, Yale University Press.
Lange, D. (1937) 'Letter to Roy Stryker,' Farm Security Administration Correspondence, Oakland Museum of California.
Lauter, P. (1996) 'More Working Class Studies,' *Radical Teacher*, 48, pp. 15–26.
Lichtenstein, N. (1982) *Labor's War at Home: The CIO in World War II*, Cambridge, Cambridge University Press.
Lichtenstein, N. (2003) *State of the Union: A Century of American Labor*, Princeton, Princeton University Press.
Leipzig, A. (2005) *On Assignment with Arthur Leipzig*, Brooklyn, Long Island University Press.
Levi Strauss, D. (2003) *Between the Eyes: Essays on Photography and Politics*, New York, Aperture.
Linfield, S. (2010) *The Cruel Radiance: Photography and Political Violence*, Chicago, University of Chicago Press.
Linkon, S. and Russo J. (2005) *New Working-Class Studies*, Ithaca, Cornell University Press.
Linkon, S. and Russo, J. (2012) 'Border Crossings: Interdisciplinarity in New Working-Class Studies,' *Labor History*, 53, 3, pp. 373–387.
'Lumberjack in Singer's Canadian Forest.' (1953) *Singer Light*, 23, 1, pp. 8–12.
Melosh, B. (1991) *Engendering Culture: Manhood and Womanhood in New Deal Public Art and Theater*, Washington D.C., Smithsonian Press.
Meltzer, M. (1978) *Dorothea Lange: A Photographer's Life*, New York, Farrar, Strauss and Giroux.
Metzgar, J. (2000) *Striking Steel: Solidarity Remembered*, Philadelphia, Temple University Press.

Milkman, P. (1997) *PM: A New Deal in Journalism*, New Brunswick, Rutgers University Press.
Montgomery, D. (1987) *The Fall of the House of Labor: The Workplace, the State, and American Labor Activism*, Cambridge, Cambridge University Press.
Newhall, B. (1964) *The History of Photography*, New York, Museum of Modern Art.
New York Times. (1956) 'Camera Notes,' x15.
Nye, D. (1988) *Image Worlds: Corporate Identities at General Electric, 1890–1930*, Cambridge, MA, MIT Press.
Phillips, C. (1989) 'The Judgment Seat of Photography,' in Bolton, R. (ed.) *The Contest of Meaning*, Cambridge, MIT Press.
Photo Booth. (2017) *New Yorker*, available at www.newyorker.com/culture/photo-booth/eight-photographers-on-their-favorite-image-from-robert-franks-the-americans.
Photo Notes, (1948), 7.
Plattner, S. (1983) *Roy Stryker USA, 1943–1950: The Standard Oil of New Jersey Photo Project*, Austin, University of Texas Press.
Quirke, C. (2010, 2011) Leipzig, A. and Leipzig, M. Oral History Interview.
Quirke, C. (2012) *Eyes on Labor: News Photography and America's Working Class*, New York, Oxford University Press.
Quirke, C. (2018) 'Imagining Racial Equality: Local 65s Union Photographers, Postwar Civil Rights, and the Power of the Real, 1940–1955,' *Radical History Review*, 18, 3, pp. 96–125.
Riis, J. (1888) 'Flashes from the Slums,' *The Sun*.
Riis, J. (1890) *How the Other Half Lives*, New York, Scribner's and Sons.
Rosler, M. (1989) 'In, Around, and Afterthoughts on Documentary Photography,' in Bolton, R. (ed.) *The Contest of Meaning*, Cambridge, MIT Press.
Saretzky, G. (2000) Libsohn, S. Interview, available at: www.visitmonmouth.com/oralhistory/bios/LibsohnSol.htm. Accessed March 9, 2018.
Schocket, E. (2002) 'Introduction,' *Rethinking Marxism*, 14, 3, pp. 25–48.
Schocket, E. (2006) *Vanishing Moments: Class and American Literature*, Ann Arbor, University of Michigan Press.
Sekula, A. (1974) 'On the Invention of Photographic Meaning,' *Artforum*, pp. 2–21.
Stein, S. (1983) 'Making Connections with the Camera: Photography and Social Mobility in the Career of Jacob Riis,' *Afterimage*, 11, 10, pp. 9–16.
Stott, W. (1973) *Documentary Expression and Thirties America*, New York, Oxford University Press.
Strangleman, T. (2008) 'Sociology, Social Class, and New Working Class Studies,' *Antipode*, 40, 1, pp. 15–19.
Tagg, J. (1993) *The Burden of Representation; Essays on Photographies and Histories*, Minneapolis, University of Minnesota Press.
Tedlow, R. (1979) *Keeping the Corporate Image: Public Relations and Business, 1900–1950*, Greenwich, CT, JAI Press.
Tucker, A. (1994) 'A History of the Photo League: The Members Speak,' *History of Photography*, 18, 2, pp. 174–184.
Yochelson, B. (1989) *Arthur Leipzig: A Retrospective*, Brookville, NY, Long Island University Press.
Zandy, J. (1990) *Coming Home: Working-Class Women's Anthology*, New Brunswick, Rutgers University Press.
Zandy, J. (2004) *Hands: Physical Labor, Class, and Cultural Work*, New Brunswick, Rutgers University Press.
Zandy, J. (2013) *Unfinished Stories: The Narrative Photography of Hansel Mieth and Marion Palfi*, Rochester, Rochester Institute of Technology Press.

24
Mapping working-class art

Janet Zandy

> Some of the freak journals are making a fuss over the refusal of the door keepers at the Metropolitan Museum to admit into the Museum a plumber in his working clothes. It appears that the plumber was working near by, and, having some of his nooning to himself, determined to have a look at the Museum. This was a laudable determination, but he should have removed his overalls before attempting to carry it out. … For him to attempt to visit the Museum in such a guise and without removing traces of his toil argues either mere carelessness or lack of self-respect. It was probably the former, for it seems that when the impropriety was brought to his notice by the refusal to let him in he retired without making any fuss, leaving it to the freak journals to make the fuss. This they promptly proceeded to do, and their doing it is a very contemptible performance. It is to be hoped that they have misjudged their readers in imagining that any considerable number of them maintain that an American citizen ought to have the right of entering any public institution no matter in how filthy a condition he may happen to be.
>
> *New York Times*, Editorial, Thursday, February 4, 1897[1]

This chapter recognizes and recovers 'traces of toil' on art making, on audiences, and on the history of art. While the language of 'filth,' 'fuss,' 'freak' in this 1897 editorial may be a relic of another century, class assumptions about who is interested in art, who has access to art making, and who writes about art and for what audience still linger in the fissures of art production.

Consider also the plumber's perspective and how working-class people see themselves *in* museums, not only as representations in paintings hung on museum walls, but as people looking, observing, and studying inside museum spaces. Contemporary working-class scholar Sarah Attfield (2016) recalls her trips to galleries in London on those days when admission was free:

> Very rarely did I come across a work that represented me, or the people I knew. … How many successful artists have working-class backgrounds? Working-class people may visit galleries on school visits at an early age, but could the lack of working-class representation … make them feel that art is not for them? … Art is something that all humans seem

> to enjoy, but working-class people are often excluded from the production of art and from the pleasures to be gained from viewing.

Another way of realizing this elision is to ask how many curators, museum directors, not to mention board members and trustees, come from the working class. Are there implicit class assumptions in the circuitry of patronage, grants, curatorial judgments, gallery ownership, distribution, and canonical determination? What unspoken biases against depiction of laborers are harbored in the exhibit selection process as well as in the texture of art criticism? Are the uniformed guards the only consistent working-class presence in museums?

A new, incomplete map

All maps are incomplete. Maps serve interests, offer perspectives, and provide topographies. In *The Power of Maps*, Denis Wood convincingly personifies maps as working instruments of particular and masked interests (1992, 1–3). Maps, like literary canons or art histories, are necessarily selective. Any revisionist history of either is tasked with scooping up exclusions and ruminating on why they are submerged. James Elkins (2002) uses maps as a meta-historical tool to see the outlines and coastlines of art history as a story told and retold. He acknowledges the impossibility of telling any whole story.

This art historical map has a specific perspective and intention: seeing workers and acknowledging class relationships. It is admittedly inconclusive and incomplete, biased toward American, British, and European perspectives—and relying on paper rather than electronic or virtual media. What is missing invites further and future studies. This is a limited intervention and partial answer to the question of how workers are presented aesthetically and from their own perspectives and interests. *The strategy of this map making—and structure of this essay—has two directions: discerning some of the shaping elements of working-class art and locating methods and practices of particular artists in relation to the working classes.* A modest, alternative continuum, it seeks to show how art creation emerges out of material circumstances, in response to social and political conditions, and from a human's own desire for beauty.

'No classless society can arise without a cultural base,' declares Stefan Szczelkun in *The Conspiracy of Good Taste* (1993, 1). To see an evolving, diverse—albeit inconsistent and fractured—working-class base in the history of art making is the challenge of this essay. It is at once a process of architectural building and archeological excavating. It recognizes working-class epistemology, ways of knowing and relating, that, though inseparable from economic forces, still fuel art making of agency, resistance, and liberation. This impulse is larger than a particular artist, artwork, or movement. It is more than reductive representation. It is a dynamic process of answerability, not as transaction or exchange, but as new circuitry. It is less about 'decisive' moments, and more about 'alterable' moments, more about communicating than 'capturing.' It is resistance to enclosure. It is an opening, an aperture, a map toward self and societal re-creation. It can take many forms, but in the global world of capital it is 'a struggle at the roots of the mind … confronting a hegemony in the fibres of the self' (Williams, 1977, 212). At its best, working-class art making is a decolonizing and liberating process.

Ways of seeing workers

Are they in the field or the foundry? In the foreground or background? Alone or wedged in a crowd? Are they objects of personal or collective memory or symbols of struggle? Are they sentimental or cutting? What is the hierarchy of representation? Who is diminutive and who is larger than life? Are the figures scaled according to their social importance? 'One is concerned,' as T. J. Clark observes, 'with what prevents representation as much as what allows it; one studies blindness as much as vision' (1973, 15).

In *The Working American*, Patricia Hills offers a brief, cogent, synopsis of the history of art in relation to (not exclusively American) working-people's representations.

> [F]rom the time of cave painting to the present—artists have represented … the everyday life of working people. In Egypt … scenes of workers [were] carved into the walls within private tombs. … During the twelfth and thirteenth centuries, the Church hired carvers to decorate the surfaces of newly erected cathedrals with small scenes, some of which represent workers engaged in tasks appropriate to the seasons or the months. In the fifteenth century, European nobility commissioned hand-painted prayer books which contained scenes of labor to symbolize times of the year, such as planting and harvest. In the Netherlands and Flanders during the sixteenth and seventeenth centuries, the merchant class … decorated their homes with small paintings of peasants and urban workers relaxing and behaving comically. In all of these instances the everyday events had importance to the class who commissioned or purchased the artists' work, because such scenes served the existing social order by teaching moral or religious lessons or by amusing a newly rich merchant class.
>
> *(Hills 1979, 1)*

Representations of workers, laborers, slaves, peasants, servants, sowers, planters, and reapers are not missing from art histories. What is missing or hidden are the power relationships beneath the representations. *That is a critical first acknowledgment.* Listing sightings and sites of worker representations is important, but not enough. How artists expose power relationships is one element of working-class representation. How audiences with questioning eyes can see whether workers are covered, concealed, or uncovered and revealed is another.

How does working-class art *work*?[2] What are the shaping elements? How does it create a circuitry of recognition and understanding outside the interests of capital and markets as well as distinct from property-owning aesthetic tastes? How does it reflect, perhaps serve, the interests of ordinary people? How can we see art making through the lens of a working-class perspective?

These key questions risk murky answers. Rather than impose a restrictive ideology, I offer these theoretical observations with brief examples followed by specific instances of worker-conscious art making. This is a project of exploration and query, not fixed borders.

What to look for: Intersecting and shaping elements

Beauty

Let us begin, not with 'filth' and 'fuss,' but with the desire for, and appreciation of, *beauty*.

> … in the end—after you've got a roof, food and warmth—all you can buy is beauty.
>
> *(Hockney and Gayford 2016)*

> [M]y real motive for choosing my subjects almost exclusively from the life of the workers was that only such subjects gave me in a simple and unqualified way what I felt to be beautiful. For me the Koenigsberg longshoremen had beauty; the Polish jimkes on their grain

> ships had beauty; the broad freedom of movement in the gestures of the common people had beauty. Middle class people held no appeal for me at all.
>
> *(Kollwitz 1988, 43)*[3]

We are concerned here not with buying beauty but in seeing it. The German painter, printmaker, and sculptor Kaethe Kollwitz (1867–1945) saw beauty in the lives and bodies of workers. She witnessed their struggle to survive and their inherent dignity, not only in facing loss, but also in sustaining human relationships. Her artwork is inseparable from her consciousness of history, war, loss, literature, motherhood, and the small joys and many defeats of ordinary lives. Conveying a sense of interiority in the human figure is more than copying forms and shapes. Kollwitz, in her hundreds of drawings, etchings, lithographs, and woodcuts, understood the power an artist can unleash in the line, the gesture, and the mark. A Kollwitz hand is recognizable—for its size and its inherent history of work.[4] Her work gives visual voice to grief, loss, and unexpected death. Always a searching worker artist, she saw beauty where it was not expected—and where it is not usually claimed in the history of art.

What is not overtly conveyed in Kollwitz's powerful prints and portraits is whether her subjects saw and shaped beauty for themselves.

In her 1861 story 'Life in the iron mills,' Rebecca Harding Davis turns a voyeuristic tour of a rolling iron mill into a confrontation between wealth and power and mill labor degradation (see Davis 1985).[5] Davis demands that her middle-class readers 'look deeper' and see the furnace-tender Hugh Wolfe as a human being and as an artist (14).[6] Wolfe had within him 'a fierce thirst for beauty—to know it, to create it' (25). Out of blocks of korl ('a light, porous substance, of a delicate, waxen, flesh-colored tinge'; 24), Wolfe, during his breaks from the furnace, would sculpt 'strangely beautiful' figures. A particular one, huge, of a woman crouched on the ground, 'her arms flung out in some wild gesture of warning' caught the attention of visiting observers. What does it mean, they asked. 'She be hungry,' Wolfe responded, for 'summat [something] to make her live' (33).

The working-class writer Tillie Olsen, who recovered that lost story, understood well how class oppression blights lives and thwarts artistic expression. She knew that beauty is no one's special domain. Perceiving and presenting beauty as a class-conscious aesthetic is one element of working-class art; that is, art made out of the lives and by the hands of the working and poverty classes. It's a reminder that there's bread hunger and there's hunger for roses.

Physicality of labor

Is the subject work itself or is it the worker? In *Work and Struggle: The Painter as Witness 1870–1914*, Edward Lucie-Smith and Celestine Dars (1977) reproduce paintings depicting male laborers as field harvesters, weavers, glassmakers, cobblers, quarry men, miners, tanners, and gleaners, as well as paintings of female laborers such as Max Liebermann's *Women Working at a Canned Food Factory* (1879), Abraham Archipov's *Laundry Women* (1901), and Ernest Duez's *Wet Nurses Feeding the Sickly Infants at the Maternity Hospital* (c. 1895) (25–56). These highly skilled salon paintings were, according to Lucie-Smith and Dars (1977), quite popular, appealing to the curious middle and upper classes. Perhaps like Rebecca Harding Davis's owning class visitors to the iron mills? Or perhaps like a trip to a zoo? As John Berger astutely observed: 'Visitors visit the zoo to look at animals. They proceed from cage to cage, not unlike visitors in an art gallery who stop in front of one painting, and then move on to the next or the one after next' (1980, 21). Were these pictorial laborers viewed (unconsciously?) as human subspecies, observed briefly, and then, without further acknowledgment, passed over?

Picturing working lives

A life as a picture: a *bildung*—a process as well as an object. The process—autodidactic, developmental, formational, and the outcome—an object/person shaped and reshaped—whose life story becomes a *bildungsroman*. Whether secular or religious or nationalistic, these are all permutations of the deeply rooted German concept of *bildung*. James Elkins draws this useful connection between interior development and exterior presentation: '*Bildung*—a kind of aesthetic education that polishes a person by making him into a picture (that's the literal meaning of the German word)' (2002, 86).

But what if pictures of workers trigger class discomfort? Is there prejudice against seeing working and poverty classes of all races and geographies on their own terms instead of framed by privileged preconceptions? It's a cutting question, difficult to measure how class affiliations shape ocular experiences. Images of workers are acceptable subjects if they do not disturb the ideological order. Richard Avedon's aesthetically framed, white backgrounded, a-contextual portraits of working people are valued because the subject is the photographer's own artistic skill, not the anonymous people in front of his camera (see Avedon 1985). There is no visual disruption to class order. But that was not the case of the gold watches.

The Lowell Girls, Yankee farmers' daughters, became the first generation of female factory workers in New England mill towns (approximately1840–1845). They exemplify *bildung*, as polished image and as personal development. Hard-working, self-educated, striving, saving—soon to leave the mills driven out by worsening working conditions and replaced by immigrant labor—some of these young workers disrupted the class order by wearing gold watches. Daguerreotypes of men and women in their Sunday best, employees of Amoskeag Manufacturing, show some women wearing gold watches (c. 1844). What a muddle—working girls and class-privileged daughters looked similar! One observer noted

> How sadly the world has changed! The time was when the *lady* could be distinguished from the *no-lady* by her dress .... Even gold watches are now no *sure* indication—for they have been worn by the lowest, even by 'many of the factory girls.'
>
> *(Eisler 1998, 184–185)*

Such is the discomfort when the working classes appropriate objects or styles that the bourgeoisie assumes it owns.

The narrative impulse and historical consciousness

There are many serving hands, severed from thinking minds, in the long history of art. Representations of labor are contained within larger secular and religious narratives. Medieval images of *Labours of the Months* (*les travaux des mois*) depict peasants in relation to the cycles of the seasons. Likewise, the illuminated 15th-century calendar pages, *The Occupations of the Month*, (*Tres Riches Heures*, c. 1416) artistically reflect a reassuring social order of labor. But a series of images of laboring bodies is not a subjective working-class story. Visual stories for working-class audiences emerge out of history, struggle, and connection to communities. One of the best visual storytellers of the 20th century, combining history and the immediacy of daily lives, is Jacob Lawrence (1917–2000) (see Hills (1986; King-Hammond (2000, 67–85); Hills (2009).

Jacob Lawrence got his start at the Harlem Art Center. Sculptor Augusta Savage took him to the WPA/Federal Art Project, where he developed, in his distinctive 'expressive cubism' style, paintings about the lives and history of black people. His heroic biographical series *Toussaint L'Ouverture*, on the revolution of Haitian slaves, was followed by *Frederick Douglass, Harriet Tubman*, and *John Brown*. Lawrence's distinctive sense of line, form, and space—his signature style—works in harmony with his capacious vision. Whether his subject was black migration north, or life aboard a warship, or the work of builders and carpenters, or the prosaic rhythms of Harlem streets, libraries, hospitals, and pool halls, or the not so simple struggles of everyday people, especially black women's labor, Lawrence's figures are inseparable from his sense of community. Struggle is a key word for Lawrence: 'When you don't feel struggle, there is no passion. It's true in civil rights and in art' (quoted in Hills 2009, 270).

Communal sensibility

Working-class artists, whether born into the laboring classes or politically affiliated with them, may create art alone but are grounded in communities, neighborhoods, workplaces, and shared struggles. Jacob Lawrence is one example; Alice Neel is another. Alice Neel's Spanish Harlem portraits, for example, convey her consciousness of the individual in relationship to community.

> I love you Harlem … what a treasure of goodness and life shambles thru the streets, abandoned, despised, charged the most, given the worst/I love you for electing Marcantonio, and him for being what he is. And for the rich deep vein of human feeling buried under your fire engines your poverty and your loves.
>
> *(Neel, quoted in Allara 2000, 127)*

Sculptor, printmaker, American, Mexican, activist, and cultural worker, Elizabeth Catlett (1915–2012) is a figure of convergent artistic influences and great communal imagination. She wanted to take art to people who do not usually go to museums. 'Art has to belong to everyone,' she said. Catlett led a long, artistically fruitful, and politically productive life with many geographic and cultural intersections. In 1947 she moved to Mexico, and there she absorbed the 'visual politics' of the great Mexican muralists and printmakers producing her first linocut series, *The Negro Woman* (Herzog 2005, 73). Like Kaethe Kollwitz and Jacob Lawrence, Catlett threaded her individual artistry with collective consciousness: 'I have always wanted my art to service my people—to reflect us, to relate to us, to stimulate us, to make us aware of our potential,' as told to Samella S. Lewis (quoted in Lewis 1990, 134).[7]

Representations of alienated labor or good work

In a fragmentary piece written in 1844 but not published until 1927, Karl Marx defines alienated labor as work that is extraneous to the worker, where the worker is personally unfulfilled, where he (or she) feels homeless at work, and experiences himself as a stranger who loses personal identity. 'The alienated character of work for the worker is shown by the fact that the work he does is not his own, but another's, and that at work he belongs not to himself, but to another.'[8]

There is no shortage of alienated labor depictions—in film, Charlie Chaplin's *Modern Times* (1936), in literature, Thomas Bell's *Out of This Furnace* (1941[1976])—in painting, Peder Severin Kroyer's *The Iron Foundry Burmeister and Wain* (1885) (which pictures laborers struggling to manage a swinging cauldron as visitors observe; reprinted in Lucie-Smith and Dars 1977, 58). There are resistances to alienation as well, in, for example, Jules Adler's *The Strike* (1899) (reprinted in Lucie-Smith and Dars 1977, II).

John Barrell, in *The Dark Side of the Landscape* (1980), analyzes preindustrial paintings of rural labor by parsing the differences between idealized pastoral settings, suitable for privileged drawing rooms, and actual lives of toil. Barrell reads class relationships in British landscape paintings, noting that '[t]he labourers do not step between us and the landscape—they keep their place, and it is a very small place, a long way away' (1980 134). In contrast, the physicality of peasants looms large in Jean-Francois Millet's paintings of sowers, planters, gleaners, and winnowers. Millet is respectful of labor, empathetic, not revolutionary. He saw depictions of rural penury as possibly disturbing the Salon-attending public 'in their contentment and leisure' (Berger 2015, 221).

Are there portrayals of un-alienated labor that are not distant, quaint, precious, exquisite, or, worst of all, according to some critics, sentimental? The answer is yes in the work of painter, photographer, printmaker, and activist Marilyn Anderson. In her bilingual *Guardianes de Las Artes: Guardians of the Arts* (2016), Anderson presents her own woodcut print depictions of Guatemalan craft workers as makers—weavers, knotters, embroiderers, hatmakers, paper cutters, stone carvers, tile makers, silversmiths, mask makers, and many other forms of 'slow art.' Anderson lived in Guatemalan villages, photographed villagers and their crafts, especially women, and learned techniques of back-strap weaving. Her woodcuts of process and products, of making by hand—hats, hammocks, pots, sandals, masks, marimbas—emerge from her subjects' generational memory and show un-alienated, though threatened, labor.

Intent and audience

Intention, instrumentality, and audience are immeasurable elements of working-class representation. Yet some forms of working-class visual expression are fairly clear in their intentions and audience. Posters, whether as polished graphics or handwritten biting social commentary, are usually straightforward. True, posters can be right-wing propagandistic tools, but they are also, powerfully, a plebian art of resistance, wit, accessibility, and creative graphic beauty. The best posters embed themselves in our visual memories, and artists continue to carry and bend their meanings (see Cushing and Drescher 2009).

Paintings are a different matter, especially in relation to audience within the architectonics of galleries and museums. Later in her life, the pioneering *Life* photographer Hansel Mieth (1909–1998) created large representational paintings of field workers and laboring families. Subjects she knew well as a photographer but also from her own early impoverished life as a migratory laborer. Museums and galleries declined to exhibit her work. And she had ambiguous feelings about exhibiting.

> I thoroughly hate the fake and pretense of the world of art … and yet, I know the paintings must get out and live and fight for their existence, even as the people they portray are fighting for their existence in our world.
>
> *(Mieth, quoted in Zandy 2013, 57–58)*

In a small gallery in San Francisco, Mieth found an audience for her massive four-by-eight-foot representational paintings. 'The rooms of the gallery were filled with these outspoken pictures. … And many people came, some of them had never been to a gallery or museum before, and they understood' (Mieth, quoted in Zandy 2013, 58).

Visual languages and representational forms

The work of this chapter is to observe and connect. The first part offered critical observations with examples of working-class artistic representation. This second part elaborates and connects those observations by focusing primarily on paintings, printmaking, and photographs. Future research might explore public working-class representations as evidenced in sculpture, monuments, and murals, 'outsider' and folk art, cartoons, threaded art making, especially by women, in the form of tapestries, quilts, and *arpilleras*, and intersections of technology and working-class representation, such as installations that particularize working-class lives. It's a large, ongoing excavation.

Paintings and workers

Historically, paintings, especially oil portraits, were for and about the aristocracy, the monarchy, the church, and, with a spreading mercantile world, the bourgeoisie. We glimpse the lives of peasants, servants, sowers, artisans, and the indigent in genre paintings. Pieter Bruegel the Elder (1525–1569) painted cinematic scenes of peasant lives and events, such as *Peasant Wedding* (1566–1569). But the humans in most generic paintings do not have Bruegel the Elder's existential complexity. Generic human figures—men, women, and children—offered the merchant class amusement, and reassurance of an ordered and stratified world.[9]

Unambiguous class relationships are stunningly detailed and materially determined in 17th-century Dutch paintings. For example, in Jacob Ochtervelt's *Street Musicians at the Door* (1665), five figures are each positioned in gradations of class identity: the illuminated matron/mother, the aproned servant, the female child, and, at the threshold, two dark-clothed street musicians. The child desires the music; the musicians with their ingratiating smiles are eager to play. Will the matron say yes so they can be monetarily rewarded and the child can have some fun? (Baer 2015).

There are pitfalls in reading art too literally as social history (Clark 1973). Better to ask how material, cultural, and political circumstances *work on* the artist and the art-making process. If we keep to the metaphor of the map, we can follow certain shifts and fissures in representation. By the mid 19th century, we see peasants as people, individualized, yet static, as in the work of Jean-Francois Millet (1814–1875, previously noted). We have to look more deeply to see the disconnect between the aesthetics of his oil paintings and the actuality of peasant penury, the necessity of gleaning itself, the urgent need to retrieve remnants from the harvest.

Look for disturbances in the landscape. Gustave Courbet (1819–1877) was one such disturber. John Berger begins his portrait of Courbet by

> clean[ing] off some of the mud that has stuck. Because Courbet was uncompromising in his convictions, because his work and his way of life 'vulgarly' proved that art was as relevant to the back-parlour, the workshop, the cell, as to the drawing room, because his paintings never offered the slightest possibility of escape from the world as it was, he was officially rejected in his lifetime and has since been only grudgingly admitted.
>
> *(2015, 226)*

Berger interprets Courbet as

> opposing art to any hierarchical system or to any culture whose function is to diminish or deny the expression of a large part of what exists. He was the only great painter to challenge the chosen ignorance of the cultured.
>
> *(2015, 235)*

See worker representations as oppositional to the classed convenience of willed ignorance. It is not the sameness of experience that matters, but the capacity for imaginative empathy, and for recognizing what is experientially unknown or unknowable. The word Reality is damaged, hijacked. John Berger sees reality as 'inimical to power' (2015, 267). Agreed, but even Berger cannot rescue Reality from patronizing academic categorization, not to mention political and pop culture obfuscation. I prefer James Agee's more modest observation of approaching 'human actuality,' (in Agee and Evans 1941[1980], xvi). The difference is an embodied understanding of labor. Vincent van Gogh (1853–1890) had that sense; he grasped the process of making. Here's Berger on van Gogh:

> Nothing appeared more sacred to Van Gogh than work. He saw the physical reality of labour as being, simultaneously, a necessity, an injustice, and the essence of humanity throughout history. The artist's creative act was for him only one among many such acts. He believed that reality could best be approached through work, precisely because reality itself was a form of production.
>
> [...] A chair, a bed, a pair of boots. His act of painting them was far nearer than that of any other painter to the carpenter's or the shoemaker's act of making them. He brings together the elements of the product ... as though he too were fitting them together, *joining* them, as if this *being joined* constituted reality.
>
> *(2015, 263, 268)*

In the millennial year 2000, the Whitney Museum of American Art presented *The American Century in Art and Culture, 1900–2000.* The great working-class painter Ralph Fasanella was not included in the exhibit or the two-volume catalog. Why not?

Like Jacob Lawrence,[10] Ralph Fasanella's art is bardic—a visual troubadour telling a communal story. A tough street kid, a talker, a union organizer, a Southern Italian-American, a garage attendant, an autodidact, a volunteer for the Abraham Lincoln brigade, a husband, father, son, Ralph Fasanella painted the lives, work, neighborhoods, games, politics, and values of working-class people (mostly New Yorkers) in a broad context of American history and culture. Fasanella's paintings challenge bourgeois aesthetics: 'My paintings look easy, but they're very complicated. That's why they're so big; that's why people like them' (quoted in Zandy 2004, 157). His subjects—family suppers, baseball games, labor parades, demonstrations, union meetings, garment workers, May Day parades—speak the language of working-class solidarity. His paintings are composed, designed (like Jacob Lawrence's work) as a built environment of parts in relation to the whole, an architectonics of relationships and tensions. His human figures may appear diminutive in relation to the power structures of church, state, and work that dominate them, but through his painterly body gestures and facial expressions, Fasanella affirms working-class lives as complex and varied, not small. Fasanella' paintings are an epic visual narrative—largely a story of wealth and power on one side and the struggle for a decent life by the little guy on the other side—a working-class story. Fasanella's democratic vision never faltered: 'And the point I'm trying to make is, great human leaders have this compassion .... You've got to have that feeling. It's a kind of artistry' (quoted in Zandy 2004, 169).

Graphic arts and workers

The working classes, according to Stefan Szczelkun, are 'denied a community of intellectual thought' because of limited access to resources and because of 'denial of our intellectual capacity which is at the heartless core of class oppression' (1993, 1). The graphic arts as pioneered in Mexico in the 1920s, as supported in the United States through the Works Progress Administration, Federal Art Project (WPA/FAP) in the 1930s and 1940s, and as practiced by individual artists of great empathetic imagination, like Kaethe Kollwitz and Elizabeth Catlett or, more recently, Sue Coe, a contemporary graphic artist of deep political consciousness, resist that kind of communal and intellectual denial.[11]

Mexican revolutionary printmaking

Mexico has a long print tradition, beginning in 1539 with religious book illustrations. Lithography flourished in the 19th century, blending national identity and indigenous culture. After the Mexican Revolution of 1910, the visual language of murals and prints inspired and spread the language of revolutionary ideas to the peasant and working classes. In the 1920s and 1930s, *Los Tres Grandes*—Jose Clemente Orozco (1883–1949), Diego Rivera (1886–1957), and David Alfaro Siqueiros (1896–1974)— produced stunning lithographs, some based on the murals that made their reputations in Mexico and for which they are famous abroad. Printmaking schools, open and non-elitist, welcomed those usually excluded and laid the groundwork for the great collaborative printmaking workshop—*The Taller de Grafica Popular* (TGP—The People's Print Workshop). TGP emphasized the collaborative, highly skilled, anti-fascist ethos of the workshops: 'workers can also realize that art is a career and a social activity that is useful, and not the idle pastime that the bourgeois philosophers pretend it is' (Wechsler 2006, 16). TGP championed the ideal of art serving the people and reflecting the lived reality of their lives (see Williams (2006).

WPA/FAP (Works Progress Administration/Federal Art Project)

There are political and stylistic differences between Mexican and American versions of government-supported art making, but both had in their sights the lives of ordinary people as well as the opening of art ownership to the masses. With the establishment of the graphic division of the WPA/FAP in 1937, the art of printmaking was rejuvenated—artists had small salaries, connections to other artists and audiences, larger print runs, and access to equipment and new techniques, to produce, in the words of Rockwell Kent, 'multiple originals' (O'Connor 1973, 139). Printmaker Elizabeth Olds envisioned the idiom of art prints as cultural literacy, through 'picture textbooks' on a wide range of subjects, places, and people, putting access to art on the same level as public education (O'Connor, 1973, 143).[12]

Photography and workers

It is small wonder that portrait painters feared for their economic survival when the technology of photographic reproduction emerged in 1839. For ordinary people, though, the camera was not a threat, but a means and a tool for self-representation. Photography expanded worker self-representation and, perhaps, worker consciousness.[13]

Class relations and the aesthetic of worker representation are under-theorized in the history and practice of photography. Consider how the wealth of Alfred Stieglitz (1864–1946) and the near poverty of Lewis Hine (1874–1940) affected the reception of their photographs. Alan Trachtenberg parses the differences between the two in 'Camera work/social work' (in Trachtenberg 1989) through a probing look at the intentionality of Stieglitz and Hine. The operative word is *work*. Stieglitz was intent on securing space on museum walls for pictorial and modernist photography, and on advancing his reputation as a connoisseur of fine art photography: 'Nothing charms me so much as walking among the lower classes,' remarked Stieglitz (quoted in Trachtenberg 1989, 184). As Trachtenberg astutely observes, Stieglitz 'narrowed the range of aesthetic possibility' (1989, 174).

Lewis Hine, in contrast, broadened aesthetic possibilities. In his 'human documents' of girl textile workers, coal mining 'breaker boys,' Ellis Island immigrants, Pittsburgh East European steel workers, and the sky boys/men building the Empire State Building, Hine showed how aesthetics and labor are not mutually exclusive. There is no better starting place for working-class representational studies than the photography of Lewis Hine (see *America and Lewis Hine*, published in 1977).[14]

The photographic collective and the individual imaginary

Workers photograph each other and the conditions of their lives. One useful starting point to explore this vein of working-class studies is the Association of German Worker Photographers, where photography was a tool for proletarian struggle *and* artistic expression during the Weimar Republic (1919–1933). Willi Munzenberg, publisher of *Arbeiter-Illustrierte Zeitung* (AIZ, *The Workers Pictorial Newspaper*), was catalytic in organizing German working-class amateur photographers. They were encouraged to photograph 'working-life at the grass-roots, and above all in the factories, where professional photographers could not gain entry' (Guttsman 1997, 166).[15]

The New York-based Photo League (1936–1951) was a growing community of photographers ready to teach, learn, experiment, and hang out together. Its members embraced the work of photographing neighborhood streets and people. For a small membership fee, photographers got access to darkrooms, workshops, newsletters, curriculum, print competitions, critique, lectures, and documentary projects as well as to each other. It was a fluid learning community of hundreds of photographers.[16]

The communal, photographic integrity of the Photo League was endangered in 1947 when it was listed as a 'subversive' organization by Attorney General (and later Supreme Court Justice) Tom C. Clark. Lasting until 1951, the Photo League became one more casualty of McCarthyism, a right-wing ideology that hovers just under the surface, shapeshifting with different scare tactics and enemies in today's image-saturated culture.

The Photo League was not the only photo club in town. Imagine a social context where worker culture could flourish. District 65 UAW, a local of the United Retail and Wholesale Employees of America, built a vibrant union in the 1930s, 1940s, and 1950s that integrated worker cultures into labor and civil rights struggles. Photography was key to union building. Workers were the subjects, creators, producers, and consumers of images about … workers. They created a visual balance between documenting labor struggle and celebrating worker power and culture. These union photographers shared a visual vernacular and a recognizable working-class approach to knowing the world (Zandy 2010; Quirke 2012).[17]

Clerks, cooks, nurses, tailors, building supervisors, cashiers, immigrants, and hundreds of others participated in Unseenamerica (trademark of Bread and Roses Local 1199 SEIU), a contemporary multifaceted project of worker photographic representation, now expanded nationally and internationally.[18] As one photographer/worker wrote:

> There is a whole second part, a second soul to everybody here that nobody seems to know about. Unfortunately, a lot of people will assume that you are what your job is: taking out garbage or fixing plumbing. They don't realize there's an artful soul to everyone.
>
> *(Cohen 2006, 17)*

Culture and no conclusion

Seeing an expressive art relationship between workers and communities involves another ground of artistic being—and, perhaps, some hegemonic insecurity. Begin with Raymond Williams's simple (but not simplistic) observation: 'Culture is ordinary: that is where we must start' (1989, 4–5). Williams insists on two meanings of the word culture: as a 'whole way of life' and 'the arts and learning—the special processes of discovery and creative effort' (1989, 4). Williams has in mind a 'working-class way of life' (understood from his Welsh childhood, but not limited to it), with 'its emphases of neighborhood, mutual obligation, and common betterment' (1989, 8).

Raymond Mason (1922–2010), self-described as 'a working-class boy living in the simplest of working-class areas in Birmingham, England' (in Farrington and Silber 1989, 11), became a great public sculptor whose life and work demonstrate Williams's ideas about culture. Mason had a sculptor's eye for the crowd, human density, as seen in multiple sculptures and settings. Artistry, respect for the inherent dignity of his subjects, a capacity to carry his birthplace with him, consciousness of community, and a great love for beauty mark his life. He called beauty, 'the great subject' itself (in Farrington and Silber 1989, 13). He resolved, 'never to turn my back on the community at large, standing hungry for art and beauty' (in Farrington and Silber 1989, 13).

Art, walls, and resistance to walls

John Berger speaks to the ideology of walls:

> The present period of history is one of the Wall. When the Berlin one fell, the prepared plans to build walls everywhere were unrolled. Concrete, bureaucratic, surveillance, security, racist walls. Everywhere the walls separate the desperate poor from those who hope against hope to stay relatively rich. The walls cross every sphere, from crop cultivation to health care. They exist too in the richest metropolises of the world. The Wall is the front line of what, long ago, was called the Class War.
>
> *(2015, 350)*

Unstoppable Chinese artist Ai Weiwei answers political walls with art walls. Good Fences Make Good Neighbors is a Public Art Fund project of over 300 artworks/installations/sculptures through the five New York boroughs, with three large sculptures in Central Park, Washington Square, and around the Unisphere in Flushing Meadows Corona Park in Queens—made from metal security wire. It is an intervention and a reminder of the millions and millions of people in motion, in camps, at borders, displaced and forced from their homes (see Loos 2017; Scott 2017).

The commons as an alternative to the wall

The word 'common' has a range of meanings: a class slur, a shared experience, and a physical space. The commons is also a site of political struggle—in the square, the maidan, the zocalo, or as occupied space. These are instances of *commons* as a noun, fenced or unfenced. What if we imagine working-class studies as a process of *commoning*, a verb and action that enlarges space? Consider working-class art as an expansion of the commons.[19]

It is time to enlarge the map.

Notes

1 As referenced in Dorothy Moss, 'The worker in the art museum,' in Ward and Moss (2017) *The Sweat of Their Face: Portraying American Workers*. See the original editorial in TimesMachine, February 4, 1897, NYTimes.com.

2 See John Berger (1985) 'The *work* of art' in *The Sense of Sight*.

3 *The Diary and Letters of Kaethe Kollwitz* (1988, 43). For biographical interpretation, see Martha Kearns (1976); for analysis of her art in relation to her life see Klein and Klein (1972). Note as well that John Berger as a young artist in postwar England drew studies of builders and fishermen (Sperling 2018, 24).

4 Future studies might trace how visual representations of the human hand reveal larger working-class histories. Kollwitz is a good starting point; so is Charles White (1918–1979). See his powerful drawings and paintings such as *Native Son No. 2* (1942) and *Our Land* (1951) (in Oehler 2018).

5 For a visual reference, see A. von Menzel's painting *The Steelworks* (date unknown) Lucie-Smith and Dars (1977, plate IV).

6 Rebecca Harding Davis's 'Life in the iron mills' was originally published in *The Atlantic Monthly* (1861). These quotations are from the reprinted edition, *Life in the Iron Mills and other Stories*, with a biographical interpretation by Tillie Olsen (Davis 1985, 14, 23–25, 33).

7 This Catlett summary rests on the scholarship and biographical interpretation of Melanie Anne Herzog's *Elizabeth Catlett: In the Image of the People* (2005) and Herzog's *Elizabeth Catlett: An American Artist in Mexico* (2000). An analytical juxtaposition of Kaethe Kollwitz and Elizabeth Catlett could be an evocative dialogue for future writing on working-class art.

8 www.marxists.org/archive/marx/works/1844/manuscripts/labour.htm.

9 John Berger draws a parallel between Pieter Bruegel the Elder's paintings and Bertolt Brecht's poetry and, despite the centuries between them, their prophetic sensibilities: 'They both want it understood that not to resist is to be indifferent, and that to be indifferent is to condone' (Berger 2015, 41–43).

10 In 2016–2017 the Met Breuer staged *Kerry James Marshall: MASTRY, a Major Retrospective* (October 2016–January 2017), that included 72 paintings depicting the lives of Black Americans, contextually, in barbershops, hair salons, and housing. Marshall's use of flat black paint paradoxically suggests an interior, personal and cultural, that is rarely seen through the screen of whiteness. Marshall (once a student of Charles White), who rightly claims a link to Western art history, observes, 'Extreme blackness plus grace equals power' (Pinckney 2017, 40). This is an actuality that is more than technique or style. The generational linkages of form, content, and narration between Charles White, Jacob Lawrence, Kerry James Marshall, and Meleko Mokgosi are worthy of future study. In a talk at the Memorial Art Gallery, Rochester, New York (February 23, 2017), Meleko Mokgosi commented, 'You have to know the history of painting, but you also have to know how to negate that history.'

11 'To think and act as a human being in a system set up for profit is to be classified as a criminal' (Sue Coe, *Police State*, 1987).

12 A 1989 exhibit of 'Black Printmakers and the WPA' underscores the importance of community art centers. The Philadelphia Center was committed to the technical and artistic development of printmaking led by Black artists—Dox Thrash (1893–1965), Claude Clark (1915–2001), Raymond Steth (1918–1997), and Samuel Brown (1907–1994), among others. Dox Thrash headed the graphic arts division that included three other artists—all white. Curator Leslie King-Hammond describes Thrash as a 'virtuoso printmaker' whose visual lyricism reveals 'a vast range of tonal variation … enhancing an emotional depth and sensitivity not seen before in Black portraiture in this country' (1989, 7). Why is his work and others not better known today? Ernest Crichlow (1914–2005), a Harlem-based artist, answers by noting, 'there were no Black curators at that time who went about to save and preserve this work. I have no idea where my work is now' (8).

13 Tintypes are undervalued examples of worker self-representation. Affordable and transportable, tintypes were popular among (particularly American) workers from about 1856 to 1900. In Michael L. Carlebach's *Working Stiffs* (2002) we see workers with their tools—hammers, tongs, mallets, tinsnips, brooms, milk pails, paint cans, brushes, wrenches, screwdrivers, hatchets, ice tongs, cooper's adzes, pitchforks, chisels, saws, etc. The tools denote a relationship, aesthetic as well as utilitarian; the tools add balance to the portraits, and both show the pride of labor. These workers still hold their skills in their own hands and are not yet the alienated laborers of the new industrialism (Zandy 2010, 34–35). How do tintypes contrast today with selfies? Instagrams? Has a sense of community and collectivity been lost to self-promoting individualism? Questions for a new generation of scholars.

14 Always the teacher, Hine saw art as a process of 'social seeing' within the larger context of societal change. Art, according to John Dewey and practiced by Hine, is intrinsically part of the experience of making a life. Trachtenberg claims Hine's photographs and texts as *monuments* in the best sense, as testaments to human lives (1989, 202). Preferring 'interpretative photography' to social photography, Hine called for 'the intelligent interpretation of the world's workers.' Situate contemporary photographers David Bacon (2016) and Earl Dotter (2018) within this Hine legacy.

15 Worker photographers were urged to go beyond visual evidence 'to bring out underlying relationships and show the contradictions of social reality' (Guttsman 1997, 166). Look to photographers like Tina Modotti, Paul Strand, Robert Capa, and Kata Kalman to see international links between worker photographs and organizations like New York's Photo League. See also the conversation between Jorge Ribalta and Guy Lane at 'Worker photography movement,' *FOTO8* (www.foto8.com/live/worker-photography-movement/); and *A Hard, Merciless Light: The Worker-Photography Movement, 1926–1939*, Museo Nacional Centro de Arte Reina Sofia, Madrid, 2011, curated by Jorge Ribalta.

16 Some members were better known than others, some more politically motivated than others. They included Sid Grossman (one of the founders), Walter Rosenblum, Aaron Siskind, Paul Strand, John Vachon, Jerome Liebling, Arthur Rothstein, and women—Rosalie Gwathmey, Ruth Orkin, Sonia Handelman Meyer, Lucy Ashjian, Helen Levitt, Consuela Kanaga, Vivian Cherry, Marion Palfi, and Berenice Abbott. See Klein and Evans (2011) and Tucker et al. (2001).

17 See also District 65 archives at The Tamiment Library & Robert F. Wagner Labor Archives, NYC, in Zandy (2010), 'Seeing dirt, seeing beyond dirt.'

18 Unseenamerica 'disrupts and challenges a hidden and pervasive cultural narcissism that lies beneath the rhetoric of the aesthetic. An ideology of expressive individualism … impedes an imaginary for a photographic aesthetic of relationships' (Zandy 2010, 37).

19 See Peter Linebaugh's distinction between commons as natural resource and as an activity that expresses relationships in society and to nature. That is, 'resistance to the reality of a planet of slums, gated communities, and terror without end' (2008, 279).

References

Agee, J. and Evans, W. (1941[1980]) *Let Us Now Praise Famous Men*, Boston, Houghton Mifflin.

Allara, P. (2000) *Pictures of People: Alice Neel's American Portrait Gallery*, Hanover, NH, Brandeis University Press/University Press of New England.

Anderson, M. (2016) *Guardians de Las Artes: Guardians of the Arts*, Antigua, Guatemala, Ediciones del Pensativo/Coleccion Vesarte.

Attfield, S. (2016) 'Art for whose Sake? Working-Class Life in Visual Art,' *Working-Class Perspectives*, April 25.

Avedon, R. (1985) *In the American West*, New York, Harry N. Abrams.

Bacon, D. (2016) *In the Fields of the North: En los campos del norte*, Oakland, CA, University of California Press.

Baer, R. (2015) *Class Distinction: Dutch Painting in the Age of Rembrandt and Vermeer*, Boston, MFA Publications.

Barrell, J. (1980) *The Dark Side of the Landscape: The Rural Poor in English Painting 1730–1840*, Cambridge, Cambridge University Press.

Bell, T. (1941[1976]) *Out of This Furnace*, Pittsburgh, University of Pittsburgh Press.

Berger, J. (1980) *About Looking*, New York, Pantheon.

Berger, J. (1985) *The Sense of Sight*, New York, Pantheon.

Berger, J. (2015) *Portraits: John Berger on Artists*, edited by T. Overton, London, Verso.

Carlebach, M. (2002) *Working Stiffs: Occupational Portraits in the Age of Tintypes*, Washington, DC, Smithsonian Institution Press.

Chaplin, C. (1936) *Modern Times*, Director Charlie Chaplin.

Clark, T.J. (1973) *Image of the People: Gustave Courbet and the Second French Republic 1848–1851*, Greenwich, CT, Graphic Society, Ltd.

Coe, M. (1987) *Sue Coe, Police State*, texts by Mandy Coe, essays by Donald Kuspit and Marilyn Zeitlin [catalog], Anderson Gallery, Virginia Commonwealth University.

Cohen, E. (ed.) (2006) *Unseen America: Photos and Stories by Workers*, New York, Regan Books.

Cushing, L. and Drescher, T. (2009) *Agitate! Educate! Organize! American Labor Posters*, Ithaca, ILR Press.

Davis, R.H. (1985) *Life in the Iron Mills and Other Stories*, with a Biographical Interpretation by Tillie Olsen, New York, The Feminist Press.

Dotter, E. (2018) *Life's Work: Fifty Year Photographic Chronicle of Working in the USA*, Falls Church, VA, American Industrial Hygiene Association.

Eisler, B. (ed.) (1998) *The Lowell Offering: Writings by New England Mill Women (1940-1845)*, New York, Norton.

Elkins, J. (2002) *Stories of Art*, New York, Routledge.

Farrington, J. and Silber, E. (eds.) (1989) *Raymond Mason: Sculptures and Drawings*, London, Lund Humphries in association with Birmingham City Museum and Art Gallery.

Guttsman, W.L. (1997) *Art for the Workers: Ideology and the Visual Arts in Weimar Germany*, Manchester, Manchester University Press.

Herzog, M. (2000) *Elizabeth Catlett: An American Artist in Mexico*, Seattle, University of Washington Press.

Herzog, M. (2005) *Elizabeth Catlett: In the Image of the People*, Chicago, The Art Institute of Chicago, and New Haven, Yale University Press.

Hills, P. (1979) *The Working American*, Washington, DC, Smithsonian Institution.

Hills, P. (1986) 'Jacob Lawrence's Expressive Cubism,' in Wheat, E.H., *Jacob Lawrence, American Painter*, Seattle, University of Washington Press.

Hills, P. (2009) *Painting Harlem Modern: The Art of Jacob Lawrence*, Berkeley, University of California Press.

Hine, L.W., Trachtenberg, A. and Brooklyn Museum (1977) *America & Lewis Hine: Photographs 1904–1940* [exhibition], New York, Aperture.

Hockney, D. and Gayford, M. (2016) *A History of Pictures*, New York, Abrams.

Kearns, M. (1976) *Kathe Kollwitz: Woman and Artist*, New York, The Feminist Press.

King-Hammond, L. (1989) *Black Printmakers and the W.P.A.*, Bronx, NY, Lehman College Art Gallery.

King-Hammond, L. (2000) 'Inside-Outside, Uptown-Downtown: Jacob Lawrence and the Aesthetic Ethos of the Harlem Working-Class Community,' in Nesbett, P. and DuBois, M. (eds.) *Over the Line: The Art and Life of Jacob Lawrence*, Seattle, University of Washington Press.

Klein, M. and Evans, C. (2011) *The Radical Camera: New York's Photo League 1936–1951)*, New York, The Jewish Museum, Columbus, Ohio, Columbus Museum of Art, New Haven, Yale University Press.

Klein, M.C. and Klein, H.A. (1972) Kaethe Kollwitz: Life in Art, New York, Holt, Rinehart and Winston.

Kollwitz, H. (ed.) (1988) *The Diary and Letters of Kaethe Kollwitz*, translated by Richard and Clara Winston, Evanston, IL, Northwestern University Press.

Lewis, S. (1990) *African American Art and Artists*, Berkeley, University of California Press.

Linebaugh, P. (2008) *The Magna Carta Manifesto: Liberties and Commons for All*, Berkeley, University of California Press.

Loos, T. (2017) 'Barnstorming the Boroughs,' *New York Times*, October 6, pp. C13–C19.

Lucie-Smith, E. and Dars, C. (1977) *Work and Struggle: The Painter as Witness 1870–1914*, New York, Paddington Press.

O'Connor, F.V. (1973) *WPA Art for the Millions: Essays from the 1930s by Artists and Administrators of the WPA Federal Art Project*, Greenwich, CT., New York Graphic Society.

Oehler, S. K. and Adler, E. (eds.) (2018). Charles White: A Retrospective, Chicago, Art Institute of Chicago.

Pinckney, D. (2017) 'The Genius of Blackness,' *New York Review of Books*, January 19, pp. 40–42.

Quirke, C. (2012) *Eyes on Labor: News Photography and America's Working Class*, New York, Oxford University Press.

Scott, A. (2017) 'Fall Preview,' *The New Yorker*, August 28.

Sperling, J. (2018) The Life and Work of John Berger, New York, Verso.

Szczelkun, S. (1993) *The Conspiracy of Good Taste*, London, Working Press.

Trachtenberg, A. (1989) *Reading American Photographs: Images as History, Mathew Brady to Walker Evans*, New York, Hill and Wang.

Tucker, A., Cass, C. and Daiter, S. (2001) *This Was the Photo League: Compassion and the Camera from the Depression to the Cold War*, Chicago, Stephen Daiter Gallery and Houston, John Cleary Gallery.

Ward, D.C. and Moss, D. (2017) *The Sweat of Their Face: Portraying American Workers*, Washington, DC, Smithsonian Institution.

Wechsler, J. (2006) 'Propaganda Grafica: Printmaking and the Radical Left 1920–1950,' in Ittmann, J. (ed.) *Mexico and Modern Printmaking: A Revolution in the Graphic Arts, 1920 to 1950*, Philadelphia, Philadelphia Museum of Art.

Williams, L. (2006) 'Evolution of a Revolution: A Brief History of Printmaking' in Mexico,' in Ittmann, J. (ed.) *Mexico and Modern Printmaking: A Revolution in the Graphic Arts, 1920 to 1950*, Philadelphia, Philadelphia Museum of Art.

Williams, R. (1977) *Marxism and Literature*, New York, Oxford University Press.

Williams, R. (1989) *Resources of Hope*, London, Verso.
Wood, D. (1992) *The Power of Maps*, New York, Guilford.
Zandy, J. (2004) 'Ralph Fasanella: Epic Painter of the Working Class,' in *Hands: Physical Labor, Class, and Cultural Work*, New Brunswick, Rutgers University Press.
Zandy, J. (2010) 'Seeing Dirt, Seeing Beyond Dirt: Photographs By and About Workers,' *exposure*, Fall, pp. 33–40.
Zandy, J. (2013) *Unfinished Stories: The Narrative Photography of Hansel Mieth and Marion Palfi*, Rochester, NY, RIT Press.

25

'Things that are left out'

Working-class writing and the idea of literature

Ben Clarke

In his 1939 article 'A critique of proletarian literature,' R. W. Steadman surveyed texts published in the United States after Michael Gold's *Jews Without Money* (1930/2004), the book he argued had 'heralded the birth of the entire proletarian movement in the arts' (Steadman 1939, 143). He concluded that although this movement had produced '[s]ome fifty novels, several hundred poems, and a dozen plays,' the 'quality of it all is not very high' (144). Langston Hughes had 'added to the store of American verse' (151), but few other authors had written anything of lasting significance. Steadman was particularly critical of the novelists, who did not have 'the shadow of an idea of what constitutes literature' and considered it sufficient to 'yell about the woes of workers and farmers' (152). Most proletarian literature was not literature at all but polemic or reportage that had adopted literary forms. The problems were apparent from the outset; the ending of Gold's novel, according to Steadman, read 'like a soap-box harangue' (146). Proletarian literature was always flawed, an attempt to use literature for other ends.

Steadman's article exemplifies a number of ideas that still shape critical attitudes to working-class writing. This chapter argues that these claims are founded on a particular, limited understanding of what constitutes literature that is so pervasive as to seem natural. The judgements it sustains appear to be passive acts of identification in which the critic simply recognizes the value of a text. This narrative obscures the ways in which evaluation is informed by broader ideological narratives that marginalize certain kinds of writing and experience. The act of differentiation is not a neutral exercise but makes implicit claims about the functions of literature and the people who can participate in its production and interpretation. It is consequently a political matter in the sense identified by Jacques Rancière, in that it is concerned with 'a partition of the sensible, of the visible and the sayable, which allows (or does not allow) some specific data to appear; which allows or does not allow some specific subjects to designate them and speak about them' (Rancière 2010/2012, 152). This chapter argues that the study of working-class writing demands a broader model of the literary that makes visible previously ignored forms of value and significance, just as working-class literature makes visible what Jack Hilton calls those 'many things that are left out when art falls on its knees to make the lady in the villa a nice cup o' tea' (Hilton, JH/1/1/24/1/3). This will involve reading differently as well as reading different things and, in particular, recognizing the distinct ways in which working-class authors use the resources made available by the dominant literary culture.

The exclusion of working-class texts from literary histories, syllabi, and publishers' lists is justified by the claim that they are not literature but examples of other, less prestigious forms, such as reportage or propaganda. The argument depends on a number of intersecting ideas about what defines literature, and it is best understood by focusing on a single, key claim, that literature must be concerned with the individual. Working-class writing, in contrast, is represented as focusing on collective struggles and, as a consequence, as Raymond Williams insists, a 'degraded establishment criticism would have us believe' that those who write about working-class life are necessarily 'more interested in sociology than people' (Williams 1980/1989, 222). As Jeremy Hawthorne observes, critics see an inherent 'conflict between the interest that the novel takes in the individuality of its characters and their predicaments, and the working-class sources of ... material,' which means that for 'some people, "working-class novel" is a contradiction in terms' (Hawthorne 1984, vii). The position Hawthorne describes depends upon a circular logic; a novel cannot be working class, because to be a novel it must accept bourgeois forms and focus on the individual. Texts that fail to do this are not novels but something else.

Though false, the argument that working-class texts neglect the personal is valuable insofar as it reveals a series of intersecting critical assumptions. It not only implicitly constructs individuality as a middle-class quality, defined in opposition to the essentially collective nature of the working class, but assumes an opposition between the personal and the social, obscuring what Williams calls the 'distinctive truth' that 'the lives of individuals, however intensely and personally realized, are not just influenced but in certain crucial ways formed by general social relations' (Williams 1980/1989, 221). As Marx argues, society is not the antithesis of individuality but its precondition; '[m]an is in the most literal sense a *zoön politikon*, not only a social animal, but an animal which can individuate itself only in society.' (Marx 1857/1996, 129) Individuality is constructed rather than expressed, the product of shifting relations between the self and others rather than the realization of a stable, inherent identity. Working-class writers are often acutely conscious of this process of social production, of what Janet Zandy calls the 'multiple, competing, contradictory, and demanding voices that inhabit the "we" inside the individual writer's "I"' (2004, 90).

Dismissing working-class texts as sociological rather than literary because of their concern with social structures limits literature to the parameters established by a historically and class-specific model of the personal. The acceptance of a dominant bourgeois understanding of the autonomous individual, the independent agent of the capitalist marketplace, becomes synonymous with a concern with 'people' as such and a defining characteristic of art. The resultant model of literature insists that it is antithetical to politics, not simply in the narrow sense of a concern with institutions, parties, and movements, but in the broader terms described by Rancière of a

> struggle that is waged about such original issues as: 'where are we?,' 'who are we', 'What makes us a we', 'what do we see and what can we say about it that makes us a we, having a world in common?'
>
> *(2009, 116)*

The insistence on this division is a consistent element of the various critical structures that exclude working-class writing and persists despite what Graeme Turner calls the widespread 'academic performance' of political engagement (2012, 159).

Individualism is not the only concept the serves to marginalize working-class texts, and not all working-class writers emphasize social and communal structures. Many focus on the experience and thoughts of particular characters and their attempts to fashion distinct identities despite their restrictive environments and limited resources. Their texts do not ignore the personal but interrogate its established forms and recognize that people, like societies, 'make their own history, but they do not make it just as they please in circumstances they choose for themselves; rather they make it in present circumstances, given and inherited' (Marx 1852/1996, 32). Philip Callow's early work demonstrates this critical relation to dominant narratives, questioning not only ideas of the individual but also the artistic conventions founded upon them.

Callow was born in Stetchford, near Birmingham, in what he later described as 'a tidy, law-abiding slum' (2002, 2), and was a lathe apprentice before publishing his first novel, *The Hosanna Man* (1956). He was one of a generation of iconoclastic working-class authors who began their writing careers in the 1950s, but despite critical praise (Penelope Mortimer wrote that 'the first forty pages' of Callow's *Common People* (1958) 'are the most brilliantly successful account of English working-class life I have ever encountered in any medium' (1958, 7)), he never achieved the prominence or commercial success of contemporaries such as Alan Sillitoe and John Braine. He is now little read and rarely republished, but his work illustrates the innovative ways in which working-class writers used and adapted inherited forms and techniques. In particular, it explores ideas of individual identity and the forces that constrain it, from economic inequality to family and communal traditions. In *Common People*, the protagonist Nick Chapman's pursuit of a 'new life' in which he could be 'a poet, or an artist of some kind' challenges the conventions of the Künstlerroman even as it uses them (Callow 1958, 99). Nick questions the roles he nonetheless pursues, disliking even 'the word "poet" intensely', because 'it sounded so foppish, and so far removed from life as I knew it' (49). His competing desires and restricted circumstances prevent him from achieving the autonomy and agency with which narratives of artistic development normally conclude. At the end of the text he has not achieved independence and his 'inner and outer life' are 'just as incompatible as before' (241).

The difficulties Nick experiences in trying to realize himself demonstrate the inability of received forms to accommodate working-class experience. Early in the novel he attempts one conventional path to liberation, leaving Woodfield for the 'magic centre' (95) of London. He hopes that moving will make him 'free of the past' so that a 'new life would somehow begin for me' (99), but he is drawn back, convinced that he can only achieve his desire 'to love a woman, to be married and to know common joys' (180) in Woodfield, which stubbornly remains home despite its flaws. The novel does not follow the misogynistic tradition of representing his lover as a trap, retarding his development; Jessie tells him that they would be 'better as lovers' (208) and is only convinced to marry him after he 'kept prising away with words, stubbornly, with all the selfishness of love' (209). Nick is instead shaped by his desire to inhabit a coherent working-class culture, which he sees as centered on the family; when Jessie gives birth, he questions the 'good of it all … painting, philosophy, religion' compared to this 'elemental fact' (231). He is also conscious that his circumstances mean that this desire prevents him from dedicating himself to art. He retains an 'itch to wander' (243) and create, but gets a job in an insurance office. When he tells Jessie that he still wants to '[p]aint … [w]rite poetry', she points out that 'you wanted to marry' and questions how he expected 'us to live' (240). The material forces often ignored in the Künstlerroman or contained by ideas of bohemian poverty shape the structure of the novel, which is circular rather than tracing a process of ascent.

Common People questions the conventions it uses, a process repeated by other working-class writers. Its representation of the personal is not a passive submission to existing forms but an active process that adapts them to represent neglected kinds of experience and the systems that shape it. In revising and extending the Künstlerroman, it challenges the ideological narratives upon which it depends, including ideas of individualism that cannot recognize the material and social complexities of working-class life under advanced capitalism. The friction between Callow's subject and the techniques available to him demands formal innovation. Not all working-class writing is experimental, but the structural tension between its subject matter and existing forms prevents a simple identification with established representational strategies.

Analyzing the idea of individuality and its critical deployment illustrates the political implications of processes of definition. It demonstrates that the attempt to reinterpret working-class writing must involve an engagement with the concept of literature as well as the reinterpretation of specific works. Plenty of working-class writers are neglected despite meeting existing standards of literary value, but the broader task is to challenge the ways in which definitions of literature dismiss or misinterpret many of their characteristic concerns and the forms they employ. The incorporation of working-class authors in literary history demands a revision of the criteria that structure the field rather than the identification of texts that already enact them; it is not simply a matter of finding what Jonathan Rose calls a 'modernist in overalls' (2002, 141).

Unfinished business: Working-class writers and the 'canon wars'

In most instances, working class writers are absent from British literary histories rather than denigrated in them; their texts are invisible, excluded before critical analysis not because of it. Virginia Woolf's argument that if one were to '[t]ake away all that the working class has given to English literature ... that literature would scarcely suffer' exemplifies the long-standing view that there is little working-class literature to assess (Woolf 1940/1966, 168). The statement emphasizes that working-class people rarely have access to the material and cultural resources necessary for artistic production but also suggests that actually existing working-class writing does not achieve the condition of literature. The conviction shapes Woolf's encounters with working-class texts. In her introduction to *Life as We Have Known It, by Co-operative Working Women*, she argues that considered 'as literature,' the collected accounts have 'many limitations' and the 'writing, a literary critic might say, lacks detachment and imaginative breadth.' The prose might have 'some qualities ... the literate and instructed might envy' (Woolf 1931/1977, xxxix–xxxx), but these are not sufficient for it to be defined as literature; the word 'some' qualifies as well as acknowledges its value. The argument represents such texts as excluded by their own limitations rather than the categories within which they are evaluated, which remain outside analysis.

Woolf's judgment represents itself as working backwards from a canon of literary texts rather than outwards from a set of critical premises. She implicitly shares Orwell's position that '[u]ltimately there is no test of literary merit except survival,' and sees the absence of working-class texts from such narratives as demonstrating a lack of working-class literature. The use of survival has an apparent democratic logic (Orwell argued that it was 'merely an index to majority opinion' (1998, 57)), but obscures the ideological forces that shape literary history and consequently the reproduction of texts, not only in cultural terms, as the objects of criticism, but also materially, in new editions. These forces operate most conspicuously through the education system and particularly the universities, which are still instrumental in defining literary hierarchies. Working-class texts may get good reviews in newspapers and literary journals and even win major awards, but few establish a stable position on reading lists; David Storey's *Saville* (1976) and James Kelman's *How Late It Was, How Late* (1994) both won the Booker Prize, but neither is widely taught.

Inclusion on syllabi remains important to the long-term prospects of a text, because reading lists and critical articles inform not only the teaching of literature at other levels but also decisions about re-publication. University departments remain privileged ideological spaces in which the canon is reproduced along with the critical assumptions that legitimize it. They are also sites of dispute and conflict in which histories and definitions can be contested and revised. Whilst questions of class have been neglected in recent decades (as Peter Hitchcock observes, '[m]ost literary critics visibly wince at the mention of working-class representation as a significant component of cultural analysis' (2000, 20)), theoretically-sophisticated analyzes of the ways in which questions of gender, race, and sexuality have shaped literary hierarchies provide models for effective critical intervention. The attempt to reinterpret and revaluate working-class texts does not occur in a vacuum, but often involves the adaptation of existing strategies for different ends, a process that can strengthen solidarities between interlocking emancipatory projects.

As Woolf's comments demonstrate, the absence of working-class texts from the canon is used to justify their marginalization; their failure to gain entry is sufficient to prove their inadequacy. There are conspicuous parallels between this argument and the dominant logic of the capitalist society within which it is articulated, which also insists that value is recognized through a process of free competition, a position that assumes open, objective comparison and evaluation. The argument is familiar from its use to oppose attempts to recover other neglected texts, such as those by women. As a consequence, as Michelle Tokarczyk insists, feminism provided working-class studies with 'a model of a literary criticism that could critique hegemony' (2011, 4). It not only exposed the assumptions used to exclude particular traditions of writing from literature but also shows the strategies that could be used to successfully challenge them.

In 'Dancing through the minefield,' Annette Kolodny recalls being told by a colleague that if 'Kate Chopin were really worth reading ... she'd have lasted—like Shakespeare' (1980, 7). The fact that Chopin now regularly features on syllabi, that her work is included in influential textbooks such as the *Norton Anthology of American Literature* (Hungerford et al. 2017), and that there are multiple, competing editions of *The Awakening* (first published in 1899), including several critical editions, demonstrates the possibility of making the kind of critical intervention Kolodny advocates. The attention to Chopin's work is not the consequence of its reinterpretation within existing categories, a belated recognition that it always possessed qualities already valued by the critical establishment, but the result of sustained interpretative labor that succeeded in transforming the terms of debate and the institutions, from literature departments to publishers, in which they were embodied. Rachel Donadio argues that the fact that many literature syllabi include previously ignored works by 'women and minority writers' demonstrates that 'multiculturalists won the canon wars' (2007, 16); but the benefits did not extend to working-class authors, whose work still rarely features in anthologies or on reading or publishers lists. This includes the writing of working-class women and minority writers; novels such as Ethel Carnie Holdsworth's *This Slavery* (1925/2011) and Buchi Emecheta's *Second-Class Citizen* (1974/1975) are rarely amongst the texts recovered by publishers and scholars.

As this suggests, an increased attention to working-class writing does not demand a diminished concern with questions of gender, ethnicity, and sexuality but a renewed critical engagement with them. As John Russo and Sherry Linkon argue, 'the phrase "working class"' has too often 'operated as a code for talking about white men' (Russo and Linkon 2005, 3), and there is no competition or even division between the interests of the working class and those of other marginalized groups, in literary studies or elsewhere. The reinterpretation and revaluation of working-class literature not only draws upon the strategies of feminist and postcolonial criticism but extends these fields, insisting, as Zandy argues, 'that any analysis of race, gender, sexuality, even disability, cannot be complete if class is excluded' (2004, 91). Working-class studies is, as Tokarczyk insists, necessarily a form of 'intersectional analysis' (2011, 3), its diversity founded, in the last instance, on that of the working class itself. As Owen Jones argues, the working class is 'far more ethnically mixed than the rest of the population' (2011, 243); those from minority groups are, like women, disproportionately likely to do working-class jobs. The myth that the working class can be identified with white men serves particular interests, limiting radical critical and political practice by contributing to what Sally Munt calls the 'fragmentation of sympathetic discourses' (2000, 7). It legitimizes not only the neglect of working-class studies, by representing it as indifferent to questions of gender, sexuality, and ethnicity, but also the marginalization of groups such as working-class women, by implying that their interests have already been addressed by a feminist movement still dominated by middle-class intellectuals, academics, and activists.

Reading differently: The idea of literature

As Jane Tompkins argues, whilst 'the term "literary excellence" or "literary value" remains constant over time, its meaning—what literary excellence turns out to be in each case— does not' (Tompkins 1985, 192). Reevaluating neglected work means challenging the social and historical narratives that determine its reception and interpretation and, at the level of textual analysis, reading differently, rather than simply extending existing critical practices to new material. In particular, it demands a return to texts previously dismissed as crude, trivial, or didactic. The reconsideration of such works has the potential to redefine the literary itself. As Nicholas Coles and Janet Zandy argue, working-class literary studies must understand 'the concepts of "literature" and "working class" in elastic, expansive ways' (2007, xix). Their anthology, *American Working-Class Literature*, is one of a number of recent collections that insist on the significance of a wide range of marginalized texts and makes them available to a broader readership. Like volumes of critical essays—such as John Lennon and Magnus Nilsson's *Working-Class Literature(s)* (2017), Nicholas Coles and Paul Lauters' *A History of American Working-Class Literature* (2017), John Goodridge and Bridget Keegan's *A History of British Working-Class Literature* (2017), and Michael Pierse's *A History of Irish Working-Class Writing* (2017)—Coles and Zandy seek both to extend the canon and to challenge the model of literature that shapes and legitimizes it.

As Tompkin argues in *Sensational Designs: The Cultural Work of American Fiction, 1790–1860* (1985), definitions of literature have long served to exclude political texts, in the broad sense of the term. The texts she discusses were dismissed partly due to their concern with 'transitory issues' such as 'revolution ([Charles] Brockden Brown), consolidation ([James Fenimore] Cooper), revival ([Susan] Warner), and abolition ([Harriet Beecher] Stowe)'; they were represented as 'closer to propaganda than to art' and consequently as 'material for the historian rather than the literary critic' (186). There are obvious parallels between this and the treatment of working-class writers, including the insistence that an attempt to intervene directly in social and political debates makes a text propaganda rather than literature.

The idea of literature regulates the production and reception of texts, limiting their range and functions. Despite this, the critical challenge is to redefine the literary rather than abandon it. The concept remains necessary because, as Tompkins argues, we 'are always making choices, and hence value judgments, about which books to read, teach, write about, recommend, or have on our shelves' (1985, 193), and must reflect on the bases and implications of these decisions, but also because, as Richard Hoggart argues, the word 'literature' attempts to name a kind of writing that 'provides … a form of distinctive knowledge about society' (1970b, 19). The idea of the literary has historically served a distinct ideological function, constructing a hierarchy that marginalizes certain kinds of text, including working-class writing, but the response to this cannot be to abandon the concept itself as so compromised as to be unusable. The interpretation of working-class texts as just political or sociological documents reproduces the logic of the system that excludes them, implicitly constructing art as a middle-class category. As Eagleton argues, '[t]he "aesthetic" is too valuable to be surrendered without a struggle to the bourgeois aestheticians,' even if it is 'too contaminated by that ideology to be appropriated as it is' (1976/1995, 187). The task is to recognize the value and complexities of working-class texts and their implications for the concept of literature, a process that would transform the idea of aesthetic whilst exposing the values it currently encodes.

As the history of feminist criticism demonstrates, any project seeking to reinterpret and reevaluate neglected texts must be wide-ranging in its concerns and pursue material as well as interpretative changes. It needs to recover texts physically as well as critically, to ensure that they are available for people to borrow, purchase, and teach. The proliferation of feminist publishers and lists beginning in the early 1970s, from long-running imprints such as Virago to shorter-lived series such as Macmillan's 'Women in Society,' demonstrates the possibility of such an intervention. Disseminating texts also involves contesting the anthologies that now dominate lower-division university literature teaching, particularly in the US; the canon is not simply embodied in critical discourse, but concretely in a small number of widely used collections. These anthologies have become an important site of critical intervention for American scholars of working-class literature, who have not only emphasized writing currently excluded from textbooks in their criticism but also produced alternative volumes, such as Nicholas Coles and Janet Zandy's *American Working-Class Literature* (2007) and Paul Lauter and Ann Fitzgerald's *Literature, Class, and Culture: An Anthology* (2001). The texts offer a different vision of American literary history and also enable this to be taught, introducing to undergraduates texts previously only available to researchers. At the level of interpretation, reading working-class texts involves an engagement with everything from style to genre, from the structure and tone of specific sentences and paragraphs to the forms writers inherit, use, and adapt. It demands a significant revision of existing critical strategies and different emphases and principles of analysis. These material and interpretative practices are interdependent; working-class literary studies must be understood as a wide-ranging political project rather than just another analytical school.

Changing the 'distribution of the sensible': Working-class writing and form

The remaining section of this chapter briefly outlines some possible starting points for a new approach to working-class literature that would consider the ways in which writers use available resources to achieve a different 'distribution of the sensible' (Rancière 2009, 121) Working-class literature is not simply bourgeois literature with different content, significant only because it focuses on mines and the means test rather than drawing rooms and dinner parties; it also disrupts, adapts, and extends the conventions of literary language. Its analysis requires a close attention to tone, to the syntax and diction of prose as well as its subject matter. Hoggart's argument that the 'movement' and 'voice' of the opening passage of D. H. Lawrence's *Sons and Lovers* (1913/2006) are those of a 'working-class man who had become articulate and—instead of acquiring rhythms foreign to his deep-rooted ways of feeling—had kept the rhetoric of his kind and so (this is the point) could better say what *he* had to say' (Hoggart 1970a, 197–198) suggests a distinct sensibility visible in the formal strategies of working-class writing. The contrast he draws with the first paragraph of E. M. Forster's *A Passage to India* (1924, 2005), which uses the 'voice of a civilized, literate, English middle-class observer' (Hoggart 1970a, 195), suggests that the attempt to communicate 'the peculiar feel of experience as working-class people live it' (199) produces different kinds of prose. Such experimentation is sometimes conspicuous, as in the case of James Kelman, whose shifting, frequently oblique styles not only explore the variety of working-class speech but also the limits of its intelligibility, directly addressing what Rancière identifies as a central political question of 'who speaks and who makes noise' (Rancière 2009, 115). Often it is more subtle; in his introduction to James Hanley's *Men in Darkness*, John Cowper Powys argued that Hanley's technical radicalism lay in his 'bald, bleak, stripped, winnowed and harrowed style, bare of every kind of literary "purple patch"' (1931/1932, x). What might appear as the kind of simplicity or crudeness often attributed to working-class writers marked Hanley's contribution to 'the most modern school of aesthetics' (Powys 1931/1932, x–xi) as his attempt to find a new form appropriate to his subject matter. In all these examples, style is used to extend the 'visible and the sayable' to include those conventionally excluded from discourse, those whose presumed inarticulacy structures the existing political as well as representational order. This kind of formal analysis does not seek to identify a stable working-class mode of writing, but rather the multiple strategies writers use to question and extend the forms they inherit.

The effort to develop new kinds of writing also demands the adaptation of existing generic forms. As Pierre Macherey argues, 'the work never "arrives unaccompanied"; it is always determined by the existence of other works,' which means that 'novelty and originality, in literature as in other fields, are always defined by relationships' (1966/1986, 100). For Macherey, criticism must analyze a process of production that uses existing materials rather than accept a fantasy of spontaneous creation, recognizing that the text is 'the product of a certain labour' and specifically the 'work of a labourer, not of a conjurer or showman' (41). In the case of working-class literature, this means abandoning the search for an autonomous tradition and considering instead the ways in which writers used and reinterpreted received forms for new purposes. As Williams argues, the established structures of the novel operate at 'a distance from working-class life' (1980/1989, 219), and writers have consequently been forced to adapt them in order to address new problems and forms of experience. Jack Common's use of the Bildungsroman in *Kiddar's Luck* (1951/1990) illustrates this kind of critical engagement with an existing genre. The son of a Newcastle train driver, Common was a significant figure in the working-class literary culture of the 1930s, serving as the assistant editor and, from 1935 to 1936, editor of *The Adelphi* (1923–1955), to which he regularly contributed, publishing an important collection on work and unemployment (*Seven Shifts*, 1938/1978) as well as a volume of his own essays (*Freedom of the Streets*, 1938/1988), and establishing friendships with a number of prominent writers and intellectuals, most famously George Orwell. *Kiddar's Luck* appeared in 1951, but by this time conditions had changed, and although he published one more novel, *The Ampersand* (1954), three years later, he could not find a publisher for his third, *In Whitest Britain*. As Keith Armstrong observes, *Kiddar's Luck* 'won critical acclaim' but was not a 'commercial success' (2009 146), and although the 1950s saw a renewed attention to working-class writers, Common was unable to secure the kind of access to presses and journals he had enjoyed before the Second World War.

Kiddar's Luck is best understood as a working-class Bildungsroman, a critical revision of an established genre that exposes its ideological implications. As Helena Feder argues, the Bildungsroman is 'the narrative of the individual coming into culture' (2014, 21). It represents the acquisition of knowledge and the consequent development of authority; a broadly conceived process of education establishes individual agency, albeit within existing cultural systems, and texts frequently end when the main character achieves at least a measure of independence. As *Kiddar's Luck* demonstrates, this assumes a bourgeois protagonist, for the working class acculturation involves a submission to social and economic discipline. Willie Kiddar experiences not a steady progress towards autonomy but attempts to curtail this, to reintegrate him into the 'masses.' He resists with varying degrees of success. In fantasies, he sees himself 'as an apprentice planter in Malaya; as a wireless telegraphist aboard ship; as the youngest astronomer in a Moroccan observatory; as librarian to an eccentric earl in Morayshire; as a mystery man of Fleet Street,' but he recognizes that his 'heritage' excludes him from the geographical and economic mobility embodied in these roles and that he is instead expected to accept 'the routine of the factory or some similar industrial hour-glass regularly turning the sands of uncelebrated and nearly-unconsequenced labour' (Common 1951, 141). Despite his intellectual ability, his main experience of education is of a training in 'being bored,' a 'negative capability' necessary to working-class children if they are to 'put up with the jobs they are going to get, most of them, on leaving school' (32). The linear structure of the conventional Bildungsroman, in which a growing authority is demonstrated through an increasing capacity to exercise choices, is replaced by a circular form in which social forces act like fate, imposing an identity and function determined at birth. The letter Kiddar 'might have written' at the end of the text suggests the extent to which his environment confirms him in the role established with his conception in a 'working-class suburb in Newcastle-upon-Tyne' (5); addressing himself to a potential employer, he notes that '[m]y parents are working-class, my environment is working-class, the school I have just left is working-class, and with your kind assistance I feel qualified to become working-class myself' (143). In this context, '[w]hat is important about a man is not how able he is, nor how hard-working, but what's his luck' (144). Kiddar cannot alter his origins, which determines his future as it does that of the conventional hero whose 'coming greatness hangs like a halo over the cradle' (4). Imagining his conception as a 'blunder' (4), a failure to take the 'golden opportunities' (5) available to him, comically emphasizes the absurdity of dominant ideas of agency. Common exposes the ideas of self-determination integral to both the traditional Bildungsroman and the broader ideological narratives that legitimize capitalism as bourgeois fantasies.

The Bildungsroman enables Common to organize what Pickering and Robins call the 'strongly autobiographical' material of his text and avoid its reduction to an exclusively personal narrative (1984, 79). As Williams argues, life-writing has long been the 'most accessible' (1980/1989, 219) prose form available to working-class writers, and they have produced an extensive and varied body of work, as John Burnett, David Vincent, and David Mayall's three-volume critical bibliography, *The Autobiography of the Working-Class* (1984), demonstrates. The form is valuable because it not only insists on an individuality conventionally denied to working-class people but also enables an analysis of the conditions under which it is formed, the 'constitution of the individual human subject within the class and patriarchal structure of social relations' (Pickering and Robins 1984, 78–79). Despite acknowledging the extent to which *Kiddar's Luck* draws on his own experience (79–80), Common does not work within this tradition. His decision to write a novel fulfils distinct artistic and political functions, challenging the idea of a working-class insensibility to the implications of form. It enables him to establish a narrative distance from his protagonist, Willie Kiddar, and insists on the text as a structured aesthetic object rather than a record of experience. Common's use of the Bildungsroman is critical rather than passive, and he frequently challenges the conventions he employs, a process that exposes both the particular constraints on working-class lives and the class values and assumptions implicit in the genre.

Kiddar's Luck illustrates the challenges as well as the critical possibilities of a renewed critical engagement with working-class texts. Although arguably one of the better-known twentieth-century British working-class novels, it seldom features in literary histories or on syllabi, and is sometimes regarded as significant solely because of its subject matter. Its representation of Northern working-class life in the early 20th century is important, exposing the limitations of dominant cultural narratives, their implicit assumption that certain subjects and people do not merit artistic representation, but emphasizing its autobiographical foundations and careful attention to historical detail risks constructing it as a documentary rather than literary text. This obscures its formal complexities and the ways in which it uses these to achieve a new 'distribution of the sensible.' *Kiddar's Luck* is innovative not only in its adaptation of generic conventions but also in its style, which draws on vernacular traditions of comedy and storytelling to reconfigure the relationship between text and audience. The process is political in the broad sense identified by Rancière, insisting on the presence and legitimacy of voices and perspectives conventionally excluded from literature.

Jack Common and Philip Callow are both concerned with the mechanisms that integrate individuals into existing material and cultural systems. *Kiddar's Luck* and *Common People* use established genres, particularly the Bildungsroman, to explore this process, but their focus on working-class protagonists reveals the implicit class content of these forms. The friction between their subject matter and the conventions they employ results in a series of critical innovations that extend the political and aesthetic possibilities of the genre, enabling it to expose the ways in which advanced capitalism restricts personal agency and to explore experiences previously excluded from literature. Recognizing the significance of these productive adaptations depends on a broader conception of the literary that, amongst other things, is not constrained by bourgeois individualism but admits a concern with the communal, with collective experiences and struggles. It also depends on access to the texts themselves. There is a recent American edition of *Common People*, but the majority of Callow's fiction has not been re-published. *Kiddar's Luck* is the only one of Common's books currently in print and its continued availability depends partly on its status as a regional novel; it was reissued by the Northumberland press Bloodaxe. Other working-class authors have been similarly reliant on their local affiliations; the most recent edition of Simon Blumenfeld's *Jew Boy* (1935/2011) was issued by London Books, and the first complete version of George Garrett's *Ten Years on the Parish* (2017), by Liverpool University Press. Many important texts are still out of print; none of Jack Hilton's work has been reissued, and his remarkable autobiography, *Caliban Boswelling*, like Common's *In Whitest Britain*, has never been published. The recovery, reinterpretation, and reevaluation of neglected texts demands both analytical and material changes, an ability to obtain texts and read them differently. Feminist literary criticism provides a model for this kind of critical intervention and demonstrates the possibility of its success; it changed the methods as well as the objects of analysis. At its best, its aim was not just to add books by women to existing reading lists but to challenge the ideas that had excluded them and establish the material apparatus necessary to sustain a broader understanding of literature. It also demonstrated that, if these things are achieved, some of those previously dismissed as having no 'idea of what constitutes literature' are capable of extending and enriching the category, enabling readers to the see 'things that are left out.'

References

Armstrong, K. (2009) *Common Words and the Wandering Star: A Biographical Study of Culture and Social Change in the Life and Work of Writer Jack Common (1903–1968)*, Rainton Bridge, University of Sunderland Press.

Blumenfeld, S. (1935, 2011). *Jew Boy*, London, London Books.

Burnett, J., Vincent, D. and Mayall, D. (1984) *The Autobiography of the Working-Class: An Annotated Critical Bibliography* (3 volumes), Brighton, Harvester.

Callow, P. (1956) *Hosanna Man*, London, Jonathan Cape.

Callow, P. (1958) *Common People*, London, Heinemann.

Callow, P. (2002) *Passage from Home: A Memoir*, Nottingham, Shoestring Press.

Chopin, K. (1899) *The Awakening*, Chicago, Herbert S. Stone & Company.

Coles, N. and Lauter, P. (eds.) (2017) *A History of American Working-Class Literature*, Cambridge, Cambridge University Press.

Coles, N. and Zandy, J. (eds.) (2007), *American Working-Class Literature: An Anthology*, Oxford, Oxford University Press.

Common, J. (ed.) (1938/1978) *Seven Shifts*, Wakefield, E. P. Publishing.

Common, J. (1938/1988) *Freedom of the Streets*, London, People's Publications.

Common, J. (1951/1990) *Kiddar's Luck*, Highgreen, Bloodaxe.

Common, J. (1954) *The Ampersand*, London, Turnstile Press.

Donadio, R. (2007) 'Revisiting the Canon Wars,' *New York Times Book Review*, pp. 16–17.

Eagleton, T. (1976/1995) *Criticism and Ideology: A Study in Marxist Literary Theory*, London, Verso.

Emecheta, B. (1974/1975) *Second-Class Citizen*, New York, G. Braziller.

Feder, H. (2014) *Ecocriticism and the Idea of Culture: Biology and the Bildungsroman*, Farnham, Ashgate.

Forster, E. M. (1924/2005) *A Passage to India*, London, Penguin.

Garrett, G. (2017) *Ten Years on the Parish*, Liverpool, Liverpool University Press.

Gold, M. (1930/2004) *Jews Without Money*, New York, Carroll & Graf.

Goodridge, J. and Keegan, B. (eds.) (2017) *A History of British Working-Class Literature*, Cambridge, Cambridge University Press.

Hawthorne, J. (1984) 'Preface,' in Hawthorne, J. (ed.), *The British Working-Class Novel in the Twentieth Century*, London, Edward Arnold.

Hilton, J. *Caliban Boswelling*, University of Nottingham Manuscripts and Special Collections.

Hitchcock, P. (2000) 'They Must Be Represented? Problems in Theories of Working-Class Representation,' *PMLA*, 115, 1, pp. 20–32.

Hoggart, R. (1970a) 'A Question of Tone: Problems in Autobiographical Writing,' *Speaking to Each Other: Volume Two: About Literature*, New York, Oxford University Press.

Hoggart, R. (1970b) 'Literature and Society,' *Speaking to Each Other: Volume Two: About Literature*, New York, Oxford University Press.

Holdsworth, E. (1925/2011) *This Slavery*, Nottingham, Trent Editions.

Hungerford, A. et al. (2017) *The Norton Anthology of American Literature: Ninth Edition*, New York, Norton.

Jones, O. (2011) *Chavs: The Demonization of the Working Class*, London, Verso.

Kelman, J. (1994) *How Late It Was, How Late*, London, Secker & Warburg.

Kolodny, A. (1980) 'Dancing Through the Minefield: Some Observations on the Theory, Practice and Politics of a Feminist Literary Criticism,' *Feminist Studies*, 6, 1, pp. 1–25.

Lauter, P. and Fitzgerald, A. (2001) *Literature, Class, and Culture: An Anthology*, New York, Longman.

Lawrence, D. H. (1913/2006) *Sons and Lovers*, London, Penguin.

Lennon, J. and Nilsson, M. (eds.) (2017). *Working-Class Literature(s): Historical and International Perspectives*, Stockholm, Stockholm University Press.

Macherey, P. (1966/1986) *A Theory of Literary Production*, London, Routledge.

Marx, K. (1852/1996) 'The Eighteenth Brumaire of Louis Bonaparte,' in Carver, T. (ed.), *Marx: Later Political Writings*, Cambridge, Cambridge University Press.

Marx, K. (1857/1996) 'Introduction to the *Grundrisse*,' in Carver, T. (ed.), *Marx: Later Political Writings*, Cambridge, Cambridge University Press.

Mortimer, P. (August 10, 1958) 'A White Hope?,' *The Sunday Times*, p. 7.

Munt, S. (2000) 'Introduction,' in Munt, S. (ed.), *Cultural Studies and the Working Class: Subject to Change*, London, Cassell.

Orwell, G. (1998) 'Lear, Tolstoy and the Fool,' in Davison, P. (ed.), *It Is What I Think: 1947–1948*, London, Secker & Warburg.

Pickering, M. and Robins, K. (1984) 'A Revolutionary Materialist with a Leg Free: The Autobiographical Novels of Jack Common,' in Hawthorn, J. (ed.), *The British Working-Class Novel in the Twentieth Century*, London, Edward Arnold.

Pierse, M. (ed.) (2017) *A History of Irish Working-Class Writing*, Cambridge, Cambridge University Press.

Powys, J. (1931/1932) 'Preface,' in Hanley, J. *Men in Darkness*, New York, Alfred Knopf.

Rancière, J. (2009) 'A few remarks on the method of Jacques Rancière,' *Parallax*, 15, 3, pp. 114–123.

Rancière, J. (2010/2012) 'The Politics of Literature,' *Dissensus: On Politics and Aesthetics*, London, Continuum.

Rose, J. (2002) *The Intellectual Life of the British Working Classes*, New Haven, Yale Nota Bene.

Russo, J. and Linkon, S. (2005) 'What's New about New Working-Class Studies?,' in Russo, J. and Linkon, S. (eds.), *New Working-Class Studies*, Ithaca, Cornell University Press.

Steadman, R. W. (1939) 'A Critique of Proletarian Literature,' *North American Review*, 247, 1, pp. 142–52.

Storey, D. (1976) *Saville*, New York, Harper & Row.

Tokarczyk, M. (2011) 'Introduction,' in Tokarczyk, M. (ed.), *Critical Approaches to American Working-Class Literature*, New York, Routledge.

Tompkins, J. (1985) *Sensational Designs: The Cultural Work of American Fiction, 1790–1860*, Oxford, Oxford University Press.

Turner, G. (2012) *What's Become of Cultural Studies?* London, Sage.
Williams, R. (1980/1989) 'The Welsh Industrial Novel,' *Problems in Materialism and Culture*, London, Verso.
Woolf, W. (1931/1977) 'Introductory Letter to Margaret Llewelyn Davies,' in Davies, M. L. (ed.), *Life as We Have Known It, by Co-operative Working Women*, London, Virago.
Woolf, V. (1940/1966) 'The Leaning Tower,' in Woolf, L. (ed.), *Collected Essays: Volume Two*, London, Hogarth.
Zandy, J. (2004) *Hands: Physical Labor, Class, and Cultural Work*, New Brunswick, Rutgers University Press.

26

Lit-grit

The gritty and the grim in working-class cultural production

Simon Lee

Although working-class culture holds no monopoly on the word, 'gritty' has become a customary adjective to describe working-class cultural production. It would be strange to hear of a high-society narrative referred to as 'gritty,' but it would be stranger to hear of a working-class narrative *not* described that way. Yet, when used as a noun, 'grit' is more equivocal and contingent, frequently signaling perseverance—a trait sometimes associated with the working-class notion of 'getting by.' Academics in the field of working-class studies regularly focus on the concept of perseverance—especially in the social sciences, with work by Beverly Skeggs, Lynsey Hanley, and Lisa Mckenzie underscoring the prevalence of tenacity in working-class culture.[1] However, contemporary representations of working-class life in cultural production suggest that there is much work to be done in terms of mining the finer details of technique within the narrative arts. Critics like Pam Fox and Sherry Lee Linkon have helped us trace the contours of working-class cultural production more broadly, yet discrete formal effects also warrant close scrutiny. This chapter, then, seeks to advance ways of thinking about working-class representation by considering how cultural traits such as grittiness operate as technical effects of narrative, raising questions about their role in the formation and reiteration of cultural identities.

Grit infers character and resolve—specifically as it relates to persistence in oppressed or subjugated states. But, as a term that eludes precision and transcends class boundaries, grit warrants inquiry when deployed in relation to contemporary working-class cultural production. To that end it is wise to study the representational interplay between grit as an industrious character trait, and 'aesthetic grit'—the grittiness and grime associated with sites of labor. The term can be parsed along three representational paths: the depiction of working-class environments (the grit and grime of industry); the doggedness of surviving such spaces as part of a community (tenacity and solidarity); and more individualized notions of grit presented as a means of escape (ambition and autonomy). As working-class texts tend to interlace these paths as part of their structure, setting takes on profound valence—especially in the way characters respond to and articulate their position in relation to it. Looking to 1950s British social realism as a moment when working-class texts amplified the significance of space in narrative, this chapter considers contemporary representations of grit and grittiness as a method by which to better comprehend legitimacy.[2] Consequently, it underscores the term's slippery nature, calling on the working-class scholar to address the way the term (and terms like it) are circulated through culture.

Neoliberal individualism's embracing of grit as an estimable character trait has led to a conspicuous increase in its usage from the 1960s to the present moment.[3] Yet, when mobilized as kudos, the term invites imprecision, celebrating an individual's capacity to overcome adversity while failing to account for circumstances involved. This can be understood as the kind of 'pull yourself up by the bootstraps' language which (falsely) assumes a level playing field with equal opportunities for all. Furthermore, success stories of grit and tenacity tend to reflect individual success rather than success achieved as part of a community or a collective, with 'grit' characterized more as a component of successful upward mobility. A news story of a working-class person rising above will most likely focus on the individual rather than their community, lessening the contributions of others and inferring the importance of the self over the collective. In this model, the role that community may have played in the person's success is shadowed by the success itself.

Fictional narratives, by design, follow suit in that they also tend to elevate the individual above the group.[4] Working-class narratives are no different in that the construction of the protagonist is predicated on differentiating the character from the community, often relegating the community to stereotypes while the protagonist is given greater dimension.[5] As such, representations of working-class communities tend to fall back on forms of nostalgia and sentimentality to produce this effect, romanticizing the notion of community through shared values and symbols of sameness.[6] What is important to note here is that in much working-class cultural production, the main character can be read as an appendage of the space they inhabit, but one that is potentially distinct from it. As the result, the trait of individual tenacity produces tension when contrasted against the aesthetic grit of the industrial setting, and the interplay between them provides grist for the literary scholar's mill.

The impact of the environment on proletarian subjects can therefore be read as a bridge between gritty aesthetics and grit as survival instinct; yet the notion of grit as personal triumph over class-based adversity is somewhat of a rarity in working-class representation as it suggests class migrancy—a relatively taboo topic in working-class culture.[7] In this regard, Richard Hoggart's 'them and us' binary merges with the dogged tradition of 'making do' to produce a distinctly working-class feature of perseverance informed directly by gritty aesthetics.[8] The upshot is that, aesthetic representations of grit and shared struggle function as two sides of the same coin, but the term's usage bears a tenuous connection to the kind of neoliberal individualism associated with personal ambition and social ascension. Given this, when narratives emphasize a protagonist, it is wise to assess whether the protagonist is distinguished from their community as a technical effect associated with the form (to develop a character), or whether the novel seems to promote separation or alienation from the community (to explore existential crises), allowing the working-class scholar to question why that might be the case.[9] We might approach working-class representation as heavy on the adjectival use of 'grit' through depictions of spaces of labor, but somewhat volatile in terms of the noun form, with working-class characters often torn between surviving oppressive conditions or rising above them. Once more, close analysis of the way this term is mobilized in a particular text can reveal a great deal about the intent and purpose of the text itself.

Gritty space

What undergirds the enigmatic appeal of a working-class environment is the polysemous notion of grit—not the dirt or the residue of industrial production, but the way such spaces are characterized by customs and traditions emanating from the physical conditions themselves.

Shelagh Delaney, the author of the 1958 play *A Taste of Honey*, described her hometown of Salford, in North West England, in such a manner, noting how the region possessed a magnetic quality, largely based on a shared sense of community in relation to conditions of existence (Russell 1960). Delaney's account of working-class space reflects the way an established community seeks to assuage the more oppressive aspects of industrial environs through persistence akin to Emile Durkheim's notion of the collective conscience.[10] Durkheim (1893) argues that social groups thrive through their ability to defend internal characteristics, especially in the face of oppression or adversity. Working-class communities frequently adopt a similar stance, and that stance can be identified in the space itself through representations of literal and figurative grittiness.[11] This kind of identification, however, relies on knowledge of class signifiers associated with such spaces. The kind of working-class representation that Delaney fashioned—exemplified by the late 1950s movement known as kitchen sink realism—deployed class signifiers as a method by which to celebrate the extraordinary within the ordinary, offering insight into aspects of British culture generally ignored within the arts.[12]

The techniques of spatial representation advanced in the postwar years exemplify a fairly specific set of protocols that serve to foreground space as a critical component of gritty working-class representation. Texts of this period tend to portray the same environment multiple times, allowing such descriptions to function as rhythmic pauses in the narrative, but also to serve as a continual and insistent reminder of the repressive conditions of working-class life. Such spaces are often shown from manifold angles, fleshing out details with resolute, documentary-style precision. And, in light of the kitchen sink movement's allegiance to social-realist verisimilitude, the way characters navigate, interact with, and are impacted by the environments they inhabit is especially instructive. For example, representations of working-class domestic spaces tend to emphasize the notion of limitation and restriction, barely offering any refuge from the noisy industrial atmosphere outside.[13] Given the ethical thrust of much working-class production—to illuminate conditions of class-conscious texts of the late 1950s are rarely set in open or pastoral spaces, shifting representation from the poetic and romantic landscapes of early-20th-century working-class writing toward spaces in which factories and industrial production dominate. Closed confines (be it rooms or institutional spaces) are matched by claustrophobic vicinities (environs and communities that appear hemmed in or marked by aesthetic grit), so oppressive limitations and abstract boundaries made manifest through spatial representation are foregrounded as a theme consistent throughout the era.

If social class is to be considered as the culmination of a series of power relations, then a comprehension of the way spaces reveal power flows and dynamics can help clarify how class is constructed, reiterated, and potentially contested through working-class cultural production. Henri Lefebvre establishes how space is developed socially and is therefore open to transformation through cognitive displacement. For Lefebvre, conceptions of space are comprehended as the product of interactions broken down into three categories. 'Perceived space' encompasses the physical materiality of space—the commonly held understanding of the way a particular space exists in society (Lefebvre 1974, 38). In its most refined form, perceived space is the physical plane of reality. 'Conceived space,' however, exists as imagined space, or the intended function conceptualized by architects or planners prior to a space's material formation (Lefebvre 1974, 39). 'Lived space' refers to the experience of space that is socially constructed (Lefebvre 1974, 39), but also the sort of space that an individual may view as adaptable for their own needs. Lefebvre insists, however, that these categories should not be considered discretely; instead, they function dialectically, and any attempt to parse a space in the world should account for all three.

The problem, according to Lefebvre, is that lived space is difficult to quantify due to its subjective nature whereas physical and conceived space can be grasped with little effort. The reason for this difficulty, he notes, is because we conceive of space primarily as a material construct—something that exists in reality with no deeper meaning beyond its physical presence. Space, in this regard, appears like a stage; it exists only to contain the actions we bring to bear on it. Lived space emerges in response to perceived and conceived space, understood through negotiation and compromise. For instance, if a space or region has been promised government support to help address some of its more pressing issues—yet the problems still persist because the funds were misappropriated—then lived experience is informed by this injustice with behavior following suit. On the one hand, Lefebvre's conception of what is sometimes referred to as a socio-spatial triad posits that there is far more to a space than meets the eye; on the other, it suggests that space is subject to social manipulation and is, by extension, open to our own manipulation of it.[14]

In terms of representation in cultural production, such an approach to spatial analysis can provide a constructive way of parsing class-based issues, and the use of aesthetic grit in describing such spaces serves as a key to unlock the kind of tensions outlined by Lefebvre. To illustrate, when homes are imagined as sanctuary from factory life, yet fail to live up to their intended purpose due to their grim conditions or meagre resources, class dynamics are revealed as expressions of lack. Similarly, when local facilities or municipal services are presented in a state of dereliction, tension between a space's intent and its reality underscores the dire straits of classed lives and the sense of alienation felt in many working-class communities. In this regard, an analysis of spatial production helps elucidate the way represented space impacts characters and shapes behavior, granting additional insight into how gritty environments function to reiterate class boundaries. It might be presumed that working-class cultural production that tends to the complex intricacies of 'grit' is more likely to explore class from an ethical perspective rather than simply relying on surface aesthetics or the superficial, helping the reader gauge authorial motives and legitimacy as the result.

Yet, if grit is so multivalent within working-class cultural production, the question may be raised as to why a focus on gritty aesthetics should suffice as a method by which to evaluate class representation. For one thing, such an approach provides consistency—the vast majority of working-class cultural production deploys instances of grit by design. For another, if we conceive of class as mutable in that the specific contours of what it means to be working-class are fluid and unstable across different time periods, then an emphasis on space *over* time sidesteps the restrictions of chronological analysis. In this sense, whereas working-class attitudes and experiences may fluctuate, spatial analysis offers a more robust approach in that the impact of working-class conditions—conditions characterized by grit and limitation—bear similarities from place to place as well as from time period to time period. For example, the kind of struggles experienced in Victorian slums is relatively commensurate to the environmental conditions of precarity experienced by working-class people today. In other words, an emphasis on representational grit and gritty space allows for a more stable, anchored way to evaluate working-class cultural production.

Commodified grit

The upshot of approaching grit as shorthand for working-class culture is that it lends credence to the way working-class culture itself is increasingly fetishized and commodified through nostalgic signifiers. This is where the slippery conflation of aesthetic grit and gritty characteristics converge to produce a consumable product primed for 21st-century exploitation. In a 2002 essay, Karen Bettez Halnon introduced the term 'poor chic' to describe the consumption of working-class symbols as a means to establish oneself as 'upmarket.' This trend, Halnon argues, permeates contemporary culture in ways that seem anodyne ('shabby chic' decor is one of the examples she provides). Lately, more egregious examples of class fetishism have emerged, following the seemingly innocuous rise of 'lad culture' in the 1990s to the wave of 'poverty porn' television shows developed throughout the 2000s. Whereas these kinds of trends tend to borrow cosmetic signifiers from working-class culture in ways that blur the line between celebration and appropriation, recent examples of cultural production have rendered such exploitation unambiguous. Nonetheless, reprobate depictions of working-class life are not always quite as brazen, requiring cautious scrutiny to fully assess their intent.

Gritty working-class environments, I would argue, are fetishized in contemporary culture to stand in for a loose set of working-class traits which ordinarily resist such commodification due to their immateriality. For instance, to market a product as structured upon the characteristics of a social demographic would require essentialism and stereotyping, but fetishizing working-class space is far less onerous—especially given that such spaces have been historically romanticized in past cultural narratives. Contemporary working-class representation, however, is prone to a more direct flattening of space and character through the polysemous use of grit, suggesting that the exploitation of space conveniently masks the exploitation of a social demographic while sidestepping the need to reference the demographic itself. The use of grit as shorthand for working-class culture, then, can potentially be understood as a furtive method of class profiling—the mobilization of stereotypes based on spatial conflation rather than on individuals or individual characters. This produces a dilemma: how to differentiate between working-class aesthetic representation that exploits working-class people and that which celebrates and elevates them. Analysis of the way a text utilizes the multivalent notion of grit can help the reader grapple with this issue, specifically whether such an approach reduces gritty attributes into a single form or explores their potential to produce tension.

For example, the British soap opera *Coronation Street* played a critical role in cementing postwar working-class representational motifs, specifically in terms of TV programming and the sustenance of the British New Wave.[15] Written by Tony Warren, and first broadcast in December of 1960, Coronation Street sustained gritty kitchen sink aesthetics through the remainder of the century while establishing a blueprint for a host of other popular soap operas that would dominate British households for decades to come. Originally conceived as a kitchen sink drama, the show demonstrates the way the spatial aesthetics of the kitchen sink movement were quickly commodified and repackaged for easy consumption.[16] The show's use of rhetorical devices to appeal to specific emotional needs of the British populace—largely one anxious about shifts in the built environment—suggests an adaptation of working-class representation developed in the late 1950s.[17] Rather than sustaining the kitchen sink realists' commitment to balancing aesthetic and ethical impulses, Coronation Street evacuates the political, turning instead on superficial depictions of working-class life in which subversive objectives are diminished in lieu of an easily consumable product. In this case, gritty spatial aesthetics and the grit of persistence are reduced with little representation of the kind of grit that suggests social elevation. Characters' social status rarely shifts; instead, they accept their limited social position and shared acquiescence in a passive manner—a rhetorical device that mirrors patterns of passive consumption performed by the show's target audience. Aesthetic grit and the grit of tenacity are unified to produce a strong sense of community akin to kitchen sink texts, yet the movement's insurgent and political imperatives are attenuated. *Coronation Street*'s success can be understood, in part, through the show's willingness to romanticize images of working-class life and render them palatable. While distinct from the kind of pure exploitation seen in 'poverty porn' programming, *Coronation Street* points toward the lucrative capacity of commodified identities when grit is sanitized and then mobilized as a prevailing characteristic.

In contrast, Irvine Welsh's 1993 novel *Trainspotting* signals a turn to hyperbolic representations of working-class grit, acting as somewhat of a precursor to a style that would emerge in the late 1990s and early 2000s. With parallels to the American writer Chuck Palahniuk, Welsh relies upon hard-hitting, visceral narratives that bludgeon the reader into the decaying demimondes the narrative produces.[18] Like *Coronation Street*, *Trainspotting* borrows heavily from mid-century writing, but further emphasizes gritty space in a number of ways. The rough, run-down environments usually seen in working-class fiction are exploded in the opening scene in which the Edinburgh Festival—a space metaphorically designated for high-brow culture—is contrasted against what has become known through Danny Boyle's 1996 film adaptation as the 'worst toilet in Scotland' scene of the novel. Here, every possible violation of hygiene is mobilized in detail, suggesting that a character like Mark Renton has no place in civil society and is relegated to the basement, slipping and falling in puddles of human waste. Since this scene occurs early in the text, it is evident that Welsh uses space to set the tone of social ostracism that the novel advances throughout.

Whereas the gritty spaces of *Coronation Street* retain a degree of poetic romanticism, in *Trainspotting*, spaces are cast more as abject, underscoring the severity of division in society in a manner that differs from collective congeniality and perseverance. In this case, working-class tenacity is rendered impossible by the visceral filth of the setting, so aspirational grit supersedes in Renton's desire to leave for Amsterdam, and a notable tension between aesthetic and characteristic grit is rendered clear. Here, working-class persistence is supplanted by ambition as the upshot of the uninhabitable conditions; the neoliberal individualism model of elevation becomes the grit of survival in spaces like Muirhouse, by necessity.[19] While Muirhouse is commensurate with a range of estates developed in the 1950s that were subsequently abandoned by governing bodies, Welsh's hyperbolic amplification of social neglect brings such concerns to the forefront of the cultural imaginary as a persistent and recurring problem. In this regard, Welsh's work balances the aesthetic of chaos and disorder with the political imperative of illuminating its effects on the population, emerging therefore as a text that offers an authentic portrayal of working-class inequality with none of the sanitation required for easy consumption.

Similarly, Richard Milward's 2007 novel *Apples* signifies the shift in working-class representation toward a hyperreal barrage of grit. But whereas the characters of *Trainspotting* navigate gritty space, Milward's characters succumb to them, functioning more as flattened extensions of the environment. Bearing in mind that Milward was the same age as many of the kitchen sink writers when he published his first novel, it is possible to think of a text like *Apples* as conveying a similar youthful exuberance to a play like *A Taste of Honey*. However, the novel is more closely aligned to the aesthetics of In-Yer-Face theater and TV shows like *Shameless*, depicting little of the youthful optimism of a writer like Delaney and relying instead on bleak pessimism administered largely through spatial metaphors.[20] While kitchen sink texts were hardly uplifting affairs, and working-class representation that followed throughout the 1970s and 1980s emphasized grit to such a degree that optimism was simply something that existed in other genres, Milward's novel reflects the more commercial strain of class representation that seems to portray working-class people in a stereotypical manner. Ultimately, the environment depicted in *Apples*—a housing estate in Middlesborough—hosts a diverse set of interactions while emphasizing the sameness of the space.[21] Characters do not merely struggle to elevate themselves from a maligned social status; they succumb to and perpetuate cultural stereotypes as the result of their own limited worldview as well as their limited options to escape their milieu. Whereas *Trainspotting* stages individual grit as a necessity of survival, the characters in *Apples* neither escape nor survive the space and are pummeled and broken down by it.

Verisimilitude is clearly Milward's goal, but the rapidity and barrage of social ills that the novel presents through the space itself reads more as a catalog of tabloid stereotypes than as a text seeking productive identification. Its heightened emphasis on gritty space and environment surpasses the tenacity of community, and the characters demonstrate little in the way of individual aspiration. In essence, the characters and the space are conflated, resulting in a gestalt effect rather than revealing dynamic tension or exchange. While there is no questioning the level of realism that *Apples* provides through its emphasis on setting, its contribution ends there—an act of cultural mimesis, grounded almost entirely in the aesthetic and marketed as such. While the novel was a relative commercial success, the text represents a contemporary trend in working-class representation that seeks to transform cultural identity into a horror-show spectacle based on the sensationalizing of class as a subcultural form.

Evaluating gritty aesthetics

One of the challenges of addressing legitimacy in working-class cultural production is that attempts to police authorial ethos can result in essentialism and literary ghettoization. But when working-class culture is so easily commodified through representational methods, it behooves us to think about authenticity in new, pressing ways. By focusing on the way gritty aesthetics are deployed in relation to working-class representation, it is possible to elucidate authorial motives and, therefore, evaluate the success of the work as representative of working-class legitimacy. Analysis of spatial production can help identify the tension between aesthetic grit and the kind of grit that represents a character's interactions with the space itself. Doing so grants access to an evaluative framework of working-class representation that does not rely upon identity or biographical experience, sidestepping the kind of limits that may emerge from such an approach.

The function of grit in working-class texts, despite appearing as lazy shorthand for working-class culture, can convey authenticity as long as representations take into consideration the term's polysemous nature. When a text appears to reduce grittiness to a single, overarching signifier, it might be assumed that the aim is to produce an easily consumable image or identity. But when a text explores the tension between aesthetic space and characteristic grit, it would appear that a greater attempt is underway to represent working-class culture as complex and dynamic rather than monolithic or stereotypical. Therefore, an analysis of gritty representation forges a new way of thinking about legitimacy that bypasses the kind of essentialism associated with biographic authenticity. In this regard, working-class grit—comprised of representations of gritty space alongside a full comprehension of the way working-class characteristics adapt to that space—signifies authenticity through aesthetic representation, but also through character development in which working-class traits and traditions are conveyed through space in honest, deferential ways.

Notes

1 Mckenzie suggests that tenacity is rooted in 'passed-down knowledge' in which working-class people share information on how to make the most of less-than-ideal conditions (2015, 47). For Hanley (2007), exposure to such conditions begets an increased tolerance of them, with the comfort and security of the familiar helping to insulate the working-class individual from the world beyond the immediate community. Skeggs (2004) shows how tenacity augments self-identification, allowing working-class people to define themselves, in part, through their resilience.

2 It should be noted that while concerns raised in this chapter are transnational, the emphasis here on UK working-class culture allows for a more precise focus for the purposes of this particular argument. Recent collections like *Working-Class Literature(s): Historical and International Perspectives* (Lennon and

Nilsson 2017) allude to characteristic parallels across national lines, but a survey of global proportions is beyond this chapter's purview.

3 Neoliberal individualism can be understood as the preferred posture of a consumer society, one generally characterized by solipsistic, utopian fantasies. Radical self-interest, oftentimes at the expense of others, is a central tenet of such a position. While working-class culture saw signs of segmentation coinciding with the rise of late 1950s subculture, the kind of individualism of the 1980s was structured around meritocracy and competition. Although ngram reports of the word 'grit' connote relative instability (aside from a notable increase in the period following industrialization), 'gritty' shows a demonstrable and sharp increase of use through the 1980s.

4 There have been, of course, plenty of exceptions to such production. For example, actuality films and the cinéma-vérité movement decentered the individual through nontraditional narrative, but such production was relatively niche. A film like Mike Leigh's *Life is Sweet* (1990) centers on the plight of numerous characters, but tends to emphasize community spirit as a dominant force overall.

5 Fox suggests how working-class writing subverts traditional narratives, arguing that the genre grants access to modes of being that counter dominant and hegemonic cultural narratives (1994, 19). Furthermore, Zandy (1993) discusses working-class writing as cultural artifact, noting that this kind of work is often imbued with authenticity that stems from experience or committed empathy. While both of these claims are true, I would argue that working-class narratives still align to formal characteristics associated with more traditional cultural production and literary techniques.

6 One example might be the way public spaces or institutions are represented in a text as a space that connotes shared status and characteristics of those who frequent the space. A common example of this effect can be seen in George Orwell's famous account of mining communities in *The Road to Wigan Pier* (1972).

7 It is worth noting that the recent anthology of essays on working-class life, *Know Your Place: Essays on the Working Class by the Working Class* (Connolly 2017), offers a different perspective on the notion of migrancy as social elevation, arguing rather that class delineations are too blurred for such a rigid set of class dynamics to hold. Instead, social ascension is described more as the movement of class contours.

8 Hoggart's discussion of 'them and us' is a key chapter in his *The Uses of Literacy: Aspects of Working-Class Life* (1957), outlining how working-class people self-identify in relation to other social classes as well as positions of authority and expertise. Character and tradition, in this regard, is a culmination of what one is as well as what one is not. Such a rigid binary seems potentially problematic, raising questions as to the way working-class communities embrace immiseration in the process of self-definition.

9 To provide examples, the novels of John Braine (*Room at the Top*, 1957), Alan Sillitoe (*Saturday Night and Sunday Morning*, 1958), and David Storey (*This Sporting Life*, 1960) all feature alienated protagonists who vacillate between working-class and middle-class life. This is a feature of the particular genre and period, with novels exploring issues of class migrancy and the failure of the British welfare state to meet the needs of the populace.

10 The term emerged from Emile Durkheim's *Division of Labour in Society* (1893) and was later developed by Georg Lukács and others. For Durkheim, preservation instincts inform the notion of collective consciousness in that the beliefs and values of a particular group are to be maintained for the group to survive shifts in culture and society. Values and beliefs pertaining to a specific group, then, act as a stabilizing factor and as a mechanism that sustains a group in perpetuity.

11 An example might be a local pub or working-man's club, designed to serve a specifically classed region. Such spaces often lack the ornamentation of Edwardian- or Victorian-style pubs, aimed instead at community engagement and copious drinking. Although a number of working-class institutions serve similar roles, the pub is probably the most ubiquitous in British culture, often playing a key role in working-class cultural production as well.

12 The movement's name stemmed from a 1954 review in *Encounter* by the art critic David Sylvester that argued that the domestic realism of painters like Jack Smith and John Bratby celebrated insignificant lives in a cheerless manner. Yet what this particular movement produced was a renewed interest in environmental representations of working-class culture—an attempt to characterize aesthetic grit in a way that incorporated gritty character traits as well. In doing so, the kitchen sink realism movement helped develop the foundation for understanding the way spatial representation and aesthetic grit can work together to communicate more cumulative goals.

13 When spaces that represent non-working-class environs are depicted, they are oftentimes deployed as sites of reverie or reflection—generally a retreat into nature or a similar site beyond ideological confines. These sites tend to serve as breaks in the plot, but they can also be read as sites of insurgent potentiality.

14 Like Lefebvre, Harvey (2006) considers how the environment analogizes manifestations of capital, and the use of aesthetic grit amplifies such distinctions. Harvey picks up where Lefebvre left off, developing the link between urbanism and capitalism to uncover differential spaces of contention. Whereas Lefebvre posited space as the result of a dialectical triad, Harvey develops this concept further by adding three more categories to merge with perceived, conceived, and representational space, resulting in a nine-way matrix. By complicating his original approach, Harvey offers a more nuanced way of conceiving of Lefebvre's slippery 'lived space' category—the immaterial component of space structured upon social interactions and negotiations.

15 The British New Wave is the cinematic counterpart to the literature and theater production of the kitchen sink movement. Many of the novels and films of the period were transformed into screenplays by the original writers, teaming up with directors like Lindsay Anderson, Karel Reisz, and Tony Richardson. *Room at the Top* (1959), *Look Back in Anger* (1959), *Saturday Night and Sunday Morning* (1960), and *A Taste of Honey* (1961) all balanced aesthetic interests with social and ethically minded intent.

16 As discussed prior, and well outlined in work by Higson (1996) and Lay (2002), kitchen sink texts built on documentary motifs as well as the use of taboo subject matter. However, I would argue that kitchen sink texts amplify the use of space and setting to place working-class characters into stark relief for close analysis.

17 Whereas the kitchen sink movement was arguably more political than commercial, *Coronation Street* shows how those two roles can be flipped, in that the show served to pacify rather than agitate. Considering that the show centered on working-class people's lives, actual scenes of labor were astonishingly rare. Given the fact that the show aired in the evenings, this choice suggests that the writers sought to appeal to viewers who had recently returned home from work themselves and wanted to be entertained rather than reminded of their own working-class status.

18 Duff has argued that the barrage effect of such texts stems from cultural trends dominant at the time, specifically responding to the vestiges of punk subculture and the drug-driven hedonism of 1990s raves (2014, 52). Duff also points out that the characters in *Trainspotting* are products of their surroundings—the Muirhouse housing estate of the text—relegating individuals to types commonly marked as working class (2014, 53).

19 Whereas working-class representation tends to veer toward individuals 'making do' in spaces that lack resources, Muirhouse is presented as a direct threat—largely based on the fact that HIV ran rampant there with 51% of the population testing positive.

20 Although not discussed in this chapter, both In-Yer-Face theater and *Shameless* are characterized by visceral, confrontational subject matter. 'In-Yer-Face' was the term Aleks Sierz used to describe the kind aggressive plays written by Mark Ravenhill (*Shopping and Fucking* 1996) and Sarah Kane (*Blasted* 1995). Paul Abbott's *Shameless* (2004–2013) adopted a similarly aggressive tone in terms of the way it depicted the various families living on a council estate in Manchester. Whereas kitchen sink texts engaged taboo topics readily, In-Yer-Face theater and *Shameless* pushed the envelope further in terms of shocking content.

21 Broadly speaking, the kind of environments presented in these kinds of texts do not vary much from one another. But this is also true for a number of working-class regions in general, in which the home, the pub, and the factory are the primary destinations. In a number of cases, these spaces are physically linked with pubs built into council estates and older housing terraces connected to (or at least close by) the means of production.

References

Abbott, P. (2004–2013) *Shameless*, London, Company Pictures.

Anderson, L. (1959) *Room at the Top*, London, British Lion Films.

Boyle, D. (1996) *Trainspotting*, Los Angeles, Miramax.

Braine, J. (1957) *Room at the Top*, London, Methuen Publishing.

Connolly, N (2017). *Know Your Place: Essays on the Working Class by the Working Class*, Liverpool, Dead Ink.

Delaney, S. (1958) *A Taste of Honey*, London, Methuen Publishing.

Duff, K. (2014) *Contemporary British Literature and Urban Space*, London, Palgrave Macmillan.

Durkheim, E. (1893) *The Division of Labor in Society*, Florence, The Free Press, 1984.

Fox, P. (1994) *Class Fictions: Shame and Resistance in the British Working Class-Novel, 1890–1945*, Durham, Duke University Press.

Halnon, K. B. (2002) 'Poor Chic: The Rational Consumption of Poverty,' *Current Sociology*, 50, 4, pp. 501–516.
Hanley, L. (2007) *Estates: An Intimate History*, London, Granta.
Harvey, D. (2006) 'Space as a Keyword,' in Castree, N. and Gregory, D. (eds.) *David Harvey: A Critical Reader*, Hoboken, Wiley-Blackwell.
Higson, A. (1996) *Dissolving Views: Key Writings on British Cinema*, London, Cassell.
Hoggart, R. (1957) *The Uses of Literacy: Aspects of Working-Class Life*, London, Penguin Classics, 2009.
Kane, S. (1995) *Blasted*, London, Methuen Drama.
Lay, S. (2002) *British Social Realism: From Documentary to Brit Grit*, New York, Wallflower Press.
Lefebvre, H. (1974) *The Production of Space*, translated by Donald Nicholson-Smith, Wiley-Blackwell, 1992.
Leigh, M. (1990) *Life is Sweet*, New York, Criterion Collection.
Lennon, J. and Nilsson, M. (2017) *Working-Class Literature(s): Historical and International Perspectives*, Stockholm, Stockholm University Press.
Linkon, S. L. (2018) *The Half-Life of Deindustrialization*, Ann Arbor, Michigan University Press.
Mckenzie, L. (2015) *Getting By: Estates, Class, and Culture in Austerity Britain*, Bristol, Policy Press.
Milward, R. (2007) *Apples: A Novel*, Edinburgh, Canongate.
Orwell, G. (1937) *The Road to Wigan Pier*, San Diego, Harcourt, 1972.
Ravenhill, M. (1996) *Shopping and Fucking*, London, Methuen Drama.
Reisz, K. (1960) *Saturday Night and Sunday Morning*, London, Bryanston Films.
Richardson, T. (1959) *Look Back in Anger*, Woodfall Film Productions.
Richardson, T. (1961) *A Taste of Honey*, London, British Lion Films.
Russell, K. (1960). 'Shelagh Delaney's Salford,' *Monitor*.
Sillitoe, A. (1958) *Saturday Night and Sunday Morning*, London, W. H. Allen Ltd.
Skeggs, B. (2004) *Class, Self, and Culture*, London, Routledge.
Storey, D. (1960) *This Sporting Life*, London, Longman.
Sylvester, D. (1954) 'The Kitchen Sink,' *Encounter*, 18, pp. 61–63.
Warren, T. (1960) *Coronation Street*, Manchester, Granada Television.
Welsh, I. (1993) *Trainspotting*, New York, W. W. Norton & Company.
Zandy, J. (1993) *Calling Home: Working-Class Women's Writings—An Anthology*, New Brunswick, Rutgers University Press.

27

Mass incarceration, prison labor, prison writing

Nathaniel Heggins Bryant

Mass incarceration is a global phenomenon resting on a complicated nexus of labor and class issues that must be addressed. There are many reasons why we need to highlight the intersections of prison, class, and labor. US prisons are spaces where chattel slavery has in some ways never ended; prison activists routinely evoke current prison labor conditions to slavery. Numerous labor activists and theorists—from Peter Kropotkin, Sacco and Vanzetti, Emma Goldman, and Antonio Gramsci to recent Chinese organizer Meng Han—have been incarcerated for their efforts.[1] Some penal spaces simultaneously rely on exploitative, coercive convict labor on the one hand and powerful unionized prison guard labor on the other. While prison industries have generally mirrored the broader trends of declining industrial labor and increased service-industry work, some penal industries have also provided cheaper pools of labor than northern Mexican *maquilas* and Southeast Asian sweatshops, marking a strange return of industry and manufacturing to the United States (Pimpare 2008, 189). Although some monographs—including Sherry Lee Linkon and John Russo's *Steeltown U.S.A.: Work and Memory in Youngstown* (2002)—have begun to highlight how prisons await laborers after decades of deindustrialization and the overt criminalization of the informal economy, penal spaces are nevertheless largely understudied and undertheorized in working-class and labor studies.[2]

This critical omission is partly because most work on US prisons rightfully foregrounds race, given the patently racialized dynamics of American incarceration practices affecting communities of color. This is most striking given the overrepresentation of African American, Native American, and Latinx prisoners in some form of correctional supervision, which includes pre-trial detention to post-prison parole and probation.[3] Recently, there has been an increased examination of gender and sexuality in prison, because the incarceration rates of women and LGBTQ+ individuals have skyrocketed over the last thirty years; both populations endure indifference, abuse, and violence in institutions predicated upon the young, cisgendered, able-bodied male prisoner of color as the ideal inmate. But we must remember that prisons are institutions that rest upon a concatenation of racialized (and patently racist), gendered (often misogynistic and queerphobic), *and* classist state actions, and they should always be examined along these intersectional axes. As an institution, prison is an inevitability for those who have endured a process of hyper-policing, jailing, and judicial practices that disproportionately affect both minority communities and the poor. The targeted policing of certain neighborhoods, the controversial seizure of private property upon arrest, and the inordinately high costs for both bail and adequate legal defense—in contrast to the overworked state-appointed public defenders that most indigent offenders receive—are some of the factors leading poor people in legal trouble down an inexorable path to prison. (This is best summed up in Jeffrey Reiman and Paul Leighton's textbook *The Rich Get Richer and The Poor Get Prison*, now in its 10th edition, 2012.) As should be evident from this brief overview, it is imperative that we understand how class and labor intersect with carceral practices. To this end, this chapter—which centers on the United States because it establishes global carceral trends—seeks to contribute to that work by outlining a history of prison labor and the rationales behind it before considering dimensions of contemporary US prison writing and literature as forms of intellectual labor and as potential sources of resistance.

A brief history of penal labor

Penal labor history spans Michel Foucault's (1995) famous distinction between regimes that punished and those that discipline. Prison labor, in fact, remains a notable continuity in a process otherwise marked by the slow decline of sovereign, royal power and the uneven transition to ostensibly democratic practices. It may even outlive the current penological systems: science fiction is rife with hard-labor penal colonies, which is itself a telling commentary on our utter lack of imagination when rethinking penal alternatives.[4]

What has not been constant is the nature of prison labor itself, for it has not always resulted in the production of goods or services and the generation of capital. As late as the Victorian period, some prison administrators forced English prisoners to endure hard labor that had very little overt economic worth. Beyond the proverbial rock-breaking associated with 19th-century convict labor, these make-work activities also included walking the treadmill; turning the crank; participating in the shot drill; and picking oakum. All were rarely economically useful. And anecdotal evidence abounds of similar make-work routines in the United States, like the ones made famous in the film *Cool Hand Luke* (1967), in which guards force the eponymous character to dig a grave-sized hole only to fill it up and start all over again.

Ostensibly, this hard work only had two purposes: degrading and brutalizing convicts. On the spectrum between discipline and punishment, these seemingly unproductive activities are clearly more punitive. But even this labor has a productive potential. Strenuous exercise is often heavily repetitive, but this regularity also has the capacity to insinuate a new sense of time and rhythm within the convict's mind and body. Even unproductive make-work schemes could, hypothetically, instill in the body a new mechanical work-discipline. The prisoner tired from breaking rocks has been forcefully, violently docilized, but through sheer repetition he might become accustomed to labor, engendering what Foucault describes as a 'pedagogy of work' (1995, 121). Thus, the cumulative 'economic effect' of hard penal labor is the production of 'individuals mechanized according to the general norms of an industrial society'—the proletarianization of convicts into new workers (1995, 242).[5]

For much of the 19th and 20th centuries in the United States, the restriction of convict labor to public works and the limitation of prison-made goods to state or government use were the two dominant models of production and consumption informing prison labor. Perhaps the most notable example of public-work labor was the construction of New York's Sing Sing prison in 1825, built almost exclusively by one hundred already-incarcerated convicts (Melossi and Pavarini 1981, 136). During the 19th century, labor laws were drafted to keep prison-made goods off the free market, because labor unions rightly contended that prison-manufactured goods would undercut waged labor. This maintains the long-standing labor principle of 'less eligibility,' which utilitarian Jeremy Bentham (1791) defined thus: 'the ordinary condition of a convict doomed to punishment [...] ought not to be made *more eligible* than that of the poorest class of subjects in a state of innocence and liberty' (original emphasis, 122–123).[6] But despite the sentiment, as an 1887 document put it, that 'the hard-working and honest mechanic is insulted by having felons put on an equal footing with him' (quoted in Hawkins 1983, 96), laws intended to protect free labor were routinely flouted until the Great Depression. Then, in the face of global economic devastation, several federal legislative acts—the Hawes-Cooper Act (1929), the Ashurst-Sumners Act (1935), and the Walsh-Healy Act (1936)—and a host of state laws across the country would truly restrict the use of convict labor (90). Though it was bookended by increased patriotic convict productivity supporting both world wars, the stagnation of convict labor that occurred during the Depression would remain the status quo until 1979, when politicians adopted the first legislation to reintroduce labor as a comprehensive part of the corrections process, creating the Prison Industries Enhancement Certification (PIE) Program (91).

Prisoner-made goods were limited to state-use-only for a better part of the 20th century—think of soldiers' helmets (Lamothe 2016) or furniture used by state governments and even state universities (Britto 2015)—but these now constitute a small corner of the prison-labor landscape since states began providing private companies unprecedented access to their prisoners. This process began in earnest in 1984, when penologists, policymakers, and politicians met in two separate conferences to rethink and redesign incarceration, which rapidly increased under the Reagan administration. More than 800 people attended the second conference, 'Factories with Fences: The Prison Industries Approach to Correctional Dilemmas,' which resulted in a national task force seeking to expand prison industries across the nation (Burger 1985, 756).

In 1985, Supreme Court Chief Justice Warren Burger weighed in, contending that prison administrations must make prison sites of production, and this evolution would occur by repealing laws governing prison-made goods and the integration of prison labor with free-market business practices (Burger 1985, 755). The short essay in which he articulates this plan, entitled 'Prison industries: Turning warehouses into factories with fences,' is a remarkable piece of 1980s pro-business rhetoric. This is apparent from the introduction when Burger asks, 'What business enterprise could conceivably succeed with the rate of recall of its products that we see in the "products" of our prison?' (1985, 754). He frames deregulation as a noble effort to introduce more 'freedom' in the free market at the same time that he scapegoats labor unions and their protectionist policies. In arguing 'This great country of ours—the most voracious consumer society in the world—will easily absorb the production of all the inmates who can be trained without displacing private workers' (1985, 755), he attempts to refute the long-standing criticism that prison-work programs undermine free labor. And yet, at the same time Burger and others were shaming unions publicly, unions were daily losing any leverage and negotiating power they once had—and the nation itself was hemorrhaging jobs—precisely because of the same deregulation he promoted.

Perhaps the only thing Burger correctly predicted was our willingness to 'easily absorb the production of all the inmates' we now warehouse (1985, 755). But in every other capacity he was wrong. It took about a decade for the federal government to craft new laws overturning Depression-era statutes limiting the impact of convict labor. They did so partly with the aid of powerful lobbying bodies and at the behest of policy think tanks like the obscure but influential American Legislative Exchange Council (ALEC), a controversial nonprofit organization comprised of conservative politicians and free-market businessmen working together to churn out bills in various state legislatures. Mike Elk and Bob Sloan (2011) enumerate ALEC's impact on recent legal and incarceration trends, which include the movement it spearheaded to change parole by privatizing the process, thereby increasing the private bail bond industry as well as its lobbying efforts to build new for-profit prisons. ALEC members have also had a profound impact on prison labor. In 1993, Texas adopted a proposal crafted by ALEC member and State Representative Ray Allen that sought to expand Texas's modest PIE program; it proved successful and resulted in the drafting of the Prison Industries Act in 1995, a legislative template for state politicians to adopt, adapt, and revise depending on local conditions and state economies. The Prison Industries Act in turn accelerated prison industries across the country, as it provided a legislative blueprint for states to adopt similarly worded laws and mandates governing the access of private business to prison labor.

We can trace the ideological roots of the current situation in the United States back to the burgeoning neoconservative movement under the Nixon administration's demands for increased law and order, demands answered by the Reagan and Bush administrations' War on Drugs and tougher sentencing for crimes. But the Clinton administration also expanded the carceral state when it passed the Violent Crime Control and Law Enforcement Act in 1994, the same year that the North American Free Trade Agreement (NAFTA) began. It is no accident that in the same year politicians signed both a controversial economic treaty ultimately resulting in tens of thousands of lost working-class jobs for Americans and a robust, far-reaching piece of crime legislation. In what followed, we witnessed the deliberate construction of carceral spaces in both deindustrial and former agricultural communities as a means of providing stable forms of employment to a select few while warehousing many others who lost their jobs. In the conflict over the prison boom outside of Youngstown, Ohio, one United Steelworkers spokesman worried about former 'steelworkers guarding steelworkers' (quoted in Linkon and Russo 2000, 62). Elsewhere, California's Central Valley, an important agricultural space, underwent a boom in new prison construction on increasingly worthless land that began in the 1980s and accelerated in the 1990s. As family farming gave way to increasingly mechanized, monoculture-oriented agribusiness conglomerates, many farmworkers lost their jobs and the value of land plummeted, to the extent that California 'bought land sold by big landowners' and 'assured the small, depressed towns now shadowed by prisons that the new, recession-proof, non-polluting industry would jump start local redevelopment' (Gilmore 1998, 184).[7] In general, since the mid-1990s, the rapid development and expansion of carceral spaces has coincided and overlapped with the equally rapid decline in industrial jobs and wage-based, unionized work in the United States; a sharp rise in low-wage, service-oriented labor; and the formulation of a globalized 'risk society,' in which the welfare state's social security nets have either been underfunded or eliminated in favor of 'flexibilized,' precarious work relations that have attended global neoliberal economic practices (Beck 2000, 3). The German sociologist Ulrich Beck notes that in the United States, 'We also have a social net, only it is four times more expensive than the German one. It is called prison' (117). Most recently, the War on Terror and increased anti-immigration law enforcement have expanded the modes, spaces, and means of incarceration, rendering what was once a uniquely American problem into a global prison-industrial complex.

But what is the 'prison-industrial complex'? First coined in 1995 by Mike Davis, the term is a direct reference to President Dwight D. Eisenhower's 1961 warning about the military-industrial complex, a national economy predicated upon weapons development and proliferation, military buildup, and war that posed a dangerous threat to democratic principles and global peace. Davis was one of the first observers to note how increased incarceration rates and prison construction translated to more jobs, higher wages, and increased property values in rural, depressed areas of California. He also carefully documented how the political power and economic contributions of prison-guard labor unions, like the California Correctional Peace Officers' Association, managed to influence states' political legislative processes by donating considerable money to law-and-order politicians and by lobbying for longer, tougher sentencing. Davis condemned the reallocation of state resources away from educational opportunities and community services to fund the prison-construction frenzy, and he was not alone in calling attention to the ways this emerging complex overwhelmingly affected the young, the poor and working-class, and communities of color. Perhaps no better articulation exists of the prison-industrial complex than the vignette he provides of Calipatria, a small town that underwent a 'micro-renaissance' after two new prisons were constructed in Imperial County (Davis 1995, 231). The 1,100 new jobs revitalized a depressed downtown that looked 'like the forlorn set of *The Last Picture Show*,' and one citizen confessed that she was not sure 'if the city could have afforded to light the Little League field without tax revenue from the cornucopia of prison wages' (231).

Since 1995, the term prison-industrial complex has become the dominant metaphor for American mass incarceration, and if anything, the situation has become more acute since Davis first named it. California's prison-guard union has become richer and more powerful; Peter Moskos observes that it now represents 'thirty thousand workers in a $7-billion-a-year industry and has a war chest of about $22 million,' wryly contending that the union's ability to manipulate policy for tougher sentencing has made contemporary prisons 'a new Works Progress Administration without any of the constructive infrastructure, education, or culture' that accompanied original Works Progress Administration endeavors (2011, 78). But perhaps the most significant difference between 1995 and now is the increased exploitation of state prisoners' labor by private corporations. Linda Evans and Eve Goldberg describe this situation succinctly:

> For private business prison labor is like a pot of gold. No strikes. No union organizing. No health benefits, unemployment insurance, or workers' compensation to pay. No language barriers, as in foreign countries. [...] Prisoners do data entry for Chevron, make telephone reservations for TWA, raise hogs, shovel manure, and make circuit boards, limousines, waterbeds, and lingerie for Victoria's Secret, all at a fraction of the cost of 'free labor.'
>
> *(2009, 13)*

What is notable about the current climate of coercive penal labor is not only the sheer variety of manufacturing work accomplished in prison, but also that it has successfully mimicked, in some capacity, the changing dynamics of free labor outside the institution. Service-oriented positions (like phone receptionists) have increased in and out of prison, as have more tech-oriented and ostensibly 'white-collar' work, including data entry and circuit-board construction.

Since the initial naming of the prison-industrial complex, the United States has also experienced the emergence and swelling influence of private, for-profit prisons. Angela Davis, among others, has noted the historical similarities of the private prison and the convict-leasing arrangements during the Reconstruction,[8] but she is quick to note that the problem is not as simple as the dubious ethics of a state paying private companies like Corrections Corporations of America (now called CoreCivic) or the GEO Group to house, feed, and work its prisoners (2003, 93–95). For-profit prison companies, in conjunction with organizations like ALEC, have successfully spearheaded legislative change to continually fill their beds and their coffers, taking a page out of the prison-union playbook: 'the CCA [Corrections Corporations of America] and other private prison groups lobby for and even help draft tough anti-immigration laws, such as Arizona's controversial SB-1070' (Moskos 2011, 81).[9] Private prison corporations have thus created their own niche market by effecting policy change and then offering up their services as convenient warehouses for deportees, funneling people out of already overfull state and federal prisons. But the problems run even deeper. Some of these same companies are now 'public,' insofar as they have listings on the international stock market in which the public can invest. What was once largely a local concern—taxes generated by increased wages helping to light Little League baseball fields—has become a global one: anyone across the world can literally buy stock in warehoused human misery.[10] What else is this but the direst of neoliberal labor situations?

Prison writing

One other dynamic requires our attention: we must consider prison writing in all its various forms—including prison literature—as a specific category of prison-based intellectual labor. According to the United Nations, the control of one's labor is a protected human right: Article 23 of the UN's Universal Declaration of Human Rights begins, 'Everyone has the right to work.' The philosophy that informs this declaration is, in part, that individuals have the right to manage their own labor, which entails the 'control over time, energy, attention, and effort' as all 'vital to one's being able to live a life on one's own terms'; a person should 'be free to determine when to employ it, with whom, under what conditions, and in exchange for what benefits' (Lippke 1998, 536). When compared to other categories of (often compulsory) work available to prisoners, the intellectual labor they elect to do often has more personal, social, economic, and even existential and epistemological values, precisely because of the agency and autonomy it affords them.

However, we should be leery of the term 'prison literature,' and prison abolitionist Dylan Rodríguez provides the best reason why this is the case. The problems with prison literature are twofold. The first is of reification (Rodríguez 2006, 82). There is a political necessity in appending the unique site of production (prison) to our identification of the mode of writing (literature), since doing so refers to the material and existential difficulties faced by individual writers. Nevertheless, calling something 'prison literature' often unintentionally 'legitimizes and reproduces the discursive-material regime of imprisonment,' because it erases any and all kinds of historical, social, and economic specificity: 'to the extent that "the prison" becomes a homogenizing modifier, designating the institutional location of the writer's labor, the genre equilibrates state captivity with other literary moments and spatial sites in civil society, or the free world' (84). In other words, in locating the site of production in an over-generalized, dehistoricized institutional setting, we tend to treat all prison-produced texts in the same way, regardless of the differences that mark various penal institutions, and sometimes we even treat prison-produced texts on par with those works produced in the free world. Embedded in this process of homogenization, one supported by academics and publishers alike, is also 'a discursive gesture toward order and coherence where, for the writer, there is generally neither' (85), as prisons are disruptive, destabilizing, and often traumatizing institutions for their inmates.

The second issue that I want to caution us against, one only implied in Rodríguez's critique, is the tendency to fetishize 'prison literature' and prison culture. This is especially true given the relatively recent appeal and proliferation of popular US prison narratives, including *Oz*, *Prison Break*, *Orange Is the New Black*, and the documentary *13th*, as well as a burgeoning fascination with prison cultures in other places, such as Russia (in fiction films like *Eastern Promises* and *Deadly Code* or the documentary *The Mark of Cain*), Latin America (*Carandiru* and the Netflix series *Narcos*), and elsewhere (the British-Danish film *Bronson*, the Australian film *Chopper*, the French film *Un prophète*, and the Iranian film *Day Break*). Prison literature has a dual appeal: on the one hand, the best of this work has all the trappings of high culture, aesthetic appeal, and, perhaps, transcendence. Like all great art, prison literature's success confirms something about the indomitability of the human spirit in the face of adversity, our infinite capacity for creativity and intelligence no matter the circumstances, and the like. On the other hand, prison literature has, for lack of a better term, a kind of slum appeal for middle- and upper-class (and usually white) consumers. We expect, consume, and thereby often fetishize prison texts based on markers of class-based realism; depictions of sex (especially homosexual rape or consensual lesbian encounters), drugs and addiction, tattoo culture, and violence (particularly overtly racialized prison-gang violence) result in 'gritty,' 'tough,' 'real' texts. This fetishization usually happens uncritically, without much thought as to why audiences desire these elements in prison texts, and, most problematically, these desires inform the production of new texts that feature more of the same. Yes, addiction and rape are a part of prison life, but how recognizable (and at the same time disappointing, and *boring* even) would it be to watch a prison film that documents a different facet of prison life, like the sheer tedium of living in a permanent state of lockdown—23½ hours of no human contact—in a federal supermax? And, as Rodríguez points out, we also give little thought to the individuals who produced these texts and to the psychological ramifications of living through these events. The logic of late capitalism makes it so that anyone investing in a retirement package through the stock market may benefit from mass incarceration, but this same logic is manifested even in the desires we have about prison literature: we require rape and murder from those texts, and we expect that its producers render the world of violence and oppression legible, which also renders it consumable, fungible, and clichéd.[11]

Despite these caveats, prison writing is one of the only means by which we have access to convicts' perspectives and voices and also to those working in prison, to guards who bear prison stigmas and do 'a life sentence in eight-hour shifts' (Conover 2000, 21). If acquiring literacy in the institution itself is a form of work—renowned poet Jimmy Santiago Baca likens his process of becoming literate, days 'of looking up words and writing,' to the physical exhaustion of running 'ten miles' (2001, 185)—then surely the writing they produce should be conceived of as such, too. We can and should look to prison writing—the literary and the non-literary, even the mundane and everyday—as both a form of labor and as a kind of active participation and even resistance to those greater discourses in which prison writers are interpolated and defined, the legal, juridical, and popular narratives told *about* but rarely *by* prisoners. Fyodor Dostoyevsky, a famous ex-prisoner in his own right, once claimed 'The degree of civilization in a society is revealed by entering its prisons' (1860/1957, 76). Since our entrance to prisons is usually barred, prison writing is one way to breach the walls, and, as Nigerian playwright and former political prisoner Wole Soyinka eloquently puts it, 'A breach is worth all in confinement' (1988, 82–83).

In highlighting these dynamics—of prison labor and prison writing—I have two larger desires, two challenges to labor and working-class studies regarding prison. The first, a practical desire, is that continued work in these areas might usefully expand the parameters of prison labor to include education and writing as necessary steps in decarceral and even abolitionist efforts. We must convincingly articulate the different ways that intellectual engagement is individually and even socially valuable, even if it does not necessarily produce wealth or goods, because these efforts are the ones most likely to be defunded as extraneous under the rubric of less eligibility. The second, a more philosophical issue, is that in some small way, we must galvanize a new kind of solidarity between workers of all varieties on both sides of the prison wall. If we recognize the sheer variety of what it means to be productive beyond simply producing *things*, we might be better able to appreciate the ways that all of us act as workers in this world. In other words, I hope that this chapter and future work in the intersections of prison studies, prison activism, and working-class studies helps to redefine, and thus reclaim, what it means to work. This project is motivated in part by André Gorz's call to 'recognize that *real work is no longer what we do when "at work"*: the work, in the sense of *poesis*, which one *does* is no longer [...] done "at work"' (original emphases, 1999, 3). We must, he says, 'exit from "work" and the "work-based society" in order to recover a taste for, and the possibility of, "true" work' (3). Many notable prison-based writers and activists—from Gramsci, George Jackson, Angela Davis, and Mumia Abu-Jamal to less notable activists like David Resendez Ruíz or the activists in the Free Alabama Movement and the Incarcerated Workers Organizing Committee—have taken up these labor issues in their work in different degrees; their lessons might help us to rethink our current moment.[12] The time has come where the principle of less eligibility—that the lowliest worker should always be on a better footing than the prisoner—no longer should apply. After all, a fine line exists between our freedom and others' captivity, and it is diminishing every day. Perhaps by redefining what work is or could be, we could also help to reverse that trend as well.

Notes

1 Peter Kropotkin (1842–1921) was a major anarchist writer and revolutionary who was imprisoned in Russia in 1874 and escaped two years later; he lived in political exile for the rest of his life. Nicola Sacco (1891–1927) and Bartolomeo Vanzetti (1888–1927) were two Italian anarchists arrested and eventually executed by the state of Massachusetts for an armed robbery that many thought they had not committed. Emma Goldman (1869–1940) was a Russian anarchist who was arrested numerous times in the United States for her anti-war and pro-birth control writing and activism, and she was eventually deported in 1917. Antonio Gramsci (1891–1937) was a leading Italian Marxist philosopher jailed for nearly eleven years by the fascist government for his Communist writing and activism, and who died as a result of health deterioration and neglect he experienced while in prison. In November 2016, Meng Han, a labor activist at the Panyu Workers' Centre in Guangdong, was sentenced to twenty-one months in jail for using collective bargaining to secure unpaid compensation for shoe factory workers (Hui 2016).

2 One exception to this trend is sociologist Devah Pager's *Marked: Race, Crime, and Finding Work in an Era of Mass Incarceration* (2007). Pager's study involved pairing up young men with nearly identical profiles and resumes, randomly assigning them criminal backgrounds, and sending them out in search of work in Milwaukee. She gauged success rates by the number of employer callbacks these 'workers' received, and found that the stigma of prison reduced an applicant's potential for callbacks by half (for white applicants) to a third (for African Americans). Perhaps the most surprising finds are that a white applicant *with* a criminal background was slightly more likely to receive a callback than a black applicant *without* a criminal background (17 percent to 14 percent), and that African Americans with a criminal background had an exceptionally low callback rate of 5 percent.

3 The term 'Latinx' is increasingly used as a gender-neutral and queer-inclusive alternative to the terms Latino, Latina, and Latin@; it circumvents the tendency in Spanish grammar to default to masculine forms of words as universal forms. Historically, for instance, we would refer to all people of Latin American descent as Latinos, ending with the masculine 'o,' thereby erasing the presence of Latinas.

4 The penal colony is a ubiquitous science fiction trope. Robert Heinlein depicts a lunar penal colony in *The Moon is a Harsh Mistress* (1966). *Star Trek VI: The Undiscovered Country* (1991) features a Klingon hard-labor colony. *Alien 3* (1992) is set on the remnants of an off-world lead-smelting operation employing prison labor that is owned by a private galactic corporation.

5 The most trenchant critique of Foucault's *Discipline and Punish* (1995) is that his history generally only applied to white men; discipline-based techniques were generally not applied to African and African American slaves and were, at best, unevenly employed against those living under colonial regimes across the world. According to Joy James, Foucault does not account for 'the bodies of nonmales and nonwhites' in *Discipline and Punish* (1996, 26). This means that the variety of other 'abnormal' subjectivities such as 'gay men, lesbians, bisexuals, the poor, women, children, and dark-skinned peoples' are left out of his account (27).

6 The principle of less eligibility is still the prevailing sentiment regarding prisons today, embedded in the complaints about everything from prison educational programs to access to three meals a day; it is at the core of every policy that seeks to reduce so-called amenities and make prisons more punitive and cost-effective.

7 For a more specific description of how these processes played out, see Linkon and Russo's examination of Youngstown, Ohio in *Steeltown, U.S.A.* and Ruth Wilson Gilmore's *Golden Gulag: Prisons, Surplus, Crisis, and Opposition in Globalizing California* (2007).

8 Michelle Alexander (2010) has made a similar claim in *The New Jim Crow: Mass Incarceration in the Age of Colorblindness*, and filmmaker Ava DuVernay echoes these claims in her documentary *13th* (2016), named after the 13th Amendment to the U.S. Constitution, which prohibits slavery except for those people duly convicted of crimes. This provision effectively created a loophole that legally preserved slavery in the United States since the end of the Civil War.

9 Moskos notes that states, like New York and Illinois, with particularly strong prison-guard unions have effectively blocked the use of private prisons, not out of altruism but because of the threat these companies pose to their livelihoods (2011, 79).

10 Since the global market crash in 2008–2009, these stocks have steadily declined; cash-strapped states are considering alternative forms of sentencing that do not involve prison terms, which has negatively impacted private prisons' profits (Takei 2013). Profits decreased further when the Obama administration phased out the federal government's use of private facilities, but the Trump administration rolled back those Obama-era decisions, much to the delight of private prison companies. At the time of this writing, these companies are expecting to profit greatly under Trump, especially given his regime's hard-line immigration practices (Brittain and Harwell 2017).

11 Michelle Brown details this dynamic in *The Culture of Punishment: Prison, Society, and Spectacle*, where she examines 'penal spectatorship,' a cultural phenomenon predicated upon observation, safe voyeurism, and consumption (including tourism) of the incarcerated by those who are free (2009, 10–12).

12 David Resendez Ruíz was a notable Chicano prison activist and jailhouse lawyer who wrote a civil rights complaint regarding his treatment in Texas prisons. In 1979, his complaint was joined with six others into a class-action lawsuit against the state of Texas, resulting in the case *Ruiz v. Estelle*. The case determined that the entire system was cruel and unusual because of systemic guard violence, overcrowding, limited access to healthcare, and the like. Importantly, some of Ruíz's earliest activism started as a result of being forced to work on Texas prison farms—he mutilated himself by cutting his Achilles tendon in protest of the coercion—and during the trial many other prisoner participated in work stoppages in solidarity with Ruíz and the other defendants (Perkinson 2010, 251–285). In 2016, the Free Alabama Movement, in conjunction with the Industrial Workers of the World's Incarcerated Workers Organizing Committee, organized a massive strike against 'prison slavery,' involving upwards of 24,000 prisoners across twenty-four states, beginning on September 9, the 45th anniversary of the Attica prison uprising (Kim 2016).

References

13th, Director Ava Duvernay, 2016.

Alexander, M. (2010) *The New Jim Crow: Mass Incarceration in the Age of Colorblindness*, New York, The New Press.

Alien 3, Director David Fincher, 1992.

Baca, J. (2001) *A Place to Stand*, New York, Grove.

Beck, U. (2000) *The Brave New World of Work*, translated from German by P. Camiller, Malden, Polity Press.

Bentham, J. (1791) 'Panopticon, or the Inspection-House,' in J. Bowring (ed.), *The Works of Jeremy Bentham*, Vol. 4, Edinburgh, William Tait.

Brittain, A. and Harwell, D. (2017) 'Private-Prison Giant, Resurgent in Trump Era, Gathers at President's Resort,' *Washington Post* [online], 25 October. Available at: www.washingtonpost.com/politics/with-business-booming-under-trump-private-prison-giant-gathers-at-presidents-resort/2017/10/25/b281d32c-adee-11e7-a908-a3470754bbb9_story.htmlutm_term=.a9d7d6f8e8c5 [Accessed 10 January 2018].

Britto, B. (2015) 'State Inmates Build Furniture for UMD Buildings,' *The Diamondback* [online]. Available at www.dbknews.com/archives/article_1c3defd0-f1db-11e4-9775-b7dfa005d178.html [Accessed 12 May 2018].

Bronson, Director Nicolas Winding Refn, 2008.

Brown, M. (2009) *The Culture of Punishment: Prison, Society, and Spectacle*, New York, New York University Press.

Burger, W. (1985) 'Prison Industries: Turning Warehouses into Factories with Fences,' *Public Administration Review*, 45, pp. 754–757.

Carandiru, Director Héctor Babenco, 2003.

Chopper, Director Andrew Dominik, 2000.

Conover, T. (2000) *Newjack: Guarding Sing Sing*, New York, Vintage.
Cool Hand Luke, Director Stuart Rosenberg, 1967.
Davis, A. (2003) *Are Prisons Obsolete?* New York, Seven Stories.
Davis, M. (1995) 'Hell Factories in the Field: A Prison-Industrial Complex,' *The Nation*, 260, 7, pp. 229–234.
Day Break, Director Hamid Rahmanian, 2005.
Deadly Code, Director Gabriele Salvatores, 2013.
Dostoyevsky, F. (1860) *The House of the Dead*, Reprint 1957, translated from Russian by C. Garnett, New York, Grove Press.
Eastern Promises, Director David Cronenberg, 2007.
Elk, M. and Sloan, B. (2011) 'The Hidden History of ALEC and Prison Labor,' *The Nation* [online]. Available at: www.thenation.com/article/hidden-history-alec-and-prison-labor/ [Accessed 25 February 2014].
Evans, L. and Goldberg, E. (2009) *The Prison Industrial Complex and the Global Economy*, Oakland, PM Press.
Foucault, M. (1995) *Discipline and Punish: The Birth of the Prison*, translated from French by A. Sheridan, New York, Vintage.
Gilmore, R. (1998) 'Globalisation and U.S. Prison Growth: From Military Keynesianism to Post-Keynesian Militarism,' *Race & Class*, 40, 2/3, pp. 171–188.
Gilmore, R. (2007) *Golden Gulag: Prisons, Surplus, Crisis, and Opposition in Globalizing California*, Berkeley, University of California Press.
Gorz, A. (1999) *Reclaiming Work: Beyond the Wage-Based Society*, translated from French by C. Turner, Cambridge, Polity.
Hawkins, G. (1983) 'Prison Labor and Prison Industries,' *Crime and Justice*, 5, pp. 85–127.
Heinlein, R. (1966) *The Moon is a Harsh Mistress*, Reprint 1997, New York, Orb Books.
Hui, E. (2016) 'Throwing Labor Activists in Jail Won't Solve China's Structural Problem,' *Quartz* [online] 14 November. Available at: https://qz.com/827623/throwing-labor-activists-like-meng-han-in-jail-wont-solve-chinas-structural-problems/ [Accessed 14 January 2018].
James, J. (1996) *Resisting State Violence: Radicalism, Gender, and Race in US Culture*, Minneapolis, University of Minnesota Press.
Kim, E. (2016) 'A National Strike Against "Prison Slavery,"' *The New Yorker* [online] 3 October. Available at: www.newyorker.com/news/news-desk/a-national-strike-against-prison-slavery [Accessed 24 January 2018].
Lamothe, D. (2016) 'Inmates Made Defective Combat Helmets for U.S. Troops—and No One Was Prosecuted,' *Washington Post* [online] 17 August. Available at www.washingtonpost.com/news/checkpoint/wp/2016/08/17/inmates-made-defective-combat-helmets-for-u-s-troops-and-no-one-was prosecuted/?noredirect=on&utm_term=.76ce705a662e&wpisrc=nl_daily202&wpmm=1 [Accessed 12 May 2018].
Linkon, S. L. and Russo, J. (2002) *Steeltown, U.S.A: Work and Memory in Youngstown*, Lawrence, University of Kansas Press.
Lippke, R. (1998) 'Prison Labor: Its Control, Facilitation, and Terms,' *Law and Philosophy*, 17, 5–6, pp. 533–557.
The Mark of Cain, Director Alix Lambert, 2000.
Melossi, D. and Pavarini, M. (1981) *The Prison and the Factory: Origins of the Penitentiary System*, translated from Italian by G. Cousin, Totowa, Barnes and Noble.
Moskos, P. (2011) *In Defense of Flogging*, New York, Basic Books.
Narcos, Created by Chris Bracato, Carlo Bernard, and Doug Miro, 2016–2017.
Orange is the New Black, Created by Jenji Kohan, 2013–2019.
Oz, Created by Tom Fontana, 1997–2003.
Pager, D. (2007) *Marked: Race, Crime, and Finding Work in an Era of Mass Incarceration*, Chicago, University of Chicago Press.
Perkinson, R. (2010) *Texas Tough: The Rise of America's Prison Empire*, New York, Metropolitan Books.
Pimpare, S. (2008) *A People's History of Poverty*, New York, New Press.
Prison Break, Created by Paul Scheuring, 2005–2017.
Reiman, J. and Leighton, P. (2012) *The Rich Get Richer and the Poor Get Prison*, 10th ed., London, Routledge.
Rodríguez, D. (2006) *Forced Passages: Imprisoned Radical Intellectuals and the US Prison Regime*, Minneapolis, University of Minnesota Press.
Soyinka, W. (1988) *The Man Died: Prison Notes of Wole Soyinka*, New York, Noonday.

Star Trek VI: The Undiscovered Country, Director Nicholas Meyer, 1991.
Takei, C. (2013) 'Anonymous Exposes U.S.'s Biggest Private Prison Company as a Bad Financial Investment,' *Blog of Rights* [online] 9 July. Available at www.aclu.org/blog/mass-incarceration/anonymous-exposes-uss-biggest-private-prison-company-bad-financial [Accessed 22 October 2013].
'Universal Declaration of Human Rights.' *United Nations* [online]. Available at: www.un.org/en/universal-declaration-human-rights/ [Accessed 16 April 2014].
Un prophète, Director Jacques Audiard, 2009.

28

Marketing millennial women

Embodied class performativity on American television

Jennifer H. Forsberg

In 2017, media worldwide was inundated with conversations of sexual assault in show business. The ongoing testimony of female actors, producers, and writers in the industry encouraged public outcry in campaigns like the #MeToo and #Timesup Movements to acknowledge systematic gender subordination across workplaces and institutions globally. As a moment dedicated to remedying gender discrimination, it is crucial to call attention to the fact that many characterizations of these abusive and/or demeaning practices of gender disparity are tied to a central narrative of economic volatility. In order to address the relationship between sexual, social, and economic susceptibility, scholars of gender and class must provide perspective on how hierarchical and dominating systems of stratification are made normative, in this case within in the media. Within show business, this process encompasses not only the behind-closed-doors conversations in audition rooms, but also the engineered production of highly curated content distributed by networks worldwide.

Millennial television is a key site for examining working-class identity, because it corresponds with a current media moment where women are producing testimony regarding predatory workplace decorum. In particular, these testimonies speak to the endangered wages, bodily harm, and restricted opportunities that arise from unequal treatment. Despite these calls for change, there remains an active circulation of narratives that make normative the gendered systems that perpetuate gender inequality. However, unlike previous generations, this programming is being consumed by increasing audiences via digital streaming technologies. As platforms like Amazon, Netflix, and Hulu provide a growing catalog of broadcast television and premium cable programming to growing audiences in worldwide markets, the everyday nature of television can inspire patterns of bingeworthy consumption seldom critiqued for problematic representational politics.

While academic interest in television is not new, a study that prioritizes the immense power of gender and class representations on contemporary audiences is needed. This chapter aims to situate the study of representation in not only a millennial economy, but also a new media landscape that circulates notions of gendered global politics in the digital age. As Elizabeth Faue argues in *New Working Class Studies*, the integration of working-class studies and labor history has been a decades-long development that requires ongoing intersectional analyses with which to characterize and illustrate working women's experience (2005). In order to articulate women's experience in a millennial era saturated with mass media, gendered experience—including representations in mass media narratives—must be examined for their 'cultural and political expression of class' drawing on both cultural studies and women's studies (Faue 2005, 20).

An examination of the cultural production of working-class representations in mass media exists across mediums, including popular print publications in the 19th century and the contemporary modes streaming digitally in film and television. As Kathy M. Newman's work attests, representations of class and gender have great social, political, and personal impact on mass-media audiences and scholars should be examining working-class texts that fall outside of activist expectations (2017, 374–375). For instance, Newman's analysis of working-class stories in mid-20th century women's magazines highlights the 'ideological containment' of working-class women by magazines hoping to 'sell products … without heightening [their working-class] collective consciousness' (2002, 236, 231). Newman argues that the magazine *True Story*, in particular, circulated 'parables of working-class identity' which valorized class *im*mobility through 'anti-consumer morality tales' that punished women for class-climbing (2002, 232). Punishments, as Newman describes, were often embodied by women through pregnancy, or presented through domestic disruption (infidelity) and/or familial dispersal (adoption, runaways, imprisonment, etc.) (2002, 235).

In modernizing the media, millennial television circulates a similar 'anti-consumer morality tale' to a new century, facilitating an 'ideological containment' to millennial workingwomen. These 'tales' feature female subjects, often emphasize consequence on the female body, and maintain audience engagement by 'affirm[ing] working-class values, while at the same time containing working-class desire' (Newman 2002, 232). By shifting Newman's argument from mass periodicals to television, millennial mass media participates in the continued containment of women's working experience in a new era characterized by a self-aware struggle for equality, while showcasing that women's bodies remain a central site for envisioning class debates in the United States. For instance, studies like *Reacting to Reality Television: Performance, Audience and Value* suggest that women on television—especially reality television—are seen as accessing new forms of capital through the performance of gender on television, making women 'subject to public judgment' for their 'ability to use the performances of their bodies … to their own material advantage' (Skeggs & Wood 2012, 6, 2). These practices make class visible on the female body, illustrating millennial women's fraught financial status and need for *any* form of capital in a neoliberal market. Like Newman's study of *True Stories*, the mimetic guise of the study of reality television has advanced innovative critical apparatuses for examining contemporary media. However, the critical study of representation and performance—of gender and class identity—requires study of the crafted *fictional* narratives and morality tales that circulate in media too. Previous scholars have spent substantial time studying sitcoms like *Roseanne* (1988–1997; 2018) and *Grace Under Fire* (1993–1998) that proletarianize the plight of the white woman in a bygone era. Yet, the present representational economies of gender and class in millennial sitcoms benefits from the study of and millennial influence of reality television more recently, in order to address the characterization of millennial working-women whose bodies are placed in subordinate positions by hegemonic ideologies of containment from within the contemporary rhetoric of agency and awareness.

The millennial working-class figure of the post-recession period is female, young, unmarried, without children, and underemployed. Most importantly, her entrepreneurial potential is defined by her body and its erotic capital. Millennial sitcoms dramatize not only the self-conscious performance of gender and class seen within reality television, but become the normalizing sites of working-class representations that are consumed by audiences with little attention paid to their oppressive class ideologies. Millennial sitcoms such *The Big Bang Theory* (2007–2019), *New*

Girl (2011–2018), and *Crazy Ex-Girlfriend* (2015–2019) construct and perpetuate conservative and often problematic intersections of gender, race, and class identity that romanticize the universality of youthful economic struggle when class fantasy and a desire for predictability exerts unspoken pressures on a new generation of the American population.

These contexts will be examined in three millennial television shows: *2 Broke Girls* (2011–2017), *Young & Hungry* (2014–2018), and *Girls* (2012–2017) to display how highly-performative female bodies are represented as vulnerable to obscure class stratifications in the millennial age. In these shows, the millennial female body is dramatized in episodes of bad luck, which mask social and economic volatility in an effort to stress lifestyle choices that relate bodily regulation to entrepreneurial potential. These representations depict working-class identity as a female body on display for capitalized object consumption, valuation, and judgment. These narratives circulate ideologies of containment for millennial women, and by proxy the American working class, foregrounding bodily self-consciousness in an effort to stave off subjectivity and class consciousness.

Precarious post-feminist fantasies and embodied regulation

Millennial television participates in a long-standing social tradition wherein working-class women are defined by their bodies, often depicted as 'the hopeless underclass … [t]he polyester-class, overweight occupants of the slow track. Fast food waitresses, factory workers, housewives—members of the invisible pink-collar army' (King, quoted in Skeggs 1997, 100). When millennial sitcoms showcase the working female body through these stereotypes, they communicate neoliberal assertions of sexual capital but overlook gendered debates of labor inequality and economic strife. These practices make class visible on the female body, illustrating millennial women's fraught financial status and need for *any* form of capital in a neoliberal market.

Guy Standing's notion of the 'precariat' helps to further theorize these millennial figures as young 'class-in-the-making' that arises from the global impact of neoliberalism and the loss of labor-related securities (2011, vii.).[1] Television codes the impact of this new material reality on the millennial generation by projecting economic precarity on the female body, featuring *girls*, not women, who are *broke* or *hungry* in an effort to construct a value claim of sexual capital in place of economic vulnerability. While television fashions the 'precariat' within contexts of 'youthful struggles against the dictates of subordinated labour,' it evacuates the political consciousness necessary for changing a highly gendered status quo (Standing 2011, 9). Instead, these television programs prove that economic precarity in a post-recession United States is inseparably tied to the sexual precarity of the female body.

The circulation of precarious representations are part of contemporary marketplace practice that aligns women's bodies with what Jessica Ringrose and Valerie Walkerdine call a 'postfeminist fanta[sy]' (2008, 232). The postfeminist fantasy advises women to 'retain their femininity' from within the 'processes of regulation … individual adaptation and entrepreneurship' (Ringrose & Walkerdine 2008, 232). Regulation may include anything regarding the appearance of the female body, including but not limited to hair, makeup, fashion, and weight. In gender studies, bodily regulation has been mapped onto neoliberal sites like television, which prioritizes 'the sexy female body … [as] hyper-thin' concluding that 'sexiness is leveraged through the way that control is marked on the body' (Winch 2016, 902). Control, and its facade of subjectivity, may be marked by restrictive diets, workout regimens, or plastic surgery to project what is socially valued as sexy (Winch 2016, 902).

Women able to access and maintain regulation of the body 'harness their sexuality for empowerment within a normative paradigm' that is policed by a homosocial female 'gynaeopticon' (Winch

2016, 899, 901). This normative paradigm issues judgments of valuation based on 'respectable' forms of femininity that arise from restriction in order to achieve material gain or capitalize on entrepreneurial potential (Skeggs 1997, 100). Respectability is characterized by the performance of a normative or hegemonic femininity that accumulates capital by devaluing other forms of femininity, which includes working-class femininity. As an abjectified femininity, working-class women have been historically represented through '[d]irt and waste, sexuality and contagion, danger and disorder, [or] degeneracy and pathology,' making gendered respectability specifically class situated (Skeggs 2004, 4). Televised characterizations of respectable femininity perpetuate the benefits of bodily regulation in contained contexts, but also privilege sexual capital as the method for earning economic capital.[2]

Networking the bawdy in America

The CBS show *2 Broke Girls* (2011–2017) follows two twenty-something women: Max Black (Kat Dennings), a sardonic waitress from a broken working-class family who has two jobs, and Caroline Channing (Beth Behrs), a former well-to-do socialite and business student who has been catapulted from her elite life after her father is caught in a financial scandal. The two meet at an out-of-date diner in Brooklyn where Caroline has taken her first ever job alongside Max, a seasoned career waitress.

The dire material situation implicated in the show's title presents Max and Caroline's embodied class characterizations in a post-recession United States. Max contributes real-world advice about work, living frugally, and speaking one's mind in a precarious economy. Meanwhile, Caroline possesses skilled training in business and the importance of self-care. These forms of capital, the social and the cultural, are presented through the female body. Max is stuck in a dead-end service economy job, her curvy body comfortably contained by a tight polyester uniform. Caroline wears the same uniform, but adorns it with a flashy necklace and is vocal about the fact that she gets hives from the cheap fabric. But Caroline's inability to embody her position at the diner also translates to a dire bodily vulnerability: the danger of being homeless. In an early episode, Max finds Caroline sleeping on the subway. Max wakes her and is tased by a startled Caroline. Max falls to the ground comically, struggling to return to her feet as the passengers of the subway car look away from the scene indifferently.

> *Caroline:* Are you all right?
> *Max:* What the hell were you doing?!
> *Caroline:* I didn't know it was you! I thought I was being raped.
> *Max:* That's not what rape feels like.
>
> ('Pilot' 2011)

This early exchange shows Caroline equating a loss of status with the fear of rape, a definitive indicator of how precarious economic positions are represented through embodied female vulnerability on millennial television.

Caroline's character is defined by a privileged life of high fashion, self-care and respectability. Her concern with social acceptance and appearances makes her embarrassed and self-conscious about the decline in her economic status and social reputation. Caroline's overt concern with the control of her body's value assumes her initiation into the world of waitressing work is a testament of a decrease in bodily integrity, one that puts her at risk for not only vulnerability but also violation. For example, Caroline tells Max: 'don't mess with my hand sanitizer. I've already caught poverty this year and I refuse to catch the flu' ('And the Kosher Cupcakes' 2012). For

Caroline, entry into a working-class life as a waitress is problematically equated to poverty and coded as a contagion. In this context, Caroline's primary concern is retaining bodily control—her health *and* her respectability—despite her sudden precarity.

Max, by contrast, is bawdy and defined by her unreserved body. She has no filter when she speaks, makes explicit comments about sex, and purposefully commands sexual attention with her voluptuous figure. Max recognizes that rape is Caroline's biggest fear, yet makes jokes about it in order to ridicule the gendered respectability foreclosed to working-class femininity. The many references to rape throughout the first season become a testament to the show's central plot antagonism: gendered respectability amid economic precarity.

Max consistently addresses Caroline in reference to rape, communicating the inevitability of her interpellation. When responding to Caroline's complaint about the heat, Max says 'Stop fighting it, just give in to it. I don't know why I'm quoting a rapist' ('And Strokes of Goodwill' 2011). When Caroline needs to find an affordable dentist, Max warns: 'If you go back there with him, you'll need a bite guard and a rape guard' ('And the Rich People Problems' 2011). Max's level of comfort joking about rape culture may stir a frenzied response across numerous critical camps, but her discourse can be linked to women of a new era. For instance, contemporary television writer and director Jill Solloway argues that the only people who can make rape jokes are 'women, and men that we decide. It's like the Supreme Court and porn, only we know when it's funny or not funny and we'll tell you' (quoted in Romano 2012). This makes the discussion of rape proprietary content that serves as an exercise in social and gender respectability as it classifies the female body.

Max and Caroline call attention to a provocative tendency for millennial women to use the regulation of the female body as a status marker for homosocial containment in relation to class identity. Characterizing the economic inequality central to each female protagonist renders Max's frequent reference to rape a new socioeconomic reality for millennial women. The pairing of economic precarity to bodily vulnerability represents the millennial woman in the context of gendered violence in the United States.[3] Max's outspoken and unapologetic working-class body serves as a counterpoint to Caroline's attempts for rigid self-protection. By embodying the precarity of the times, Max attempts to earn a sense of power by articulating a dangerous morality tale that uses rape jokes to over-determine the female working-class body. This leverages power based on impropriety or unrespectable femininity, utilizing social and psychological class warfare and the 'gynaeopticon' against class-mobile figures like Caroline (Winch 2016, 899).

Max frequently capitalizes on Caroline's inner-most fear of rape by presenting a general desensitization to the potential dangers of her own precarious position. For example, when Max's romantic interest, Johnny, knocks on her apartment window in the middle of the night, the following exchange takes place:

> *Caroline:* What is Johnny doing here at 3:00 a.m.? I thought it was a rapist or something.
> *Max:* Rapists don't knock and wave. And if they looked like that, we wouldn't call them rapists.
>
> ('And Hoarder Culture' 2011)

Max's response to Caroline shows the complexity of the using the body as class representative. While Caroline equates any unexpected or dangerous situation as the threat of rape, Max utilizes the vulnerable female body to showcase her own sexual appetite. Max's refusal to exhibit self-control initiates the embodied class demeanor of the show, which introduces Caroline's upper-class worldview to the precarity of a working woman's social position.

2 Broke Girls conflates sex, sexuality, and the regulation of the body to display how liberated and empowered femininity has become a marketable commodity saturated with class codes in the millennial era. These codes promote the economic implication of *broke girls* to audiences as the failure of female respectability and bodily regulation, overlooking the material reality of economic inequality.

Cable TV dinners: As American as apple pie

While *2 Broke Girls* presents working-class identity through embodied precarity and regulation, Free Form Television's *Young & Hungry* explores working-class representation through heteronormative associations with economic security. The show opens in a San Francisco penthouse as millennial food blogger Gabi Diamond (Emily Osment) arrives at the front door of Josh Kaminski (Jonathan Sadowski), a young technology mogul and self-made millionaire seeking a personal chef. In a hurry because she can only afford to park her car for 12 minutes, a naïve Gabi is asked by Kaminski's housekeeper to enter through the service entrance to interview ('Pilot' 2014). Unaware of her subordinate position as potential employee and lack of qualifications against other professionals, Gabi manages to charm Josh with her folksy personality and secures a test dinner. When Josh's dinner date breaks up with him, he and Gabi are left to eat the meal she has prepared, and she earns the job. Yet hours of drunken commiserating over failed romance results in Gabi and Josh sleeping together. This immediately connects Gabi's employment her role as sexual object in the show.

Gabi's story serves as not only a working-class morality tale, but also a testament of how the millennial economy reinforces normative control over the female body in the power differential between employer and employee. Gabi's precarious position as employee and sexual partner puts her in danger of both losing her job and her bodily autonomy. This concern is showcased by Gabi's roommate Sofia (Aimee Carrero), a high-energy and ambitious Latina para-professional who fears she will have to cover Gabi's rent *again*. Sofia's response equates Gabi's choice to have sex with her boss a precarity that moves beyond financial burden.

> *Gabi:* …I left my chef knives there [at the penthouse]. They cost more than my car.
> *Sofia:* Well you better go get them, we're gonna need them if we're gonna live on the streets.
>
> ('Pilot' 2014)

Sofia connects Gabi's failure of bodily regulation to a heightened economic hardship of not just unemployment, but homelessness and the danger of living on the streets. Sofia's response repurposes the professional tools Gabi uses for work into potential weapons to keep their bodies safe in a tailspin of downward mobility that is imminent with the loss of a single paycheck. Sofia's character relays the power of female respectability and is often depicted as the voice of reason, telling Gabi to conduct herself—and more importantly her body—'like your job and paying our electric bill depend on it' ('Young & Ringless' 2014).

When Gabi returns to the penthouse for her knives, she apologizes for her poor behavior. Josh surprisingly responds, 'I'm not firing you. A lawyer said I couldn't.' Gabi shows relief because she retains her wage-earning potential ('Pilot' 2014). While Gabi's entrepreneurial spirit accomplishes becoming employed, it also provides a false sense of security based on systematic subordination by her employer, her presence and labor merely ornamental. Problematically, Gabi's work arrangement exploits her female body, making her precarious employment secured by her sexuality and not her professional skill.

The penthouse becomes a setting for an embodied and normative femininity where Gabi's employment requires her to perform an objectified femininity that performs respectability through class fantasy: playing house with her boss, who pays the rent and buys the groceries. While Gabi knows that that Josh is 'way out of [her] league' and considers herself 'an expired Twinkie' in comparison to his usual 'fancy chocolate éclair' girlfriends ('Pilot' 2014), the show presents an on-again-off-again desire for Gabi to become Mrs. Kaminski and transform her paid employment into unpaid domestic labor. Skeggs & Wood argue that these 'complex forms of exchange … [allow women to] produce a return through the exchange relation of marriage to access economic security' (2012, 8). Gabi's employment and vision of gendered respectability is recalibrated by the demands of a service industry position in the millennial age. *Young & Hungry* informs Gabi's body-based service work through reference to her gender and working-class stereotyped parents, a waitress mother and mechanic father. Their service positions intimate the lack of class mobility in America, denoting how the next generation of millennial women must learn to serve the marketplace, only now through entrepreneurial bodily capital in an economy of predatory one-percenters looking to strengthen the status quo.

For instance, the Season One DVD promotes Gabi in a short skirt and apron, holding an apple pie to impress her Americana-connections upon global audiences, as well as the international business dinners that Josh hosts ('Young & Ringless' 2014). As a personal chef, Gabi's relationship to the pie allows her to capitalize on her millennial femininity by drawing on classic American stereotypes of waitress and housewife, both of which are rooted in the presentation of rigid mid-century class and gender roles. Gabi's correlation to this form of femininity allows the show to celebrate the benefits of performing traditional gender roles as a competitive edge for women in a neoliberal marketplace. Ironically, Gabi's class-climbing associations act as a direct affront to gendered respectability, finding these performative roles degrading when Sofia approaches her with a job prospect while she bakes in her leisure time.

> *Sofia:* So all we have to do is wear cute outfits and get guys to drink. Like we do on weekends anyway, but now we'll get paid!
>
> *Gabi:* I don't know. It sounds kind of sexist. I mean, why don't you just throw us back to the '50s where women were stuck in the kitchen slaving away for their men. (Bell dings) Ooh, Josh's apple pie is done!
>
> ('Young & Punchy' 2014)

Gabi and Sofia's discussion of a potential paycheck is also a debate about how to capitalize on the female millennial body. Their conversation suggests that everything has a price, in this case $500 for one night of work, and proves that economic need overrules notions of internally dictated gendered respectability.

The façade of autonomous choice in a neoliberal market—whether or not to capitalize on the body—is presented to obscure the oppressive politics of Gabi's sexual objectification throughout the first season. This becomes abundantly clear when Gabi thinks she may be pregnant after her encounter with Josh. In a marketplace that rewards normative regulation of the female body, unplanned and unwed pregnancy becomes a loss of economic potential and a testament to caste-like millennial class divisions. Gabi asks Sofia to bring a pregnancy test to the penthouse, which she reports is delayed because 'I didn't have enough cash, so I had to go home shake down our couch' ('Young & Pregnant' 2014). Unable to afford either the pregnancy test or the impact of pregnancy and childrearing on her career, Gabi finds herself at odds with the success of her thin, well-styled female body. While her sexual encounter with Josh may have had fantasy-driven promise for domestic bliss, her potential pregnancy indicates a momentary lack of regulation that threatens her financial stability and professional aspirations. While waiting for the test results, Gabi confesses: 'I finally got my dream job. And it was gonna lead to my dream career … And now all of it could be ruined because of one stupid drunken mistake' ('Young & Pregnant' 2014). The precarity of Gabi's statement notes the difficulty of millennial women to advance in the neoliberal marketplace with children. Specifically, the show perpetuates the notion that pregnancy and motherhood interrupts if not derails upward moves from a job to a career, retaining precarious economic context rather than stable ones. Gabi's character makes visible the difficult social position of millennial women, who must use their feminine body as a form of capital but in doing so are taxed by forms of bodily regulation that include not only appearance but reproductive health as economic classifiers ('Young & First Time' 2015).

The containment of Gabi's working-class character indicates the realities of female subordination and dependence on male economies, offering embodied morality tales of class climbing. By performing respectable femininity through bodily regulation, Gabi represents how the millennial generation self-consciously conflates domestic service with sexual objectivity as entrepreneurial potential, when it offers only the precarious promise of social mobility.

Reproducing the laboring female body

While not a sitcom, HBO's critically acclaimed drama *Girls* (2012–2017) is central to a conversation of millennial women on television. *Girls*' female cast navigates the pressures and politics of contemporary existence, romantic relationships and professional aspirations in New York City. Lead character Hannah, played by creator Lena Dunham, is presented as comfortable in her often un-regulated body, often dressed in short and revealing clothing, unselfconscious of her appearance. Hannah's character is unapologetic about her presence in body and mind, her disregard for bodily regulation, gendered respectability, and the valuation of taste a provocative conclusion to the ways that class is projected on the female body in American television.

Television critic David Hinckley (2012) notes that the youthful ensemble of *Girls* presents a working-class version of the bourgeois New York experience of *Sex in the City* (1998–2004). The less-affluent female experience of the millennial cast of *Girls* is contextualized by the precarity of a post-recession economy, characters like Hannah seen relying on the social capital of parents and friends to remedy economic ills. These parameters elaborate on Hinckley's claim, to acknowledge how *Girls* embodies these class codes as fantasies of a post-feminist, neoliberal marketplace. Like Gabi in *Young & Hungry*, Hannah never *really* seems at risk of losing her apartment or being unable to eat. And while Hannah may take on a service economy job like Max or Caroline in *2 Broke Girls*, it is in a modern coffee shop that requires little responsibility or quality customer service, allowing her flexible time to pursue her creative writing.

Hannah and her cast of friends exemplify what *New York Times Magazine* writer Wesley Morris calls 'an alternative realm—a kind of "whatever" class' in millennial television (2016). This 'whatever class' depicts 'almost everybody belong[ing] to the same generic, vaguely upper-class class' despite their 'actual job' (Morris 2016). This predominantly white, millennial representation 'tend[s] to fetishize labor,' and exchanges work for a wage for *work on the self* (Morris 2016). This implicates a neoliberal method where female bodily regulation is featured as the primary method for attaining the elusive fiction of economic security, shifting conversations of class identity into the presentation and performance of gender.

In *Girls*, work on the self provides a nuanced form of self-regulation wherein the respectability of the female body is collapsed with the personal and professional gains of a millennial economy. The pressures of these classifying practices culminate in *Girls*' series finale, 'Latching' (2017), which presents Hannah pregnant in her last trimester and having moved, on her own, from Brooklyn to upstate New York. She has taken a teaching position at a local college and has rented a large two-story house with nice furnishings. Friend Marnie (Allison Williams) breaks into Hannah's house in the middle of the night, crawls into Hannah's bed, and begs to help with the baby. Marnie's plea, pitched as a friendly obligation, offers unpaid domestic service in exchange for a sense of security after she has lost her apartment and is economically volatile for the first time in her privileged life. After Hannah gives birth, this three-person household: Hannah, Marnie, and son, Grover, exist in a queer family unit riddled with domestic and gendered antagonism for control. As the sole parent and provider, Hannah is in a constant competition with Marnie, relegating her to a subordinate position of servitude. Overwhelmed, Marnie calls Hannah's mother Loreen (Becky Ann Baker) for assistance, and she also moves into the house. The show quickly constructs Marnie and Loreen as the providers of live-in housework and childcare, allowing Hannah to care for herself and pursue her career.

The episode 'Latching' articulates a post-feminist and neoliberal crossroads for young women on television. Hannah's status as a member of the 'whatever class' not only over-determines her economic stability based on a rare academic appointment in a precarious humanities field, but characterizes her as an independent, middle-class, single-mother that can take on a breadwinner role by having other women perform her domestic service. Hannah's entrepreneurial role commands new forms of regulation on her female body. When she cannot breastfeed her son but refuses to buy formula for anti-consumerist reasons, her body becomes defined by a social-lifestyle imperative rooted in respectable femininity, as well as a mis-regulated site of a sex-related biological function.

Hannah is absent from the house for much of the episode, escaping the pressure of Marnie and Loreen's gynaeopticon on her unproductive, reproductive body. After being scolded by them one too many times, Hannah hastily dresses in an oversized hooded sweatshirt and baggy blue jeans—clothes that obscure her femininity—and roams the neighborhood one afternoon. The episode frames Hannah as out of place: in her new middle-class neighborhood and in her own body, which is still recovering from childbirth. Wandering into the night, Hannah encounters a teary teenaged girl who runs by her in only a tee-shirt, hooded sweatshirt and underwear. Hannah pleads with the girl to stop, the scene implying sexual assault. The girl stops, but evades Hannah's questions. Hannah removes her pants and shoes and dresses the girl with them, she herself now standing vulnerable in the street, barefoot and in her underwear. Now clothed and calmer, the girl reveals that she has had a fight with her mother over homework. Shocked and sympathetic to the responsibilities of parenthood, Hannah demands her clothes back, but the girl runs away comically in the oversized pants and shoes. Defeated, Hannah begins to walk home, nearly naked, when an African-American police officer in a patrol car stops to ask if she is all right. Hannah explains that she lives in the neighborhood and the officer slowly follows her with his headlights shining in the road to ensure her safety. Hannah arrives home to find Marnie and Loreen bonding on the front porch. Hannah hears her son cry and goes inside to tend to him after a day away. After weeks of failed attempts, Hannah successfully breastfeeds, but only after Marnie and Loreen have already fed the baby formula.

This multilayered ending to the series prioritizes not only the female body in the millennial era, but also the class fantasies projected upon the laboring female body as it moves from a diminutively object-driven *girl* to a subjectivity-possessing *woman*. When Hannah strips herself to protect the body of a young, vulnerable girl, she exhibits an interesting class resiliency able to expose her own body without fearing its vulnerable state. This watershed moment allows Hannah's newly maternal body to inhabit a variety of performative positions: she is coded as a tom-boy whose abject femininity conveys working-class stereotypes, an overbearing middle-class mother, and, most provocatively, an absent breadwinning father. But it isn't until Hannah places herself in the vulnerable and ambiguous class position of the young girl—standing half-naked on the street requiring the protection of a police watch—that she can embrace the distinctly white and privileged fantasy of bodily regulation as a form of security in the millennial era. In the end, Hannah's 'whatever class' body and 'vaguely upper class' worldview align to construct an embodied respectability that is credentialed by the bodily capital of breastfeeding. It is not Hannah's employment or neighborhood status that indicates her millennial class status, but rather the insecurity of her body in the series finale.

The representation of millennial women as girls relies on heteronormative contexts that emphasize the potential capital of the female body as a subjectivity-desiring corporeal object within ideologies of containment. As providers of a performative femininity, millennial programming reproduces female subordination in service roles or domestic labor that are often unpaid or underpaid to reaffirm the façade of white, *middle-class* heteronormativity in America. This practice results in the systematic subordination of women in precarious economic situations in the 21st century, rendering the female body a highly regulated object with the façade of entrepreneurial agency in America. In this system, female subjectivity—and thus the fantasy of economic stability—can only be earned through bodily regulation, or a woman's ability to capitalize on her body through regulatory control. Consequently, this emphasis on respectability also results in blame-oriented rhetoric that abjectifies any refusal or failure to capitalize on bodily regulation. This neoliberal impasse holds women accountable for their status roles in an unpredictable economic marketplace, while overlooking 21st-century forces that impair or impede women's control over their bodies.

As nations across the globe celebrate the claiming of women's rights in an effort to actualize gender equality, mass-marketed American television circulates entrepreneurial narratives that gloss over the embodied effects of economic inequality in the United States. Working-class studies scholars interested in the representation of class identity possess the methodology with which to identify the racial and gendered components of narratives that perpetuate the female body as sexually and socially vulnerable in lieu of exposing economic volatility. These facets are crucial to the growth of the contemporary moment since such representations overlook labor devaluation, racial privilege, and sexual violence in the millennial era, and instead celebrate a fantasy-driven form of social mobility divorced from material conditions. While the rationale of a neoliberal marketplace has provided an opportunity for women to become participants in economic markets that have otherwise excluded them for centuries, contemporary television often undermines the material effects of gendered class inequality. This results in the further objectification of the status and struggle of working women as opportunistic female bodies who are contained by a middle-class, heteronormative morality perpetuated by popular media.

Notes

1 Standing suggests that 'the precariat consists of people who lack the seven forms of labour-related security: ... Labour market security, Employment security, Job security, Work security, Skill reproduction security, Income security and Representation security. ... Not all those in the precariat would value all seven forms of security, but they fare badly in all respects' (2011, 9–11).

2 For instance, compare *Here Comes Honey Boo Boo*'s (2012–2014) Mama June Thompson and her televised rise to middle-class respectability after major weight lost and a makeover in 2017. Media outlets judged Thompson for attempting to mask her working-class origins. However, upper-class women like Paris Hilton and Nicole Richie are celebrated for slipping their thin, regulated bodies into overalls and factory uniforms for their poverty tourism reality show *The Simple Life* (2003–2007).

3 In 2015, the National Sexual Violence Resource Center reported that one in five women in the United States are sexually assaulted in their lifetime.

References

2 Broke Girls. (2011–2017) Creators Whitney Cummings and Michael Patrick King.
'And Hoarder Culture.' (2011) *2 Broke Girls*. Series 1, episode 8. CBS, 7 November 2011.
'And the Kosher Cupcakes.' (2012) *2 Broke Girls*. Series 1, episode 17. CBS, 20 February 2012.
'And Strokes of Goodwill.' (2011) *2 Broke Girls*. Series 1, episode 3. CBS, 3 October 2011.
'And the Rich People Problems.' (2011) *2 Broke Girls*. Series 1, episode 4. CBS, 10 October 2011.
The Big Bang Theory. (2007–2019) CBS.
Crazy Ex-Girlfriend. (2015–2019) The CW.
Faue, E. (2005) 'Gender, Class, and History,' in Russo, J. and Linkon, S. L. (eds.) *New Working Class Studies*, Ithica, Cornell University Press.
Girls. (2012–2017) Creator Lena Dunham.
Grace Under Fire. (1993–1998) ABC.
Here Comes Honey Boo Boo. (2012–2014) TLC.
Hinckley, D. (2012) 'Lena Dunham's "Girls" Looks at "Sex and the City" World Through Young Working-Class Eyes.' *New York Daily News*, www.nydailynews.com/entertainment/tv-movies/lena-dunham-girls-sex-city-world-young-working-class-eyes-article-1.1059927 (Accessed 14 June 2017).
'Latching.' (2017) *Girls*. Series 6, episode 10. HBO, 16 April 2017.
Morris, W. (2016) 'TV's Dwindling Middle Class.' *The New York Times Magazine*. www.nytimes.com/2016/05/01/magazine/tvs-dwindling-middle class.html (Accessed 14 June 2017)
National Sexual Violence Resource Center. (2015) 'Statistics About Sexual Violence.' www.nsvrc.org/sites/default/files/publications_nsvrc_factsheet_media-packet_statistics-about-sexual-violence_0.pdf (Accessed 14 June 2017).
New Girl. (2011–2018), Fox.
Newman, K. M. (2002) 'True Lies: *True Story Magazine* and Working-Class Consumption in Postwar America,' *The Minnesota Review*, 55–57, pp. 223–244.
Newman, K. M. (2017) 'The Labor Plot: One Hundred Years of Class Struggle on the Silver Screen,' in Cole, N. and Lauter, P. (eds.) *A History of Working-Class American Literature*. Cambridge, Cambridge University Press.
'Pilot.' (2011) *2 Broke Girls*. Series 1, episode 1. CBS, 19 September 2011.
'Pilot.' (2014) *Young & Hungry*. Series 1, episode 1. Free Form, 25 June 2014.
Ringrose, J. and Walkerdine, V. (2008) 'Regulating The Abject,' *Feminist Media Studies*, 8, 3, pp. 227–246.
Romano, T. (2012) 'Rainn Wilson, "2 Broke Girls," and the Rise of the Rape Joke.' *The Daily Beast*. www.thedailybeast.com/rainn-wilson-2-broke-girls-and-the-rise-of-the-rape-joke (Accessed 14 June 2017).
Roseanne. (1988–1997; 2018) ABC.
Sex in the City. (1998–2004) HBO.
The Simple Life. (2003–2005) FOX.
The Simple Life. (2006–2007) E!
Skeggs, B. (1997) *Formations of Class & Gender: Becoming Respectable*, London, Sage.
Skeggs, B. (2004) *Class, Self, Culture*, New York, Routledge.
Skeggs, B. and Wood, H. (2012) *Reacting to Reality Television: Performance, Audience and Value*, London, Routledge.
Standing, G. (2011) *The Precariat: The New Dangerous Class*, London: Bloomsbury Academic, eBook Academic Collection EBSCO*host* (Accessed 14 June 2017).
Winch, A. (2016) '"I Just Think It's Dirty and Lazy": Fat Surveillance and Erotic Capital,' *Sexualities*, 19, 8, pp. 898–913.
'Young & First Time.' (2015) *Young & Hungry*. Series 2, episode 5. Free Form, 22 April 2015.
Young & Hungry. (2014–2018) Creator David Holden.
'Young & Pregnant.' (2014) *Young & Hungry*. Series 1, episode 4. Free Form, 16 July 2014.
'Young & Punchy.' (2014) *Young & Hungry*. Series 1, episode 6. Free Form, 30 July 2014.
'Young & Ringless.' (2014) *Young & Hungry*. Series 1, episode 2. Free Form, 2 July 2014.

Part VI

Activism and collective action

Section introduction

Activism and collective action

Scott Henkel

In the final scene of the 1954 film *Salt of the Earth*, the sheriff and two deputies of Zinctown, New Mexico—a company town owned by the Delaware Zinc company—attempt to evict the film's main characters, Esperanza and Ramón Quintero, from their home. By this point, the film's characters have been on strike against Delaware Zinc for several months. The police, who act on the company representatives' orders, plan to use the eviction as a provocation to arrest the strikers and, therefore, to beat the strike.

As the police throw the Quinteros' possessions on the lawn, nearby people shout 'Eviction! Eviction!' and their voices travel like call and response through Zinctown and the surrounding communities (Wilson 1993, 84). These calls bring a multitude of people—women and men, miners and other workers, Mexican-Americans and Anglos, adults and children—into the street in front of the Quinteros' house. For a moment, the police continue to throw the Quinteros' possessions into the yard, until some of the women simply pick them up and put them back into the house. The police are puzzled by the women's actions, until they notice the crowd, which has grown to a hundred or more people, staring fiercely back at them. The crowd's solidarity stops the eviction, and in the face of a strongly implied threat from that crowd, the police retreat. The characters do not yet know it, but stopping the eviction means that they have also won the strike.

This crowd's multiracial, gender-inclusive, cross-age solidarity did not just materialize from the air in the film's final scene. One of the film's main storylines is how difficult it is to build such solidarity by breaking down traditional gender, race, and class divisions (Camacho 2008). *Salt of the Earth* is a fictional retelling of an actual strike in Grant County, New Mexico, in 1951, in which the male miners, who were mostly Mexican-American, were forced by a Taft-Hartley injunction either to give up the strike or to continue and, thus, break the law. Instead of choosing between those two bad options, the miners' spouses and sisters propose to take over the picket line (Wilson 1993). When they do—after much debate and hostility, even from their spouses and friends—their activism builds new bonds of solidarity, which becomes the basis of their power and also the reason why they win the strike.

The story of *Salt of the Earth* shows a range of problems and possibilities for working-class activism and collective action. What forms does activism take? What does it mean to take action with others? Who takes part in what actions, and when they do, what particular risks do they face? What is the nature of institutionalized power? What is the nature of the collective power of people working together to achieve common goals? Important works of scholarship (Zweig 2011) and the daily experience of workers show that in comparison to the concentrated power of corporations and states, an individual worker has much less power. Yet people act collectively around the basis of many identities and aspects of their lives, and when they do, they multiply their power and have the possibility to build it to such a degree that it can balance or even outweigh the concentrated power of employers and legislators (Montag 1999).

While that situation may seem straightforward, it is complicated by an almost-endless number of factors. Consider again the women activists of *Salt of the Earth*: most of them work tireless hours, unwaged, in their homes, which they do not own—Zinctown is a company town, and all the property is owned by that company. Ramón, like many of the men in the film, has a near-unquestioned role as the household's head when the story begins. Therefore, a range of cultural and structural prohibitions make the women's activism difficult: the women must confront the sexism of people who ought to be their allies, and in the process, they must grow into roles many have never played before; the male miners must confront their gendered privileges or else lose the strike. On the picket line, the women endure a range of intimidation by the police, from lewd taunts to physical attacks (Wilson 1993). The men's union has a constitution that prohibits non-members—thus, all the women in the community—from voting in a union meeting (Wilson 1993).

What *Salt of the Earth* shows, in other words, is how traditional, hierarchical relationships of gender, race, and class are obstacles to activism and collective action, and how the renegotiation of those relationships along more equal lines is one key to effective, even transformational, activism. As Deborah Silverton Rosenfeldt writes, the film represents Esperanza as a strong female lead,

> a female hero who not only struggles and suffers but grows and wins. And she gains not simply in self-knowledge, not simply through wrestling a piece of her own turf from an unchanged society; rather, her victory represents the shared triumph of the community.
>
> *(1993, 93)*

Esperanza's activism is not only personally liberating—her collective action with her community has the potential to be tremendously powerful. *Salt of the Earth* shows the anatomy of a successful struggle, waged by people whose solidarity has not come easily. Even though that solidarity has had to be built in painstaking ways, once it is built, the characters find that they can accomplish remarkable things and achieve goals that they could not have won alone.

Scenes like these from *Salt of the Earth* have played out in many different working-class struggles, in a variety of ways. Debates and theories about activism and collective action in working-class studies are parts of several scholarly fields, from literature to critical race and gender theory,[1] history,[2] philosophy,[3] sociology,[4] anthropology, and economics. Questions about the nature of power—the power to overpower others and the power of human brains and muscles—have been a continuous source of philosophical debate from Enlightenment thinkers like Spinoza up to the present day (Henkel 2017). There are many forms of activism, such as subtle actions like slowing the pace of work (Shotwell 2006), online activism (Srinivasan 2017), critical work that produces ideas to build constituencies (Robin 2016), critiques of academic labor (*Workplace: A Journal of Academic Labor*), mass actions like general strikes (Luxemburg 2007), and mass movements that realign whole populations (Du Bois 1998). Often the very names of these actions are debated—what some call riots, others call rebellions (Gutierrez 2017). Likewise, there are many organizations for collective action: unions, community organizations, political parties, consciousness-raising study groups, spontaneous gatherings.

This chapter first gives an overview of the theoretical and scholarly conversations about activism and collective action, with a focus on debates about its methods and organizational forms, in a broad historical scope. Next, this chapter sketches the range of responses to collective action: the ways in which activism and collective action have been hindered historically, by law and by force. The chapter concludes by previewing the essays in this section.

What are activism and collective action in working-class studies?

Perhaps the first response to this question is to clarify the terms: activism and collective action in working-class studies most often mean the intent to act and to cooperate with others in pursuit of common goals. This consensual relationship can be deliberate or spontaneous, like the careful, methodical efforts of building a union's membership, which has been argued recently and persuasively by Jane F. McAlevey (2016) in her book *No Shortcuts: Organizing for Power in the New Gilded Age*, for example, or the last-straw action that sends people out into the streets without any advance planning, as shown in the recent film *Detroit* (2017).[5] It is often difficult to distinguish between deliberate and spontaneous collective action: even bureaucratic forms of organization can act unpredictably at times. Spontaneity is not the creation of something from nothing, but rather the emergence of something into view, like simmering water that comes to a boil. Therefore, whether deliberate or spontaneous, collective action implies the affirmative choice of a group of people to work together to achieve an end that they would not be able to achieve alone.

Furthermore, the terms to use are themselves a matter of some debate. The film *Detroit* builds from the events in July 1967 in that city, in which a group of African Americans were arrested in a bar. As their arrest proceeded, people began to gather in the street outside, protesting the arrest. From there, the events escalated into one of the most significant, large-scale collective actions in recent American history. Most newspaper writers covering the event at the time called it a race riot (Gutierrez 2017). Participants in that event called it 'The Great Upheaval,' as do Dan Georgakas and Marvin Surkin in their book *Detroit, I Do Mind Dying: A Study in Urban Revolution* (2012).

In *Black Reconstruction in America, 1860–1880*, W. E. B. Du Bois (1998) uses the term 'general strike' to describe the mass movement of emancipated black workers from the southern plantations to the Federal army camps. What Du Bois calls the General Strike, therefore, is the two-part mass movement, in the years following 1862, of black workers to defect from southern plantations as soon as they could break their chains and then align their labor with the Union army as it moved through the South. This mass movement, which was not centrally organized or planned, had the effect of depriving the slaveocracy of its primary source of labor while simultaneously bolstering the forces of abolition. Du Bois writes that the general strike

> was not merely the desire to stop work. It was a strike on a wide basis against the conditions of work. It was a general strike that involved directly in the end perhaps a half million people. They wanted to stop the economy of the plantation system, and to do that they left the plantations.
>
> *(1998, 67)*

This strike, Du Bois argues, was the decisive event of the war. Much of the scholarship on *Black Reconstruction* questions whether the term 'general strike' is adequate or accurate to describe the unplanned, leaderless leaving of the plantation en masse when the wartime conditions made it possible to break the bonds of enslavement (Foner 2013; Robinson 1977; Villard 1936). Perhaps the questions about Du Bois' use of the term general strike arise because the planned, concerted strike action is the most widely recognized form of activism and collective action by working people. The classic book on the topic is Jeremy Brecher's *Strike!* (2014), which has recently been re-released in an updated and expanded edition.

The proper form of organization for working-class collective activism has historically been a subject of much debate. The bigotry and exclusiveness of many craft unions in the U.S. during the 19th and 20th centuries are well documented (Roediger 2007). Nevertheless, the importance of organizing in order to build collective power is recognized by activists and theorists like Du Bois, who wrote in 'The black man and the unions,' referring to the exclusion of African American workers from craft unions, that

> beyond the hurt of mine own, I have always striven to recognize the real cogency of the Union argument. Collective bargaining has, undoubtedly, raised modern labor from something like chattel slavery to the threshold of industrial freedom, and in this advance of labor white and black have shared.
>
> *(1986, 1174)*

The structure of those organizations has also been subject to debate. Through the 19th century and first half of the 20th century, the vanguard party, comprised of a few visionary leaders who lead the movement, carried much weight, from Che Guevara's cadres (2007) to the Black Panther Party (Spencer 2016). In the mid-20th century, that form of organization came under much-needed criticism by thinkers like C. L. R. James (1999, 2010) and Jo Freeman (1972–3).

In her important essay 'The tyranny of structurelessness,' Freeman (1972–3) critiques both these rigidly hierarchical forms of organization and the organizations that evolved as an antithesis to them. Her analysis of so-called 'structureless' groups, and her suggestions for critical thinking about how an emancipatory organization should be organized—what she calls 'the principles of democratic structuring' (162)—have had a profound influence on recent political movements like Occupy Wall Street and the Movement for Black Lives.

Recent movements, like the Zapatista movement in Mexico, the workplace cooperative movement in Argentina, Occupy Wall Street, and the Movement for Black Lives, built structures that are less dependent upon centralized leadership and, therefore, distribute power more broadly throughout the movement. As Marina Sitrin writes in *Horizontalism: Voices of Popular Power in Argentina*, as the movement uses it, the term 'horizontalism'

> does not imply just a flat plane for organizing or non-hierarchical relationships in which people no longer make decisions for others. It is a positive word that implies the use of direct democracy and the striving for consensus, processes in which everyone is heard and new relationships are created. [...] As its name suggests, *horizontalidad* implies democratic communication on a level plane and involves—or at least intentionally strives towards—non-hierarchical and anti-authoritarian creation rather than reaction.
>
> *(2006, vi, 3)*

These alternatives to traditional, hierarchical forms of organization are attracting scholarly attention in fields relevant to working-class studies, like economics and sociology. Elinor Ostrum (1990) won the Nobel Prize in 2009 for work in this field; Bruno Latour (2007) develops what he calls Actor Network Theory in books like *Reassembling the Social: An Introduction to Actor-Network-Theory.*

Efforts to hinder activism and collective action

As the above examples show, the collective power of people cooperating to achieve shared goals has the potential to remake the world: to win a safer and fairer workplace, to gain civil and human rights, to overthrow oppressive governments. But recognizing this, employers and states have often responded by hampering, hindering, or repressing altogether the possibility to build the solidarity that makes activism and collective action possible. To paraphrase a letter Karl Marx (1843) sent to Arnold Ruge, people who care about building a better world benefit from paying attention to such reactionary efforts. E. P. Thompson (1966) analyzed the British Combination Laws that prohibited organizing and collective bargaining; Erik R. Seeman's book *Death in the New World: Cross-Cultural Encounters 1492–1800* (2010) charts how laws put limits on the number of enslaved people who could congregate in any place in a given time, in order to prevent them from rebelling. In our era in the United States, the proliferation of so-called 'Right to Work' laws have attempted—often successfully—to limit a people's ability to act collectively (O'Donnell 2013).[6] The significant degree to which employers and states have attempted to thwart activism and collective action is an indication of its importance.

Of equal importance is the fact that, in the U.S. in particular, but by no means exclusively, the history of racism, sexism, and classism is also the history of attempts to segregate groups from one another and, thus, to reduce their potential for collective power. Knowing that history, and working to counteract it, should be among the starting points for any activist who is serious about working-class collective action. As Keeanga-Yamahtta Taylor writes in *From #BlackLivesMatter to Black Liberation*, 'the American working class is female, immigrant, Black, white, Latino/a, and more. Immigrant issues, gender issues, and antiracism *are* working class issues' (2016, 216, emphasis in original). To provide this list is not to suggest that all struggles are the same or that their histories can be smoothed over or lumped together. To the contrary, recognizing that working-class struggles against racism, sexism, and other injustices have unique histories provides the opportunity to learn about the complex ways these injustices work. There is strength in diversity. Any effort to obscure that fact, any attempt to portray a homogenous or exclusively white working class, is a disservice to working people who struggle for a freer, fairer world.

One branch of this scholarship that charts this exclusionary history follows from David Roediger's work on critical whiteness studies in books like *The Wages of Whiteness: Race and the Making of the American Working Class* (2007).[7] Another branch of this scholarship considers the theory of intersectionality—how various struggles for racial, gender, and class justice intersect one another. Among the key texts in this line are Kimberle Crenshaw's essays 'Mapping the margins: Intersectionality, identity politics, and violence against women of color' (1991) and 'Demarginalizing the intersection of race and sex' (1989); Crenshaw is generally credited with popularizing the term 'intersectionality,' although many writers, like Audre Lorde, in books like *Sister Outsider: Essays and Speeches* (1984), write about the idea without using the term as such.

Conclusion

This section of the *Routledge International Handbook of Working-Class Studies* explores past and present initiatives that have given voice to working-class people's struggles and their efforts to mobilize movements across geographical borders, periods, and generations. Chapters include a diverse array of examples of collective actions, focusing on the intersections of class and race; questions of activism in community college classrooms; food justice; post-Fordist affect; precarity; the working conditions of day laborers and housing; and Indigenous labor history. These contributions expand notions of the efficacy of protest and collectivity in advocating for economic, political, and social justice, and they also illustrate the problems and possibilities of activism and collective action in working-class studies. As the essays that follow show, there are many examples, both successes and failures, of people attempting to make the world a better place in which to live and to work through their activism and collective action.

Terry Easton's chapter illustrates ways that oral history and photography research methods can be used to collapse university and community borders while building mutually beneficial collaborations. Through his local history projects on working- and poverty-class populations in Atlanta—day laborers and affordable housing activists—Easton presents voices, images, and reflections on moving across race, class, and national boundaries in a deep-South U.S. city. Michele Fazio's chapter also draws upon the use of oral history to capture lived experience, revealing a wide range of stories about individual perseverance and collective struggle. Outlining a two-year service-learning project, the essay explores how the changing workforce of Robeson County, North Carolina, shapes the lives of Lumbee elders who lived during the growth and decline of manufacturing in the American South. The essay's interviews represent a chapter of American Indian labor history, an important aspect of working-class life that has largely been ignored in the field of working-class studies.

Karen Gaffney argues that we should center the community college when considering activism and explore the relationship between academic confidence, belonging, and activism. When we do, she shows, the idea of activism confidence can then emerge. As Leslie Hossfeld, E. Brooke Kelly, and Julia F. Waity demonstrate, local food movements such as farmers' markets and community-supported agriculture and food sovereignty efforts move toward food justice in an often unjust food system. Yet, some of these approaches face criticism for primarily serving those who are white and middle class.

Joseph Varga's chapter uses examples of labor contention to examine how unions and members of the working class and their supporters have adapted, or not adapted, establishing repertoires of contention to meet the needs of contemporary struggles over worker's rights in the post-Fordist, or postindustrial period. Race and class are different structures of power, Michael Zweig argues, but they are mutually determined. His chapter traces the ways in which the imposition of racial slavery in the U.S. in the late 17th century and 18th century served as an instrument of social control exercised by economic elites through the technique of 'divide and conquer' to subordinate European-American labor as well as African-Americans, to the material detriment of both parts of the working class.

Isabel Roque's chapter argues that in the 21st century, a new class power is being rebuilt in the service sector, especially among those who work with digital platforms. She shows how, in 2011, several anti-austerity and new digitally enabled movements arose on an international scale, creating a massive impact on the Portuguese society amongst trade unions and workers' organizations. It brought new strategies and tactics of organization and resistance, creating a greater degree of awareness by social struggle and also liberating individuals to shape a new autonomy and reclaim power.

We can build from the essays in this section to ask many more questions: what tactics and strategies are best for a given situation? How has activism changed, and how should it adapt now, in light of changes in work and capitalism? Why have movements in the U.S. failed to form, or chose not to form, a political party to represent their interests when workers in many countries have done so successfully? When are small-scale forms of activism more appropriate? What new forms of collective action may develop in response to changing forms of economic, racial, or gendered exploitation and domination? How can particular populations like prison laborers or migrant workers organize themselves, given, on the one hand, their enforced isolation, and on the other, their high mobility? How can allies assist in that activism?

As answers to these questions about the future continue to provoke further debate, the study of past actions and movements can be instructive. The abolition of slavery, the right to form a union or to join one, the hope for greater future gains—these things have been accomplished, and likely will be accomplished, because groups of people will have forged a solidarity that is inclusive. To do so is an exceptionally difficult task, but it is also a difficult task for an employer to command an employee, for police to check a crowd of protesters, or for the few to repress the many. The relative power of corporations, governments, or traditional cultural norms in comparison to the power of people cooperating in pursuit of common goals is a balance or an imbalance well worth testing, the outcome of which is by no means certain.

Notes

1 The *Journal of Working-Class Studies* is the official journal of the Working-Class Studies Association and is interdisciplinary and international in scope. See https://workingclassstudiesjournal.com/.
2 *Labor: Studies in Working Class History* is the official journal of the Labor and Working Class History Association. Seewww.lawcha.org/labor-studies-in-working-class-history/.
3 The American Philosophical Association keeps a list of course syllabi approved by the organization's Committee on Inclusiveness in the Profession; while not thematically housed under the category 'working class,' the resources have an intersectional relevance. See www.apaonline.org/members/group_content_view.asp?group=110430&id=380970.
4 The Section on Labor and Labor Movements of the American Sociological Association keeps a current bibliography of relevant research on its website. See http://asalabormovements.weebly.com/research.html.
5 It is important to note that collective action, in the broadest sense of that term, is part of the human condition. People have always gathered together for a variety of reasons, in a variety of ways. That fact is why Aristotle, in the *Politics* (2009), calls a person a political animal—not in the modern sense of caring for electoral politics or the like, but rather in the sense that we gather together in communities, because we derive many benefits from those communities. A more recent, and intriguing, body of scholarship on that situation builds from Jane Jacobs' book *The Death and Life of Great American Cities* (1992), especially its final chapter, 'The type of problem a city is.' It is notable that Jacobs' book, and her efforts in New York City, have had a significant influence on the activism about city planning and the resistance to gentrification.
6 Patrick S. O'Donnell's 'Workers, the World of Work & Labor Law: A Basic Bibliography' is an exhaustive and recent resource. Seewww.lawcha.org/2013/08/13/patrick-s-odonnell-workers-the-world-of-work-labor-law-a-basic-bibliography/.
7 The most recent edition of *The Wages of Whiteness*, listed in this essay's references, includes a selection of major related scholarly works as an appendix.

References

Aristotle. (2009) *Politics*, Oxford, Oxford University Press.

Brecher, J. (2014) *Strike!* Oakland, PM Press.

Camacho, A. S. (2008) *Migrant Imaginaries: Latino Cultural Politics in the U.S.-Mexico Borderlands*, New York, NYU Press.

Crenshaw, K. (1989) 'Demarginalizing the Intersection of Race and Sex: A Black Feminist Critique of Antidiscrimination Doctrine, Feminist Theory and Antiracist Politics,' *The University of Chicago Legal Forum*, 1, pp. 139–167.

Crenshaw, K. (1991) 'Mapping the Margins: Intersectionality, Identity Politics, and Violence Against Women of Color,' *Stanford Law Review*, 43, 6, pp. 1241–1299.

Detroit, Director Kathryn Bigelow, 2017.
Du Bois, W. E. B. (1986) 'The Black Man and the Unions,' *Writings*, New York, Library of America.
Du Bois, W. E. B. (1998) *Black Reconstruction in America, 1860–1880*, New York, Free Press.
Foner, E. (2013) 'Black Reconstruction: An Introduction,' *South Atlantic Quarterly*, 112, 3, pp. 409–418.
Freeman, J. (1972–3) 'The Tyranny of Structurelessness,' *Berkeley Journal of Sociology*, 17, pp. 151–164.
Georgakas, D. and Surkin, M. (2012) *Detroit: I Do Mind Dying: A Study in Urban Revolution*, Chicago, Haymarket Books.
Guevara Che, E. (2007) *The Che Guevara Reader: Writings on Politics and Revolution*, North Melbourne, Ocean Press.
Gutierrez, M. P. (2017) 'Detroit 1967: There's Still a Debate over What to Call It,' *NPR*, 28 July. www.npr.org/sections/codeswitch/2017/07/28/539748145/50-years-after-detroit-s-july-67-unrest-there-s-still-a-debate-over-what-to-call.
Henkel, S. (2017) *Direct Democracy: Collective Power, the Swarm, and the Literatures of the Americas*, Jackson, University Press of Mississippi.
Jacobs, J. (1992) *The Death and Life of Great American Cities*, New York, Vintage.
James, C. L. R. (1999) *Marxism for Our Times: C. L. R. James on Revolutionary Organization*, Jackson, University Press of Mississippi.
James, C. L. R. (2010) 'Every Cook Can Govern,' *A New Notion: Two Works by C. L. R. James*, Chicago, Kerr.
Latour, B. (2007) *Reassembling the Social: An Introduction to Actor-Network-Theory*, Oxford, Oxford University Press.
Lorde, A. (1984) *Sister Outsider: Essays and Speeches*, Trumansburg, NY, Crossing Press.
Luxemburg, R. (2007) 'Introduction to *The Mass Strike*,' in Scott, H. (ed.) *The Essential Rosa Luxemburg: Reform or Revolution and the Mass Strike*, Chicago, Haymarket Books.
Marx, K. (1843) 'Marx to Ruge: Letters from the Deutsch-Französische Jahrbücher,' www.marxists.org/archive/marx/works/1843/letters/43_05.htm.
McAlevey, J. (2016) *No Shortcuts: Organizing for Power in the New Gilded Age*, New York, Oxford University Press.
Montag, W. (1999) *Bodies, Masses, Power: Spinoza and His Contemporaries*, New York, Verso.
O'Donnell, P. S. (2013) 'Workers, the World of Work & Labor Law: A Basic Bibliography,' 13 August www.lawcha.org/2013/08/13/patrick-s-odonnell-workers-the-world-of-work-labor-law-a-basic-bibliography/.
Ostrom, E. (1990) *Governing the Commons: The Evolution of Institutions for Collective Action*, Cambridge, Cambridge University Press.
Robin, C. (2016) 'How Intellectuals Create a Public,' *Chronicle of Higher Education*, 22 January. www.chronicle.com/article/How-Intellectuals-Create-a/234984.
Robinson, C. (1977) 'A Critique of W. E. B. Du Bois' *Black Reconstruction*,' *The Black Scholar*, 8, 7, pp. 44–50.
Roediger, D. (2007) *The Wages of Whiteness: Race and the Making of the American Working Class*, New York, Verso.
Rosenfeldt, D. S. (1993) 'Commentary,' *Salt of the Earth*, New York, Feminist Press/CUNY.
Salt of the Earth, Director Herbert J. Biberman, 1954.
Seeman, E. R. (2010) *Death in the New World: Cross-Cultural Encounters, 1492–1800*, Philadelphia, University of Pennsylvania Press.
Shotwell, G. (2006) *Workers Will Rule When They Work to Rule—From a Speech Made at Labor Notes Conference, 5-8-06*. https://labornotes.org/files/pdfs/shotwellWorkToRule.pdf.
Sitrin, M. (ed.) (2006) *Horizontalism: Voices of Popular Power in Argentina*, Oakland, AK Press.
Spencer, R. C. (2016) *The Revolution Has Come: Black Power, Gender, and the Black Panther Party in Oakland*, Durham, Duke University Press.
Srinivasan, R. (2017) *Whose Global Village? Rethinking How Technology Shapes Our World*, New York, New York University Press.
Taylor, K. (2016) *From #BlackLivesMatter to Black Liberation*, Chicago, Haymarket.
Thompson, E. P. (1966) *The Making of the English Working Class*, New York, Vintage.
Villard, O. (1936) 'Black Controversy,' *The Saturday Review of Literature*, 18 January.
Wilson, M. (1993) 'Screenplay,' *Salt of the Earth*, New York, Feminist Press/CUNY.
Workplace: A Journal of Academic Labor, Petrina, S. and Ross, E. W. (eds.) https://ices.library.ubc.ca/index.php/workplace/index.
Zweig, M. (2011) *The Working Class Majority: America's Best Kept Secret*, Ithaca, Cornell University Press/Industrial and Labor Relations Press.

29

From stigma to solution

Centering the community college through activism in the classroom and the community

Karen Gaffney

In their introduction to *New Working-Class Studies*, editors John Russo and Sherry Lee Linkon write, 'Ultimately, new working-class studies is not just an academic exercise. Rather, we strive to advance the struggle for social and economic justice for working-class people' (2005, 15). In pursuing this 'struggle for social and economic justice,' there are many directions to explore, but I am focusing on the issue of activism in a location that receives minimal attention: the community college. Instead of perpetuating a culture that tends to stigmatize the community college, I seek to highlight the community college not despite—but because of—its considerable working-class student population. This approach can provide us with new insight that follows the example of working-class studies, which shifts our perspective so that 'we look at all classes in society from the point of view of working people—their lives, experiences, needs, and interests' (Zweig 2004, 4). Shifting from, as bell hooks puts it, 'margin to center' (2000) can alter the power dynamics so that we don't replicate an oppressive power structure by leaving it unexamined and unchanged. Rather, centering the community college can reveal the dynamics of 'economic and political power' (Zweig 2004, 4), the very focus of working-class studies.

I want to begin by acknowledging my own proximity to power. I am a white, cisgendered, heterosexual, able-bodied, neurotypical, middle-class female who is a tenured full professor. I have taught in the English Department at Raritan Valley Community College in New Jersey since 2003. I acknowledge the privilege that comes with my identity and faculty status that allows me the opportunity to write this piece and use my privilege to highlight the issue of activism at an often-stigmatized institution, the community college. Community colleges are, by definition, colleges meant to serve the community. They are open-access (available to anyone with a high school diploma or its equivalency), likely the most affordable college option, and often nonresidential. All of these attributes can translate into powerful beliefs that community colleges are not 'real' colleges.

In terms of campus activism, one would likely get the impression it didn't exist at community colleges based on mainstream media or even academic research. For example, recent articles in *The Atlantic* (Anderson 2015), *The New York Times* (Ellin 2016), and the *Chronicle of Higher Education* (Ruff 2016) that focus on campus activism feature prestigious public and private universities. Likewise, while there are several scholarly articles that provide valuable analysis of student activism, they generally study campuses of four-year colleges and universities, though Fernandez (2010) and Miller and Schwartz (2016) are notable exceptions. Furthermore, an entire book titled *'Radical Academia?': Understanding the Climates for Campus Activists* (Broadhurst and Martin 2014) did not include any chapters addressing student activism at community colleges, and a special issue of *Journal of Diversity in Higher Education* (Warnock and Hurst 2016) devoted to college student activism included very few references to, much less any sustained focus on, community colleges.

Is there not much activism on community college campuses? Or is it just not getting much attention because the institution itself is so often stigmatized? One study compared students with an associate's degree (a two-year college degree) and those with a bachelor's degree (a four-year college degree) and found that students with a four-year degree tended to have a higher level of 'civic engagement' than students with a two-year degree, who tended to have a higher level of 'civic engagement' than students with a high school diploma (Newell 2014). While this study is a good start, it's quite limited, and even this study acknowledges that there are 'large gaps in the literature on the engagement of students at 2-year colleges' (Newell 2014, 67). Another study states, 'we know very little about the extent and ways in which community colleges develop the civic capacities of their students' (Kisker et al. 2016). While 'civic capacities' and 'engagement' are not exactly the same as activism, there is overlap, and these statements reinforce the lack of much-needed research.

I propose that the answer may lie somewhere in between, meaning that more activism exists at community colleges than we hear about but perhaps less activism than documented at four-year institutions. Centering the community college in this discussion reveals several things that need our attention: 1) why the community college is such a critical site of potential activism for social change, 2) obstacles to activism that do exist at community colleges, 3) a strategy of focusing on the classroom as a site of activism, and 4) a recommendation that community college faculty, in particular, are well positioned to engage in public scholarship as a form of activism.

Why the community college is such a critical site of potential activism for social change

Given how little attention community colleges receive when it comes to higher education in general (not to mention activism on campus), it may come as a surprise that 'half of all undergraduate students are enrolled at a community college' (Newell 2014, 70). Moreover, in applying the working-class studies lens to higher education, we must recognize the working-class student demographic at community colleges, which

> enroll a higher percentage of low-income students than 4-year institutions .... In fact, compared with all types of higher education institutions, community colleges enroll most students from the lowest socioeconomic quintile.
>
> *(Martin et al. 2014)*

Furthermore, 'the majority of Black and Hispanic undergraduate students in the United States study at a community college' (Newell 2014, 70). Therefore, when we take into account a focus on 'economic and political power' at the heart of a working-class studies approach, we can see the need to feature rather than stigmatize the community college because it serves the most racially and economically disenfranchised.

Focusing on the community college as an opportunity rather than as an institution overcome with challenges can be a challenge itself. As a community college faculty member, I can certainly acknowledge that I've contributed to discussions about community college where we focus on problems, like state and county budget cuts making it impossible to hire enough full-time faculty and provide enough much-needed resources for our students. The teaching load of full-time faculty (usually five courses per semester) is demanding and exhausting, which doesn't even begin to speak to the challenges faced by adjunct faculty, who often teach more classes than that, spread out over multiple institutions and with different course requirements, with little to no job security and no benefits (see, for example, Soria 2016). Community colleges and their employees are stretched very thin. However, given that we serve college students with the least amount of power and therefore with the greatest need for justice, how might we reimagine this institution as an opportunity to be at the center for social change?

We tend to emphasize the narrative of individual community college students attending community college in order to elevate their individual relationship to the class structure, as in the publicity about how community college graduates can get higher-paying jobs than high school graduates. While I am not discounting the importance of financial security for our students, focusing on individuals climbing the class structure doesn't change that structure. If we center the community college and reimagine the community college as a site of opportunity for social change, then that allows us to focus on changing an oppressive class structure rather than on changing individuals' relationships to it.

Interestingly, research about working-class students' experiences in higher education explicitly reveals obstacles to organizing working-class students at four-year institutions. For example, Deborah Warnock and Allison Hurst studied organizing among 'low-income, first-generation, and/or working-class' students, who were in the minority at 'a predominantly wealthy and elite liberal arts college campus' (Warnock and Hurst 2016, 265–266). Their study found that it was 'difficult to organize around an already stigmatized identity' (Warnock and Hurst 2016, 266) because of that stigma and also because of the limited amount of time such students have available. Organizing working-class students on elite campuses is important and should be supported. After all, recent evidence shows that

> Students at elite colleges are even richer than experts realized, according to a new study based on millions of anonymous tax filings and tuition records. At 38 colleges in America, including five in the Ivy League–Dartmouth, Princeton, Yale, Penn and Brown–more students came from the top 1 percent of the income scale than from the entire bottom 60 percent.
>
> *(Aisch et al. 2017)*

Working-class students at elite institutions are very much in the minority and need as many resources as they can get, but this research can also point to the conclusion that elite colleges and universities may be perpetuating the class structure rather than being in a position to subvert it.

However, if we shift our attention to institutions with more working-class students, how might that change the way this population navigates class, and open up opportunities for activism? One study takes us in that direction by comparing the experiences of 'lower income students' from an 'elite college' to those at a 'state college' and found that the former

> faced more class-related challenges and difficulties than students at the state college.... The disparities of wealth between students at the prestigious college heightened awareness of social class, whereas greater homogeneity in class backgrounds at the state college made class less salient.
>
> *(Aries and Seider 2005, 438–439)*

While this study does not include community college students, I suggest we continue to follow the path of looking at institutions with higher proportions of working-class students, as this framework makes clear how community colleges provide key insights about class structure. For example, another study focuses on an institution where the majority of students are low-income, specifically San Bernadino Community College. The results find campus 'involvement levels higher than anticipated' and reveal how 'a campus that is not stratified by income may prove to be more welcoming for low-income students and students of color' (Bell et al. 2016, 10–11). Furthermore, 'It only makes sense that feeling safe, secure, and comfortable is a precursor to student involvement and engagement' (Bell et al. 2016, 12). These results support the approach that we may focus on the community college as an opportunity, as a space for social justice and change, because the higher numbers of economically and racially disenfranchised students form a critical mass that may create a more supportive space for activism that critiques oppressive structures of race and class.

Obstacles to activism at community colleges

While the community college may be a critical site for social change, we need to acknowledge a series of logistical obstacles to community college campus activism, which in turn will lead to my recommendation about teaching activism within the classroom. For example, many community colleges provide little to no on-campus housing, so the residential experience that might prompt and support activism at four-year college campuses wouldn't exist in the same way at community colleges. Furthermore, many students attend community colleges so that they can live at home, often with various family and work commitments. Community college students may want to spend more time on campus getting involved in events and activism, but their schedules do not allow them the same time as students at more elite institutions, who have more flexibility and financial resources to devote to campus engagement. For example, one article used survey data to analyze 'civic outcomes' for community college students and found that the more students worked off-campus, 'the less likely they are to exhibit Civic Capacity, Civic Agency, or Civic Knowledge' (Kisker et al. 2016). This study can point to the idea that if students are not able to engage in campus activism that requires their own free time, perhaps there is even a greater need to incorporate activism into the classroom, a space that all students have access to.

Furthermore, since community colleges generally provide freshman- and sophomore-level courses, community college students are usually considered freshmen and sophomores and don't become juniors and seniors until they transfer to four-year institutions. Students may not come into their own as activists until they are juniors and seniors, so while that might occur, it doesn't necessarily happen on the campus or in the classrooms of the community college. Moreover, at four-year institutions, freshmen and sophomores are surrounded by juniors and seniors who may serve as unofficial activist mentors, likely prompting freshmen and sophomores to engage in activism more readily and at an earlier point in their college career than they would at a community college. As a result, community college students, as freshmen and sophomores, may again benefit from activism incorporated into the classroom to provide a foundation.

What does incorporating activism into the classroom look like, and what types of obstacles to activism emerge there? The journal *Radical Teacher* devoted a special issue to 'Teaching Black Lives Matter,' and articles highlighted many different ways instructors could integrate information about Black Lives Matter into the classroom, facilitate opportunities for students to study and engage with this movement, and encourage students to contribute to the movement through various papers, projects, and engagement in social media. One article concluded:

> Radical teachers therefore play a critical role in disrupting 'business as usual' when it comes to discussions of authority, discipline, and related phenomena like the carceral state, state violence, police brutality, representation, and framing. Whether it be by juxtaposing past and present, rewriting the narrative on black lives, or challenging the ways they are represented, students must be reminded of their ability to influence their lives by seizing their story and their voice.
>
> *(Cumberbatch and Trujillo-Pagán 2016, 84)*

In order to highlight injustices and work toward justice, students must be able to 'seize their story and their voice.' But how does this challenging work occur?

Students who already have the most power (i.e. white, middle- and upper-class students at prestigious colleges and universities) might feel the most comfortable in raising their voice, but how do we encourage a similar outcome at community colleges? More specifically, what happens when students don't feel that their story matters or that nobody wants to listen to their voice? This problem relates directly to the power structure of our society, a structure built on capitalism, patriarchy, and white supremacy that privileges the voices and perspectives of the wealthy, of men, and of white people and tends to silence the voices of the poor, of women, and of people of color. If community colleges tend to have a higher proportion of students who come from groups that have historically been silenced, then it is important to consider how this power imbalance impacts the ease with which students at community colleges will 'seize their story and their voice.'

For example, I have heard students from marginalized communities ask, in class discussions about student activism, 'Why would anyone care what I think?' or 'Why would anyone listen to my suggestion?' Further, especially under the Trump administration, students may feel at risk to engage in any activism, for fear of attracting attention to themselves, a serious concern if they or their family members are undocumented, for example. Therefore, in addition to the other obstacles that may prevent community college students from engaging in campus activism, students' marginalized status (by class, race, citizenship status, sexual orientation, ability, religion, gender identity, etc.) may also make this engagement more challenging and riskier.

It might be helpful, then, if we connect these obstacles to student activism to the challenge of limited 'academic confidence,' because these issues can often negatively affect the same marginalized students. In the article 'Experiences of earned success: Community college students' shifts in college confidence,' the authors 'define academic confidence as students' certainty in their ability to meet the academic and social demands of college' (Bickerstaff et al. 2017, 501). In other words, students with less academic confidence can have a more challenging time in college because they don't believe they are capable of being academically successful. Bickerstaff et al. write:

> [D]ominant cultural narratives and persistently low expectations of certain groups of students, particularly working class students and students of color, are associated with poor academic performance .... These expectations have been shown to shape academic identity, the dimension of self-concept tied to academic motivation, achievement, and future expectations.
>
> *(Bickerstaff et al. 2017, 502)*

My anecdotal experience teaching the same course (English composition) at a large public university and at a community college supports the claim that low academic confidence disproportionately affects community college students, and I would go so far as to speculate that one of the biggest differences between students at community colleges and students at four-year colleges and universities is academic confidence. My first college teaching experience occurred when I was in graduate school at the University of Delaware teaching first-year composition. Students who were unhappy with a B, for example, appeared comfortable sharing that concern, and students readily asked questions about what they didn't understand. I didn't really think much of that behavior until I started teaching the same course at my community college. Instead of complaining about a B, students often express relief at getting a C, or even a D (which is technically passing). They frequently share doubts about their ability to complete an assignment. They will also sometimes skip class (or stop attending class) when they feel overwhelmed and don't complete the work. One student even told me she almost dropped out of school because she couldn't find her class on the first day of the semester.

Focusing on the classroom as a site of activism

Although research about low academic confidence might lead us to lose hope in the possibility for community colleges to make a difference, research shows otherwise, reinforcing my point that we can reimagine community colleges as sites of opportunities. Researchers recognize that 'college confidence is not static. Students experience shifts and changes in their perceptions of themselves as students as they engage with the college environment' (Bickerstaff et al. 2017, 507). This conclusion is really critical because it means that what faculty do in the classroom matters. We can have a profound impact, for better or for worse, depending on how we set up our courses, the classroom environment, and student feedback. This leads me to make some recommendations for incorporating student activism into the community college classroom, based on a combined understanding of the challenges that community colleges may face in the interrelated areas of academic confidence and what we might call 'activism confidence.'

While I have experience incorporating student activism into Introduction to Women and Gender Studies (which I discuss in an article I co-wrote titled 'Navigating the gender box: Locating masculinity in the Introduction to Women and Gender Studies Course'; Gaffney and Manno 2011) and into Race in American Literature and Popular Culture (which I discuss in my blog (dividednolonger.com) and my book *Dismantling the Racism Machine: A Manual and Toolbox* 2018), I will focus here on a special topic section I designed for English Composition II, 'Inequality, the American Dream, and the 99%'—a second-semester composition course required of most degrees and programs that establishes a foundation in critical reading, critical writing, and critical thinking. The first unit in the course established an introduction to economic inequality in order to provide students with basic concepts to explore in their writing, before we even discussed action. Texts included a documentary film, nonfiction, autobiography, and songs in order to provide a range of theoretical concepts, research, and lived experiences, such as Robert Reich's documentary film *Inequality for All* (2013), Michael Zweig's introduction to *What's Class Got To Do With It?* (2004), Elizabeth Warren's 'The vanishing middle class' (2004) Linda Tirado's 'Why poor people stay poor' (2014), Billy Joel's 'Allentown' (2014) and Eminem's 'Rock Bottom' (2014).

The second unit asked students to apply the broader concept of economic inequality from the first unit to the system of education, with questions like: What is the relationship between access to education and class? How does inequality impact access to education and the educational experience? We began by reading a *New York Times* article 'Who gets to graduate?' (Tough 2014) which highlights challenges that working-class students experience in college, from cost to expectations, and it explicitly discusses the concept of academic confidence, especially in relation to math. Other readings included essays about homeless students, adjunct faculty on food stamps, lack of guidance counselors for high school students in under-resourced schools, the stigma of community college, working-class students' experiences, and the relationship between racism, xenophobia, poverty, and student learning. Authors and artists included Michelle Tokarczyk (2004), Barbara Jensen (2004), Gloria Anzaldúa (1987), Ernesto Quiñonez (2000), and Tracy Chapman. While students' points of entry into the material varied, they consistently made direct connections between their experiences and the course material, which emerged in group activities and discussion in class as well as in their writing. Students became invested in the material, which became the moment I introduced activism. The first time I taught the course, I didn't introduce activism until later in the semester, and given the reluctance and concern students expressed about engaging in activism, even writing a letter to an official, I changed the course to incorporate activism much earlier when I taught the class again.

While the second essay assignment required students to primarily focus on creating an argument about education and economic inequality using two of the assigned readings, the assignment also asked them to address one specific obstacle to student learning that inequality can cause and to devote at least one paragraph of their paper to recommend a solution to this problem. The assignment directions stated, 'I'm not asking you to carry out this solution, but I'm asking you to recommend a solution as practice for later in the semester when I will ask you to take action on a solution you are recommending.' Here, my goal was to gradually pave the way to activism by helping the students establish their academic confidence through a clearly structured assignment and to build their activism confidence by imagining an action without actually having to take it. As one researcher argues, community college courses should provide students with 'critical tools needed for participation in collaborative transformations of society' (Hougaard 2013, 46). More specifically,

> Transformation in this context is defined as being directed by an agenda of social justice and points towards the need for education to allow students to engage not only the contradictions in the college, but being able to place their own current struggles in the college within a larger societal context.
>
> *(2013, 33)*

My goal was to provide these 'critical tools' early on so that they would be better prepared for the action assignment later. Students then pursued a systemic approach by connecting poverty to other oppressions, especially those based on race, sexual orientation, and gender, through creative work that included Patricia Smith's poem about Hurricane Katrina 'What to tweak' (2011), Tupac's song 'Changes' (2014), and a personal narrative by Dorothy Allison (1994). Essay assignments asked students to create an argument about how poverty and another form of oppression impact each other, compounding each other in a vicious cycle.

All of the work done so far culminated in the final paper set up as a problem/solution paper so students could make an argument explaining why one specific aspect of economic inequality is a serious problem and how we might go about solving it. The paper required an action component, which meant the students needed to personally carry out one specific small piece of the student's solution rather than only write about it. The students could create a social media post to raise awareness about the problem they were researching, they could send a letter or email to an elected official or someone else responsible for the problem, or they could propose an alternative type of action. We talked about how the action needed to stand alone and speak for itself and how they needed to write for an audience they identified.

The first semester I taught this course, many of the students balked and expressed serious reluctance about the action component to the assignment. They asked questions like: 'Why do

I have to send the letter—why can't I just show it to you?' Even though I had been teaching at my community college for some time and was well aware of their challenges with academic confidence, I was still not prepared for their hesitation. The second semester I taught the course, I was much more deliberate about the process, and it was more successful. In addition to asking students to imagine (but not carry out) an action in their second assignment halfway through the semester, having a course Tumblr page was also very helpful. This social media site was especially popular at the time, so with student input, I created a page to showcase student work from both semesters (the site is still accessible at: http://rvccgaffneyeng2.tumblr.com/). I posted information about the action assignment as well as some information about the activities leading up to it and, with permission, the students' actions.

While all students focused on some aspect of economic inequality, the site reveals the significant range in topics, from immigration and the DREAM Act to homeless veterans to campaign finance reform. At the end of the semester, in the anonymous course evaluations, students provided positive open-ended comments: 'connects modern-day issues to course,' 'focused on a great topic; awesome way to focus on real-world issues,' and 'keep up the good work in inspiring students to think for themselves.' I taught this course for two consecutive semesters (Fall 2014 and Spring 2015). It's only been in retrospect as I've researched the topic of activism at community colleges and begun plans for teaching the course again in Spring 2019 that I've started to think more carefully about whether my students actually gained 'activism confidence' during the course. And, if so, would it transfer to another course or situation? At the time, I did not have the foresight to ask students to reflect on their 'activism confidence' or to measure it, even in an unofficial way. I can say that anecdotally, I observed that some students who wanted to use social media for their action still expressed initial hesitation about taking this step for fear that their friends wouldn't agree with them, but once they carried out the action, they seemed positive about the experience. Moreover, even after the semester concluded, some students contacted me about how they were still pursuing their action item, which leads me to conclude that requiring a small action can lead some students to engage in future action, unprompted by an assignment.

This course's official learning outcomes do not include activism since all sections need identical outcomes not only within our institution but also within community colleges in New Jersey, and these outcomes focus on the writing process, analysis, evidence, and research. However, what I wish I had done, and what I will do next time, is to give students an opportunity to reflect on their relationship with activism before we even begin to focus on it and then to do the same thing at the end of the semester, with additional measures of 'activism confidence' along the way, perhaps giving them particular scenarios to respond to.

Community college faculty and public scholarship as a form of activism

While I encourage community college faculty to consider integrating activism into teaching, we can't stop there. What better way to model activism in the classroom than to show how we're taking our work into the community? As community college faculty, we are uniquely well positioned to engage the public in our research. As Russo and Linkon put it, 'What does it mean to be a socially responsible academic? As many others have said before us, our role must be not merely to interpret the world but to change it' (2005, 15). Limiting our work to the classroom is not enough if we want to transform oppressive power structures. One area of activism that is perhaps most realistic for faculty is what has become known as 'public scholarship.' It essentially means taking the work we do inside the academy and making it accessible outside of the academy. In the recent book *Going Public: A Guide for Social Scientists*, Arlene Stein and Jessie

Daniels provide a step-by-step process for teaching social scientists to write for the public. Stein and Daniels explain the need for this work:

> When those who possess in-depth training and expertise are excluded from public debates about pressing issues such as climate change, work-family balance ... such discussions are likely to be shaped by corporations, wealthy businessmen with vested interests such as the Koch brothers or celebrities.
>
> *(2017, 5)*

A working-class studies approach reminds us that if the economic elite are guiding such work, then the status quo will be perpetuated, maintaining oppression.

However, faculty are not often trained or comfortable with a public role. Linda Stamato, in *Inside Higher Ed*, writes, 'We develop expertise in our disciplines, often with a narrow, even detached, focus that can dissuade us from speaking publicly, let alone advocating actively' (2017). I would argue that this is more likely the case at a research university and much less likely the case at a community college. Community college faculty tend to be more experienced at teaching our subject area to people relatively new to the field, due to our student population of freshmen and sophomores, who are presumably more representative of the public than the graduate students in a specialized seminar, so let's become leaders in public scholarship. Evidence of public scholarship can be seen not only in the social sciences, but also in the humanities. For example, the 2018 Modern Language Association Conference hosted a panel devoted to the concept of the 'Public Humanities,' where humanities faculty explained how they took their expertise into the public arena, through websites, blogs, podcasts, books, workshops, and other venues aimed at sharing their research with the general public.

Another valuable example of scholars taking their work public is the blog *Working-Class Perspectives*, which provides 'commentary on Working-Class Culture, Education, and Politics' (available at https://workingclassstudies.wordpress.com/). Recently, editor Sherry Linkon wrote on this very topic in a post titled 'Going public with working-class studies,' where she concludes:

> no matter how insightful and critical our academic work is, if we want to influence politics and culture, we need to reach wider audiences. We need to translate our scholarly analyses into forms and styles that will engage more people, and we need to go public with our stories.
>
> *(2018)*

A recent example of my public scholarship includes co-organizing a public film screening and discussion of Reich's *Inequality for All*. Scholars take for granted basic concepts of economic inequality, but the public is often unaware of these ideas. While the Occupy movement popularized the concept of the '1%,' many community members at this screening expressed surprise and confusion about how laws, court decisions, stagnant wages, union busting, and other events over the past few decades have dramatically increased the gap between the rich and the poor.

Likewise, in my book *Dismantling the Racism Machine: A Manual and Toolbox*, my primary goal is to translate scholarship about race and racism into an accessible format for beginning college students and the general public, creating an introduction to race and racism with tools for action. A profound gap exists between what scholars consider long-established and what is familiar to the general public when it comes to fundamental concepts of race, including, for instance, the concept that race is a social construct and not biological. Community members I work with are often shocked to hear that race is an invention, that racial categories like whiteness are not natural or biological. As a white anti-racist educator, I found that one contribution I could make is to help bridge this gap. If faculty scholarship and expertise about analyzing power and oppression remain within the confines of the academy, how is it going to have an impact on our power structure in order to fight against oppression? I'm not suggesting that public scholarship is the only valuable type of expertise that is necessary for activism, but it can make an important contribution in effecting change in and outside of the classroom.

However, one major obstacle that can hamper faculty getting involved in public scholarship and community service is that if colleges and universities do not count this work toward tenure and promotion, it will be additional work, and it's unrealistic to ask faculty to do more than they're already doing. It's far more common to count service in the community as part of service in the promotion and tenure process at community colleges than at four-year colleges and universities. For example, Peter Monaghan writes in the *Chronicle of Higher Education* that 'At two- and four-year teaching colleges, service matters more' than at research institutions (Monaghan 2017). While serving on department or college-wide committees is part of service, giving workshops at your local public library should likewise count toward service, as should being a member of your local community anti-racism coalition. There needs to be institutional support for public scholarship for it to be effective and meaningful. Faculty members who are contingent, who are graduate students, or who are untenured need to be able to engage in this work with confidence that it will support their career, not impede it. If graduate students and then faculty just climb the existing structure, it won't change. We need to empower ourselves to transform an oppressive structure to create justice. Several universities are focusing explicitly on public scholarship, including The New School for Social Research's Center for Public Scholarship, Brown University's John Nicholas Brown Center for Public Humanities and Cultural Heritage, and the University of Washington's Simpson Center for the Humanities. Likewise, many states sponsor public scholars programs, like the one I recently joined, New Jersey Council for the Humanities.

Let's again take the lead from community colleges, where service counts, and service often includes both college service and community service. In the *Chronicle of Higher Education*, college leaders Nancy Cantor and Steven D. Lavine write an article titled 'Taking public scholarship seriously' where they argue: 'We must think boldly about what we define as knowledge, what we regard as interesting, and whom we call "scholars." The future demands it' (Cantor and Lavine 2006). As we think about analyzing power structures in our academic work and in the teaching that we do, we need to think seriously about how we can take that work outside of the academy. If we're asking our students to engage in activism, how can we not engage in it ourselves? If we're asking students to question an oppressive power structure, how can we not do the same by making the boundary between the academy and the public more permeable?

Centering the community college allows us to look to the community college not as a stigma but as a solution, which in turn reveals a multitude of possibilities that are often otherwise invisible. Incorporating activism into the classroom can provide students with tools and confidence for transformative change. Encouraging faculty to engage in public scholarship can likewise lead to social change through advocacy and information sharing. Community college faculty and leadership alike need to cultivate the confidence we're asking our students to develop. We say we have a social justice mission of open access education, but we need to speak up much more loudly and clearly about that mission and have the confidence in that mission so that community colleges can become leaders of social change.

References

Aisch, G., Buchanan, L., Cox, A. and Quealy, K. 'Some Colleges Have More Students From the Top 1 Percent Than the Bottom 60. Find Yours,' *The New York Times*, January 18, 2017. https://nyti.ms/2jRcqJs.

Allison, D. (1994) *Skin: Talking About Sex, Class and Literature*, Ithaca, Firebrand Books.

Anderson, M. (2015) 'The Other Student Activists,' *The Atlantic*, November 23.www.theatlantic.com/education/archive/2015/11/student-activism-history-injustice/417129/.

Anzaldúa, G. (1987) *Borderlands/La Frontera: The New Mestiza*, San Francisco, Aunt Lute Books.

Aries, E. and Seider, M. (2005) 'The Interactive Relationship Between Class Identity and the College Experience: The Case of Lower Income Students,' *Qualitative Sociology*, 28, 4, pp. 419–443, Complementary Index, EBSCO*host*, viewed April 22, 2018.

Bell, D. A., Hackett, C. D., and Hoffman, J. L. (2016) 'Student Satisfaction and Success in a Low-Income Community College Environment,' *Journal of Applied Research in the Community College*, 23, 1, pp. 1–13, Supplemental Index, EBSCO*host*, viewed April 22, 2018.

Bickerstaff, S., Barragan, M. and Rucks-Ahidiana, Z. (2017) 'Experiences of Earned Success: Community College Students' Shifts in College Confidence,' *International Journal Of Teaching And Learning In Higher Education*, 29, 3, pp. 501–510, ERIC, EBSCO*host*, viewed April 22, 2018.

Broadhurst, C. J. and Martin, G. L. (eds.) (2014) *'Radical Academia?' Understanding the Climates for Campus Activists: New Directions for Higher Education*, Number 167, Somerset, John Wiley & Sons. Available from: ProQuest Ebook Central, viewed April 22, 2018.

Cantor, N., and Lavine, S. D. 'Taking Public Scholarship Seriously,' *Chronicle of Higher Education*, June 9, 2006,www.chronicle.com/article/Taking-Public-Scholarship/22684.

Cumberbatch, P. and Trujillo-Pagán, N. (2016) 'Hashtag Activism and Why #BlackLivesMatter In (and To) the Classroom,' *Radical Teacher*, 106, pp. 78–86. https://doi.org/10.5195/RT2016.302.

Ellin, A. (2016) 'Meet the New Student Activists,' *The New York Times*, February 1.ww.nytimes.com/2016/02/07/education/edlife/the-new-student-activists.html.

Eminem. 'Rock Bottom,' *AZ Lyrics*, 2014,www.azlyrics.com/lyrics/eminem/rockbottom.html.

Fernandez, K. (2010) 'Planet Activism: Students Further Their Environmental Passions through Clubs and Groups,' *Community College Journal*, 81, 2, pp. 34–36, ERIC, EBSCO*host*, viewed April 22, 2018.

Gaffney, K. (2018) *Dismantling the Racism Machine: A Manual and Toolbox*, New York, Routledge.

Gaffney, K. and Manno, A. (2011) 'Navigating the Gender Box: Locating Masculinity in the Introduction to Women and Gender Studies Course,' *Men and Masculinities*, 14, 2, pp. 190–209. https://journals.sagepub.com/doi/abs/10.1177/1097184X11407046.

hooks, b. (2000) *Feminist Theory: From Margin to Center*, Cambridge, South End Press.

Hougaard, N. B. (2013) 'Making Sense of the Community College: Interrogating Belongingness,' *Outlines: Critical Practice Studies*, 14, 2, pp. 29–53. SocINDEX with Full Text, EBSCO*host*, viewed April 22, 2018.

Inequality for All, Director Jacob Kornbluth, 2013.

Jensen, B. (2004) 'Across the Great Divide: Crossing Classes and Clashing Cultures' in Zweig, M. (ed.) *What's Class Got To Do With It? American Society in the Twenty-First Century*, Ithaca, Cornell University Press.

Joel, B. 'Allentown,' *Billy Joel*, 2014,www.billyjoel.com/song/allentown-12/.

Kisker, C. B., Weintraub, D. S. and Newell, M. A. (2016) 'The Community Colleges' Role in Developing Students' Civic Outcomes,' *Community College Review*, 44, 4, pp. 315–336. https:/doi.org/10.1177/0091552116662117.

Linkon, S. 'Going Public with Working-Class Studies,' *Working-Class Perspectives*, April 9, 2018. https://workingclassstudies.wordpress.com/2018/04/09/going-public-with-working-class-studies/.

Martin, K., Galentino, R. and Townsend, L. (2014) 'Community College Student Success: The Role of Motivation and Self-Empowerment,' *Community College Review*, 42, 3, pp. 221–241. https://doi.org/10.1177/0091552114528972.

Miller, B. and Schwartz, J. (2016) 'The Intersection of Black Lives Matter and Adult Education: One Community College Initiative,' *New Directions for Adult and Continuing Education*, 150, pp. 13–23. https://doi.org/10.1002/ace.20182.

Monaghan, P. (2017) 'Making Committee Service Count,' *Chronicle of Higher Education*, February 12.www.chronicle.com/article/Making-Committee-Service-Count/239165.

Newell, M. A. (2014) 'What's a Degree Got to Do With It? The Civic Engagement of Associate's and Bachelor's Degree Holders,' *Journal Of Higher Education Outreach and Engagement*, 18, 2, pp. 67–89, ERIC, EBSCO*host*, viewed April 22, 2018.

Quiñonez, E. (2000) *Bodega Dreams*, New York, Vintage.

Ruff, C. (2016) 'The Mental and Academic Costs of Campus Activism,' *Chronicle of Higher Education*, March 16.www.chronicle.com/article/The-MentalAcademic-Costs/235711.

Russo, J. and Linkon, S. L. (2005) 'What's New about New Working-Class Studies?,' in Russo, J. and Linkon, S. L. (eds.) *New Working-Class Studies*, Ithaca, Cornell University Press.

Smith, P. (2011) 'What to Tweak,' in Reichard, W. (ed.) *American Tensions*, Oakland, New Village Press.

Soria, K. (2016) 'Working-Class, Teaching Class, and *Working* Class in the Academy,' in Hurst, A and Nenga, S. (eds.) *Working in Class: Recognizing How Social Class Shapes Our Academic Work*, Lanham, Rowman & Littlefield.

Stamato, L. (2017) 'Making Research Matter: A Public Challenge to Scholars,' *Inside Higher Ed*, October 12.www.insidehighered.com/views/2017/10/12/scholars-need-use-their-research- more-effectively-weigh-public-issues-day-essay.

Stein, A. and Daniels, J. (2017) *Going Public: A Guide for Social Scientists*, Chicago, University of Chicago Press.

Tirado, L. (2014) 'Why Poor People Stay Poor,' *Slate*, December 5. https://slate.com/.

Tokarczyk, M. M. (2004) 'Promises to Keep: Working Class Students and Higher Education' in Zweig, M. (ed.) *What's Class Got to Do With It? American Society in the Twenty-First Century*, Ithaca, Cornell University Press.

Tough, P. (2014) 'Who Gets to Graduate?' *The New York Times*, May 15. https://nyti.ms/1gjJOoU.

Tupac. 'Changes,' *AZ Lyrics*, 2014,www.azlyrics.com/lyrics/2pac/changes.html.

Warnock, D. M. and Hurst, A. L. (2016) '"The Poor Kids' Table": Organizing around an Invisible and Stigmatized Identity in flux,' *Journal of Diversity in Higher Education*, 9, 3, pp. 261–276. https://doi.org/10.1037/dhe0000029.

Warren, E. (2014) 'The Vanishing Middle Class,' in Weinstein, L. (ed.) *Money Changes Everything*, Boston, Bedford St. Martin's.

Zweig, M. (ed.) (2004) *What's Class Got to Do With It? American Society in the Twenty-First Century*, Ithaca, Cornell University Press.

30

Border crossing with day laborers and affordable housing activists

Terry Easton

Like many of you reading this chapter, I am interested in understanding the roles that work plays in people's lives. Peter Oresick and Nicholas Coles offer a perspective from which to think about this. In their introduction to *Working Classics: Poems on Industrial Life*, they suggest that the collected poems offer 'in the way good poems do,' ways to explore the meanings of work in our lives, such as 'what we get out of work, what work takes out of us, how work got to be this way, and how it might be different' (1990, xxvii). Their ideas provide impetus for two distinct though intertwined lines of documentation and analysis in working-class studies: the rewards and pain of work, and the desire to improve working conditions. These modes of inquiry offer a framework for understanding how to link scholarship with community engagement. In my projects on day laborers and affordable housing advocates, I used oral history and photography as activist approaches to working in the academy. Workers' and activists' voices and images illuminated economic and political circumstances that shaped their lives while unveiling actors responsible for the conditions under which they labored and lived in a deep-south US city at the turn of the twenty-first century.

Because I sought to recover histories that could have gone unrecorded due to the habitus marginalized lives embody, notions of 'hidden histories' shaped my perspective. Oral history creates opportunities for people to articulate their own interpretations of history, especially for those whose experiences might otherwise have been 'hidden from history' (Perks and Thomson 1998, ix). I embraced Michael Frisch's notion of shared authority in oral history, 'the history-making offered by both interviewer and narrator' (Shopes 2003, 103; Frisch 2011, 127).[1] Staughton Lynd has another name for this democratic vision, 'accompaniment,' a phrase borrowed from Latin American activists. Lynd suggests that during oral history interviews,

> the *accompagnateur* and the person accompanied are equals; each brings to their encounter a particular expertise based on professional training or life experience and as they come to form through their shared experience a vision of a better world, each has an obligation to be faithful to that dream.
>
> *(2012, 7)*

Lynd emphasizes not only that each collaborator brings expertise to the interview, but also that each is responsible to the other for initiating action based on the interview.[2] In short, oral histories should 'do something.'

To augment oral history and archival research, I used photographs for visual evidence. Known primarily for his occupational hazard photography, Earl Dotter's photos served as the central inspiration for the ways that I portrayed people working or waiting for work. His photographs, whether full frontal, framed from the shoulders up, or bodies in motion, capture what I now understand as workers' dignity.[3] 'If I am successful,' he states, 'the viewer will be better able to stand before the photograph and feel the intensity of the moment as I felt it myself' (1998, 153). David Bacon also influenced my photographic vision. Largely known for his agricultural labor and migrant worker photographs, Bacon, like Dotter, seeks to enact change by teaching viewers to see.[4] His images lead viewers into worksites, homes, and communities. Refusing to conform to purported objectivity in photojournalism, Bacon acknowledges his partisan position: 'As a photographer documenting poverty, migration and deportation, neutrality is not really possible ... I don't claim to be an unbiased observer' (2016, 22). Because he believes that images and words together can have a power that neither possesses alone, Bacon employs an approach that combines photographs with interviews and personal histories to capture 'complex social reality, as well as people's ideas for changing it' (2016, 24, 32). Bacon's oeuvre, like Dotter's, includes photographs of marches and protests, visual prompts of the vitality of collective action. Echoing their thematic strategies, I too recorded these kinds of events in Atlanta.

Day labor in a global south

The rise of temporary work in the 1970s, coupled with Ronald Reagan's fiscal and social policies of the 1980s, created particularly hard times for low-wage workers in the closing decades of the twentieth century in Atlanta and beyond. Increasing globalization and economic uncertainty since the 1990s promised that wages, rights, and protections of low-wage workers would become even more tenuous. During this period, the Atlanta metropolitan region was transformed into a convention, tourist, and employment destination. The construction and renovation of office towers, shopping malls, universities, sports arenas, airports, hotels, homes, and venues for the 1996 Olympic Games significantly altered the size, shape, and scope of Atlanta's place in the national and international economies.

Geographer Saskia Sassen's research on cities in the late twentieth century demonstrates that in many large metropolitan areas with highly developed global processes, the gap between rich and poor widened through the simultaneous development of a large low-wage informal or service economy and a high-income commercial or business economy. In these 'transnational spaces within national territories,' new socio-spatial economic configurations increased inequality, especially in cities already devastated by manufacturing decline (Sassen 1994, xiii). Historically a transportation hub, Atlanta was never a major manufacturing center, but in this deeply divided, class-based social and racial context, the growth of advanced producer services benefited only certain segments of the labor force, while increasing numbers joined the contingent workforce, day laborers and homeless people among them.

Trying to find good wages, safe and clean working conditions, and possibly a full-time position with a regular schedule and employment benefits, day laborers conducted their daily search for work from 1980 to 2005 by determining which employment strategy would most likely fulfill their employment goals. Atlanta's African American, Latino, and White day laborers used for-profit temporary staffing agencies, street corners, and nonprofit hiring halls to secure work. Experience taught the men that the likelihood of meeting all their employment goals was unrealistic.[5] Most knew that even if they wanted full-time, regular employment, finding it was possible but difficult. They also knew that they might find themselves working in an unpleasant or dangerous environment. Still they turned out each day (or whenever they could or wanted to turn out) and waited for the opportunity to work. By 2006, there were roughly thirty for-profit temporary manual labor staffing agencies, forty street corner-waiting areas, and two nonprofit hiring halls in Atlanta.

Depending upon factors such as skill, training, experience, age, race, ethnicity, English language proficiency, and the particular day labor employment strategy deployed, Atlanta's day laborers were likely to be engaged to work at a construction site, conference center, sports arena, hotel, or private residence. At these work sites, day laborers performed some of the most dangerous and physically demanding work in Atlanta: they operated machines, demolished buildings, dug ditches, tended lawns, moved stock in and out of warehouses, set up and took down special event seating, loaded and unloaded trucks, worked on assembly lines, and helped build homes, apartments, offices, and shopping centers. Some of these men lived in homes; others lived on the streets or in homeless shelters. Some found refuge in low-rent daily, weekly, or monthly rental units; others shared cramped quarters in apartments and sent money to their families in Mexico and Central America.

Temporary staffing agencies

In temporary staffing agencies (commonly called labor pools), men were generally required to sign up for work each day as early as five o'clock in the morning. A dispatcher, usually separated from workers by a partition with an opening or a window, controlled the assignment of work. If assigned a job for the day, labor pool workers were employees of the labor pool, not the client company, so the labor pool paid them at the end of each day. Grim working conditions generally characterized Atlanta's labor pools. Take-out fees for safety equipment and the cost of lunch and transportation often brought day laborers' wages below minimum wage. Labor pool workers generally earned minimum wage or just above, so additional take-out fees meant that workers rarely went home with enough money to support themselves with ample food, clothes, and shelter. After eight hours of work and three to four hours of travel time across a large metropolitan region, labor pool workers' days frequently averaged ten to fourteen hours.

Men used this type of day labor employment for several reasons: they avoided the pushing and shoving associated with street corner pickup sites; they were covered by workers' compensation insurance if they were injured at a job site; their pay could increase if they used power tools or performed skilled work; their employment was 'on the books' and therefore fully legal in terms of tax and social security deductions; and barring unusual circumstances, they did not get 'stiffed' for their daily labor. Atlanta's labor pools provided men on demand. Relationships between bodies, labor power, and contingent work were often inscribed within the names of the labor pools: Temporary People, Manpower Temporary Services, Labor Guys Staffing, Add-A-Man Labor Service, and Right Hand Man. Emmanuel Killen, an African American man who worked at numerous Atlanta labor pools since the early 1980s spoke with vitriol about them: 'They are part of the discrimination against lower income or no income or homeless people. I feel like they are nothing but a trap' (Killen 2003).

Danny Solomon described what it was like using a labor pool to secure work.

> 'If you didn't have a full-time job, that was your only means of supporting yourself or getting any kind of money. You know, I worked on jobs all day long on construction sites, and digging ditches, and stuff like that, and just being *dirty* and smelly, and *garbage*

Image 30.1 Danny Solomon, Atlanta, Georgia, 2005
Source: photo by Terry Easton

> and stuff like that, and work eight hours and come back and get paid twenty-five to thirty dollars. But the labor pool might have made one hundred and some dollars off me that day. Day laborers is just exactly what it is, day labor, *labor*, meaning slave work man, hauling trash, sweeping, mopping, construction clean up, the *hard work*, I mean the hard work that has to be done, lifting heavy boxes, which there's no skill involved in that. I've been on construction clean-up jobs where I've just pushed a broom all day. All day long eight hours just pushin' a broom. Physically exhausting, emotionally exhausting.
>
> (Solomon 2005)[6]

I met Danny when he was living at Open Door Community, a residential Christian Community grounded in the tradition of Catholic Worker houses (see Image 30.1). At Open Door, hospitality joined Civil Rights Movement-style political action. Homeless and housing-challenged day laborers frequented Open Door's breakfasts, lunches, clothes closet, and showers. I learned about Open Door through archival research revealing co-founder Reverend Ed Loring's efforts to call attention to and ameliorate labor pool working conditions. I began serving weekly at the Monday Morning Breakfast and subsequently interviewed day laborers and Loring. I also talked to day laborers in informal situations when cleaning up after breakfast, transporting people from a homeless shelter to Open Door for holiday meals, and sometimes taking them to purchase items unavailable at Open Door. Additionally, I joined Open Door in street actions, including events to bring attention to Atlanta's policies harmful to homeless people and low-wage workers.

Because of my steady hand serving breakfast and holiday meals, transporting homeless visitors to Open Door, and documenting day laborer's lives, Loring felt comfortable participating in my research. Having had many years of experience visiting labor pools and writing about them, Loring held deep convictions. As a method to collaborate on the production of knowledge, during one of our interviews, I asked him to comment on photographs that documentary photographer Tom Rankin had taken of labor pools in the 1980s for *Hard Labor: A Report on Day Labor Pools and Temporary Employment* (Williams 1988). Rankin's extraordinary images of people and places comprising the day labor scene invoke exigencies of hard-pressed lives. With a

Image 30.2 Dispatcher (right) talking to worker, 1988
Source: photo by Tom Rankin

doctorate in African American history and deep knowledge of Christianity through theological training, Loring used a wide lens to analyze the photographs.

This is an edited excerpt of our conversation about one of the photographs (shown in Image 30.2).

> *TE:* Is that a scene that is familiar to you?
> *EL:* It certainly is.
> *TE:* What is it that you see there that is particularly interesting or revealing?
> *EL:* I think those hands show the hunger and the desire for work. I think it is a breaking down of the stereotypical way that the poor are described as lazy and not wanting to work. I think it also shows the disproportion of power in our society. This person [the dispatcher] is a king in that he has access to labor. He is a very powerful person in these people's lives, and he makes decisions that shape these people's lives. Also, from my background as a historian and as a theologian and ethicist, I see slavery. And although I see that all [people] here are African American, I know that what lies behind this is a White system of capitalism that requires us to keep a pool of unskilled, unemployed people to keep the minimum wage low—below a living wage—and this creates the desperation of these [day laborers].
>
> (Loring 2006)[7]

Street corners

Street corner waiting areas were unregulated labor pickup sites. 'Connected' sites were located near home improvement stores; 'unconnected' sites were in locations without a designated home improvement store nearby but had high traffic flow, good visibility, and a safe means of exiting and entering the roadway. These sites were prone to change depending upon factors including city regulations, police harassment, Immigration and Naturalization Service (INS) raids, and vehicular traffic.

Advantages of using catch-out corners included workers being able to negotiate their hourly wage directly with a potential employer; wages were generally three to five dollars more per hour than what workers received at labor pools; expenses such as transportation costs and safety equipment fees were not deducted from their wages; it was a more active approach to securing work compared to waiting at a labor pool; workers could conceivably work more than one job per day; workers who wished to remain anonymous or 'invisible' due to their undocumented status were better able to do so. Disadvantages at street corner pickup sites included having to push and shove when competing for work; not getting paid for work performed; possibly not having workers' compensation insurance if an injury occurred; and making oneself an easy target for police and INS harassment.

Imagined and real economic opportunities spurred men from Mexico and Central America to journey to Atlanta searching for work in the 1980s and 1990s. For these men, the push of destitution and the pull of opportunity resulted in transnational lives that shaped and were shaped by local customs, national laws, and international politics (see Image 30.3). While Atlanta's businesses and consumers benefited from the arrival of a steady supply of low-wage workers, many Latino day laborers, vulnerable because of their immigration status, labored at what Grace Chang calls the 3D jobs: 'dirty, dangerous, and degrading' (2000, 180). Exposure to hazardous chemicals and dangerous machinery, lifting heavy loads, and working several stories from the ground were day laborers' constant companion. Day laborers often feared coming from the shadows to report crimes against them. Atlanta Attorney David Moskowitz reports that the abuse of illegal immigrants remains, like the workers themselves, undocumented (Abkowitz 2005, 32). In addition to being stiffed for their pay, day laborers faced the possibility of being beaten or robbed. In 2004, suburban Atlanta high school students lured a day laborer into their truck with an offer of work. They drove him to a remote location, beat him with fists and clubs, yelled racial epithets, and robbed him.

Attorney Jennifer Gordon expresses the complexity inherent in seeking workplace justice in the 'new sweatshops' found scattered in pockets of suburban sprawl where, she reports, 'long hours, illegally low wages, and staggering rates of injury' are found (2005, 2). Entangled in globalization, these 'suburban sweatshops' are sites where small and mobile, low-overhead, cash-economy employers leave few traces and travel below the radar (24). Despite the difficulties inherent in seeking justice in these areas, activists sought to improve working conditions for day laborers in Atlanta's vast suburban landscape. To ameliorate the problems day laborers faced when securing work at street corners, I collaborated with Tisha Tallman, the Southeast Regional Counsel of the nonprofit advocacy organization the Mexican American Legal Defense and Educational Fund (MALDEF), and Remedios Gomez Arnau, consul general of the Mexican Consulate in Atlanta, on a project designed to document and prevent workplace abuse. I had created a map of street corner, labor pool, and nonprofit hiring hall day labor sites in Atlanta. At Tallman and Gomez Arnau's request, we traveled to multiple sites across the metro region to collect information about the problems street corner day labors faced, to enact possible interventions (see Image 30.4).

After learning from day laborers at street corner sites and synthesizing what I had collected through oral history and photography, Gomez Arnau and Tallman produced fliers and wallet-sized cards to distribute at day labor pickup sites throughout metro Atlanta. These tracts contained a list of telephone numbers and help hotlines such as the Labor Department, the

Image 30.3 Work secured at a street corner, Decatur, Georgia, 2005
Source: photo by Terry Easton

Occupational Safety and Health Administration, the Mexican Consulate, and MALDEF. The flyer featured images and words explaining workers' rights in the United States. These materials also contained space for day laborers to document employers' names, telephone numbers, license plate numbers, agreed-upon wages, dates and hours of employment, names and phone numbers of other workers, work performed, and the tools used. The larger fliers, printed in Spanish and English, featured pictorials explaining workers' rights in the United States and what to do if injured on the job. The fliers stressed the importance of reporting robberies, unpaid work, and violent attacks. This information provided evidence for the identification of employers when day laborers sought redress for employment abuse. They distributed cards and flyers at day labor sites. After only a short time, Tallman reported positive results from the project (2006).

Nonprofit hiring halls

Non-profit hiring halls and labor pools functioned similarly in that they both provided a place for day laborers to wait for work in a building that shielded them from intemperate climate. Unlike labor pools, non-profit hiring halls did not make money in their intermediary role of connecting workers to employers. Latinos comprised the majority day labor population at these hiring halls; generally, homeowners and contractors in the landscaping and construction industries comprised the client base. The primary goal of hiring halls was to offer day laborers a safe place to wait for work: a place that shielded them from extreme temperatures and a place where they were less likely to experience nonpayment or underpayment of wages. The men established

Image 30.4 Tisha Tallman (left) and Remedios Gomez Arnau (center) learn about day labor conditions, Sandy Springs, Georgia, 2005
Source: photo by Terry Easton

a minimum wage rate of roughly twice the federal minimum wage. More than just a place to wait for work, some hiring halls offered coffee, English classes, health workshops, full-time job announcements, immigration and human rights information and workshops, table games, and access to computers.

Hiring hall coordinators worked on behalf of day laborers to ensure that workers were paid the full sum of their promised wages. The primary tactic to prevent such abuse was requiring employers to leave their name and contact information at the hiring hall before securing a worker. A secondary tactic was to mediate on workers' behalf should employers not pay them. Workers' regard for hiring halls was measured by their frequent return to them. As evidenced by their comments, the hiring hall was a safe place to wait for work. Thomas Alcantara used a hiring hall instead of the street for many reasons: 'The street is very unorganized. I don't like that everybody shoves and pushes, and somebody can hurt you. I like the list here. I like the order. Everybody communicates with everybody very strongly' (Alcantara 2003). Thomas's comments illuminate the atmosphere of respect cultivated at the hiring hall. Javier Lopez used the hiring hall instead of a street corner to find work because, as he says, 'Over here it is easier. Over there everybody runs and I'm not aggressive enough. I don't like that' (Lopez 2003). He also enjoyed talking to the other men and eating the fifty-cent breakfast soups. Guillermo Hernandez said that he liked waiting for work at the hiring hall because the men 'fool around and have fun' when they waited for work (Hernandez 2003). Pickup soccer games, for example, were an established part of the waiting process at one of the hiring halls.

Following Eva Villafañe's advice (the coordinator at one the nonprofit hiring halls), I printed individual and group photos for the men to send to their families back home. She suggested that this was one of the ways that I could soothe some of the pain they experienced being so far away from their families. In a more practical way, and approved through the Review Board of my institution, I gave every interviewee a gift card for a local chain store. More informally, I arrived at sunrise with a cooler of cold drinks that I shared as they faced the day's heat. Over the roughly two months that I visited this hiring hall, I became part of the scenery. When Eva had to leave unexpectedly one day, she trusted me to run the list, the check-in and check-out system the men had designed to ensure a fair, orderly system of attaining work (see Image 30.5). At another nonprofit hiring hall that I had visited numerous times over the course of two years and where I had conducted interviews, the coordinator and three day laborers came to my class to talk to students about day laborers' working lives in the context of local, national, and international political economies. This kind of boundary crossing also occurred when Tisha Tallman, David Moskowitz, and a representative from the Mexican Consulate participated in a panel that I organized for a Southern Labor Studies Association conference in Atlanta. Later, Tallman gave a campus-wide talk about Latinos in the South, and a labor attorney visited my classroom to inform us about immigrant workers from Mexico and Central America laboring in low-wage, high-risk occupations in the United States.

Marches and protest

According to historian Susan Davis (1986), in the contested terrain of the streets, public events such as marches build and challenge social relations. Atlanta Latinos demonstrated that they would

Image 30.5 Eva Villafañe, nonprofit hiring hall, Canton, Georgia, 2003
Source: photo by Terry Easton

Image 30.6 Marchers on the street, Doraville, Georgia, 2004
Source: photo by Terry Easton

not acquiesce to abuse, exploitation, and disempowerment. Construction and landscaping offered a seemingly endless supply of work for Atlanta's Latino day laborers; however, as a perceived foreign workforce, they sometimes bore the brunt of Southern (in)hospitality. At street corner pickup sites, some local business owners and residents viewed day laborers with suspicion, scorn, and fear. As a result, local city councils and county commissions passed ordinances designed to forbid day laborers from congregating in designated areas. A local county commissioner urged landlords to check the immigration status of tenants and declared English the county's official language. Governor Purdue signed a bill that allowed local police to check the immigration status of Latinos. Former consul general of the Mexican Consulate in Atlanta, Teodoro Maus, called these kinds of actions 'wanting the hands, but not the body' (Ahmed 2001, D1). At the state capitol and on the streets, I photographed people asserting their rights and fighting for dignity in marches and protests across Atlanta's urban and suburban landscapes (see Image 30.6).

Affordable housing development

Protestors also took to the streets when they fought for affordable housing, which dwindled rapidly in the 1980s as Atlanta emerged as an international metropolis. In a defiant act to foreground economic disparity, activists and homeless people illegally took over Atlanta's abandoned Imperial Hotel in 1990. With nearly 10,000 homeless people in the city, the Imperial, empty and in severe disrepair, was emblematic of the larger failure of city leadership to provide ample affordable housing. People for Urban Justice (PUJ), the activist group that initiated the occupation, began their work with ameliorating brutal labor pool working conditions, but the closing of a city-run shelter and the increasing destruction of low-cost, single-room occupancy (SRO) housing propelled them on a different path: affordable housing development.[8] Formed in early 1990, PUJ was a collaborative social justice movement comprising people from Open Door Community, Concerned Black Clergy, Metro Atlanta Task Force for the Homeless, and other faith-based and secular organizations. They were angered and frustrated that political and business leaders promoted and funded glamorous projects such as sports stadiums and entertainment centers at the cost of disenfranchising Atlanta's poor people.[9]

Stanley Gibson, a homeless person who participated in the occupation, describes how SRO housing was an important option for low-wage workers: 'It was like a stepping stone. It was a place to start. It was a base of operations. You could get yourself focused, get your money going, have a place inside with running water, a place to sleep that was safe, and then go ahead and move to the next phase' (Gibson 2005). Robert Dobbins, a labor pool worker and homeless person who participated in the occupation, points out, 'By the time the occupation was going on, the most boomin' jobs was the labor pools' (Dobbins 2005). With only fifteen to twenty-five dollars in their hands for a long day's work, labor pool workers could not afford housing with a long-term rental agreement and security deposit, but they could afford ten bucks for a room in an SRO.

Activists broke into the hotel before daybreak on June 18 with a commitment to taking their Christian and civil rights era-inspired beliefs to the streets. In late morning, they unfurled a banner from the top floor windows with the message 'House the Homeless Here!' (see Image 30.7). They expected to be removed and arrested by noon, but police, city officials, and the hotel's owner, noted Atlanta architect John Portman, had simply let them be. PUJ decided to remain in the hotel until their demands for affordable housing were met or until they were forcibly removed. In the meantime, they opened the hotel to homeless people, and they all stayed through the night. That one night became the sixteen nights of the Imperial Hotel occupation; during this period, roughly three hundred people slept in the rooms at night and agitated on the sidewalks and streets during the day.

When reflecting on the place of this occupation in the history of activism in Atlanta, historian Charles Steffen characterized this action as a social movement 'without precedent' and 'one of the most dramatic street actions in Atlanta since the student-led civil rights protests of the 1960s' (2012, 760, 756). In my book, *Raising Our voices, Breaking the Chain: The Imperial Hotel Occupation as Prophetic Politics* (2016), I document the dramatic events that occurred during those sixteen remarkable days, primarily from the perspective of PUJ activists and those aligned with their interests. I also demonstrate how this event spurred affordable housing development in the 1990s and beyond, including the transformation of the Imperial Hotel itself into affordable housing in 1996 and its renovation in 2014.

During the sixteen days of the occupation, community was created among activists, homeless people, and sympathetic participants and observers. They shared food, water, and song. They spoke with resolve to the press. Solidarity inside the hotel was torn asunder when Mayor Maynard Jackson's assistant, future two-term mayor Shirley Franklin, negotiated clandestinely with leaders of homeless people in the hotel. Franklin promised homeless occupants jobs, temporary housing, and a commitment to the development of 3,500 units of affordable housing; in exchange, the hotel occupants agreed to leave. Some PUJ activists refused to leave the hotel, seeking a stronger commitment to develop 5,000 affordable housing units. In the end, six were arrested.

The long-term legacy of the occupation included affordable housing; the short-term legacy included a series of surprises that demonstrated that prophetic politics, or 'foot theology,' as described by Loring, can be a vital tool in civic engagement. Bill Jones, a homeless participant in

Image 30.7 Imperial Hotel occupation with banner, Atlanta, Georgia, 1990
Source: photographer unknown; photo courtesy of Open Door Community

the occupation, exclaimed that the takeover had done more in two weeks for homeless people than committees had done in seven years (Sherman and Smith 1990). Craig Taylor, a long-time developer of affordable housing, called the occupation a 'lightning strike' (Taylor 2013). The takeover energized the development of affordable housing during the 1990s and beyond. Roughly 1,000 units built during this period are rooted in the Imperial occupation: the takeover spurred developers, influenced politicians, and tapped financial streams (see Image 30.8). If we consider what was accomplished under the circumstances presented, the Imperial Hotel occupation can be described as successful, even though 3,500 affordable housing units were not developed as promised. Put another way, as framed by social movement theorists Frances Fox Piven and Richard Cloward, 'The relevant question to ask is whether, on balance, the movement made gains or lost ground; whether it advanced the interests of [poor] people or set back those interests' (1979, xiii). Clearly, the interests of poor and working-class people were advanced, at least minimally: affordable housing *was* developed.

Oral historian Todd Moye contends that *Raising Our Voices, Breaking the Chain* tells the story of one of the most fascinating and important chapters in Atlanta's recent history. He places my work in the radical camp of progressive-minded oral historians and remarks, 'An oral history … begins with the interviewer's respectful approach to a would-be interviewee and the words (be they spoken or unspoken), "I think you're important. I would like to learn from you."' Moye adds, 'this kind of knowledge generation and sharing can document the stories of those who challenge power, which in turn leads to social change.' Signaling the use-value of *Raising Our Voices*, he suggests that it will prove beneficial for organizers who need to know 'what hasn't worked in situations similar to their own as well as what has, what pitfalls they need to look out for, [and] what goals are unrealistic but worth fighting for anyway' (2017, 5).

Image 30.8 Supporters of the Imperial Hotel occupation, Atlanta, Georgia, 1990
Source: photographer unknown; photo courtesy of Open Door Community

Moye's description of the book characterizes how it achieves a goal of working-class studies, to promote scholarship that actively involves and serves the interests of working-class people ('What We Do' n.d.).

Research accessibility

As a form of community engagement, I released my research in accessible ways: the day labor project through an open-access, online journal; the affordable housing project through readers' option of a free or low-cost book, with any funds collected going directly to the community organization that published it. Akin to the long history of progressive-minded educators and documentarians, elements of my projects can be described as 'participatory documentary,' where the 'mode of effect' hinges on 'participation, arousal, and engagement' (Hale 2018, 102). In my 2006 dissertation on day laborers, I reveal how African American, Latino, and White day laborers experienced Atlanta's transformation to an international metropolis from 1980 to 2005.[10] In addition to documenting the conditions under which day laborers worked and lived, the project also tells larger stories about power, resistance, and reform by showing how activists, attorneys, legislators, and union members sought to improve day laborers' working conditions. To make the research accessible, I published an abbreviated version of the dissertation in *Southern Spaces*, an online journal exploring spaces and places of the American South. I included audio clips, images, ephemera, and maps. Through this multimedia format, day laboring and the issues surrounding it are richly presented with aural and visual appeal. From December 21, 2007, to March 29, 2020, 'Geographies of hope and despair: Atlanta's African American, Latino, and White day laborers' was viewed 9,667 times by 7,729 unique readers.[11]

In my 2016 book, *Raising Our Voices, Breaking the Chain: The Imperial Hotel Occupation as Prophetic Politics*, I detail how a four-hour street action to bring attention to the dearth of affordable housing turned into a sixteen-day homeless and activist occupation of an abandoned hotel in 1990. After gaining Ed Loring's trust through my service at Open Door Community and having interviewed him for day labor research, he asked me to write a history of the occupation. There were times when I thought that I could not finish the project; however, my dedication to Open Door Community ushered its completion. The book is published by Open Door Community Press, a small, local press that Loring wanted to use, partially because Open Door Community would have control over distribution. Because the press is not a university press or another kind of equal stature, the book will likely not figure prominently in my next workplace promotion. I am fine with this: my dedication to the project and loyalty to Loring outweigh any disruptions to my workplace promotion.

Some of the most rewarding labor I have completed is associated with this project. This includes giving away nearly 500 books since its publication. I worked with Open Door to mail free copies of the book to public and private libraries, local and state politicians, participants in the occupation, and Open Door donors. I also gave free books to the current owner and manager of the Imperial for distribution among employees and housing residents. I donated books to participants of the annual Georgia Supportive Housing conference, where local and national practitioners chart the future of affordable housing.[12] Through a blog entry titled 'A "lightning strike" in the history of Atlanta's affordable housing development,' I published key insights of the book in *Atlanta Studies*, an open-access, online journal for analysis of Atlanta's past and present aimed at diverse public audiences (Easton 2017).

The highlight of my working life is the book signing I organized at the renovated Imperial Hotel, now a ninety-unit affordable housing structure called The Commons at Imperial. Occupation participants, current residents, a reporter who covered the hotel takeover, a politician who fought for the hotel renovation, and affordable housing developers and architects, including the current owner and manager of the hotel, attended this event. We toured the building, talked about its history, discussed the future of affordable housing, and concluded with an uplifting rendition of the Civil Rights anthem 'This little light of mine.'[13]

Working-class studies as border crossing

As a worker in the production of knowledge ensconced in a public university in the United States South with a demanding teaching load and sizeable portion of first-generation students, and as someone whose scholarly pursuits formally began later than traditional trajectories, I am aware of the indomitable qualities of time. Ethically sound oral history and photography projects achieved through meaningful relationships, though inherently time-consuming, enact aims of working-class studies: to create partnerships that link scholarship with activism in labor, community, and other working-class social justice organizations ('What We Do' n.d.).

This is not to suggest that my foray into documentary scholarship has not included blunders, especially along the lines of race and class. In terms of positionality, I grew up working class in racially integrated housing projects in a small Illinois town in the 1960s to 1980s. I am White. I felt the sting of classism at a young age, and that set the stage for what I now recognize as a life-long commitment to challenging top-down perceptions of working-class people. Even though I was vigilant about recognizing my racial advantage and situational middle-class status, I made mistakes. These included impelling a weary day laborer for a photograph (he justifiably responded after the photograph, 'there, you got what you wanted'); asking a day laborer how he felt about growing up in a 'bad' neighborhood (he rightfully told me he did not consider it bad); varying how I 'cleaned up' interviewees' speech patterns (generally along lines of class and race) and failing to offer all interviewees an opportunity to review interview transcripts (with homeless or transient participants getting fewer opportunities).

I acknowledge my errors in documentary engagement not only to signal the problematic nature of well-meaning border crossing, but also to raise the idea that, overall, the benefits generally outweigh the risks. I recall my dissertation advisor responding to my anxiousness about textures of power in day labor research. After acknowledging the realities of this power and the potential for paralysis (and suggesting ways to reduce the distance between interviewer and interviewee), he asked if it was better to have collected nothing at all or at least something that illuminated marginalized voices, however problematic. I chose the latter. Twenty years later, this conversation still informs my thinking about documentary scholarship.

Local oral history and photography offer opportunities to learn from and with working-class people across racial, ethnic, and classed terrain. These methods also enact activist routes for economic and political power. As my writing of this chapter concludes, I am teaching a course on Latino workers in the United States. Students—ten of them connected to migrant farm work in some fashion—examine agricultural worker oral histories and interpret historical, fictional, photographic, and filmic accounts of labor and migration. Interdisciplinary research and pedagogy enrich the scope of working-class studies.[14] As the field thrusts more completely toward international reach, border-crossing narratives rooted in collaborative documentary scholarship await our embrace.

Notes

1 Shopes captures Frisch's significant contribution to oral history when she observes that Frisch's 'shared authority' concept 'neatly captures that which lies at the heart of both the method and the ethic—or perhaps one should say the politics—of the oral history enterprise: the dialogue that defines the interview process itself and the potential for the dialogue to extend outward—in public forums, radio programs, dramatic productions, publications, and other forms—toward a more democratic cultural practice' (2011, 103).

2 I am indebted to Daniel Kerr for introducing me to Lynd's ideas about oral history interviews. See his 2016 essay 'Allan Nevins is not my grandfather: The roots of radical oral history practice in the United States' in *The Oral History Review*.

3 Joseph Entin's comments about Milton Rogovin's photographs are helpful when thinking about the relationship between photographer, subject, and audience: 'his photographs are grounded in and make manifest forms of reciprocity and collaboration that challenge the one-sided dynamics of traditional liberal-reformist documentary image-work, which tended to reaffirm the privilege of well-to-do viewers by presenting pity-inducing depictions of social subordinate subjects' (2018, 155).

4 Bacon's and Dotter's work, and their impetus to teach viewers to see, is directly linked to early-twentieth-century photographer Lewis Hine. For an engaging discussion of post-World War II documentary photography, see the introduction to *Remaking Reality: U.S. Documentary Culture after 1945* (Sara Blair, Joseph B. Entin, and Franny Nudelman, editors, 2018). See Janet Zandy's *Unfinished Stories: The Narrative Photography of Hansel Mieth and Marion Palfi* (2013) for theoretical and gendered perspectives on documentary photography. For additional David Bacon and Earl Dotter photographs, see their websites at http://dbacon.igc.org/ and https://www.earldotter.com/.

5 A small percentage of women and men of other races and ethnicities day-labored in Atlanta during the period I studied. Knowing the experiences of these women and men would enrich our understanding of Atlanta's day laboring social and political economies. However, since they comprised a small segment of the day-laborer population, and because I needed to tighten the focus of the dissertation, I excluded them from study. If we are to have a more complete portrait of day labor in Atlanta, these populations need to be studied. At a nonprofit hiring hall, for example, a hiring hall coordinator had a list of women available to do day labor such as house cleaning and other domestic duties on an on-call basis. The women did not wait for work at the hiring hall.

6 One of Danny's evocative statements during one of our interviews was 'They just want a body … they don't care nothin' 'bout you.' You can hear an excerpt of our interview at https://doi.org/10.18737/M7H608. Also, I worked for four days as a day laborer through a temporary labor agency when I conducted research. I, too, spent some time as a 'clean-up' person. A situation I recall most vividly is when a supervisor berated me intensely throughout the day in what I interpret as a method of asserting psychological dominance.

7 You can see this photograph and other Tom Rankin day labor photographs in my *Southern Spaces* essay titled 'Geographies of hope and despair: Atlanta's African American, Latino, and White Day Laborers' (2007): https://doi.org/10.18737/M7H608.

8 For an instructive account of the destruction of SRO and low-income housing in Atlanta, see Steffen (2012).

9 I am borrowing material in this section of this essay from a blog post I published on April 6, 2017: 'A "lightning strike" in the history of Atlanta's affordable housing development: Revisiting the 1990 Imperial Hotel occupation' (Easton 2017).

10 This dissertation, *Temporary Work, Contingent Lives: Race, Immigration, and Transformations of Atlanta's Daily Work, Daily Pay* (2006), is the recipient of the 2007 Constance Coiner Dissertation Award of the Working-Class Studies Association.

11 The essay was published on December 21, 2007. In 2019, the most recent full year of viewing statistics, there were 379 views by 279 unique readers. I would like to thank Madison Elkins, Managing Editor of *Southern Spaces*, for providing readership statistics. This essay can be accessed at https://doi.org/10.18737/M7H608.

12 I also gave away books at a book-signing hosted by the Metro Atlanta Democratic Socialists of America. I have given away more than twenty books to faculty and students on my campus. Whenever possible, I take books to academic conferences to give away. Additional opportunities to give away books occurred when I appeared three times on Atlanta public radio stations to talk about the book.

13 A blog entry about this book signing can be accessed at https://nationalchurchresidences.blog/2016/12/05/new-book-tells-story-of-imperial-hotels-16-day-occupation/.

14 In my research and teaching, I believe that I am practicing a tenet of working-class studies, to 'Promote interdisciplinary, multi-disciplinary, and disciplinary approaches to studying and teaching about the lived experience of working-class people' ('What We Do' n.d.). I also believe that implicit in this chapter is another tenet of working-class studies: to 'Facilitate conversations and critical debate engaging diverse intellectual and political approaches to scholarship, teaching, and outreach in working-class studies' ('What We Do').

References

Abkowitz, A. (2005) 'Invisible man: A Hispanic immigrant chases the American dream—and falls,' *Creative Loafing*, 34, 30, 1 December, pp. 28–32.

Ahmed, S. (2001) 'Chains of diplomacy broken,' *Atlanta Journal and Constitution*, 15 February, pp. D1.

Alcantara, T. [pseudonym] (2003) Interviewed by Terry Easton, interpreted by Eva Villafañe, 5 August.

Bacon, D. (2016) *In the Fields of the North / En los Campos del Norte*, Oakland/Tijuana, University of California Press/El Colegio de la Frontera Norte.

Blair, S., Entin, J.B., and Nudelman, F. (eds.) (2018), *Remaking Reality: U.S. Documentary Culture after 1945*, Chapel Hill, University of North Carolina Press.

Chang, G. (2000) *Disposable Domestics: Immigrant Women Workers in the Global Economy*, Cambridge, South End Press.

Davis, S. (1986) *Parades and Power: Street Theatre in Nineteenth-Century Philadelphia*, Berkeley, University of California Press.

Deggans, E. (6 August 2018) '"This Little Light of Mine" Shines On: A Timeless Tool of Resistance.' Available from: www.npr.org/2018/08/06/630051651/american-anthem-this-little-light-of-mine-resistance. [accessed 23 March 2020].

Dobbins, R. (2005) Interviewed by Terry Easton, 25 November.

Dotter, E. (1998) *The Quiet Sickness: A Photographic Chronicle of Hazardous Work in America*, Fairfax, American Industrial Hygiene Association.

Easton, T. (2006) *Temporary Work, Contingent Lives: Race, Immigration, and Transformations of Atlanta's Daily Work, Daily Pay*. PhD dissertation, Emory University.

———. (2007). 'Geographies of hope and despair: Atlanta's African American, Latino, and White day laborers,' *Southern Spaces*, https://doi.org/10.18737/M7H608.

———. (2016) *Raising Our Voices, Breaking the Chain: The Imperial Hotel Occupation as Prophetic Politics*, Atlanta, Open Door Community Press.

———. (2017) 'A "lightning strike" in the history of Atlanta's affordable housing development: Revisiting the 1990 Imperial Hotel occupation,' *Atlanta Studies*, 6 April. https://doi.org/10.18737/atls20170406.

Entin, J.B. (2018) 'Working photography: Labor documentary and documentary labor in the neoliberal age,' in Blair, S., Entin, J.B., and Nudelman, F. (eds.) *Remaking Reality: U.S. Documentary Culture after 1945*, Chapel Hill, University of North Carolina Press.

Frisch, M. (2011) 'From *a shared authority* to the digital kitchen, and back,' in Adair, B., Filene, B., and Koloski, L. (eds.) *Letting Go? Shared Historical Authority in a User-Generated World*, Philadelphia, The Pew Center for the Arts & Heritage; Walnut Creek, Left Coast Press.

Gibson, S. (2005) Interviewed by Terry Easton, 26 September.

Gordon, J. (2005) *Suburban Sweatshops: The Fight for Immigrant Rights*, Cambridge, Harvard University Press.

Hale, G.E. (2018) 'Participatory documentary: Recording the sound of equality in the Southern civil rights movement,' in Blair, S., Entin, J.B., and Nudelman, F. (eds.) *Remaking Reality: U.S. Documentary Culture after 1945*, Chapel Hill, University of North Carolina Press.

Hernandez. G. [pseudonym] (2003) Interviewed by Terry Easton, interpreted by Eva Villafañe, 12 August.

Kerr, D. (2016) 'Allan Nevins is not my grandfather: The roots of radical oral history practice in the United States,' *The Oral History Review*, 43, 2, pp. 367–391.

Killen, E. (2003) Unrecorded Interview by Terry Easton, 10 October.

Lopez, J. [pseudonym] (2003) Interview by Terry Easton, interpreted by Eva Villafañe, 8 August.

Loring, E. (2006) Interview by Terry Easton, 11 February.

Lynd, S. (2012) *Accompanying: Pathways to Social Change*, Oakland, PM Press.

Moye, T. (2017) 'Radical oral history—*raising our voices, breaking the chain: The Imperial Hotel occupation as prophetic politics*,' *Hospitality*, February–March, 36, 2, p. 5.

Oresick, P. and Coles, N. (eds.) (1990) *Working Classics: Poems on Industrial Life*, Urbana, University of Illinois Press.

Perks, R., and Thomson, A. (eds.) (1998) *The Oral History Reader*, London, Routledge.

Piven, F.F., and Cloward, R.A. (1979) *Poor People's Movements: Why They Succeed, How They Fail*, New York, Vintage Books.

Sassen, S. (1994) *Cities in a World Economy*, Thousand Oaks, Pine Forge Press.

Sherman, M., and Smith, B., III (1990) 'Six squatters at old hotel are arrested,' *Atlanta Journal*, 3 July.

Shopes, L. (2003) 'Commentary: Sharing authority,' *The Oral History Review*, 30, 1, pp. 103–110.

Solomon, D. (2005) Interview by Terry Easton, 19 April, 22 April.

Steffen, C. (2012) '(Dis)empowering homeless people: The battle for Atlanta's Imperial Hotel, 1990–1991,' *Journal of Urban History*, 38, 4, pp. 753–776.

———. (2016) 'The rise and fall of Atlanta's skid row,' *Atlanta Studies*, 6 December. https://doi.org/10.18737/atls20161206.

Tallman, T. (2006) Interview by Terry Easton, 11 February.

Taylor, C. (2013) Interview by Terry Easton, 23 December.

'What We Do' (n.d.) *Working-Class Studies Association*. Available from: https://wcstudiesassociation.wordpress.com/what-we-do/ [accessed 3 March 2020].

Williams, R. (1988) *Hard Labor: A Report on Day Labor Pools and Temporary Employment*, Atlanta, Southern Regional Council.

Zandy, J. (2013) *Unfinished Stories: The Narrative Photography of Hansel Mieth and Marion Palfi*, Rochester, RIT Press.

31

Finding class in food justice efforts

Leslie Hossfeld, E. Brooke Kelly, and Julia F. Waity

Farming in the U.S. has shifted toward large-scale agricultural production and increased mechanization. California, where most of the produce consumed in the U.S. is grown and harvested, serves as an example of these trends. Yet, such crops are still harvested by hand by farmworkers who make some of the lowest wages in the U.S. economy, leading to an enduring paradox: that those who labor to plant and harvest crops essential to a healthy diet, such as lettuce, spinach, and broccoli, find themselves unable to include those foods at their own tables (Fuller 2016). This is certainly not new to contemporary farming. Indeed, the contradictions of farmworkers' circumstances have been poignantly captured in John Steinbeck's writings as far back as the 1930s (*In Dubious Battle*, 1936, *Of Mice and Men*, 1937, and *The Grapes of Wrath*, 1939). And again years later, as articulated by farmworker activist and co-founder of the National Farm Workers Association Cezar Chavez (1927–1993), who captured this painful reality when he wrote: 'It's ironic that those who till the soil, cultivate and harvest the fruits, vegetables, and other foods that fill your tables with abundance have nothing left for themselves.'

Nevertheless, more recent changes in the food system have, perhaps, exacerbated the circumstances of farmworkers and others from the working class. Zweig (2004) defines the working class as those who find themselves lacking power and authority at work and as citizens. As the above example of farmworkers illustrate, this can include those living below the poverty line and those in the working poor. In this chapter, we consider the ways the working class, broadly defined, lack power and authority over food and food systems as both laborers and consumers. Globalization and policies, such as the North American Free Trade Agreement (NAFTA), have undermined the position of workers within the current food system. We also focus on the ways food serves as a site of resistance, highlighting examples of actions and calls to action to ameliorate food and class inequalities and promote food justice.

Food workers and labor

The circumstances of farmworkers, food vendors, and restaurant workers highlight the vulnerable position of the workers who grow, harvest, process, and prepare our food. To understand some of the dramatic and complex changes in food production and how these have negatively affected the working class, we begin with farms and small farmers. Since the 1940s there has been a marked decrease in the number of small family farms, once the mainstay of U.S. food production. For example, in North Carolina, a state located in the Southeast region of the U.S. with a history in rural agriculture and farming, more than 250,000 farms have gone out of business since 1950 (USDA [U.S. Department of Agriculture] Economic Research Service, cited in Thompson 2002, 59). Increased mechanization, urbanization, and changes in agricultural practices and policies precipitated the shift from small farms to large-scale agricultural production (Hossfeld, Kelly, and Waity 2015).

African American farmers have lost ground at an alarming rate, with the number of African American farm owners dropping to around 18,000 from more than a million in 1920. Systematic discrimination against African Americans by the Farmers Home Administration, the federal agency responsible for providing credit to small farmers, as acknowledged by the 1999 U.S. Supreme Court ruling in *Pigford v. USDA*, contributed to the dwindling number of African American farm owners. Historically, African American farmers faced many hurdles in acquiring land, and land lost among African Americans in agriculture is rarely regained (Smith and Poff 1997, cited in Thompson 2002: 64). When slaves were freed after the end of the Civil War, many became sharecroppers or tenant farmers, but rarely did they become landowners. Poor whites also worked as sharecroppers, caught in a cycle of debt and repayment, and remained dependent on the landowning class (Thompson 2002). Historically, government funded agricultural programs have done little to combat the racial inequalities found in agricultural practices (Benson 2011). Despite recent strategies to remedy past discriminatory practice through program expansions to include socially disadvantaged growers, and increased diversity in the USDA workforce, inequalities in farming and accessing farmer programs remain (Hossfeld, Rico-Mendez, and Russell 2018).

Today, many small farmers find themselves estranged from their land and labor, trapped in a state of debt and/or contracting out their labor after losing their land. The global agricultural marketplace increasingly consists of large-scale agribusiness, making it more difficult for small farmers to compete. Indeed, about ten companies control most of the U.S. food production (Hoffman 2013). As large farms replace small farms, farmers lose control over the land and instead begin selling their labor (Hossfeld, Kelly, and Waity 2015). Farm subsidies and policies in the U.S. impact farmers there and abroad. For example, because of U.S. subsidies on corn, U.S. corn farmers are able to sell their corn on the international market under the cost of production. Large amounts of cheap U.S. corn in Mexico have displaced many Mexican farmers. As a result, many of those displaced farmers crossed the border to the U.S. in search of work as laborers on U.S. farms. With the passage of NAFTA, the percentage of migrant farmworkers that are undocumented rose from 7 percent to 50 percent (Albritton 2013).

Within the U.S., an example of farmers losing control of their land and selling their labor is seen with corporate-owned contract farms, which have been replacing family operations in agricultural communities nationwide at a fast pace (Heffernan 2000). Contract farms are often operated by individuals that previously controlled their own farm businesses, often on the very same land, but have become, in essence, 'hired hands' for large agribusiness entities (Schlosser 2001, cited in Hossfeld, Kelly, and Waity 2015). One example of this is poultry farming in the Southeastern U.S. In such arrangements, farmers sign their farms over to banks to build entirely new poultry houses for corporate entities, such as Perdue, who dictate how the chickens are farmed from egg to market (Thompson 2002). Though these farmers may own the land and poultry, they lack control over it and the food they produce. In a Marxian sense, these farmers have lost control of the means of production—their land—and find themselves alienated from their labor, their farms, and their livelihood.

Despite the decline in small family farms and the increase in large-scale agribusiness, the myth of the small family farm remains a prominent image and icon, particularly in efforts to sell food to consumers in supermarkets. While farmers and farms may be misrepresented in this sense, the representation of farming usually entirely excludes those who have and continue to engage in labor essential to bringing produce to the market. In more recent U.S. history, much of the invisible labor necessary to stock grocery shelves has come from Mexico. The U.S. Guest Worker program began in the 1940s as a temporary worker program to assuage labor shortages experienced during World War II. However, this program expanded primarily with increased Mexican guest worker labor to American farmland and farm businesses. The program has expanded and gone through various iterations since the 1950s, particularly during NAFTA, and more recently with the Border Security, Economic Opportunity, and Immigration Modernization Act of 2013 and H-2A and H-2B workers. Though only about 10 percent of farm jobs are filled by H-2A programs, U.S. agriculture relies heavily on labor from outside the U.S. to ensure farm production.[1] The National Center for Farmworker Health found that 72 percent of all farmworkers are foreign-born, with 68 percent coming from Mexico.[2] The push factor for Mexican labor out of Mexico to the U.S., particularly with the 1994 implementation of NAFTA which flooded heavily subsidized corn into Mexico, compelled Mexican laborers to leave their own farms and move to the U.S. as cheap, temporary labor. The problem continues, and new Trump-era proposed cuts to scrap NAFTA leave U.S. farmers worried about who will work their land, and farm workers about how they will eat.

The vast majority of fruit and vegetable crops in the U.S. are harvested by hand, despite increased mechanization in farming. Farmworkers, whose hands engage in the labor of planting, cultivating, harvesting, and preparing crops for market or storage, deal with difficult and physically demanding working conditions for some of the lowest pay in the U.S. Farm work is seasonal by nature, leading to inconsistencies in hours and availability of work. For example, farmworkers spend, on average, about 66 percent of the year working at farm work (National Center for Farmworker Health). Though some farmworkers settle in one area more permanently, the necessity to move for work is common, with about 42 percent moving at least 75 miles for work (National Center for Farmworker Health). Migrant farmworkers[3] (about 14 percent of farmworkers) move as a regular practice, following work and crops. Though some families migrate together, in other cases this migration leads to the separation of family members from each other. It can also present major challenges to the education of migrant youth. Indeed, the average level of formal education completed by all farmworkers is eighth grade.[4]

While farmworkers' labor and lives remain almost entirely invisible to the elite and middle class, recent news events, such as the viral video of a man tipping over a Los Angeles street vendor's food cart (Florido and McEvers 2017) illustrate the way such exclusion may also elicit more visible class, race, and anti-immigrant tensions. The relatively recent advent of the food truck has become a symbol of 'foodie' culture and gentrification, a middle-class icon of food consumption creativity. In a Chicago case study, Martin (2014) contrasts this with the often overlooked and sometimes loathed street vendors, who also serve food on the street and have been a part of the city fabric for much longer.

In contrast to the more recent phenomena of food trucks, working-class immigrant street vendors, selling traditional Mexican street food in carts that are often quite ramshackle, are said to be a public health risk and a traffic nuisance. Vending has been criminalized in much of the city, with carts confiscated by police. In contrast to food trucks, they 'embody economic and social marginality that is not "cool," "hip," or "creative"' (Martin 2014, 1872). Many venders have previously struggled with poor working conditions in manufacturing and service jobs. Street vending offers workers more control over the conditions of their work. Nonetheless, vendors struggle to find a space on the street. For decades, immigrant (mostly Mexican) street vendors fought without success to change Chicago city ordinances that prohibited the sale of prepared foods. But, in less than two years, food truck vendors were able to get the Chicago City Council to pass an ordinance allowing the preparation and sale of food in food trucks. Food truck owners are viewed by politicians as creative entrepreneurs vital to attracting young urban professionals to the city. Of this disparity in discourse, Martin (2014) asks, whose creativity is valued by those in power? Whose consumption preferences are valued: those of gentrifying neighborhoods or those of working-class immigrants? Whose efforts to shape the city and the food sold there are legitimized and whose voices are marginalized?

Like street vendors and farmworkers, 'the restaurant workers who make our food, bring it to our tables, or wash the dishes it is cooked and served on, live on some of the lowest wages in the U.S. and face segregation and exploitation at the workplace' (Délano 2014, 343). The food service industry is one of the fastest-growing sectors of the U.S. economy. The wages for servers, bussers, and runners has been frozen at $2.13 for over 20 years. Food servers in the U.S. suffer poverty rates three times the rest of the U.S. workforce and use food stamps twice as much (Restaurant Opportunity Center 2012, cited in Jayaraman 2014, 348). The industry is the largest employer of people of color and the second-largest employer of immigrants, and workers of color are disproportionately represented in the industry's lowest-paid positions (Restaurant Opportunity Center 2013, cited in Jayaraman 2014). These jobs also represent some of the lowest quality in terms of wages and benefits. Ninety percent of restaurant workers report not having sick days. Because of fear of losing their jobs and/or out of economic necessity, two-thirds report cooking, preparing, and serving food when sick with such illnesses as the flu, H1N1, and typhoid fever, presenting dangers to public health. According to the Center for Disease Control, 50–90 percent of outbreaks of norovirus (the winter stomach flu) can be tracked to sick restaurant workers (Jayamaran 2013, cited in Jayamaran 2014). Additionally, restaurant workers face segregation by race and gender, with immigrants and people of color relegated to the lowest-paying positions, as bussers instead of waiters, and dishwashers instead of cooks. They are also found in the lowest-paying areas: fast food instead of fine dining (Jayamaran 2014).

Calling attention to the working conditions that restaurant workers face and the public health concerns such conditions present also illuminates class-based assumptions about the problems with our food system. Movements of the middle class and elite to promote local and sustainable food focus primarily on where our food comes from and how it is grown, largely ignoring the conditions of the workers who grow, cook, and bring our food to the table. As Jayaraman (2014, 350) explains, 'No matter how locally sourced, organic, biodynamic, vegetarian, or otherwise positively presented food might be, as long as workers are too poor to be able to care for themselves and their families, or sick while cooking and serving that food, it cannot be healthy or sustainable.'

Focusing on the position of the working class as laborers within the food system reveals their often invisible and overlooked work: the hands that harvest and pick crops, process and prepare food in restaurants, push street carts, and clean and bus tables. As Metzgar (2012) contends, such labor is often excluded from or undervalued in elite and middle-class consciousness. Uncovering such labor also illuminates the conditions under which this labor takes place, such as the physical strain, irregular hours, low pay, and limited, if any, benefits. Such circumstances of the working class as laborers within the food system are inextricably linked to their position as consumers of food.

Working-class consumers

Food is essential to life, and a most basic human need. Yet, in our contemporary society, we largely experience food as consumers in a marketplace where the myth of the small family farm is used to sell products and the hands of those who harvest the food are invisible. Consumers wield power through choices and access. Does one have access to food? How much? What sorts of foods? Although choices are often presented as limitless on grocery store shelves, those choices available are produced by a food system that is further limited by social class.

Members of the working class do not have unlimited access and choice in what they eat. Farmworkers and others from the working class disproportionately experience food insecurity, lacking the economic resources to secure adequate food and a healthy diet. Those with limited resources are also more likely to live in food deserts, areas where residents have limited access to places where healthy food can be purchased, such as full-service grocery stores. They also experience higher rates of obesity, in what is often noted as a paradox of the poor, as well as higher rates of diabetes. American adults overall are 24 pounds heavier today than they were in 1960[5] (Center for Disease Control 2017), with more than half of American adults considered obese. Obesity does affect some groups more than others: non-Hispanic African Americans have the highest rates, and non-Hispanic Asians have the lowest rates. What we do know is that obesity prevalence decreases as level of education increases, primarily in urban areas (Jackson, Doescher, et. al. 2005). In rural areas, the relationship between education and obesity prevalence exists, but not as strongly as in urban areas where increasing educational attainment reduces likelihood of obesity.

Changes in food production help explain some of these apparently contradictory health outcomes related to food access and 'choice.' U.S. farm policy since World War II has increasingly focused on supporting commodity production, driving down the costs of commodities such as corn and soybeans through government subsidies and support. One of the results of large-scale agricultural production and the increase in commodity production has been the introduction of fructose corn syrup and hydrogenated vegetable oils into the American diet. These products have made the costs of snacks, soda, candy, and fats very inexpensive and economical for consumers. Farm policy that buttresses the cheap production of these products in recent years has, at the very same time, provided very few subsidies for fruits and vegetables, and this has driven up the costs of these healthier foods options. It is much easier, and indeed cheaper, to buy low-nutrition, long shelf life, mass-produced food. This type of food is omnipresent and found at every corner store, at every convenience store, and on grocery store shelves across the nation. When the USDA Farm Bill (in essence, farm policy) supports, through large subsidies, the proliferation of commodity foods while also increasing the price of fresh fruits and vegetables, it becomes abundantly clear that farm policy has very little relationship to health policy (Hossfeld, Kelly, and Waity 2018). Such shifts in production and the cost of food help explain the way food policies and family budgets structure economic choices about food purchases and higher rates of obesity and diabetes by social class. When sugar and carbohydrates become cheaper than fruits and vegetables, then those with limited budgets are more likely to choose the former.

While farm policy clearly impacts food access and choices, there are other factors that contribute to what we eat, and how and why we eat; this is what has come to be known as foodways (Hossfeld, Kelly, O'Donnell, and Waity 2017). Coles and Zandy (2007) address social class identity as lived experience, as a set of relationships. Research on social class and food illustrates a complex relationship between material conditions and culture that shapes lived experience. For example, a recent study of parents and adolescents across the class spectrum suggests that to understand whether and why parents buy their adolescent children junk food, we need to examine the material contexts within which these parents make food choices and the symbolic meaning they attach to food (Fielding-Singh 2017). For parents who operate within a context of material abundance, denying their children Cheetos and soda symbolizes care by teaching their children how to delay gratification and modeling healthy eating habits. In contrast, for parents who operate within a context of material scarcity, where parents often have to deny their child's requests for non-food items, food comes to symbolize a realm where a parent can demonstrate care by honoring a child's request. Though expensive shoes and other indulgences may be out of reach, a bag of Cheetos may be financially accessible (Fielding-Singh 2017).

In a new book by Bowen, Brenton, and Elliott (2019), the 'mythical status' of home-cooked meals and the 'foodie' ideals and nostalgic notions of dinner around the table are examined through the lens of working-class families trying to 'put food on the table.' The authors examine the challenges and complexities of meeting this 'ideal' food notion and the reality of household food production and food choices that have to be made. The reality includes not only access to food or cost of food, but the basic concerns around time needed for food preparation and ensuring well-stocked kitchens to support food production in the home, as well as the gendered notions about food production (being a 'good mother' through cooking). The 'foodie' culture of being a good mother and good provider through food production in the home negates and obscures the burden of working mothers trying to make ends meet.

Thus, food choices are structured by a complex relationship between material conditions and culture that shapes the meaning of food. The symbolic significance of food can also be connected to class identity. Among farmworkers, most of whom are of Mexican descent, there is a cultural preference for sugary drinks and filling but high-calorie foods like tacos and tamales (Fuller 2016). Similarly, though there is not agreement among those who are Mexican or Mexican American, interviews with those who frequent food carts in Chicago suggest that a cultural nostalgia about Mexico motivates customers to buy popsicles, ice cream, and other traditional Mexican snacks (Martin 2014), illustrating Coles and Zandy's (2007) point about the connection between social class and identity. Though material conditions place restrictions on food options, individuals still make choices about food. In some cases, food can serve as a site of resistance and social action.

Local food movements and food sovereignty

Local food movements such as farmers' markets and community-supported agriculture (CSA) have been seen as a way to establish food justice. Food justice is defined as 'ensuring that the benefits and risks of where, what, and how food is grown and produced, transported and distributed, and accessed and eaten are shared fairly' (Gottlieb and Joshi 2010, 6). Proponents of local food movements point to a variety of benefits, including more healthful food for consumers, less of a harmful impact on the environment, and more equality and justice than what is generally found in a traditional food system (Schupp 2017). Farmers' markets vary in size and duration, but they all provide farmers the opportunity to sell the products that they grow directly to the consumer. They are generally considered to be the 'flagship' of local food movements (Hinrichs, Gillespie, and Feenstra 2004). CSAs are another way for consumers to get access to fresh, local food while at the same time helping farmers achieve a steady source of income. Participants sign up for the CSA program at the beginning of a growing season and pay the cost to the farmer, who then uses that money to grow crops; the participant then gets a weekly basket of produce from that farmer, whatever is in season.

Despite the worthy goals of local food movements, there are numerous criticisms of them based on race and class exclusions (Guthman 2008a, 2008b; Holt-Giméénez and Wang 2011; Kato 2013; Schupp 2017). Too often they exclude those who are low-income due to a focus on the elite and middle-class consumer base (DuPuis and Goodman 2005). In the way food movements are currently conceptualized, working-class community members can be left out. While more recent research looking at macro-level geographic location data has shown this to be less common than previously thought, the majority of farmers' markets are located in affluent areas, which creates an access barrier for lower-income individuals (Schupp 2016). Thus, CSAs are sometimes seen as only accessible to the elite. Although programs to provide low-income households with CSA shares have been effective (Andreatta, Rhyne, and Dery 2008), these have been limited in scope.

There are deep segmentations in the local food movement along race lines in addition to class (Holt-Giméénez and Wang 2011). Guthman (2008d) has criticized the 'whitened cultural practices' that she found in alternative food movements (434). A great deal of current research examines the ways in which local food movements have class- and race-based limitations, and it is argued that the food movement is 'grounded in the social base of predominately white, middle-class consumers' (Kato 2013; Holt-Giméénez and Wang 2011, 85). Indeed, this is certainly how it is portrayed in the media. Farmers' markets have been criticized for being located in predominately white areas and focusing on the involvement of whites (Guthman 2008b). While local food movements have been successful, these criticisms suggest a need to involve people of color and those with low incomes to create a more inclusive food movement. To address this issue, food sovereignty movements seek to include all classes in the food movement, not just the elite. A lack of attention to issues surrounding food sovereignty—defined as the right to healthy, culturally appropriate food—can lead to failure for some of these movements in addressing food justice issues for low-income communities (Kato 2013).

The food sovereignty movement began with La Via Campesina, a peasant organization responding to the globalization of the food system (Block et al. 2012). At the local level, food sovereignty allows for local communities to have control over their local food system (Block et al. 2012). Food sovereignty involves the entire community to address issues of food insecurity and strive towards food justice. Food insecurity differs from food sovereignty in that it accounts for people not being able to access food consistently. This is described by Coleman-Jensen et al. (2017, abstract): 'at times the food intake of one or more household members was reduced and their eating patterns were disrupted because the household lacked money and other resources for obtaining food.' Households with lower incomes are more likely to experience food insecurity. The goal of food sovereignty is to address hunger, but also to involve people as more than just consumers in the food system.

In order to address issues of food insecurity, turning to food sovereignty movements can be helpful for working-class households. While these movements have generally come from less-developed nations, there are parallels between them and what is going on in some parts of the U.S. today. Researchers studying low-income food insecurity have suggested a food sovereignty approach as a way to address these issues (Alkon and Mares 2012; Carney 2012; Hossfeld, Kelly, O'Donnell, Waity 2017). These movements add social justice and equity components to traditional food movements that might not benefit this population otherwise.

However, even within the food sovereignty movement, the needs of the working class are often ignored. In discussing limited participation in alternative food systems among people of color, Guthman (2008c, 388) notes,

> It may also be the case that working class, or more likely, less formally educated whites do not participate equal to their numbers either, but neither have they been subject to the same sort of scrutiny regarding their food provisioning practices, including attempts to enroll them in alternative food practice.

This group has been widely left out of the alternative food movement, and future research should study the issues around working-class people and food that have been largely ignored. Many of those in the working class occupy a space that is too poor to be considered the main consumers for farmers' markets and CSAs, but too affluent to be targeted with programs that give away CSA shares or double-buck Supplemental Nutrition Assistance Program (SNAP) spending at farmers' markets. This limited position excludes members of the working class from many of the efforts described above. One possible reason for the exclusion of the working class from food movements is a lack of resources related to time and money. As described in the previous section, both the wages and work schedules associated with many jobs that the working class hold may preclude them from being active in food movements. While there may also be a lack of efficacy that members feel and a powerlessness to change their local food system, working-class individuals are finding ways to engage in food activism and work toward food justice.

Food activism/food justice at work

Working-class individuals are using food as sites of resistance and action—resistance in not adhering to middle-class expectations and in participating and creating food sovereignty practices that give voice and power to those in the poor and working class. What follows is a brief overview of projects and movements currently underway that illuminate community response to food injustice through the current food system.

Local food systems initiatives are gaining traction across the country and indeed are becoming fairly mainstream in some parts of the U.S. Viewed as 're-localization' and a return to local community food production, these movements are a direct response to the development of big agriculture and the dramatic change in food production since World War II. Also known as the Farm to Table movement and community foods systems, these initiatives have, at their core, localized responses to food production, distribution, and consumption. Community food systems, in particular, are more concerned with issues of equity and social justice, and grounding this work in community concerns around sustainability, food security, and food access.

Successful initiatives across the U.S. have begun to focus on labor within the food system, as well as racial equity and food justice. The Coalition of Immokalee Workers' Fair Food Program, that began in 2011, is just such an initiative that 'ensures humane wages and working conditions for workers who pick fruits and vegetables.'[6] It is a partnership between famers, farmworkers, and retail food companies, that is worker driven, consumer powered, and fair food certified. The success of this project is reflected in participating buyers that include food retailers such as Whole Foods and Trader Joe's, and restaurant chains such as Chipotle. This program was hailed by the United Nations Office of the High Commissioner for Human Rights as a model to be used globally to leverage change and protect workers.[7]

A similar campaign that addresses workers' rights that grew out of fast-food worker employment is the Fight for $15 movement, that began in 2012.[8] Based in New York City, fast-food workers organized to address the reality of not being able to live on minimum wage pay. The movement has grown across the U.S. to include low-wage and underpaid workers in many sectors, including child care, teachers, adjunct professors, and retail workers as well as fast-food workers.

Food sovereignty programs have developed across the U.S. as an effort to address food access and food insecurity among working-class and high-poverty communities. Wholesome Wave, a nonprofit formed in 2007, is a leader in bringing together farmers, underserved consumers, SNAP recipients, farm to school programs, and community groups to create systematic change in communities and regions to address healthy food access needs. Wholesome Wave was commended by the Obama Administration as a key group in making a difference in childhood obesity. According to its website, Wholesome Wave 'empowers underserved consumers to make healthier food choices by increasing affordable access to fresh, local food.'[9] Working primarily with SNAP recipients in doubling the amount of fresh fruits and vegetables SNAP consumers purchase through incentives at point of purchase, this program works with small-scale and mid-size farmers and vendors at over 1,400 farmers' markets, through CSA programs, and in USDA Promise Zones (low-income communities) in 48 states across the nation. They seek to expand this work in their outreach areas through creative projects that include: the Fruit and Vegetable Prescription program (or FVRx), that empowers doctors to write prescriptions for fruits and vegetables; the Double Up Food Bucks SNAP program, that doubles the amount of fresh produce SNAP recipients can purchase with their SNAP dollars; and expanding networks and linking community groups to participate in these projects and change outcomes in communities in terms of accessing healthy, affordable foods, particularly for working-class and working-poor families.

Other examples of this type of work include the U.S. Food Sovereignty Alliance (USFSA), whose mission is to 'rebuild local food economies and assert democratic control over the food system.'[10] USFSA began in 2010 based on the principle that food and water is a basic human right. Some of the key alliances this organization has built focus on immigration rights, particularly for farm workers and fisherpeople; land and resource rights; land reform; and food sovereignty, particularly as it relates to sustainability and environmental protection. This national umbrella organization serves as an organizing mechanism for community-based projects that focus on food sovereignty in their communities.

A good example of a local-level, grassroots food system and food sovereignty initiative is The North Bolivar Good Food Revolution in the Mississippi Delta. This is one of the poorest places in the U.S. with high unemployment, low educational attainment, and embedded, rural, persistent poverty. It is an agricultural area where soybean and corn production thrive, yet there are few outlets for fresh fruits and vegetables or healthy foods. The Bolivar County Good Food Revolution is a multi-sector collaboration led by the Delta Fresh Foods Initiative that has brought together growers, community organizers, healthy food advocates, and funders to redress the food system in the county. The community-based initiative has created a food sovereignty mobile market program that delivers locally grown fresh food to key stakeholder sites in three neighboring communities. The cornerstone of the project is to build community capacity, embedding youth development and training throughout the enterprise. Youth Ambassadors receive local and national training on food systems development and food justice training, and in partnership with a local demonstration farm and Alcorn State University, are receiving new and beginning farmer training. Local stakeholders are part of the Advisory Board that ensures the success of the program, and nutrition classes and demonstration healthy cooking programs have developed. Famers, food-insecure community members, elected officials, and local leaders are central to the work of the project. Building community buy-in has been a central feature of the successful initiative (Hossfeld, Kerr, and Belue 2019).

Many communities seek to develop programs and initiatives to address hunger and food access for their members and are turning to food policy councils and state-wide projects that concentrate on creating a food movement and food systems projects that link hunger, working people, and healthy, affordable food.[11] The problem remains, however, when organizations simply replicate and replace the function of the state in solving social problems (Alkon and Mares 2012). The critique of food policy councils is that they reflect a white, middle-class experience, often led by white middle-class professionals. One important way for food policy councils to be successful is to ensure racial equity and racial justice, and *class* justice too, in the design and implementation of place-based projects (Harper, Shattuck, Holt-Gimenez, et al., 2009).

The explosion of food banks and food pantries across the nation has been noteworthy. Food pantries were initially established as *emergency* food sources for families, yet they are now considered routine food sources for many working-class families (Johnson et al. 2017). Pantry providers face increased demand and increased usage along with endless challenges in meeting growing community needs. Across the U.S., food pantries and food banks are seeing an increased number of patrons from working-class and chronically poor families who are seeking ways to make ends meet. Feeding America, a nationwide network of food banks, has examined this crisis and the increase in working families seeking assistance.[12] It has found that despite working, families struggle to put food on the table and turn to food pantries and food banks to supplement, and often to provide the main source for, their families' food needs.

On college campuses across the U.S. a number of projects raise awareness about class disparities in the food system and address food justice through volunteer opportunities, service-learning, community-based projects, and partnerships with national and regional efforts. As students are increasingly saddled with debt, food can be something that doesn't make the cut in student budgets. Student food insecurity reminds working-class scholars of the material obstacles that low-income, first-generation, and working-class students face.[13]

The number of campus food pantries are growing rapidly, as campuses become more aware that food insecurity can be a problem for college students (Price and Sampson 2018). Pantries serve as a means for students to take action in addressing food justice, and their presence on campuses helps raise awareness about food insecurity among their fellow classmates. Price and Sampson's research on 141 campus food pantries across the U.S. found a variety of approaches, all emphasizing protection of the privacy and dignity of students relying on pantries. Service-learning projects are one way to simultaneously facilitate learning and support such initiatives. For example, a poverty class at the University of North Carolina (UNC) Pembroke surveyed students across campus using a USDA food insecurity measure. Students in the class gained research experience and a better understanding of the extent of food insecurity across campus. Working on the project helped dispel stereotypes among the student surveyors, as they learned that: 'Hunger doesn't have a face; you can't look at a student and know whether they are hungry or not.' Through the survey process, students also raised awareness about the newly opened campus food pantry, since many of those surveyed were unaware it existed. The data collected helped demonstrate a need for the campus food pantry and has been used as a rationale for future funding and resources. Campuses and faculty are increasingly assessing student food insecurity to inform knowledge, awareness, and programming. For example, through the Southeastern Consortium for Research on Food Insecurity, researchers across the Southeast have collaborated to create and implement a common food security measure. This is used by campuses across the region to assess regional variation and patterns in student food security and to inform programming on individual campuses.

Two additional examples of campus engagement illustrate efforts to raise awareness about food justice. The Real Food Challenge[14] campaign is a student-driven initiative on college campuses to urge campus dining to move toward the goal of purchasing real food. Real food, defined on the Real Food Challenge website as food that 'truly nourishes everyone: producers, consumers, communities, and the earth,' moves beyond efforts to purchase local food to also ensure food is produced in a way that is fair and humane to animals, workers, and the environment. Students start by collecting baseline data on the percentage of real food currently purchased at their institution. This is to raise awareness and interest in moving toward increasing the share. Student efforts also include advocating for farmworkers and making them more visible. Student Action with Farmworkers (SAF) is a nonprofit organization whose mission is to 'bring students and farmworkers together to learn about each other's lives, share resources and skills, improve conditions for farm workers, and build diverse coalitions working for social change.'[15] Among other programs, SAF helps students organize events for National Farmworkers Awareness Week in late March. For example, as part of an interdisciplinary service-learning course at UNC Pembroke, students organized events for Farmworkers Awareness Week, including an information table in the university center, a clothing drive, a documentary film screening, and an event that brought twelve migrant youth to campus to learn about life on a college campus.[16] Such campaigns hold the potential to raise students' awareness about food systems and food justice and to empower them by showing that they hold the potential to promote change.

Finding class in food justice efforts

Food, the most basic need of all humans, is one of the most contested resources on the globe, and this is certainly evident in the U.S. No individual should have to make choices about whether they eat, pay the rent, or keep the electricity going. Working-class families struggle to provide healthy food for their families, often while laboring at jobs that produce, process, and/or serve food to others. Many workers cannot afford the food they produce or serve at their jobs. Much of the food Americans eat is increasing our likelihood of developing diabetes, becoming obese, and experiencing myriad health problems that develop from the type of unhealthy food the food system produces. Accessing healthy, affordable food should not be a challenge, yet it is one of the greatest struggles Americans face today. Working-class studies provides a theoretical frame and lens to scrutinize and critique the current food system, and we suggest that class-based food sovereignty programs provide the greatest likelihood of achieving food justice in the U.S., and across the globe, today.

Notes

1 Brookings Institute: www.brookings.edu/research/immigration-facts-temporary-foreign-workers/, accessed December 15, 2017.

2 National Center for Farmworker Health: www.ncfh.org/uploads/3/8/6/8/38685499/fs-migrant_demographics.pdf, accessed December 15, 2017.

3 Note that a guest worker is one who gained access to the US through the Guest Worker program, discussed above. Migrant farmworkers may or may not be guest workers. Migrant farmworkers are those who move regularly to follow crops and work at agricultural labor.

4 National Agricultural Workers Survey 2013–2014 (from Student Action with Farmworkers fact sheet).

5 Center for Disease Control: www.cdc.gov/obesity/data/prevalence-maps.html, accessed October 27, 2017.

6 www.fairfoodprogram.org/

7 www.fairfoodprogram.org/recognition/
8 https://fightfor15.org/about-us/
9 www.wholesomewave.org
10 http://usfoodsovereigntyalliance.org/
11 https://communityfoodstrategies.com/
12 www.feedingamerica.org/research/hunger-in-working-america/from-paycheck-to-pantry.pdfp, accessed October 15, 2017.
13 https://workingclassstudies.wordpress.com/2017/11/13/food-insecurity-and-the-costs-of-college/
14 http://realfoodchallenge.org/
15 www.saf-unite.org/content/vision-mission-goals
16 For syllabi and other information about the class projects addressed, please contact the authors.

References

Albritton, R. (2013) 'Between Obesity and Hunger: The Capitalist Food Industry,' in Counihan, C. and Van Esterik, P. (eds.) *Food and Culture: A Reader*, 3rd edition, New York, Routledge.

Alkon, A. and Mares, T. (2012) 'Food Sovereignty in U.S. Food Movements: Radical Visions and Neoliberal Constraints,' *Agriculture and Human Values*, 29, 3, pp. 347–359.

Andreatta, S., Rhyne, M. and Dery, N. (2008) 'Lessons Learned from Advocating CSAs for Low-Income and Food Insecure Households,' *Southern Rural Sociology*, 23, 1, pp. 116–148.

Benson, P. (2011) *Tobacco Capitalism: Growers, Migrant Workers, and the Changing Face of a Global Industry*, Princeton, Princeton University Press.

Block, D. R., Chávez, N., Allen, E. and Ramirez, D. (2012) 'Food Sovereignty, Urban Food Access, and Food Activism: Contemplating the Connections through Examples from Chicago,' *Agriculture and Human Values*, 29, pp. 203–215.

Bowen, S., Brenton, J., and Elliot, S. (2019) *Pressure Cooker: Why Home Cooking Won't Solve Our Problems and What We Can Do about It*, Oxford, Oxford University Press.

Carney, M. (2012) 'Compounding Crises of Economic Recession and Food Insecurity: A Comparative Study of Three Low-Income Communities in Santa Barbara County,' *Agriculture and Human Values*, 29, pp. 185–201.

Coleman-Jensen, A., Rabbitt, M. P., Gregory, C. A. and Singh, A. (2017) *Household Food Security in the United States in 2016*, ERR-237, US Department of Agriculture Economic Research Report Number 237, 1–33.

Coles, N. and Zandy, J. (eds.) (2007) *American Working-Class Literature: An Anthology*, New York, Oxford University Press.

Délano, A. (2014) 'Introduction: The Food Business and the American Dream: Gateway or Obstacle?' *Social Research: An International Quarterly*, 81, 2, pp. 343–346.

Du Puis, E. M. and Goodman, D. (2005) 'Should We Go Home to Eat? Toward a Reflexive Politics of Localism,' *Journal of Rural Studies*, 21, 3, pp. 359–371.

Fielding-Singh, P. (2017) 'A Taste of Inequality: Food's Symbolic Value Across the Socioeconomic Spectrum,' *Sociological Science*, 4, 17, pp. 424–448.

Florido, A. and McEvers, K. (2017) 'Viral Video of Man Tipping Over LA Street Vendor's Cart Fuels Protest.' *National Public Radio*, July.

Fuller, T. (2016) 'In a California Valley, Healthy Food Everywhere but on the Table,' *New York Times*, November.

Gottlieb, R. and Joshi, A. (2010) *Food Justice*, Cambridge MA and London, The MIT Press.

Guthman, J. (2008a) 'Neoliberalism and the Making of Food Politics in California,' *Geoforum*, 39, 3, pp. 1171–1183.

Guthman, J. (2008b) 'Thinking Inside the Neoliberal Box: The Micro-Politics of Agro-Food Philanthropy,' *Geoforum*, 39, 3, pp. 1241–1253.

Guthman, J. (2008c) '"If They Only Knew": Color Blindness and Universalism in California Alternative Food Institutions,' *The Professional Geographer*, 60, 3, pp. 387–397.

Guthman, J. (2008d) 'Bringing Good Food to Others: Investigating the Subjects of Alternative Food Practice,' *Cultural Geographies*, 15, 4, pp. 431–447.

Harper, A., Shattuck, A., Holt-Gimenez., E., Alkon, A. and Lambrick. F. (2009) *Food Policy Councils: Lessons Learned*, Institute for Food and Development Policy.

Hefferman, W. D. (2000) 'Concentration of Ownership and Control in Agriculture,' in Magdoff, F., Foster, B. J. and Buttel, F. (eds.) *Hungry for Profit: The Agribusiness Threat to Farmers, Food and the Environment*, New York, Monthly Review Press.

Hinrichs, C., Gillespie, G. and Feenstra, G. (2004) 'Social Learning and Innovation at Retail Farmers' Markets,' *Rural Sociology*, 69, 1, pp. 31–58.

Holt-Giméénez, E. and Wang, Y. (2011) 'The Pivotal Role of Food Justice in the U.S. Food Movement,' *Race/Ethnicity: Multidisciplinary Global Contexts*, 5, 1, pp. 83–102.

Hoffman, B. (2013) *Behind the Brand: Food Justice and the Big Ten Food and Beverage Companies*, Oxfam Briefing Paper, Oxford, Oxfam. www.behindthebrands.org/images/media/Download-files/bp166-behind-brands-260213-en.pdf. Accessed January 10, 2019.

Hossfeld, L., Kelly, E. B., O'Donnell, E. and Waity, J. (2017) 'Food Sovereignty, Food Access, and the Local Food Movement in Southeastern North Carolina,' *Humanity and Society*, 41, 4, pp. 446–460.

Hossfeld, L., Kelly, E. B. and Waity, J. (2015) 'Towards Economies That Won't Leave,' in Fitzpatrick, K. and Willis, D. (eds.) *A Place-Based Perspective of Food in Society*, London, Palgrave MacMillan.

Hossfeld, L., Kelly, E. B. and Waity, J. (eds.) (2018) *Food and Poverty: Food Insecurity and Food Sovereignty among America's Poor*, Nashville, Vanderbilt University Press.

Hossfeld, L., Kerr, L .J. and Belue, J. (2019) 'The Good Food Revolution: Building Community Resiliency in the Mississippi Delta,' *Social Sciences: MDPI*, 8, 2, pp. 1–10.

Hossfeld, L., Rico-Mendez, G. and Russell, K. (2018) *Accessing Government Assistance for Socially Disadvantaged Farmers*, Prepared for the Socially Disadvantaged Farmers and Ranchers Policy Research Center, Alcorn State University.

Jackson, E., Doescher, M., Jerant, A. and Hart, G. (2005) 'A National Study of Obesity Prevalence and Trends by Type of Rural County,' *Journal of Rural Health*, 21, 2, pp. 140–148.

Jayaraman, S. (2014) 'Feeding America: Immigrants in the Restaurant Industry and Throughout the Food System Take Action for Change,' *Social Research: An International Quarterly*, 81, 2, pp. 347–358.

Johnson, K., McKinley, K., Hossfeld, L., Oliver, B., Jones, C., Kerr, L. J. and Trinh, M. (2017) '"God Always Provides": Challenges and Barriers in Food Assistance Delivery in Mississippi,' *Community Development*, 49, 1, pp. 2–17.

Kato, Y. (2013) 'Not Just the Price of Food: Challenges of an Urban Agriculture Organization in Engaging Local Residents,' *Sociological Inquiry*, 83, 3, pp. 369–391.

Martin, N. (2014) 'Food Fight! Immigrant Street Venders, Gourmet Food Trucks and the Differential Valuation of Creative Producers in Chicago,' *International Journal of Urban and Regional Research*, 38, 5, pp. 1867–1883.

Metzgar, J. (2012) 'President's Letter.' *Working-Class Notes*. Fall.

Price, C. and Sampson, N. (2018) 'Food Pantries on College and University Campuses: An Emerging Solution to Food Insecurity,' In Hossfeld, L, Kelly, E. B. and Waity, J. (eds.) *Food and Poverty: Food Insecurity and Food Sovereignty among America's Poor,* Nashville, Vanderbilt University Press.

Schupp, J. L. (2016) 'Just Where Does Local Food Live? Assessing Farmers' Markets in the United States,' *Agriculture and Human Values*, 33, 4, pp. 827–841.

Schupp, J. L. (2017) 'Cultivating Better Food Access? The Role of Farmers' Markets in the U.S. Local Food Movement,' *Rural Sociology*, 82, 2, pp. 318–348.

Thompson, C. (2002) 'Layers of Loss: Migrants, Small Farmers, and Agribusiness,' in Thompson, C. and Wiggins, M. (eds.) *The Human Cost of Food: Farmworkers' Lives, Labor, and Advocacy*, Austin, University of Texas Press.

Zweig, M. (2004) 'Introduction—The Challenge of Working Class Studies,' in Zweig, M. (ed.) *What's Class Got to Do With It? American Society in the Twenty-First Century*, Ithaca, NY, Cornell University Press.

32

The mutual determination of class and race in the United States

History and current implications

Michael Zweig

The 2016 election of Donald Trump as U.S. president brought class to the forefront of American political and social commentary. This is especially true in references to white (i.e. European American) people in the working class, usually referred to as 'the white working class.' Once again, quite spontaneously and naturally, discussion of class has been linked with discussion of race, another indication that one cannot talk productively about either one without the other.[1]

'Race' and 'class' are abstract categories. Each distills from the complex reality of people's lives one particular aspect for definition and investigation. They are distinct but not fully separate. Speaking of 'race,' 'class,' or 'gender' as if these abstractions are the same in life as they appear in study, necessarily is to simplify and therefore distort reality. At some point, understanding these categories cannot deepen while still holding them in isolation from each other. That point has long since passed in the United States.

To get closer to the rich meaning of these social and personal categories, we need to consider their complex mutual determination in lived experience. To have true effect in the political process, the abstractions of history and social analysis we use must connect back with the personal lives of those involved in the political process in such a manner that they 'get it' and come to see their own experiences in a new light, conscious of the ways in which race and class form what political scientist Jeffrey Lustig (2004) has called a 'tangled knot.'

In this chapter, I begin with the historical origins of racism and white supremacy as an instrument of social control dating back to early English colonial rule. I move next to consider the post-Civil War period of Reconstruction and its betrayal, placing the rise of the AFL (American Federation of Labor) and the suppression of class-based labor organizing in this context. I turn next to the Depression-era resurgence of class-based attempts at union organizing, thwarted after World War II by anti-communism that also, paradoxically, turned against the racial oppression of Jim Crow. We then look at the betrayal of this Second Reconstruction and its consequences for the labor movement, civil rights, and American politics leading up to Donald Trump's 2016 victory. The chapter concludes with reflections on the implications of this history and Trumpian political alignment for class-based organizing, in labor as well as civil rights arenas.

Historical origins of white supremacy and racism

In the United States, the history of racism and white supremacy extends back to the English colonies in the seventeenth century. Bonded laborers were transported to the colonies, some from England, some from Africa. At first they worked under common terms that limited their time of servitude, usually from four to seven years, before they were set free. Because these bond servants were bound to their masters who could sell them to others to hold for the duration of their bond obligation, they were sometimes called slaves. But this was not slavery in the sense that it came to be: it was not for life, it did not extend to the life of the children born of the bond servants, and it was not racially based.

As historian Theodore W. Allen has documented, by the last quarter of the 1600s the English began to impose a new system of race-based chattel slavery in the colonies, led especially by legislatures in Virginia, Maryland, and South Carolina. This didn't happen in one stroke (Allen 2006, 2012). It took nearly a century, into the late 1700s, to invent and consolidate this system of racial slavery and the stripping of rights from free blacks. In the process, not only did the English authorities encounter resistance from the black population, they also met, and severely punished, resistance from white people, especially those who assisted runaway slaves or entered into any common cause with a black person. The brutal and forced imposition of racial slavery required decades to consolidate across generations of whites as well as blacks, demonstrating that there was nothing 'natural' or 'innate to human nature' about racism, or the system of white supremacy that racist attitudes justify.

The system of racial slavery arose in the Anglo-American colonies under specific social circumstances. It was invented and imposed by English elites to disrupt and pacify rebellions against harsh laboring conditions and terms of service, rebellions that brought bond laborers of English and African origin together in common cause. The most troublesome of these was Bacon's Rebellion in 1676 Virginia, after which the English ruling elites began to systematize racial slavery.

Creating racial slavery brought two benefits to the English ruling elites. First, by enslaving the African American while allowing European Americans to keep their freedoms, degraded as they were for working people, racial slavery divided the rebels in the ancient and well-known process of 'divide and conquer.'

But racial slavery had a further powerful effect, especially in the southern colonies where slave-based plantation monocultures in tobacco, rice, and cotton prevailed. There, the plantation owners mobilized the European-American laboring population into militias that put down slave revolts, captured runaway slaves, and enforced the racial oppression entailed in the slave system. Poor European laborers and small farmers, previously self-identified as English, Irish, and Scots, were reimagined together with plantation and governing elites as 'the white race.' Thus redefined, they became the primary instrument of social control in slave society. Throughout U.S. history, this process has continued, as repeated waves of immigrants or their children learned to become white, or to become black if they were African, Afro-Caribbean, or Afro-Hispanic (Ignatiev 2008; Jacobson 1999; Roediger 2005).

Repressive local militias were vital to the secure functioning of the slave system, but participation in them did nothing to improve the actual living and working conditions of poor white people. Because the large plantations took the best land, ordinary white farmers were restricted to marginal land for subsistence farming in the hills and up in the mountains. The planter elite had no interest in advancing the economic or social prospects of poor laboring whites. Instead, they were supposed to be happy with what W.E.B. DuBois named 'a psychological wage.' As DuBois put it: '[T]he white group of laborers, while they received a low wage, were compensated in part by a sort of public and psychological wage. They were given public deference and titles of courtesy because they were white' (DuBois 1965, 700).

In the course of establishing this hierarchy, white people became what Bill Fletcher has termed 'the relevant population' in political, economic, and social affairs, all others having been marginalized and rendered irrelevant to the values and norms of the race-based country (Fletcher 2004). The exclusion of black people and Native Americans from economic, social, and cultural standing certainly created a circumstance in which white workers, even the poorest among them, were materially somewhat better off compared to black and Native people, but not in absolute terms. As Virginia legislator George. W. Summers explained to his colleagues in 1832, speaking of the militias as Patroles, 'In the character of Patroles ... the poor white ... is thus made to fold to his bosom the adder [a poisonous snake] that stings him' (quoted in Allen 2006, 17).

Reconstruction and its aftermath

By the time of the Declaration of Independence and the writing of the U.S. Constitution, one hundred years after Bacon's Rebellion, racial slavery was a bedrock element of the new country, with racism deeply engrained. Patriarchy and male chauvinism also remained entrenched, although, as the nineteenth century unfolded, it was vigorously challenged by the Suffragist Movement.

The decade following the Civil War were years in which the states of the Confederacy were occupied by the Union Army and a period of Reconstruction was imposed on the South. There is not space here to explore the rich history of this period and its experiences of racial unity as well as division (DuBois 1965; Foner 2014). I will only note the most important elements of the story as they relate to the subject of this chapter.

Under the policies of Reconstruction and the protection provided by the Union Army, blacks in some places gained access to land, entered into skilled craft occupations with training and experience they had gained as slaves, and participated in the political process. Blacks from South Carolina, Mississippi, and other states of the Confederacy were elected to state legislatures and to the U.S. Senate and House of Representatives—with support from white voters as well as blacks.

But the implementation of Reconstruction was inconsistent and violently resisted. By December 1865, only months after the war's end, Confederate officers founded the Ku Klux Klan (KKK) in Tennessee. The Klan grew in size and reach, engaging in murder and intimidation throughout the South, and beyond, directed at free blacks and white supporters of Reconstruction. Furthermore, the Republican Party that administered Reconstruction policies included many open racists who, while opposing the secession that founded the Confederacy, had no sympathy for the freed slaves.

In this period, some white-led labor organizations welcomed black workers in an explicit effort to bridge racial differences for the purpose of greater strength. William Silvis of the Iron Moulders' International Union and president of the National Labor Union (not itself a union, but a confederation of unions) told the NLU convention in 1866 that racial antagonism would 'kill off the trades' unions unless the two [black and white workers] could be consolidated' (quoted in Nicholson 2004, 99). Yet Silvis and black labor leader Isaac Myers could not persuade white unions in the NLU to accept black members. By 1869 the Colored National Labor Union had organized separately, with Myers as its first president. The Knights of Labor, the most powerful labor organization in the twenty years following the Civil War, also promoted racial unity. But as has been typical in U.S. history, these leadership attempts failed to take root broadly among white workers. The legacy of racism was too strong. The chance to build a united working-class movement failed to bear fruit.

The U.S. presidential election of 1876 provided the opportunity to scuttle Reconstruction altogether. The Republican Rutherford B. Hayes won and by the middle of 1877 had made good on his pledge to end Reconstruction—a promise he had given to win Southern support. The call for 'states' rights' grew out of anti-Reconstruction attitudes that continued long after the Civil War.

In 1886, cigar maker and English immigrant Samuel Gompers led the formation of the AFL. With failure of class-wide organizing by the NLU and Knights of Labor, the AFL took an opposite approach: organize workers by specific skill to protect individual craftsmen as much as possible from the harsh discipline of capitalist labor relations. Gompers was a socialist, at first personally opposed to racial exclusion in labor generally, although he did support the Chinese Exclusion Act in 1882. But the logic of AFL strategy, vigorously enforced by white craftsmen, limited numbers of workers in the craft to increase union members' bargaining power with employers. In this context, Gompers came to endorse widespread racist practices. Whereas the Knights of Labor had included black workers as well as white, AFL unions explicitly barred blacks from membership.

Two major attempts by workers to form a class-based anti-racist labor movement arose in the first part of the twentieth century. The Industrial Workers of the World (IWW, known as the Wobblies) was formed in 1905 and developed by, among others, class-conscious miners and lumber, textile, and agricultural workers (Dubofsky 2000; Chester 2014). It accepted all workers – black, white, native-born, and immigrants of all nationalities, as well as both men and women – and explicitly challenged capitalism. They saw in an organized, united working class, black and white together, the force required to replace it with a worker-controlled society.

These radical assertions of working-class power and unity called forth fierce repression. Local, state, and federal law enforcement agents, sometimes working with private security companies and vigilante mobs, broke up meetings, attacked strikers, and jailed Wobbly organizers. Joe Hill went before a Utah firing squad in 1915 after conviction on what are now widely conceded to have been trumped-up charges. U.S. Attorney General A. Mitchell Palmer ordered the arrest of some 10,000 radical union organizers, most of them white, in the infamous Palmer Raids in seventy cities in twenty-three states on January 2, 1920. Widespread open repression coupled with internal divisions crippled the IWW after the mid-1920s.

The second major attempt at class-based labor organizing emerged in the middle of the Great Depression in 1935 with the Congress of Industrial Organizations (CIO), a new federation that brought together unions based in the workforces of auto, steel, rubber, electrical equipment, textile, slaughterhouse and meat packing plants, and other mass-production sectors. The effect would bring the collective strength of the whole workforce, black and white, men and women, of all nationalities to bear in a common battle against their common employer.

Perhaps the high water mark of labor's political power came in the midst of Franklin Roosevelt's New Deal. The National Labor Relations Act (sometimes called the Wagner Act, after its main author, New York Senator Robert F. Wagner) passed in 1935. For the first time in U.S. history, it gave federal legal protection to workers trying to organize unions in their workplaces. But racial differences were built into the law, greatly limiting relief to black workers even for these protections. To gain support from Southern legislators, New Deal leaders explicitly excluded from union protection government, agricultural, and household laborers, who were the vast majority of black workers at the time. The exclusion applied as well to the reach of the minimum wage, overtime pay, and other worker protections enacted in the period—a practice continued after World War II in the G.I. Bill that gave Jim Crow states and racist local officials control over the distribution of the bill's benefits.

The New Deal not only excluded the overwhelming majority of black workers; it also left millions of Southern white agricultural workers—sharecroppers—without protection. Earlier in the 1930s, the Alabama Sharecroppers Union, led by the Communist Party, attempted to organize on an interracial basis but ran into fierce resistance from planters and local authorities who implemented murderous repression and played on racist fears of whites to keep them from participating (Law 2016). The Southern Tenant Farmers' Union met a similar fate (Naison 1996). White supremacy was again the adder that came back to poison the lives of poor white people.

Post-World War II anti-communism and the Second Reconstruction

It is no surprise that employers and their political representatives again sought to crush the gains of workers. With the Taft-Hartley Act of 1947, Congress outlawed many of the most effective organizing tools unions had, such as mass picketing and certain types of boycotts. It restricted strikes and allowed states to pass so-called 'right-to-work' laws preventing unions from collecting dues from workers they must represent but who are not union members. The law stripped all protections in the Wagner Act from unions with communists in any elected position, a direct assault on the class-conscious leadership at the forefront of anti-racist organizing.

Beyond legislation, Congress came at union power through committee investigations that sought to discredit communist and socialist influences and intimidate union officials and rank-and-file workers from harboring any sympathies for a class-conscious labor strategy. Most famously, the 'Hollywood 10,' screenwriters and directors blacklisted for their leftist views, ran afoul of the House Un-American Activities Committee (HUAC) in 1947 hearings where they refused to answer questions about their political opinions. Many spent a year in federal prison and couldn't find regular work for more than a decade afterwards. HUAC's interest in Hollywood followed a militant strike in 1945 against major studios by the Conference of Studio Unions, representing thousands of carpenters and other craft workers on movie sets.[2]

But as historian Ellen Schrecker has pointed out:

> The entertainment industry's blacklist was the most visible of the economic sanctions of the McCarthy era, but it was hardly unique. Most of the politically motivated dismissals affected Communists and ex-Communists and tended to be concentrated in industries where Communist-led unions had been active. … Steelworkers, teachers, sailors, lawyers, social workers, electricians, journalists, and assembly line workers were all subject to the same kinds of political dismissals and prolonged unemployment as show business people. And the experience was just as devastating. … Industrial workers also faced dismissals and blacklists, especially if they were active in the locals of left-wing unions.
>
> *(Schrecker 1994)*

In the context of this fierce anti-communist atmosphere in the early post-World War II Cold War years, coupled with government and company attacks on left-wing, class-conscious unions and their leaders and activists, the CIO and many of its constituent unions cooperated by purging from leadership anyone who had sympathy for communists. The CIO threw out left-led unions that refused to go along, raiding their members into anti-communist unions claiming to represent workers in the same industry.

To be sure, class-oriented unions also often faced resistance from white workers. In Detroit, for example, in the first six months of 1943 there were as many as a dozen 'hate strikes' in which white workers walked out in response to the promotion of black workers into what they felt were 'white jobs.' The most serious, in June 1943, saw twenty-five thousand white workers walk out of a Detroit Packard plant manufacturing wartime materiel. The Ku Klux Klan had been organizing white workers in the plant since 1941, challenging the union as a communist organization that promoted race mixing. The FBI and Congressional committees considered union support for civil rights as proof of communist infiltration. The United Auto Workers union leadership opposed all these reactionary walkouts and, with the assistance of the federal government, secured the promotions for black workers and pushed the strikers back to work (Meier and Rudwick 1979, 109–110, 162–174).

Over time, with the initial coercion coupled with a dedicated campaign of persuasion, almost all white workers in American industry came to accept integration in the plant. Yet outside the workplace, where the pressure to integrate was absent, racial segregation continued in housing patterns, social interactions, and the preferences of most white people (Lichtenstein 2002).

The Detroit experience shows again that racism is not innate but arises in the socialization process that young people experience. At the time, Detroit had a Polish population larger than every city in Poland except Warsaw, with thousands working in auto plants. Polish immigrants who went into the plants on first arriving in the United States worked well with black workers and lived harmoniously in integrated neighborhoods near the plants in Hamtramck. But by the time the children of these immigrants grew up, they had learned to be 'white' and often expressed virulent racism (Meier and Rudwick 1979, 178).

The twenty-year period following World War II involved the implementation of a Second Reconstruction. Beginning in 1948 with President Harry Truman's order to integrate the U.S. military, culminating in the 1964 passage of the Civil Rights Act and the 1965 Voting Rights Act, the legal foundations of Jim Crow were largely disabled. White Southern resistance was turned back in the courts and through federal legislation. And, as in the post-Civil War era, Southern resistance was sometimes met with the mobilization of federal troops in coordination with local African-American social movements. Little Rock, Birmingham, and Oxford, Mississippi, are among the most important examples.

In these early decades of the Cold War, racism was gradually decoupled from anti-communism. As the United States took the world stage as 'the leader of the Free World,' corporate and political elites attuned to the international arena came to see that Jim Crow had to be dismantled, at least as a legal framework. There was no other way to sustain the U.S. claim to be the guardian of democracy, in competition with the Soviet Union in Eastern Europe, the Middle East, Latin America, and the emerging countries of Africa and Asia. Indigenous struggles there for independence and opposition to colonial domination included political maneuvering, and even proxy civil wars, involving the two competing superpowers. Whereas demands for racial equality were once deemed part of communist subversion of the American Way of Life, by the early 1960s these demands, now viewed as democratic, came to be adopted as a central pillar of the anti-communist posture of the United States around the world.

These changes in official policy were in part driven by, and in part gave opening to, the civil rights movement of the 1950s and 1960s, itself consciously energized by the anti-colonial struggles of African and Southeast Asian peoples. By 1967, even Rev. Martin Luther King, Jr. spoke out publicly against the U.S. war in Vietnam, challenging the 'triple evils' of militarism, racism, and poverty. He called on the country to get on 'the right side of history,' the side of the national liberation movements challenging capitalist domination across the Third World (King 1967). Though not within the scope of this chapter, it must be acknowledged that during the Second Reconstruction, the Second Wave feminist movement organized its own powerful challenge to the established order, whose effects are felt to this day.

As the black freedom struggle took on more militant, more anti-war, and more anti-capitalist directions with the Black Power movement, the Black Panthers, and militant black caucuses in many unions, most of the labor movement distanced itself. Many of the old AFL unions in the building trades and the Teamsters supported Nixon in 1968 and helped fan racist sentiments among their white members.

Popular culture has contributed to shaping public understanding of the working class in negative ways. The documentary film *Class Dismissed* (2005) shows how it worked in television. For example, Archie Bunker came to represent the working class in the sit-com *All in the Family* (1971–1979). The show contributed to a reinvention of the relationship between race and class in political and economic commentary in the United States and to the rise of identity politics to replace class identity. From the angle of progressive supporters of civil rights and women in the popular culture and dominant political discourse, the working class came to mean white men, who were caricatured as hopelessly reactionary buffoons. For many who identified the importance of the three-part mix of 'race, class, and gender,' class came to mean 'the poor,' who were identified as women and minorities.

In both approaches, class as such disappeared, replaced by combinations of race and gender: white men, or women and minorities. In progressive analysis and organizing, separation grew between the receding concept of class on the one side and vibrant race and gender on the other. Black workers were taken to be black; women workers taken to be women; each stripped of their class character. For all the attention now paid to 'the white working class,' one almost never hears about the 'black working class' or the 'female working class,' or the 'multiracial working class.'

Betrayal of the Second Reconstruction

The Second Reconstruction that followed World War II, with strong support from many white people and predominantly white unions, met its own fierce betrayal. In the years after Richard Nixon's election in 1968, the most derogatory terms for African Americans were banished from polite speech in the United States as black people again rose in political office and business affairs. Yet at the same time Richard Nixon inaugurated the Republicans' 'Southern Strategy' in the 1968 election with calls for 'law and order,' a direct challenge to urban uprisings and Black Power. Just as the imposition of racial slavery and the betrayal of post-Civil War Reconstruction had taken decades to consolidate, so this second betrayal was not instantaneous. More than a decade passed before Ronald Reagan took further steps along the path. He could telegraph no clearer signal than staging his first 1980 presidential campaign event in Philadelphia, Mississippi, seat of Neshoba County where three civil rights workers—two white, one black—had been murdered during the 1964 Freedom Summer campaign for voter registration. Reagan promised a return to a states' rights agenda, morally and politically equivalent to the withdrawal of the Union Army over one hundred years earlier.

Early in his administration, Reagan intensified the 'War on Drugs' that Nixon and New York governor Nelson Rockefeller had initiated a decade earlier. Reagan's policies consolidated the era of mass incarceration of African Americans. His initiatives began well before the crack epidemic of the mid-1980s and formed the backbone of what Michelle Alexander has called the New Jim Crow. With deliberate purpose, over the following twenty years harsh criminal justice policies directed at African Americans, especially young men, deprived millions of ex-felons of the right to vote for life, restricted their access to jobs, housing, jury duty, the right to bear arms, and social safety net programs. The result is legally prescribed, structural second-class citizenship status, in effect reproducing Jim Crow times (Alexander 2012).

As is so often the case, Reagan's hostility to civil rights matched his hostility to organized labor. Within months of taking office, he fired over 11,000 mostly white striking air traffic controllers to break PATCO, the union of professional air traffic controllers. Ironically, PATCO had endorsed Reagan in the 1980 campaign, another example of white workers clasping the poisonous adder of white supremacy to their breast.

President Clinton's support for legislation in the mid-1990s to 'end welfare as we know it,' which imposed long minimum sentences for drug-related crimes and mandated life in prison in 'three strikes, you're out' cases, intensified the betrayal of the Second Reconstruction in bi-partisan fashion. By 2016, 7.44 percent of adult blacks were barred from voting because of their court record. And once again the policies of white supremacy adversely affected whites. The non-African-American adult disenfranchisement rate was 2.47 percent, only one-third the rate for blacks but still numerically affecting far more whites than blacks (Sentencing Project 2018).

Repression directed at poor and working-class African Americans coincided with the rise of a few others into the bourgeoisie. For example, Clarence Thomas was appointed to the U.S. Supreme Court. Condaleezza Rice became Secretary of State. Barack Obama was president for eight years. Jeh Johnson was Secretary of Homeland Security, and Eric Holder and Loretta Lynch were Attorneys General. In January 2015, there were five black CEOs of Fortune 500 companies; among the Dow 30 there were two (Wallace 2015). This constituted a considerable advance from the times in which E. Franklin Frazier described the black bourgeoisie as morticians, storekeepers, and people in stable employment in the postal service (Frazier 1957). The United States has also seen a significant growth of black participation in occupations of the professional middle class, such as lawyers, doctors, accountants, and professors.

Important though these advances are, they do not signal the success of the Second Reconstruction. Racial income inequalities persist for ordinary people as well as at the highest economic ranks. In 2015, the overall U.S. poverty rate was 13.5 percent (43.1 million). For non-Hispanics whites, the rate was 9.1 percent (17.8 million). For blacks alone, the rate was 24.1 percent (10.0 million); for Hispanics 21.4 percent (12.1 million); and for Asian alone 11.4 percent (2.1 million) (U.S. Census Bureau 2017).

A truer insight into economic inequality comes from looking at wealth comparisons, the accumulated consequence of annual income inequalities. The U.S. Census Bureau's most recent survey of wealth finds that the median net worth of all U.S. households was $80,039 in 2013. Excluding equity in homes it was $25,116. Whites had a net worth of $103,963 ($34,755, excluding home equity) while black households had a net worth of $9,211 ($2,725, excluding home equity). Net worth among black households in 2013 was about 12 percent of the median U.S. household's net worth and only 7 percent of white wealth (U.S. Census Bureau 2014). With the growth of a true black bourgeoisie has come increasing inequality of income in the black community since the year 2000. Yet income distribution has become even more unequal among whites, as top white incomes have grown more quickly than top incomes among blacks (Akee et al. 2016, 4).

Organizing in the Trump era

Donald Trump came to the White House as an apparent champion of white workers, continuing the racist drumbeat of white supremacy. But his administration is a disaster for white workers, as it is for the entire working class. Open white supremacists were a small part of Trump's electoral base. The willingness of millions of white people to overlook Trump's racism in hopes of some gain for themselves was the far greater problem. Once again the adder came to the breast of white working people.

We have seen in the Trump base that 'whiteness' continues to have a powerful grip. But if we look at the privileges white workers have gotten in relation to blacks in this historical context, these privileges have not served the interests of the working class, not even white workers. Here we come back to the divide-and-conquer role that the imposition of racial slavery fulfilled. Convincing poor and working-class whites to align themselves with white plantation owners and capitalists on the basis of their common skin color was central to the creation of an alliance based on race across class lines. This cross-class alliance simultaneously disrupted and condemned to failure a united working-class challenge to corporate power across racial lines, resulting in losses for white as well as black workers. Indeed, where racist practices have been the most entrenched, in the antebellum South, we find some of the highest poverty rates for whites, their lowest levels of wealth, lowest levels of unionization, and greatest dependence on government support programs such as food stamps and Medicaid.

As the cross-class alliance of whites unfolded over the centuries, it became impossible to speak of a uniform class experience across racial lines, even though class differences were manifest within racial communities, black as well as white. The use of racial difference to disrupt class unity has made race and class inseparable in life, distinct though they are conceptually.

Successful organizing on racial or class lines requires making this dynamic conscious so that workers recognize it in their own lives, turn away from racism and its illusions as they would from a poisonous snake, and grow into the class solidarity required to advance worker interests.

Corporate resistance and internal confusion have reduced the labor movement to its weakest state since the 1920s. The black community is also reeling in the deepening betrayal of the Second Reconstruction. To fire up a Third Reconstruction (Barber and Wilson-Hartgrove 2016), each community needs the other to address the common power arrayed against them. In some aspects it is principally a problem of class; in some aspects, principally race. But no adequate appreciation or effective response can come in either arena until the mutual determination of race and class becomes the basis for understanding and action.

U.S. race/class history embodies two contrary trends. Dominant power has lain in the institutions of white supremacy and their ideology—racism—which have been systematically imposed and enforced by ruling elites. These have been taken up by broad swaths of the European-American population, eager to embrace their status as white people. But there has also always been resistance to white supremacy, with occasional significant but partial gains through abolitionist, civil rights, and Black Power movements, led and drawing their highest energy from within the African-American population. Yet European-Americans who reject racism and work to undermine white supremacy have always been part of these movements.

What explains white participation in civil rights campaigns for African-American equality? How can these impulses gain strength in coming years as the Third Reconstruction unfolds? These are inescapable and urgent questions once we grasp that 'civil rights' is not just a 'black issue' but in significant measure a 'white issue' as well, requiring white people to challenge, among other white people, racism and structures of white supremacy.

If we look at what historically has prompted white resistance to white supremacy, several elements emerge that can guide current and future efforts. Religious sentiment has led many whites to embrace all people as 'children of God' requiring equal treatment and compassion. To be sure, other interpretations of the same religious sources have reinforced the most brutal repression and murder of black people. From this we can conclude that racism infects all aspects of cultural, religious, and political life but is also subject to challenge from within those realms.

For those people for whom religion is a beacon to thought and practice, religious belief is an arena for white people to engage their racist coreligionists.

Others accept the U.S. Declaration of Independence, that it is indeed 'self-evident that all men are created equal.' This belief can reinforce religious sentiments, or stand independent of them for the nonreligious, to give a patriotic meaning to racial equality. But patriotism has also been interpreted to be a major force for white supremacy and racial exclusion, from slavery at the founding of our country to the America First agenda of Donald Trump and millions of his white followers. So, as with religion, patriotism is an arena for challenges to white supremacy, sometimes presented in the rhetorical question 'What kind of a country are we?'

Historically, commitment to class-wide organizing among working people has led many white socialist and communist activists to challenge racism. They have encouraged other whites to set aside racist attitudes to embrace class unity in a common battle against capitalists and their political establishments. Often appealing to moral and patriotic sentiments as well as class analysis, these leaders have helped to broadly change the racial environment in unions and in progressive political activist circles.

But even here there have been important limits to progress. Appeals to class-wide unity have too often resulted in willingness, if not a felt imperative, to downplay demands for racial justice related to the specific conditions of African-American people. Some class-conscious leaders fear alienating whites, and thereby 'splitting' the desired class unity, by supporting affirmative action, the Movement for Black Lives, criminal justice reform, and other issues that appear to be unrelated to, or even to challenge, the lives of white people. Calls for class solidarity made equally to white and black workers on issues of common concern too often reject calls for the redress of specific racial injustices. Even the left-led Operation Dixie, the CIO campaign to organize the South after World War II, muted its call for racial equality to avoid alienating white workers. Within class analysis, as within religious and patriotic realms, there is no uniform response to white supremacy. For class analysis to confront white supremacy among white people, moral and patriotic elements must play some role, as well as a more refined understanding of class interests in a racially divided country.

This understanding does not come automatically. Although reading history and class-conscious works can help, real learning happens for most people in the course of confronting daily problems, whether through struggles at work or over social policy. As Gabriel Kristal has put it: '[P]eople often only make the effort to challenge their prejudices when they are engaged in struggle with others' (Kristal 2017).

As long-time union leader Jeff Perry summed up from his years in Local 300 of the National Postal Mail Handlers Union in the Bulk Mail Facility in North Jersey, the union had to pay consistent attention in its weekly newsletters and regular union meetings to ways in which white supremacy operates at work. Perry confirmed the general rule that there is no substitute for one-to-one conversations, adding that the presence of white as well as black workers as leaders of the process is critical. In Local 300, attention fell to the disparate assignment of light duty, overtime, and workplace discipline. The union made progress by stressing to white workers that they had more to gain by uniting with black workers than siding with white managers in these and other disputes (Perry 2017). He reported:

> If [racism] goes unchallenged, the group tends to be monolithic in its understanding [of white supremacy]. But if it is challenged, the thing can fracture a little bit, and the racism doesn't have such a pervasive hold.
>
> *(LaBotz 1991, 170)*

Organize we must, but there should be no expectation that in the process we will win over many staunch racists and militant defenders of white supremacy. We should be guided by an old organizing prescription: unite the advanced, win over the intermediate, isolate the backward. What Perry describes above is such a process, in which 'the thing can fracture a little bit.'

One example of the opposite approach is the 2017 decision of the United Federation of Teachers in New York City to refuse to endorse the Black Lives Matter movement for fear of alienating many of the union's white members. When the union declined to give official support to such a profoundly important and consequential uprising, it turned the organizing method on its head, uniting with the backward to isolate everyone else.

When I wore a Black Lives Matter button in gatherings of friends who were Trump supporters, I was greeted with challenging claims that 'white lives matter' and 'blue lives matter.' I found that some space opened up when I acknowledged the truth of those claims but insisted that in this country that's old news. The news flash now is that black lives matter, or, I asked, do you think black lives do not matter?

When we organized the bi-annual How Class Works conferences at SUNY Stony Brook from 2002 to 2016, we made sure that leading African-American scholars participated in the planning and presentations of intellectual matters concerning race and class intersections, as well as other explorations of the role class dynamics play in culture, politics, and the economy.

The First Reconstruction arose out of the logic of the defeat of slavery. The Second Reconstruction arose out of the logic of the Cold War. Each was driven by powerful mass movements; each was betrayed to the detriment of all workers. As we seek to launch a Third Reconstruction, its own logic will arise from the struggle, which already includes the Movement for Black Lives and a third wave of feminism in the #TimesUp and #MeToo uprisings. In all these struggles, people can learn that racism and white supremacy are institutions, not just personal preferences. Class-based education in the course of struggle can make it clearer that we are fighting institutionalized corporate power operating as a common oppressor on class as well as racial lines.

This can be the basis for white workers to understand that for their own class interests, as well as on moral and patriotic grounds, they must oppose the institutional repression black people face. Perhaps the most obvious example is the need to resist all attempts at voter suppression aimed at black and Hispanic people as Republicans seek to consolidate their power by disenfranchising those who would likely vote against them. The policy agenda that comes with this suppression seeks to limit Medicaid and other healthcare services. It seeks to cripple union power. It seeks to turn every public service, from schools to bus lines to jails and prisons, into cash cows for private corporations – all to the pain and suffering of working people of all races and ethnicities.

This approach, based in an explicit analysis of power relations, has nothing in common with the all-too-typical appeal to 'white guilt' over past oppression of blacks. The foundation for a progressive future requires a patriotic, morally based, class-conscious movement that unites all segments of the working class, with due respect and support for freedom movements within oppressed communities of race, gender, and nationality.

Notes

1 U.S. Department of Labor data show that in 2010 non-Hispanic whites were 70 percent of the employed labor force and 65 percent of the working class; blacks were 11 percent of the labor force and 13 percent of the working class. Also, 58 percent of non-Hispanic whites were in the working class compared with 73 percent of blacks (Zweig 2012 pp. 33–34).

2 Ronald Reagan, the only former union president ever elected as President of the United States, was president of the Screen Actors' Guild in Hollywood at this time. He wholeheartedly supported the blacklist, as did many others anxious to show their patriotism by promoting anti-communism and the suppression of class-conscious understandings of society.

References

Akee, R., Jones, M.R., and Porter, S.R. (December 21, 2016) *Adding Insult to Injury: Racial Disparity in an Era of Increasing Income Inequality*, Washington, D.C., U.S. Census Bureau.

Alexander, M. (2012) *The New Jim Crow*, New York, New Press.

All in the Family, Creator Norman Lear, 1971–1979.

Allen, T.W. (2006) *Class Struggle and the Origin of Racial Slavery*, Stony Brook, NY, Center for Study of Working Class Life. Also available at http://clogic.eserver.org/2006/allen.html.

Allen, T.W. (2012) *The Invention of the White Race* (2 vols.), London, Verso.

Barber, W.J., Rev., and Wilson-Hartgrove, J. (2016) *The Third Reconstruction: How a Moral Movement Is Overcoming a Politics of Division and Fear*, Boston, Beacon Press.

Chester, E. (2014) *The Wobblies in Their Heyday: The Rise and Destruction of the Industrial Workers of the World During the World War I Era*, Portsmouth, NH, Praeger.

Class Dismissed: How TV Frames the Working Class, Director Loretta Alper, 2005.

Dubofsky, M. (2000) *We Shall Be All: A History of the Industrial Workers of the World* (Abridged edition – Joseph McCartin editor), Urbana, University of Illinois Press.

DuBois, W.E.B. (1965) *Black Reconstruction in America: An Essay Toward a History of the Part Which Black Folk Played in the Attempt to Reconstruct Democracy in America, 1860–1880*, New York, The Free Press.

Fletcher, W., Jr. (2004) 'How Race Enters Class in the United States,' in Zweig, M. (ed.), *What's Class Got to Do with It? American Society in the Twenty-First Century*, Ithaca, Cornell University ILR Press.

Foner, E. (2014) *Reconstruction: America's Unfinished Revolution, 1863–1867*, updated edition, New York, Harper Perennial.

Frazier, E.F. (1957) *Black Bourgeoisie*, Glencoe, IL, Free Press.

Ignatiev, N. (2008) *How the Irish Became White*, New York, Routledge.

Jacobson, M.F. (1999) *Whiteness of a Different Color: European Immigrants and the Alchemy of Race*, Cambridge, Harvard University Press.

King, M.L., Jr. (April 4, 1967) 'Beyond Vietnam.' http://kingencyclopedia.stanford.edu/encyclopedia/documentsentry/doc_beyond_vietnam.

Kristal, G. (August 10, 2017) 'A Working Class Strategy for Defeating White Supremacy,' *In These Times*. http://inthesetimes.com/working/entry/20411/Unions-organizing-fighting-racism-white-supremacy-Donald-Trump-left-progres.

LaBotz, D. (1991) *A Troublemakers Handbook: How to Fight Back Where You Work – and Win!* Detroit, Labor Notes.

Law, M.K. (2016) 'Alabama Sharecroppers Union,' in *Encyclopedia of Alabama*, www.encyclopediaofalabama.org/article/h-2477.

Lichtenstein, N. (2002) *State of the Union*, Princeton, Princeton University Press.

Lustig, J. (2004) 'The Tangled Knot of Race and Class,' in Zweig, M., (ed.) *What's Class Got to Do With It: American Society in the Twenty-first Century*, Ithaca, Cornell University Press.

Meier, A. and Rudwick, E. (1979) *Black Detroit and the Rise of the UAW*, Oxford, Oxford University Press.

Naison, M.D. (1996), 'The Southern Tenant Farmers' Union and the CIO,' in Lynd, S. (ed.) *We Are All Leaders*, Urbana, University of Illinois Press.

Nicholson, P. (2004) *Labor's Story in the United States*, Philadelphia, Temple University Press.

Perry, J.B. (July 13, 2017) author interview.

Roediger, D. (2005) *Working Toward Whiteness: How America's Immigrants Became White*, Boston, Basic Books.

Schrecker, E. (1994) 'Black Lists and Other Economic Sanctions,' in *The Age of McCarthyism: A Brief History with Documents*, Boston, St. Martins. www.english.illinois.edu/maps/mccarthy/schrecker5.htm.

Sentencing Project (June 2018) 'Fact Sheet: Trends in U.S. Corrections.' www.sentencingproject.org/publications/trends-in-u-s-corrections/.

U.S. Census Bureau (2014) 'Median Value of Assets for Households, by Type of Asset Owned and Selected Characteristics: 2013' in *Survey of Income and Program Participation, 2014 Panel, Wave 1*, Table 1. www.census.gov/data/tables/2013/demo/wealth/wealth-asset-ownership.html.

U.S. Census Bureau (2017) 'Historical Poverty Tables: People and Families – 1959 to 2015,' in *Poverty Status of People by Family Relationship, Race, and Hispanic Origin: 1959 to 2015*, Table 2. www.census.gov/data/tables/time-series/demo/income-poverty/historical-poverty-people.html.

Wallace, G. (January 29, 2015) 'Only 5 Black CEOs at 500 Biggest Companies,' *CNNMoney*. http://money.cnn.com/2015/01/29/news/economy/mcdonalds-ceo-diversity/index.html.

Zweig, M. (2012) *The Working Class Majority: America's Best Kept Secret* (2nd ed.), Ithaca, Cornell University ILR Press.

33

Documenting Lumbee working-class history

A service-learning approach

Michele Fazio

In the book *Someplace Like America: Tales from the New Great Depression* (Maharidge 2011), writer Dale Maharidge along with photographer Michael S. Williamson revisit the study of poverty and homelessness that comprised the focus of their groundbreaking *Journey to Nowhere: The Saga of the New Underclass* (1985). Tracing the lives of Americans across the country surviving 'decades of economic assault' (3), the book details how everyday citizens have endured the spiraling effects of job loss and economic precarity since the 1980s. As Bruce Springsteen describes in the foreword to *Someplace Like America*, 'It is the story of the deconstruction of the American dream, piece by piece, literally steel beam by steel beam, broken up and shipped out south, east, and to points unknown, told in the voices of those who've lived it' (2011, x). Places like Detroit, Michigan, and Youngstown, Ohio, as well as many other industrial cities nationwide were economically devastated by the outsourcing of American manufacturing, forcing those who were laid off to relocate south and west to look for work while others remained at home cloaked in the 'dark grip' of economic precarity (Maharidge 2011, 9).

I encountered this situation face to face when I moved to North Carolina in 2009 soon after the global financial crisis, fortunate to have landed a full-time position in academia and at an institution that embraced community engagement—it was a component listed in the job description. Driving past abandoned factories nestled among fields of overgrown wildflowers and dilapidated barns on my way to work, I was immediately struck by the incongruity between the natural and industrial landscapes. The buildings ranged in size from the sprawling Converse, Inc. plant, which once employed thousands of workers, to the smaller apparel manufacturers such as Sara Lee Knit Products, Inc. and Gerber Childrenswear, Inc. Since their closures between 1995 and 2003, these buildings—ghostly remnants of the past—have stood eerily quiet next to posted 'For Sale' signs, undisturbed for years. While I anticipated learning a great deal about life in the South, I did not figure on finding textile mills like the ones where I grew up in the northeast, located in such cities as Fall River and Lawrence, Massachusetts. These former work sites told a story about job creation and loss in the U.S., of how the rise of manufacturing and its decline in the rural South—brought about by northeastern industries seeking cheaper labor and nonunion shops during the mid-20th century and, later, by the elimination of U.S. jobs as a result of the North American Free Trade Agreement (NAFTA) during the 1990s and 2000s—impacted individuals and families in this region for decades.[1]

The stories Maharidge recounts in *Someplace Like America*, portraits of workers' experiences after their jobs have permanently left, resonate in the rural space of the southeastern U.S. where I teach. It is clear that NAFTA hit Robeson County hard; it remains a region marked by persistent poverty and record unemployment—the loss of nearly 10,000 manufacturing jobs 'resulted in a total reduction in regional unemployment of 18,345 jobs' between 1993 and 2003 (Hossfeld, Legerton, Dumas, and Keuster 2004, 5).[2] Double-digit unemployment rates in the county rose as high as 15.3% in July 2011, peaking again at 13.6% in October 2016, and have since declined to an average of 5.9% in 2018.[3] The state overall felt a similar impact: 'From 1994 to 2015, the Labor Department certified that more than 216,000 workers in North Carolina were displaced … making it the hardest-hit state in the country' (Kromm 2016). This chapter, drawing upon Maharidge and Williamson's work as a framework, outlines the creation of a multi-semester service-learning oral history project designed to recover the work histories of Lumbee elders to understand how (de)industrialization shapes their lives.

Race and class in the southeast

Robeson County—one of North Carolina's largest and poorest counties—is the most ethnically diverse rural county in the U.S. with its predominantly American Indian population; it is home to the University of North Carolina at Pembroke (UNCP) and to the Lumbee Tribe.[4] The Lumbee, according to the tribe's website, consists of 55,000 members and is the largest tribe in North Carolina, the largest east of the Mississippi River, and the ninth largest in the nation.[5]

Even though the tribe has been recognized by North Carolina since 1885 and by the federal government since 1956, the Lumbee continue to fight for full federal recognition. UNCP's rich historical origins are uniquely tied to the Lumbee. Originally established as the Croatan Normal School in 1887 and later called the Indian Normal School of Robeson County in 1911, the school was founded to train American Indian public school teachers. It underwent several name changes from Pembroke State College to Pembroke State University until it officially became a part of the University of North Carolina system in 1996.[6] The first white student graduated in 1954 and the first African American student in 1969. This timeline reflects the social, cultural, and political shifts taking place regionally and nationally, namely desegregation and economic growth.

As historian Malinda Maynor Lowery (Lumbee) explains, American Indian tribes are 'linked by kinship, culture, and economy, but also by race, class, gender, and inequality' (2010, 255). The question of land is inextricably tied to American Indian tribal identity and cultural survival. U.S. federal policies such as the Indian Reorganization Act in 1934, which aimed to restore land and tribal sovereignty, were fraught with racist ideology that continues to have cultural, political, and economic ramifications for tribal nations today. Jim Crow laws—the legalization of racial segregation in the American South—and the onset of the Depression in the 1930s brought about economic changes for the Lumbee that decreased Indian-owned land. For example, 'about 200 Indian families owned land, but only twenty-five of those were "independent farmers" who "had money in the bank"' (Maynor Lowery 2010, 67). Many others (approximately 1,800) sustained themselves through the 'restrictive system' of tenant farming and sharecropping, that kept harvest profits in the hands of landlords (Maynor Lowery 2010, 69). Pembroke Farms, a community project in Robeson County created out of the New Deal's Farm Security Administration's resettlement program, resulted in seventy-five farmers establishing individual farms (Anderson 1999). This economic initiative 'included far-reaching efforts to resettle landless tenant farmers onto more productive land on which they might crawl out of the agricultural depression that had hit the South in 1920' (Maynor Lowery 2010, 135).[7] Post-World War II American society, however, amid the rise of industry, provided rural farming communities the opportunity to seek 'public work' in manufacturing plants that opened during the 1960s and 1970s (Thompson 2002, 61). The rise of agribusiness and the practice of mechanized farming also led to a decrease in the number of smaller family-run farms, creating what Charles D. Thompson, Jr. calls a 'silent exodus' (2002, 69): 'In 1960 there were 212,000 farms in North Carolina. By 1980 there were 93,000, a loss of six thousand farms each year for twenty years' (68). As Thompson further explains, 'individual farmers ... who could not afford the technology became farm laborers or left agriculture altogether' (62). Amidst these changes, a new generation of industrial workers emerged.

The socioeconomic realities of Robeson County and its connection to the Lumbee Tribe make the study of class and culture a critical subject to explore in advancing an understanding of American Indian labor history—a topic virtually absent in the field of working-class studies. As Alice Littlefield and Martha C. Knack argue, 'Studies of North American Indian economic life have largely ignored the participation of indigenous people in wage labor, even though for over a century such participation has often been essential for the survival of Native individuals and communities' (1996, 3). As an outcome of European contact and not solely a result of federal policies and urban relocation programs (5), American Indian wage labor existed 'long before the twentieth century, frequently at their own initiative, in rural areas, and as a critical portion of their economic lives' (Littlefield and Knack 1996, 6). Work and working-class culture are not separate from but are an integral part of indigenous peoples' lives, shaping kinship and community across generations. The field of working-class studies with its 'clear focus on the lived experience and voices of working-class people' embraces an intersectional analysis 'that link class with race, gender, ethnicity, and place' (Russo and Linkon 2005, 14); and, together, the Lumbee Tribe and Robeson County comprise a vital chapter of southeastern working-class history.

Taking it to the streets: Student learning redefined

The idea for this service-learning project emerged out of class discussions in my first-year writing and literature courses during the first two years I taught on campus, where I noted several instances of subtle and not-so-subtle racial tension exhibited toward the Lumbee (linguistically, culturally, and socially). As a newcomer to the South, I was largely unaware of the region's local history, but my students quickly filled in the gaps by sharing comments they heard on campus and on social media, such as the Lumbee are 'crazy' and not 'real Indians'. Unfortunately, the proliferation of negative media headlines like 'Robeson County—A Deadly County' have helped to fuel misconceptions about the Lumbee Tribe given the region's high poverty and crime rates (see Hayes 2015). Tackling race as a subject in the classroom has its own set of challenges, but it was even more difficult to ignore the ways these long-held beliefs disrupted, at times, dialogue and interaction among students at UNCP—the most racially diverse campus in the UNC system with a student population of approximately 13% American Indian, 31% Black/African American, and 38% white.[8]

In keeping with UNCP's history as a school created by and for American Indians, I charged my students with the task of putting into practice the university's mission statement of cultivating an appreciation of American Indian history and demonstrating a commitment to serving the local region.[9] I accomplished this through academic service-learning—a pedagogical practice that is more than volunteering or participating in community service; it is a teaching method that integrates course content and civic engagement with the goal of building long-term relationships with community partners and fostering students' awareness of social justice issues (Einfeld and Collins 2008; Grobman and Rosenberg 2015).[10] At its core is reflection. In other words, students would perform a service for a community partner (in this case, the

Lumbee Tribe); they would also be directly involved with strengthening community ties, writing reflective and analytical essays that incorporated research and their learning experiences while taking on leadership roles to implement social change. Service-learning 'opens up new ways for students to make sense of the dissonances, gaps, and similarities between real and imagined lives', enabling students to engage directly with class and racial injustice at the local level (Grobman and Rosenberg 2015, 1).

My campus' Office of Community and Civic Engagement provided contact information for the Elder Services of the Lumbee Tribe, and it took a significant amount of time to determine the scope of the interviews and topics to be explored, a combination of cultural interests and labor history, as well as to generate protocol guidelines. I knew I wanted to work with the elder population because of the historical context they could provide my students on the relations between the local community and the campus. My access to elders, however, was not immediate. It took months to arrange multiple meetings, prior to the project's implementation, with tribal leaders and elders' groups to discuss course logistics. In an effort to build trust with the Lumbee and accountability among my students, project transparency at every stage was crucial, from reviewing (and revising) the Institutional Review Board (IRB) application and observing student interactions with elders to approving interview transcripts and analyzing data. As an outsider (not a Southerner or Lumbee), I sought to develop—and have maintained since then—strong relationships with the community, based on a shared belief that civic engagement and activism enhance student learning. Natascha Tilson, then director of Elder Services, and members of her staff accompanied me during several visits to Lumbee Heritage Group sites to show their support. At the time of this project (2011–2012), over 500 tribally enrolled Lumbee elders gathered weekly at these community spaces to design crafts to sell at local powwows and to socialize more generally. There, I pitched my idea to collect their work histories, explaining that, too often, students simply drove to and from campus without any thought of the Lumbee except that they should be avoided, and that I hoped to change this perception. I also explained my interest in working-class studies and shared my family's background working in factories and what it meant for them to experience unemployment and underemployment. My decision to preserve close ties with tribal leaders throughout the research process made clear from the beginning that the project would be long term, inclusive, and beneficial in offering a service to the Lumbee Tribe.[11]

Teaching a service-learning course with as many moving parts as this project requires flexibility. Each iteration of the course (three different sections of first-year writing and one contemporary literature section offered consecutively during 2011–2012) began with an introductory writing exercise to explore how, in the face of despair or perhaps in spite of it, working-class people find a way to get by. The following prompt taken from the required textbook, *Someplace Like America*, guided students in small groups to consider the hardships of contemporary working-class life.

> Some say that Americans are no longer able to stand up to tough times the way the 'greatest generation' of the 1930s Depression and World War II did. But this is so very wrong. We are wounded as a culture today, certainly, and many of us are soft, bewildered, made numb by loss. Yet something is going on. We are at the front end of a process. People will rise to the challenge of these hard times. We have a long way to go before the transformation occurs, but it will happen.
>
> *(Maharidge 2011, 3)*

From the outset, students were intent on drawing the past's connection to the present—of understanding how massive layoffs, federal trade policies, and the decline of U.S. manufacturing persistently impact both the local economy and future regional developments. Other informal writing responses included examining popular culture and media representations of American Indians, which led to thoughtful discussion of how much (or little) they knew about the Lumbee. Students also compiled their own records of employment, noting the intersections between gender and class in the kinds of work performed. As we read through the remaining chapters of *Someplace Like America*, students immediately identified with the stories from across the country of displaced workers, contingent labor, and homelessness—tales of struggle and broken dreams that resembled their own working-class backgrounds. They also expressed concern over the increasing division between the rich and the poor, asking questions about future work opportunities and whether they will be able to combat this disparity in their lifetime. Part of the 'transformation' Maharidge suggests, I posed in class, could begin with the recovery of oral histories—stories rooted in community and family life that honor individual experiences and the collective meaning of work.

The resulting service-learning project required all parties—students, members of the Lumbee Tribal Council, and elders in the community—to work together, and since this was a newly developed course, I intentionally left several weeks open on the syllabus to accommodate the coordination of students' schedules and site visits. After introducing the project's parameters, students also studied best practices for oral history as defined by the Oral History Association.[12] Tilson served as a guest speaker to discuss tribal history and review project goals from the perspective of the community partner. Additional course readings included bell hooks' *Where We Stand: Class Matters* (2000), Studs Terkel's *Working: People Talk about what they Do All Day and How they Feel about what they Do* (1974), including Harvey Pekar's graphic adaptation (2009), as well as the documentary *People Like Us: Social Class in America* (2001). These materials enabled students to discuss multiple forms of privilege and helped them understand what it would mean to interact with those from different racial and class backgrounds. Lastly, we reviewed the project's logistics from consent forms to the guidelines set forth from the IRB to study human subjects. Students practiced interviewing in several class sessions so they could better understand their own position of power as university students and as research assistants asking questions.

While this preliminary work provided an opportunity to examine the concepts of racial and class oppression at the local level, it moved the conversation beyond theoretical debates alone to make a significant difference in how students and elders viewed one another. As Einfield and Collins state, 'service learning is more than a means for those in power to serve the less fortunate, but rather provides students with a "multicultural education" whereby they begin to understand local issues from a different perspective' and 'witness inequality' toward the purpose of 'explor[ing] their understanding of citizenship and responsibility to society' (2008, 97, 102, 108). Despite these intentions, not every student embraced my 'take it to the streets' activist approach. Some of them had never left campus before and expressed genuine concern over leaving the security of the classroom and crossing the railroad tracks that border campus; likewise, a few Lumbee students expressed doubt that our presence would be welcomed in the community. In reality, the majority of elders were excited to be involved. One woman told me that they had 'waited a long time for this moment'. This service-learning project also challenged my own teaching, making clear how necessary it is to embrace uncertainty and give up my own authority in implementing innovative curricular changes. As proponents of service-learning argue, this strategy puts students at the center, creating active citizens who 'challenge cultural norms and stereotypes' (Grobman and Rosenberg 2015, 25) and 'deconstruct pre-conceived assumptions' in their academic careers and beyond (Cole and Zhou 2014, 110).

Someplace like Pembroke: From the fields to the factory

Over the course of two years, my students and I traveled to and from campus (sometimes a forty-mile round trip) throughout Robeson County to visit Lumbee Heritage Group sites. Our initial visits introduced elders, men and women, to the overall research question driving the project: to consider the kinds of labor—wage, domestic, and unpaid—they performed in their lives. Students recruited interested participants (overall, fifty-five volunteered), and as they conducted interviews, students also learned how to quilt as the elders shared stories and prepared food. This interaction, which enriched the analysis of the significant relationship among community, family life, and economic developments in the students' final projects, began a long overdue conversation about cultural and generational differences that helped to close the gap between the university and the local communities it serves.

It is important to underscore the amount of time students spent collecting these oral histories. As Alessandro Portelli reminds us, 'An interview is not a question-and-answer session; rather it is the opening of a narrative space, which the interviewer's presence and questions or comments encourage the interviewee to explore and navigate' (2009, 30). This project, designed on the basis of relationship-building and reciprocity, required students to return to sites (sometimes outside of class time) to meet with elders to ensure the accuracy of the information transcribed. In other words, the questions asked were not just answered in a single visit; we worked at cultivating relationships with each participant to emphasize service-learning as a long-term, transformative endeavor, which empowered both the students and elders (Einfeld and Collins 2008). Some of the questions we asked focused on participants' earliest memories of work and how the meaning of work has changed over time; and their responses documented the dramatic changes children of farmers experienced in leaving the fields for factories. For example, students asked elders what their favorite or least favorite job was and to describe their work ethic, and additional questions prompted reflections on regional history and cultural heritage. Many of the elders reminisced about the old days of quilting, cooking, picking cotton, curing tobacco, caring for children, and feeding hogs, as these work experiences were tied to their cultural identity and families. We also learned what they did not like about farm work: cleaning up animal pens, milking cows, and plowing the fields. As one woman put it, 'We were hard workers because we had to be'.[13]

Factory work offered an alternative to tenant farming and an opportunity to earn wages, but as the elders remarked, they faced difficulties working on assembly lines because the jobs were too fast and hard to complete. One elder professed: 'Farm work is better. It's freedom. It was less stressful and a lot healthier. Working in [factories] is like a prison.' The search for work after the end of World War II also resulted in many Lumbee relocating to urban centers, such as Baltimore, where they maintained a close community of 'several thousand' (Maynor Lowery 2010, 233). For instance, one man we interviewed said he worked for thirty-two years at General Motors in Detroit, forging steel 'down the line' to make axles, cranks, and piston rods. He observed:

> The work can't stop, you know. I've seen a person drop dead on the line. They pulled his weight from the machine and got the nurse working on him, and brought somebody else in to keep the machine running.

These comments impressed upon my students the pressures of adapting to mechanized assembly lines and the reality of worker expendability. Despite these challenges, the pride in having held these positions in manufacturing for as long as twenty-five to thirty years was evident in the individuals we interviewed, which made the factory closings all the more disruptive to their lives.

In the wake of crippling job loss during 1993–2003, participants experienced downward mobility as they entered the retail and service industries, working part-time and temporary jobs at minimum wage. Many rural displaced workers, particularly women, experienced more long-term unemployment than their younger counterparts (Hossfeld, Legerton, Dumas, and Keuster 2004, 10; Hossfeld, Kelly, McTague, and Wadsworth, 2012). One worker stated that when the factories closed, 'it took our livelihood away. We left the tobacco fields and went to work to make money. It was the beginning of the end'. A few elders also spoke about gender inequity in the workplace: 'There's a lot of difference in pay, but a woman can do a man's job'. Another woman who embraced the physicality of cutting lumber acknowledged, 'It was a man's job, and I loved it'. Not all elders, however, worked in manufacturing. Many pursued other occupations in education and healthcare and served in the military and local government. The Lumbee, my students realized, were a lot like their own parents and grandparents who experienced similar circumstances at work or in becoming unemployed.

Other common threads emerged in the interviews, yielding a greater understanding of how the past remains rooted in the present. The most notable concern related to preserving cultural traditions and community relations. Many spoke about the devastating effects that massive layoffs since the 1990s still had on their own lives and, subsequently, on future generations, and whether their grandchildren would be able to remain in the area or have to leave to find work. My students learned firsthand that the Lumbee are hardworking people who persevered through decades of job growth and decline as they adapted to a rapidly changing workforce. This realization shattered the illusion of meritocracy and illustrated, quite plainly, NAFTA's long-standing consequences leading up to and following the 2009 recession. As one elder stated simply yet forcefully, 'More industry needs to return here to keep families together'.

Class reflections

While this project broadened an understanding of Lumbee history and culture, it also stressed the importance of student engagement—of strengthening academic skills while encouraging students to become more productive citizens on and off campus. My students' involvement went beyond simply earning a grade for the course, as they gained confidence in public speaking and demonstrated greater responsibility in their writing; they also developed cultural sensitivity and advocacy skills. As co-producers of knowledge, they took on the responsibility of recording the voices of the Lumbee in their own words, creating an historical snapshot of the past. These learning outcomes are essential to developing a working-class studies activist approach to service-learning. The interview process emphasized the importance of documenting lived experience and provided an opportunity for students to explore their own relationship to work and academic careers, as evidenced by one student who noted:

> From the first meeting, I've been deeply touched. The town of Pembroke *has* practically withered away to nothing because of the outsourcing of jobs. My elder hit home when she said that she worked at two of the major factories that used to keep this area thriving. She suffered being laid off and had to find work on her own.
>
> *(Emphasis original)*

Another student reflected:

> This service-learning project has started to have an impact on me already. I feel so important that we are being [asked to take] part [in] such a wonderful project that will help record my people's history. It feels like an honor and gives me hope for the future.

Another concluded that the Lumbee are still experiencing 'hardship and oppression' and 'their stories need to be told and retold', echoing the call to end the silence surrounding American Indian labor.[14] As Lowery states,

> The myth of U.S. history—that we are a nation of immigrants, struggling to find common ground and expand freedoms for all—leaves no place for Native nations. Excluding Native peoples, or telling only their stories of dispossession, does not honor the complexity of those communities or of American history.
>
> *(2018, xiv)*

In benefiting both the local community and student life, service-learning advocates for a deeper appreciation of social responsibility beyond the classroom, and this project transformed the lives of students and elders alike. One elder admitted during her interview, 'I didn't know I had so much to say about my family and culture. You're making me remember why I'm proud to call myself Lumbee'. As Portelli explains, oral history 'bring[s] into the vision of history aspects of experience that have been ignored and left out, and at the same time … challenge[s] and stimulate[s] the historical self-awareness of the people … interview[ed]' (2009, 30). This 'self-awareness' of class and race is present throughout the interview archive (now housed at the offices of the Lumbee Tribe). The memories the Lumbee shared about their homeland document the historical and social realities of the rural southeast, where the 'legacy of deindustrialization remains' (Cowie and Heathrow 2003, 6). Furthermore, the study of deindustrialization beyond a focus on white workers advances the field of working-class studies by recognizing the workforce contributions of communities of color—critical steps to take in achieving a fuller picture of working people in the U.S.

Making working-class life public

This service-learning project brought together intellectual inquiry, activism, and community engagement, and it enabled students, more than any textbook could, to examine the intersections among race, gender, and class within the context of American Indian labor history. As sociologist Tim Strangleman (2019) writes,

> in studying the past we chart both what we had and what we have lost. But we also ask critical questions as to why, not so long ago, ordinary working-class people could enjoy conditions at work that gave them dignity, confidence, and hope that their lives were getting better, decade by decade, and that the children's lives would be better still.

Wrestling with the story of deindustrialization in the rural South—of widespread job loss and downward mobility—sparked a great deal of interest both on campus and within the community and culminated in two multimedia projects. The first was 'Someplace like Pembroke: Work Histories of the Lumbee' (2013), inspired by 'Worker Portraits: Faces of

Strength,' the Mahoning Valley steel town work history project coordinated by Sherry Linkon and Alyssa Lenhoff at Youngstown State University's Center for Working-Class Studies (2007). This exhibit featured twenty panels consisting of photographs of elders and local landscapes along with excerpts of interviews that illustrated many of the major themes outlined above. Together, they portrayed a chapter of American labor history that ought to be recognized—less visible, but equally compelling stories that bring American Indians to the forefront of the study of working-class culture and life. The second project, *Voices of the Lumbee* (2014), an award-winning feature-length documentary film that I co-wrote and co-produced, incorporates the elders' work histories and highlights local social justice organizations' efforts to initiate positive change in the region.[15] The documentary, produced in cooperation with the Lumbee Tribe and supported by internal institutional grants, involved nearly one hundred students enrolled in service-learning courses at UNCP. Both the exhibit and film have been viewed at universities and cultural centers across the U.S., sparking interest about the urgency in continuing the preservation of family and local history centered around the subject of work.

As this service-learning project has shown, making working-class life public is an integral part of preserving labor history and culture. I hope it may serve as a model, inspiring others to incorporate this practice in their teaching and in organizing community events. Robeson County is a region filled with hard-working people—like many families across the U.S.—who were displaced by and survived economic decline.[16] The study of deindustrialization makes clear how the story of job creation and loss is more than percentages and the bottom line: 'People experience the effects in immediate and personal ways' (Linkon 2018, 3), and their 'shared memory … create[s] and maintain[s] relationships' (4). Reflecting about this past in the college classroom has increased student awareness about the nature of work—its impact on the local community and what potentially lies in store for them after graduation. The service provided to the Lumbee Tribe also made the study of work personal, prompting many of my students to explore their own work history and obtain a greater understanding of their relationship (and that of their family) to class. On a greater level, more work needs to be done to bridge the divide between class and race in order to capture indigenous communities' contemporary working-class lives. As I told my students, this project contributes to a larger, critical undertaking of considering the lived history of the rural deindustrialized South, not as a fixed representation of the past but as one that informs our present and future.[17] With the passage of time, we stand to lose a connection to those who lived through these experiences and what might be gained in privileging their memories about the meaning of work. The recovery of these voices could serve not only as sources of struggle, pride, and hope, but also as stories to heed as the precariousness of work in today's economy continues to increase.

Notes

1 Since its passing, NAFTA eliminated one million jobs (*Public Citizen* 2013). Robeson County serves as the middle point in moving northeastern manufacturing to the southeast and, later, to Mexico and China, establishing a pattern of displacing workers seeking cheaper labor and expanding profit margins in a growing global, competitive market (Hartford 1996; Koistinen 2002). As textile operations moved south, the anti-unionism at these new locations all but diminished the power of workers' collective bargaining rights (Hartford 1996; Koistinen 2002; Minchin 2013).

2 See North Carolina Department of Commerce (2018) and U.S. Bureau of Labor Statistics (n.d.) for more information about regional job loss and growth.

3 See U.S. Bureau of Labor Statistics (n.d.) for unemployment rates in Robeson County.

4 With a population of 132,606, Robeson County has a 29% poverty rate (U.S. Census Bureau n.d.). According to the 2010 census, the county is 38% American Indian, 29% White, 24% African American, and 8% Latino (Census Viewer n.d.). See also Hossfeld, Kelly, McTague, and Wadsworth (2012) and Martin (2014) for additional information on job loss and growth in the region.
5 See Lumbee Tribe of North Carolina (n.d.) for more information.
6 See UNCP (n.d.-a) for a complete description of the school's history. I am using the term 'American Indian' to follow the language of my institution, which has an American Indian Studies program.
7 See Lowery's chapter, 'Pembroke farms: Gaining economic autonomy' in *Lumbee Indians in the Jim Crow South: Race, Identity, and the Making of a Nation* (2010). This book, along with her recently published *The Lumbee Indians: An American Struggle* (2018), outlines the tribe's history of racial and social inequality, and its survival.
8 See UNCP (n.d.-b) for additional institutional data.
9 The university's full mission statement can be found at UNCP (n.d.-c).
10 This definition is also informed by the UNCP's Office of Civic Engagement (n.d.).
11 I would like to thank Natascha Tilson and other staff members of the Lumbee Tribe who made this oral history project possible, and all the elders who participated, especially Annie Lowery, Mabel Cummings, Lottie Locklear, and Dr. JoAnn Lowery for their collaboration and enthusiasm over the years. I remain deeply honored by their friendship and trust in this community-based project. I am also grateful to all the students who participated and appreciate their extraordinary passion and professionalism, particularly research assistants Moe Gazali and Sandra Torres, whose involvement from conducting interviews to the creation of an exhibit and research for the documentary was both instrumental and inspiring.
12 For more information, see Oral History Association (n.d.).
13 Per the IRB application, consent was granted by participants to use excerpts for educational purposes. All subsequent quotes are from unpublished interviews conducted by students enrolled in my first-year writing and literature courses.
14 Student comments originated from class discussion and course evaluations.
15 *Voices of the Lumbee* received the North Carolina Folklore Society Hudson-Brown Award and earned First Place in the Broadcast Education Association District 2 Production Faculty Video Award. The film opened the 20th Annual American Indian Heritage Celebration at the North Carolina Museum of History in Raleigh, and it was awarded the Working-Class Studies Association's Studs Terkel Award in Journalism and Media. For more information on the film and cultural exhibit, please visit: www.voicesofthelumbee.com.
16 Even with the region's current unemployment rate hovering under 5%, job loss is still occurring; for example, the Alamac American Knits' closure in 2017 placed 150 people out of work (the plant originated in Indian Orchid, Massachusetts in the 1940s and relocated south in 1962). In its place will emerge a renewable energy plant with the promise of only fifty jobs (Douglas 2019). For a fuller picture of Robeson County's economic profile, see the sources provided in Note 2.
17 Additional recent oral history projects on Lumbee culture can be found at Southern Foodways Alliance (n.d.) and at the Southern Oral History Program (n.d.) at the Center for the Study of the American South at the University of North Carolina at Chapel Hill. See also Jessica R. Markey Locklear's ongoing digital history project on Lumbee's post-World War II migration to Philadelphia (Markey Locklear n.d.).

References

Anderson, R. K. (1999) 'Lumbee Kinship, Community, and the Success of the Red Banks Mutual Association', *American Indian Quarterly*, 23, 2, 39–58.

Census Viewer. (n.d.) http://censusviewer.com/county/NC/Robeson. Accessed February 9, 2019.

Cole, D. and Zhou, J. (2014) 'Do Diversity Experiences Help College Students Become More Civically Minded? Applying Banks' Multicultural Education Framework', *Innovative Higher Education*, 39, pp. 109–121.

Cowie, J. and Heathcott, J. (2003) 'The Meanings of Deindustrialization', in Cowie, J. and Heathcott, J. (eds.), *Beyond the Ruins: The Meanings of Deindustrialization*. Ithaca, NY, ILR Press. https://digitalcommons.ilr.cornell.edu/cgi/viewcontent.cgi?article=1035&context=cbpubs. Accessed February 9, 2019.

Douglas, D. (2019) 'Renewable Energy Plant Lands in Robeson County', *Laurinburg Exchange*. www.laurinburgexchange.com/news/24793/renewable-energy-plant-lands-in-robeson-county. Accessed February 15, 2020.

Einfeld, A. and Collins, D. (2008). 'The Relationship between Service-Learning, Social Justice, Multicultural Competence, and Civic Engagement', *Journal of College Student Development*, 49, 2, 95–109.

Grobman, L. and Rosenberg, R. (2015) 'Introduction: Literary Studies, Service Learning, and the Public Humanities', in Grobman, L. and Rosenberg, R. (eds.) *Service Learning and Literary Studies in English*, New York, Modern Language Association.

Hartford, W. F. (1996) *Where Is Our Responsibility? Unions and Economic Change in the New England Textile Industry, 1870–1960*, Amherst, University of Massachusetts Press.

Hayes, T. (2015) 'Robeson County: A Deadly County'. *WMBF News*, January 29. www.wmbfnews.com/story/27972828/robeson-county-a-deadly-county/. Accessed December 1, 2015.

hooks, b. (2000) *Where We Stand: Class Matters*, New York, Oxford.

Hossfeld, L., Kelly, E. B., McTague, T. and Wadsworth, A. (2012) 'Gender and Job Loss in Rural North Carolina: The Costs of Carework', *Sociation Today*, 10, 1. www.ncsociology.org/sociationtoday/v101/jobloss.htm. Accessed February 9, 2019.

Hossfeld, L., Legerton, M., Dumas, C. and Keuster, G. (2004) 'The Economic and Social Impact of Job Loss in Robeson County North Carolina 1993–2003', *Sociation Today*, 2, 2. www.ncsociology.org/hossfeld.htm. Accessed February 9, 2019.

Koistinen, D. (2002) 'The Causes of Deindustrialization: The Migration of the Cotton Textile Industry from New England to the South', *Enterprise & Society*, 3, 3, 482–520.

Kromm, C. (2016) 'Trade Deals Have Hit North Carolina Harder Than Michigan', *Facing South: A Voice for a Changing South*, March 10. www.facingsouth.org/2016/03/trade-deals-have-hit-north-carolina-harder-than-mi. Accessed March 6, 2020.

Linkon, S. L. (2018) *The Half-Life of Deindustrialization: Working-Class Writing about Economic Restructuring*, Ann Arbor, University of Michigan Press.

Linkon, S. L. and Lenhoff, A. (2007). 'Worker Portraits – Faces of Strength', Center for Working-Class Studies, Youngstown State University. https://ysu.edu/center-working-class-studies/worker-portraits-faces-strength. Accessed February 9, 2019.

Littlefield, A. and Knack, M. (1996) (eds.) *Native Americans and Wage Labor: Ethnohistorical Perspectives*, Norman, University of Oklahoma Press.

Lowery, M. M. (2010) *Lumbee Indians in the Jim Crow South: Race, Identity, and the Making of a Nation*, Chapel Hill, University of North Carolina Press.

Lowery, M. M. (2018) *The Lumbee Indians: An American Struggle*, Chapel Hill, University of North Carolina Press.

Lumbee Tribe of North Carolina. (n.d.) 'Culture – Tradition – History'. www.lumbeetribe.com. Accessed March 20, 2019.

Maharidge, D. and Williamson, M. (1985) *Journey to Nowhere: The Saga of the New Underclass*, New York: Hyperion.

Maharidge, D. and Williamson, M. (2011) *Someplace Like America: Tales from the New Great Depression*, Berkeley, University of California Press.

Markey Locklear, J. R. (n.d.) 'About'. https://sites.temple.edu/jessicamarkey/. Accessed March 4, 2020.

Martin, E. (2014) 'This is the Place', *Business North Carolina*. https://businessnc.com/this-is-the-place/. Accessed February 9, 2019.

Minchin, T. J. (2013) *Empty Mills: The Fight Against Imports and the Decline of the U.S. Textile Industry*, Lanham, MD, Rowan & Littlefield Publishers, Inc.

North Carolina Department of Commerce. (2018) 'Country Profile: Robeson County (NC)', Labor & Economic Analysis Division. https://accessnc.nccommerce.com/DemoGraphicsReports/pdfs/countyProfile/NC/37155.pdf. Accessed February 26, 2020.

Office for Community and Civic Engagement. (n.d.) 'Academic Service-Learning', *University of North Carolina at Pembroke*. www.uncp.edu/campus-life/community-and-civic-engagement/academic-service-learning. Accessed March 20, 2019.

Oral History Association. (n.d.) 'Principles and Best Practices'. www.oralhistory.org/about/principles-and-practices-revised-2009/. Accessed March 20, 2019.

Pekar, H. (2009) *Studs Terkel's Working: A Graphic Adaptation*, in Buhle, P. (ed.) New York, The New Press.

People Like Us: Social Class in America. Directors Louis Alvarez and Andrew Kolker, 2001.

Portelli, A. (2009) 'What Makes Oral History Different', in Del Giudice, L. (ed.), *Oral History, Oral Culture, and Italian Americans*, New York, Palgrave.

Public Citizen. (2013). 'NAFTA's Broken Promises 1994–2013: Outcomes of the North American Free Trade Agreement'. www.citizen.org/article/naftas-broken-promises-1994-2013-outcomes-of-the-north-american-free-trade-agreement/. March 15. Accessed March 6, 2020.

Russo, J. and Linkon, S. L. (2005) (eds.) *New Working-Class Studies*, Ithaca, Cornell University Press.

Southern Foodways Alliance. (n.d.) 'Oral Histories'. www.southernfoodways.org/oral-history/work-and-cook-and-eat-lumbee-indians-of-north-carolina/. Accessed March 4, 2020.

Southern Oral History Program. (n.d.) https://sohp.org. Accessed March 4, 2020.

Springsteen, B. (2011) 'Foreword', in Maharidge, D. and Williamson, M. *Someplace Like America: Tales from the New Great Depression*, Berkeley, University of California Press.

Strangleman, T. (2019) 'Why Can't It Be Like that Now? Remembering What We Had and Could Have Again', *Working-Class Perspectives*, July 8. https://workingclassstudies.wordpress.com/2019/07/08/why-cant-it-be-like-that-now-remembering-what-we-had-and-could-have-again/. Accessed December 1, 2019.

Terkel, S. (1974) *Working: People Talk about What they Do All Day and How they Feel about What they Do*. New York, Pantheon Books.

Thompson, C. D. (2002) 'Layers of Loss: Migrants, Small Business and Agribusiness', in Thompson, C. and Wiggins, M. (eds.) *The Human Cost of Food: Farmworkers' Lives, Labor and Advocacy*, Austin, University of Texas Press.

University of North Carolina at Pembroke. (n.d.-a) 'About', www.uncp.edu/about/history. Accessed March 2, 2020.

University of North Carolina at Pembroke. (n.d.-b) 'Campus Profile', www.uncp.edu/sites/default/files/2019-09/Campus%20Profile%202019%20Electronic_2.pdf. Accessed February 15, 2020.

University of North Carolina at Pembroke. (n.d.-c) 'Mission Statement', www.uncp.edu/about/mission-statement. Accessed October 1, 2015.

U.S. Bureau of Labor Statistics. (n.d.) 'Unemployment Rate in Robeson County, NC' [NCROBE7URN], retrieved from FRED, Federal Reserve Bank of St. Louis. https://fred.stlouisfed.org/series/NCROBE7URN. Accessed February 26, 2020.

U.S. Census Bureau. (n.d.) 'Robeson County, North Carolina', www.census.gov/search-results.html?searchType=web&cssp=SERP&q=Robeson%20County,%20NC. Accessed February 9, 2019.

Voices of the Lumbee, Director Jason Hutchens, 2014.

34

Precarious workers and social mobilization in Portuguese call centre assembly lines

Isabel Roque

Introduction

The digital revolution of the 21st century brought new challenges for the world of work, including social, economic and technological dimensions. Tertiarization, feminization and the dissemination of flexible forms of employment are significant trends in the recent evolution of employment in Europe. Sizable changes in knowledge acquisition, sharing and distribution, and massive ripple effects in the workplace allowed employees to perform their tasks outside the office as a consequence of computer networks (Andreessen 2011). Clients are also relying increasingly on digital, mobile and social-media tools (OECD 2009, 2011). Today's information and communication technologies are holding down employment, and the technological progress is eliminating the need for many types of jobs. This outcome is a result of structural changes in the economy, leaving the typical worker in precarious working conditions, especially due to the fact that the type of skills stipulated by employers demand continuous change and training for workers to keep up with new information and communications technology (ICT) skill requirements and multitasking, even those in low-skilled jobs (Katz 2010; Rotman 2013; Brynjolfsson and McAfee 2014; Autor 2015; Bessen 2015; Deming 2015).

Nevertheless, the growing army of the precariat, a symbol of globalization, electronic life and alienated work, performs unsafe work and is incapable of receiving an occupational identity or desired career (Standing 2011, 15). According to Standing, precarious workers share a common situation in the social structures (job, market, politics and culture) with a relative degree of vulnerability, instability, and uncertainty without employment security (2011, 8). As a result, most are excluded from the legal protections and labour rights achieved by the labour movements (Vosko 2010, 2; Milkman and Ott 2014, 8).[1] They are considered as the 'new proletariat of the modern times' of the service sector, facing few opportunities for training and professional development, low salaries, and the imminent risk of dismissal (Scott 1994, 236; Casaca 2005). In order to survive, the precariat is forced to accept jobs below their competence or outside their professions, doing work-for-labour, which is neither recognized nor remunerated, especially within zero-hours contracts and shift work, losing non-wage benefits, and lowering their social income and their long-term earnings. In this sense, the precariat experiences not only the loss of acquired labour but also cultural, civil, social, economic, and political rights, even begging to maintain or to get a job (Standing 2016).

Call centre workers, also known as the precariat, infoproletariat, cyber-proletariat and/or cybertariat, are caught up in a cybernetic vortex, being treated as disposable labour by temporary work agencies that provide them with ephemeral linkages to the main service companies (Marx and Engels 1992; Huws 2003; Antunes and Braga 2009; Standing 2011; Dyer-Witheford 2015). Workers' mobilization connected with digital labour has been emerging in Portugal since 2006. In 2011, the 'newest social movements' or 'new digitally enabled social movements', at an international scale, arose with specific protest actions aiming the struggle against austerity measures, triggered by the financial and economic crisis (Feixa et al. 2009, 438). Just as alternative media activists in the late 1960s and 1970s incorporated video technologies, nowadays workers' mobilizations communicate and disseminate their messages mainly through social media and digital technologies (Raymond 1999; Hamelink 2000; Edwards 2001; Postigo 2012; Campos et al. 2016). Social protest movements such as Precários Inflexíveis (Inflexible Precariat), Mayday, Indignados, Ferve (Tired of Green Receipts), Geração à rasca (Troubled Generation), Plataforma 15 de Outubro, Que se Lixe a Troika (Screw Troika), and more specifically in the call centre area, Pt Precariacções (Portugal Telecom Precarious Actions) and the Call Centre Workers' Trade Union (STCC), which are analyzed in this paper, are some of the examples of 'virtual-real' activism, working as a powerful weapon at the service of media activists to support their actions and struggles. Trade unions have become excessively bureaucratized and anachronistic regarding the labor market, being poorly equipped to meet the needs of the precarious workers. In many cases, they work alongside political organizations within a vertical organization structure, being mere representatives of the employees and not handling the precarious workforce situations in the best way possible (Estanque 2010; Milkman and Ott 2014). In this sense, social movements can be considered networked social movements, liberating individuals to shape a new autonomy, reclaiming power, and also shaking the political scene. Fueled by indignation, these workers mobilize, leading to social change expressed in revolts and personal projects anchored in multidimensional experiences (Castells 2013).

Precariousness includes not only precarity of employment but also precarious work and labour conditions, intermittence, uncertainty, and uprootedness as a general life experience (Kalff 2017; Lorey 2015). In an ongoing process of economic restructuring, flexibility becomes imperative for labour, work organization and life, forming precarious biographies (Berardi 2009). Between 2008 and 2016, the author of this paper conducted fifty semi-structured interviews with former and present call centre workers in Portugal, as well as with trade union delegates and activists from workers' mobilizations. The majority of the interviewees, ranging between 30 to 54 years old, underscored the fact that the majority of call centres consisted of female workers holding academic degrees. Most of them had been working in call centres for several years, while others were dismissed or were living abroad, looking for better life opportunities.[2]

This study concentrates mainly on trade unions and social mobilization within the Portuguese call centre service. Sections will focus on call centre workers' working conditions and their labour profile as well as the set of occupational risks they are subject to, in order to provide an analysis of trade unionism and virtual collective action in call centres. Such a focus is crucial for the debate in working-class studies, which encompasses a definition of class that goes beyond the notions of race, gender, and power relations in production, and which is also influenced by politics and culture (Weber 1978; Huws 2003, 2006; Wright 2005; Fuchs 2010; White 2012; Dyer-Witheford 2015; Woodcock 2016). These subjects have been studied in the last years as part of working-class and employment relations research, concerning incidence and trends in advanced capitalist societies as well as psychosocial consequences for individuals' health (Huws 2009; Vosko 2010; Standing 2011; McKay et al. 2012).

Call centre assembly lines

The proliferation of the call centre industry has often been linked to the spread of rapid service deliveries (Mukherjee and Malhotra 2006), representing the fastest developing form of electronic work. Call centres are a symbol of the modern service economy where services are available all around the clock and delivered from almost any spot (Paul and Huws 2002). Within the neoliberal system, these companies engage in forms of outsourcing to foreign countries where costs are lower and labour is cheaper. The location of call centres varies widely in different parts of the world, reflecting diversities in terms of technology and culture (Bonnet 2002). There are also different types of call centre services that provide information to callers, connect consumers to third parties, sell goods/products/services over the telephone, and supply emergency services and helplines (Glucksmann 2004).

Paul and Huws (2002) have characterized call centres as 'information processing factories' or 'modern-day sweatshops,' illustrated by images of call handlers 'chained to cage-like workstations' by their headphones. In this sense, call centre work is stigmatized, presenting the highest levels of electronic performance monitoring (EPM) (Taylor et al. 2002) and limitless worker surveillance (Ajunwa et al. 2017), which affect workers' psychological and emotional health (Collins 1991; Van Jaarsveld and Poster 2013). Call centre work is electronically managed without any privacy or autonomy, lowering job satisfaction, increasing stress and leading to low-trust, negative work relationships (Schumacher 2011) and to poor working conditions (Moore et al. 2017). According to Brophy (2009), the neo-Taylorist mode of production provides workers with low wages, high stress, precarious employment, rigid management, draining emotional labour, and pervasive electronic surveillance—i.e. call centres represent one of digital capitalism's fastest-growing professions (Baldry et al. 1998; Callaghan and Thompson 2000; Head 2003; Mulholland 2002; Taylor and Bain 1999; Brophy 2009).

Call centres are organized as a social hive, assuming themselves as a totalitarian institution, and managed by internal rules where each one performs an individual role with the others (Goffman 1959). This illustrates the relationship between 21st-century technologies and 19th-century labour conditions, submitting the worker to Toyotist flexibility and control techniques stemming from Taylorism (Antunes and Braga 2009), where flexible production and efficiency are maximized without any waste (Paugam 2000; Kovács 2002, 2005)

Call Centre Workers

According to Danilo Moreira, STCC's President, until 2008, the majority of Portuguese call centre workers were academic students (a highly skilled workforce) and women, working on a part-time basis.

> In the late nineties, when I started working in call centres, there were more women and students with a part-time job. With the emergence of call centre lines related with banks, technical lines related with technologies of information and communication, more men were hired. With the 2008 crisis, the age group became older because of dismissals and company closures, forcing people to face new realities and new means of life. Nowadays, we see mostly people with 30 and 40 years of age, but also unemployed people with 50 and more, some of them working in part-time regime in call centres as an addition to their basic pension.

This shift in the European labour market, which saw an increase in the number of men and older workers from their 40s on, can be seen working in call centres. In 2016, a Portuguese study revealed that the turnover rate amongst the banking and the telecommunications call centre workers was around 13% and the annual dismissal rate was around 30%. This situation reveals the fragile working conditions where workers can be easily dismissed and replaced by new and cheaper acquisitions, especially through temporary work agencies.[3] Call centre companies are increasingly adopting outsourcing strategies to reduce costs, subcontracting through temporary work agencies, which leads to high levels of job rotation (turnover) and dismissals.

Call centre workers are also knowledge workers (Drucker 1959) who perform abstract/immaterial work (Marx 1990), organizing and redirecting information, performing the virtual delivery of products, and managing the relationship between capital and the service sector clients. The existence of these workers is characterized by gestures and tasks that prevent them from developing their mental capabilities and creative potential—i.e. they become a mere extension of the computer. The workers' identity is deconstructed, in the sense that they feel unable to identify with the role of call centre operators, preventing them from achieving a professional career or attaining a sense of belonging to the company (Huws 2003).

Emotional labour is demanded of workers in order to sell more products and/or services and to secure customer loyalty. In this sense, workers practically ignore all verbal forms of aggression, always smiling down the phone through the use of their voices (Hochschild 1983; Callaghan and Thompson 2000; Taylor and Tyler 2000; Taylor et al. 2002; Roque 2016). Apart from speaking with the customers, workers must be able to register, in a virtual application, all the actions undertaken during the call, as they are also responsible for software development, electronic file updating, and the delivery of tasks related to the telephone operator. Inside the call centre, workers are restrained to a small cubicle in a room, sometimes without any windows or natural light, having access to a shared keyboard, chair, headset and mouse; the space is not properly cleaned, and the room temperature is often inadequate. They must also be fast, attentive, friendly, emotionally balanced and flexible—i.e. be able to deal with unexpected situations and act pleasantly with clients when they are subject to moral harassment and verbal aggression. According to Moreira, more than 80% of call centre workers experience precarious and temporary working contracts with temporary work agencies and do not have access to their full rights regarding parental license and sick leaves. In this sense, these workers will never benefit from the same social and labour rights that a full-time worker is entitled to. For these reasons, STCC is getting more workers involved in their struggle for the recognition of call centre worker as a profession in the the Standard Classification of Occupations.

One of the female interviewees, a 43-year-old, mentioned that being a supervisor gave her no satisfaction in the work she does nor in the wage she receives. She is submitted to extra hours and her wage depends upon her team's performance. Even though she has been working in the Telecommunications' service and in the same call centre for more than twenty years, her contract is precarious as it is established with a temporary work agency.

> Before I became a supervisor, I was happy because I took it as a professional evolution that doesn't exist. It's just a status. I consider myself a precarious person. Nowadays, I think that the majority of people are precarious, but they don't realize that. Being precarious is being disposable. Basically, we are machines.

Another male interviewee, 30 years of age, who has been working in call centres for four years in the charity service, revealed how his daily routine was leading him into psychological problems.

> I think that working in a contact centre can definitely create a precarious mind, especially if you work full-time or unsociable hours. You just want to shut down and to be as mindless as possible because the work isn't sociable at all. You are being treated like a machine and you are just literally acting as a command voice. You are always speaking to someone, always calling. It is always just work, work, work and your breaks are very, very short.

Employee well-being in the workplace is related to working conditions. Poor physical and psychosocial working conditions can increase the risk of work disability, retirement, and early exit from working life (Lahelma et al. 2012; Keenan 2015).

Social mobilization and trade unionism in call centres

The trade union movement arrived quite late in Portugal, being established with the democratic revolution of 25 April 1974, the so-called Carnation Revolution. This process radically changed the social and political landscape and paved the way for the emergence of social movements inspired by left-wing parties, such as the Portuguese Communist Party. In 1972, the biggest Portuguese trade unions, CGTP-Intersindical (General Confederation of Portuguese Workers-National Trades Union)[4] and UGT (Workers General Union),[5] joined the political scenario. UGT was identified as a reformist trade union, linked to the centre and right-wing political parties PS (Socialist Party) and PSD (Social Democracy Party), and was considered a privileged partner for social dialogue. CGTP-Intersindical was always connected to the left-wing parties. Nevertheless, by the end of the 1980s, with neoliberal globalization and the expansion of the third sector, the service class rose to the detriment of the working class, leading to a decrease in the unionization rate (Estanque 2005; Costa 2012). The strong influence of political parties did not allow trade unions to adjust ideologies and modes of action to the current Portuguese labour context. Progressively, trade unions lost touch with new forms of employment contracts, ignoring the degrading conditions of the vulnerable and disqualified workforce.

Trade unions have become more active in institutional regulation, negotiating with the state and other social partners, changing their scope of action and becoming mere instruments of regulatory action (Estanque and Ferreira 2002). As a result, trade unions are struggling to organize and represent the emergent precarious workforce, especially as a consequence of their inability to deal with atypical, non-regulated and flexible working conditions, prompted by service companies such as call centres (Brophy 2017). The ability to organize and represent the emergent precarious workforce faces many challenges, as Moreira states:

> Nowadays, the majority of workers are discredited concerning trade unions' role, so there is a high level of individualism. Trade unions should make the first move towards workers. Only when trade unions begin to show practical examples of their ideas and advance into action [will] workers will start to feel firmness and support and want to collaborate.
>
> (Danilo Moreira, STCC's President)

According to the senior interviewees, most Portuguese call centre workers, especially in the 1990s, consisted of students who perceived their labour experiences as temporary or transient. Regarding the traditional role of trade unions, there is still some mistrust among workers, as well as a sense of fear of affiliating. The interviews conducted revealed disappointment and lack of confidence and recognition in the traditional trade unions' leadership. As one female travel agency call centre worker, 28 years of age, put it,

> My colleagues and I were motivated to join a trade union to do something regarding our problems. Since I was a socially active person, I was a member of Precários Inflexíveis, [and] I wanted to be part of a change and help my colleagues. In this sense, I managed to get a meeting with the vice-president of Sinttav Trade Union, where I was affiliated. When I spoke with him, it was like I was talking about something that he knew nothing about. We received no information about the changes in the labour code or concerning strikes. Me and my colleagues started questioning the reason for this affiliation, the reason for giving them part of our salaries every month and not seeing any practical help and information.

Nowadays, most call centre workers see their labour experience as a permanent occupation, especially as a consequence of the precarious labour market which cannot offer them alternatives with a contract or a fixed monthly salary. Nevertheless, short-term contracts and the high turnover of workers in call centres presents a real and difficult obstacle for workers' organization or even social mobilization.

In terms of Portuguese call centre trade unions, SIESI (The South and Islands Electric Industries' Trade Union)[6] was the first, stemming from the former electricians' trade union and being affiliated with CGTP-Intersindical. It is linked to Electricity of Portugal (EDP) call centres and its foundation goes back to 1939, to the beginning of the Electricians' National Trade Union. The National Trade Union of Postal and Telecommunication Workers (SNTCT)[7] was created in Lisbon on 5 March 1974, with more than 10,000 workers of the Postal and Telecommunications Public Company of Portugal. The Democratic Union of Media and Communication Workers (SINDETELCO)[8] represents postal, telecommunications, graphics, logistics and new economy workers. It was created in 1981 and is affiliated with CGTP-Intersindical. The National Trade Union of Telecommunications and Audiovisual (SINTTAV)[9] was created in 2006 and is affiliated with UGT. In terms of force, in the first months of 2017, STCC and SNTCT have been very prominent in their actions, especially STCC with their involvement with other social protest movements and trade unions, not only planning them on the internet but on the streets too.

Virtual collective action in call centres

Cyberspace has contributed greatly to social action and to the democratization of the Portuguese workers' movement. Since 2011, several social protest movements have appeared on the Portuguese scene, like Geração à Rasca (The Desperate Generation), Mayday (Emergency), 15M or Indignados (Indignant), Podemos (We Can), Ferve (Tired of the False Green Receipts), Precários Inflexíveis (Inflexible Precariat) and Pt Precariacções (Portugal Telecom Precarious Actions). Following transnational forms of activism (Tarrow 2011)—i.e., against austerity measures and for participatory and deliberative democracy social protest movements—a series of Portuguese demonstrations started taking place, bringing remarkable changes in the organizational structure of Portuguese mobilizations, especially in terms of their impact aside from the traditional trade unions, leading to new social protest movements connected with digital labour (Baumgarten 2013).

The most relevant organizational consequence of these social protest movements in Portugal was the emergence of Precários Inflexiveis, an organization created in 2007 that includes members of all the aforementioned protest movements. They were one of the first cyber platforms operating a website, a blog, and a Facebook page aimed at helping precarious workers and trade unions. Above all, their major aim has always been to inform workers and unemployed people about their labour and civic rights. These social protest movements were followed by trade unions which called for their own protests and strikes, especially CGTP-Intersindical. In this sense, in Portugal, the general strikes were accompanied by demonstrations involving trade unions, activist groups, and social protest movements (Baumgarten 2013).

Until 2014, according to a trade union delegate from SINTTAV and also a founding member of a call centre workers' organization, the telecommunications' trade union sector was in a state of apathy and conformity. This situation led to a 'rebellion' and a feeling of discontent among the workers, who relied on very low wages and uncertain working conditions. As a result, a group of workers in Coimbra in central Portugal (of which the author was a part, as she was working at a telecommunications' call centre in 2006) started to gather in coffee shops, activists' houses and cultural neighborhood associations. The activities planned by the groups of workers were aimed at raising public awareness of the unhuman atrocities and precarious working conditions that call centre workers were exposed to. Between 2006 and 2013, this movement was disseminating information through the distribution of flyers outside call centres, by word of mouth, but also via the internet with the development of a blog and a Facebook page.

Nevertheless, between 2006 and 2013, Precariacções Inflexiveis organized several social mobilizations of call centre workers at the telecommunications' company Portugal Telecom in Coimbra. Precariacções made anonymous appearances near the workplaces, placing posters and banners in front of every major call centre in order to bring attention to the exploitation of call centre workers. According to a 27-year-old member, in July 2009 Precariacções organizers were questioned during a police raid at the main telecommunications' call centre.

> During the night we placed some banners outside the main call center denouncing the company's president, and the next morning they called the police, who raided the call centre, asking every [Precariacções] delegate who was responsible for it. Nevertheless, we did not stop our actions because we wanted to denounce the inefficient approach that trade unions have towards our problems.

In 2013, most of *Precariacções'* members went to Lisbon (in central Portugal) and others to Braga and Porto (in northern Portugal), where they distributed flyers and leaflets outside every major call centre, providing concrete information about call centre workers' issues. These actions allowed the building of trust and informal networks between colleagues while also developing class-conscious ways of fighting back or sabotaging work.

As a result of these experiences with 'virtual real' activism and interactions with call centre workers, in September 2014, *Precariacções* activists decided to formalize their struggle by forming the STCC. Since then, STCC has been working as a union, organizing general workers' assemblies and issuing several strike, involving both their members and other unaffiliated call centre workers. Their statutes were written and published by the Installation Committee constituted with call centre operators who work on a voluntary basis. In 2015, they elected their first female president, Paula Lopes, one of the very few women leading a trade union in Portugal. After Lopes's two-year term ended, Danilo Moreira was elected president. He has worked in several call centres over twenty years as a supervisor, operator and quality technician, and he currently works in two inbound and outbound call centres. All union officers are unpaid and currently work as call centre workers. STCC now has nine delegates located in the major call centres across Portugal. In this sense, the range of action has broadened, opening up opportunities to cooperate with other trade unions, social movements, and even various political parties at national and international levels. In cyberspace, this trade union manages a web page, a blog, and a Facebook page and Youtube pages (Tás Logado) where call centre workers can pose questions related to labour and legal concerns, interact with the leaders and delegates, and collect information on trade union activities and labour rights. Besides the official trade union email, a mobile help line was created in 2017. There are frequent negotiation meetings with companies and workers' committees, and delegates are offered training as well. Workshops are also available for workers.

One of the main goals of STCC was the approval of a petition (E-petition), submitted on 12 October 2016, to the Portuguese Parliament to recognize call centre work as a 'high-stress occupation' and to have it included in the Standard Classification of Occupations. In the near future, they aim to create a multidisciplinary team to deliver psychological support to workers, with the help of specialized staff in Psychology and Hygiene and Safety at Work.

They are also establishing synergies with call centre workers in Brazil, Poland, Spain, Cabo Verde and Angola, trying to create a similar trade union with the same cyberspace strategies as STCC. As a result, workers feel more empathetic, aware of their problems and struggles, while acquiring a sense of belonging to a trade union that, unlike the vast majority, deals with their specific questions and is led by workers like them. STCC also aims to increase the number of associates, to consolidate the bonds between media, legal authorities, and other call centre trade unions in support of workers' commissions and active social movements fighting precarity.

Conclusion

From the qualitative analysis of the interviews and through informal conversations, it was concluded that prior to 2010, Portuguese workers were living under a dialectics of consent and resignation, revealing isolated, vulnerable and alienated identities. Most of the interviewees weren't unionized, and the degree of participation in social protest movements and strikes were low, characterized by the fear of iminent dismissal. Nevertheless, the new social movements that appeared led to a new vision of social intervention that was supported by social media and promoted by the media.

This study has shown the ways in which cyberspace is reviving Portuguese trade unionism. TIC works as forms of recruitment and mobilization, contributing to the revitalization of the trade union movement (Diamond and Freeman 2002). Cyberspace communication is crucial for labour organizing, as it overcomes communication constraints geographically, physically and linguistically. Social networks also provide a sense of community for dialogue between delegates and workers, where they can discuss and anonymously pose questions and receive community-oriented messages. In fact, according to Danilo Moreira, this was the first trade union to perform digital unionizing and to address specific questions raised by call centre workers. This was possible because STCC is made up only of call centre workers; their experiences ranged from seeing a class-in-the-making (Standing 2011) to a bigger sense of class for itself, in the Marxian sense.

This new trade union has emphasized workers' class consciousness in order to struggle for better working conditions alongside other social actors, such as academia and other trade unions and social protest movements. These actions had an impact on society, and it was noticeable that the other trade unions started to worry much more about workers' rights, and their flyers started to focus more on precarity and unionization than they had ever before. They also started to call for strikes through the internet, such as on 30 June 2017 when SNTCT and CGTP-Intersindical demanded higher salaries and permanent contracts. An outcome was participation in the Dockers' trade union strike in May 2017 in Lisbon, with the presence of workers, trade union delegates and Portuguese academics who had been studying this subject. STCC supported this strike for better wages right from the beginning, posting on social media and delivering flyers, but also attending the workers' plenary sessions. In this sense, and according to an interview with Danilo Moreira, participating in the Docker's strike involved a sharing of struggle strategies that transported their struggle into the wider society in order to bring more people into activism.

STCC does not receive any financial support from political parties, nor does it have any attachments to any central union; this offers the perfect degree of freedom to engage in parallel activities, strikes and social mobilizations that might not be directly related to call centres. Solidarity unionism stands in opposition to 'business' or 'service-provider' unionism—that is, workers carry out their own organizing and every worker has an equal say in the union's actions. In this sense, there is direct participation in the union's struggle, allowing members to become more focused and effective, especially since workers have good proximity with the board in terms of class consciousness and mobilizing for working-class solidarity through workers' assemblies (Lynd 2015). Nevertheless, STCC's weaknesses might result from the fear that companies have inflicted on workers regarding unionization and the lack of recognition by other trade unions, especially due to the fact that they are not financially dependent on political parties.

Since call centres are considered by many academics as one of the biggest representatives or icons of digital work, it is crucial to learn how it is enabling the working class to progressively gain media and government attention and to have a strong impact on the international realm. Associations are being established with Brazilian, African and European trade unions as well as with precarious workers' social movements. The latter includes feminist, environmental, LGBTQ, and anti-racist social movements. In this sense, gathering several organizational structures and sharing new strategies that empower oppressed people can lead to a more forceful democratic, open and independent trade unionism in the 21st century. As Woodcock states, 'The future success of trade unions in call centres will depend in no small measure on their ability to contest and redefine the frontiers of control on terms desired by their members' (2016, 118). This requires a break from the perception of unions as service providers to a shrinking base of members and a move towards seeing them as strong organizations that are focused on workplace struggle.

Notes

1 Such as the lack of control over the pace and content of their work and sharing a basic powerlessness in relation to the authority of the owner and the owner's representatives who supervise and control them, and the lack of community support in times of need, lack of assured enterprise or state benefits, and lack of private benefits to supplement money earnings.

2 Finding interviewees was a relatively easy task since the author had already worked in several Portuguese call centres and has been involved in social protest movements and trade unions. Various other informants were also identified through snowball sampling.

3 www.conferenciaapcc.org/2016/pdf/APCC_Estudo_Benchmarking_2016.pdf

4 www.cgtp.pt/

5 www.ugt.pt/

6 www.siesi.pt/

7 www.sntct.pt/o-sindicato/historico/

8 www.sindetelco.pt/

9 http://sinttav.org/joomla/

References

Ajunwa, I., Crawford, K. and Schultz, J. (2017) 'Limitless Worker Surveillance', *California Law Review*, 105, 3. Available at http://ssrn.com/abstract=2746211.

Andreessen, M. (2011) 'Why Software is Eating the World', *The Wall Street Journal*, August 20. www.wsj.com/articles/SB10001424053111903480904576512250915629460.

Antunes, R. and Braga, R. (eds.) (2009) *Infoproletários: Degradação Real do Trabalho Virtual*, São Paulo, Boitempo.

Autor, D. (2015) 'Why Are there still so Many Jobs? The History and Future of Workplace Automation', *Journal of Economic Perspectives*, 29, 3, pp. 7–30.

Baldry, C., Bain, P. and Taylor, P. (1998) '"Bright Satanic Offices": Intensification, Control and Team Taylorism', in Thompson, P. and Warhurst, C. (eds.), *Workplaces of the Future*, Basingstoke: Macmillan.

Baumgarten, B. (2013) 'Geração à Rasca and Beyond: Mobilizations in Portugal after 12 March 2011', *Current Sociology*, 61, 4, pp. 457–473.

Berardi, F. (2009) *The Soul at Work: From Alienation to Autonomy*, Los Angeles, Semiotext(e).

Bessen, J. (2015) *Learning by Doing: The Real Connection between Innovation, Wages, and Wealth*, New Haven, Yale University Press.

Bonnet, N. (2002) 'The Establishment of Call Centres in France: Between Globalism and Local Geographical Disparateness', *NETCOM*, 16, pp. 75–78.

Brophy, E. (2009) 'Resisting Call Centre Work: The Aliant Strike and Convergent Unionism in Canada', *Work Organisation, Labour and Globalisation*, 3, 1, pp. 80–99.

Brophy, E. (2017) *Language Put to Work. The Making of the Global Call Centre Workforce*, London, Palgrave Macmillan.

Brynjolfsson, E. and McAfee, D. (2014) *The Second Machine Age: Work, Progress, and Prosperity in a Time of Brilliant Technologies*, New York, W.W. Norton.

Callaghan, G. and Thompson, P. (2000) 'Proceeding to the Paddling Pool: The Selection and Shaping of Call Centre Labour', Open Discussion Papers in Economics, No. 15, Milton Keynes, Open University.

Campos, R., Pereira, I. and Simões, J. (2016) 'Activismo Digital em Portugal: Um Estudo Exploratório, Sociologia', *Problemas e Práticas*, 82, pp. 27–47.

Casaca, S. (2005) 'Flexibilidade de Emprego, Novas Temporalidades de Trabalho e Relações de Género: A Reconfiguração da Desigualdade nos Novos Sectores dos Serviços', Lisboa, ISEG, Universidade Técnica de Lisboa, Dissertação de Doutoramento.

Castells, M. (2013) *Redes de Indignação e Esperança: Movimentos Sociais na era da Internet,* São Paulo, Zahar.

Collins, C. (1991) 'Bill Would Require Notices When Bosses Snoop on Employees', *Los Angeles Times*, March 11. Available at http://articles.latimes.com/1991-11-03/business/fi-1400_1_employee-performance. Accessed March 30, 2018.

Costa, H. (2012) 'From Europe as a Model to Europe as Austerity: The Impact of the Crisis on Portuguese Trade Unions', *Transfer – European Review of Labour and Research*, 18, 4, pp. 397–410.

Deming, D. (2015) 'The Growing Importance of Social Skills in the Labor Market, *NBER Working Paper*, No. 21473.

Diamond, W. and Freeman, B. (2002) 'Will Unionism Prosper in Cyberspace? The Promise of the Internet for Employee Organization, *British Journal of Industrial Relations*, 40, 3, pp. 569–596.

Drucker, P. (1959) *Landmarks of Tomorrow*, Harper, New York.

Dyer-Witheford, N. (2015) *Cyber-Proletariat: Global Labour in the Digital Vortex*, London, Pluto Press.

Edwards, R. (2001) 'Digital Activism in the Independent Media Center Movement', *Spectator*, 21, 2, pp. 82–94.

Estanque, E. (2005) 'Trabalho, Desigualdades Sociais e Sindicalismo', *Revista Crítica de Ciências Sociais*, 71, pp. 113–140.

Estanque, E. (2010) 'Sindicalismo e Movimentos Sociais: Ação Coletiva e Regulação Social No Contexto Europeu e Português', *Revista Lutas Sociais*, 8, 23. Revista do Núcleo de Estudos de Ideologia e Lutas Sociais da PUC. São Paulo.

Estanque, E. and Ferreira, A. (2002) 'Transformação No Mercado Laboral e Novos Desafios No Sindicalismo Português', *Revista Crítica de Ciências Sociais*, pp. 151–159.

Feixa, C., Pereira, I. and Juris, J. (2009) 'Global Citizenship and the "New, New" Social Movements: Iberian Connections', *Young—Nordic Journal of Youth Research*, 17, 4, pp. 421–442.

Fuchs, C. (2010) 'Labor in Informational Capitalism and on the Internet', *The Information Society*, 26, 3, pp. 179–196.

Glucksmann, M. (2004) 'Call Configurations: Varieties of Call Centre and Divisions of Labour', *Work, Employment and Society*, 18, 4, pp. 795–811.

Goffman, E. (1959) *The Presentation of Self in Everyday Life*, New York, Anchor.

Hamelink, C. (2000) *The Ethics of Cyberspace*, London, Sage Publications.

Head, S. (2003) *The New Ruthless Economy: Work & Power in the Digital Age*, Oxford, Oxford University Press.

Hochschild, A. (1983) *The Managed Heart: Commercialization of Human Feeling*, Berkeley, University of California Press.

Huws, U. (2003) *The Making of a Cybertariat: Virtual Work in a Real World*, Monthly Review Press, New York.

Huws, U. (2006) 'The Spark in the Engine: Creative Workers in a Global Economy', *Work Organisation, Labour and Globalisation*, 1, 1, pp. 1–12.

Huws, U. (2009) 'Working at the Interface: Call Centre Labour in a Global Economy', *Work Organisation, Labour and Globalisation*, 3, 1, pp. 1–8.

Kalff, Y. (2017) 'The Knowledge Worker and the Projectified Self: Domesticating and Disciplining Creativity', *Work Organisation, Labour & Globalisation*, 11, 1, pp. 10–27. 10.13169/workorgalaboglob.11.1.0010.

Katz, L. (2010) 'Long-term unemployment in the great recession', Presented to U.S. Congress Joint Economic Committee. www.jec.senate.gov/public/index.cfm?a=Files.Serve&File_id=e1cc2c23-dc6f-4871-a26a-fda9bd32fb7e.%2520.

Keenan, D. (2015) 'Is Another Unionism Possible? Solidarity Unionism in the Industrial Workers of the World in the U.S. and Canada', *WorkingUSA, The Journal of Labor and Society*, 18, 2, pp. 211–229.

Kovács, I. (2002) *As Metamorfoses do Emprego: Ilusões e Problemas da Sociedade de Informação*, Oeiras, Celta Editora.

Kovács, I. (2005) *Flexibilidade de Emprego*. Riscos e Oportunidades, Oeiras, Celta Editora.

Lahelma, E., Laaksonen, M., Lallukka, T., Martikainen, P., Pietiläinen, O., Saastamoinen, P., Gould, R. and Rahkonen, O. (2012) 'Working Conditions as Risk Factors for Disability Retirement: A Longitudinal Register Linkage Study', *BMC Public Health*, 12, 309.

Lorey, I. (2015) *State of Insecurity: Government of the Precarious*, London, Verso.

Lynd, S. (2015) *Solidarity Unionism: Rebuilding the Labor Movement from Below*, second edition, United States, PM Press.

Marx, K. (1990) *Capital. A Critique of Political Economy*, Volume One (trans. Ben Fowkes), London, Penguin Books.

Marx, K. and Engels, F. (1992) *The Communist Manifesto*, Oxford, Oxford University Press.

McKay, S., Jefferys, S., Paraksevopoulou, A. and Keles, J. (2012) *Study on Precarious Work and Social Rights*, Final Report prepared for the European Commission, Working Lives Research Institute, London UK, Faculty of Social Sciences and Humanities, London Metropolitan University.

Milkman, R. and Ott, E. (2014) *New Labor in New York: Precarious Workers and the Future of the Labor Movement*, Ithaca, NY, ILR Press.

Moore, P., Upchurch, M. and Whittaker, X. (eds.) (2017) *Humans and Machines at Work: Monitoring, Surveillance and Automation in Contemporary Capitalism, Dynamics of Virtual Work*, Cham, Switzerland, Palgrave Macmillan.

Mukherjee, A., and Malhotra, N. (2006) 'Does Role Clarity Explain Employee-Perceived Service Quality? A Study of Antecedents and Consequences in Call Centres', *International Journal of Service Industry Management*, 17, 5, pp. 444–473.

Mulholland, K. (2002) 'Gender, Emotional Labour and Teamworking in a Call Centre', *Personnel Review*, 31, 3, pp. 283–303.

OECD (2009) *Rethinking e-Government Services: User-Centred Approaches*, Paris, OECD Publishing. http://dx.doi.org/10.1787/9789264059412-en.

OECD (2011) *M-Government: Mobile Technologies for Responsive Governments and Connected Societies*, Paris, OECD Publishing. http://dx.doi.org/10.1787/9789264118706-en.

Paugam, S. (2000) *Le Salarié de la Précarité*, Paris, PUF.

Paul, J. and Huws, U. (2002) *2nd Draft Report for the Tosca Project*, Analytica Social and Economic Research Ltd, August.

Postigo, H. (2012) *The Digital Rights Movement*, Cambridge MA, The MIT Press.

Raymond, E. (1999) *The Cathedral and the Bazaar, Musings on Linux and Open Source by an Accidental Revolutionary*, Sebastopol, O'Reilly Media.

Roque, I. (2016) 'Psychosocial Risks at the Portuguese Contact Centres', in Arezes, P., Baptista, J., Barroso, M., Carneiro, P., Cordeiro, P., Costa, N., Melo, R., Miguel, A. and Perestrelo, G. (eds.), *Occupational Safety and Hygiene IV*, London, CRC Press.

Rotman, D. (2013) 'How Technology is Destroying Jobs', *MIT Technology Review*, June 12. www.technologyreview.com/featuredstory/515926/how-technology-is-destroying-jobs/.

Schumacher, S. (2011) 'What Employees should Know about Electronic Performance Monitoring', *ESSAI*, 8, 38, pp. 138–144. Available at http://dc.cod.edu/cgi/viewcontent.cgi?article=1332&context=essai. Accessed February 15, 2017.

Scott, A. (1994) 'Gender Segregation in the Retail Industry', in Scott, A. M. (ed.). *Gender Segregation and Social Change, Men and Women in Changing Labour Markets*, Oxford, Oxford University Press.

Standing, G. (2011) *The Precariat: The New Dangerous Class*, London, Bloomsbury Academic.

Standing, G. (2016) 'Meet the Precariat, the New Global Class Fueling the Rise of Populism', *World Economic Forum*, 9, November.

Tarrow, S. (2011) *Power in Movement. Social Movements and Contentious Politics*, Cambridge, Cambridge University Press.

Taylor, P. and Bain, P. (1999) 'An Assembly Line in the Head: Work and Employee Relations in the Call Centre', *Industrial Relations Journal*, 30, 2, pp. 101–117.

Taylor, P., Mulvey, G., Hyman, J. and Bain, P. (2002) 'Work Organisation, Control and the Experience of Work in Call Centres', *Work, Employment and Society*, 16, 1, pp. 133–150.

Taylor, S. and Tyler, M. (2000) 'Emotional Labour and Sexual Difference in the Airline Industry', *Work, Employment and Society*, 14, 2, pp. 77–95.

Van Jaarsveld, D. and Poster, W. (2013) 'Call Centers: Emotional Labor Over the Phone', in Grandey, A. A., Dieffendorff, J. M. and Rupp, D. E. (eds.), *Emotional Labor in the 21st Century: Diverse Perspectives on Emotion Regulation at Work*, New York, Routledge.

Vosko, L. (2010) *Managing the Margins: Gender, Citizenship, and the International Regulation of Precarious Employment*, Oxford, Oxford University Press.

Weber, M. (1978) *Economy and Society: An Outline of Interpretive Sociology* (trans. Ephraim Fischoff et al.), Berkeley, CA, University of California Press.

White, A. (2012) *The Digital Labour Challenge: Work in the Age of New Media*, Working Paper, Geneva, International Labour Office.

Woodcock, J. (2016) *Working the Phones Control and Resistance in Call Centres*, London, Pluto Press.

Wright, E. (2005) *Approaches to Class Analysis*, Cambridge, Cambridge University Press.

35

Post-Fordist affect

Unions, the labor movement, and the weight of history

Joseph Varga

American workers have always contested their exploitation under the capitalist system. Like workers around the globe, they have developed historically located modes of contestation, backed by theory and tested in practice. The modes of struggle and resistance, or *repertoires of contention*, challenge the control of capitalist owners and achieve gains for workers (Silver 2003; Tilly 2006; Tarrow 2013). But, of course, workers never struggle for better conditions under circumstances of their own choosing. As capital has come to dominate in all corners of the global economy, workers have adapted existing repertoires, and have developed area-specific, and historically specific, modes of struggle (Laurie 1997; Lichtenstein 2002; Luce 2014). One can observe a pots-and-pans-banging noise demonstration in Portland, Maine, and a corporate campaign highlighting the private failings of a corporate leader in La Paz, and recognize each as adapted to local conditions (Evans 2014).

Of course, not all repertoires and modes of struggle translate, and some are never very effective in their places of origin. A factory occupation without the backing of a strong local community will quickly collapse. Likewise, a public relations campaign where all modes of media are controlled by the bosses and their allies may not be effective. In addition, state-sponsored market capitalism has proven to be resilient, pliant, adaptive, clever, and often violently resistant. Unfortunately for workers, they neither control large amounts of capital nor, in many instances, have much effective political power. Thus, workers and their institutions and organizations are often reactive, moving to resistance, adaption, and accommodation based on changes at the level of investment, movement of capital, and the legal/juridical structure (Harvey 2007). In other words, things change, and workers are often forced to change in catch-up mode, utilizing existing repertoires of contention while updating and adapting them to meet new conditions.

There is an extensive literature on what constitutes an effective mode of struggle for workers, and for the general cause of social justice, broadly defined (Hurd, Milkman, and Turner 2003; Lambert 2005; Burns 2011; Geoghagan 2014; McAlevey 2015). Many activists and scholars still view the role of workers, and the working class in general, as key to building a more just and equitable system (Clawson 2003; Engeman 2014). For these, the extraction of surplus value and the reproduction of labor power under capital remain the key point around which justice, and, indeed, injustice, turn (Arrighi 2010; Silver 2014: Della Porta 2015). Thus, how workers, as ad hoc groups in neighborhoods, or as organized collectives in the workplace, or as actors in the public sphere and political system adapt and adjust their modes or repertoires of contention will often be determinate for such indices of social justice as economic inequality, civil rights, and political participation. To put it simply, the ability of workers to organize against exploitation will be an important determining factor for the overall health of any system (Rosenfeld 2014).

In this contribution to the study of the working class, I examine how unions and their members in the American Midwest have changed, and often not changed, in response to alterations in the capitalist mode of accumulation. As Zweig points out, 'Workers have historically been slow to adjust to such changes with new organizing strategies' (2016, 15). Thus, it is vital to both the study of working-class activism and to that activism itself to examine ways that the failure to adjust hinders and discourages innovation in tactics and strategies. It makes sense that unions and labor movement leaders would call upon the repertoires developed during the period of union expansion and influence. Yet those same repertoires can serve to prevent organized labor from facing the realities of changes in the labor process.

By studying what ethnographers have termed post-Fordist affect, we can see how existing frames and structures of labor activism, developed in the period of postwar prosperity, are adapted to contemporary conditions, often to the detriment of workers themselves. Post-Fordist affects are those remnants of these registers and intensities that congeal during the period from the 1980s to the 2000s, when some semblance of a national economy and culture held over from the period of mythical post-War consensus shape and structure cultural production and political claim-making. For example, workers and their allies in the South Central Indiana region continue to call upon modes of industrial relations and community that harken back to the perceived social contract of the Fordist era (1946–1973), modes that survived in altered and often diluted forms through the period of transition away from the Fordist and Keynesian labor market regime. This chapter looks at the variety of ways that lingering visions of a strong state, economic stability, robust unionism, and a common public sphere influence, encourage, and at times inhibit and repress forms of labor militancy and activism. Based on interviews and research on deindustrialization in the region, I explore how several instances of struggle over labor rights in South Central Indiana demonstrate how post-Fordist modes of claim-making in the era of neoliberalism are rendered ineffectual and how the affectual registers of the industrial past weigh on the present (Varga 2013, 2014).

General Electric lies. Does it matter?

Shortly after General Electric (GE) announced in the spring of 2014 that it would lay off 160 of its 600 production workers from the company's facility in Bloomington, Indiana, members of the International Brotherhood of Electrical Workers Local 2140 organized a series of public actions meant to highlight GE's role as a poor corporate citizen. Demonstrations were held in front of the plant with signs highlighting the fact that GE was announcing layoffs two years after making a commitment to expansion *and* after accepting both federal stimulus funding and Tax Increment Financing aid from local government. The public demonstrations were meant to build support for GE workers in their struggle against an employer they presented as a poor neighbor and uncaring member of the local community. Of the remaining 600 workers at the plant, more than 80% had been on the job for more than 20 years as of 2014, and were the rump of a factory workforce that had peaked in the 1980s at approximately 3,400 (Varga 2014).

As the crowd marched and chanted on the sidewalk, some passing cars honked in support. Many kept silent, and many drivers looked annoyed at the spectacle. As GE workers would point out one year later during a different episode, many local people, including hourly wage workers, considered the GE employees to be a 'labor elite.' For many, the GE workforce was overpaid and had brought on their own problems by demanding too much from their employer. Bill Fairbairn, a longtime employee, who would soon be elected president of the International Brotherhood of Electrical Workers local at the plant, carried a sign that echoed the sentiment of many of his fellow workers: 'GE Lied.' While many of his coworkers agreed, it was uncertain, in the 2014 environment of South Central Indiana, how loud the echo of his claims would be for the public. Further, to describe the claim as echoing might be even more appropriate, considering that the stage on which this claim was being made might have been empty. The claims of the GE workers raised several questions, not just about their employer, but also about the public sphere and the ability of workers to effectively make demands.

There was little doubt over the substantive nature of the charge that 'GE Lies.' The company had promised to expand production at the Bloomington plant, and was now reneging on that promise. The question was did anybody care? Or perhaps more accurately, how, in the era of neoliberalism, rampant consumerism, union decline, and the retreat of the effective welfare state, could a small group of workers make people take their claims seriously? Was the tactic of publicly charging a multinational corporation with misbehavior toward their workforce ineffective in the contemporary environment?

South Central Indiana has seen numerous examples of protests over the closing of factories, from the shuttering of the Whirlpool facility in Evansville in 2009 to striking limestone workers in Oolitic in 2011 to demonstrations over proposed layoffs at the GE plant in Bloomington in 2013, the repertoires are similar. Most of the stories follow a familiar pattern: the employer seeks to increase profits or cut losses by moving or closing a facility and demanding reductions in the workforce or give-backs/wage freezes and benefit cuts in a contract. The reactions are patterned as well; while negotiators and politicians hit the meeting rooms and media outlets, the workers hit the streets, bringing their message to the public. But what publics are there to absorb their message? Do messages accusing a multinational corporation with varied interests in the global economy of dishonesty and greed still resonate in an effective manner? And how do such accusations rely on assumptions regarding the relationships between corporations, workers, political leaders, and the public?

It is possible that workers and unions invested in lingering visions of a strong state, economic stability, robust unionism, and a common public sphere influence, encourage, and at times inhibit and repress forms of labor militancy and activism. Here, post-Fordist affect describes the various material and cultural artifacts, such as mass-production facilities, banners and signs, bullhorns, sidewalks, American flags, union jackets and shirts, detached single-family homes, and chanting, that coalesce and disperse to structure forms of public protest and contestation. Post-Fordist affect is not necessarily the things in themselves, but the registers and intensities that operate in the contested meanings of these objects in action (Muelebach and Shoshan 2012).

Affect and action

Labor protests are emotionally laden and can cause a variety of reactions. For some, the sight of workers on strike will evoke intensely personal feelings of pride and commitment to a certain understanding of rights. For others, the same workers can evoke feelings of revulsion, with connections to forms of collective organization that suggest loss of freedoms, or worse. For still others, the sight can evoke apathy, the feeling that if the actions do not directly involve the individual, then they have little or no stake (Madland and Walter 2010). These emotions, bound up in material conditions and ideological understandings, do not fully constitute affect. Rather, affect refers to the ongoing and shifting meanings and relations that are formed and re-formed based on reactions and interpretations of subjective and collective positions. Indeed, that is their point, for both pro- and anti-labor activists. The evocative emotions of public actions are meant to appeal to notions of fairness, justice, economic prosperity, and civil rights, of both protestors and their object of protest, which in the case of labor actions is often the owner of private capital in various forms (Weldon 2014). The emotions are the desired result: intentional, patterned, and part of the strategy (Weston 2012).

Lauren Berlant, in her essay 'Nearly utopian, nearly normal: Post-Fordist affect in *La Promesse and Rosetta*,' describes affect as the unqualified/nonconscious intensities that exist under or beyond meaning (2007). In Berlant's telling, affect, and affective registers, are deeply tied to forms of production, and each mode of capitalist production engenders its own. The contention here is that affects, as a set of intensities and registers, are the underlying, deeply felt but not acknowledged sets of material objects and relations that structure the emotional attachments and reactions described above. Thus we can see repertoires of contention, among other phenomena, as remnants, holdovers, whose effectiveness is severely inhibited by the changing nature of both state and capital (Arruzza 2014). Under these conditions, acquired forms of political contention take on the aspects of specters, haunting the present with dreams of a past that never really existed. As Berlant puts it, contemporary instances of struggle become the 'scene of constant bargaining with normalcy in the face of conditions that can barely support even the memory of fantasy' (2007, 278).

The relative stability of the Fordist period engendered certain affective registers, the linkage of certain emotional conceptions of what was just and fair, and what constituted a decent standard of living, with certain practices and representations. Taken together, the imagery and material production of the Fordist period constitute what Muehlbach and Shoshan, in their *American Quarterly* special edition on post-Fordist affect, describe as the 'affect factory' (2012, 332) of the postwar era. They point out, through Gramsci, how the true nature of Fordism was only partially about productions, but more generally entailed organizing the 'affective capacities of citizens, their deepest desires, longings and feelings' (Muehlbach and Shoshan 2012, 333).

The post-Fordist period was characterized by industrial job loss, closed factories, free trade agreements, and the rise to dominance of finance. The notion that those who 'worked hard and played by the rules' could still celebrate morning in America guided the repertoires of labor contention, despite the relentless drive of globalization (Tabb 2004, 43). For many American workers during this period, the belief that there was no longer any commitment, at either the level of the firm, or in national political ideologies, to any notion of protecting or preserving domestic prosperity for wageworkers, was outside of the realm of the narrative that drove and sustained the postwar regime of bargaining and compromise (Dudley 1994; Strangleman 2013). For many of these workers, even amid massive job relocation, the basic principles of national strength, fair remuneration for hard work, and commitment to stable communities was the normalcy that sustained them as conditions changed beneath their feet. Thus, as Massumi (1995) works out in 'The autonomy of affect,' the reception of the evidence that America was gone, or never existed, was always tempered by an embodied sense that the story of progress had to continue (Dudley 1994). As Massumi states of the embodied reception of intensities and reactions to negative content and why workers could ignore or transform them, 'The reason may be that they are associated with expectation, which depends on consciously positioning oneself in a line of narrative continuity' (1995, 85). The narrative continuity here, the story of working-class America entering the realm of prosperity, remains so strong in the post-Fordist era as to solidify in place repertoires of contention more suited to a different regime.

Several assumptions structure this narrative continuity. The first vestigial assumption from the Fordist period is that profit is derived from production, and thus workers play a key role as commodified labor. Along with this goes the notion that the health of the firm is linked upwards to the health of the nation and downwards to the stability of the community. Relatedly, if those factors prevail, the state, at all levels, would then maintain some commitment to some semblance of balance in the relationship between capital and labor, and perform the same regulatory functions, such as support for organizing and domestic labor markets, that were the hallmark of the postwar period. Further, and perhaps most critically, workers and their advocates maintain the belief that their actions as collective citizens, such as public protest, resonate with both political representatives and corporate executives, and act in concert with the previously described links to national health and community stability (Tabb 2004; Rosenfeld 2014).

Yet the history of the post-Fordist period is the history of the slow dissolution of these relationships, and their collective emergence in altered forms that render the repertoires formulated and shared under post-Fordism ineffective at best, counterproductive at worst (Roberts 2015). The financialization of the economy has severed the long-standing ties between worker productivity and wages. Globalization has rendered obsolete the upward relations of firm and national body and the downward relations of firm and community (Fine 2014). International shifts in geopolitical alliances have reversed the positive relationship between working-class citizen and state—no longer does the national economy rely upon the protection of its own workers (and their concomitant training and education), but now, rather, depends upon opening their labor markets to the competitive pressures of global labor in order to attract investment (Lazonick 2014). This long-term process of the destruction of labor market security leads to Berlant's question, 'What happens when the economic and social promise of a state becomes privatized like everything else, redistributed through emerging nonstate institutions and formal and informal economies?' (2007, 91).

States and claims

The affective intensities that structure the assumptions about public action, effectiveness, and claim-making derive, in part, from the relative success of labor movement activism in the Fordist period. In this sense, recognition that the state, embodied in a strong post-New Deal federal government, needed workers as part of its overall strategy, drove the labor movement to advocate as much for legal rights as for workplace power. Following theorists like Charles Tilly and Karl Polyani, the form of the state is affected by the demands of workers and their unions. It was Tilly's contention that the ability of interest groups, based in class struggle, to make strong claims for political and economic rights, served to shape the nature of the governing system (Tilly 2006). The ability of workers in the growing industrial system starting in the 1870s, to use strikes, walkouts, boycotts, shutdowns, and sit-ins, to demand better conditions, structured the expansive and, indeed, intrusive state and federal apparatus of the New Deal governing system. Workers, through their unions, literally forced a more activist stance on state and federal institutions.

The relative loss of labor power in the economic and political sphere has had the opposite effect since the economic crisis of the 1970s. The inability of workers to maintain their collective strength in numbers in the face of the onslaught of attacks on labor market stability has meant a shift in governing outlook and philosophy. This decline in the influence that organized labor has been able to exert over the political process has left unions with difficult decisions on how to respond to pressures exerted on their members by shifts in manufacturing and the outsourcing of jobs (Mishel 2012; Berger 2014). With viable options limited, most unions have cast their lot with the Democratic Party, despite decreasing returns, and relied on outmoded or ineffective modes of contention based in frayed relationships (Schmitt and Mitukiewicz 2011).

Returning to South Central Indiana, the results of these shifts in governing philosophy and in workers' collective power can be seen in three incidents of labor activism: the closing of the Whirlpool plant in Evansville in 2009; the strike by limestone workers at Indiana Limestone Company in 2011; and the long, slow dissolution of the Bloomington GE factory between 2010 and 2016, introduced in the opening section of this chapter. In each instance, a traditional union workforce, employed in well-established lower Rust Belt industries, contested the loss of employment and the weakening of their bargaining power through established contentious methods. They appealed in turn to fellow union members, to the local community, and to the court of public opinion. They accompanied this with demands for redress from local, state, and national political representatives. The repertoires deployed harkened back to a time that may have never existed, when large manufactures could be swayed by appeals to national and local concerns, when communities rallied around local workers, and when those workers exercised political influence powerful enough to persuade representatives to back their claims. It is a process seen not only in South Central Indiana, but across the wider Midwest region and beyond (Broughton 2015; Loomis 2015; Chen 2015).

Whirlpool Corporation located one of their main production plants in Evansville, Indiana, in the southwest region of the state near the Illinois and Kentucky borders, in 1956. The plant primarily produced refrigerators for the U.S. market, and it employed, at its peak production in the 1980s, upwards of 800 wageworkers. The wage labor force was organized by IUE-CWA Local 808 (IUE-CWA 2010). Like most durable goods manufacturers, Whirlpool was subject to increasing competition from non-U.S. producers, and struggled to maintain sales levels. In addition, the company itself was subject to the pressures of shareholder/investor demands for ever-increasing returns in the face of falling sales, sending the company in search of cost-cutting measures. Like many manufacturers, Whirlpool suffered from a lack of demand in the wake of the 2007–2008 economic crisis. The company took advantage of federal programs meant to stimulate the consumer economy, including federal rebates to consumers for 'energy-efficient' purchases and a grant from the Department of Energy totaling 19 million dollars for energy-efficient products. After taking stimulus finance, Whirlpool announced in summer of 2009 that it would close the Evansville production plant, while moving the refrigerator production to their plant in Monterrey, Mexico (Courier Press 2010a).

Workers and leadership from Local 808 fought back, but largely utilized the time-tested, and time-worn, repertoire of actions meant to shame the corporation. This included ad buys in the local paper, billboards in Whirlpool's corporate home in Benton Harbor, Michigan, letters to the editor denouncing the move, a petition campaign demanding Whirlpool stop being, in the words of IUE-CWA President Jim Clark, a 'bad corporate citizen,' and a solidarity rally on February 26, 2010, attended by AFL-CIO President Richard Trumka (Courier Press 2010b). Local 808 appealed to citizens of Evansville and the surrounding area to put pressure on Whirlpool, citing the union's crucial role in the development of the local economy and reminding local politicians and residents that the wages earned by their members were largely returned to the local economy in the form of spending and taxes. The union received the support of many in the community, whose statements seemed to summon the bygone days of the Keynesian/Fordist economic model. Local restaurant owner Tom Vinnedge reminded locals that 'More unemployed neighbors mean less customers who can afford a meal out' but also more need for the 'free meal' program at Thanksgiving. Vinnedge summed up the new economic model of outsourcing as 'just madness' (Courier Press 2010c). Local minister Phil Hoy wrote that he was 'appalled by Whirlpool's disregard for the community' and by the 'apathy of local politicians' toward the working families of Evansville (Courier Press 2010d). A crowd estimated at 4,000 union members and supporters attended the February 26 rally, lining the side of the highway that ran by the plant and marching to the union hall for speeches, replete with music, American flags, and union banners from locals in Gary, Indiana, Ohio, and Illinois.

Far from acknowledging the protest or negotiating with the union, the company doubled-down in their insistence on their right to dispense with corporate assets to increase shareholder value. Leadership in Benton Harbor cited the cost of the company's recent acquisitions of Maytag, Amana, and other brands as well as their expansion of plants in Ames, Iowa, and their long history of providing employment and living wage packages for its U.S. workforce. The company pointed out that the acceptance of federal stimulus in no way obligated them to keep jobs at any location that was not profitable (Matuszak 2010). Meanwhile, on the local level, plant executive Paul Coburn inflamed worker sentiment by warning workers, in a written memo circulated on February 24th, that 'these negative activities will only hamper employees when they look for future work' (Coburn 2010). Whirlpool felt no obligation to justify their actions beyond the need to increase shareholder value. As in many other cases, the legal environment favored the company, while the shifting cultural environment had already accepted that there were no American corporations and that workers were on their own. In a small but telling measure of the ineffectiveness of the post-Fordist repertoire of struggle, despite the efforts of the Local and supporters, an editorial in the Evansville *Courier Press* (2010b) on the day of the rally asked, in stark terms, 'Why Bother?'

For the members of Carpenters Local 8093, it was a forced strike in winter, 2011 that drove the union to initiate its own post-Fordist repertoire. Indiana Limestone Company (ILC) was one of the oldest survivors of the unique limestone quarries and fabricators of the limestone belt in southern Indiana. Financial pressures of competition from cheaper materials, the cyclical nature of building construction, and other factors had driven the limestone companies into periodic fits of consolidation and sell-offs. By the 1990s the formerly family-owned ILC had been purchased by an outside firm, which in turn sold to an investment company, Resilient Capital Partners (RCP), in 2010 (Dixon 2012). In the initial contract negotiation with RCP, the new investors pressured the union to make concessions in key contract provisions. These included calling for changes in seniority rules and attendance policy, and alterations of 'just cause' dismissal and discipline, in addition to a wage freeze and increases in health and pension costs. After unanimously turning down the offer, Local 8093 agreed to continue working and meet again in two weeks. On November 15, company negotiators presented their last, best and final proposal, identical to the rejected offer. Feeling pressed, Local 8093 took a strike vote on November 15, which passed with over 90% approval (O'Donnell 2012).

The strike commenced on November 16, with two picket lines set up, one at the main entrance and another at a little-used rear gate. Millworkers Local 8093 were joined on the picket by members of the Machinist Local and the Stonecutters Local. Strikers set up two lines at entrances to the plant, erected shelters, brought homemade signs, and settled in for the grueling work of picketing. During the workday, a presence of roughly 20–30 workers was maintained at the two gates. The local United Way chapter provided food from donations collected from local union groups and food banks. United Auto Workers Local 440 from nearby Bedford provided picket support, as did United Steel Workers members, who were engaged in their own struggle in nearby Mitchell, Indiana, with C&M Conveyor. The main organizing event was a labor summit convened in Bedford on November 22, organized in part by CWA 4730 local president Bryce Smedley and attended by officers from six local unions and a dozen local activists. While all participants in the summit agreed to continue to support picketing, ideas about how to bring negative publicity and other forms of public and private pressure were also discussed. It was from this and other meetings among non-Local 8093 activists that activities around RCP, and local trucking companies and stone factories supplying replacement labor, were coordinated (O'Donnell 2012).

At each stage of the contract dispute and subsequent work stoppage, Local 8093 members and their allies engaged in established labor repertoires intended to build community support and damage the public standing of the company, to force ILC back to the bargaining table. Workers appeared on the picket line with their family members, including children, who carried picket signs appealing to the decency of the ownership group and the health of the community. Limestone workers carried signs proclaiming, 'Men of stone don't scab,' aiming to shame replacement workers from crossing the picket line. The picket messages and the messages at public rallies made similar appeals, calling on ILC and RCP to rescind the call for concessions and settle with the workers, not just for the sake of the company but in the name of decency and for the health of the local economy and community. While pressure was brought on members of management who lived locally, the ultimate decisions regarding the contract, and future of the company, were made by executives at RCP headquarters in Cleveland, Ohio, for a company with an established pattern of buying struggling companies and selling them after maximizing profits. While Local 8093 workers' concerns remained local, they struggled with a management group that they also assumed had the health of the local community as at least a consideration in company operations. While the contract dispute was settled in early 2012, by 2014 ILC was officially bankrupt, allowing RCP to rid itself of the unionized workforce, debts they had run up, and pension obligations. The rump of the company would be sold to Wynnchurch Capital of Chicago, who resumed a pared-down operation without union workers (Reschke 2014).

The wage workforce at ILC was drawn almost exclusively from 'the belt,' the area producing Indiana limestone in a roughly 20 by 30 mile stretch around the towns of Bedford, Stinesville, Oolitic, and Bloomington. For most of these local workers, millwrights, carvers, and quarries, the skills they utilized on the job were generational and transferrable from quarry to quarry. At times of robust growth in the demand for limestone, the local businesses would expand hiring, and local revenues from increased wages and taxes would increase. In other words, for the locals, the strength of the regional economy depended on the health of the industry. For RCP, no such relationship existed. Ultimately, the surviving company, known as Indiana Limestone Company, uses no union labor and a small crew of nonunion quarries. It outsources much of the work that previously was performed at its Oolitic facility. In 2014, in one of its first post-bankruptcy contracts, ILC agreed to supply Indiana University with material for a new building on the Bloomington campus, voted one of the most beautiful grounds among American universities due mainly to its limestone buildings. The stone was quarried in Oolitic, then shipped to China for fabrication and returned to Indiana for final construction (Reschke 2016).

In each case, appeals were made for solidarity to fellow union members and labor movement activists. For the region that the three union locals operated in, such appeals would have, at one time, resonated with a dense union workforce. Union density, at a peak of nearly 40% in the 1960s, had plunged to 11% in private sector workplaces. In addition to there being fewer union workers in an absolute sense, the plunge in density also meant that family connections and community bonds with organized labor were also reduced drastically. By the post-recession period, labor strikes were rare occurrences, and while most people, if pressed, could recall a union member or two in the family, most had little direct connection to labor activism. When the threatened workers took their case to the public, there were many sympathetic citizens, but many more believed that unions played little role in the contemporary economy. When workers made their case for redress to elected officials, they found few representatives above the city council level willing to directly challenge the right of capitalist firms to direct their workforce and investment capital to where profit was maximized (Varga 2013; 2014; Lafer 2013; Hogler, Hunt, and Weiler 2014; Cooper and Mishel 2015).

The unions inevitably assumed that the health and well-being of their membership was tied to and important for their respective employers and community. The tactics employed by the unions—public rallies, peaceful pickets, letter-writing and post petitioning, appeals to friendly political figures, accusations leveled against their employers—were embedded in a repertoire established in the Fordist period, when foreign competition was limited, U.S. domestic markets supported increasing profits and expanding markets, and the assumption that the well-being of wageworkers was tied to increasing productivity and community health were generally accepted (Gordon 2014, Picketty 2017). Brief local strikes could disrupt a regional economy at both the production and retail levels, affecting businesses and individuals beyond the immediate firm. Labor solidarity, including calls for primary boycotts, resonated beyond the immediate labor force to the larger union environment. Public appeals, often based in patriotic notions of a deserving working class and the assumption of responsibility by 'American' companies, could sway public opinion in favor of workers (Dray 2010).

The 2007–2008 financial crisis, that was spurred by the collapse of the U.S. real estate market, effectively severed the last remnants of the weak post-Fordist labor movement. For far too many union members and supporters, the supposed end of organized labor was rooted in the perception that effective unions needed to conform to the Fordist model, and post-Fordist remnants, of industrial organization centered in factory production. The reality was that the working class was still large, still a majority, and still exploited, only not primarily engaged in industrial production. By the post-Great Recession period, working-class labor was often nonwhite, engaged in service work, and in dire need of workplace influence (Bacon 2014; Schmitt and Warner 2009). In addition, talk of protecting 'American' factory jobs often ignored the hard reality of computer-based processes that increased worker redundancy and reduced workers' collective ability to influence labor conditions (Kristal 2013).

As a result, workers and labor movement activists have been forced to rethink and re-conceptualize the basics of workplace and community activism (Compa 2015; Moody 2016). One major thrust of the re-conceptualization has been to acknowledge that the decline of industrial-based unions did not mean the 'death of labor.' Rather it signaled that labor movement activists and organizers needed to move beyond the post-Fordist paradigm and recognize that the women and minority workers in the service, healthcare, and retail workplaces were still exploited workers who needed representation and a voice to secure a decent living. Organizers have also looked beyond the narrow vision of organizing factory by factory and have worked with community partners and allies to push for higher local wage levels, rules regarding scheduling and start times, and the misclassification of workers as 'contractors.' And perhaps most importantly, new labor organizing is recognizing the threat posed by increased labor redundancies due to technological advances and starting to explore potential solutions such as guaranteed basic incomes (Godard and Frege 2013; Firestein, King, and Cabrera 2010; Schneider 2015).

Images of the heroic era of labor struggles, with workers facing off with armed guards, standing bravely with Old Glory waving, helped define a positive image for workers struggling for a decent life. Similarly, the image of the loyal union man, lunchbox in hand, returning to his single-family home with a decent paycheck secured by his union, is a powerful image that defines the era of the so-called labor accord and the New Deal coalition. Both are based in repertoires of contention that helped to secure advances made by American workers. While the images can inspire, they also can inhibit a progressive vision of labor struggle that takes full stock of the changes in workplaces, labor market economics, legal regulations, and political allegiances.

This does not mean that public rallies, strikes, and other actions that harken back to the advances of the past are never effective. But it does suggest that changing conditions call for changing repertoires and that strategies and tactics need to be constantly evolving to meet the challenges workers face, now and in the future (Kalleberg 2009; NESRI 2010; Schmitt and Warner 2009).

There is no shortage of analysis of labor's failings in the post-Fordist period; neither is there a lack of works detailing new directions for organizing and mobilization. The so-called 'crisis of labor' dates to at least the late 1990s, and it inspired works like that of Fantasia and Voss (2004), who promoted social movement unionism, the integration of workplace labor struggles with broader issues affecting the working poor, as the path to revitalization. Subsequently, works like Getman (2010) and Lambert (2005) have used historical perspective to advocate for broad coalitions that can support more militant action, such as increased use of the strike. More recently, labor movement scholar-activists such as Fine (2006) have supported the increasing use of worker centers that mobilize low-wage immigrant workers by providing them space for organizing and education. Similarly, Milkman (2006) looks to immigrant labor as a revitalizing force, rightly viewing the service sector as the potential growth field for unions. In two excellent collected volumes, Katz and Greenwald (2012) compile historically informed approaches to labor revitalization while Milkman and Ott's (2014) collection looks at ways to organize and mobilize among younger precarious workers in the new urban economy. Finally, Geoghegan (2014) suggests radical policy-based approaches, such as bargaining away the union shop at the national level in exchange for recognition of organizing as a civil right, while Quigley (2015) details the on-the-ground experiences of activists fighting to organize, and even winning, in a labor-hostile, right-to-work state.

For those scholars and activists interested in learning from the hard experiences of the post-Fordist period, it is important to set aside the nostalgic vision of heroic union members battling corporate behemoths and to turn a critical eye to the repertoires of contention utilized in the struggle for decent living standards and workplace voice. In particular, the period from the initial shocks of deindustrialization through the relative prosperity of the 'tech boom' (1980–2000) witnessed major shifts in how investment capital was deployed, while only certain sectors of labor adjusted to changing conditions. Most labor actions remained mired, in this crucial period, in traditional modes of contention. When the shocks of the Great Recession hit, unions from the UAW down had little choice but to accept the terms offered by capital, agreeing to closings and tiered wage systems and losing right-to-work battles in key industrial states. Scholars of working-class activism, union organizing, and working-class culture need to take a hard look at the post-Fordist period, and determine what worked and what did not, and what types of representations of working-class life reinforced the values of compromise and called upon the affectual residues of the Fordist period to the detriment of new organizing and new ways of viewing an ever-changing working class.

References

Arrighi, G. (2010) *The Long Twentieth Century: Money, Power, and the Origins of Our Times*, London: Verso.

Arruzza, C. (2014) 'The Capitalism of Affects,' *Public Seminar*. www.publicseminar.org/2014/08/the-capitalism-of-affects/#.Wb2NqK2ZOb8 (accessed July 8, 2015).

Bacon, D. (2014) *The State of Labor Twenty Years after NAFTA*, Institute for Transnational Social Change.

Berger, S. (2014) 'How Finance Gutted Manufacturing,' *Boston Review*, April 1.

Berlant, L. (2007) 'Nearly Utopian, Nearly Normal: Post-Fordist Affect in *La Promesse* and *Rosetta*,' *Public Culture*, 19, 2, pp. 273–301.

Broughton, C. (2015) *Boom, Bust, Exodus: The Rust Belt, The Maquilas, and a Tale of Two Cities*, New York, Oxford University Press.

Burns, J. (2011) *Reviving the Strike: How Working People Can Regain Power and Transform America*, Brooklyn, NY, Ig Publishing.

Chen, V. (2015) *Cut Loose: Jobless and Hopeless in an Unfair Economy*, Oakland, University of California Press.

Clawson, D. (2003) *The Next Upsurge and the New Social Movements*, Ithaca and London, Cornell University Press.

Coburn, P. (2010) 'A Letter from Paul Coburn,' *Whirlpool Evansville Advantage*, Whirlpool Corporation, February 24.

Compa, L. (2015) 'Careful What You Wish For: A Critical Appraisal of Proposals to Rebuild the Labor Movement,' *New Labor Forum*, October 15.

Cooper, D. and Mishel, L. (2015) 'The Erosion of Collective Bargaining Has Widened the Gap Between Productivity and Pay,' *Economic Policy Institute*, January 6.

Courier Press. (2010a) 'Whirlpool Rally Fills Labor Hall,' *Evansville Courier Press*, February 27.

Courier Press. (2010b) 'Editorial: Whirlpool Rally,' *Evansville Courier Press*, February 26.

Courier Press. (2010c) 'Letter to Editor,' *Evansville Courier Press*, February 28.

Courier Press. (2010d) 'Letter to Editor,' *Evansville Courier Press*, March 2.

Della Porta, D. (2015) *Social Movements in Times of Austerity: Bringing Capitalism Back into Protest Analysis*, Cambridge, UK, Polity Press.

Dixon, T. (2012) 'Indiana Limestone Company – Going Forward Into Another Century of Growth,' *Slippery Rock Gazette*, October, 35. http://slipperyrockgazette.net/index.cfm/pageID/615/.

Dray, P. (2010) *There is Power in a Union: The Epic Story of Labor in America*, New York, Anchor Books.

Dudley, K. (1994) *The End of the Line: Lost Jobs, New Lives, in Post-Industrial America*, Chicago, University of Chicago Press.

Engeman, C. (2014) 'Social Movement Unionism in Practice: Organizational Dimensions of Mobilization in the Los Angeles Immigrant Rights Marches,' *Work, Employment, and Society*, 29, 3, pp. 444–461.

Evans, P. (2014) *National Labor Movements and Transnational Connections: Global Labor's Evolving Architecture under Neoliberalism*, IRLE Working Paper 116-14. http://irle.berkeley.edu/workingpapers/116-14.pdf.

Fantasia, R. and Voss, K. (2004) *Hard Work: Remaking the American Labor Movement*, Berkeley, University of California Press.

Fine, B. (2014) 'Financialization from a Marxist Perspective,' *International Journal of Political Economy*, 42, 4, pp. 47–66.

Fine, J. (2006) *Worker Centers: Organizing Community at the Edge of a Dream*, Ithaca, NY, Cornell University Press.

Firestein, N., King, D. and Cabrera, L. (2010) 'New Approaches to Organizing Women and Young Workers,' *Labor Project for Working Families*, July.

Geoghegan, T. (2014) *Only One Thing Can Save Us: Why America Needs a New Kind of Labor Movement*, New York, The New Press.

Getman, J. (2010) *It Takes a Movement: Restoring the Power of Unions*, New Haven, Yale University Press.

Godard, J. and Frege, C. (2013) 'Labor Unions, Alternative Forms of Representation, and the Exercise of Authority Relations in U.S. Workplaces,' *ILR Review*, 66, 1, pp. 142–168.

Gordon, R. (2014) *The Rise and Fall of American Growth: The U.S. Standard of Living since the Civil War*, Princeton, NJ, Princeton University Press.

Harvey, D. (2007) *A Brief History of Neoliberalism*, Oxford, Oxford University Press.

Hogler, R., Hunt, H. and Weiler, S. (2014) 'Killing Unions with Culture: Institutions, Inequality, and the Effects of Labor's Decline in the United States,' *Employer Responsibility and Rights*, 27, pp. 63–79.

Hurd, R, Milkman, R. and Turner, L. (2003) 'Reviving the American Labor Movement: Institutions and Mobilizations,' *European Journal of Industrial* Relations, 9, 1, 99–117.

IUE-CWA. (2010) 'Whirlpool Building New Plant in Mexico to Take 900 U.S. Jobs,' Press Release, February 20.

Kalleberg, A. (2009) 'Precarious Work, Insecure Workers: Employment Relations in Transition,' *American Sociological Review*, 74, 1, pp. 1–22.

Katz, D. and Greenwald, R. (2012) *Labor Rising: The Past and Future of Working People in America*, New York, The New Press.

Kristal, T. (2013) 'The Capitalist Machine: Computerization, Workers' Power, and the Decline in Labor's Share within U.S. Industries,' *American Sociological Review*, 78, 3, pp. 361–389.

Lafer, G. (2013) *The Legislative Attack on American Wages and Labor Standards, 2011–2012*, Economic Policy Institute Working Paper, October 31.

Lambert, J. (2005) *If the Workers Took a Notion: The Right to Strike and American Political Development*, Ithaca, IRL Press.
Laurie, B. (1997) *Artisans into Workers: Labor in Nineteenth-Century America*, Chicago, University of Illinois Press.
Lazonick, W. (2014) 'Profits without Prosperity,' *Harvard Business Review*, September. https://hbr.org/2014/09/profits-without-prosperity.
Lichtenstein, N. (2002) *State of the Union: A Century of American Labor*, Princeton, Princeton University Press.
Loomis, E. (2015) *Out of Sight: The Long and Disturbing Story of Corporations Outsourcing Catastrophe*, New York, The New Press.
Luce, S. (2014) *Labor Movements: Global Perspectives*, Malden, MA, Polity Press.
Madland, D. and Walter, K. (2010) 'Why is the Public Suddenly Down on Unions?' *Center for American Progress*. www.americanprogressaction.org/issues/economy/reports/.
Massumi, B. (1995) 'The Autonomy of Affect,' *Cultural Critique*, 31, pp. 83–109.
Matuszak, J. (2010) 'Whirlpool to Workers: Don't Protest Outside Plant,' *Southwest Michigan Herald-Palladium*, February 26.
McAlevey, J. (2015) 'The Crisis of New Labor and Alinsky's Legacy: Revisiting the Role of the Organic Grassroots Leaders in Building Powerful Organizations and Movements,' *Politics and Society*, 43, 3, pp. 1–27.
Milkman, R. (2006) *L.A. Story: Immigrant Workers and the Future of the U.S. Labor Movement*, New York, Russell Sage.
Milkman, R. and Ott, E. (2014) *New Labor in New York: Precarious Workers and the Future of the Labor Movement*, Ithaca, NY, Cornell University Press.
Mishel, L. (2012) 'Unions, Inequality, and the Faltering Middle Class,' *Economic Policy Institute*, Policy Brief, August 29.
Moody, K. (2016) 'U.S. Labor: What's New, What's Not,' *Against the Current*, May 1, 19.
Muehlebach, A. and Shoshan, N. (2012) 'Introduction to Special Issue on Post-Fordist Affect,' *Anthropological Quarterly*, 85, 2, pp. 317–345.
NESRI (National Economic and Social Rights Initiative). (2010) *Toward Economic and Social Rights in the United States: From Market Competition to Public Goods*, Joint Submission to the UN Human Rights Council Universal Periodic Review of the United States of America.
O'Donnell, D. (2012) Interview by author, Oolitic, Indiana, November 24.
Picketty, T. (2017) *Capital In the Twenty-First Century*, New York, Belknap Press.
Quigley, F. (2015) *If We Can Win Here: The New Front Lines of the Labor Movement*, Ithaca, NY, Cornell University Press.
Reschke, M. (2014) 'Limestone Industry Making Strong Comeback,' *The Herald-Times*, June 27.
Reschke, M. (2016) 'Local Stone to be Shipped to China and Back Before Being Used on New Informatics Building,' *The Herald-Times*, July 10.
Roberts, A. (2015) 'Wage Inequality and the Liberalization of Industrial Relations in the United States,' *Research and Policy Brief*, 38, November, Los Angeles, Institute for Research on Labor and Employment.
Rosenfeld, J. (2014) *What Unions No Longer Do*, Cambridge, MA, Harvard University Press.
Schmitt, J. and Mitukiewicz, A. (2011) *Politics Matter: Changes in Unionization Rates in Rich Countries, 1960–2010*, Washington, D.C., Center for Economic and Policy Research.
Schmitt, J. and Warner, K. (2009) *The Changing Face of Labor, 1983–2008*, Washington, D.C., Center for Economic and Policy Research.
Schneider, N. (2015) 'Why the Tech Elite is Getting Behind Universal Basic Income,' *Vice*, January 6.
Silver, B. (2003). *Forces of Labor: Workers Movements and Globalization since 1870*, New York, Cambridge University Press.
Silver, B. (2014) 'Theorizing the Working Class in Twenty-First Century Global Capitalism,' in Atzeni, M., (ed.) *Workers and Labor in a Globalized Capitalism*, Basingstoke, Palgrave McMillan.
Strangleman, T. (2013) 'Smokestack Nostalgia, Ruin Porn, or Working Class Obituary? The Role and Meaning of Deindustrial Representation,' *International Labor and Working Class History*, 84, Fall, pp. 23–37.
Tabb, W. (2004) *Economic Governance in the Age of Globalization*, New York, Columbia University Press.
Tarrow, S. (2013) 'Contentious Politics,' in *Encyclopedia of Social and Political Movements*, New York, Wiley-Blackwell.
Tilly, C. (2006) *Regimes and Repertoires*, Chicago, University of Chicago Press.
Varga, J. (2013) 'Breaking the Heartland: Creating the Precariat in the Lower Rust Belt,' *Global Discourse*, 3, 3–4, pp. 430–446.

Varga, J. (2014) 'Dispossession is Nine-Tenths of the Law: Right-to-Work and the Making of the American Precariat,' *Labor Studies Journal*, 39, 1, pp. 25–45.
Weldon, K. (2014) 'Public Attitudes Towards Labor Unions, 1936-Today,' *Huffpost*, August 29. www.huffingtonpost.com/kathleen-weldon/public-attitudes-about-la_b_5716177.html.
Weston, K. (2012) 'Political Ecologies of the Precarious,' *Anthropological Quarterly*, 85, 2, pp. 429–455.
Zweig, M. (2016) 'Rethinking Class and Contemporary Working Class Studies,' *Journal of Working-Class Studies*, 1, 1, pp. 14–21.

Conclusion

Michele Fazio, Christie Launius, and Tim Strangleman

We set out on a journey a number of years ago to create the volume in front of you. We came together to work on this project because each of us, Christie, Michele and Tim, have built our careers within and around the field of working-class studies and have benefited enormously from the personal and professional relationships and opportunities that the field has brought to us. For each of us, our lives would look very different without the presence of this field. This project is a recognition that we owe a debt to those who created the field and began to call themselves working-class studies scholars and activists. This volume represents a way of paying it forward, for it not only celebrates the work of the field's founders, many of whom are still writing, and whose work is published within these pages, but it also brings to print work by a new generation of working-class studies practitioners who are building on the foundation erected over the last two decades or more.

We three editors are very aware of our place in this field, representing a pivotal generation who came of age when the certainties of working-class life were shifting. We bridge the gap between a set of people and scholars who were formed by the politics, culture, and conditions of the long boom, and those who came of age into an era of precarious work shaped by the processes of deindustrialization and economic globalization. In generational terms, we come after the baby boomers and before millennials. This gives us a privileged vantage point to appreciate the ideas and inspiration of those who began the field while, simultaneously, understanding many of the issues and challenges of those who came later. Here at the end of the second decade of the 21st century, the gulf between the haves and the have-nots continues to widen, accompanied by the rise of nationalism as well as ethnic and racial conflict. At the same time, social movements such as the Fight for $15, the Poor People's Campaign, and Black Lives Matter illuminate the intersections among class, race, and gender, particularly as they pertain to income inequality and the wealth gap.

Like any field, working-class studies has had its challenges, and like any it needs to be aware that however important its origins and original members are, we need to remain fresh and alive to change and new developments. Toward that end, the three of us convened and facilitated a roundtable session at the 2018 conference of the Working-Class Studies Association in an effort to solicit a broad, loose, and inclusive set of reflections from conference attendees about future directions of the field. We posed the following questions: What is the field of working-class studies to you? What do you want and need working-class studies to be in the coming decades? Going forward, what is your role in creating the field that you want and need? The discussion that ensued was spirited and lively, and we have tried to incorporate many of the suggestions, insights, and points of tension that surfaced during the session into this concluding section.

One of the recurring threads of the conversation that day had to do with strategies for building the field and increasing its visibility, both among the public and within the academy across disciplinary lines. Several people present spoke of the importance of self-identifying as a practitioner of working-class studies in all of our work, whether in our institutions (for those of us who are academics), in our community engagement and activism, in disciplinary settings (such as conferences), and in our writing. More specifically regarding our writing, whether for a scholarly or public audience, there is a growing recognition about how important it is to be deliberate and intentional about our citational practices; that is to say, how important it is to cite the work of those in the field. The three of us feel strongly about this and have explicitly asked all of the contributors to this volume to cite relevant texts from within the field wherever appropriate.

More generally, the working class has been an object of intense interest and scrutiny since Brexit and the 2016 presidential election in the US, but these media treatments of the working class are frequently instances of so-called parachute journalism and rarely feature the voices of actual working-class people. Also problematic is the persistent conflation of 'working class' with whiteness, all demographic evidence to the contrary. The task for practitioners of working-class studies is to relentlessly insert themselves into this ongoing discourse whenever possible to problematize stereotypical and harmful representations of the working class that obscure and misconstrue its composition and politics. But more urgently, we need to build our confidence to speak up on working-class issues. In the US, UK, and across the EU, populist politicians, often from very elite backgrounds, have no qualms in speaking for their imagined working-class constituents. As a field, we need the capacity to engage in the conversation from a basis of rooted knowledge of working-class life, community, and culture. We do not aim to speak on behalf of, but rather as part of a diverse and complicated group. This is an urgent matter. Those that would speak for the working class have no real connection nor long-term interest in the working class.

Another theme that emerged at the conference is that the work of building interdisciplinarity never ends. Most academics in working-class studies have discipline-specific training and teach and publish in that 'home' discipline as well as in working-class studies. Self-identifying as practitioners of working-class studies, and being deliberate about our citational practices, is part of the work of building interdisciplinarity, but that work extends to bringing working-class studies back to our 'home' disciplines by, for example, proposing conference panels on working-class studies at disciplinary conferences. Working-class studies continually works in and against disciplinary traditions and politics, and stages scholarly and political conversations across disciplinary boundaries. This work, a special aspect of the field, is perhaps most visible at our conferences, and it is something we are committed to continuing to nurture in the future.

The challenge then is one of relevance; the need to retain a focus on the continuities of working-class life while seeking out the 'whys' and 'hows' of change. The experience of class has always been differentiated by way of country, region, trade, occupation, and work role. Identities of ethnicity, race, gender, age, and sexuality have formed important contours of the classed experience. Working-class studies has always sought to problematize its own roots and to recognize diversity, difference, and conflict within the working class. This is its strength. It is equally important that we realize that these features of the working class are not static, and never were.

Class is a dynamic process and experience that we struggle to conceptualize and appreciate. The power of our field is that we are often, but not always, products of the phenomena we study—its streets, communities, industries, workplaces, schools, homes, prisons, pubs, clubs, and bars. Coming to terms with class tells us part of a rich fragmentary story, but only a part. Our job is to recognize the strengths and limits of these fragments in being able to tell a much larger narrative about the working-class experience as a whole.

Methodologically, working-class studies has always been inter- and cross-disciplinary. The sections and chapters in this collection speak to that plurality and diversity. Michael Zweig has often talked about the 'mosaic' of class, but perhaps we need a metaphor that captures the multi-dimensional nature of class experience and the way in which class is apprehended through an appreciation of movement, interaction, and reaction across time and space. As a field, and at many of our conferences, social scientists, artists, poets, activists, historians and humanities scholars, and organizers each capture moments of experience, both past and present, that speak to future possibilities. Perhaps the best we can do is to ensure that the 'now' we speak of reflects, as best we are able, the scope of working-class experience in all its guises.

We wanted this collection to do a number of things. First, we wanted it to show a maturing field in all its breadth—methodologically, theoretically, and substantively. It was intended to capture a sense of how the field began and why it looks as it does today, and hopefully this is apparent in general and in the detail of the texts. But we also wanted each section, and each chapter, to set some kind of agenda for a way we can think about class in the future. In practical terms, we hope that this volume can serve as a useful introduction to the field for those learning about it for the first time, even as it also intervenes in and carries on conversations that have been ongoing over time. We also hope that it creates a space for future discussions on the role of class and the presence of working-class people in movements for immigrant rights and environmental justice, and in the fields of queer studies, memory studies, and ethnic studies among others.

Any intervention like this is a place marker; it captures a moment in time and reflects the preoccupations and biographies of those who write. But we hope it has set people to thinking about what the working-class experience was, is, and may be yet. We want this volume to act not as a time capsule but as a point of reference, a point of departure, a book to learn from and argue with, and as a spur to engage more fully with growing precarity and new and emerging class formations. We can only do this if we are creatively brave in reaching out to new individuals, organizations, and groups who look different from us. The WCSA's recent conference in the UK brought together participants from over twenty countries; as an international organization and field, this gathering at the University of Kent is a sign of a growing critical mass—one that positions the subjects of work and working-class culture as central to the study of class in order to understand labor and power relations both historically and in the present.

Finally, when we were planning this volume, we were conscious that the field was approaching its quarter century in 2020. As the field continues to broaden public discourse and civic engagement in classrooms, in workplaces, and on the streets, we must persist in increasing an understanding of how the historical trajectories of working-class life will be shaped over the course of the next twenty-five years and beyond. As we complete the final edits of this handbook, all three editors are under lockdown due to the Covid-19 pandemic. This pandemic is both revealing and exacerbating the income and wealth gap globally, and it will undoubtedly have a profound and lasting impact on the working-class landscape for the foreseeable future. There will be a huge cost in terms of jobs and livelihoods in both the public and private sectors. It is clear already that working-class people and communities (especially working-class people and communities of color) are suffering more than the middle and upper classes due to fewer material resources and lack of access to appropriate healthcare, and their ability to recover in the medium to long term will also undoubtedly be restricted. If we are to try and see a positive side, we could point to the way the pandemic reminds us of the vital jobs working-class people do around the globe—the health and social care staff, logistics and delivery workers, and low-paid shop workers, all of whom are now designated key workers, essential to the economy. What comes out of the current crisis—the increased visibility of workers and the risks they take on the job—makes working-class studies even more necessary now than it was a quarter of a century ago.

Index

'the 1%' 418–19, 421
1vyG (Ivy League schools) 95
2 Broke Girls 395–7
9/11 205–7

Aamann, Iben Charlotte 17
academia *see* first-generation college students; working-class studies
academic confidence 417–18, 419–20
academic performance: achievement gap 108, 154; the impact of excessive testing and assessment on learner identities 135–7; interventions 146–8; tracking and the invidious consequences of being in the bottom sets 131–5; the working-class student 144–5
academics: community colleges 414–15; as guides to academic culture 124; positionality 25–6, 438–9; public scholarship 420–2; research accessibility 437–8; of working-class roots 84–8, 92–4, 99–101, 231–3
academies *see* college
access *see* college admissions
accessibility, of community research 437–8
accomplishment of natural growth parenting approach 153, 243
achievement *see* academic performance
achievement gap 108, 154
activism 7, 405–11; class cultures 262–72; community colleges 410, 413–22; day labourers in Atlanta 433–4; efforts to hinder 409; food justice 447–9; gaming 320–2; General Electric 493–4; intellectual 5; occupational disease movement 196–7; post-Fordist affect 493–501; precarious work 481; recent movements 186–7; 'social haunting' 217, 218–20; virtual collective action in call centres 485–7; in working-class studies 407–9
activism confidence 410, 418–20
Actor Network Theory 409
admissions, college 46, 157
advocacy, occupational disease movement 196–7
affect: and action 494–6; post-Fordist 492–501; 'social haunting' 213–22
affective histories 217, 220
affordable housing activists 434–7
African Americans: historical origins of racism in the US 456–7, 459; marriage 184; methods of research 71; teenager counselling case study 252–3; unemployment 182
Agee, James 327
agency: first-generation college students 49, 50, 51, 54; personal narratives 27–8
agriculture: farm work vs. factory work 470, 473; food justice 442–52; food workers and labour 442–5; New Deal 469–70
alienated labour 348–9
Alkobaisi 295
Allen, Theodore W. 456
American culture 234–5
American dream: classism 259; cognitive dissonance 258; deconstruction of 468; education as gatekeeper 83, 151; *The Great Gatsby* 125–6; social reproduction 151–2; working-class studies 119, 121
American Federation of Labour (AFL) 455, 458, 461
American Indians 469, 470–6
American Legislative Exchange Council (ALEC) 383–4
American literature 125–6
analytical narratives 15
Anarchist groups 267, 270
'anarchist process' 269
Anderson, Marilyn 349
'anecdotalism' 65
answerability 35
anthropology: ethnographic fieldwork 59–61; 'social haunting' 221; working-class studies 73
Apples 376–7
Armstrong, Richard 305
Arnau, Gomez 430
art: mapping working-class art 291, 343–54; visiting galleries 343–4
Arts and Humanities Research Council Connected Communities (AHRCCC) projects 213, 217

asbestos 193, 194
assembly lines, Portuguese call centres 482–8
assessment: achievement gap 154; the impact of excessive testing and assessment on learner identities 135–7; tracking and the invidious consequences of being in the bottom sets 131–5
Atlanta: affordable housing activists 434–7; oral history - border crossing with day labourers 426–34; tracking and the invidious consequences of being in the bottom sets 131–5
Attfield, Sarah 343
audience, working-class art 349
the Australian working-class: historical context 274–6; in popular culture 276–82
authority, attitudes towards 247, 266, 268, 269–70
auto-ethnography 3–4, 63, 64; *see also* personal narratives
automation, economic dislocation and trauma 185–6

Baca, Jimmy Santiago 387
Bacher 295
Bacon, David 426
Badalov, Rahman 298
Bangladeshi labour migrants 295
Barker, Pat 291
Barrell, John 349
beauty, in art 291, 345–6, 354
Beck, Ulrich 1, 384
'becoming', as middle-class expectation 231–2, 245
'belonging' 231–2, 245; *see also* community belonging
Bentham, Jeremy 383
Berger, John 350–1, 354
Berlant, Lauren 495
Bidinger, Elizabeth 28–9
Biehl, Joao 68
Black Lives Matter 408, 416–17, 465
Blessed 279–80
blue-collar workers: economic dislocation and trauma 180; precarity's affects 202–3; US postwar documentary photography 336; working-class cultures 227–8
Bluestone, Barry 2
bodies: marketing millennial women 392–401; and school 110–12; work-health cultures, risk and the body 193–4, 198
Boebel, Chris 69–70
Boehmer, Elleke 307
bogan (slang) 277–8
Boler, Megan 50
Bondi, Marina 21
Boos, Florence S. 290
Bourdieu, P.: class analysis 2; class cultures 243; cultural capital 153; digital storytelling, voice, and power 48; education 83–4; influence on working-class studies 228; *Sketch for a Self-Analysis* 64
Bowles, S. 152
Boynton 300
The Boys , Blackrock and Snowtown 279
brain drain 81
Brandt, Maria F. 289
Brecher, Jeremy 172, 408
Brexit: populism 506; reactionary politics 203; 'social haunting' 213–14, 220–1; and the working-class 5, 171
Bridgewater State University, Class Beyond the Classroom (CBtC) group 96–101
Britain: deindustrialization as 170; English classrooms 130–9
Brooks, Cathleen 126
Broomfield, Nick 316
Brown University, 1vyG 95
Burger, Warren 383
Bush, Perry 172
Butler, Judith 206–7

call centre assembly lines 481–8
Call Centre Workers Trade Union (STCC) 485, 486–8
Callow, Philip 361–2, 368
campus activism 413–22
Canada: deindustrialization 170, 171–3; environmental health movement 198; globalization 2; injured workers movement 197; virtual gaming 320
Cantor, Nancy 421
capitalism: civil rights movement 39–40; living labour 39–41; Marxist theories 33; precarity 37; struggle and resistance 492–3; unemployment 182–3
capitalist accumulation 37
Capps, Lisa 66–7
careers, middle-class conception of 235–8
Carnation Revolution 484
Carter, P. 156
The Castle 280
Chakrabarty, Dipesh 39
Chambers, Claire 299
Chapman, Nick 361
chav (slang) 278
Chicago, USA, Exit Zero Project 61, 64–7, 69
child labour 315, 317
childrearing practices *see* parenting style
China: internal migration 315–16; Wal-Mart manufacture 319
Chopin, Kate 363
Christopher, Renny 20, 118, 122, 288, 289
cinema *see* film
cities 426
citizenship status, and race 109, 461
City of Life 302–8
civic outcomes 416
civil rights movement 39–40, 460–2

Civil War, US 457
Clarke, Ben 291
class *see* social class; working-class
Class Action 96
Class Beyond the Classroom (CBtC) group 96–101
class blindness 234–9
class cultures 242–9; activist groups 262–72; importance 246–8; meaning of 243; origins 243–4; variation by class 244–6
class positioning 17
class sensitivity 87, 107–8, 112–13, 145
class speech codes 264–5
class straddlers 16
classism 258–9
'classless society' 119, 228, 344
Clinton, Bill 462
coalfields, 'social haunting' 213–22
Coalition of Immokalee Workers' Fair Food Program, 449
Cobb, Johnathan 227, 228
cognitive dissonance 257–8
Cohen, Esther 353
Coiner, Constance 289
Cole, Darnell 472
Coles, Nicholas 364, 425
collective action 7, 405–11; cognitive dissonance 258; efforts to hinder 409; occupational disease movement 196–7; post-Fordist affect 494–6; virtual collective action in call centres 485–7; in working-class studies 407–9
collective memory 214; *see also* 'social haunting'
'collective sensibility' 122
college: academic confidence 417–18, 419–20; activism confidence 410, 418–20; activism in community colleges 413–22; as a collaborator 85–8; employment prospects with a degree 238; escalator model of education 80–2, 84, 86; gatekeeping 83–5, 86; pedagogy of class 118–28; Real Food Challenge 452; universal access 80; whether it is worthwhile 79; the working-class student 123–5, 141–8; *see also* first-generation college students
college admissions 46, 157
college-educated activists 262–72
Collins, Peter 221
Collins, R. 151
colonialism: ethnographic fieldwork 60–1; historical origins of racism 456–7
commodified 'grit' 374–7
Common, Jack 366, 367–8
'commons' 354
communal sensibility 348
communism 81
communities of practice 26–7
community belonging: interdependent vs. independent cultural model 143–4; mismatch between social class cultures in college 92–4, 141–2; psychological importance 143; social mobility 155–6; and work 163–7; working-class culture 231–2
community colleges: activism through 410, 413–16; the classroom 418–20; faculty and public scholarship as a form of activism 420–2; obstacles to activism 416–18
community organizing groups 267, 268
community ownership 172–3
community partnership programme, Lumbee working-class history 470–6
community-supported agriculture (CSA) 447–51
Community Tarot technique 218
concerted cultivation parenting approach 153, 243
Congress of Industrial Organizations (CIO) 458, 459
Connell, R.W. 279
consumerism: food justice 446–7; foodie culture 444, 447; television 292
Coronation Street 375, 376
Corrections Corporations of America (CCA) 385
correspondence principle 152
cortisol study of stress 144
counternarratives 63
Courbet, Gustave 350–1
Covid-19 pandemic 507–8
Cowie, Jefferson 164, 170, 175
craft unions 408
Crane, Stephen 287
crime: the Australian working-class in popular culture 278–9, 281; prison labour 381–6; prison writing 292, 381–2, 386–8
critical pedagogy 112–13
critical social theory 50–1
critical theory 336
critical whiteness 409
cross-disciplinarity 288
cultural capital: first-generation college students 46; popular culture 280; professionals 239; schools 153
cultural norms: education 86; mismatch between social class cultures in college 92–4, 141–8; pedagogy of class 118; working-class and academic success 84–5; working-class bodies 110–12, 114
cultural omnivores 244–5
cultural persistence vs. erasure 173–5
cultural univores 244–5
culturally relevant pedagogy 112–13
culture shock 124, 157, 242, 262
curriculum: inclusion of social class 114; marginalization of working-class knowledge 137–9; vocational education 132
cyber-proletariat 481
cybertariat 481

Daniels, Jessie 420–1
Dars, Celestine 346
Davis, Angela 385

Davis, Mike 298, 317, 384–5
Davis, Rebecca Harding 346
death: grievability 205–7; living with 195–6
Declaration of Independence 457, 464
deficit culture 233
degrees, employment prospects 238; *see also* college
deindustrialization: consequences for industrial workers 169–76; cultural persistence vs. erasure 173–5; economic downturn 468–9; Exit Zero Project 61, 65; as global trend 170; 'half life' 61, 166, 174; multimedia conversations 69; multimedia projects 475–6; post-Fordist affect 495–6; precarity's affects 201–9; smokestack nostalgia 164–5, 175; sources and limits of resistance 171–3
deindustrialization studies 170
Delaney, Shelagh 373
Denning, Michael 302, 335
demographics, millennials 127
Depression Era 288
deproletarianization 182
Detroit 407
Detroit, hate strikes 459–60
Dewey, John 132
di Donato, Pietro 287
dialect 264–5; *see also* language use
dialogic research 27
Dickens, Charles 290
diet, working-class consumers 446–7
difference-education intervention 146–8
digital storytelling, first-generation college students 14, 15, 16, 47–55
disability: living with 195–6; oral history 191, 198
disempowerment 265–6
dislocation, economic change 180–7
dispositions, variation by class 246
'distribution of the sensible' 359, 365–8
diversity: academics of working-class roots 101; dominant cultures 235; working-class 33, 35–6; working-class studies 119–20
division of labour 37, 180–7
division of non-labour 186
documentaries 291; migrant labour 315–16; poverty 315; recycling and waste 316–18; US postwar documentary photography 325–40; Wal-Martization 319
domestic labour 191
dominant cultures 234–5
dominated culture 233
Dotter, Earl 426
Du Bois, W. E. B. 407–8, 456–7
Dubai Dreams 295–6, 297, 299–308
Dubai, Indian labour migrants 295, 297–308
Dudley, Kate 165

ecomuseums 175
Economic and Social Research Council 3
economics: dislocation and trauma 180–7, 204–5; transformation of work 166; *see also* capitalism
education 6, 79–80; college as a collaborator 85–8; English classrooms 130–9; escalator model 80–2, 84; first-generation college students 45–55; 'five principles for change' 113–15; investment in 154–5; social reproduction 151–9; understanding how education remains a gatekeeper 83–5; universal access 80–2, 87
egalitarianism, in Australian history 274–6
electronic performance monitoring (EPM) 482
Elkins, James 344, 347
embodied experiences 16, 47, 87
emotional labour 483
emotions: first-generation college students 50–1; positioning 52; precarity in employment 256
empathy, personal narratives 24–5
employee ownership 172–3
employment *see* the workplace
employment prospects: call centres 482–3; career cultures and job cultures 235–9; contemporary context 238; day labourers 426–34; degrees 238; deindustrialization and its consequences 169–76; food workers and labour 442–5; standards of living 238–9; *see also* precarity
English classrooms 130–9; the impact of excessive testing and assessment on learner identities 135–7; marginalization of working-class knowledge 137–8; tracking and the invidious consequences of being in the bottom sets 131–5
English coalfields, 'social haunting' 213–22
English working-class culture 227
entanglement, affect/imagination 213–22
Entin, Joseph 13, 15
entrepreneurship culture 185
environmental issues, cinema of the precariat 316–18
epistemology 12–13
erasure 173–5
Eribon, Didier 64
escalator model of education 80–2, 84, 86
ethics: belonging 267; class as predictor 238; personal narratives 28–9; work ethic 154, 193, 197; working-class studies 438; working-class values 93, 110
ethnographic fieldwork 15, 59–61, 214
Evans, Linda 385
Evans, Walker 325–6
everyday integration of working-class studies 125–7
Ewers 300
Ewick, P. 51–2
Exit Zero Project 25, 27, 61, 64–7, 69
extracurricular activities 247

factory jobs: deindustrialization and its consequences 169–76; dislocation and trauma 180–7
faculty members *see* academics
family: access to college 157; accomplishment of natural growth vs, concerted cultivation approach 153–4; activism 266; individual educational choice 83; mismatch between social class cultures in college 141–8; parenting style 153–4, 243; social reproduction 155; unemployment 184; worldviews 245
Farabundo Martí National Liberation Front (FMLN) 265
Farm to Table movement 449
farmers' markets 447–8
Fasanella, Ralph 351
fast-food 449–50
Faue, Elizabeth 392–3
Federici, Silvia 37
feminist movement 269, 363–5
'feminist process' 269
feminist theory 67–8
fictional narratives 393
film: activism and collective action 405–6; the Australian working-class 277–80; habitus 69; migrant labour 295–6, 297–308, 314–15; multimedia conversations 69–73; the precariat 313–22; prison culture 386–7; representations of the working-class 289, 290–1, 461
financial crisis (2008) 500
Finn, Patrick J. 123
first-generation college students: breaking silences on class 50–1; challenges faced by 45–6, 142–7, 148; Class Beyond the Classroom (CBtC) group 96–101; digital storytelling 45–55; digital storytelling, voice, and power 47–50; mismatch between social class cultures 92–4; narratives as subversive stories 51–3; programs in support of 94–6; research context 91–2; stories for equity and justice 53–4; the working-class student 123–5
First in Our Families 48, 52, 54, 96
Fischer, Claude 235
fishing industry 332–3
Fiske, Susan T. 119–20
'five principles for change' 113–15
Flanagan, Micky 131
flexible work 33–4, 480–5; *see also* precarity
Foley, Barbara 288
food banks 451
food justice 442; food workers and labour 442–5; local food movements and food sovereignty 447–9; social class 452; at work 449–52; working-class consumers 446–7
food pantries 451
food sovereignty 447–9
foodie culture 444, 447
football 276
Fordism 33, 493, 495, 500
Forsberg, Jennifer 292
Foucault, Michel 50, 382
Frank, Robert 336, 338–9
Freeman, Jo 408
funding, working-class studies 3
furniture industry 201
futurity, loss of 203–5

gaming 320–2
Gardner, Andrew 297–8
gatekeeping, education as 83–5, 86
Geertz, Clifford 60
gender: the Australian working-class in popular culture 279–80; class dynamics 63–4; domestic labour 191; Lumbee working-class history 474; marketing millennial women 392–401; occupational health 193–4, 195; status of theory 67–8; stereotypes 71, 292; working-class women's writing 288–9, 363–4
gender studies 11–12, 394, 418
General Electric (GE) 493–4
generational differences: marketing millennial women 292, 392–401; millennial concept of class 127; the workplace 165–6
gentrification 173, 184, 278, 318, 444
Ghosh, Amitav 290, 295–6, 298, 299–300
Ghost Labs 215–16, 217–22
gig economy 125, 166, 260; *see also* precarity
Gintis, H. 152
Girls 399–401
Global South, day labourers 426–34
globalization: economic dislocation and trauma 185–6; flexible workforce 33–4; food justice 442; Marxist theories 33, 36; post-Fordist affect 496; the precariat 313–14; social class 32; transnational corporations 33–4; Wal-Martization 318–20; working-class literature 290
Goldberg, Eve 385
Gompers, Samuel 458
Goodridge, John 289–90
Gordon, Avery 214–15, 216, 220
Gordon, Jennifer 430
Gorz, André 387–8
Gosh, Amitav 296, 298, 299
grade point averages (GPAs) 145–7, 156; *see also* academic performance
Graduate Record Examinations (GRE) 146
graphic arts 351–2
The Great Gatsby 125–6
Green, Jonathon 338
grievability 205–7
Grimes, M. D. 92
'gritty': commodified grit 374–7; evaluation gritty aesthetics 377; spaces 291–2, 372–4; in working-class cultural production 371–2

Grobman, Laurie 472
Gulf states 296–7; *see also* Dubai, Indian labour migrants
gynaeopticon 394–5, 396, 400

habitus 69, 263, 266, 425
'half life', deindustrialization 61, 166, 174
Hall, Stuart 277
Halnon, Karen Bettez 374–5
Hanley, James 365–6
Hanley, Lawrence 119
Hapke, Laura 121–2
hard individualism 243–4, 247
Harikrishnan 297
Harrison, Bennett 2
Harvey, David 34
hate strikes 459–60
Hawthorne, Jeremy 360
Hayes, Rutherford B. 458
health *see* illness; mental health; occupational health; physical health
health cultures 190–91, 193–5
Heathcott, Joseph 164, 175
heritage, deindustrialization 174–5
Hermeston, Rod 290
Herzog, Werner 298
heteronormativity 205, 401
hierarchy, attitudes towards 247, 266, 268, 269–70
higher education *see* college; first-generation college students; universities
Hills, Patricia 345
Hilton, Jack 359
Hinckley, David 399
Hine, Lewis 327, 352–3
historical consciousness 347–8
Hitchcock, Peter 35
Hoad 306
Hoggart, Richard: 'gritty' narratives 372; personal narrative 20; working-class cultures 227; working-class literature 364, 365
Holland, Dorothy 54
The Honeymooners 292
hooks, b. 55, 413, 472
'horizontal process' 269
horizontalism 408
Hoskins, B. 132–3
Hossfeld, Leslie 469, 474
housing, affordable housing activists 434–7
human suffering 259–60
Hunt 295
Hurst, Allison L. 16–17, 415
Hutton, Barry 131
Hyland, Ken 21

identity: the Australian working-class 275–6; community colleges 415; first-generation college students 51, 53, 54; food choices 447; illness 195, 197; the impact of excessive testing and assessment on learner identities 135–7; intersectionality 4–5; mismatch between social class cultures in college 92–4, 141–8; narratives as subversive stories 51–2; race and being working-class 86–7, 108–9; seriality 38–9; social class as fluid 158; as working-class 119–20, 121–3; working-class bodies 110–12, 114
illness: deindustrialization and job loss 197; living with 195–6; occupational disease movement 196–7; oral history 190–3; work-health cultures, risk and the body 193–4; the working-class student 143–4
imagination/affect, 'social haunting' 213–22
imposter syndrome 144–5
imposterism 93
income inequality: achievement gap 154
independent cultural model 143–4
Indian labour migrants 290, 295, 297–308
Indiana Limestone Company (ILC) 498, 499
Indigenous Australians 275, 277, 279, 281–2
Indigenous (Native) Americans 457, 469, 470–6
Indignados 187
individual imaginary 353
individualism: class cultures 243–4, 245; 'gritty' 372; in schools 247; working-class writing 360–2
industrial workers: class and race 455–65; consequences of deindustrialization 169–76; farm work vs. factory work 470, 473; Lumbee working-class history 468–76; physicality of labour 346; 'social haunting' in English coalfields 213–22; US postwar documentary photography 325–40
inequality: class cultures 242–9; contemporary context 260; escalator model of education 80–2; impacts on health 254; 'the 1%' 418–19, 421; wealth and race 462
inferiority, sense of 131–5
infoproletariat 481
information gap 157
intellectual activism 5
intent, working-class art 349
interactional styles 247
interdependent cultural model 143–4
interdisciplinarity: recent publications 3–4; representations of the working-class 307–8; working-class studies 288, 506, 507; working-class writing 289
intersectionality: activism and collective action 409; the mutual determination of class and race 455–65; personal narratives 63–4; representations of the working-class 307–8; social class 158; working-class studies 4–5, 13; working-class writing 363–5
interventions, higher education 146–8
interviewing: class straddlers 16–17; first-generation college students 47; Lumbee working-class history 473, 474–5; oral history 190–8

investment, in education 154–5
The Iron Ministry 316
Isenberg, Nancy 119

Jackson, Phoebe S. 289
Jaggar, Alison 50
James, Daniel 171
Jensen, Barbara: becoming and belonging 231–2; personal narrative 21, 22, 24, 25, 26–7; the working-class student 124
job complaining 236
jobs *see* employment prospects; the workplace
journals 3, 4

Kapiszewski, Andrzej 298
Kara, H. 52
Keegan, Bridget 289–90
Kelly, Jeff 322
Kelman, James 365
Kenny 280
Keynesianisn 493
Khalaf 295
King, Martin Luther 39–40
Knack, Martha C. 470
knowledge: epistemology 12–13; ethnographic fieldwork 60; marginalization of working-class knowledge 137–8; occupational health 193
knowledge production: art as 52; first-generation college students 52; 'situated' 62; 'social haunting' 215, 216; working-class studies 4
Kollwitz, Kaethe 346
Kolodny, Annette 363
Kristal, Gabriel 464
Kromm, Chris 469
Ku Klux Klan (KKK) 457, 460

La Via Campesina 448
Lavine, Steven D. 421
labour see migrant labour; the workplace
Labour and working-class Studies Project 1
labour, physicality of 346
labour pools 427–9
labour strikes: call centres 486, 487–8; post-Fordist affect 494–5, 498–501; working-class studies 407–8
labour migration *see* migrant labour
labour movements 266–7, 268, 496–501
laissez-faire approach 246
Langton, Marcia 281–2
language use: class identity 23–4; class speech codes 264–5; making speeches 270; multilingual film 303; variation by class 246, 247; visual languages and representational forms 349–52
Lareau, Annette 153
Last Train Home 315–16
Latour, Bruno 408–9
Lauter, Paul 35, 289, 290, 326
Lawrence, D. H. 291, 365
Lawrence, Jacob 347–8, 351
leadership, activist class cultures 267–71
Lee, Simon 291
Lefebvre, H. 373–4
Lehmann, W. 92, 93
Leipzig, Arthur 327–36, 339–40
Leipzig, Mimi 327, 335, 336
Leonard 297
Lerner, Michael 255
Lichterman, P. 268
Lindquist, J. 50
Linkon, Sherry: defining class 4, 13; deindustrialization 290; diversity 35–6; lived experience of class 12; Lumbee working-class history 476; personal narrative 15, 62; public scholarship 421; researcher positioning 17–18; social justice 14; socially responsible academics 420; 'struggle for social and economic justice' 413; working-class studies 289, 421, 470
literary radicalism 307–8
literature *see* working-class literature; working-class studies
Littlefield, Alice 470
living class 16, 47, 50
living labour 39–40
living standards *see* standards of living
Lixin Fan 315–16
local food movements 447–9
Long, Vicky 196
low income *see* poverty; socioeconomic status
Lowell, Massachusetts 174–5
Lowery, Malinda 469, 473, 475
Lucie-Smith, Edward 346
Lumbee working-class history 469–76
Lutz, Cathy 67–8
Lynd, S. 425–6

Macherey, Pierre 366
macho culture: illness, disability and death 195–6; occupational health 193–4; overworking 182
MacKenzie, Lawrence 123–4
Maharidge, Dale 468, 469, 471–2
Malacrida, Claudia 191
Malecki 300
managerial approach 246
manufacturing decline *see* deindustrialization
maps 344
Marcuse, Herbert 187
marginalization: working-class knowledge 137–8, 139; working-class writing 363
Marinara, Martha 126
marketing millennial women 392–401
marriage 184
Marx, Karl 32, 360, 409
Marxist theories: capitalism 33; reconceiving class 32–41; working-class studies 15

masculinities: the Australian working-class 275–6; the Australian working-class in popular culture 278–9; illness, disability and death 195–6; occupational health 193–4; precarity in employment 257–8
Mason, Raymond 354
mass incarceration 381; *see also* prison writing
McAlevey, Jane F. 407
McCray Beier, Lucinda 190–1
McGrath, John 297
McLarney, Ellen 300–01
media: the Australian working-class in popular culture 276–82; multimedia conversations 69–73; research methods 16; working across media 59; working-class portrayal 4, 5, 7
memory: collective/social memory 214; oral history 190–8; personal narratives 29
mental health: cognitive dissonance 257–8; human suffering 259–60; oral history 198; precarity in employment 255–60; the working-class student 142–3
meritocracy, educational inequalities 47, 83, 153, 158–9
methods of research 11–18; class analysis from the inside 20–30; ethnographic fieldwork 15, 59–61; getting personal 15, 61–5; multimedia conversations 69–73; oral history 192–3
#MeToo 392, 465
Metzgar, Jack: personal narrative 20, 23, 25–7; working-class epistemology 12; the workplace 164, 167
Mexican-Americans 71, 155, 156, 405
Mexico: food choices 447; revolutionary printmaking 352; Zapatistas 265, 408
Mezzadra, S. 36–7
Michigan, First-Generation College Students 94
middle-class: activist class cultures 262–72; distinction from working-class culture 227, 231–3; education 107, 111; epistemology 12–13; 'one right way' 234–9
middle-class imperialism 234–5
middle-class researchers 17
migrant labour: China 315–16; in film 295–6, 297–308, 314–15; Indian labour migrants and taxi topographies 290, 295–308; oral history - border crossing with day labourers 425–34, 437–8; working-class studies as border crossing 438–9
Mikulincer, Mario 255, 256
mill colonialism 175
millennials: inequality 260; marketing millennial women 292, 392–401; working-class identity 127, 292
Millet, Jean-Francois 349, 350
Milward, Richard 376–7
mining, 'social haunting' in English coalfields 213–22
Miyamoto Walters, Melody M. 126
mobility *see* social mobility
Monaghan, Peter 422
moral worth 79
Moreira, Danilo 482
Morgan, Nicky 137
Morris, J. M. 92
Morris, Wesley 399
Mostafa, Ali F. 297, 302–8
Moye, Todd 436–7
multiculturalism: service-learning approach 472; working-class studies 13
multimedia authoring 45
multimedia conversations 69–73
multimedia projects, Lumbee working-class history 475–6
Munif, Abdelrahman 296
Murad, Maurice 315
Murrow, Edward R. 314–15
museums: dress code for entry 343; industrial heritage projects 174–5; working-class art 343–54
music 244–5, 276–7, 289

narrative analysis 198
narrative impulse 347–8
narratives *see* personal narratives; stories
Nash, Robert J. 21, 22
NASPA (Student Affairs Administrators in Higher Education Foundation) 95–6
National Labour Union (NLU) 457
National Trade Union of Postal and Telecommunication Workers (SNTCT) 485
Native Americans 457, 469, 470–6
Neel, Alice 348
neoliberalism: economic dislocation 180–7, 205; education 83; 'gritty' 372; marketing millennial women 394–5, 398–401
New Deal 458–9, 469–70, 496
Newhall, Beaumont 327
New New Journalism 300
new social movements 267
New Working-Class Studies 216–17
New York, Willets Point 317–18
'newest social movements' 481
Newman, Kathy M. 393
Nichols and Stone, Gardner, Massachusetts 201–9
Nixon, Richard 461
nonprofit hiring halls 431–3
North American Free Trade Agreement (NAFTA) 442, 468–9
North Bolivar Good Food Revolution 450
nostalgia *see* smokestack nostalgia
novels *see* working-class literature
nutrition, working-class consumers 446–7

Oakes, J. 152
Obama, Michelle 120
obesity 446

occupational health: history of 191–2; living with illness, disability and death 195–6; occupational disease movement 196–7; work-health cultures, risk and the body 193–4
Occupy Wall Street 187, 421
Ochs, Elinor 66–7
oil industry 295, 296–7, 299–302
Open Door Community 428, 438
Opening the 'Unclosed Space' project 217, 218
oral history: activism and collective action 410; affordable housing activists 434–7; border crossing with day labourers 425–34, 437–8; contribution of 198; deindustrialization and job loss 197; illness 190–3; living with illness, disability and death 195–6; Lumbee working-class 469–76; as method 192–3; occupational disease movement 196–7; precarity 205–7; research accessibility 437–8; work-health cultures, risk and the body 193–4; working-class studies as border crossing 438–9
Oresick, Peter 425
Orwell, George 362, 366–8
Ostrum, Elinor 408
outsourcing 468–9, 474–5
overworking 182, 185

paintings, working-class art 343–54
Pakistani labour migrants 295
parenting style: accomplishment of natural growth vs, concerted cultivation approach 153–4; activism 266; class cultures 243; worldviews 245
parents: access to college 157; individual educational choice 83; the working-class student 123
participant observation: ethnographic fieldwork 59–61; meaning of 60; as method 64–5
participatory research: Ghost Labs 215–16; multimedia authoring 45
patriotism 464
Paul, Ronald 297
pedagogy of class 118–28
People for Urban Justice (PUJ) 434–7
Perera, Sonali 36, 290, 307–08
performance in education *see* academic performance
performativity 292, 393–4, 398–401
Perry, Jeff 464–5
perseverance in working-class culture 371; *see also* 'gritty'
personal freedom 313
personal narratives: agency 27–8; class analysis from the inside 20–30; education 122; integrating working-class studies 126–7; as method 61–5; oral history 190–8; research methods 15, 62; researcher positioning 17–18, 25–6; as signature genre 62, 63; subjectivity of working people 12
personhood, 'social haunting' 214
petroculture 296–7, 299–302
the Photo League 328, 335, 336, 353
photography: oral history - border crossing with day labourers 426, 428–31, 438–9; research methods 410; US postwar documentary photography 325–40; working-class art 352–3
physical demands, the working-class student 143–4
physical health 254
physicality of labour 346
platform economy 166
poetics, 'social haunting' 221
poetry 425
politics: 'five principles for change' 113–14; impact of working-class studies 5; public discourse 32–3; resistance to deindustrialization 171–3; white working-class 110
Polletta, Francis 55
Polyani, Karl 496
popular culture: the Australian working-class 276–82; prison culture 386–7; representations of the working-class 287–92, 461
populism 336
Portelli, Alessandro 171, 473, 475
portrayal *see* media; popular culture; representations of the working-class
Portuguese call centre assembly lines 480–8
positionality, as an academic 25–6, 438–9
positioning: narratives as subversive stories 51–2; as researcher 17–18, 25–6
post-Fordist affect 492–501
post-traumatic stress disorder (PTSD) 252–60
Potter, D. 153–4, 158
Pouliot, Tracie 203–4
poverty: documentaries 315; 'five principles for change' 113, 114; following outsourcing 468–9; food justice 450, 451; food workers and labour 445; integrating working-class studies 126; investment in education 154–5; precarity in employment 255; wealth and race 462; *see also* socioeconomic status (SES)
'poverty porn' 375
power: collective action 496–7; disempowerment 265–6; ethnographic fieldwork 60; first-generation college students 47–50; middle-class imperialism 234–5; personal narratives 27, 29; 'social haunting' 214; white supremacy 463–4
the precariat, as term 313–14
precarity 37, 166; cinema of the precariat 313–22; contemporary context 260, 480–1; economic dislocation and trauma 180–7; effects of 201–9; entrepreneurship culture 185; following outsourcing 468–9; marketing millennial women 394–5, 396; Portuguese call centre assembly lines 481–8; post-traumatic lives 254–60; temporary staffing agencies 427–9, 431–3; throughout history 181–2; working-class culture 229

primitive accumulation 33
principles of research 11–18
printmaking 352
'prison-industrial complex' 384
prison labour 381–6
'prison literature' 386–7
prison writing 292, 381–2, 386–8
privilege: college students 46; marketing millennial women 395, 400, 401; picturing working lives 347; positionality 413, 505; race 463; universities 362–3
productivity of labour 37
professional career paths 235–9
professional middle-class (PMC) 262–72; *see also* middle-class
professors *see* academics
progressive education 82
proletarian literature 359; *see also* working-class literature
the proletariat 36–8
psychological demands: post-traumatic lives 252–60; the working-class student 142–3, 148
public scholarship 420–2
Puri, Shamlal 290, 295–6, 297, 299–308

Rabinowitz, Paula 288–9
race: activism and collective action 408, 409; activist groups 267, 271; the Australian working-class in popular culture 279; capitalism 40; civil rights movement 39–40; class dynamics 63–4; craft unions 408; day labourers 426–7, 437–8; food justice 443; historical origins of racism 456–9; incarceration 381–2; intersectionality 4–5; Lumbee working-class history 469–70; the mutual determination of class and race in the US 455–65; public scholarship 421–2; in schools 108; social mobility 155–6; stereotypes 71; unemployment 182; US postwar documentary photography 338–9; wealth divide 462; working-class bodies 111–12; and working-class identity 86–7, 108–9
Radhakrishnan 298
Rancière, Jacques 359, 360
Rankin, Tom 428
Reagan, Ronald 461–2
Real Food Challenge 452
reality television 281
Reardon, S. F. 154
Reay, Diane 16–17, 51, 86
'reciprocal visibility' 13
recycling, cinema of the precariat 316–18
Redfern Now 282
reflexivity, personal narratives 62
religion: attitudes towards hierarchy 269–70; white supremacy 463–4
representations of the working-class 287–92; the Australian working-class in popular culture 276–82; film 289, 290–1, 461; 'gritty' 371–7; US postwar documentary photography 325–40; working-class art 343–54
research *see* working-class studies
research accessibility 437–8
researcher positioning 17–18, 25–6
residual culture 233
resistance: capitalism 492–3; deindustrialization 171–3; *see also* activism; collective action
'retrospective radicalism' 300–1
revolutionary printmaking 352
Rhodes, James 173
Riis, Jacob 327
Ringrose, Jessica 394
risk: dislocation and trauma 205; work-health cultures, risk and the body 193–5
Robeson, Lumbee working-class history 469–76
robotization 185–6
Rodríguez, Dylan 386–7
Roediger, David 307
Roksa, J. 153–4, 158
Romper Stomper 278, 279
Roosevelt, Franklin 458
Rosenberg, Roberta 472
Ross, Andrew 313
Rubin, Lillian 254, 257–8
Rubin, Rachel Lee 289
Rugby League 276
Russo, John: defining class 13; lived experience of class 12; social justice 14; socially responsible academics 420; 'struggle for social and economic justice' 413; working-class studies 289, 470
Rust Belt 171, 172

Salt of the Earth 405–6
Sander, Libby 125
Sartre, Jean-Paul 38
Sassen, Saskia 34, 426
Savoie, Guy 204–5, 208
Schocket, Eric 326–7
scholarly personal narratives 20–30
schools: class cultures 244; the impact of excessive testing and assessment on learner identities 135–7; interactional styles 247; marginalization of working-class knowledge 137–8; race 108; segregation within and among 152–3; social reproduction 151–9; tracking and the invidious consequences of being in the bottom sets 131–5; working-class bodies 110–12, 114; the working-class student 123
Schrecker, Ellen 459
Schuster, Leslie A. 127
self-care 395
self-disclosure 16
self-initiative 185
self-reflection 16
Seligman, Martin 255, 256, 257

selves 59
Sennett, Richard 227, 228
The Sentimental Bloke 278
seriality 38–41
service-learning approach, Lumbee working-class history 469–76
sexual abuse 258
sexual capital, marketing millennial women 394–401
sexual violence 279
sharing economy 166
Sharma, Sarah 304
Shor, Ira 121, 123
Silbey, S. 51–2
silence, social class in education 46, 50–1, 55
Silverstein, Morton 314–15
Simmons, Robin 131
sitcoms 393–4
situated knowledges 68
Skeggs, 393, 395
skilled labour 257
slang language 278
slavery 456
Smith, Adam 130
smokestack nostalgia 164–5, 175
Smyth, John 131
social change, stories of 55
social class: bodies and school 110–12; contemporary meaning 506–7; critical pedagogy 112–13; in the curriculum 114; definitional issues 13; English perception 130; as fluid 158; globalization 32; hierarchies in schools 114; popularized constructions 110; reconceiving class 32–41; relevance to modern world 1–2
'social haunting' 213–22
social history 350
social justice: English classrooms 139; struggle and resistance 492–3; working-class studies 14
social memory 214; *see also* 'social haunting'
social mobility: achievement gap 154; belief in 145; challenges faced 155–6; education 79, 84, 121, 123; English classrooms 139; escalator model of education 80–2, 84, 86; norms and social reproduction 151–2; segregation within and among schools 152–3; social class as fluid 158
social mobilization, Portuguese call centre assembly lines 481, 484
social movements: activism and collective action 405–11; activist class cultures 262–72; Atlanta protests 435; civil rights movement 39–40, 460–2; contemporary context 505; disempowerment 265–6; food sovereignty 447–9; precarious work 481; virtual collective action in call centres 485–7
social reproduction: cultural choices 237; in education 79, 151–9; gatekeeping role of education 83–5, 86; the workplace 40–1
socioeconomic status (SES): segregation within and among schools 152–3; stereotypes 145–6; the working-class student 142–6; see also inequality; poverty
soft individualism 243–4, 247
Solomon, Danny 427–8
Song Lines: Creating Living Knowledge through Working with Social Haunting 213–14, 218
Southeast Chicago Historical Museum 70–3
space, 'gritty' 291–2, 372–4
spatial representation 373
speech 23–4
speech codes 264–5; *see also* language use
speech performances 270
sports 245, 276
Springsteen, Bruce 468
Stamato, Linda 421
Standard Assessment Tests (SATs) 135–6
standards of living: employment prospects 238–9; inequality 260; recent history 228; 'the 1%' 418–19, 421; working-class culture associations 232, 233; *see also* socioeconomic status
Standing, Guy 166, 301, 313, 394
The Stanley Parable 321
Stanton, Cathy 174–5, 176
the state 496
Steadman, R.W. 359
Steedman, Carolyn 20, 23, 24
steelworkers 71–2
Stefan Szczelkun 344
Stein, Arlene 420–1
Steinbeck, John 287, 288, 314
stereotype threat 145–6, 148
stereotypes: careers 237–8; gender 71, 292; multimedia conversations 71–2; socioeconomic status 145–6
Stewart, Kathleen 221
Stieglitz, Alfred 352–3
stigmatization: implications of 249; socioeconomic status 142; stereotype threat 145; unemployment 184–5; vocational education 132
stories: analytical narratives 15; contribution to theory 65–9; digital storytelling 14, 15; first-generation college students 47–54, 96–101; multimedia conversations 69–73; narratives as subversive stories 51–3; 'social haunting' in English coalfields 216, 217–21; and theory 12–13; working across media 59; *see also* personal narratives
Story Center 47
Stout, Linda 264, 266
Strangleman, Tim 475
street corner waiting areas 429–30
stress: cortisol study 144; occupational mental health 198; psychological demands 142–3, 148
strikes see hate strikes; labour strikes
Struggle Street 281
Student Action with Farmworkers (SAF) 452

student activism 413–22
student community partnership programme, Lumbee working-class history 470–6
students see college; first-generation college students; universities
subjectivity, personal narratives 12, 25–6, 29
subversive stories, narratives as 51–3
Suchocki, Barbara 205–8
suicide: precarity's affects 201, 204, 257; teenager counselling case study 252–3
superiority 246–8
surplus population 182

Tablante, Courtney B. 119–20
Taft-Hartley Act 459
Taksa, Lucy 174
Tallman, Tisha 430–1
tastes, variation by class 244–5
Tate, Gary 120
Taylor, Keeanga-Yamahtta 4–5
'tech boom' 501
technology: robotization 185–6; transformation of work 166
television: the Australian working-class in popular culture 280–2; consumerism 292; 'grit' 375–7; marketing millennial women 392–401; migrant labour 314–15
temp workers 322; *see also* precarity
temporary staffing agencies 427–9, 431–3
tenacity in working-class culture 371; *see also* 'gritty'
testing: achievement gap 108, 154; the impact of excessive testing and assessment on learner identities 135–7; tracking and the invidious consequences of being in the bottom sets 131–5
textual analysis 14
theory of stories 12–13, 65–9
Thompson, Charles D. Jr. 470
Thompson, E. P. 35, 227
Tilly, Charles 496
#Timesup 392, 465
Tokarczyk, Michelle M. 118, 363
Toomelah 279
tracking in English schools 131–5
trade unions: activist class cultures 264, 270; call centres 482, 484–5, 487–8; deindustrialization 171–3; labour strikes 407–8; occupational disease movement 196–7; occupational health 194; post-Fordist affect 493, 494–5, 499–501; precarious work 481; recent movements 186–7
Trainspotting 376
transmedia, Exit Zero Project 61, 69
transnational corporations 33–4
transnational working-class 34
trauma: economic dislocation 183–5; living with illness, disability and death 195; post-traumatic lives 252–60; precarity's affects 203–9
TRIO Programs 95
Trow, Martin 81–2
Trump, Donald: organizing in the Trump era 462–5; populism 506; reactionary politics 203; white supremacy 455; and the working-class 5, 173

underemployment: dislocation and trauma 180–7; effects of 257–8
underground economy 183
unemployment: deindustrialization and illness 197; dislocation and trauma 180–7; effects of 257–8; Lumbee working-class history 474
unions *see* trade unions
United Kingdom: English classrooms 130–9; English coalfields, 'social haunting' 213–22; English working-class culture 227; globalization 2
United States: deindustrialization and its consequences 169–76; food justice 442–52; globalization 2; marketing millennial women 392–401; the mutual determination of class and race 455–65; postwar documentary photography 325–40; Trump's presidency 173, 455, 462–5, 506
universal access, education 80–2, 84, 87
universities: academic confidence 417–18, 419–20; as a collaborator 85–8; culture shock 124; education as gatekeeper 83–5; escalator model of education 80–2, 84, 86; the working-class student 123–5, 141–8; *see also* academics; first-generation college students
University of North Carolina at Pembroke (UNCP) 469, 470–6
Updike, John 300
urban imaginaries 302–4
US Food Sovereignty Alliance (USFSA) 450
US Rust Belt 171, 172

values: belonging 267; English perception 130; investment in education 154–5; work ethic 154, 193, 197; of the working-class 93, 110
Van Galen, Jane: digital storytelling 14–15, 16, 96, 97; "first person" readings 126–7
van Gogh, Vincent 351
Vance, J. D. 110, 127, 154–5
Victorian prison labour 382
Victorian working-class 290
video, multimedia conversations 69–73; *see also* film
virtual gaming 320–2
visual languages 349–52
Vivienne, S. 14, 48, 49, 53, 54
vocational education 132
Vohra, Anchal 301
voice, first-generation college students 47–50
voluntarily downwardly mobile (VDM) 267, 270

wages: post-Fordist affect 499; risk and occupational health 194; *see also* precarity
Wal-Martization 318–20
Walley, Charles William 61–2, *62*
Walley, Christine J. 12–13, 14–15, 22–4, 25, 27, 28
walls, ideology of 354
Walkerdine, Valerie 394
Walonen, Michael K. 296
War on Terror 384
Warnock, Deborah 415
waste, cinema of the precariat 316–18
wealth and race 462
Weber, Max 313
Weimar Republic 353
Weiner, Dan 336–8, 339–40
Welsh, Irvine 376
Wenzel, Jennifer 296
Whirlpool Corporation 497–9
white supremacy 455, 456–7, 462–4
white trash (slang) 278
whiteness: the Australian working-class 275, 276; community belonging 155–6; critical whiteness 409; intersectionality 4–5; Trump's leadership 455, 462–3; working-class identity 108–10
Whitman College First Generation club 94–5
Whitman, K. 275–6
Whitson, Carolyn 288
Wholesome Wave 450
Willets Point, New York 317–18
William Dow 308
Williams, Raymond: culture 344, 354; retrospective radicalism 300–1; 'social haunting' in English coalfields 221; working-class cultures 227; working-class writing 360
Williamson, J. 277
Williamson, Michael S. 468, 469
Willis, Paul 155
Wilson, Nicola 296
Winch 394, 396
Wood 393
Wolfe, Hugh 346
women's studies 11–12, 418
Woolf, Virginia 362–3
working-class: definitional issues 4, 121; diversity 33, 35–6; epistemology 12–13; in recent history 2–3; relevance to modern world 1–2
working-class and first-generation (WCFG) *see* first-generation college students
working-class art 291, 343–4
working-class bodies 110–12, 114
working-class culture 6–7, 227–30; academic success 84–5; class blindness 234–9; class cultures 242–9; meaning of 227, 231–3; mismatch between social class cultures in college 92–4, 141–8; in research 2
working-class literature: 'canon wars' 291, 362–4; defining 362; 'distribution of the sensible' 359, 365–8; exclusion of working-class texts 360; 'gritty' narratives 371–7; as idea 364–5; Indian labour migrants 297–308; meaning of 35, 120, 288; oil industry 296–7; recent publications 3–4; representations of the working-class 287–90, 291; 'things that are left out' 359–62, 368
working-class studies: 'classless society' 228; contemporary context 505–8; culture 228–9; evolution of 119; as field 2–3, 5; funding 3; future directions of the field 505–6; integrating 125–7; interdisciplinarity 506, 507; intersectionality 4–5, 13; journals 3, 4; methods and principles of research 6, 11–18; migrant labour 296–308; New Working-Class Studies 216–17; personal narratives 20–5; political impact 5; recent publications 3–4; reconceiving class in 32–41
Working-Class Studies Association (WCSA) 1, 3, 4, 91
working-class writing: 'canon wars' 291, 362–4; 'distribution of the sensible' 365–8; individualism 360–2; meaning of 35, 288, 290; oil industry 296; personal experience 122; prison writing 292, 381–2, 386–8; 'things that are left out' 359–62, 368; by women 288–9, 363–4
Working with Social Haunting project 217
the workplace 6; in art 346–7, 348–9, 350–2; cinema of the precariat 313–22; and community 163–7; deindustrialization and its consequences 169–76; dislocation and trauma 180–7; flexible work 33–4, 480–5; food justice 442–5, 449–52; job complaining 236; Marxist theories 33, 37, 39; oral histories 190–8, 425–34; performance monitoring 482; physicality of labour 346; Portuguese call centre assembly lines 481–88; post-traumatic lives 254–60; precarity 37, 166; 'social haunting' in English coalfields 213–22; social reproduction 40–1; US postwar documentary photography 325–40; working-class literature 290; *see also* employment prospects
Works Progress Administration, Federal Art Project (WPA/FAP) 351–2
World War II 325, 444, 455, 458, 459–60, 461
worldviews, variation by class 245
writing *see* working-class writing

Yezierska, Anzia 287
Young & Hungry 397–9
Yuval-Davis, Nira 307

the Zabbaleen 317
Zandy, Janet: educational practices 119; multiculturalism 13; personal narrative 20–1, 26, 28; photography 326; representations of the

working-class 287–8, 289, 326; social justice 14; subjectivity of working people 12; working-class art 291; working-class identity 122, 128; working-class literature 35, 364

Zaniello, Tom 277, 289, 290–1
Zapatistas 265, 408
Zhou, Ji 472
Zweig, Michael 4, 413, 507